LOVE, GUILT AND REPARATION AND OTHER WORKS 1921-1945

The Writings of Melanie Klein

Under the general editorship of
Roger Money-Kyrle
in collaboration with
Betty Joseph, Edna O'Shaughnessy
and Hanna Segal

Volume I

LOVE, GUILT AND REPARATION
AND OTHER WORKS

*

Volume II

THE PSYCHO-ANALYSIS OF CHILDREN

*

Volume III

ENVY AND GRATITUDE
AND OTHER WORKS

*

Volume IV

NARRATIVE OF A CHILD ANALYSIS

The Writings of Melanie Klein

Volume I

LOVE, GUILT AND REPARATION AND OTHER WORKS 1921-1945

by
Melanie Klein

With an Introduction by
R.E. Money-Kyrle

THE FREE PRESS
A Division of Macmillan, Inc.
New York

Copyright © 1975 by The Melanie Klein Trust

The Free Press
A Division of Macmillan, Inc.
866 Third Avenue, New York, N.Y. 10022

The Free Press Edition 1984

Printed in the United States of America

printing number

1 2 3 4 5 6 7 8 9 10

Library of Congress Cataloging in Publication Data

Klein, Melanie.
   Love, guilt, and reparation, and other works, 1921-1945.

   (The Writings of Melanie Klein; v. 1)
   Bibliography: p.
   Includes index.
   1. Psychoanalysis—Addresses, essays, lectures.
2. Personality in children—Addresses, essays, lectures.
3. Child analysis—Addresses, essays, lectures.
I. Title. II. Series: Klein, Melanie. Works. 1984 ;
v. 1.
BF173.K4825 1984   150.19′52   84-13766
ISBN 0-02-918420-7

CONTENTS

PREFACE

MELANIE Klein's works were produced over a period of about forty years, some as books, some in books with contributions from other authors, and some as papers which have not previously been collected in book form. Moreover, as would be inevitable in any creative effort spread over so long a time, her ideas were subject to a constant process of extension, amendment and clarification. It is therefore not easy for the student, confronted with this fairly large mass of literature, to discover what were Melanie Klein's most mature ideas or how she had arrived at them. For this reason, in bringing out a new edition of her complete works, a major aim was to indicate the position of the main themes in each work in relation to her earlier and later thought on the same topic by means of explanatory notes. These notes are collected at the end of each volume except Volume IV, *Narrative of a Child Analysis*, which already has Melanie Klein's own notes.

Although this was the chief aim of the new edition, once it was decided to bring it out, an opportunity arose to make certain improvements: the translation of one book, *The Psycho-Analysis of Children*, originally published in German, has been largely revised; all references to earlier editions of Freud's works have been amended to refer to the *Standard Edition*; and as far as possible this is also true of references to other works of which there are now more recent editions. Moreover, new indices have been prepared for Volumes I, II and III, bringing them into harmony with one another for ease of cross-reference.

The work required to implement these aims has been carried out by different groups of people.

The preliminary negotiations with the publishers were undertaken by Professor Elliott Jaques, who was generously met, and assisted, by Mr Masud Khan as Editor of the International Psycho-Analytical Library. Professor Jaques has also written a Preface to Volume IV, *Narrative of a Child Analysis*.

The Explanatory Notes have been prepared by Mrs Edna O'Shaughnessy in consultation with Dr Hanna Segal, Miss Betty Joseph and myself, who thus share with her the responsibility but not the real work. Meanwhile, Dr Hans Thorner, assisted by his daughter-in-law, Mrs Prudence M. Thorner, and in the initial stages also by Dr Stephen Smith, had undertaken to revise the translation of *The Psycho-Analysis of Children*; and he, in turn, submitted the draft of each chapter to Mrs Strachey who had made the original translation. One paper, 'Inhibitions and Difficulties at Puberty', which has not previously appeared in English, was translated by Dr Claud Wedeles. The difficult task of checking and standardizing all references was undertaken by Miss Ann Hutchinson, and that of preparing, rewriting and amending the indices by Mrs Barbara Forryan.

It remains for me to express my gratitude to these friends and helpers for the sustained and devoted effort which they have put into the production of *The Writings of Melanie Klein*. On behalf of the trustees of the Melanie Klein Trust, which has sponsored this work, I also wish to thank The Institute of Psycho-Analysis which, in collaboration with The Hogarth Press, has already published many of Melanie Klein's works, for now publishing the complete collection of them in four volumes.

R. E. MONEY-KYRLE

INTRODUCTION

MELANIE Klein, née Reizes, was born in Vienna in 1882, the fourth and youngest child of parents who were of Jewish origin but no longer strict in religion, in which they seem to have been tolerant agnostics. There is evidence of a good deal of heritable ability on both sides; and certainly the setting for the children's growing up was a highly intellectual one. What is more important, in Melanie Klein's own recollection, was that her family was very united, held together by strong ties of love. It did not, however, escape periods of acute sadness when, first, her favourite sister died and, later, the older brother whom she had enormously admired—a tragedy which in after years was repeated when one of her own grown sons was killed in a climbing accident.

To come now to the beginning of Melanie Klein's professional life, she was about fourteen when she conceived a strong desire to study medicine, and with her brother's help quickly learnt enough Latin and Greek to pass into the Gymnasium. Her prospects of a medical career, however, came to an end when she got engaged at the early age of seventeen. Four years later, in 1903, she was married and became in due course the mother of three children.

It was not until the first world war that she was able to return, in a new form, to her interrupted career. She had come across a book by Freud and felt that she recognized in it something she had always vaguely been looking for. She was then in Budapest and able to start analysis with Ferenczi, who encouraged her to specialize in the analysis of children; and, indeed, she had already begun to do so in Budapest before the end of the war. At that time the analysis of young children, apart from Freud's 'Little Hans' and some preliminary work by Dr Hug-Hellmuth, was an unknown field, soon also to be entered from a somewhat different direction by Anna Freud. After the war, in 1921, Melanie Klein went to Berlin, at the invitation of Dr Karl Abraham, to continue her work with children, and soon introduced significant and new concepts into analysis. Her innovations were encouraged and supported by Abraham, with whom she also had further analysis from the beginning of 1924 until it was terminated by his early death in 1925. It was while she was in Berlin and

¹ For longer biographical accounts see H. Rosenfeld, *International Encyclopedia of the Social Sciences*, and John A. Lindon, 'Melanie Klein's Theory and Technique: Her Life and Work', in *Tactics and Techniques in Psychoanalytic Therapy*, ed. Peter L. Giovacchini (New York: Science House; London: Hogarth Press, 1972).

her husband in Sweden that their marriage, not a wholly happy one, came to a final end. In 1926 she came to London, at the invitation of Ernest Jones, who also gave her much support, and she remained there, gradually increasing the proportion of adult patients, particularly training cases, in her practice, until her death in 1960. It is worth noting that, like Freud himself and many others, she practised self-analysis, so the works she published were almost certainly the result of analytic observations made both on her patients and on herself, cross-checked against each other.

In her clinical work, which aroused a good deal of controversy, she assumed from the outset that a child analysis was to be conducted in exactly the same way as an adult one—except that the analysis of verbal association was to be supplemented by the analysis of play. She assumed that a transference was possible, observed that a super-ego, though a more rudimentary one, was present, and believed that no moral or educational pressure was to be exerted by the analyst. In other words, she adopted Freud's transference analysis both for adults and children; and if she later introduced any changes at all these were in the direction of purer transference analysis, her rôle becoming more and more confined to interpretation. A characteristic which was perhaps the most specific for her technique was that, from the beginning, she always gave preference to the interpretation of unconscious anxiety based on unconscious phantasy wherever she could see it—even when the first results of this appeared to be an increase of anxiety.

It was this technique which brought up and enabled her to record many hitherto unseen patterns in the psyche, so that her theory of the mind and what could go wrong with it, originally taken from Freud, underwent a continuous development. It would be unnecessary and redundant to summarize this here, since Melanie Klein's own writings, especially if read in conjunction with the Explanatory Notes, should speak for themselves. One point, however, deserves stressing. In introducing the concepts of the paranoid-schizoid and depressive positions, Melanie Klein also clarified the distinction between two vitally different types of morality which innately tend to develop successively in human beings. The child's earliest super-ego, containing his own projected destructiveness turned against himself, is a paranoid-schizoid construction which, as Freud discovered, operates as an archaic internal god with an archaic morality of an eye-for-an-eye kind. This is not ego-syntonic, and a major aim of analysis is to weaken it. But around four months old the appearance of the depressive position ushers in the possibility of a different and far more ego-syntonic morality based no longer on a specific form of a paranoid delusion, but on depressive guilt at the injuries inflicted both in reality and phantasy on loved objects outside and inside the self in the earlier paranoid-schizoid position. In so far as these damaged loved objects are mourned, they are felt to come alive inside as internal mentors who help and sustain the ego in its struggle against remaining bad objects inside and real external enemies. It is certainly not true that Melanie Klein used any kind of moral pressure to foster this kind of morality in her patients; but it is true that in so far as she was able to lay bare the delusions behind the archaic morality and also behind various forms of manic defence against both persecutory and depressive guilt, the second type of morality did tend of its own accord progressively to predominate in them. This change was considered by her as one of the factors indicating a change towards integration and maturity.

Although the theory which Melanie Klein eventually developed —and in particular the distinction between the paranoid-schizoid and depressive position—seems capable of explaining at least the main facts of both normal and abnormal mental life, it would be a mistake to regard her theory as a closed one. She herself added to it almost to the end of her life. And no one knows what future modification or addition may be required. As in physics, so in psychology ultimate truth is perhaps of infinite complexity, to be approached only by an infinite series of approximations.

R. E. Money-Kyrle

THE DEVELOPMENT OF A CHILD

(1921)

I

THE INFLUENCE OF SEXUAL ENLIGHTENMENT AND RELAXATION OF AUTHORITY ON THE INTELLECTUAL DEVELOPMENT OF CHILDREN

Introduction

THE idea of enlightening children in sexual matters is steadily gaining ground. The instruction introduced in many places by the schools aims at protecting children during the age of puberty from the increasing dangers of ignorance, and it is from this point of view that the idea has won most sympathy and support. The knowledge obtained by psycho-analysis, however, indicates the necessity, if not of 'enlightening', at least of bringing up children from the tenderest years in such a fashion as will render any special enlightenment unnecessary, since it points to the completest, most natural enlightenment compatible with the rate of development of the child. The irrefutable conclusions to be drawn from psycho-analytic experience demand that children shall, whenever possible, be protected from any over-strong repression, and thus from illness or a disadvantageous development of character. Alongside the certainly wise intention of countering actual and visible dangers with information, therefore, analysis aims at avoiding dangers that are equally actual, even if not visible (because not recognized as such), but which are much commoner, deeper, and therefore call much more urgently for observation. The results of psycho-analysis, which always in every individual case leads back to repressions of childish sexuality as the causes of subsequent illness, or of the more or less operative morbific elements or inhibitions present even in every normal mentality, indicate clearly the path to be followed. We can spare the child unnecessary repression by freeing—and first and foremost in ourselves,—the whole wide sphere of sexuality from the dense veils of secrecy, falsehood and danger spun by a hypocritical civilization upon an affective and uninformed foundation. We shall let the child acquire as much sexual information as the growth of its desire for knowledge requires, thus depriving sexuality at once of its mystery and of a great part of its danger. This ensures that wishes, thoughts and feelings shall not—as happened to us—be partly repressed and partly, in so far as repression fails, endured under a burden of false shame and nervous suffering. In averting this repression, this burden of superfluous suffering, moreover, we are laying the foundations for health, mental balance and the favourable development of character. This incalculably valuable result, however, is not the only advantage we can expect for the individual and for the evolution of humanity from an upbringing founded upon unqualified frankness. It has another and not less significant consequence—a decisive influence upon the development of the intellectual powers.

The truth of this conclusion drawn from the experiences and teachings of psycho-analysis has been clearly and irrefutably borne out by the development of a child with whom I have occasion to be much occupied.

Previous History

The child in question is a boy, little Fritz, the son of relations who live in my immediate neighbourhood. This gave me the opportunity to be often in the child's company without any restraint. Further, as his mother follows all my recommendations I am able to exercise a far-reaching influence on the child's upbringing. The boy, who is now five years of age, is a strong healthy child of normal but slow mental development. He only began to speak at two years of age and was more than three and a half before he could express himself consecutively. Even then especially remarkable sayings, such as one hears at a very early age sometimes from gifted children, were not observed. In spite of this he gave the impression both in looks and behaviour of an alert and intelligent child. He mastered a few individual ideas very slowly. He was already more than four years old before he learnt to distinguish colours, and almost four and a half before he became familiar with the conceptions of yesterday, today and tomorrow. In practical things he was distinctly behind other children of his age. Although he was often taken shopping, it seemed (from his questions) rather incomprehensible to him that one should not get things as a present from people who had a number of them, and it was very difficult to make him understand that things had to be paid for, and at various rates according to their value.

On the other hand, his memory was remarkable. He remembered and remembers comparatively remote things in every detail and he is completely master of ideas or facts that he has once understood. Speaking generally, he has asked few questions. When he was about four and a half years old a more rapid mental development and also a more powerful impulse to ask questions set in. A this time too the feeling of omnipotence (what Freud has called the 'belief in the omnipotence of thought') became very marked. Anything that was being spoken of—any skill or handicraft—Fritz was sure that he could do perfectly, even when the contrary was proved to him. In other instances, when in reply to questions he was told that papa and mamma too were ignorant of much, it did not seem to shake his belief in his own omnipotence and in that of his environment. When he could defend himself in no other fashion, even under the pressure of proof to the contrary, he would assert, 'If I am shown how just once, I can do it quite well!' So in spite of all proof to the contrary he was convinced he could cook, read, write and speak French perfectly.

Onset of the birth-question period

At the age of four and three quarters, questions concerning birth set in. The conclusion was forced upon one that hand-in-hand with this there went a striking increase in his need to ask questions in general.

Here I would remark that the questions put by the little fellow (with which he mostly came to his mother or me) were always answered absolutely truthfully and, when necessary, on a scientific basis suited to his understanding, but as briefly as possible. Questions once answered were never referred to again, neither was a new subject introduced unless he either repeated one or spontaneously started a new question.

After he had once put the question,[1] 'Where was I before I was born?' it cropped up again in the form of 'How is a person made?' and recurred almost daily in this stereotyped fashion. It was clear that the constant recurrence of this question was not due to lack of intelligence, because he evidently fully understood the explanations that were given him about growth in the maternal body (the part played by the father was not referred to as he had not at that time asked directly about it). That a certain 'pain', an unwillingness to

[1] The question was occasioned by the chance remarks of an older brother and sister, who on different occasions said to him, 'You were not born then.' It seemed also to be based on the evidently painful feeling of 'not always having been there', as immediately on being informed and repeatedly afterwards he expressed his satisfaction by saying that he had been there before all the same. It was evident that this was not the only instigation for the question, however, as in a short time it cropped up in the altered form of 'How is a person made?' At four and a quarter years another question recurred frequently for a time. He would ask, 'What is a papa needed for?' and (more seldom), 'What is a mamma needed for?' The reply to this question, of which the meaning was not recognized at the time, was that one needed a papa to love and to take care of one. This was visibly unsatisfactory, and he frequently repeated the question until he gradually let it drop.

accept (against which his desire for truth was struggling) was the determining factor in his frequent repetition of the question was shown by his conduct—his absent-minded, somewhat embarrassed behaviour when the conversation had hardly started and his visible endeavour to be quit of the subject he himself had begun. For a short time he stopped putting this question to his mother and me and addressed himself with it to his nurse (who shortly afterwards left) and his elder brother. Their replies, that the stork brought the babies and God made people, contented him however only for a few days, and when he later came back to his mother again with the question, 'How is a person made?' he seemed at last more inclined to accept her reply as the real truth.[1]

To the question, 'How is a person made?' his mother once more repeated the explanation given him often before. This time he became more talkative and told her that the governess had told him (he seems to have heard this previously too from someone) that the stork brought babies. 'That is only a story,' said his mother. 'The L. children told me that the Easter hare did not come at Easter but that it was the governess who hid the things in the garden.'[2] 'They were quite right,' she replied.—'There isn't such a thing as an Easter hare, is there? That is only a story?'—'Of course.'—'And is there no Father Christmas either?'—'No, there is none either.'—'And who brings and arranges the tree?'—'The parents.'—'And there are no angels either, that is only a story too?' —'No, there are no angels, that too is only a story.'

This knowledge was evidently not easily assimilated, for at the conclusion of this conversation he asked, after a short pause, 'But there are locksmiths, aren't there? They are real? For else who would make boxes?' Two days later he tried the experiment of a change of parents, announcing that he was taking Mrs L. for his mamma, and her children for his brothers and sisters, and he kept up this arrangement for a whole afternoon. He came home repen-

---

[1] At the same time he grasped some other ideas that had been repeatedly discussed in the period immediately preceding the birth questions, but that also apparently had not been thoroughly cleared up. He had even sought to defend them in a way; for instance, he had tried to prove the existence of the Easter hare by saying the L. children (playmates) possessed one too, and that he had himself seen the devil in the distance in the meadow. It was much easier to convince him that what he thought he had seen was a foal than it was to persuade him of the lack of foundation for belief in the devil.

[2] Apparently he had only been convinced in the matter of the Easter hare by this information supplied by the L. children (although they often told him untruths). It was this too perhaps that instigated him to investigate more closely the answer—so often demanded but as yet not assimilated—to the question, 'How is a person made?'

tant in the evening.[1] His question next day to his mother immediately after his morning kiss, 'Mamma, please, how did you come into the world?' showed that there was a causal connection between his deliberate change of parents and the preceding enlightenment that had been so difficult to assimilate.

After this he also showed much more pleasure in really coming to grips with this subject, to which he repeatedly returned. He enquired how it happened in dogs. Then he told me that recently he had 'peeped into a broken egg' but had failed to see a chicken in it. When I explained the difference between a chick and a human child and that the latter remains in the warmth of the maternal body till it is strong enough to thrive outside of it, he was manifestly pleased. 'But then who is inside the mother to feed the child?' he asked.

The next day he asked me, 'How do people grow?' When I took a little child of his acquaintance as an example, and as further examples for different stages of growth, himself, his brother and his papa, he said 'I know all that, but how does one grow at all?'

In the evening he had been reprimanded for disobedience. He was perturbed about it, and endeavoured to make it up with his mother. He said, 'I shall be obedient to-morrow and the next day and the day after . . .' suddenly pulling up, he thought for a moment and asked, 'Please, mamma, how long does the day after go on coming?' and when she asked exactly what he meant, he repeated, 'For how long does a new day still come?' and immediately after, 'Mamma, doesn't the night always belong to the day before and early in the morning is a new day again?'[2] His mother went to fetch something and when she came back into the room he was singing to himself. On her entering the room he stopped singing, looked at her closely and said, 'If you said now that I wasn't to sing I should have to stop singing?' When she explained that she would never say anything like that, because he could always do as he wished except when it could not be allowed for some reason and gave him examples, he seemed satisfied.

Conversation about the existence of God

On the following day it rained. Fritz regretted this because he wanted to play in the garden, and asked his mother, 'Does God

---

[1] He had run away from home just about two years before this, but his reason for doing so was not discovered. He was found in front of a watchmaker's shop carefully observing the display in the window.

[2] The conception of time that he had found so difficult seemed now to have become clear to him. Once when the increased pleasure in asking questions had already set in, he said, 'Yesterday is what has been, today is what is, tomorrow is what comes!'

know for certain how long he will let it rain?' She replied that God did not make the rain but that rain came from the clouds and explained the matter to him. Next morning he received her again with a question that had been given up for a long time, 'How is a person made?' His mother tried to discover what exactly he had not understood in her previous explanations and the child said, 'About the growing.' When she tried once more to explain how the little head and limbs, etc. grew, he said, 'Please, mamma, but how—where do the little head and the little tummy and all the rest come from?' On her reply that they are already present quite tiny inside the little egg, like the little flower in the bud, he asked no more. A little later he enquired, 'How is a chair made?'[1] In the meantime his mother had dressed him. Quite spontaneously he then asked, 'It isn't God who makes it rain? Toni' (the maid) 'said that God made the rain!' After her reply he asked, 'Is it only a story that God makes the rain?' On her replying in the affirmative, he continued, 'But there really is God?' His mother replied a little evasively that she had never seen him. 'One doesn't see him but he is really up in the sky?'—'In the sky there are only air and clouds.'—'But there is really God,' he asked again. There was no escape; so she came to a decision and said, 'No, child, he is not real.'—'But, mamma, if a real grown-up person says that God is real and lives in the sky—isn't it true even then?' Her reply was that many grown-up people did not know rightly about things and could not tell about them correctly. He had now finished his breakfast and stood at the door leading into the garden and looked out. He was thoughtful. Suddenly he said, 'Mamma, I see what is, and what I see really is there, isn't it? I see the sun and the garden—but I can't see Aunt Marie's house and yet it is there too, isn't it?' She explained to him why he could not see his Aunt Marie's house and he asked, 'Mamma, can't you see her house either?' and showed his satisfaction at her denial. Immediately afterwards however he enquired further, 'Mamma, how did the sun get right up there?' and when she said a little pensively, 'You know, it has been like that for a very, very long time already...'—'Yes, but how much longer before, how did it get up there?'

I must here explain his mother's somewhat uncertain behaviour

---

[1] He repeated this question afterwards for a time on occasions when details of growth which he had difficulty in understanding were being discussed. 'How is a chair made?' and the answer, with which he was quite familiar and which was no longer replied to for this reason, seems therefore to have been a sort of help to him, to be used as a standard or comparison for the reality of whatever he had just newly heard. He uses the word 'really' in the same way, and with this exchange the use of 'How is a chair made?' decreased and gradually ceased.

towards the child over the question of the existence of God. The mother is an atheist. Nevertheless, in the upbringing of the older children her convictions had not been put into practice. The children were, it is true, brought up quite independently of the confessional, and were also told very little about God, but the God which their environment (school, etc.) presented to them ready-made was never repudiated by her; so that even if he were little spoken of he was implicitly present for the children and occupied a place among the fundamental conceptions of their minds. The husband, who himself held a pantheistic conception of the deity, quite approved of the introduction of the idea of God into the children's education, but nothing definite had been decided on in this matter between the parents. By accident it happened that on that day she had no opportunity to discuss the situation with her husband, so that when in the evening the youngster suddenly asked his father, 'Papa, is there really a God?' he simply answered 'Yes.' Fritz retorted, 'But mamma said there was really no God.' Just at this moment his mother entered the room and he asked her at once, 'Mamma, please, papa says there really is a God. Does God really exist?' She was naturally rather taken aback and answered, 'I have never seen him and do not believe either that God exists.' At this juncture her husband came to her assistance and saved the situation by saying, 'Look here, Fritz, no one has ever seen God and some people believe that God exists and others believe that he doesn't. I believe that he does but your mamma believes that he doesn't.' Fritz, who throughout had looked from one to the other with great anxiety, now became quite cheerful and explained, 'I think too that there is no God.' After an interval however he apparently had doubts all the same and he asked, 'Please mamma, if God does exist does he live in the sky?' She repeated that there were only air and clouds in the sky, whereupon he repeated quite cheerfully and definitely, 'I think too that there is no God.' Immediately afterwards he said, 'But electric cars are real, and there are trains too—I was once in one, once when I went to Grandmamma's and once when I went to E.'

This unforeseen and improvised solution of the deity question had perhaps the advantage that it was adapted to diminish the excessive authority of the parents, to weaken the idea of their omnipotence and omniscience, since it enabled the child to ascertain —as had not before occurred—that his father and mother held different opinions about a matter of importance. This weakening of authority might possibly have fostered a certain sense of insecurity in the child; but this was, I think, quite easily overcome because a sufficient degree of authority still remained to afford him a sense of support, and at any rate I have not been able to observe in his general behaviour any trace of such an effect, either as a sense of insecurity or as a shattered trust in either of his parents. All the same, a little remark that was made about two weeks later may have had some connection with this. During a walk his sister had requested him to ask someone the time. 'A gentleman or a lady?' he enquired. He was told it was of no consequence which. 'But if the gentleman says twelve o'clock and a lady says a quarter-past-one?' he asked thoughtfully.

The six weeks subsequent to this conversation about the existence of God seemed to me to some extent to form the conclusion and climax of a definite period. I find his intellectual growth during and since this period to have been so much stimulated and so changed both in intensity and in direction and kind of development (compared with earlier conditions), as to enable me to distinguish three periods so far in his mental development, dating from his being able to express himself fluently. The period preceding the onset of questions about birth, the second period beginning with these questions and ending with the solution of the idea of the deity, and the subsequent third period which had just begun.

Third period

The need to ask questions which was so marked in the second period has not become any less but takes a somewhat different line.

He certainly often returns even now to the subject of birth, but in a way that shows he has already incorporated this knowledge into the general body of his thought. His interest in birth and connected things is still strong but decidedly less ardent, as is shown by his asking less but making more certain about it. For instance, 'Is a dog made too by growing inside its mummy?' or another time, 'How does a deer grow? Just like a person?' On receiving a reply in the affirmative, 'It grows inside its mummy too?'

Existence

Out of the question, 'How is a person made?' which is no longer put in this form, there has developed an enquiry concerning existence in general. I give a selection from the wealth of questions of this kind asked in these weeks. How teeth grow, how eyes stay in (in the orbit), how the lines on the hand are made, how trees, flowers, woods etc. grow, whether the stalk of the cherry grows with it from the beginning, whether unripe cherries ripen inside the stomach, whether picked flowers can be replanted, whether seed gathered unripe ripens afterwards, how a spring is made, how a river is made, how ships get on to the Danube, how dust is made;

further, about the manufacture of the most various articles, stuffs and materials.

Interest in faeces and urine

In his more specialized questions ('How can a person move, move his feet, touch something? How does the blood get inside him? How does a person's skin come on him? How does anything grow at all, how can a person work and make things,' etc.?), and also in the way he pursues these enquiries, as well as in the constantly expressed need to see how things are made, to get to know their inner mechanism (closet, water system, pipes, revolver—in all this curiosity there seems to me to be already the need to examine what interests him to the very bottom, to penetrate into the depths. The unconscious curiosity concerning the father's share in the birth of the child (to which as yet he had not given direct expression) may perhaps have been partly responsible for this intensity and profundity. This showed itself too in another kind of question that for a time came much to the fore, which, without his having previously spoken of it, was really an enquiry about the differences in the sexes. At this time there recurred repeatedly the question whether his mother, I and his sisters had always been girls, whether every woman when she was little was a girl—whether he had never been a girl[1]—also if his papa when he was little was a boy, whether every one, every papa was little at first; once too when the birth question was becoming more real for him, he asked his father whether he too had grown inside his mamma, using the expression 'in the stomach of' his mamma, an expression that he used occasionally although the mistake had been corrected. The affectionate interest in faeces, urine and everything connected with them that he had always displayed has remained very active and his pleasure in them is openly shown on occasion. He gave his wiwi (penis) of which he was very fond a pet name for a time, called it 'pipatsch' but otherwise often 'pipi'.[2] Once too he said to his father as he gripped the latter's walking-stick between his legs, 'Look papa what a great big wiwi I have.' For a time he often spoke of his beautiful fine 'kakis' (faeces) occasionally bestowing much contemplation upon their shape, colour and quantity.

---

[1] At the age of about three he showed a peculiar interest in articles of jewellery, particularly his mother's (this interest is maintained) and would say repeatedly, 'When I am a lady I shall wear three brooches at once.' He would frequently say, 'When I am a mamma. . . .'

[2] Once when he was three he saw his elder brother in the bath quite naked and called out quite rejoiced, 'Karl has a pipi too!' He then said to his brother, 'Please ask Lene if she has a pipi too!'

9

Once, on account of an indisposition, he had to have an enema, a very unusual proceeding for him, which he always strenuously resists; he takes medicine too only with great difficulty, particularly in pill form. He was very much surprised when instead of a solid motion he felt a fluid coming away.He asked whether the 'kaki' was coming from the front now or was that 'wiwi' water? On its being explained to him that it was happening just as usual only that it was fluid, he asked, 'Is it the same with girls? Is it the same with you?'

Another time he referred to the processes in the bowel that his mother had explained to him in connection with the enema, and asked about the hole where the 'kakis' came from. While doing so he told me that recently he had looked, or wanted to look in at this hole.

He asked whether the toilet paper was for the others too? Then ... 'Mamma, you make kakis too, don't you?' When she agreed he remarked, 'Because if you didn't make kakis nobody in the world would make them, would they?' In connection with this he talked about the size and colour of dog kakis, of those of other animals and compared his own with them. He was helping to shell peas and said that he gave the pod an enema, opened the popo and took out the kakis.

Reality sense

With the onset of the questioning period his practical sense (that, as already stated, was very poorly developed before the questions about birth which rendered the little fellow backward as compared with other children of his age) showed a great improvement. While the struggle with his tendency to repression was going on he could only with difficulty, but therefore all the more vividly, distinguish various ideas as unreal in contrast to real ones; now however he manifested a need to examine everything in this respect. Since the close of the second period this has come to the fore, particularly in his endeavour to enquire into the reality and proof of things long familiar to him, of activities he has practised and observed over and over again, and of things he has known for ages. In this way he attains independent judgements of his own from which again he can draw his own deductions.

Obvious questions and certainties

For instance, he ate a piece of hard bread and said, 'The bread is very hard'; after he had eaten it, 'I too can eat very hard bread.' He asked me what was it called that was used to cook upon in the kitchen (the word had escaped him). When I told him he stated, 'It is called a range because it is a range. I am called Fritz because I am Fritz. You are called auntie because you are auntie.' At a meal he had not chewed a morsel properly and for this reason could not swallow it. On continuing his meal he said, 'It wouldn't go down because I did not chew it.' Immediately afterwards, 'A person can eat because he chews.' After breakfast he said, 'When I stir the sugar in the tea it goes into my stomach.' I said, 'Is that certain?'— 'Yes, because it doesn't stay in the cup and it goes into my mouth.'

The certainties and facts acquired in this fashion obviously serve him as a standard of comparison for new phenomena and ideas offering themselves for elaboration. While his intellect was struggling with the elaboration of newly acquired conceptions and endeavouring to estimate those with which he was already acquainted and to get hold of others for comparison, he was led on to the scrutiny and registration of those he had already acquired and to the formation of new ideas.

'Real', 'Not real'—words that he had already been in the habit of using now obtained quite another meaning from the way in which they were used. Immediately after he had recognized the stork, Easter hare, etc., as fairy-tales and had decided that birth from the mother was something less beautiful but plausible and real, he said, 'But the locksmiths are real, for who would make boxes then?' Again, after he was relieved of the compulsion to believe in a, for him, incomprehensible and incredible invisible, omnipotent and omniscient being, he asked, 'I see what is, don't I . . . and what one sees is real. I see the sun and the garden, etc.' So these 'real' things had acquired for him a fundamental meaning that enabled him to distinguish all visible, actual things from those (however beautiful but unfortunately not true, not 'real') which occur only in wishes and phantasies. The 'reality-principle'[1] had established itself in him. When after the conversation with his father and mother he sided with the unbelief of his mother, he said, 'Electric cars are real and trains too, for I have ridden in them,' he had found, to begin with, in tangible things the standard by which to measure also the vague unreliable things that his feeling for the truth made him reject. To begin with, he measured them only against tangible physical things, but already when he said, 'I see the sun and the garden, but I don't see Aunt Marie's house and it does exist, doesn't it?' he had taken a further step along the road that transforms the actuality of what is only seen into the actuality of what is thought. He did this by establishing as 'real' something that on the basis of his intellectual development at the time seemed illuminating—and only something acquired in this way—and then adopting it.

The powerful stimulation and development of his reality sense

---

[1] Freud, 'Formulations on the Two Principles of Mental Functioning', *S.E.* **12.**

occurring in the second period were maintained undiminished in the third, but, doubtless as a result of the great mass of newly acquired facts, principally took the form of a scrutiny of earlier acquisitions and at the same time as a development of new ones; that is, elaboration of them into knowledge. The following examples of this are taken from questions and remarks he let fall at this time. Shortly after the conversation about God, he informed his mother once on being wakened that one of the L. girls had told him that she had seen a child made of china that could walk. When his mother asked him what that kind of information was called, he laughed and said, 'A story.' When she brought him his breakfast immediately afterwards he remarked, 'But breakfast is something real, isn't it? Dinner too is something real?' When he was forbidden to eat cherries because they were still unripe, he asked, 'Isn't it summer now? But cherries are ripe in summer!' During the day it was said that he should hit back when struck by other boys. (He was so gentle and unaggressive that his brother thought it necessary to give him this advice). In the evening he asked, 'Please, mamma, if a dog bites me can I bite him back again?' His brother had poured out a glass of water and had stood the glass on its somewhat rounded edge so that it spilled. Fritz said, 'The tumbler does not stand well on that border' (he calls every defining edge, all boundaries in general, for instance the knee-joint, a 'border'). 'Mamma, if I wanted to stand the glass on its border I should want to spill it, shouldn't I?' An earnest and frequently expressed wish of his is to be allowed to take off the little trousers that are the only articles of clothing he wears in the garden during the great heat, and to be able to be quite naked. As his mother really could not allege any very cogent reason why he must not do so, she replied that only quite tiny children go naked, that his playmates the L. children do not go naked, because it is not done. Whereupon he begged, 'Please let me be naked, then the L. children will say that I am naked and they will be allowed and then I shall be naked too.' Now too at last he showed not only comprehension of but also interest in money matters.[1] He repeatedly announced that one gets money for what one works at, and for what one sells in shops, that papa gets money for his work, but must pay for what is done for him. He also asked his

[1] The enlightenment that had evidently removed inhibitions and allowed his complexes to become more conscious probably determined the interest and understanding for money now appearing. Although his coprophilia had so far been expressed fairly frankly, it is probable that the general tendency to break down repressions now occurring would also make itself felt in reference to his anal erotism and thus give an impulse to the possibility of its sublimation — to an interest in money.

12

mother whether she gets money for the work she does in the house (housekeeping). When he again begged once for something that was not to be had at that time, he asked, 'Is it still war?' When it was explained that there was still a shortage of things and that they were dear and therefore difficult to buy, he asked, 'Are they dear because there are few of them?' Later he wanted to know which things for instance are cheap and which dear. Once he asked, 'When one gives a present one doesn't get anything for it, does one?'

Definition of his rights. Will, must, may, can

He showed too very obviously his need to have the limitations of his rights and powers clearly defined. He started this on the evening that he put the question, 'How long will a new day always come again?' when he asked his mother whether he must cease singing if she forbade him. At the time he showed at first lively satisfaction with her assurance that she would as far as possible let him do whatever he pleased, and he endeavoured to make himself understand by means of examples when this would and would not be possible. A few days later he got a toy from his father with the remark that it belonged to him when he was good. He told this to me and asked, 'Nobody can take away from me what belongs to me, can they? Not even mamma nor papa?' and was very content when I agreed with him. On the same day he asked his mother, 'Mamma you don't just forbid me to do things—only for a reason' (using approximately the words she had employed). He once said to his sister, 'I can do everything that I am able—whatever I am clever enough to do and what I am allowed.' Another time he said to me, 'I can do everything I want to, can't I? Only not be naughty.' Further he once asked at table, 'May I never eat naughtily then?' And on being consoled that he had eaten naughtily often enough already he remarked, 'And now I may not eat naughtily ever again?'[1] He frequently says when at play or at other times about things he likes doing, 'I do this—don't I—because I want to.' It is thus apparent that during these weeks he completely mastered the ideas of will, must, may and can. He said of a mechanical toy in which a cock jumps out of a little cage when the door that holds him in is opened, 'The cock jumps out because it must.' When the dexterity of cats was being discussed and it was remarked that a cat can clamber upon the roof, he added, 'When she wants to.' He saw a goose and asked whether it could run. Just at that moment the

[1] He repeatedly begs his sister to be very naughty again just for once and promises to love her very much for this. The knowledge that papa or mamma occasionally do something wrong also gives him great satisfaction, and on one such occasion he said, 'A mamma can lose things too, can't she?'

goose began to run. He asked, 'Is it running because I said it?' On this being denied, he continued, 'Because *it* wanted to?'

Omnipotence feeling

The decline of his 'omnipotence feeling' that had been so remarkably apparent some months previously seemed to me intimately associated with the important development of his reality sense that had already set in during the second period, but that had made still more noticeable progress since then. On different occasions he showed and shows a knowledge of the limitations of his own powers, just as he does not now demand so much from his environment. All the same his questions and remarks show over and over again that it is only a diminution that has occurred, that struggles still take place between his developing reality sense and this deep-rooted omnipotence feeling—that is to say, between the reality-principle and the pleasure-principle—frequently leading to compromise formations, but often decided in favour of the pleasure-principle. I adduce some questions and remarks from which I drew these inferences. One day after he had settled the matter of the Easter hare, etc., he enquired of me how his parents arrange the Christmas tree and whether the tree is made or really grows. Then he asked whether his parents could not decorate and give him a forest of Christmas trees at Christmas time? On the same day he begged his mother to give him the place B. (where he is to go in the summer), so that he could have it at once.[1] He was told early one morning that it was chilly and therefore he must be more warmly clad. Afterwards he said to his brother, 'It is cold, therefore it is winter. It is winter, therefore it is Christmas. To-day is Christmas eve. We shall have chocolates and nuts to nibble from the tree.'

Wishing

In general he often wishes and begs whole-heartedly and persistently for possible and impossible things, displaying much emotion and also impatience, which do not otherwise come much to the fore, as he is a quiet, unaggressive child.[2] For instance, when America

[1] At this time too he begged his mother, who was busy in the kitchen, to cook the spinach so that it would become potatoes.

[2] In his demonstrations of affection he is very tender, especially towards his mother but also towards others of his environment. He can at times be very stormy but is generally rather affectionate than rough. For a little time past however there has been a certain emotional element in the intensity of his questions. His love for his father showed somewhat exaggeratedly at about one and three-quarter years of age. At that time he loved him distinctly more than he did his mother. A few months previous to this his father had come home after an absence of almost a year.

was being spoken of: 'Mamma, please, I should like to see America—but not when I am big—I would like to see it at once, now.' He often uses this 'not when I am big—I want it at once, now', as a tag to wishes that he assumes will be met with the consolation of deferred fulfilment. But now he usually shows an adaptation to possibility and reality, even in the expression of wishes that at the time when his omnipotence belief was so much in evidence seemed utterly uninfluenced by any discrimination of their being realizable or unrealizable.

In asking to be given a forest of Christmas trees and the place B. as he did on the day following the conversation disillusioning him of so much (the Easter hare, stork, etc.), he was perhaps attempting to find how far the parental omnipotence, which was certainly much impaired by the loss of these illusions, did nevertheless still extend. On the other hand, when he tells me now what lovely things he will bring me from B. he always adds, 'If I can' or 'What I can', while formerly he never showed himself in the least influenced by the distinctions of possibility or impossibility in the formulation of wishes or promises (of all the things he would give me and others when he was big). Now when acquirements or handicrafts of which he is ignorant are being discussed (for instance, bookbinding), he says that he cannot do it and begs to be allowed to learn. But often it only requires a little incident in his own favour to render his omnipotence-belief active again; for instance, when he declared that he could work with machines like an engineer because he had got to know a little toy machine at his friend's, or when he often adds to his admission that he does not know something, 'If it is shown to me properly I shall know it.' In such cases he frequently enquires whether his papa is ignorant of it too. This clearly shows an ambivalent attitude. While the answer that papa and mamma too do not know something seems at times to content him, at other times he dislikes this knowledge and tries to modify it by proofs to the contrary. The servant once answered 'Yes' to his question whether she knew everything. Although afterwards she withdrew this claim, still for a time he would address the same question to her, trying by flattering remarks about her skill that had led him to this belief to get her to adhere to her original assertion of 'omniscience'. He had recourse once or twice to the assertion that 'Toni knows everything' (while all the time he was certainly convinced otherwise that she knew much less than his parents) when he was told that papa and mamma too could not do something, and it was evidently unpleasant for him at the time to believe this. He once begged me to uncover the water-pipe in the street because he wanted to see it from the inside. On my replying that I could neither do this nor put it to rights afterwards, he sought to put the objection aside by saying, 'But who would do such things if only the L. family and he and his parents were alone in the world?' He once told his mother that he had caught a fly and added, 'I have learnt to catch flies.' She enquired how he had learnt to do this? 'I tried to catch one and managed it and now I know how.' As he immediately afterwards enquired whether she had learnt 'to be a mamma' I think I am not mistaken in considering that—perhaps not quite consciously—he was making fun of her.

This ambivalent attitude—explained by the fact that the child puts himself in the place of the powerful father (which he hopes to occupy at some time), identifies himself with him but yet on the other hand would fain also do away with the power that restricts his ego—is certainly also responsible for this behaviour in reference to the omniscience of the parents.

The struggle between the reality and pleasure principles

From the way, however, that his increased reality sense obviously assists the decline of his omnipotence-feeling, and the way that the little fellow only gets the better of the latter by distinctly painful efforts under the pressure of his impulse for investigation, it seems to me to follow that this conflict between reality-sense and omnipotence-feeling also affects the ambivalent attitude. When the reality-principle gets the upper hand in this struggle and maintains the necessity for limiting the boundlessness of one's own omnipotence-feeling, a parallel need arises to discover a mitigation of this painful compulsion in detraction from parental omnipotence. If, however, the pleasure-principle conquers, it finds in parental perfection a support that it tries to defend. This might perhaps be one reason why the child, whenever it is apparently possible, makes attempts to rescue his belief both in his own and in his parents' omnipotence.

When, moved by the reality-principle, he attempts to make painful renunciation of his own boundless omnipotence-feeling, there probably arises in association with this the need, so obvious in the child, of defining the limits of his own and of parental power.

It seems to me as though in this case the child's urge to knowledge, being earlier and more strongly developed, had stimulated his feebler reality-sense and compelled him by overcoming his tendency to repression to make sure of the acquisition which was so new and so important to him. This acquisition, and especially the impairment of authority which went with it, will have renewed and so strengthened the reality-principle for him as to enable him to carry on successfully the progress in his thinking and knowing that began simultaneously with the influencing and overcoming of the omnipotence-feeling. This decline of the omnipotence-feeling that is brought about by the impulse to diminish parental perfection (which certainly assists in establishing the limits of his own as well as of their power) in turn influences the impairment of authority, so that an interaction, a reciprocal support would exist between the impairment of authority and the weakening of the omnipotence-feeling.

Optimism. Aggressive tendencies

His optimism is strongly developed, associated of course with his but little shaken omnipotence-feeling; it was formerly peculiarly noticeable but is even yet apparent on various occasions. Parallel with the decrease in his omnipotence-feeling, he has made great strides in adaptation to reality, but his optimism is very often stronger than any reality. This was particularly evident on the occasion of a very painful disillusionment, probably, I imagine, the severest of his life so far. His playmates, whose pleasant relations with him had been disturbed by external causes, displayed a completely altered behaviour towards him, instead of the love and affection hitherto shown. As there are several of them and they are older than he, they let him feel their power in every way and mocked and insulted him. Being unaggressive and gentle he tried persistently to win them back again by friendliness and entreaties, and for a time did not seem to admit their unkindness even to himself. For instance, although he could not but recognize the fact, he was absolutely disinclined to acknowledge that they told him lies, and when his brother had occasion once more to prove it to him and warned him not to believe them, Fritz pleaded, 'But they don't always tell lies.' Now, however, occasional if infrequent complaints showed that he had decided to recognize the wrongs done him. Aggressive tendencies now appeared quite openly; he spoke about really shooting them dead with his toy revolver, about shooting them in the eye; once too he spoke of striking them dead when he had been struck by the other children, and showed his death-wishes in this and other remarks as well as in his play.[1] At the same time, nevertheless, he did not give up his attempts to win them back again. Whenever they play with him again he seems to have forgotten all that has passed and to be quite content, though occasional remarks show that he is perfectly aware of the changed relations. As he is particularly affectionately attached to one of the little girls he suffered visibly in this affair, but carried it off with calm and great optimism. Once when

[1] He had earlier too, though very seldom, spoken of shooting dead and striking dead when he was very angry with his brother. Recently he has often enquired whom one may shoot dead, and declares, 'I may shoot dead anyone who wants to shoot me.'

he heard about dying and it was explained to him at his own request that everyone must die when they are old, he said to his mother, 'Then I shall die too, and you too and the L. children too. And then we shall all come back again and then they will be good again. It may be—perhaps.' When he found other play-fellows—boys—he seemed to have got over the whole thing and now declares repeatedly that he does not like the L. children any more.

The question of the existence of God. Dying

Since the conversation about the non-existence of God he has mentioned this matter only seldom and superficially and in general has not referred again to the Easter hare, Father Christmas, angels, etc. He did mention the devil again. He asked his sister what was in the encyclopedia. When she told him that one could look up in it everything that one did not know, he enquired, 'Is there anything in it about the devil?' To her reply, 'Yes, it says that there is no devil,' he made no further comment. He seems to have constructed only one theory about death, as first appeared from his remarks about the L. children, 'then we shall come back again'. On another occasion he said, 'I would like to have wings and be able to fly. Have the birds got wings when they are still dead? One is dead already, isn't one, when one isn't there yet?' In this case he did not wait for any answer and passed straight on to another subject. He made up phantasies at times afterwards about flying and having wings. When on one such occasion his sister told him about air-ships that take the place of wings for human beings, he was not very pleased. The subject of 'dying' gave him much preoccupation at this time. He once asked his father when he would die; he also told the servant that she would die some day, but only when she was very old, he added consolingly. In connection with this he said to me that when he died he would move only very slowly—like this (moving his index finger very slowly and very little)—and that I too when I died would only be able to move as slowly as that. Another time he asked me whether one never moves at all when asleep, and then said, 'Don't some people move and some not?' He saw a picture of Charles the Great in a book and learnt that he had died a long time ago. Thereupon he asked, 'And if I were the Emperor Charles would I have been dead already a long time?' He also asked if one did not eat for a very long time would one have to die then, and how long would it take before one died from it.

Pedogogic and psychological perspectives

New vistas open before me when I compare my observations of this child's greatly enhanced mental powers under the influence of his newly acquired knowledge with previous observations and experiences in cases of more or less unfavourable development. Honesty towards children, frank answering of all their questions, and the inner freedom which this brings about, influence mental development profoundly and beneficially. This safeguards thought from the tendency to repression which is the chief danger affecting it, *i.e.* from the withdrawal of instinctual energy with which goes a part of sublimation, and from the accompanying repression of ideational associations connected with the repressed complexes, whereby the sequence of thought is destroyed. In his article 'Symbolic Representation of the Pleasure and Reality Principles in the Oedipus Myth', Ferenczi (1912) says, 'These tendencies that, owing to the cultural upbringing of the race and of the individual, have become highly painful to consciousness and are therefore repressed, drag into repression with them a great number of other ideas and tendencies associated with these complexes and dissociate them from the free interchange of thoughts or at least prevent them from being handled with scientific reality.'

In this principal injury—*i.e.* to intellectual capacity, the shutting off of associations from the free interchange of thoughts—I think the *kind* of injury inflicted should also be taken into consideration: in what dimensions thought-processes had been affected, in how far the direction of thought, namely, in extent of breadth or depth, had been definitely influenced. The kind of injury responsible at this period of awakening intellect for the acceptance of ideas by consciousness, or their rejection as insufferable, would be of importance, in that this process persists as a prototype for life. The injury might occur in such a fashion that either 'penetration downwards' or else the 'quantity' occupying the broad dimension could be involved to a certain extent independently of one another.[1]

In neither case probably would a mere change in the direction be effected, and the force withdrawn from the one dimension benefit the other. As may be inferred from all other forms of mental development resulting from powerful repression, the energy undergoing repression remains as a matter of fact 'bound'.

If natural curiosity and the impulse to enquire into unknown as well as previously surmised facts and phenomena are opposed, then the more profound enquiries (in which the child is unconsciously afraid that he might meet with forbidden, sinful things) are also repressed along with it. Simultaneously, however, all impulses to investigate

---

[1] In Dr Otto Gross's book, *Die cerebrale Sekundärfunktion* (1902), he maintains there are two inferiority types, one due to a 'flattened' and one to a 'compressed' consciousness, the development of which he refers to 'typical constitutional changes of secondary functioning'.

deeper questions in general also become inhibited. A distaste for thorough investigation in and for itself is thus established and consequently the way opened for the innate irrepressible pleasure of asking questions to take effect merely upon the surface, to lead therefore to a merely superficial curiosity. Or, on the other hand, there may evolve the gifted type of person who is met so frequently in daily life and in science who, while possessed of a wealth of ideas, yet breaks down over the profounder issues of execution. Here also belongs the adaptable, clever, practical type of person who can appreciate superficial realities, but is blind to those that are only to be found in deeper connections—who is not able to distinguish the actual from the authoritative in intellectual matters. The dread of having to recognize as false the ideas forced upon him by authority as true, the dread of having to maintain dispassionately that things repudiated and ignored do exist, have led him to avoid penetrating more deeply into his doubts and in general to flee from the depths. In these cases development may, I think, have been influenced by injury to the instinct for knowledge, and hence also the development of the reality sense, due to repression in the depth dimension.

If, however, the repression affects the impulse for knowledge in such a way that from aversion to concealed and repudiated things the uninhibited pleasure in asking about these forbidden things (and with it the pleasure of interrogation in general, the quantity of the investigating impulse) is 'bound', that is, is affected in its broad dimension, then the pre-condition for a subsequent lack of interests would be given. If therefore the child has overcome a certain inhibiting period in regard to his investigating impulse and this has either remained active or has returned, he can, hampered now by an aversion to attacking new questions, direct the whole efficiency of his remaining unfettered energy upon the profundities of a few individual problems. In this way would develop the 'researcher' type who, attracted by some one problem, can devote the labour of a lifetime to it without developing any particular interests outside the confined sphere which suits him. Another type of learned man is the investigator who, penetrating deeply, is capable of real knowledge and discovers new and important truths, but fails utterly in regard to the greater or smaller realities of daily life—who is absolutely unpractical. It does not explain this to say that being absorbed in great tasks he no longer honours the little ones with his attention. As Freud showed in his investigation of parapraxis, the withdrawal of attention is only a side-issue. It is of no import as the fundamental cause, as the mechanism by which the parapraxis came about; it can at most exercise a predisposing influence. Even if we can assume that a thinker who is occupied with great thoughts has little interest over for the affairs of daily life, yet we see him fail also in situations in which from sheer necessity he would be bound to have the requisite interest, but in which he fails because he cannot tackle them practically. That he has developed in this way is, I think, owing to the reason that at a time when he ought to have recognized as real, primarily tangible, simple, everyday things and ideas, he was hindered in this knowledge in some way—a condition which at this stage would certainly not be a withdrawal of attention in consequence of a lack of interest in what was simple and immediately at hand, but could only be repression. It might be assumed that at some earlier time, having become inhibited about the knowledge of other but repudiated primitive things surmised by him to be real, the knowledge of the things of daily life, of the original tangible things presented to him, was also drawn down into this inhibition and repression. There would remain open for him therefore—whether he turned to it at once or perhaps only after overcoming a certain period of inhibition—only the way into the depths; in accordance with the processes of childhood which constitute a prototype, he would avoid breadth and the surface. Consequently he has not trodden or become acquainted with a path that is now for ever impassable for him, and which even at a later date he cannot tread simply and naturally, as may be done without any particular interest if one is acquainted and familiar with it from early days. He has jumped over this stage, which is locked up in repression; just as, on the contrary, the other, the 'utterly practical' person, was only able to reach this stage but repressed all access to the stages that led deeper.

It often happens that children who show by their remarks (mostly before the onset of the latent period) outstanding mental ability, and seem to justify great hopes for their future, later fall behind, and ultimately, though probably quite intelligent as adults, give no evidence of intellect above the average. The causes for this failure in development might include a greater or less injury to one or other dimension of the mind. This would be borne out by the fact that so many children who by their extraordinary pleasure in asking questions, and the number of them—or who by their constant investigations of the 'how' and 'why' of everything—fatigue those around them, yet after a time give it up and finally show little interest or superficiality of thought respectively. The fact that thinking—whether affected as a whole or in one or other dimension—could not expand in every direction in them, prevented the significant intellectual development for which as children they seemed destined. The important causes of injury to the impulse for knowledge and to the reality-sense, repudiation and denial of the sexual and primitive, set repression in operation by dissociation. At the same time, however, the impulse for

21

knowledge and the reality-sense are threatened with another imminent danger, not a withdrawal but an imposition, a forcing upon them of ready-made ideas, which are dealt out in such a fashion that the child's knowledge of reality dares not rebel and never even attempts to draw inferences or conclusions, whereby it is permanently and prejudicially affected.

We are apt to lay stress on the 'courage' of the thinker who, in opposition to usage and authority, succeeds in carrying out entirely original researches. It would not require so much 'courage' if it were not that children would need a quite peculiar spirit to think out for themselves, in opposition to the highest authorities, the ticklish subjects which are in part denied, in part forbidden. Although it is frequently observed that opposition develops the powers roused to overcome it, this certainly does not hold for the mental and intellectual development of children. To develop in opposition to any one does not signify any less dependence than submitting unconditionally to their authority; real intellectual independence develops between the two extremes. The conflict that the developing reality-sense has to wage with the innate tendency to repression, the process by which (as with the acquisitions of science and culture in the history of mankind) knowledge in individuals too must be painfully acquired, together with the unavoidable hindrances encountered in the external world, all these are amply sufficient as substitutes for the opposition supposed to act as an incitement to development, without endangering its independence. Anything else that has to be overcome in childhood —either as opposition or submission—any additional external resistance, is at least superfluous, but most often injurious because it acts as a check and a barrier.[1] Although great intellectual capacity may often be found alongside clearly recognizable inhibitions, still the former will not have been unaffected by prejudicial, hampering influences at the dawn of its activities. How much of an individual's intellectual equipment is only apparently his own, how much is dogmatic, theoretic and due to authority, not achieved for himself by his own free, unhampered thought! Although adult experience and insight have found the solution for some of the forbidden and apparently unanswerable questions—which are therefore doomed to repression —of childhood, this nevertheless does not undo the hindrance to

[1] Undoubtedly every upbringing, even the most understanding, since it presupposes a certain amount of firmness, will cause a certain amount of resistance and submission. Just as it is unavoidable and is one of the necessities of cultural development and education that there should be a greater or less amount of repression. An upbringing that is founded on psycho-analytic knowledge will restrict this amount to a minimum, however, and will know how to avoid the inhibiting and damaging consequences to the mental organism.

childish thought nor render it unimportant. For even if later on the adult individual is apparently able to surmount the barriers set up before his childish thought, nevertheless the way, be it defiance or fear, in which he deals with his intellectual limitations whatever they may be, remains the basis for the whole orientation and manner of his thought, unaffected by his later knowledge.

Permanent submission to the authority principle, permanent greater or less intellectual dependency and limitation, are based on this first and most significant experience of authority, on the relationship between the parents and the little child. Its effect is strengthened and supported by the mass of ethical and moral ideas that are presented duly complete to the child and which form just so many barriers to the freedom of his thought. Nevertheless—although they are presented to him as infallible — a more gifted childish intellect, whose capacity for resistance has been less damaged, can often wage a more or less successful battle against them. For although the authoritative manner of their introduction protects them, yet these various ideas must occasionally give proofs of their reality, and at such times it does not escape the more closely observant child that everything that is expected of him as so natural, good, right and proper, is not always considered in the same light in reference to themselves by the grown-ups who require it of him. Thus these ideas always afford points of attack against which an offensive, at least in the form of doubts, can be undertaken. But when the fundamental earlier inhibitions have been more or less overcome, the introduction of unverifiable, supernatural ideas introduces a new danger for thought. The idea of an invisible, omnipotent and omniscient deity is overwhelming for the child, all the more because two things markedly favour its effective force. The one is an innate need for authority. Freud says of this in *Leonardo da Vinci and a Memory of His Childhood* (*S.E.* **11**) 'Biologically speaking, religiousness is to be traced to the human child's long-drawn-out helplessness and need of help; and when at a later date he perceives how truly forlorn and weak he is when confronted with the great forces of life, he feels his condition as he did in childhood, and attempts to deny his own despondency by a regressive revival of the forces which protected his infancy.' As the child repeats the development of mankind he finds sustenance in this idea of the deity for his need for authority. But the innate omnipotence-feeling, too, 'the belief in the omnipotence of thought', which as we have learnt from Freud and from Ferenczi's 'Stages in the Development of the Sense of Reality' (1913), are so deeply rooted and therefore permanent in man, the feeling of one's own omnipotence, welcomes the acceptance of the idea of God. His own omnipotence-feeling leads the child to assume it for his environment too. The idea of God, therefore, which equips authority with the most complete omnipotence, meets the child's omnipotence-feeling half-way by helping to establish the latter and also by assisting to prevent its decline. We know that in this respect too the parental complex is significant and that the way in which the omnipotence-feeling is strengthened or destroyed by the child's first serious affection determines his development as an optimist or pessimist, and also the alertness and enterprise, or the unduly hampering scepticism of his mentality. For the result of development not to be boundless utopianism and phantasy but optimism, a timely correction must be administered by thought. The 'powerful religious inhibition of thought' as Freud calls it, hinders the timely fundamental correction of the omnipotence-feeling by thought. It does so because it overwhelms thought by the authoritative introduction of a powerful insuperable authority, and the decline of the omnipotence-feeling which can only take place early and in stages with the help of thought is also interfered with. The complete development of the reality-principle as scientific thought, however, is intimately dependent upon the child's venturing betimes upon the settlement he must make for himself between the reality and the pleasure principles. If this settlement is successfully achieved then the omnipotence-feeling will be put on a certain basis of compromise as regards thought, and wish and phantasy will be recognized as belonging to the former, while the reality-principle will rule in the sphere of thought and established fact.[1]

The idea of God, however, acts as a tremendous ally for this omnipotence-feeling, one that is almost insuperable because the childish mind—incapable of familiarizing itself with this idea by accustomed means, but on the other hand too much impressed by its overwhelming authority to reject it—does not even dare attempt a struggle or a doubt against it. That the mind may later at some time perhaps overcome even this hindrance, although many thinkers and scientists have never surmounted this barrier, and hence their work has ended at it, nevertheless does not undo the injury inflicted. This idea of God can so shatter the reality-sense that it dare not reject the incredible, the apparently unreal, and can so affect it that the recognition of the tangible, the near-at-hand, the so-called 'obvious' things in intellectual matters, is repressed together with the deeper processes of thinking. It is certain, however, that to achieve this first stage of knowledge and inference without a check, to accept the simple as well as the wonderful only on one's own substantiations and deductions, to incorporate in one's mental equipment only what is really known, is to lay the foundations for a perfect uninhibited

[1] Freud advances a peculiarly illuminating example for this in 'Formulations on the Two Principles of Mental Functioning', *S.E.* 12.

24

development of one's mind in every direction. The injury done can vary in kind and degree; it may affect the mind as a whole or in one or other dimension to a greater or less extent; it is certainly not obviated by a subsequent enlightened upbringing. Thus even after the primary and fundamental injuries to thought in earliest childhood, the inhibition set up later by the idea of God is still of importance. It does not therefore suffice merely to omit dogma and the methods of the confessional from the child's training, although their inhibiting effects on thought are more generally recognized. To introduce the idea of God into education and then leave it to individual development to deal with it is not by any manner of means to give the child its freedom in this respect. For by this authoritative introduction of the idea, at a time when the child is intellectually unprepared for, and powerless against, authority, his attitude in this matter is so much influenced that he can never again, or only at the cost of great struggles and expense of energy, free himself from it.

II

EARLY ANALYSIS

The child's resistance to enlightenment[1]

The possibility and necessity of analysing children is an irrefutable deduction from the results of analyses of adult neurotics, which always trace back into childhood the causes of illness. In his analysis of little Hans,[2] Freud as in everything else has shown us the way —a way that has been followed and further explored by Dr Hug-Hellmuth especially, as well as by others.

Dr Hug's very interesting and instructive paper delivered before the last Congress[3] gave much information as to how she varied the technique of analysis for children and adapted it to the needs of the child's mind. She dealt with analysis of children showing morbid or unfavourable developments of character, and remarked that she considered analysis was only adapted for children over six years of age.

I shall now, however, bring forward the question of what we learn from the analyses of adults and children that we could apply in regard to the mind of children under six, since it is well known that analyses of the neuroses reveal traumata and sources of injury in events, impressions or developments that occurred at a very early age, that is, before the sixth year. What does this information yield for prophylaxis? What can we *do* just at the age that analysis has taught us is so

[1] A paper read before the Berlin Psycho-Analytic Society, February 1921.
[2] 'Analysis of a Phobia in a five-year-old Boy', *S.E.* **10**.
[3] Sixth International Psycho-Analytical Congress at The Hague.

exceedingly important, not only for subsequent illnesses but also for the permanent formation of character and of intellectual development?

The first and most natural result of our knowledge will above all be the avoidance of factors which psycho-analysis has taught us to consider as grossly injurious to the child's mind. We shall therefore lay down as an unconditional necessity that the child, from birth, shall not share the parental bedroom; and we shall be more sparing of compulsory ethical requirements in regard to the tiny developing creature than people were with us. We shall allow him to remain for a longer period uninhibited and natural, less interfered with than has hitherto been the case, to become conscious of his different instinctive impulses and of his pleasure therein without immediately whipping up his cultural tendencies against this ingenuousness. We shall aim at a slower development, that allows room for his instincts to become partly conscious, and, together with this, for their possible sublimation. At the same time we shall not refuse expression to his awakening sexual curiosity and shall satisfy it step by step, even—in my opinion—withholding nothing. We shall know how to give him sufficient affection and yet avoid a harmful superfluity; above all we shall reject physical punishment and threats, and secure the obedience necessary for upbringing by occasionally withdrawing affection. Yet other, more detailed requirements of the kind might be set up that follow more or less naturally from our knowledge and that need not be gone into particularly here. Nor does it lie within the limits of this paper to go more closely into the question of how these demands can be fulfilled within the bounds of upbringing without injuring the development of the child as a civilized creature, nor burdening him with peculiar difficulties in his intercourse with a differently minded environment.

Just now I shall only remark that these educational requirements can be carried out in practice (I have repeatedly had the opportunity of convincing myself of this) and that they are followed by distinctly good effects and by a much freer development in many ways. Much would be achieved if it were possible to make of them general principles for upbringing. Nevertheless, I must at once make a reservation. I am afraid that even where insight and goodwill would fain fulfil these requirements, the inner possibility for this might not always be present on the part of an unanalysed person. In the meantime, however, for the sake of simplicity, I shall deal only with the more favourable instance where both the conscious and the unconscious will have made these educational requirements their own and carry them out with good results. We now return to our original enquiry: in these circumstances can these prophylactic measures prevent

26

the appearance of neuroses or of prejudicial developments of character? My observations have convinced me that even with this we often only achieve a part of what was aimed at, but have often actually made use only of a part of the requirements that our knowledge places at our disposition. For we learn from the analysis of neurotics that only a part of the injuries resulting from repression can be traced to wrong environmental or other prejudicial external conditions. Another and very important part is due to an attitude on the part of the child, present from the very tenderest years. The child frequently develops, on the basis of the repression of a strong sexual curiosity, an unconquerable disinclination to everything sexual that only a thorough analysis can later overcome. It is not always possible to discover from the analyses of adults—especially in a reconstruction—in how far the irksome conditions, in how far the neurotic predisposition, is responsible for the development of the neurosis. In this matter variable, indeterminate quantities are being dealt with. So much, however, is certain: that in strongly neurotic dispositions quite slight rebuffs from the environment often suffice to determine a marked resistance to all sexual enlightenment and a repression excessively burdensome to the mental constitution in general. We get confirmation of what we learn in the analysis of neurotics from observations of children, who afford us the opportunity of becoming acquainted with this development as it takes place. It appears, *e.g.*, in spite of all educational measures aiming amongst other things at an unreserved satisfying of sexual curiosity, that this latter need is frequently not freely expressed. This negative attitude may take the most varying forms up to an absolute unwillingness to know. At times it appears as a displaced interest in something else which is often marked by a compulsive character. At times this attitude sets in only after partial enlightenment and then, instead of the lively interest hitherto displayed, the child manifests a strong resistance against accepting any further enlightenment and simply does not accept it.

In the case I discussed in detail in the first part of this paper the beneficial educational measures referred to above were employed with good results, particularly on the child's intellectual development. The child was enlightened in so far that he was informed about the development of the fœtus within the maternal body and the birth-processes, with all the details which interested him. The father's part in the birth and the sexual act in general were not directly asked about. But even at that time I thought these questions were unconsciously affecting the boy. There were some questions that kept recurring frequently although they were answered in as detailed a fashion as possible. Here are a few examples: 'Please, mamma, where do the little tummy and the little head and the rest come from?'—'How can

27

a person move himself, how can he make things, how can he work?'
—'How does skin happen to grow on people?'—'How does it come
to be there?' These and a few other questions recurred repeatedly
during the period of enlightenment and during the two or three
months immediately following that were characterized by the marked
progress in development already referred to. I did not just at first
attribute its full meaning to this frequent recurrence of these questions, which was partly due to the fact that in the general increase
in the child's pleasure in asking questions its significance did not
strike me. From the way his impulse for investigation and his intellect
seemed to be developing I considered that demands for further enlightenment on his part were inevitable, and thought I ought to
adhere to the principle of gradual enlightenment corresponding to
the questions consciously asked.

After this period a change set in, in that mainly the questions
already mentioned, and others that were becoming stereotyped, recurred again, while those due to an obvious impulse for investigation
decreased and became mostly speculative in nature. At the same
time, preponderatingly superficial, thoughtless and apparently
groundless questions put in their appearance. He would ask again
and again what different things were made of and how they were
made. For instance. 'What is the door made of?'—'What is the bed
made of?'—'How is wood made?'—'How is glass made?'—'How
is the chair made?' Some of the trifling questions were, 'How does
all the earth get under the earth?'—'Where do stones, where does
water come from?' etc. There was no doubt that on the whole he
had completely grasped the answer to these questions and that their
recurrence had no intellectual basis. He showed too by his inattentive and absent-minded behaviour while putting the questions that
he was really indifferent about the answers in spite of the fact that
he asked them with vehemence. The number of questions, however,
had also increased. It was the well-known picture of the child who
torments his environment with his often apparently quite meaningless questions and to whom no replies are of any help.

After this recent period, not quite two months in duration, of increased brooding and superficial questions, there was a change. The
boy became taciturn and showed a marked distaste for play. He had
never played much or imaginatively but had always been fond of
movement games with other children. He would often too play at
coachman or chauffeur for hours together with a box, bench or chairs
representing the various vehicles. But games and occupations of this
kind ceased, and also the desire for the companionship of other children, with whom when he did come in contact with them he no longer
knew what to be at. He finally even showed signs of boredom in his

mother's company—a thing that had never occurred before. He also expressed dislike for being told stories by her, but was unchanged towards her in his tenderness and craving for affection. The absent-mindedness that he had often shown when asking questions also became now very frequent. Although this change could not but be noticed by an observant eye, still his condition could not be described as 'ill'. His sleep and general state of health were unexceptional. Although quiet, and, as a result of his lack of occupation, naughtier, he remained otherwise friendly, could be treated as usual and was cheerful. Undoubtedly too in recent months his inclination for food had left much to be desired; he began to be particular and showed marked distaste for certain dishes, but on the other hand, ate what he liked with a good appetite. He clung all the more passionately to his mother although, as stated, he was bored in her company. It was one of those changes that are usually either not noticed particularly by those in charge or, if they are, are not considered of any importance. Adults are generally so accustomed to notice passing or permanent changes in children without being able to find any reason for them that they are in the habit of regarding such variations in development as entirely normal, and to a certain extent with justice, as there is hardly any child but shows some neurotic traits and it is only the subsequent development of these and their number that constitute disease. I was particularly struck by his disinclination to be told stories, which was so utterly contrary to his former great enjoyment of them.

When I compared the strongly stimulated zest in questioning, which followed partial enlightenment and later became partly brooding, partly superficial, with the subsequent distaste for questions and the disinclination even to listen to stories, and when besides this I also recalled a few of the questions that had become stereotyped, I became convinced that the child's very powerful impulse for investigation had come into conflict with his equally powerful tendency to repression, and that the latter in refusing the explanations desired by his unconscious had entirely obtained the upper hand. After he had asked many and different questions as substitutes for those he had repressed, he had, in the further course of development, come to the point where he avoided questioning altogether and listening as well, as the latter might, unasked, provide him with what he refused to have.

I should like to revert here to some remarks about the paths of repression that I made in the first part of this paper. I spoke there of the well-known injurious effects of repression upon the intellect, owing to the fact that the repressed instinctive force is bound and not available for sublimation and that along with the complexes thought-associations are also submerged in the unconscious. In

29

connection with this I assumed that repression might affect the intellect along the whole of any developmental path, namely, both in the breadth and depth dimensions. Perhaps the two periods in the case I observed could in some way illustrate this previous assumption. Had the path for development been fixed at a stage when the child as a result of the repression of his sexual curiosity began to ask much and superficially, the intellectual injury might have occurred in the depth dimension. The associated stage of not asking and not wanting to hear might have led to the avoidance of the surface and of width of interest and to the exclusive direction into the depths.

After this digression I return to my original subject. My growing conviction that repressed sexual curiosity is one of the chief causes for mental changes in children was confirmed by the correctness of a hint that I had received a short time previously. In the discussion following my lecture to the Hungarian Psycho-Analytical Society, Dr Anton Freund had argued that my observations and classifications were certainly analytical, but not my interpretation, as I had taken only the conscious and not also the unconscious questions into consideration. At the time I replied that I was of opinion that it sufficed to deal with conscious questions so long as there was no convincing reason to the contrary. Now however I saw that his view was correct, that to deal only with conscious questions had proved to be insufficient.

I now held it advisable to give the child the remaining information that had so far been withheld from him. One of his questions at that time so infrequent, namely, which of all the plants grew from seeds, was taken as an opportunity to explain to him that human beings too came from seed and to enlighten him about the act of impregnation. He was absent-minded and inattentive, however, interrupted the explanation with another irrelevant question and showed absolutely no desire to inform himself about details. On another occasion he said that he had heard from the other children that for a hen to lay eggs a cock was needed too. He had hardly mentioned the subject, however, before he showed the obvious desire to be quit of it. He gave the distinct impression that he had entirely failed to comprehend this quite new piece of information and that he did not wish to comprehend it. Nor did the mental change previously described seem in any way affected by this advance in enlightenment.

His mother, however, managed by a joke with which a little tale was connected to rouse his attention and win his approval again. She said as she gave him a sweetmeat that it had been waiting for him for a long time and made up a little story about it. He was greatly entertained at this and expressed the wish to have it repeated several times, and then listened with enjoyment to the story about the woman upon whose nose a sausage grew at her husband's wish. Then quite spontaneously he began to talk, and from then on he told longer or shorter phantastic stories, originating sometimes in ones he had been told but mostly entirely original and providing a mass of analytic material. Hitherto the child had shown as little tendency to tell stories as to play. In the period following the first explanation he had, it is true, shown a strong tendency to story-telling and made various attempts at it, but on the whole these had been rather exceptions. These stories, that had nothing even of the primitive art that children usually employ in their tales in imitation of adult performances, produced the effect of dreams from which the secondary elaboration was lacking. Sometimes they began with a dream of the preceding night and then continued as stories, but they were of just the same type when he began them at once as stories. He told them with enormous zest; from time to time as resistances occurred—in spite of careful interpretations—he would interrupt them, only however to resume them again in a short time with enjoyment. I give a few excerpts from some of these phantasies:

'Two cows are walking together, then one jumps on to the back of the other and rides on her, and then the other one jumps on the other's horns and holds on tight. The calf jumps on to the cow's head too and holds tight on to the reins.' (To the question what are the cows' names, he gives those of the maid-servants.) 'Then they go on together and go to hell; the old devil is there; he has such dark eyes he can't see anything but he knows there are people there. The young devil has dark eyes too. Then they go on to the castle that Tom Thumb saw; then they go inside with the man who was with them and go up into a room and prick themselves with the spin' (spindle). 'Then they fall asleep for a hundred years; then they get up and go to the king, he is very pleased and asks them—the man, the woman and the children who were with them, whether they will not stay.' (To my question as to what had become of the cows, 'They were there too and the calves also.')—Churchyards and dying were being spoken of, whereupon he said, 'But when a soldier shoots someone he isn't buried, he just lies there because the driver of the hearse is a soldier too and he won't do it.' (When I ask 'Whom does he shoot for instance?' he first of all mentions his brother Karl, but then being a trifle alarmed, various other names of relations and acquaintances).[1] Here is a dream: 'My stick went on your head, then it took the press' (tablecloth press) 'and pressed on it with that.'—On bidding good-morning to his mother he said after she had caressed him, 'I shall climb up on you; you are a mountain and I climb up you.' A little

[1] He had remarked shortly before: 'I would like to see someone die; not what they are like when they are already dead, but when they are dying, then I would see too what they are like when they are dead.'

later he said, 'I can run better than you, I can run upstairs and you can't.'—After a further period he again began to ask a few questions with great ardour, 'How is wood made? How is the window-sill put together? How is stone made?' To the reply that they had always been like that, he said discontentedly, 'But what did it come out of?'

Hand in hand with this he began to play. He now played gladly and perseveringly, above all with others; with his brother or with friends he would play any conceivable thing, but he also began to play by himself. He played at hanging, declared that he had beheaded his brother and sister, boxed the ears of the decapitated heads and said, 'One can box the ears of this kind of head, they can't hit back', and called himself a 'hanger'. On another occasion I noticed him playing the following game. The chess-men are people, one is a soldier, the other is a king. The soldier says 'dirty beast' to the king. Thereupon he is put in prison and condemned. Then he is beaten but he does not feel this because he is dead. The king enlarges the hole in the soldier's pedestal with his crown and then the soldier comes to life again; on being asked whether he will do that again, he says 'no'; then he is merely arrested. One of the first games played was as follows; he played with his trumpet and said he was an officer, a standard-bearer and a trumpeter all in one, and, 'If papa were a trumpeter too and didn't take me to the war, then I would take my own trumpet and my gun and go to the war without him.'—He is playing with his little figures, amongst which are two dogs; one of them he has always called the beautiful and the other the dirty one. This time the dogs are gentlemen. The beautiful one is himself, the dirty one his father.

His games as well as his phantasies showed an extraordinary aggressiveness towards his father and also of course his already clearly indicated passion for his mother. At the same time he became talkative, cheerful, could play for hours with other children, and latterly showed such a progressive desire for every branch of knowledge and learning that in a very brief space of time and with very little assistance, he learnt to read. He showed such avidity in this connection as almost to seem precocious. His questions lost the stereotyped compulsive character. This change was undoubtedly the result of setting free his phantasy; my only occasional cautious interpretations merely served to a certain extent as an assistance in this matter. Before, however, I reproduce a conversation that strikes me as important I must refer to one point; the stomach had a peculiar significance for this child. In spite of information and repeated correction, he clung to the conception, expressed on various occasions, that children grow in the mother's stomach. In other ways too the stomach had a peculiar affective meaning for him. He would retort with 'stomach' in an apparently senseless way on all occasions. For instance, when another child said to him, 'Go into the garden' he answered, 'Go into your stomach'. He brought reproof upon himself because he repeatedly replied to the servants when they asked him where something was, 'In your stomach'. He would sometimes too complain at meal-times, though not often, of 'cold in the stomach', and declared it was from the cold water. He also displayed an active dislike for various cold dishes. About this time he expressed a curiosity to see his mother quite naked.   Immediately afterwards he remarked, 'I would like to see your stomach too and the picture that is in your stomach.' To her question, 'Do you mean the place inside which you were?' he replied 'Yes! I would like to look inside your stomach and see whether there isn't a child there.' Somewhat later he remarked, 'I am very curious, I would like to know everything in the world.' To the question what it was he so very much wanted to know, he said, 'What your wiwi and your kaki-hole are like. I would like' (laughing) 'to look inside when you are on the closet without your knowing and see your wiwi and your kaki-hole.' Some days later he suggested to his mother that they might all 'do kaki' on the closet at the same time and over one another, his mother, his brothers and sisters and on top himself. Isolated remarks of his had already indicated his theory, clearly demonstrated in the following conversation, that children are made of food and are identical with faeces. He had spoken of his 'kakis' as naughty children who did not want to come; moreover, in this connection he had immediately agreed with the interpretation that the coals that in one of his phantasies ran up and downstairs, were his children. Once too he addressed his 'kaki', saying he would beat it because it came so slowly and was so hard.

I will now describe the conversation. He is sitting early in the morning on the chamber, and explains that the kakis are on the balcony already, have run upstairs again and don't want to go into the garden (as he has repeatedly designated the chamber). I ask him, 'These are the children then that grow in the stomach?' As I notice this interests him I continue, 'For the kakis are made from the food; real children are not made from food.' He, 'I know that, they are made of milk.' 'Oh no, they are made of something that papa makes and the egg that is inside mamma.' (He is very attentive now and asks me to explain.) When I begin once more about the little egg, he interrupts me, 'I know that.' I continue, 'Papa can make something with his wiwi that really looks rather like milk and is called seed; he makes it like doing wiwi only not so much. Mamma's wiwi is different to papa's' (he interrupts) 'I know *that!*' I say, 'Mamma's wiwi is like a hole. If papa puts his wiwi into mamma's wiwi and makes the seed there, then the seed runs in deeper into her body and when it meets with one of the little eggs that are inside mamma, then that little egg begins to grow and it becomes a child.' Fritz listened with great interest and said, 'I would so much like to see how a child is made inside like that.' I explain that this is impossible until he is big because it can't be done till then but that then he will do it himself. 'But then I would like to do it to mamma.' 'That can't be, mamma can't be your wife for she is the wife of your papa, and then papa would have no wife.' 'But we could both do it to her.' I say, 'No, that can't be. Every man has only one wife. When you are big your mamma will be old. Then you will marry a beautiful young girl and she will be your wife.' He (nearly in tears and with quivering lips), 'But shan't we live in the same house together with mamma?' I, 'Certainly, and your mamma will always love you but she can't be your wife.' He then enquired about various details, how the child is fed in the maternal body, what the cord is made of, how it comes away, he was full of interest and no further resistance was to be noticed. At the end he said, 'But I would just once like to see how the child gets in and out.'

In connection with this conversation that solved his sexual theories to a certain extent, he showed for the first time a real interest in the hitherto rejected part of the explanation which he only now really assimilated. As occasional subsequent remarks have shown, he really has incorporated this information into the body of his knowledge. From this time on too his extraordinary interest in the stomach[1] decreased greatly. In spite of this I would not care to assert that it had been entirely stripped of its affective character and that he had quite given up this theory. As regards the partial persistence of an infantile sex theory in spite of its having been rendered conscious, I once heard from Ferenczi the view that an infantile sex theory is to a certain extent an abstraction derived from pleasurably toned functions, wherefore as the function continues to be pleasurably toned a certain persistence of the theory results. Dr Abraham, in his paper before the last Congress[2] showed that the origin of the formation of sexual theories is to be sought for in the child's disinclination to assimilate knowledge of the part played by the parent of the other sex. Róheim pointed to the same source for the sexual theories of primitive peoples.

[1] Part only of the symptom 'cold in the stomach' has been removed, namely, only in so far as it referred to the stomach. Later, though only infrequently, he declared he was 'cold in the belly'. The resistance to cold dishes has also persisted; the antipathy that had appeared in the last months to various dishes was generally unaffected by the analysis, only its object occasionally varied. His bowels usually act regularly but often slowly and with difficulty. The analysis has brought about no permanent alteration in this either, only occasional variations.

[2] Sixth International Psycho-Analytical Congress at The Hague: 'Manifestations of the Female Castration Complex' (1920).

In this case the partial adherence to this theory might also have been due to the fact that I had only interpreted a part of the wealth of analytic material and that a part of the unconscious anal erotism was still active. At any rate it was only with the solution of the sexual theory that resistance to the assimilation of knowledge of real sexual processes was overcome; in spite of a partial persistence[1] of his theory, the acceptance of the actual process was facilitated. To some extent he achieved a compromise between the theory still partly fixed in his unconscious and reality, as is best shown by one of his own remarks. He related another phantasy—it was nine months later, however— in which the womb figured as a completely furnished house, the stomach particularly was very fully equipped and was even possessed of a bath-tub and a soap-dish. He remarked himself about this phantasy, 'I know that it isn't really like that, but I see it that way.'

After this solution and acknowledgement of the actual processes, the Oedipus complex came very much to the fore. I give as an example the following dream-phantasy that he told me three days after the preceding conversation and that I partly interpreted for him. He begins with the description of a dream, 'There was a big motor that looked just like an electric car. It had seats too and there was a little motor that ran along with the big one. Their roofs could be opened up and then shut down when it rained. Then the motors went on and ran into an electric car and knocked it away. Then the big motor went on top of the electric car and drew the little one after it. And then they all got close together, the electric car and the two motors. The electric car had a connecting-rod too. You know what I mean? The big motor had a beautiful big silver iron thing and the little one had something like two little hooks. The little one was between the electric car and the motor. Then they drove up a high mountain and came down quickly again. The motors stayed there in the night too. When electric cars came they knocked them away and if any one did like that' (with an arm) 'they went backwards at once.' (I explain that the big motor is his papa, the electric car his mamma and the little motor himself, and that he has put himself between papa and mamma because he would so much like to put papa away altogether and to remain alone with his mamma and do with her what only papa is allowed to do.) After a little hesitation he agrees but continues quickly, 'The big and little motors then went away, they were in their house, they looked out of the window, it was a very big window. Then two big motors came. One was grandfather, the other was just papa. Grandmamma was not there, she was' (he hesitates a little

[1] He once said at the midday meal, 'The dumplings will slide straight along the path into the canal', and another time, 'The marmalade is going straight into the wiwi' (marmalade, however, is one of his antipathies).

and looks very solemn) '. . . she was dead.' (He looks at me, but as I remain quite unmoved, he goes on.)—'And then they all drove down the mountain together. One chauffeur opened the doors with his foot; the other opened with his feet the thing that one turns round' (handle). 'The one chauffeur became sick, that was grandpapa' (again he looks at me interrogatively but seeing me undisturbed continues). 'The other chauffeur said to him, "You dirty beast, do you want your ears boxed, I will knock you down at once." ' (I enquire who the other chauffeur was?) He, 'Me. And then our soldiers throw them all down; they were all soldiers—and smash the motor and beat him and smear his face with coal and stuff coal in his mouth too'; (reassuringly) 'he thought it was a sweetie, you know, and that is why he took it and it was coal. Then everyone was a soldier and I was the officer. I had a beautiful uniform and' (he holds himself erect) 'I held myself like this, and then they all followed me. They took his gun away from him; he could only walk like this' (here he doubles himself up). He continues kindly, 'Then the soldiers gave him a decoration and a bayonet because they had taken his gun from him. I was the officer and mamma was the nurse' (in his games the nurse is always the officer's wife) 'and Karl and Lene and Anna' (his brother and sisters) 'were my children and we had a lovely house too —it looked like the king's[1] house from the outside; it was not quite finished; there were no doors and the roof wasn't on but it was very beautiful. We made for ourselves what was wanting.' (He now accepts my interpretation of the meaning of the unfinished house, etc. without any particular difficulty.) 'The garden was very beautiful, it was up on the roof. I always took a ladder to get up to it. All the same I always managed to get up to it quite well, but I had to help Karl, Lene and Anna. The dining-room was very beautiful too and trees and flowers grew in it. It does not matter, it's quite easy, you put down some earth and then the things grow. Then grandpapa came into the garden quite quietly like this' (he imitates the peculiar gait again), 'he had a shovel in his hand and wanted to bury something. Then the soldiers shoot at him and' (again he looks very solemn), 'he dies.' After he has gone on talking for a long time about two blind kings of whom he now himself says that the one is his papa and the other his mamma's papa, he relates, 'The king had shoes as long as to America, you could get inside them and there was plenty of room. The long-clothes babies were put to bed in them at night.' Subsequent to this phantasy the pleasure in play was increased and became permanent. He now played alone for hours with the same

[1] Once when his mother said endearingly to him 'my dollykins' he remarked 'say dollykins to Lene or Anna, it does better for a girl, but say "my darling little king" to me.'

amount of pleasure as it gave him to relate these phantasies.[1] He would also say straight out, 'Now I shall play what I told you,' or 'I won't tell this but just play it.' Thus while unconscious phantasies are usually ventilated in play-activities, in this case it seemed probable, as no doubt in other similar cases, that the inhibition of phantasy was the cause of the play-inhibition, both of which were simultaneously removed. I observed that the games and occupations that had been previously pursued now dropped into the background. I mean especially the endless 'chauffeur, coachman, etc.' game that had generally consisted in his shoving benches, chairs or a box, up against one another and sitting on them. He had also never given up running to the window whenever he heard a vehicle pass and was quite unhappy if he ever missed one. He could put in hours standing at the window or at the front door mainly in order to look at the passing carriages. The vehemence and exclusiveness with which he pursued these occupations led me to consider them as of the nature of compulsions.[2]

Latterly, while he was showing such marked boredom, he had given up also this play-substitute. When, on one occasion, in order to find an occupation for him, he was urged to make a carriage in a new way as this would be so interesting, he replied, 'Nothing is interesting.' When, simultaneously with making phantasies, he took to playing, or more correctly, made his first proper start at playing, some of his games which he mostly concocted with the help of little figures, animals, people, carts and bricks consisted, it is true, in drives and changes of house; but these only constituted a part of his play that was carried on in the most varied ways and with a powerful development of phantasy such as he had never previously shown. Usually it came finally to fights between Indians, robbers or peasants on the one hand and soldiers on the other, whereupon the latter were always represented by himself and his troops. It was mentioned at the end of the war when his father ceased being a soldier that he gave up his regimentals and equipment. The child was much struck by this, especially by the idea of delivering up the bayonet and rifle. Immediately afterwards he played that peasants were coming to steal something from the soldiers. The soldiers however maltreat them dreadfully and kill them. The day after the motor phantasy he played the

[1] At this time he one morning made a 'tower' as he called it out of his bedclothes, crept into it and announced, 'Now I am the chimney-sweep and sweep the chimneys clean.'

[2] The interest in vehicles as well as in doors, locksmiths and locks is still strongly maintained; it therefore merely lost its compulsive and exclusive nature, so that in this instance, too, the analysis did not affect the helpful repression but only overcame the compulsive force.

following game, which he explained to me, 'An Indian is put in prison by the soldiers. He admits that he was naughty to them. They say, "We know that you were even naughtier than that." They spit on him, do wiwi and kaki on him, put him in the closet and do everything on top of him. He screams and the wiwi goes right into his mouth. One soldier goes away and another one asks him, "Where are you going?" "To look for manure to throw on him." The naughty man does wiwi on a shovel and it is thrown in his face.' To my question as to what exactly he had done, he replied, 'He was naughty. He didn't let us go to the closet and do it there.' He then further relates that in the closet, along with the naughty person who was put there, there are two people making works of art.—At this time he repeatedly addressed the toilet paper with which he cleansed himself after a movement of the bowels in a derisive fashion, 'My dear sir, kindly eat it up.' In reply to a question he says that the paper is the devil who is to eat the kaki.—Another time he relates, 'A gentleman lost his tie, and he searched for it a lot. At last he finds it after all.'— Again he once related of the devil that his neck and his feet had been cut off. The neck could walk only when feet had been made for it. Now the devil could only lie, he could not walk on the road any more. Then people thought he had died. And once he looked out of the window; somebody held him, it was a soldier, and he pushed him out of the window and then he died. This phantasy seemed to me to account for a (for him unusual) dread that had made its appearance a few weeks earlier. He was looking out of the window and the servant had stood behind him and held him; he displayed fear and only quietened when the girl let him alone. In a subsequent phantasy the fear showed itself as the projection of his unconscious aggressive wishes[1]—in a game in which an enemy officer is killed, mishandled, and comes to life again. In reply to the enquiry as to who he is, he says, 'I am papa, of course.' Thereupon everybody becomes very friendly with him and says (here Fritz's voice becomes very gentle), 'Yes, you are papa, then please come along here.'—In another phantasy in which, in the same way, the captain comes to life again after the most varied ill-treatment including blinding and insult, he relates that after that he was quite good to him and adds, 'I just gave him back what he had done to me and then I wasn't angry with him any

---

[1] Especially recently during this period of observation, he showed occasionally both in phantasy as well as in his games a shrinking from, an alarm at, his own aggressiveness. He would sometimes say in the midst of an exciting game of robbers and Indians that he did not want to play any more, that he was frightened, and at the same time he certainly did show a tremendous effort to be brave. At that time, too, if he had knocked himself he would say, 'It's all right; that is the punishment because I was naughty.'

more. If I hadn't given it back to him I would have been angry.'—
He now very much likes to play with dough and says that he cooks
in the closet.[1] (The closet is a little cardboard box with a depression
in it that he uses in his games.) While at play he showed me once
two soldiers and a nurse and said that those were himself and his
brother and his mamma. To my question which of the two was him
he said, 'The one that has something prickly down there is me.' I
ask what is there down there that pricks? He, 'A wiwi.' 'And does
that prick?' He, 'Not in the game, but really—no, I am wrong, not
really but in the game.'—He related more and more numerous and
extensive phantasies, very frequently about the devil but also about
the captain, Indians, robbers and wild animals as well, towards
whom both in his phantasies and his accompanying games his sadism
was clearly shown, as well as on the other hand his wishes associated
with his mother. He often describes how he has put out the eyes, or
cut off the tongue, of the devil or the enemy officer or the king, and
he even possesses a gun that can bite like a water animal. He gets
stronger and more powerful all the time, he cannot be killed in any
way, he says repeatedly that his cannon is so big that it reaches to
the skies.

I did not consider it necessary to make any further interpretations
and at this time, therefore, only quite occasionally and more as a
hint, rendered this or that individual matter conscious. Moreover, I
got the impression, from the whole trend of his phantasies and games
and from occasional remarks, that part of his complexes had become
conscious or at least preconscious for himself and I considered that this
sufficed. Thus he remarked once as he sat on the chamber that he
was going to make rolls. When his mother, falling in with him, said,
'Well, make your rolls quickly then,' he remarked, 'You are pleased
if I have dough enough.' And added at once, 'I said dough instead
of kaki.' 'How clever I am,' he remarked when he had done, 'I have
made such a big person. If someone gave me dough I would make a
person out of it. I only need something pointed for the eyes and
buttons.'

Two months approximately had passed since I started to give him
occasional interpretations. My observations were now interrupted for
an interval of more than two months. During this time anxiety (fear)
made its appearance; this had already been foreshadowed by his refusing, when playing with other children, to carry on his latterly
much-beloved games of robbers and Indians. Except for a time when
he had had night-terrors between two and three years of age he had
never apparently been subject to fear, or at any rate indications of

[1] As a little child he was for a time fond of modelling in sand or earth, but not
for long or persistently.

it had not been observed. The anxiety now becoming manifest may therefore have been one of the symptoms rendered evident by the progress of the analysis. It was probably also due to his attempts at a more powerful repression of things that were becoming conscious. The release of fear was probably occasioned by listening to Grimm's fairy-tales, to which he had latterly become much attached and with which it was repeatedly associated.[1] The fact that his mother was indisposed for a few weeks and unable to concern herself much with the child, who was otherwise very habituated to her, probably facilitated the conversion of libido into anxiety and may have had something to do with it. Fear was displayed mostly before falling asleep, which was now often a lengthy business compared with formerly, and also by occasional fright-starts out of sleep. But a set-back was to be observed in other ways as well. His playing alone and story-telling had greatly decreased; he was so zealous about learning to read as to seem decidedly over-zealous, for he frequently wanted to learn for hours at a stretch and was constantly practising. He was also much naughtier and less cheerful.

When I again had an opportunity—although only occasionally— of concerning myself with the child, I obtained from him, but, contrary to what had previously been the case, only against very strong resistances, an account of a dream that had frightened him very much and of which he was still afraid even by day. He had been looking at picture-books with riders in them and the book opened and two men came out of them. He and his brother and sisters clung to their mother and wanted to run away. They came to the door of a house and there a woman said to them, 'You can't hide here.' But they did hide all the same so that the men could not find them. He told this dream in spite of great resistances that increased so much when I began the interpretation that, not to overstimulate them, I made it very brief and left it incomplete. I got little in the way of associated ideas, merely that the men had had sticks, guns and bayonets in their hands. When I explained that these meant his father's big wiwi that he both wishes for and is afraid of, he retorted that 'the weapons were hard but the wiwi is soft'. I explained, however, that the wiwi too becomes hard just in connection with what he wishes to do himself, and he accepted the interpretation without much resistance. He then further related that it seemed to him sometimes as though the one man had stuck in the other and there was only one man!

Undoubtedly the hitherto little noticed homosexual component was now coming more to the fore, as is shown too in his subsequent dreams and phantasies. Here is another dream that was not, how-

[1] Before the analysis was started he had a strong dislike to Grimm's fairy-tales, which, when the change for the better set in, became a marked preference.

ever, associated with feelings of fear. Everywhere, behind mirrors, doors, etc., were wolves with long tongues hanging out. He shot them all down so that they died. He was not afraid because he was stronger than them. Subsequent phantasies also dealt with wolves. Once when he was frightened again before falling asleep, he said about it that he had been frightened of the hole in the wall where the light peeped in (an opening in the wall for heating purposes) because on the ceiling it looked like a hole too, and a man might get up from there with a ladder on to the roof. He also spoke about whether the devil did not sit in the hole in the stove. He recounted that he saw the following in a picture book. A lady is in his room. Suddenly she sees that the devil is sitting in the hole in the stove and his tail is sticking out. In the course of his associations it is shown that he was afraid that the man with the ladder might step on him, hurt him in the belly and finally he owns up that he was afraid for his wiwi.

Not long afterwards I heard the expression, now become very infrequent, of 'cold in the belly'. In a conversation about stomach and belly in connection with this, he related the following phantasy. 'There is a room in the stomach, in it there are tables and chairs. Someone sits down on a chair and lays his head on the table and then the whole house falls down, the ceiling on to the floor, the table too tumbles down, the house tumbles down.' To my question, 'Who is the someone and how did he get inside?' he answers, 'A little stick came through the wiwi into the belly and into the stomach that way.' In this instance he offered little resistance to my interpretation. I told him that he had imagined himself in his mamma's place and wished his papa might do with him what he does with her. But he is afraid (as he imagines his mamma to be too) that if this stick—papa's wiwi —gets into his wiwi he will be hurt and then inside his belly, in his stomach, everything will be destroyed, too.—Another time he told about the dread he had for a particular Grimm's fairy-tale. It was the tale of a witch who offers a man poisoned food but he hands it on to his horse who dies of it. The child said he was afraid of witches because, all the same, it might be that it wasn't true what he had been told about there not being any witches really. There are queens also who are beautiful and yet who are witches too, and he would very much like to know what poison looks like, whether it is solid or fluid.[1] When I asked him why he was afraid of anything so bad from his mother, what had he done to her or wished about her, he admitted that when he was angry he had wished that she as well as his papa might die and that he had on occasion thought to himself 'dirty

[1] This seems to be the reason for the interest that had recently been manifested in the question how it is that water is fluid, and in general how it is that things are solid and fluid. The anxiety was probably already active in this interest.

mamma'. He also acknowledged that he was angry with her when she forbade him to play with his wiwi. In the course of the conversation, moreover, it became apparent that he was also afraid of getting poison from a soldier, and a strange soldier too, who watched him, Fritz, in front of a shop-window when he put his feet up on a cart in order to jump on to it. In connection with my interpretation that the soldier is his papa who will punish him for his naughty intentions of jumping on to the cart—his mamma—he enquired about the sexual act itself, which he had not hitherto done. How the man could put his wiwi in—whether papa would like to make another child— how big must one be to be able to make a child—whether auntie could do it with mamma, etc.? The resistance is once more lessened. To begin with, before he starts relating things he enquires quite cheerfully whether what he finds 'horrid' will, after I have explained it to him, become pleasant again for him just as with the other things so far. He also says that he is not afraid any more of the things that have been explained to him even when he thinks of them.

Unfortunately the meaning of the poison was not further cleared up, as no more associated ideas could be obtained. In general, interpretation by means of associations was only sometimes successful, usually subsequent ideas, dreams and stories, explained and completed what had gone before. This accounts, too, for my sometimes very incomplete interpretations.

In this case I had a great wealth of material that for the most part remained uninterpreted. As well as his dominant sexual theory, several other different birth-theories and trends of thought could be perceived, and while they apparently ran parallel with one another, now one, now another, was from time to time more in prominence. The witch in the last-mentioned phantasy only introduces a figure (at the time frequently recurring) that he had, it seems to me, obtained by division of the mother-imago. I see this too in the occasionally ambivalent attitude towards the female sex that has recently become evident in him. In general, indeed, his attitude towards women as well as towards men is a very good one, but occasionally I observe that he considers little girls and also grown-up women with an unreasonable antipathy. This second female imago that he has split off from his beloved mother, in order to maintain her as she is, is the woman with the penis through whom, for him also apparently, the path leads to his now clearly indicated homosexuality. The symbol for the woman with the penis is in his case too the cow, an animal he does not like, while he is very much attached to the horse.[1] To

[1] From the material obtained so far I am not yet quite clear about the meaning of the horse; it seems sometimes to represent a masculine, sometimes a feminine symbol.

give only one example of this, he shows disgust at the foam about the cow's mouth and declares she wants to spit at people with it, but that the horse wants to kiss him. That for him the cow represents the woman with the penis is unequivocally shown, not only in his phantasies but also in various remarks. He has repeatedly on urinating identified penis with cow. For instance, 'The Cow is letting down milk into the pot.' Or, as he opens his trousers, 'The cow is looking out of the window.' The poison that the witch hands him might probably be determined, too, by the theory of impregnation from eating which he also had had. Some months previously hardly anything was yet noticeable of this ambivalent attitude. When he heard someone say a certain lady was disgusting, he asked quite astonished, 'Can a lady be disgusting?'

He related another dream associated with feelings of anxiety and again with strong indications of resistance. He accounted for the impossibility of telling it by saying it was such a long one, he would need the whole day to tell it. I replied that then he would just tell me part of it. 'But it was just the length that was horrid,' was his reply. That this 'horrid length' was the wiwi of the giant about whom the dream was concerned soon dawned on him. It reappeared in various forms as an aeroplane that people brought to a building, where there were no doors to be seen and no ground all round about it, and yet the windows were crowded with people. The giant himself was hung all over with people and snatched at him too. It was a phantasy of the maternal and paternal bodies as well as the wish for the father. His birth-theory too, however, the idea that he conceives and bears his father (at other times his mother) by the anal route, is also at work in this dream. At the end of this dream he is able to fly alone, and with the help of the other people who have already got out of the train, he locks the giant into the moving train and flies away with the key. He interpreted a great deal of this dream for himself along with me. Generally he was very interested in interpreting and would ask whether it was quite 'deep inside' him where he thought all the things that he did not know about himself, and whether every grown-up could explain it, etc.

He remarked about another dream that it was pleasant but that he could only remember that there was an officer who had a big coat-collar and that he also put on a similar big coat-collar. They came out of somewhere together. It was dark and he fell. After the interpretation that it dealt again with his father and that he wanted a wiwi similar to his, it suddenly occurred to him what the unpleasant thing had been. The officer had threatened him, had held him, not let him get up, etc. Of the free associations that he gave quite willingly this time, I shall only emphasize one detail that occurred to him in reference to the question where it was that he had come out of with the officer. The yard of a shop occurred to him that he had liked because there were little laden waggons that ran in and out of it on narrow rails—again the wish to do to mamma simultaneously with papa what the latter does with her, in which however he fails, whereupon he projects upon his father his own aggressiveness against the latter. Here too it seems to me that very powerful anal-erotic and homosexual determinants (indubitably present in the numerous devil-phantasies of where the devil lives in cavities or in a peculiar house) are at work.

After this period of approximately six weeks' renewed observation, with the associated analysis, chiefly of the anxiety-dreams, the anxiety entirely disappeared. Sleep and going to sleep were once more impeccable. Play and sociability left nothing to be desired. Along with the anxiety there had been a mild phobia of street children. Its foundation in fact was that street boys had repeatedly threatened and annoyed him. He showed fear of crossing the street by himself and could not be persuaded to do so. Owing to the intervention of a recent journey I could not analyse this phobia. Apart from this, however, the child made an excellent impression; when I had occasion to see him again a few months later this impression was strengthened. In the meantime he had lost his phobia in the following way, as he himself informed me. Soon after my departure he first of all ran across the street with his eyes shut. Then he ran across with his head turned away, and finally he walked across quite quietly. On the other hand, he showed (probably as a result of this attempt at self-cure— he assured me proudly that now he was afraid of nothing!) a decided disinclination for analysis and also an aversion to telling stories and to listening to fairy-tales; this was the only point, however, on which an unfavourable change had occurred. Was the apparently permanent—as I was able to satisfy myself six months later—cure of the phobia only a result of his attempted self-cure? Or not perhaps, at least in part, a subsequent effect of the treatment after it had stopped, as may often be observed with the disappearance of one or other symptom after an analysis.

Moreover I would rather not use the expression 'completed treatment' for this case. These observations with their only occasional interpretations could not be described as a treatment; I would rather describe it as a case of 'upbringing with analytic features'. For the same reason I should not like to assert that it was ended at the point up to which I have here described it. The display of so active a resistance to analysis, and the unwillingness to listen to fairy-tales seem to me in themselves to render it probable that his further upbringing will afford occasion for analytic measures from time to time.

This brings me to the conclusion I shall draw from this case. I am of the opinion that no upbringing should be without analytic help, because analysis affords such valuable and, from the point of view of prophylaxis, as yet incalculable assistance. Even if I can base this claim only on one case in which analysis proved very helpful as an aid to upbringing, yet on the other hand I am supported by many observations and experiences that I have been enabled to make on children who were brought up without the help of analysis. I will adduce only two instances of child development[1] that are well known to me and seem suitable as examples, as they led neither to neurosis nor to any abnormal development and are therefore to be reckoned as normal. The children concerned are very well disposed and very sensibly and lovingly brought up. For instance, it was a principle of their upbringing that all questions were permitted and were gladly answered; in other respects, too, a greater degree of naturalness and freedom of opinion was allowed them than is generally the case, but, though tenderly, they were yet firmly guided. Only one of the children made use (and that only to a very limited extent) of the entire liberty to ask questions and obtain information for the purpose of sexual enlightenment. Much later—when he was almost grown up—the boy said that the correct answer given to his enquiry about birth had seemed to him completely inadequate and that this problem had continued to occupy his mind to a considerable extent. The information had probably not been complete, though it corresponded to the question asked, as it had not included the part played by the father. It is remarkable, nevertheless, that the boy, although privately preoccupied with this problem, for reasons of which he himself was not aware, should never have asked any related questions as he had no occasion to doubt the willingness to answer him. This boy in his fourth year developed a phobia of intimate contact with other people—particularly adults—and in addition a phobia of beetles. These phobias lasted for a few years and were gradually almost conquered by the help of affection and habituation. The disgust for little creatures was never lost, however. Afterwards, too, the boy never showed any desire for society, even if he no longer had any direct aversion to it. For the rest, he has developed well psychically, physically and intellectually and is normally healthy. But a marked unsociableness, reserve and retiredness into himself, as well as a few associated traits, seem to me to have remained as traces of the otherwise happily conquered phobias, and as permanent elements in the formation of his character. The second example is a girl who showed herself in her first years of life to be really unusually gifted and eager

[1] The children are brother and sister in a family with which I am well acquainted, so that I have a detailed knowledge of their development.

for knowledge. From about her fifth year, however, the child's impulse for investigation weakened[1] very much and she gradually became superficial, had no zest for learning and no depth of interest, even though good intellectual capacities were undoubtedly present and she has, so far at least (she is now in her fifteenth year) shown only an average intellect. Even if the hitherto good and approved principles of education have achieved much for the cultural development of humanity, the upbringing of the individual has nevertheless remained, as the best pedagogues knew and know, an almost insoluble problem. Whoever has an opportunity of observing the development of children, and of occupying himself more in detail with the characters of adults, knows that often the most gifted children suddenly fail without any discoverable cause and in the most various ways. A few who till then were good and amenable become shy and difficult to manage or downright rebellious and aggressive. Cheerful and friendly children become unsociable and reserved. With others whose intellectual gifts promised the rarest inflorescence, this is suddenly nipped in the bud. Brilliantly gifted children often fail over some little task and then lose courage and self-confidence. It often happens of course, too, that such difficulties of development are happily overcome. But the lesser difficulties, that are often smoothed away by parental affection, frequently appear again in later years as great insuperable ones that may then lead to a breakdown or at least to much suffering. The injuries and inhibitions affecting development are countless, not to speak of those individuals who later fall victims to neurosis.

Even if we recognize the need for introducing psycho-analysis into upbringing, this does not entail throwing over hitherto good and approved principles of education. Psycho-analysis would have to serve education as an assistant—as a completion—leaving untouched the foundations hitherto accepted as correct.[2] Really good pedagogues have at all times striven—unconsciously—towards what

[1] This child never asked for sexual enlightenment at all.

[2] In my experience I found that outwardly little in education was changed apparently. About eighteen months have elapsed from the date of the close of the observations here retailed. Little Fritz goes to school, adapts himself excellently to its requirements and is looked upon there as elsewhere as a well-brought-up child, who is quite unembarrassed and natural and behaves appropriately. The essential difference, hardly noticeable to the uninitiated observer, lies in a completely altered basic attitude as regards the relations of teacher and child. Thus while an absolutely frank and friendly relationship has evolved, pedagogic demands which otherwise often only prevail by the exercise of great authoritative emphasis and with difficulty are quite easily carried out, since the child's unconscious resistances to this have been overcome by the analysis. The result, therefore, of education with the help of analysis is that the child fulfils the usual educational requirements but on the basis of entirely different presuppositions.

was right, and have endeavoured by love and understanding to get into touch with the deeper, sometimes so incomprehensible and apparently reprehensible, impulses of the child. Not the pedagogues but their expedients were to blame if they were unsuccessful or only partly successful in this endeavour. In Lily Braun's beautiful book, *Memoiren einer Sozialistin*, we read how, in the endeavour to win the sympathy and confidence of her stepsons (boys, I think, of about ten and twelve years of age), she tried, taking as starting-point her approaching confinement, to enlighten them about sexual matters. She is saddened and helpless when she meets with open resistance and refusal and has to abandon the attempt. How many parents whose greatest endeavour is to preserve their children's love and trust are suddenly faced with a situation where—without understanding it— they have to acknowledge they have never really possessed either.

To return to the example that has here been described in detail. Upon what grounds was psycho-analysis introduced into the up-bringing of this child? The boy was suffering from a play-inhibition that went hand in hand with an inhibition against listening to or telling stories. There were also an increasing taciturnity, hyper-criticalness, absent-mindedness and unsociableness. Although the child's mental condition as a whole could not at this stage have been described as an 'illness', still one is justified in making assumptions by analogy about possible developments. These inhibitions as regards play, story-telling, listening, and further, the hypercriticalness about trifles and the absent-mindedness, might at a later stage have developed into neurotic traits, and the taciturnity and unsociability into traits of character. I must here append the following as significant: the peculiarities indicated here had to some degree been present —though not so noticeably—since the child was very small; it was only as they developed and as others were added that they afforded the more striking impression that led to my regarding the interference of psycho-analysis as advisable. Before this, however, and also afterwards, he had an unusually thoughtful expression which, as he began to speak more fluently, had no relation to the normal, but in no way strikingly clever, remarks to which he gave utterance. His cheerful chattiness, his marked need for companionship, not only with child-ren but also where adults are concerned, with whom he converses equally gladly and freely, are now all in marked contrast with his former character.

I was, however, able to learn something else from this case; namely, how advantageous and necessary it is to intervene with analysis quite early in upbringing in order to prepare a relationship to the child's unconscious as soon as we can get in touch with his conscious. Then probably the inhibitions or neurotic traits could be easily removed as they were beginning to develop. There is no doubt that the normal three-year-old, probably indeed the still younger child, who so often shows such lively interests, is already intellectually capable of grasping the explanations given him as well as anything else. Probably much better than the older child, who is already affectively hampered in such matters by a more strongly fixed resistance, while the little child is far nearer to these natural things so long as upbringing has not extended its injurious influences too far. *This* would be, then, much more than in the case of this already five-year-old boy, an upbringing with the aid of analysis.

However great the hopes that might be associated with a general education of this kind for the individual and for the many, yet on the other hand a too far-reaching effect need not be feared. Wherever we find ourselves confronted with the unconscious of the quite tiny child, we shall certainly also find ourselves confronted with all his complexes complete. In how far are these complexes phylogenetic and innate, or in how far already ontogenetically acquired? According to A. Stärcke, the castration complex has an ontogenetic root for the infant in the periodical disappearance of the maternal breast, which he considers to be a belonging of his. The rejection of faeces is regarded as another root for the castration complex. In the case of this boy, where threats were never used and where pleasure in masturbation was pretty frankly and fearlessly shown, there was nevertheless a very strongly marked castration complex that had certainly developed partly on the basis of the Oedipus complex. In any case, however, in this complex and indeed in complex-formation in general, the roots lie too deep for us to be able to penetrate down to them. In the case described, the foundations for his inhibitions and neurotic traits seem to me to reach back before the time even when he began to speak. It would certainly have been possible to overcome them earlier and much more easily than was done, though not to cut off entirely the activities of the complexes in which they originated. There is certainly no reason to fear a too far-reaching effect from early analysis, an effect that might endanger the cultural development of the individual and therewith the cultural riches of mankind. However far we may press forward there is always a barrier at which a halt must be called. Much that is unconscious and entangled with complexes will continue to be active in the development of art and culture. What early analysis can do is to afford protection from severe shocks and to overcome inhibitions. This will assist not only the health of the individual but culture as well, in that the overcoming of inhibitions will open up fresh possibilities of development. In the boy I watched it was striking how greatly his general interest was stimulated subsequent to the satisfying of a part of his unconscious questions, and how greatly his impulse for investigation flagged again because further unconscious questions had arisen and drawn his whole interest upon themselves.

It is evident, therefore, that, to go more into detail, the effectiveness of wishes and instinctive impulses can only be weakened by becoming conscious. I can, however, state from my own observations that, just as in the case of the adult, so also with the young child this occurs without any danger. It is true that, beginning with the explanations and increasing markedly with the intervention of analysis, the boy showed a distinct change of character which was accompanied too by 'inconvenient' traits. The hitherto gentle and only occasionally aggressive boy became aggressive, quarrelsome, and this not only in his phantasies but in reality. Hand in hand with this went a decline in adult authority which is by no means identical with an incapacity to recognize others. A healthy scepticism, that likes to see and understand what he is asked to believe, is combined with a capacity to acknowledge the desserts or skill of others, particularly of his much-loved and admired father and also of his brother Karl. Towards the female sex, due to other causes, however, he feels somewhat superior and rather protective. He shows the decline of authority chiefly by his companionable friendly attitude, which is the same in regard to his parents. He values highly being able to have his own opinion, his own wishes, but at the same time he finds obedience difficult. He is, however, easily taught better things and is generally obedient enough to please his adored mother in spite of its often being hard for him. Taken all round, his upbringing offers no peculiar difficulties in spite of the 'inconvenient' traits that have appeared.

His well-developed capacity for being good is in no way diminished; it is, indeed, rather more stimulated. He gives easily and gladly, imposes sacrifices upon himself for people whom he loves; he is considerate and has his full share of 'kindheartedness'. Here we see, too, what we have learnt also from the analysis of adults, that analysis does not affect these successful formations in any prejudicial way but rather enhances them. Hence it seems to me permissible to argue that early analysis too will not injure existing successful repressions, reaction-formations and sublimations, but on the contrary will open up possibilities for further sublimations.[1]

Another difficulty as regards early analysis must still be mentioned. Owing to bringing into consciousness his incest-wishes, his passionate attachment to his mother is markedly shown in daily life, but no attempt is made to overstep the established limits in any way than is otherwise the case with affectionate little boys. His relationship

[1] In this case only their exaggeration and compulsive nature was overcome.

with his father is, in spite (or because) of his consciousness of his aggressive wishes, an excellent one. In this instance too it is easier to control an emotion that is becoming conscious than one that is unconscious. Simultaneously with acknowledging his incest-wishes, however, he is already making attempts to free himself from this passion and to achieve its transference to suitable objects. This seems to me to be inferred from one of the conversations quoted in which he ascertained with painful emotion that at least he would then live together with his mother. Other frequently repeated remarks also indicate that the process of liberation from the mother is already partly begun, or at least that an attempt at it will be made.[1]

It may be hoped, therefore, that he will achieve his freedom from his mother by the proper path; that is, by the choice of an object resembling the mother-imago.

I have also heard little of the difficulties that might ensue from early analysis of a child in his contact with an environment thinking otherwise. The child is so sensitive to even the gentlest rebuffs that he knows quite well where he can count on understanding and where not. In this case the boy entirely gave up, after a few slight unsuccessful attempts, confiding in anyone except his mother and myself on these matters. At the same time he remained quite confiding with others in respect to other things.

Another matter too that might easily lead to inconvenience proves to be quite manageable. The child has a natural impulse to use the analysis also as a means to pleasure. At night when he should go to sleep he will state that an idea that must be discussed at once has occurred to him. Or he tries to draw attention to himself throughout the day by the same plea and comes along at unsuitable times with his phantasies; in short he tries in various ways to make the analysis the business of life. A counsel given me by Dr Freund stood me in excellent stead in this matter. I set a certain time—even if this had occasionally to be changed—apart for the analysis, and although owing to our close daily association I was much with the child, this was steadfastly adhered to. The child acquiesced perfectly after a few unsuccessful endeavours. Similarly I firmly discouraged his attempt to vent in any other way something of the aggressiveness towards his parents and myself revealed by the analysis, and demanded the usual

---

[1] Not during the period covered by these notes but almost a year later, after a declaration of his affection for her he again expressed his regret that he could not marry his mother. 'You will marry a beautiful girl whom you will love when you are big,' she replied. 'Yes,' said he, already quite consoled, 'but she must look just like you, with a face the same and the same hair and she must be called Mrs. Walter W. just like you!' (Walter is not only his father's name but also the child's second Christian name.)

standard of manners from him; in these things he also very soon acquiesced. Although one was dealing here with a child over five years old and therefore more sensible, still I am sure that with a younger child too ways and means can be found to obviate these drawbacks. For one thing, with a younger child it will not be so much a matter of detailed conversations but rather of occasional interpretations either during play or at other opportunities, which will probably be accepted more easily and naturally than by the older child. Moreover it has always been the duty of even the hitherto customary upbringing to teach the child the difference between phantasy and reality, between truth and untruth. The difference between wishing and doing (later too the expression of wishes) can easily be linked up with these. Children in general are so teachable and culturally endowed that they will surely learn easily enough that while they can think and wish everything, only a part of this can be carried into effect.

I therefore think that there is no need for undue anxiety about these things. No upbringing is possible without difficulties, and certainly those acting rather from without inwards represent a lesser burden for the child than those acting unconsciously from within. If one is inwardly thoroughly convinced of the rightness of this method, then with a little experience the external difficulties will be overcome. I think too that a child who is psychically more robust, due to the operation of an early analysis, is able to support more easily an unavoidable trouble unharmed.

The question whether every child requires this assistance may well be asked. Undoubtedly there are a number of entirely healthy, excellently developed people and there certainly are also similar children who show no neurotic traits, or have got over them undamaged. From analytic experience it may at any rate be asserted that the adults and children to whom the above applies are comparatively few. Freud in his 'Analysis of a Phobia in a five-year-old Boy'[1] expressly mentions that no harm but only good accrued to Little Hans from becoming fully conscious of his Oedipus complex. Freud thinks that Little Hans's phobia differs from the extraordinarily frequent phobias of other children only in that it was noticed. He shows that it may give him 'an advantage over other children, in that he no longer carries within him that seed in the shape of repressed complexes which must always be of some significance for a child's later life, and which undoubtedly brings with it a certain degree of deformity of character if not a predisposition to a subsequent neurosis'. Furthermore Freud says that 'no sharp line can be drawn between "neurotic" and "normal" people—whether children or adults—

[1] S.E. 10.

51

that our conception of "disease" is a purely practical one and a question of summation, that predisposition and the eventualities of life must combine before the threshold of this summation is overstepped, and that consequently a number of individuals are constantly passing from the class of healthy people into that of neurotic patients', etc. He writes in 'From the History of an Infantile Neurosis'[1] 'It will be objected that few children escape such disorders as a temporary loss of appetite or an animal phobia. But this argument is exactly what I should wish for. I am ready to assert that every neurosis in an adult is built upon a neurosis which has occurred in his childhood but has not invariably been severe enough to strike the eye and be recognized as such.'

It would therefore be advisable with most children to pay attention to their dawning neurotic traits; if however we wish to get hold of and remove these traits, then the earliest possible intervention of analytic observation and occasionally of actual analysis becomes an absolute necessity. I think a kind of norm might be set up in this matter. If a child, at the time when his interest in himself and his environment is aroused and expressed, shows sexual curiosity and endeavours step by step to satisfy it; if he shows no inhibitions in this and fully assimilates the enlightenment received; if also in games and phantasies he lives through a part of his instinctive impulses, especially of the Oedipus complex, uninhibited; if for instance he listens with pleasure to Grimm's fairy-tales without subsequent anxiety-manifestations and shows himself in general mentally well balanced, then in these circumstances early analysis could probably be omitted, although even in these not-too-frequent cases it might be employed with benefit, as many inhibitions from which even the best-developed people suffer or have suffered would thereby be overcome.

I have particularly selected listening to Grimm's tales without anxiety-manifestations as an indication of the mental health of children, because of all the various children known to me there are only very few who do so. Probably partly from a desire to avoid this discharge of anxiety a number of modified versions of these tales have appeared and in modern education other less terrifying tales, ones that do not touch so much—pleasurably and painfully—upon repressed complexes are preferred. I am of opinion, however, that with the assistance of analysis there is no need to avoid these tales but that they can be used directly as a standard and an expedient. The child's latent fear, depending upon repression, is more easily rendered manifest by their help and can then be more thoroughly dealt with by analysis.

[1] *S.E.* **17.**

How can upbringing on psycho-analytic principles be carried out in practice? The requirement so firmly established by analytic experience that parents, nurses and teachers should themselves be analysed will probably remain a pious wish for a long time yet. Even if this wish were fulfilled, though probably we would have some assurance that the helpful measures mentioned in the beginning would be carried out, we still would not have the possibility of early analysis. I would here like to make a suggestion that is only a counsel of necessity but that transitionally might be efficacious until other times bring other possibilities. I mean the founding of kindergartens at the head of which there will be women analysts. There is no doubt that a woman analyst who has under her a few nurses trained by her can observe a whole crowd of children so as to recognize the suitability of analytic intervention and to carry it out forthwith. It may of course be objected amongst other things that in this way the child would at a very early age be to some extent withdrawn psychically from its mother. I think however that the child has so much to gain in this way that the mother ultimately would win back in other directions what she had perhaps lost in this one.

[*Note, 1947. The educational conclusions embodied in this paper are necessarily in keeping with my psycho-analytic knowledge at that time. Since suggestions regarding education do not enter to any extent into the following papers, the development of my views on education is not apparent in this volume, as is, I think, the case with the development of my psycho-analytic conclusions. It might therefore be worth while mentioning that, if I were to put forward at the present time suggestions regarding education, I would considerably amplify and qualify the views presented in this paper.*]

2

INHIBITIONS AND DIFFICULTIES
AT PUBERTY

(1922)

IT is well known that psychological difficulties and striking personality changes appear very frequently in children at the onset of
puberty. I should like here to give some thought to the problems
encountered by boys; the development of girls requires a separate
discussion.

One might think that the difficulties can be adequately accounted
for by the lack of psychic equipment at the boy's disposal for dealing
with his sexual maturation and the momentous bodily changes that
go with it. Bombarded by his sexuality, he feels himself at the mercy
of wishes and desires which he cannot and may not satisfy. Manifestly, he has to bear a heavy psychological burden. But to state this
is insufficient for a full understanding of all the deep-seated and
diverse troubles and problems so commonly met with at this age.

Some boys who have had trusting and cheerful natures until now,
suddenly or gradually become secretive and defiant, revolt against
home and school and cannot be influenced by either kindness or
severity. Some lose ambition and pleasure in learning and cause concern through scholastic failure; others are seized by an unhealthy
access of zeal. Experienced teachers are aware of the shaky or
damaged self-esteem that is behind both kinds of behaviour. Puberty
throws up a host of conflicts of varying intensities, many of which
existed before in milder guise but were lost to view; now, the most
extreme manifestations may appear, such as suicide or some criminal
act. If, as often happens, parents and teachers are unequal to the
heavy calls made on them at this period, additional damage will
naturally result. Many parents will spur their child on when what
he needs is holding back, or else fail to give encouragment when he
wants their confidence and trust. All too often, teachers, ambitious
for success in examinations, neglect to investigate glaring failure and
do not show compassionate understanding for the distress it signifies.
There can be no doubt that understanding adults are most helpful in
easing things for the child, but it is a mistake to over-estimate the
effect of environmental factors on the resolution of difficulties. The

54

most devoted efforts of loving and understanding parents may fail to help, or founder through their boy's ignorance of what torments him. Mature and insightful teachers can similarly be baffled by their lack of knowledge of what is behind the troubles.

It therefore becomes urgent to probe beyond the obvious physical and mental events into areas unknown to the tormented child or the uncomprehending adults; in other words, to pursue unconscious causes with the aid of psycho-analysis which has taught us so much about them.

Freud, in the course of treating adult neurotics, came to recognize the immense significance of infantile neurosis. Over many years of work with adults, he and his pupils gathered convincing evidence that the aetiology of mental illness is to be found far back in early childhood. It is at that time that character is determined and those pathological factors laid down which lead to illness when later triggered off by strains too great for an unstable psychic structure. Hence children who had felt or appeared quite healthy, or at most a little nervous, can suffer quite serious breakdowns as a result of even moderate extra strains. In such cases, the borderline between 'healthy' and 'ill', 'normal' and 'abnormal' had been fluid and never clear cut. That such fluidity is a general state of affairs is one of Freud's most important discoveries. He found that the difference between 'normal' and 'abnormal' is one of quantity and not of structure, an empirical finding constantly confirmed in our own work. As the result of prolonged cultural development we are all endowed from birth with the ability to repress instincts, desires and their imagery, *i.e.* to banish them from conscious awareness into the pool of the unconscious. Here they are preserved, alive and growing in effect, with a potentiality, if repression fails, to lead to the appearance of a wide range of illnesses. The forces of repression bear hardest on the most prohibited instinctual stirrings, especially on sexual ones. 'Sexual' should be understood in its widest, psycho-analytical sense. Freud's instinct theory teaches us that sexuality is active from the beginning of life, initially in the pursuit of pleasure by means of 'partial instincts' and not, as in adulthood, in the service of procreation.

Infantile sexual wishes and phantasies attach themselves at once to the most immediate and meaningful objects, *i.e.* the parents and more so to the one of the opposite sex. Every normal little boy will show a passionate love for his mother and declare his desire to marry her at least once between the ages of three and five; soon after, his sister will replace his mother as the object of his longing.[1] Such

[1] Meta Schoepp has given a beautiful example of a little boy's love affair with his mother, and his jealousy of his father, in her book *My Boy and I* (Berlin:

declarations, which nobody takes seriously, announce his very real, though unconscious, passions and desires and have great importance for his whole development. Their incestuous nature evokes severe social stricture, since their fulfilment would cause cultural regression and dissolution. They are thus destined for repression, to form in the unconscious the Oedipus complex, which Freud termed the nuclear complex of the neuroses. Mythology and poetry[1] bear out the universality of the desires that led Oedipus to kill his father and commit incest with his mother, and psycho-analytic work with ill and healthy people shows that they exist in the phantasy life of all adults.

The tempestuous uprush of instincts arising at puberty adds to the boy's difficulties in his struggle against his complexes, and he may succumb. The battle now joined between emerging desires and phantasies clamouring for recognition and the repressing forces of the ego taxes his strength excessively. The ego's failure will cause problems and inhibitions of every kind, including overt illness. In favourable circumstances the embattled elements achieve a kind of balance. The outcome of the struggle will determine for good the character of his sexual life, and hence is decisive for his future development, bearing in mind that what has to be done during puberty is to organize the incoherent partial sexual instincts of the child towards procreative functions. *Pari passu*, the boy must achieve an inner detachment from the incestuous links to his mother, though these will remain the foundation and model for later love. A measure of external detachment from his fixation to his parents is also necessary if he is to develop into a vigorous, active and independent man.

Conkordia, Deutsche Verlaganstalt, 1910—'Mein Junge und Ich'). A similar theme is treated by Geirestam in 'The Book of my Little Brother'—(Berlin–Verlag Fischer, 'Das Buch vom Bruederchen').

[1] A few quotations from the rich mine of illustrative material must suffice: 'If the little savage were left to his own devices and could match the strength and passion of thirty with the unreason of the cradle, he would break his father's neck and dishonour his mother.' (Diderot: Rameau's Nephew, transl. Goethe).

'I urged this on his growing heart: "Chastity decrees that Nature's wishes have to be abhorred—to rival father, to be the mother's mate".' (Lessing, Graugir).

Eckermann considered (Conversations with Goethe, 1827) that for a girl, only her love for her brother could be pure and sexless. 'I believe', answered Goethe 'that the love of sister for sister is even purer and chaster. For all we know, countless instances of sensual inclinations between brothers and sisters may have existed, which may have been conscious or unknown to the parties.'

'My Dearest . . . what shall I call you? I require a word that would include the meanings of all the names of Friend, Sister, Beloved, Bride and Wife.' (Letter to the Countess Auguste zu Stolberg, 26.1.1775).

These quotations are taken from Otto Rank's book *Das Inzestmotiv in Dichtung und Sage* (Leipzig and Vienna: Deutike, 1912). In it, he deals exhaustively with the influences of the Oedipus complex on myth and poetry.

It is not to be wondered at, then, that the individual, faced in his puberty with the onerous task set by his very complex psycho-sexual development, may suffer from inhibitions of a more or less lasting nature. Experienced teachers tell me that many previously difficult boys appear to suffer a diminution of their vitality, curiosity and receptiveness when they have settled down and become good, industrious and amenable.

What, then, can parents and teachers do to assist the boy in his struggles? Understanding something of the reasons for his problems will in itself have a favourable influence on the way they approach the child. The pain and irritation, understandably caused by his defiance, lack of love and objectionable behaviour, will become easier to tolerate. Teachers may come to recognize the transference to themselves of the boy's Oedipal rivalry with his father. One sees in the analyses of boys at puberty how often teachers become the recipients of excessive love and admiration, as well as of unconscious hate and aggression. Guilt and remorse caused by the latter will also play their part in the relationship with the teacher.

The confusion and obscurity of the child's emotions can cause a distaste for school, even for all learning and knowledge, sometimes to the point of martyrdom. A teacher's kindness and understanding may ameliorate matters, and his unwavering trust in the boy can strengthen the latter's tottering self-esteem and moderate his sense of guilt. An especially favourable situation is one in which parents and teachers have been able to preserve or create an atmosphere that makes for free discussion of sexual problems — should this be desired by the boy. Frightening or threatening warnings about sexual matters — especially masturbation, practically universal during puberty — are naturally to be avoided. The incalculable harm they can do is much greater than any conceivable benefit. Lily Braun, in her spendid book *Memoirs of a Socialist*, describes how she tried, during a pregnancy, to create a friendly relationship with her pubescent stepsons, in order to give them sexual enlightenment. Her attempts met with scorn and rejection and had to be abandoned; such can be the fate of the most talented attempts at sex education. Refusal or reserve may be insuperable. Missed opportunities for enlightening children at an early age may never present themselves again; but if openings can be made, many difficulties can be alleviated or even removed.

Such remedies exhausted, the resources available to parents and teachers are at an end, and more effective assistance will have to be sought. Psycho-analysis can offer this, as with its help we can look for causes of problems and remove noxious consequences. Its technique, still growing after years of experience, enables us to discover causes, render them available to the sufferer's awareness, and thereby to assist in adjusting the demands of conscious and unconscious. Expertly and correctly conducted, psycho-analysis holds no more danger for children than for adults; much successful work with children convinces me of this. The widely-felt anxiety that analysis diminishes children's spontaneity is disproved in practice. Many children have had their liveliness fully restored by analysis after losing it in the welter of their conflicts. Even very early analysis does not turn children into uncultured and asocial beings. The reverse is true; freed from inhibitions, they are now able to make full use of emotional and intellectual resources for cultural and social purposes, in the service of their development.

3

THE RÔLE OF THE SCHOOL
IN THE LIBIDINAL DEVELOPMENT
OF THE CHILD

(1923)

[*Note, 1947. This chapter is to be read in conjunction with the following chapter*—'*Early Analysis*'—*which deals with closely allied topics and is largely based on the same material.*]

I T is a well-known fact[1] in psycho-analysis that in the fear of examinations, as in examination-dreams, the anxiety is displaced from something sexual on to something intellectual. Sadger showed in his article, 'Über Prüfungsangst und Prüfungsträume' (1920), that the fear of examinations, in dreams as in reality, is the fear of castration.

The connection between examination-fears and inhibitions at school is evident. I came to recognize as inhibition the different forms and degrees of distaste for learning, from an unmistakable reluctance to what appears as 'laziness' and which could not have been recognized either by the child or by those round him as an aversion from school.

In the life of a child school means that a new reality is encountered, which is often apprehended as very stern. The way in which he adapts himself to these demands is usually typical of his attitude towards the tasks of life in general.

The extremely important rôle played by the school is in general based upon the fact that school and learning are from the first *libidinally* determined for everyone, since by its demands school compels a child to sublimate his libidinal instinctual energies. The sublimation of genital activity, above all, has a decisive share in the learning of various subjects, which will be correspondingly inhibited, therefore, by the castration-fear.

On starting school the child passes out of the environment that constituted the basis of his fixations and complex-formations, finds himself faced with new objects and activities, and must now test

[1] Cf. W. Stekel, *Conditions of Nervous Anxiety and their Treatment* (1923); Freud, *The Interpretation of Dreams* (*S.E.* **4–5**).

on them the mobility of his libido. It is, however, above all, the necessity for abandoning a more or less passive feminine attitude, which had hitherto been open to him, in order now to put forth his activity, that confronts the child with a task new and frequently insuperable for him.

I shall now discuss in detail examples from a number of analyses of the libidinal significance of the walk to school, school itself, the teacher, and of the activities employed at school.

Felix, aged thirteen, had a general dislike for school. In view of his good intellectual endowment, his apparent lack of any interest was striking. In the analysis he related a dream that he had dreamt when he was about eleven years of age, shortly after the death of the headmaster of his school. '*He was on the road to school, and met his piano mistress. The school house was on fire and the branches of the trees on the roadside were burnt off, but the trunks were left standing. He walked through the burning building with his music mistress and they came out unhurt, etc.*' The full interpretation of this dream was achieved only much later, when the significance of the school as mother, and of the teacher and headmaster as father, had resulted from the analysis. Here are one or two examples of this from the analysis. He complained that in all these years he had never learnt to overcome the difficulty he had had from the very first in standing up when he was called upon in school. He associated to this that girls stand up quite differently, and demonstrated the difference in the way boys stand up by a movement of the hands that indicated the genital region and showed clearly the shape of the erected penis. The wish to conduct himself towards the teacher as girls do expressed his feminine attitude to the father; the inhibition associated with standing up proved to be determined by the fear of castration which influenced his whole subsequent attitude towards school. The idea that occurred to him once in school that the master, who, standing in front of the pupils, had leant his back against the desk, should fall down, knock over the desk, break it in and hurt himself in so doing, demonstrated the significance of the teacher as father, and of the desk as mother,[1] and led to his sadistic conception of coitus.

[1] The maternal significance of dais and also of desk and slate and everything that can be written upon, as well as the penis-meaning of penholder, slate-pencil and chalk, and of everything with which one can write, became so evident for me in this and other analyses and was so constantly confirmed that I consider it to be *typical*. The sexual symbolic meaning of these objects has also been demonstrated elsewhere during analysis in isolated cases. Thus Sadger in his article, 'Über Prüfungsangst und Prüfungsträume', has shown the symbolic sexual meaning of desk, slate and chalk in an incipient case of paranoid dementia. Jokl in 'Zur Psychogenese des Schreibkrampfes' (1922) has also shown the symbolic sexual meaning of the penholder in a case of writer's cramp.

He related how the boys whispered and helped one another over a Greek exercise in spite of the master's supervision. His subsequent notions led to a phantasy about how he could manage to achieve a better place in his class.[1] He phantasied how he would catch up those above him, remove and kill them, and discovered to his astonishment that now they no longer appeared to him as companions, as they had just previously, but as enemies. Then when, by their removal, he had attained the first place and thus reached the master, there would be no one but the master in the class who would have a better place than himself——but with him he could do nothing.[2]

In the not quite seven-year-old Fritz,[3] whose disinclination for school extended to his walk to school, this distaste revealed itself in the analysis as anxiety.[4] When in the course of the analysis pleasure had taken the place of anxiety, he related the following phantasy: The school children climb through the window into the schoolroom to the mistress. But there was one little boy who was so fat that he could not get in at the window, and had, therefore, to learn and write his lessons in the street in front of the school. Fritz called this boy 'Dumpling', and described him as very funny. For instance, he had no idea how fat and funny he was when he jumped about, and he roused such mirth in his parents and brothers and sisters by his antics that the latter fell out of the window with laughing, and his parents bounced over and over again up and down against the ceiling with laughter. Finally, in so doing they struck against a beautiful glass bowl that was on the ceiling, which got cracked but did not break. The funny jumping 'dumpling' (also called 'Kasperle')

[1] At his school the children were seated according to the quality of one's work. His 'report', to which in his opinion his mother should attach less significance than to his place in class, signified for him as for Fritz (see below) potency, the penis, a child; the place in class was for him the place in the mother, the possibility of coitus accorded by her.

[2] The master here proves to be a homosexual wish-object. But a motive which is always significant in the genesis of homosexuality became evident, namely, that this homosexual wish was strengthened by the repressed wish to achieve coitus with the mother in spite of the father—in this case, therefore, to attain the first place in the class. In the same way, behind the wish to speak from the dais by forcing the master, alternatively the father, into the passive rôle of listener, the wish for the mother is also active, since the dais as well as the desk has a maternal meaning for him.

[3] Cf. 'The Development of a Child'.

[4] Cf. my chapter 'Early Analysis'; in that paper I worked out in more detail how Fritz's numerous phantasies about his mother's womb, procreation and birth concealed the most intense and strongly repressed wish to enter his mother's womb by means of coitus. Ferenczi has put forward the suggestion in his Congress paper, 'Thalassa' (1938), that in the unconscious, return to the maternal body seems only to be possible by means of coitus, and he has also set up an hypothesis that deduces this recurrently demonstrable phantasy from phylogenetic evolutionary processes.

proved to be a representation of the penis[1] penetrating the maternal body.

The *schoolmistress*, however, is also for him the castrating mother with the penis, and to his sore throat he associated that the schoolmistress had come and throttled him with reins and harnessed him like a horse.

In the analysis of nine-year-old Grete I was told of the deep impression made upon her on seeing and hearing a cart drive into the *school-yard*. Another time she related about a cart with sweetmeats, none of which she ventured to buy, as her schoolmistress came by just then. She described these sweetmeats as a kind of wadding, as something that interested her extremely, but about which she did not venture to find out. Both these carts proved to be screen-memories of her infantile observations of coitus, and the indefinable sugar-wadding to be the semen.

Grete sang first voice in the school-choir; the *schoolmistress* came quite close to her seat and looked straight into her mouth. At this Grete felt an irresistible need to hug and kiss the teacher. In this analysis the girl's stammering proved to be determined by the libidinal cathexis of speaking as well as of singing. The rise and fall of the voice and the movements of the tongue represented coitus.[2]

Six-year-old Ernst was shortly to start school. During the analysis-hour he played that he was a mason. In the course of the associated house-building phantasy[3] he interrupted himself and talked about his future *profession*; he wanted to be a 'pupil', and also later to go to the technical school. To my remark that this was hardly a final profession he replied angrily that he did not want to think out a profession for himself, because his mother might not perhaps agree to it and was cross with him anyway. A little later, as he continued the house-building phantasy, he suddenly asked: 'Is it really yard school or high school (technical school)?' (*Hofschule* or *Hochschule*).

These associations showed that for him to be a pupil meant to learn about coitus, but that a profession meant the carrying out of coitus.[4] Hence in his house-building (so closely associated for him with school and 'yard' school) he was only the mason who, moreover, still required the directions of the architect and the assistance of other masons.

On another occasion he piled some cushions from my divan on top

---

[1] Cf. Jones, 'The Theory of Symbolism' (1916).

[2] Cf. 'Early Analysis'.

[3] This house-building represented coitus and the procreation of a child.

[4] This unconscious meaning of 'profession' is typical. It is constantly demonstrated in analyses and assuredly contributes markedly to the difficulties in the choice of a profession.

of one another and sitting upon them he played at being a clergyman in the pulpit, who was, however, at the same time a *teacher*, for round about sat imaginary students who had to learn or guess something from the clergyman's gestures. During this performance he held up both his index fingers, then he rubbed his hands one against the other (according to his statement this meant washing clothes and chafing for warmth) and constantly jumped up and down on his knees on the cushions. The cushions, which constantly played a part in his games, had been shown in the analysis to be the (maternal) penis, and the various gestures of the clergyman to represent coitus. The clergyman, who shows the students these gestures but gives no explanation, represents the good father who instructs the sons about coitus or rather suffers them to be present during it as onlookers.[1]

I submit examples from a few analyses to show that the *school-task* signifies coitus or masturbation. Little Fritz displayed pleasure in learning and desire for knowledge before he went to school, and taught himself to read. He soon, however, developed a great distaste for school and showed a strong disinclination for all his tasks. He repeatedly made up phantasies about 'difficult tasks' that one was given to do in the penitentiary. As one of these tasks he mentioned having to build a house all by oneself in eight days.[2] He spoke, however, also of his school tasks as 'difficult tasks', and said once that a task was just as difficult as building a house. In one phantasy I too was put in prison and compelled to perform difficult tasks and, indeed, to build a house in a few days and to fill a book with writing in a few hours.

Felix experienced the severest inhibitions towards all his school tasks. He left, though with severe twinges of conscience, his home-work undone till the morning. Then he suffered lively remorse that he had not done it sooner, but nevertheless left it again till the last moment, reading the newspaper meantime. Then he did it breathlessly, taking up now one and now another lesson without completing any, and went to school, where he still hurriedly copied this and that with an unpleasant feeling of insecurity. He described his feeling about a school exercise thus: 'At first one is very frightened, and then one starts and it goes somehow, and afterwards one has a bad sort of feeling.' About a school exercise he told me that, just to be rid of it quickly, he began to write very fast and wrote faster and faster, and then got slower and slower, and finally could not get it finished. This 'fast—faster—slower—and not finishing', however, he had also described about his attempts at masturba-

---

[1] The boy had shared his parents' bedroom for years and this and other phantasies can be traced back to early infantile observations of coitus.

[2] Cf. the significance of house-building for Ernst and Felix.

tion that began at this time as a consequence of the analysis.[1] Parallel with his now becoming able to masturbate, his lessons also improved, and we were repeatedly able to determine his masturbatory attitude from the way he behaved about his lessons and school exercises.[2] Felix, too, generally managed to copy the lesson from someone else, whereby, when it was successful, he had to some extent secured an ally against the father and depreciated the value—therefore also the guilt—of his achievement.

For Fritz the 'Excellent' written by the schoolmistress on a good piece of work was a costly possession. On the occasion of a political murder he showed nocturnal anxiety. He said that assassins might suddenly attack him just as they had the murdered politician. They had wanted to rob the latter of his medals, and they would rob him of his commendation. The medals as well as commendation and also his report signified for him the penis, the potency which the castrating mother (as his schoolmistress appeared to him) returned to him.

For Fritz, when he was *writing*, the lines meant roads and the letters rode on motor-bicycles—on the pen—upon them. For instance, 'i' and 'e' ride together on a motor-bicycle that is usually driven by the 'i' and they love one another with a tenderness quite unknown in the real world. Because they always ride with one another they become so alike that there is hardly any difference between them, for the beginning and the end—he was talking of the small Latin alphabet—of 'i' and 'e' are the same, only in the middle the 'i' has a little stroke and the 'e' has a little hole. Concerning the Gothic letters 'i' and 'e', he explained that they also ride on a motor-bicycle, and that it is only a difference like another make of bicycle that the 'e' has a little box instead of the hole in the Latin 'e'. The 'i's' are skilful, distinguished and clever, have many pointed weapons, and live in caves, between which, however, there are also mountains, gardens and harbours. They represent the penis, and their path coitus. On the other hand, the 'l's' are represented as stupid, clumsy, lazy and dirty. They live in caves under the earth. In 'L'-town dirt and paper gather in the streets; in the little 'filthy' houses they mix with water a dyestuff bought in 'I'-land and drink and sell this as wine. They cannot walk properly and cannot dig because they hold the spade upside down, etc. It

[1] In consequence of a medical non-operative interference with his penis that occurred when he was three years old, he had subsequently masturbated only with severe moral scruples. When this interference was repeated at the age of ten, he completely gave up masturbating, but suffered from anxiety of touching.

[2] He repeatedly omitted the concluding sentence of his school exercise; on another occasion he forgot something in the middle of the exercise. When an improvement in this respect had already set in he compressed the whole lesson into the smallest possible compass, etc.

became evident that the 'l's' represented faeces. Numerous phantasies were concerned with other letters also.[1]

Thus, instead of the double 's', he always wrote only one, until a phantasy afforded the explanation and solution of this inhibition. The one 's' was himself, the other his father. They were to embark together on a motor-boat, for the pen was also a boat, the copy-book a lake. The 's' that was himself got into the boat that belonged to the other 's' and sailed away in it quickly upon the lake. This was the reason why he did not write the two 's's together. His frequent use of an ordinary 's' in place of a long one proved to be determined by the fact that the part of the long 's' that was thus left out was for him 'as though one were to take away a person's nose'. This mistake proved to be determined by castration-wishes against his father and disappeared after this interpretation.

Shortly after starting school, to which he had looked forward with joy, six-year-old Ernst displayed a marked distaste for learning. He told me about the letter 'i' which they were just learning, and that gave him difficulty. I also learnt that the master struck an older boy—who was to demonstrate to them on the blackboard how to write the letter 'i'—because he did not do it well enough. On another occasion he complained 'that the lessons are so hard', that he had always to make up and down strokes when writing, that in arithmetic he drew little stools and that altogether he had to make the strokes as the master—who watched him while he was doing them—wished. Marked aggressiveness was displayed after this in-formation; he tore the cushions off the divan and flung them to the other end of the room. Then he turned over the leaves of a book and showed me 'an "I" box'. A box (in a theatre) was something 'where one was alone inside'—the big 'I' is alone inside, round about are only little black letters that remind him of faeces. The big 'I' is the big '*popöchen*' (penis) that wants to be alone inside mummy, that he has not got and that therefore he must take from his papa. Then he phantasied that he cut off papa's *popöchen* with a knife and that the latter sawed his off with a saw; the outcome, however, was that he had his papa's. Then he cut off his papa's head, after which the latter could do no more to him because he could not see—but the eyes in the head saw him, nevertheless. Then he suddenly tried very busily to read and showed much pleasure in doing so—the resistance was overcome. He replaced the cushions and explained that they also had done 'up and down' once, the journey, indeed, from the divan to the other end of the room and back. To be able to carry out the coitus he had taken the penis (the cushions) from the mother.

[1] Cf. 'Early Analysis'.

Seventeen-year-old Lisa related in her associations that she did not like the letter 'i', it was a silly jumping boy who always laughed, who was not needed in the world at all and over whom she became quite enraged, incomprehensibly to herself. She praised the letter 'a' as being serious and dignified, it impressed her and the associations led to a clear father-imago whose name also began with an 'a'. Then, however, she thought that 'a' was, perhaps, after all a little too serious and dignified and should have at least something of the skipping 'i'. The 'a' was the castrated but, even so, unyielding father, the 'i' the penis.

For Fritz the dot of the 'i', as in general the full-stop and the colon, was a thrust of the penis.[1] When on one occasion he said to me that one must press hard on the full-stop, he at the same time raised and depressed his pelvis and repeated this at the colon. Nine-year-old Grete associated with the curve of the letter 'u' the curve in which she saw little boys urinate. She had a special preference for drawing beautiful scrolls that proved in her case to be parts of the male genitals—Lisa for the same reason omitted flourishes everywhere. Grete admired very much a friend who could hold her pen like a grown-up person, quite erect between her second and third fingers, and could also make the curve of the 'u' backwards.

With Ernst as well as with Fritz I could observe that the inhibition in respect of writing and reading, that is, the basis for all further school activity, proceeded from the letter 'i', which, with its simple 'up and down', is indeed the foundation of all writing.[2]

The sexual-symbolic meaning of a penholder is apparent in these examples, and becomes particularly clear in the phantasies of Fritz, for whom the letters ride on a motor-bicycle (the nib). It can be observed how the sexual-symbolic meaning of the penholder merges into the act of writing that the latter discharges. In the same way the libidinal significance of reading is derived from the symbolic cathexis of the book and the eye. In this there are at work, of course, also other determinants afforded by the component instincts, such as 'peeping' in reading, and exhibitionistic, aggressive sadistic tendencies in writing; at the root of the sexual-symbolic meaning of the

---

[1] For little Grete, too, the full-stop and comma were similarly determined. Cf. 'Early Analysis'.

[2] At a meeting of the Berlin P.A. Society, Herr Rohr dealt in some detail with the Chinese script and its interpretation on a psycho-analytic basis. In the subsequent discussion I pointed out that the earlier picture-script, which underlies our script too, is still active in the phantasies of every individual child, so that the various strokes, dots, etc. of our present script would only be simplifications, achieved as a result of condensation, displacement and other mechanisms familiar to us from dreams and neuroses, of the earlier pictures whose traces, however, would be demonstrable in the individual.

penholder lay probably originally that of the weapon and the hand. Corresponding with this too the activity of reading is a more passive, that of writing a more active, one, and for the inhibitions of one or the other of them the various fixations on the pre-genital stages of organization are also significant.

For Fritz the number '1' is a gentleman who lives in a hot country, and is therefore naked—only clothed in rainy weather in a cloak. He can ride and drive very skilfully, has five daggers, is very brave, etc., and his identity with 'General Pipi' (the penis)[1] is soon apparent. For Fritz numerals in general are people who live in a very hot country. They correspond to the coloured races, while letters are the white ones. For Ernst the 'up and down' of '1' is identical with that of 'i'. Lisa related to me that she made 'just a short scratch' for the down stroke of the numeral '1', an action again determined by her castration complex. It would therefore be the penis that is symbolically represented by the numeral '1', and that forms the basis for counting and arithmetic. In the analyses of children I observed repeatedly that the significance of the numeral '10' was determined by the number of the fingers, whereby, however, the fingers were unconsciously equated with the penis, so that the numeral '10' derived its affective tone from this source. Hence, too, were evolved the phantasies that a ten times repeated coitus or ten thrusts of the penis were necessary for the procreation of a child. The repeatedly demonstrable special significance of the numeral '5'[2] was an analogous one. Abraham (1923) pointed out that the symbolic meaning of the figure '3' from the Oedipus complex,—determined namely by the relationship, father, mother and child—is more significant than the very frequent employment of '3' for the male genitals. I shall adduce only one example of this.

Lisa considered the number '3' insupportable because 'a third person is of course always superfluous' and 'two can run races with one another'—the goal being a flag—but the third has no business there. Lisa, who had a taste for mathematics, but was very inhibited where it was concerned, told me that actually she only thoroughly understood the idea of *addition*; she could grasp 'that one joins with another when both are the same', but how were they added up when they were different? This idea was conditioned by her castration complex, it concerned the difference between the male and female genitals. The idea of the 'addition' proved to be determined

[1] Cf. 'Early Analysis'.

[2] I would point out that in the Roman system of numerals the numbers 'I', 'V' and 'X' are fundamental, the remaining numerals from 'I to X' being merely derivatives of these. The 'V' and 'X' are, however, also formed from the straight stroke of the numeral 'I'.

for her by parental coitus. She could well understand, on the other hand, that in multiplication different things were used, and that then, too, the result was different. The 'result' is the child. Where she herself was concerned she would only recognize a male genital, but left the female ones for her sisters.

Ernst brought to the analytic session a box of gaily coloured glass balls, separated them according to their colours and began to do sums with them.[1] He wanted to know how much '1 is less than 2', and tried it first with the balls, and then with his fingers. He showed me by putting up one finger, beside which the second was partly raised, that if the one finger were taken away then of course one had '0', 'but then all the same the other one' (the half-lifted one) 'is still there that one can also still take'. Then he showed me again by holding up his fingers that 2 and 1 are three, and said: 'The one is my *popöchen*, the others daddy's and mummy's *popöchen* that I have also taken for myself. Now mummy has taken two *popöchen* from her children again and I take them back from her—then I have five!'

In the analytic session, Ernst drew 'double lines' on a piece of paper, and told me that, according to the teacher, one could write better between double lines. He thought this was because then one had two lines and associated that they were two *popöchen* that he owned in this way. Then by vertical strokes he made 'double boxes' out of the double lines, and said: 'But it isn't so good in doing sums to have little double boxes, because the boxes become smaller in this way and then it is more difficult to put the numbers inside them.' He showed me too what he meant and wrote the sum '1 + 1 = 2' in the little boxes. The first little box in which he wrote the '1' was larger than the others. Thereupon he said: 'What is coming next has a smaller box.' 'It is mummy's *popöchen*,' he added, 'and' (pointing to the first "1") 'that is father's *popöchen*, and between them the "and" (+) is me.' He further explained that the horizontal stroke of the + (which he made very small too) didn't concern him at all, he and his *popöchen* were the *straight* stroke. Addition for him, too, is parental coitus.

On another occasion he started the session by the question whether he should count up 'how much "10 + 10" or "10 − 10" is'. (The castration fear pertaining to the numeral '1' is displaced on to the figure '10'.) He was reassuring himself that he had 'ten penises' (fingers) at his disposal. In connection with this question he attempted

[1] This shows clearly the anal basis of arithmetic. The castration fear pertaining to the penis was preceded by that of the loss of the faecal mass, which is indeed felt as 'the primitive castration'. Cf. Freud, 'On Transformations of Instinct as exemplified in Anal Erotism', (*S.E.* **17**).

to write on a piece of paper the most enormous numbers possible, which I was to work out. He then explained that a row of numbers that he made of several ones and noughts alternately—(10001000-1000)—was a '*gegentorische*' (*gegen* = against, *tor* = gate.—*Trans.*) kind of arithmetic. This he elucidated as follows: There was a town (about which he had already phantasied) that had very many gates because all the windows and openings were also called gates. In this town there were also lots of railways.[1] He then showed me that when he placed himself at the end of the room, a row of ever-diminishing circles, extending from the opposite wall, led up to him. These circles he called 'gates', the row of figures '1' and 'o' that he had made on the paper originated from them. He then worked out for me that one can also set up two '1's' against one another. Into the resulting figure, representing the printed letter 'M', he drew still another little circle, and explained 'There is another gate here.' The '1' alternating with the noughts represented the penis ('against the gate'). The 'o' was the vagina—there were several circles because the body also has several openings (many gates).

When he had explained this 'gegentorische' arithmetic to me, he got hold of a key-ring that happened to be there, drew a hairpin through it and showed me with some difficulty that the hairpin 'is in it at last', but that in doing this 'the ring must be divided—and be split as well', which again led to his sadistic idea of coitus. He moreover explained that this ring, that was indeed also like an 'o', was really only a straight piece that was bent round. Here as also in other ways with him was apparent the effect of the idea of the maternal penis, and indeed of one concealed in the vagina that he had to tear or destroy during coitus.[2] A particular aggressiveness appeared during the analysis, both in connection with this as well as with the preceding arithmetical phantasies. As always, it set in with his tearing the cushions off my divan, and jumping with both feet upon them, and also upon the divan—this represented, as frequently in his analysis, the castration of the mother and subsequently coitus with her. Immediately after this he began to draw.

Fritz had a marked inhibition in doing division sums, all explanations proving unavailing, for he understood them quite well, but always did these sums wrong. He told me once that in doing division he had first of all to bring down the figure that was required and he climbed up, seized it by the arm and pulled it down. To my enquiry

[1] Analogous to the phantasies of Fritz about the town traversed by rails (cf. 'Early Analysis'); for Ernst also, town signified the mother, railway the penis, and riding coitus.

[2] Cf. Boehm, 'Beiträge zur Psychologie der Homosexualität: II. ein Traum eines Homosexuellen' (1922).

as to what it said to that, he replied that quite certainly it was not pleasant for the number—it was as if his mother stood on a stone 13 yards high and someone came and caught her by the arm so that they tore it out and divided her. Shortly beforehand, however, he had phantasied about a woman in the circus who was sawn in pieces, and then nevertheless comes to life again, and now he asked me whether this were possible. He then related (also in connection with a previously elaborated phantasy) that actually every child wants to have a bit of his mother, who is to be cut in four pieces; he depicted quite exactly how she screamed and had paper stuffed in her mouth so that she could not scream, and what kind of faces she made, etc. A child took a very sharp knife, and he described how she was cut up; first across the width of the breast, and then of the belly, then lengthwise so that the '*pipi*' (penis), the face and the head were cut exactly through the middle, whereby the 'sense'[1] was taken out of her head. The head was then again cut through obliquely just as the '*pipi*' was cut across its breadth. Betweenwhiles he constantly bit at his hand and said that he bit his sister too for fun, but certainly for love. He continued that every child then took the piece of the mother that it wanted, and agreed that the cut-up mother was then also eaten. It now appeared also that he always confused the remainder with the quotient in division, and always wrote it in the wrong place, because in his mind it was bleeding pieces of flesh with which he was unconsciously dealing. These interpretations completely removed his inhibition with regard to division.[2]

In her reminiscences of school Lisa complained how senseless it was of the mistress to let such little children do arithmetic with such big numbers. It had always seemed so difficult to her to divide a quite big number by a smaller but also big one, and it was particularly hard if there was an incomplete remainder. She associated to this a horse, a horrible animal with a hanging mutilated tongue, cropped ears, etc., that wanted to jump over a fence, an idea that roused her most violent resistances. Further ideas led to a childhood memory, an old part of her native town where she was getting something in a shop. She phantasied that she bought an orange and a candle there, and suddenly thought that the earlier feeling of disgust and horror at the horse had all at once given place to a very pleasant and soothed feeling. She herself recognized the orange and the candle as the male, and the abominably mutilated horse as the female organs. The division of the big number by a smaller one was the

---

[1] The 'sense' was the penis.

[2] The next day in school, to his and his mistress's astonishment, it turned out that he could now do all his sums correctly. (The child had not become aware of the connection between the interpretation and the removal of the inhibition.)

coitus which she was to carry out with her mother in an ineffectual (impotent) manner.

Division here too proved to be a dividing up, actually a coitus at a sadistic cannibalistic stage of organization.

In reference to mathematical equations I learnt from Lisa that she could never understand an equation except with *one* unknown quantity.[1] She thought that it was quite clear that a hundred pfennigs were equal to one mark, one unknown could in that case be easily worked out. She associated to 'two unknowns' two glasses filled with water standing on the table of which she takes one and hurls it on the ground—further, horses amongst clouds and mist. The 'second unknown' proved to be the superfluous second penis, namely, the penis that in her infantile observations of parental coitus she wanted to get rid of, as she wished to possess either the father or the mother, and therefore to remove one of the two. Again, the second unknown meant also the semen which was mysterious to her, while the one unknown, that is the equation faeces = penis, she was aware of.[2]

Counting and arithmetic therefore prove also to have a genital symbolic cathexis; of the component instinctual activities that play a significant part in this we observe anal, sadistic and cannibalistic tendencies which achieve sublimation in this way, and are co-ordinated under the primacy of the genitals. For this sublimation, however, the castration-fear has a peculiar importance. The tendency to overcome it—the masculine protest—seems in general to form one of the roots from which counting and arithmetic have evolved. It then also becomes—the degree of it being the decisive factor—clearly the source of the inhibition.

For the libidinal significance of *grammar* I refer to a few examples which I adduced in my chapter on 'Early Analysis'. In reference to the analysis of sentences Grete spoke of an actual dismembering and dissection of a roast rabbit.[3] Roast rabbit, which she had enjoyed eating until disgust at it supervened, represented the mother's breast and genitals.

In Lisa's analysis I learnt that in studying history one had to transplant oneself into 'what people did in earlier times'. For her it was the study of the relations of the parents to one another and to the child, wherein of course the infantile phantasies of battles,

[1] These associations were in connection with a dream. She had to solve the problem: '$2x = 48$; what is the value of x?'

[2] Cf. also the interpretation of the 'unknown' in Sadger's paper, 'Über Prüfungsangst und Prüfungsträume'.

[3] In that paper I also substantiated the fact that oral, anal and cannibalistic tendencies also achieve sublimation in speech.

71

slaughters, etc., also played an important part, according to the sadistic conception of coitus.

I have made a detailed contribution to the libidinal determination of geography in my chapter on 'Early Analysis'. I showed there, too, that in connection with the repressed interest in the mother's womb—the basis of the inhibition of the sense of orientation—interest in the natural sciences is frequently also inhibited.

For instance, I found in the case of Felix that one of the main causes for his strong inhibition in drawing was as follows: he could not think how one sketched or drew a plan, he could not imagine at all how the foundations of a house are laid in the ground. Drawing was for him the creating of the object represented—the incapacity for drawing was impotence. I have indicated elsewhere the significance of a picture as a child or penis. It can be repeatedly demonstrated in analyses of children that behind drawing, painting, and photography there lies a much deeper unconscious activity: it is the procreation and production in the unconscious of the object represented. At the anal stage of organization it signifies the sublimated production of the faecal mass, at the genital stage the production of the child, and indeed a production by means of an entirely inadequate motor effort. Although it has attained to a higher stage of development, the child still appears to find in drawing a 'magic gesture',[1] by which he can realize the omnipotence of his thought. Drawing, however, contains also destructive depreciatory tendencies.[2] I adduce an example: Ernst drew[3] circles, using the outline of a snuff-box (which in his games had repeatedly proved to be the maternal genitals), so that they overlapped, and finally he shaded the drawings so that there was an oval in the middle, inside which again he drew a quite small circle. In this way he made 'mummy's *popöchen* smaller' (the oval instead of the circle)—then *he* had more.

Felix often told me that physics were quite incomprehensible to him. He mentioned as an example that he could not understand how sound could propagate itself. He could only comprehend how, for instance, a nail went into a wall. Another time he spoke of an air-tight space, and said that if my room were an air-tight space, then if anyone were to come in some air must enter with them too. This again proved to be determined by ideas of coitus where the air represented the semen.

[1] Cf. Ferenczi, 'Stages in the Development of the Sense of Reality' (1913).

[2] At the root of caricature there would thus be not only a mockery, but an actual unfavourable metamorphosis of the object represented.

[3] As I have stated, this drawing was associated with the marked aggressiveness liberated by the solution of the castration-fear which lay at the root of his arithmetical difficulties.

I have endeavoured to show that the fundamental activities exercised at schools are channels for the flow of libido and that by this means the component instincts achieve sublimation under the supremacy of the genitals. This libidinal cathexis, however, is carried over from the most elementary studies—reading, writing and arithmetic—to wider efforts and interests based upon these, so that the foundations of later inhibitions—of vocational inhibition as well—are to be found, above all, in the frequently apparently evanescent ones concerned with the earliest studies. The inhibitions of these earliest studies, however, are built upon play-inhibitions, so that in the end we can see all the later inhibitions, so significant for life and development, evolving from the earliest play-inhibitions. In my chapter on 'Early Analysis' I showed that, starting from the point where the pre-conditions for the capacity for sublimation are given by libidinal fixations on the most primary sublimations—which I considered to be speech and the pleasure in movement—the constantly extending ego-activities and interests achieve libidinal cathexis by acquiring a sexual symbolic meaning, so that there are constantly new sublimations at different stages. The mechanism of inhibition which I described in detail in the above-mentioned paper permits, owing to common sexual symbolic meanings, the progress of the inhibitions from one ego-activity or trend to another. Since a removal of the earliest inhibitions also means an avoidance of further ones, very great importance must be attached to inhibitions in the child of pre-school age, even when they are not very strikingly apparent.

In the paper referred to I endeavoured to show that the castration-fear was the common basis for these early and for all subsequent inhibitions. Castration-fear interferes with ego-activities and interests because, besides other libidinal determinants, they always have fundamentally a genital symbolic, that is to say, a coitus significance.

The far-reaching importance of the castration complex for the formation of the neuroses is well known. In his paper 'On Narcissism—an Introduction', Freud establishes the significance of the castration complex for character-formation, and refers repeatedly to this in his paper, 'From the History of an Infantile Neurosis'.[1]

We must refer the establishment of all the inhibitions which

[1] *S.E.* **17**. In his paper 'The Castration Complex in the Formation of Character' (1923), Alexander has shown the influence of the castration complex upon character-formation in the analysis of an adult. In an unpublished paper 'Die infantile Angst und ihre Bedeutung für die Entwicklung der Persönlichkeit', which I brought into connection with this work of Dr Alexander, I attempted to demonstrate this by material from the analyses of children, and indicated the far-reaching significance of the castration-fear for inhibitions of sport, games and study, and the inhibitions of personality in general.

affect learning and all further development to the time of the first efflorescence of infantile sexuality which, with the onset of the Oedipus complex, gives its greatest momentum to the castration-fear, that is, to the early period between three and four years of age. It is the consequent repression of the active masculine components— in both boys and girls—that provides the chief basis for inhibitions of learning.

The contribution which the feminine component makes to sublimation will probably always prove to be receptivity and understanding, which are an important part of all activities; the driving executive part, however, which really constitutes the character of any activity, originates in the sublimation of masculine potency. The feminine attitude towards the father, which is connected with admiration and acknowledgement of the paternal penis and its achievements, becomes by sublimation the basis of an understanding for artistic and other achievements in general. I was able repeatedly in analyses of boys and girls to see how important the repression of this femine attitude through the castration complex might be. As an essential part of every activity, repression of it must contribute largely to the inhibition of any activity. It has also been possible to observe in analysing patients of both sexes how, as a part of the castration complex became conscious and the feminine attitude appeared more freely, there often occurred a powerful onset of artistic and other interests. In the analysis of Felix, for instance, when after a solution of part of the castration-fear the feminine attitude to the father became apparent, the musical talent which now appeared showed itself in admiration and recognition of a conductor and composer. Only on the growth of the activity did a severer critical faculty develop, a comparison with his own capacity and consequent endeavours to imitate the achievements of others.

It is a frequently confirmed observation that in general girls do better at school than boys, but on the other hand that their later achievements are not nearly equal to those of men. I shall only briefly indicate here a few factors that seem to me to be of significance also in this respect.

Part of the inhibitions—and this is the more important for later development—resulting from the repression of genital activity directly affects ego activity and interest as such. Another part of the inhibitions results from the attitude to the teacher.

The boy is thus doubly burdened in his attitude to the school and to learning. All those sublimations which derive from the genital wishes directed upon the mother lead to an increased consciousness of guilt towards the teacher. Lessons, the effort to learn, which in the unconscious signifies coitus, leads him to dread the teacher as avenger. Thus the conscious wish[1] to satisfy the teacher by his efforts is combated by the unconscious fear of doing it, which leads to an insoluble conflict that determines an essential part of the inhibition. This conflict diminishes in intensity when the boy's efforts are no longer under the direct control of the teacher and he can exert himself more freely in life. The possibility, however, of wider activities is only present, in a greater or lesser degree, where the castration-fear has affected not so much the activities and interests themselves as the attitude to the teacher. Thus one may see very unsatisfactory pupils achieving eminence in later life; for those others, however, whose interests in themselves were inhibited, the way in which they failed at school remains the prototype for their later attainments.

In girls the inhibition due to the castration complex and affecting all activity is of particular importance. The relationship to a male teacher that can be so burdensome to the boy acts on the girl, if her capabilities are not too inhibited, rather as an incentive. In her relationship to the mistress the anxiety attitude originating in the Oedipus complex is, in general, not nearly so powerful as is its analogue in the boy. That her achievements in life do not usually attain to those of the man is due to the fact that in general she has less masculine activity to employ in sublimation.

These differences and common features, as well as the consideration of some other factors at work, require a more detailed discussion. I must here, however, content myself with short, and therefore insufficient, indications that necessarily render my presentation somewhat too schematic. Within these limits, too, it is impossible to draw even a part of the numerous theoretical and pedagogical conclusions yielded by the material here indicated. I shall only briefly touch upon one of the most important.

In what has been said we have come to regard the rôle of the school as on the whole a passive one; it proves to be a touchstone for the sexual development that has already been more or less successfully achieved. What, then, is the active rôle of the school? Can it achieve anything essential for the child's libidinal and whole development? It is clear that an understanding teacher who considers the child's complexes will diminish more inhibitions and achieve more favourable results than the non-understanding or even brutal teacher, who from the first represents for the child the castrating father. On the other hand I found in a number of analyses that even under the best conditions in school very strong inhibitions of

[1] In the unconscious this wish corresponds to the endeavour to outdo the father, to displace him with the mother, or to the homosexual wish to conquer the father by his efforts, to win him as a passive love-object.

learning occur, while very injudicious conduct on the part of the teacher is by no means always followed by inhibitions.

I will briefly sum up my conception of the teacher's part in the development of the child. The teacher can achieve much by sympathetic understanding, for he is able thereby considerably to reduce that part of the inhibition that attaches to the person of the teacher as 'avenger'. At the same time, the wise and kindly teacher offers the homosexual component in the boy and the masculine component of the girl an object for the exercise of their genital activity in a sublimated form, as which, as I suggested, we can recognize the various studies. From these indications, however, the possibilities of injury that can result from a pedagogically wrong or even brutal procedure on the part of the teacher can be deduced.

Where, however, repression of genital activity has affected the occupations and interests themselves, the attitude of the teacher can probably diminish (or intensify) the child's inner conflict, but will not affect anything essential as concerns his attainments. But even the possibility of a good teacher easing the conflict is a very slight one, for limits are set by the child's complex-formations, particularly by his relationship to his father, which determines beforehand his attitude towards school and teacher.

This, however, explains why, where more powerful inhibitions are concerned, the results even of years of pedagogical labour present no relation to the effort expended, while in analysis we often find these inhibitions removed in a comparatively short time and replaced by complete pleasure in learning. It would be best, therefore, to reverse the process; first of all, an early analysis should remove the inhibitions more or less present in every child, and work at school should start on this foundation. When it has no longer to fritter away its forces in dispiriting attacks upon the children's complexes, the school will be able to achieve fruitful work significant for the development of the child.

4

EARLY ANALYSIS

(1923)

We frequently find in psycho-analysis that neurotic inhibitions of talents are determined by repression having overtaken the libidinal ideas associated with these particular activities, and thus at the same time the activities themselves. In the course of the analysis of infants and older children, I came upon material that led to the investigation of certain inhibitions which had only been recognized as such during the analysis. The following characteristics proved in a number of cases and in a typical way to be inhibitions: awkwardness in games and athletics and distaste for them, little or no pleasure in lessons, lack of interest in one particular subject, or, in general, the varying degrees of so-called laziness; very often, too, capacities or interests which were feebler than the ordinary turned out to be 'inhibited'. In some instances it had not been recognized that these characteristics were real inhibitions and, since similar inhibitions make up part of the personality of every human being, they could not be termed neurotic. When they had been resolved by analysis we found,—as Abraham has shown in the case of neurotics suffering from motor inhibitions[1]—that the basis of these inhibitions, too, was a strong primary pleasure which had been repressed on account of its sexual character. Playing at ball or with hoops, skating, tobogganing, dancing, gymnastics, swimming—in fact, athletic games of every sort—turned out to have a libidinal cathexis, and genital symbolism always played a part in it. The same applied to the road to school, the relation with men and women teachers, and also to learning and teaching in themselves. Of course a large number of active and passive, heterosexual and homosexual determinants, varying with the individual and proceeding from the separate component instincts, were also found to be of importance.

In analogy to neurotic inhibitions, these which we may call 'normal' were evidently founded on a capacity for pleasure which was constitutionally great, and on their sexual-symbolic significance. The main accent, however, must be placed on the sexual-symbolic significance. It is this which, by effecting a libidinal cathexis, augments in

[1] Abraham, 'A Constitutional Basis of Locomotor Anxiety' (1914).

77

a degree which we cannot as yet determine the original disposition and primary pleasure. At the same time it is this which draws repression upon itself, for repression is directed against the tone of sexual pleasure associated with the activity and leads to the inhibition of this activity or tendency.

I came to see that in far the greater number of these inhibitions, whether they were recognizable as such or not, the work of reversing the mechanism was accomplished by way of anxiety, and in particular by the 'dread of castration'; only when this anxiety was resolved was it possible to make any progress in removing the inhibition. These observations gave me some insight into the relation between anxiety and inhibition, which I shall now discuss in more detail.

Light was thrown to a remarkable degree upon this inner connection between anxiety and inhibition by the analysis of little Fritz.[1] In this analysis, the second part of which went very deep, I was able to establish the fact that the anxiety (which at one time was very considerable but gradually subsided after it had reached a certain point) so followed the course of the analysis that it was always an indication that inhibitions were about to be removed. Every time that the anxiety was resolved the analysis made a big step forward, and comparison with other analyses confirms my impression that the completeness of our success in removing inhibitions is in direct proportion to the clearness with which the anxiety manifests itself as such and can be resolved.[2] By successful removal I do not simply mean that the inhibitions as such should be diminished or removed, but that the analysis should succeed in reinstating the primary pleasure of the activity. This is undoubtedly possible in the analysis of young children, and the younger the child the sooner it will happen, for the path which has to be traversed to reverse the mechanism of inhibition is less long and complicated in *young* children. In Fritz this process of removal by way of anxiety was sometimes preceded by the appearance of transitory symptoms.[3] These again were principally resolved by way of anxiety. The fact that the removing of these inhibitions and symptoms takes place by way of anxiety surely shows that anxiety is their source.

[1] Cf. 'The Development of a Child'.

[2] In Fritz it appeared in a violent form (and this seems to me very important) with the whole of the affect appropriate to it. In other analyses this was not always so. For instance, in Felix, a boy of thirteen, to whose analysis also I shall refer repeatedly in this paper, the anxiety was often recognized for what it was, but it was not lived through with so powerful an affect. In his paper, 'The Castration Complex in the Formation of Character' (1923), Dr Alexander points out the great importance of this affective 'living-through'. This is what psycho-analysis aimed at in its infancy, terming it 'abreaction'.

[3] Cf. S. Ferenczi, 'Transitory Symptom-formations during the Analysis' (1912a).

We know that anxiety is one of the primary affects. 'I have said that transformation into anxiety — it would be better to say discharge in the form of anxiety — is the immediate vicissitude of libido which is subjected to repression.'[1] In thus reacting with anxiety the ego repeats the affect which at birth became the prototype of all anxiety and employs it as 'the universally current coinage for which *any* affective impulse is or can be exchanged'.[2] The discovery of how the ego tries in the different neuroses to shield itself from the development of anxiety led Freud to conclude that 'It would thus seem not to be wrong in an abstract sense to assert that in general symptoms are only formed to escape an otherwise unavoidable generating of anxiety.'[3] Accordingly, in children anxiety would invariably precede the formation of symptoms and would be the most primary neurotic manifestation, paving the way, so to speak, for the symptoms. At the same time it will not always be possible to indicate the reason why anxiety at an early stage often does not become manifest or is overlooked.

At all events there is probably not a single child who has not suffered from *pavor nocturnus*, and we are probably justified in saying that in all human beings at some time or other neurotic anxiety has been present in a greater or lesser degree. 'We recall the fact that the motive and purpose of repression was nothing else than the avoidance of unpleasure. It follows that the vicissitude of the quota of affect belonging to the representative is far more important than the vicissitude of the idea, and this fact is decisive for our assessment of the process of repression. If a repression does not succeed in preventing feelings of unpleasure or anxiety from arising, we may say that it has failed, even though it may have achieved its purpose as far as the ideational portion is concerned.'[4] If the repression is unsuccessful the result is the formation of symptoms. 'In the neuroses processes are in action which endeavour to bind this generating of anxiety and which even succeed in doing so in various ways.'[5]

Now what happens to a quantity of affect which is made to vanish

---

[1] Freud, *Introductory Lectures on Psycho-Analysis*, S.E. **15-16**, p. 410.

[2] *ibid.*, p. 404.

[3] In several analyses I have been able to establish the fact that children often conceal from those around them quite considerable quantities of anxiety, as though they were unconsciously aware of its meaning. With boys there is also the fact that they think their anxiety cowardice and are ashamed of it, and indeed this is a reproach which is generally made if they confess to it. These are probably the motives for forgetting, readily and completely, the anxiety of childhood, and we may be sure that some primary anxiety is always hidden behind the amnesia of childhood and can only be reconstructed by an analysis which penetrates really deep.

[4] 'Repression', *S.E.* **14**, p. 153.   [5] *Introductory Lectures*, p. 410.

without leading to the formation of symptoms—I mean in cases of successful repression? With regard to the fate of this sum of affect, which is destined to be repressed, Freud says: 'The *quantitative* factor of the instinctual representative has three possible vicissitudes, as we can see from a cursory survey of the observations made by psycho-analysis: either the instinct is altogether suppressed, so that no trace of it is found, or it appears as an affect which is in some way or other qualitatively coloured, or it is changed into anxiety.'[1]

But how is it possible for the charge of affect to be suppressed in *successful* repression? It seems justifiable to assume that whenever repression takes place (not excepting cases in which it is successful) the affect is discharged in the form of anxiety, the first phase of which is sometimes not manifest or is overlooked. This process is frequent in anxiety-hysteria, and we also assume its existence where such hysteria is not actually developed. In such a case anxiety would really be present unconsciously for a time '. . . we find it impossible to avoid even the strange conjunction, "unconscious consciousness of guilt", or a paradoxical "unconscious anxiety" '.[2] It is true that in discussing the use of the term 'unconscious affects' Freud goes on to say: 'So it cannot be denied that the use of the terms in question is logical; but a comparison of the unconscious affect with the unconscious idea reveals the significant difference that the unconscious idea continues, after repression, as an actual formation in the system Ucs, whilst to the unconscious affect there corresponds in the same system only a potential disposition which is prevented from developing further.'[3] We see then that the charge of affect which has vanished through successful repression has surely also undergone the transformation into anxiety, but that when the repression is completely successful the anxiety sometimes does not manifest itself at all, or only comparatively feebly, and remains as a potential disposition in the Ucs. The mechanism by which the 'binding' and discharge of this anxiety, or disposition to anxiety, is rendered possible would be the same as that which we have seen to result in inhibition; and the discoveries of psycho-analysis have taught us that inhibition enters in a greater or lesser degree into the development of every normal individual, while here again it is only the quantitative factor which determines whether he is to be called well or ill.

The question arises: Why is it that a healthy person can discharge in the form of inhibitions that which in the neurotic has led to neurosis? The following may be laid down as the distinguishing characteristics of the inhibitions which we are discussing: (1) certain ego-tendencies receive a powerful libidinal cathexis; (2) a quantity of

[1] 'Repression', *S.E.* **14,** p. 153.
[2] 'The Unconscious', *S.E.* **14,** p. 177.   [3] *ibid.*

anxiety is so distributed amongst these tendencies that it no longer appears in the guise of anxiety but in that of 'pain',[1] mental distress, awkwardness, etc. Analysis, however, shows that these manifestations represent anxiety which is only differentiated in degree and which has not manifested itself as such. Accordingly, inhibition would imply that a certain quantity of anxiety had been taken up by an ego-tendency which already had a previous libidinal cathexis. The basis of successful repression would thus be the libidinal cathexis of ego-instincts, accompanied in this double-sided way by an outcome in inhibition.

The more perfectly the mechanism of successful repression accomplishes its work the less easy is it to recognize the anxiety for what it is, even in the form of disinclination. In people who are quite healthy and apparently quite free from inhibitions it ultimately appears only in the form of weakened or partly weakened inclinations.[2]

If we equate the capacity to employ superfluous libido in a cathexis of ego-tendencies with the capacity to *sublimate*, we may probably assume that the person who remains healthy succeeds in doing so on account of his greater capacity for sublimating at a very early stage of his ego-development.

Repression would then act upon the ego-tendencies selected for the purpose and thus inhibitions would arise. In other cases the mechanisms of the neuroses would come more or less into operation and result in the formation of symptoms.

We know that the Oedipus complex brings repression into play with quite peculiar force and at the same time liberates the dread of castration. We may probably also assume that this great 'wave' of anxiety is reinforced by anxiety already existing (possibly only as a potential disposition) in consequence of earlier repressions—this latter anxiety may have operated directly as castration-anxiety originating in the 'primal castrations'.[3] I have repeatedly in analysis discovered birth-anxiety to be castration-anxiety reviving earlier material and have found that resolving the castration-anxiety

[1] Writing of the connection between 'pain' and anxiety in dreams, Freud says (*S.E.* **15**, p. 217): 'We may suppose that what is true of undistorted anxiety-dreams applies also to those which are partly distorted as well as to other un-unpleasurable dreams, in which the distressing feelings probably correspond to an approach to anxiety.'

[2] Even in this form of successful repression, in which the transformation undergone by anxiety makes it quite unrecognizable, it is undoubtedly possible to effect the withdrawal of very large quantities of libido. I found in the analyses of a number of cases that the development of individual habits and peculiarities had been influenced by libidinal ideas.

[3] Cf. Freud, 'On Transformations of Instinct as exemplified in Anal Erotism', *S.E.* **17**; Stärcke, *Psychoanalyse und Psychiatrie*; Alexander, *loc. cit.*

dissipated the birth-anxiety. For instance, I came across the fear in a child that when he was on the ice it would give way beneath him or that he would fall through a hole in a bridge—both obviously birth-anxiety. Repeatedly I found that these fears were actuated by the far less obvious wishes—brought into play as a result of the sexual-symbolic meaning of skating, bridges, etc.—to force his way back into the mother by means of coitus, and these wishes gave rise to the dread of castration. This also makes it easy to understand how generation and birth in the unconscious are frequently conceived of as coitus on the part of the child, who, even though it be with the father's help, thus penetrates into the maternal vagina.

It seems no great step then to regard the *pavor nocturnus* which occurs at the age of two or three as the anxiety which is liberated in the first stage of repression of the Oedipus complex, the binding and discharge of which subsequently ensues in various ways.[1]

The fear of castration that develops when the Oedipus complex is repressed is now directed towards the ego-tendencies which have already received a libidinal cathexis, and then in its turn, by means of this cathexis, is bound and discharged.

I think it is quite evident that, just in proportion as the sublimations hitherto effected are quantitatively abundant and qualitatively strong, so will the anxiety with which they are now invested be completely and imperceptibly distributed amongst them and thus discharged.

In Fritz and Felix I was able to prove that the inhibitions oɪ pleasure in motion were very closely connected with those of pleasure in learning and of various ego-tendencies and interests (which I will not now specify). In both cases that which made possible this *displacement of inhibition* or anxiety from one group of ego-tendencies to another was obviously the main cathexis of a sexual-symbolic character which was common to both groups.

In the thirteen-year-old Felix, whose analysis I shall use to illustrate my remarks in a later part of this paper, the form in which this displacement appeared was an alternation of his inhibitions between games and lessons. In his first years at school he had been a good pupil, but on the other hand he was very timid and awkward in all kinds of games. When his father came back from the war he used to

[1] The result of repression then appears in a striking manner somewhat later (at the age of three or four, or rather older) in certain manifestations, some of which are fully formed symptoms—effects of the Oedipus complex. It is clear (but the fact still requires verification) that, if it were possible to undertake an analysis of the child at the time of the *pavor nocturnus* or soon after it, and to resolve this anxiety, the ground would be cut away from under the neurosis and possibilities of sublimation would be opened out. My own observations lead me to believe that analytic investigation is not impossible with children of this age.

beat and scold the boy for this cowardice, and by these methods attained the result he desired. Felix became good at games and passionately keen on them, but hand in hand with this change there developed in him a disinclination for school and all learning and knowledge. This dislike grew into an undisguised antipathy, and this he brought with him to analysis. The common sexual-symbolic cathexis formed a relation between the two sets of inhibitions, and it was partly his father's intervention, leading him to regard games as the sublimation more consonant with his ego, which enabled him to displace the whole inhibition from games to lessons.

The factor of 'consonance with the ego' is, I think, also of importance in determining against which libidinally invested tendency the repressed libido (discharged as anxiety) will be directed, and which tendency will thus succumb to inhibition in a greater or lesser degree.

This mechanism of displacement from one inhibition to another seems to me to present analogies with the mechanism of the phobias. But, while in the latter all that happens is that the ideational content gives place through displacement to a substitutive formation, without the sum of affect disappearing, in inhibition the discharge of the sum of affect seems to occur simultaneously.

'As we know, the development of anxiety is the reaction of the ego to danger and the signal preparatory to flight; it is then not a great step to imagine that in neurotic anxiety also the ego is attempting a flight from the demands of its libido, and is treating this internal danger as if it were an external one. Then our expectation, that where anxiety is present there must be something of which one is afraid, would be fulfilled. The analogy goes further than this, however. Just as the tension prompting the attempt to flee from external danger is resolved into holding one's ground and taking appropriate defensive measures, so the development of neurotic anxiety yields to a symptom-formation, which enables the anxiety to be "bound".'[1]

In an analogous fashion, as it seems to me, we might look upon inhibition as the compulsory restriction, now arising from within, of a dangerous excess of libido—a restriction which at one period of human history took the form of compulsion from without. At the outset, then, the first reaction of the ego to the danger of a damming-up of the libido would be anxiety: 'the signal for flight'. But the prompting to flight gives place to 'holding one's ground and taking appropriate defensive measures': which corresponds to symptom-formation. Another defensive measure would be submission by restriction of the libidinal tendencies, that is to say, inhibition; but this would only become possible if the subject succeeded in diverting

[1] Freud, *Introductory Lectures on Psycho-Analysis.*

libido on to the activities of the self-preservative instincts and thus bringing to an issue on the field of the ego-tendencies the conflict between instinctual energy and repression. Thus inhibition as the result of successful repression would be the prerequisite and at the same time the consequence of civilization. In this way primitive man, whose mental life is in so many respects similar to that of the neurotic,[1] would have arrived at the mechanism of neurosis, for not having sufficient capacity for sublimation he probably also lacked the capacity for the mechanism of successful repression.

Having reached a level of civilization conditioned by repression, yet being in the main capable of repression only by way of the mechanisms of neurosis, he is unable to advance beyond this particular infantile cultural level.

I would now draw attention to the conclusion which emerges from my argument up to this point: the absence or presence of capacities (or even the degree in which they are present), though it appears to be determined simply by constitutional factors and to be part of the development of the ego-instincts, proves to be determined as well by other, libidinal, factors and to be susceptible of change through analysis.

One of these basic factors is libidinal cathexis as a necessary preliminary to inhibition. This conclusion agrees with the facts which have been repeatedly observed in psycho-analysis. But we find that libidinal cathexis of an ego-tendency exists even where inhibition has not resulted. It is (as appears with special clearness in infant-analysis) a constant component of every talent and every interest. If this is so, we must suppose that for the development of an ego-tendency not only a constitutional disposition but the following considerations must be of importance: how, at what period and in what quantity—in fact, under what conditions—the alliance with libido takes place; so that the development of the ego-tendency must also depend on the fate of the libido with which it is associated, that is to say, on the success of the libidinal cathexis. But this reduces the importance of the constitutional factor in talents and, in analogy with what Freud has proved with reference to disease, the 'accidental' factor is seen to be of great importance.

We know that at the narcissistic stage the ego-instincts and sexual instincts are still united because at the beginning the sexual instincts obtain a foothold on the territory of the self-preservative instincts. The study of the transference-neuroses has taught us that they subsequently part company, operate as two separate forms of energy and develop differently. While we accept as valid the differentiation be-

[1] Cf. Freud, *Totem and Taboo*.

tween ego-instincts and sexual instincts, we know on the other hand from Freud that some part of the sexual instincts remains throughout life associated with the ego-instincts and furnishes them with libidinal components. That which I have previously called the sexual-symbolic cathexis of a trend or activity belonging to the ego-instincts corresponds to this libidinal component. We call this process of cathexis with libido 'sublimation' and explain its genesis by saying that it gives to superfluous libido, for which there is no adequate satisfaction, the possibility of discharge, and that the damming-up of libido is thus lessened or brought to an end. This conception agrees also with Freud's assertion that the process of sublimation opens up an avenue of discharge for over-powerful excitations emanating from the separate component sources of sexuality and enables them to be applied in other directions. Thus, he says, where the subject is of an abnormal constitutional disposition the superfluous excitation may find outlet not only in perversion or neurosis but also in sublimation.[1]

In his examination of the sexual origin of speech, Sperber (1915) shows that sexual impulses have played an important part in the evolution of speech, that the first spoken sounds were the alluring calls of mate to mate and that this rudimentary speech developed as a rhythmic accompaniment to work, which thus became associated with sexual pleasure. Jones draws the conclusion that sublimation is the ontogenetic repetition of the process described by Sperber.[2] At the same time, however, the factors conditioning the development of speech are active in the genesis of symbolism. Ferenczi postulates that the basis of identification, as a stage preliminary to symbolism, is the fact that at an early stage of its development the child tries to rediscover its bodily organs and their activities in every object which it encounters. Since it institutes a similar comparison within its own body as well, it probably sees in the upper part of its body an equivalent for each affectively important detail of the lower part. According to Freud, the early orientation to the subject's own body is accompanied also by the discovery of fresh sources of pleasure. It may very well be this that makes possible the comparison between different organs and areas of the body. This comparison would be subsequently followed by the process of identification with other objects—a process in which, according to Jones, the pleasure-principle allows us to compare two otherwise quite different objects on the basis of a similitude of pleasurable tone, or of interest.[3] But we are probably justified in assuming that on the other hand these objects and activities, not

[1] *Three Essays on Sexuality*, S.E. **7**.

[2] Jones, 'The Theory of Symbolism' (1919). Cf. also Rank and Sachs, *Die Bedeutung der Psychoanalyse für die Geisteswissenschaften* (1913).

[3] Jones, *loc. cit.*

in themselves sources of pleasure, become so through this identification, a sexual pleasure being displaced on to them, as Sperber supposes it to have been displaced on to work in primitive man. Then, when repression begins to operate and the step from identification to symbol-formation is taken, it is this latter process which affords an opportunity for libido to be displaced on to other objects and activities of the self-preservative instincts, not originally possessing a pleasurable tone. Here we arrive at the mechanism of sublimation.

Accordingly, we see that *identification* is a stage preliminary not only to symbol-formation but at the same time to the evolution of speech and sublimation. The latter takes place by way of symbol-formation, libidinal phantasies becoming fixated in sexual-symbolic fashion upon particular objects, activities and interests. I may illustrate this statement as follows. In the cases I have mentioned of pleasure in motion—games and athletic activities—we could recognize the influence of the sexual-symbolic meaning of the playing-field, the road, etc. (symbolizing the mother), while walking, running, and athletic movements of all kinds stood for penetrating into the mother. At the same time, the feet, the hands and the body, which carry out these activities and in consequence of early identification are equated with the penis, served to attract to themselves some of the phantasies which really had to do with the penis and the situations of gratification associated with that organ. The connecting link was probably pleasure in motion or rather organ-pleasure in itself. This is the point where sublimation diverges from hysterical symptom-formation, having hitherto run the same course.

In order to set forth more exactly the analogies and differences between symptoms and sublimation I would refer to Freud's analysis of Leonardo da Vinci. Freud takes as his starting-point Leonardo's recollection—or rather phantasy—that when he was still in his cradle a vulture flew down to him, opened his mouth with its tail and pressed its tail several times against his lips. Leonardo himself makes the comment that in this way his absorbing and detailed interest in vultures was determined for him very early in life, and Freud shows how this phantasy was actually of great importance in Leonardo's art and also in his bent for natural science.

From Freud's analysis we learn that the real memory-content of the phantasy is the situation of the child being suckled and kissed by the mother. The idea of the bird's tail in his mouth (corresponding to fellatio) is evidently a recasting of the phantasy in a passive homosexual shape. At the same time we see that it represents a condensation of Leonardo's early infantile sexual theories, which led him to assume that the mother possessed a penis. We frequently find that, when the epistemophilic instinct is early associated with sexual interests, the result is inhibition or obsessional neurosis and brooding mania. Freud goes on to show that Leonardo escaped these fates through the sublimation of this component instinct, which thus did not fall a victim to repression. I should now like to ask: How did Leonardo escape hysteria? For the root of hysteria seems to me recognizable in this condensed element of the vulture's tail in the phantasy—an element often met with in hysterics as a fellatio phantasy, expressed for instance in the globus sensation. According to Freud we have in the symptomatology of hysteria a reproduction of the capacity for displacement of the erotogenic zones which is manifest in the child's early orientation and identification. Thus we see that identification is also a stage preliminary to hysterical symptom-formation, and it is this identification which enables the hysteric to effect the characteristic displacement from below upwards. If now we assume that the situation of gratification through fellatio, which in Leonardo became fixated, was reached by the same path (identification—symbol-formation—fixation) as leads to hysterical conversion, it seems to me that the point of divergence occurs at the fixation. In Leonardo the pleasurable situation did not become fixated as such: he transferred it to ego-tendencies. He might have had the capacity to make, very early in life, a far-reaching identification with the objects in the world around him. Possibly such capacity is due to an unusually early and extensive development from narcissistic to object-libido. Another contributing factor would appear to be the ability to hold libido in a state of suspension. On the other hand we might suppose that there is yet another factor of importance for the capacity of sublimating—one which might well form a very considerable part of the talent with which an individual is constitutionally endowed. I refer to the ease with which an ego-activity or tendency takes on a libidinal cathexis and the extent to which it is thus receptive; on the physical plane we have an analogy in the readiness with which a particular area of the body receives innervation and the importance of this factor in the development of hysterical symptoms. These factors, which might constitute what we understand by 'disposition', would form a complementary series, like those with which we are familiar in the aetiology of the neuroses. In Leonardo's case not only was an identification established between nipple, penis and bird's tail, but this identification became merged into an interest in the motion of this object, in the bird itself and its flight and the space in which it flew. The pleasurable situations, actually experienced or phantasied, remained indeed unconscious and fixated, but they were given play in an ego-tendency and thus could be discharged. When they receive this sort of representation the fixations are divested of their sexual character; they become consonant with the ego and if the sublimation succeeds—if, that is to say, they are merged in an ego-tendency—they do not undergo repression. When this happens, they provide the ego-tendency with the sum of affect which acts as the stimulus and driving force of talent and, since the ego-tendency affords them free scope to exercise themselves in a manner consonant with the ego, they allow phantasy to unfold itself without check and thus are themselves discharged.

In hysterical fixation, on the other hand, phantasy holds so tenaciously to the pleasure-situation that, before sublimation is possible, it succumbs to repression and fixation; and thus, assuming that the other aetiological factors are operative, it is forced to find representation and discharge in hysterical symptoms. The way in which Leonardo's scientific interest in the flight of birds developed shows that also in sublimation the fixation to the phantasy with all its determinants continues to operate.

Freud has comprehensively summed up the essential characteristics of hysterical symptoms.[1] If we apply the test of his description to Leonardo's sublimation as seen in connection with the vulture-phantasy, we shall see the analogy between symptoms and sublimation. I think too, that this sublimation corresponds to Freud's formula that an hysterical symptom often expresses on the one hand a masculine, and on the other a feminine, unconscious sexual phantasy. In Leonardo the feminine side is expressed by the passive phantasy of fellatio; the masculine phantasy seems to me recognizable in a passage which Freud cites from Leonardo's notes as a kind of prophecy: 'The great bird will take its first flight from the back of its great swan; it will fill the universe with amazement and all literature will tell of its fame and it will be an everlasting glory to the nest where it was born.' Does not this mean winning the mother's recognition of his genital achievements? I think that this phantasy, which also expresses an early infantile wish, was represented, together with the vulture-phantasy, in his scientific study of the flight of birds and of aeronautics. Thus Leonardo's genital activity, which played so small a part as far as actual instinctual gratification was concerned, was wholly merged in his sublimations.

According to Freud the hysterical attack is simply a pantomime representation of phantasies, translated into terms of motion and projected on to motility. An analogous assertion may be made of those phantasies and fixations which, as in the artist, are represented by physical motor innervations whether in relation to the subject's own body or some other medium. This statement agrees with what

[1] 'Hysterical Phantasies and their Relation to Bisexuality, *S.E.* **9**.

Ferenczi and Freud have written on the analogies and relations between art and hysteria on the one hand, and the hysterical attack and coitus on the other.

Now as the hysterical attack uses for its material a peculiar condensation of phantasies, so the development either of an interest in art or a creative *talent* would partly depend upon the wealth and intensity of fixations and phantasies represented in sublimation. It would be of importance not only in what quantities all the constitutional and accidental factors concerned are present and how harmoniously they co-operate, but also what is the degree of genital activity which can be deflected into sublimation. Similarly in hysteria the primacy of the genital zone has always been attained.

Genius differs from talent not only quantitatively but also in its essential quality. Nevertheless we may assume for it the same genetic conditions as for talent. Genius seems possible when all factors concerned are present in such abundance as to give rise to unique groupings, made up of units which bear some essential similarity to one another—I mean, the libidinal fixations.

In discussing the question of sublimation I suggested that one determining factor in its success was that the fixations destined for sublimation should not have undergone repression too early, for this precludes the possibility of development. Accordingly we should have to postulate a complementary series between the formation of symptoms on the one hand and successful sublimation on the other—these series to include also possibilities of less successful sublimation. In my opinion we find that a fixation which leads to a symptom was already on the way to sublimation but was cut off from it by repression. The earlier this happens the more will the fixation retain of the actual sexual character of the pleasure-situation and the more will it sexualize the tendency on which it has bestowed its libidinal cathexis, instead of becoming merged in that tendency. The more unstable, too, will this tendency or interest be, for it will remain perpetually exposed to the onslaught of repression.

I should like to add a few words about the distinction between unsuccessful sublimation and inhibition, and the relations between the two. I have mentioned certain inhibitions which I termed normal and which had arisen where repression had been successful; when these were resolved by analysis, it was found that they were based in part on very strong sublimations. These had, it is true, been formed, but had been inhibited either entirely or to some extent. They had not the character of unsuccessful sublimations, which oscillate between symptom-formation, neurotic traits and sublimation. It was only in analysis that they were recognized as inhibitions; they manifested themselves in a negative form, as a lack of inclination or capacity, or sometimes only as a diminution in these. Inhibitions are formed (as I tried to show on page 78) by the transferring of superfluous libido, which finds discharge as anxiety, on to sublimations. Thus sublimation is diminished or destroyed by repression in the form of inhibition, but symptom-formation is avoided, for the anxiety is thus discharged in a manner analogous to that with which we are familiar in hysterical symptom-formation. Accordingly, we may suppose that the normal man attains his state of health by means of inhibitions, assisted by successful repression. If the quantity of anxiety which invests the inhibitions exceeds that of the sublimation, the result is neurotic inhibition, for the tug-of-war between libido and repression is no longer decided on the field of the ego-tendencies, and therefore the same processes as are employed in the neuroses to bind anxiety are set going. Whilst in unsucceessful sublimation the phantasies encounter repression on their way to sublimation and thus become fixated, we may suppose that for a sublimation to be inhibited it must have actually come into existence as a sublimation. Here again we may postulate the complementary series already inferred between symptoms on the one side and successful sublimation on the other. We may assume, however, on the other hand that in proportion as the sublimations are successful and hence little libido remains dammed up in the ego, ready to be discharged as anxiety, the less necessity will there be for inhibition. We may be sure, too, that the more successful the sublimation the less will it be exposed to repression. Here again we may postulate a complementary series.

We know the significance of masturbation phantasies in hysterical symptoms and hysterical attacks. Let me give an illustration of the effect of masturbation phantasies on sublimation. Felix, aged thirteen, produced the following phantasy in analysis. He was playing with some beautiful girls who were naked and whose breasts he stroked and caressed. He did not see the lower part of their bodies. They were playing football with one another. This single sexual phantasy, which in Felix was a substitute for onanism, was succeeded during the analysis by many other phantasies, some in the form of day-dreams, others coming to him at night as a substitute for onanism and all concerned with games. These phantasies showed how some of his fixations were elaborated into an interest in games. In the first sexual phantasy, which was only a fragmentary one, coitus had already been replaced by football.[1] This game, together with others,

[1] This meaning of football, and indeed of all sorts of games with balls, I discovered from the analyses of both boys and girls to be typical. I shall illustrate this statement elsewhere; at present I shall merely state that I came to this conclusion.

had absorbed his interest and ambition entirely, for this sublimation was reinforced by way of reaction as a protection against other repressed and inhibited interests less consonant with the ego.

This reactive or otherwise obsessive reinforcement may very well be in general a determining factor in that destruction of sublimations which sometimes occurs through analysis, though as a rule our experience is that analysis only promotes sublimation. The symptom is given up, as being a costly substitutive formation, when the fixations are resolved and other channels are opened for discharge of the libido. But the bringing into consciousness of such fixations as form the basis of sublimation has as a rule a different result: very often the sublimation is reinforced, for it is retained as the most expedient and probably the earliest substitutive channel for the discharge of libido which must remain unsatisfied.

We know that fixation to 'primal' scenes or phantasies is potent in the genesis of neurosis. I will give an example of the importance of primal phantasies in the development of sublimations. Fritz, who was nearly seven years old, recounted many phantasies about the 'Pipi-general' (the genital organ) who led the soldiers, the 'Pipi-drops', down streets; Fritz gave an exact description of the situation and lie of these streets and compared them with the shape of letters of the alphabet. The general led the soldiers to a village, where they were quartered. The content of these phantasies was coitus with the mother, the accompanying movements of the penis and the way that it took. From their context it appeared that at the same time they were masturbation phantasies. We found that they were operative in his sublimations, together with other elements, into the development of which I cannot at present enter. When he rode on his 'scooter' he attached particular importance to making turns and curves,[1] such as he had described in various phantasies also about his Pipi. For instance he once said that he had invented a patent for the Pipi. The patent consisted in being able, without touching it with his hand, to make the Pipi appear with a jerk through the opening in his knickers by twisting and turning his whole body.

[1] His great delight and skill in this pastime had been preceded originally by awkwardness and distaste. During analysis there occurred first of all an oscillation between enjoyment and distaste—which happened also in regard to his other games of movement and his sports. Later on, he attained to a lasting pleasure and skill in place of the inhibition, which had been determined by the dread of castration. The same determination became evident in regard to his inhibition (and subsequently his pleasure) in tobogganing. Here again he laid peculiar stress on the different postures assumed. We discovered an analogous attitude in him to all games of motion and athletics.

91

He repeatedly had phantasies of inventing special kinds of motor-bicycles and cars. The point of these constructions of his phantasy[1] was invariably to attain special skill in steering and curving in and out. 'Women', he said, 'can perhaps steer but they cannot swerve quickly enough.' One of his phantasies was that all children, girls as well as boys, as soon as they were born had their own little motor-bicycles. Each child could take three or four others on its bicycle and might drop them on the way wherever it liked. Naughty children fell off when the bicycle turned a corner sharply, and the others were put off at the terminus (were born). Talking of the letter S, about which he had many phantasies, he said that its children, the little s's, could shoot and drive motors when they were still in long clothes. All of them had motor-bicycles, on which they could go farther in a quarter of an hour than grown-up people could go in an hour, and the children were better than the grown-ups at running and jumping and in all kinds of bodily dexterity. He also had many phantasies about the different kinds of vehicles which he would like to have and in which he would go to school as soon as he got them, and take his mother or sister with him. At one time he showed anxiety in regard to the idea of pouring petrol into the tank of a motor, because of the danger of explosion; it turned out that in the phantasy of filling up a large or small motor-bicycle with petrol, the latter represented the 'Pipi-water' or semen, which he supposed to be necessary for coitus, while the peculiarly skilful handling of a motor-bicycle and making constant curves and turns stood for skill in coitus.

It was only quite early in life that he had given any sign of this strong fixation to the road and all interests connected with it. When he was about five years old, however, he had a marked distaste for going for a walk. At this age, too, his lack of understanding of distance in time or space was very striking. Thus, when we had been travelling for some hours, he thought he was still in his native town. Associated with his dislike of going out walking was his total lack of interest in becoming acquainted with the place where he had come to stay and the complete absence of any capacity or feeling for orientation.

A keen interest in vehicles took the form of watching carts go by for hours at a time from a window or the entrance-hall of the house and also a passion for motoring. His chief occupation was pretending to be a coachman or a chauffeur, chairs being pushed together to form the vehicle. To this game, which really only consisted in

[1] It was plain that the root of the patent devices and constructions which he phantasied lay always in the movements and functions of the Pipi, which his inventions were designed to bring to greater perfection.

his sitting there quite quietly, he devoted himself so exclusively that it seemed like a compulsion, especially as he had a total disinclination for any other kind of game. It was at this time that I began his analysis and after a few months there was a great change, not only in this respect, but in general.

Hitherto he had been free from anxiety, but during the analysis intense anxiety made its appearance and was analytically resolved. In the last stage of this analysis a phobia of street-boys manifested itself. This was connected with the fact that he had repeatedly been molested by boys in the street. He displayed fear of them and finally could not be persuaded to go into the street alone. I could not get at this phobia analytically, because for external reasons the analysis could not be continued, but I learnt that, soon after we broke it off, the phobia completely disappeared and was succeeded by a peculiar pleasure in roaming about.[1]

Hand in hand with this he developed a more lively feeling for orientation in space. At first his interest was specially directed towards stations, the doors of railway-carriages, and further to the entrances and exits of places as soon as he set foot in them. He began to take a great interest in the rails of the electric tramway and the streets through which it led. Analysis had removed his distaste for play, which had proved to have many determining factors. His interest in vehicles, which had developed early and had been of an obsessive character, now showed itself in many games, which, in contrast to the earlier monotonous game of chauffeur, were played with a wealth of phantasy. He also displayed a passionate interest in lifts and going in lifts. About this time he was ill and had to stay in bed, whereupon he devised the following games. He crept under the bedclothes and said: 'The hole is getting bigger and bigger, I shall soon get out.' So saying, he slowly lifted up the bedclothes at the opposite end of the bed, till the opening was big enough for him to climb out. Then he played that he was going for a journey under the bedclothes; sometimes he came out on one side and sometimes on the other, and he said when he got to the top that he was now 'overground', which he meant to be the opposite to an underground railway. He had been extraordinarily struck by the sight of the underground railway coming out of the ground at a terminus and continuing above ground. In this game with the bedclothes he took great care that they should not be lifted up at either side during his journey,

---

[1] When he was two years and nine months old he once ran away from home and crossed busy streets without a sign of fear. This inclination to run away lasted for about six months. Later he began to show very marked caution about motors (analysis showed that this was neurotic anxiety), and the desire to run away as well as his enjoyment in wandering off seemed to have finally vanished.

so that he only became visible when he emerged at one or other end, which he called the 'end-station'. Another time he had a different game with the bedclothes; this consisted in climbing in and out at different points. When playing these games he once said to his mother: 'I am going into your tummy.' About this time he produced the following phantasy. He was going down into the underground. There were many people there. The conductor was going quickly up and down some steps and gave the people their tickets. He was riding in the underground underneath the earth, till the lines met. Then there was a hole and there was some grass. In another of these games in bed he repeatedly made a toy motor with a chauffeur drive over the bedclothes, which he had rolled into a mound. He then said: 'The chauffeur always wants to go over the mountain, but that is a bad way to go'; then, making the chauffeur go under the bedclothes, 'this is the right way'. He was specially interested in one part of the electric railway where there was only a single line, and a loop was formed. He said about this that there had to be a loop, in case another train came in the opposite direction and there was a collision. He illustrated this danger to his mother: 'Look, if two people come in opposite directions' (so saying he ran towards her), 'they run into one another, and so do two horses, if they come like this.' A frequent phantasy of his was what he imagined his mother to be like inside: how there were all sorts of contrivances, especially in her stomach. This was followed by the phantasy of a swing or merry-go-round, on which there were a number of little people, who kept on getting on one after the other and getting off on the other side. There was somebody who pressed on something and helped them to do this.

His new delight in roaming about and all his other interests lasted for some time, but, after several months, they were succeeded by the old dislike of going for a walk. This was still there when I again began to analyse him recently. He was then nearly seven years old.[1]

During this next part of his analysis, which now went very deep, this dislike increased and showed clearly as an inhibition, until the anxiety behind it became manifest and then could be resolved. It was in particular the *way to school* which called forth this great anxiety. We found that one of the reasons why he did not like the roads along which he went to school was that there were trees on them. Roads where there were fields on each side, on the other hand, he thought very beautiful, because paths could be made there

---

[1] The boy had had a relapse, which was due in part to the fact that, in my desire to be careful, I had not taken the analysis deep enough. Part of the result obtained, however, had proved to be lasting.

and they could be turned into a garden if flowers were planted and watered.[1] His antipathy to trees, which for some time took the form of fear of woods, proved to be partly determined by phantasies of a tree being cut down, which might fall on him. The tree stood to him for his father's large penis, which he wanted to cut off and therefore feared. What his fear was on the way to school we learnt from various phantasies. Once he told me about a bridge (which existed only in his imagination) on his way to school.[2] If there had been a hole in it he might have fallen through. Another time it was a thick piece of string, which he saw lying on the path, that caused anxiety because it reminded him of a snake. At this time, too, he attempted to hop for part of the way, giving as his reason that one of his feet had been cut off. In connection with a picture which he saw in a book he had phantasies about a witch, whom he would meet on his way to school and who would empty a pitcher of ink over him and his satchel. Here the pitcher stood for the penis of the mother.[3] He then added spontaneously that he was afraid of it, but at the same time it was nice. Another time he phantasied that he met a beautiful witch and looked intently at the crown which she wore on her head. Because he stared at her so [*kuckte*] he was a cuckoo [*Kuckuck*] and she charmed away his satchel from him and turned him from a cuckoo into a dove (*i.e.* a female creature, as he thought).

I will give an instance of phantasies which occurred later on in the analysis, in which the original pleasurable significance of the road was evident. He once told me that he would quite like going to school, if only it were not for the road. He now phantasied that, in order to avoid the road, he laid a ladder across from the window of his room to that of his schoolmistress, then he and his mother could go together, by climbing from rung to rung. Then he told me about a rope, also stretched from window to window, along which he and his sister were drawn to the school. There was a servant who helped them by throwing the rope, and the children who were already at school helped too, He himself threw the rope back, 'he would move the rope', as he called it.[4]

[1] Connected with the planting of flowers was his habit of passing urine at certain definite points on the way.

[2] S. Ferenczi, 'The Symbolism of the Bridge' (1921).

[3] His associations to being soiled with ink were: oil and condensed milk—fluids which, as his analysis showed, stood for semen in his mind. It was a mixture of faeces and semen which he supposed to be in the penis both of mother and father.

[4] This was part of a very long and abundantly determined phantasy, which yielded material for various theories of procreation and birth. He also gave other associations about a machine invented by himself, by means of which he could throw the rope to different parts of the town. This phantasy again revealed his idea of being procreated by his father, amalgamated with ideas of coitus on his own part.

During the analysis he became much more active and thereupon he told me the following story which he called 'highway-robbery': There was a gentleman who was very rich and happy, and though he was quite young he wanted to marry. He went into the street and there he saw a beautiful lady and asked her what her name was. She said: 'That has nothing to do with you.' Then he asked where she lived. She said to him again that it was nothing to do with him. They made more and more noise as they talked. Then a policeman came along, who had been watching them, and he took the man to a grand carriage—the kind of carriage such a grand gentleman would have, He was taken to a house with iron bars in front of the window—a prison. He was accused of highway robbery. 'That's what you call it.'[1]

His original pleasure in roads corresponded to the desire for coitus with the mother, and therefore could not come into full operation until the castration-anxiety had been resolved. Similarly we see that, in close connection with this, his love of exploring roads and streets (which formed the basis of his sense of orientation) developed with the release of the sexual curiosity which had likewise been repressed owing to the fear of castration. I will give some examples. He once told me that, when he was urinating, he had to put on the brakes (which he managed by pressing his penis), for otherwise the whole house might fall in.[2] In this connection there were many phantasies which showed that he was under the influence of the mental image of the inside of his mother's body and, by identification with her, of his own body. He pictured it as a town, often as a country, and later on as the world, intersected by railway lines. He imagined this town to be provided with everything necessary for the people and animals who lived there and to be furnished with every kind of modern contrivance.

There were telegraphs and telephones, different sorts of railways, lifts and merry-go-rounds, advertisements, etc. The railways were constructed in different ways. Sometimes there was a circular railway with a number of stations and sometimes they were like the town-railway with two termini. There were two kinds of trains on the rails: one was the 'Pipi'-train, conducted by a 'Pipi'-drop, while

[1] This phantasy shows what determined his earlier phobia of street-boys, which had temporarily disappeared. The first analysis, which had not gone deep enough, had not succeeded in resolving sufficiently the fixations underlying the phobia and his inhibitions. This made it possible for him to relapse. This fact, taken with further experience of the analysis of children, seems to me to prove that infant-analysis as well as later analysis should go as deep as is found to be necessary.

[2] We met with these ideas in his first analysis. (Cf. 'The Development of a Child'.) As the analysis did not go deep enough the phantasies bound up with these ideas could not be released. They made their appearance only in the second analysis.

the other was a 'Kaki'-train, which was driven by a 'Kaki'.[1] Often the 'Kaki'-train was represented as an ordinary passenger train, while the 'Pipi'-train was an express or electric train. The two termini were the mouth and the 'Pipi'. In this case there was a certain place where the train had to cross a track which ran downhill and sloped away steeply at the sides. Then there was a crash, for the train which ran along this track and carried the children—the 'Kaki'-children—was run into by another. The injured children were taken to the signal-box.[2] This turned out to be the 'Kaki'-hole, which was later often introduced into phantasies as the arrival or departure platform. There was also a collision and a crash when the train came from the other direction, that is, when they got in at the mouth. This represents impregnation through eating, and his disgust at certain kinds of food was determined by these phantasies. There were others, in which he spoke of both railways having the same departure platform. The trains then ran along the same lines, branching off lower down and so leading to the 'Pipi' and the 'Kaki'-hole. How strongly he was influenced by the idea of impregnation through the mouth is seen in a phantasy which forced him to stop seven times when urinating. The idea of seven stops proved to have its origin in the number of drops of a medicine which he was taking at the time and for which he had a great repugnance, because, as his analysis showed, he equated it with urine.

There is just one more detail which I would mention in the extraordinarily rich imagery which came to light in these phantasies of a town, railways,[3] stations and roads. Another frequent phantasy was that of a station, to which he gave different names and which I will call A. There were two other stations, B and C, stuck on to the first. Often he pictured these two as a single big station. A was a very important one, because from it all sorts of goods were forwarded,

---

[1] Faeces.

[2] Here I would refer again to a phantasy narrated in 'The Development of a Child', In this phantasy the 'Kaki'-children ran down some steps from the balcony into the garden (the chamber).

[3] The circular railway which came into his phantasies appeared in all his games as well. He constructed trains which ran in a circle and he drove his big hoop round and round in a circle. His gradually increasing interest in the direction and names of streets had developed into an interest in geography. He pretended that he was going on journeys on the map. All this showed that the advance in his phantasies from his home to his town, his country and the world at large (an advance which manifested itself when once the phantasies were set free) was having its effect on his interests also, for their sphere was widening more and more. Here I should like to draw attention to the very great importance of inhibitions in play from this point of view as well. The inhibition and restriction of interests in play leads to the diminishing of potentialities and interests both in learning and in the whole further development of the mind.

and sometimes passengers got in as well, for instance, railway officials, whom he represented by his finger. A was the mouth, whence food went on its way. The railway officials were the 'Pipi', and this led back to his ideas of impregnation through the mouth. B and C were used for unloading the goods. In B there was a garden without any trees but with paths which all led into one another, and to which there were four entrances—not doors but simply holes. These turned out to be the openings of the ears and nose. C was the skull, and B and C together the whole head. He said that the head was only stuck on to the mouth, an idea partly determined by his castration complex. The stomach, too, was often a station, but this arrangement frequently varied. In all this a great part was played by lifts and merry-go-rounds, which were used only to convey the 'Kaki' and children.

As these and other phantasies were interpreted, his sense and faculty of orientation became stronger and stronger, as was plainly shown in his games and interests.

Thus we found that his sense of orientation, which had formerly been strongly inhibited but now developed in a marked manner, was determined by the desire to penetrate the mother's body and to investigate it inside, with the passages leading in and out and the processes of impregnation and birth.[1]

I found that this libidinal determination of the sense of orientation was typical and that favourable development (or, alternatively, inhibition of the sense of orientation owing to repression) depended

---

[1] In the discussion which took place at the meeting of the Berlin Society on my unpublished paper, 'Über die Hemmung und Entwicklung des Orientierungssinnes' (May, 1921), Abraham pointed out that the interest in orientation in relation to the body of the mother is preceded at a very early stage by the interest in orientation in relation to the subject's own body. This is certainly true, but this early orientation seems to share the fate of repression only when the interest in orientation in reference to the mother's body is repressed, of course because of the incestuous wishes bound up with that interest; for in the unconscious the longed-for return to the womb and exploration of it takes place by way of coitus. For instance, Fritz made a tiny dog (which repeatedly represented the *son* in his phantasies) slide along his mother's body. When doing this he had phantasies of the countries through which he was wandering. At her breast there were mountains and near the genital region a great river. But suddenly the little dog was intercepted by servants—toy figures—who charged him with some crime and said he had damaged their master's motor, and the phantasy ended in quarrelling and fighting. At another time he had further phantasies about the little dog's journeys. It had found a pretty spot where he thought he would like to settle, etc. But again it all turned out badly, for Fritz suddenly declared that he had got to shoot the little dog, because it wanted to take away his own log-hut from him. There had, too, been earlier indications of this 'geography of the mother's body'. When he was not five years old he called all the extremities of the body and also the knee-joints 'boundaries', and he called his mother a 'mountain which he was climbing'.

upon it. Partial inhibitions of this faculty, *e.g.* interest in geography and orientation, with a greater or lesser lack of capacity, proved to depend on the factors which I regard as essential to the forming of inhibitions in general. I refer to the period of life and the degree in which repression begins to operate on fixations which are destined for sublimation or are already sublimated. For instance, if the interest in orientation is not repressed, pleasure and interest in it are retained, and the extent of the development of the faculty is then proportionate to the degree of success attending the search for sexual knowledge.

I should like here to draw attention to the very great importance of this inhibition, which, not only in Fritz, radiates to the most diverse interests and studies. Apart from the interest in geography I discovered that it was one of the determining factors in the capacity for drawing[1] and the interest in natural science and everything to do with the exploration of the earth.

In Fritz I found also a very close connection between his lack of orientation in space and in time. Corresponding to his repressed interest in the place of his intra-uterine existence was the absence of interest in details as to the time when he was there. Thus both the questions 'Where was I before birth?' and 'When was I there?' were repressed.

The unconscious equation of sleep, death and intra-uterine existence was evident in many of his sayings and phantasies, and connected with this was his curiosity as to the duration of these states and their succession in time. It would appear that the change from intra-uterine to extra-uterine existence, as the prototype of all periodicity, is one of the roots of the concept of time and of orientation in time.[2]

There is one thing more which I should like to mention, which shows me that the inhibition of the sense of orientation is of very great importance. In Fritz I found that his resistance to enlightenment, which turned out to be so closely connected with the inhibition of his sense of orientation, arose out of his retaining the infantile sexual theory of the 'anal child'. Analysis showed, however, that he held to this anal theory in consequence of repression due to the Oedipus complex and that his resistance to enlightenment was not caused by an incapacity for apprehending the genital process owing to his not having yet reached the genital level of organization.

[1] Fritz, for instance, made his first attempts at drawing at this time, though it is true that they gave no sign of talent. The drawings represented railway-lines with stations and towns.

[2] In this conclusion I am in agreement with Dr Hollós ('Über das Zeitgefühl' (1922)), who arrived at the same result from a different point of departure.

Rather the converse was true: it was this resistance which hindered his advancing to that level and strengthened his fixation at the anal level.

In this connection I must again refer to the meaning of resistance to enlightenment. The analysis of children has over and over again confirmed me in my view of it. I have been forced to regard it as an important symptom, a sign of inhibitions which determine the whole subsequent development.

In Fritz I found that his attitude towards learning, too, was determined by the same sexual-symbolic cathexis, Analysis showed that his marked distaste for learning was a highly complex inhibition, determined in reference to the separate school-subjects by the repression of different instinctual components. Like the inhibition against walking, games and the sense of orientation, its main determinant was the repression, based on castration anxiety, of the sexual-symbolic cathexis common to all these interests, namely, the idea of penetrating into the mother by coitus. In his analysis this libidinal cathexis, and with it the inhibition, plainly advanced from the earliest movements and games of motion to the way to school, school itself, his schoolmistress and the activities of school life.

For in his phantasies the lines in his exercise book were roads, the book itself was the whole world and the letters rode into it on motor bicycles, *i.e.* on the pen. Again, the pen was a boat and the exercise book a lake. We found that Fritz's many mistakes (which for a time could not be overcome, until they were resolved in analysis, when they disappeared without any trouble) were determined by his many phantasies about the different letters which were friendly with one another or fought and had all sorts of experiences. In general he regarded the small letters as the children of the capital letters. The capital S he looked upon as the emperor of the long German s's; it had two hooks at the end of it to distinguish it from the empress, the terminal s, which had only one hook.

We discovered that the spoken word was to him identical with the written. The word stood for the penis or the child, while the movement of the tongue and the pen stood for coitus.

I shall just briefly mention what the analysis of children has shown me to be the general significance of libidinal cathexis for the development of infantile speech and its peculiarities, and indeed for the development of speech as a whole. In speech oral,[1] cannibalistic and anal-sadistic fixations are sublimated, more or less successfully according to the degree in which the fixations of the earlier

---

[1] I would refer here to an interesting paper by Dr S. Spielrein (1922), in which, in a very illuminating way, she traces the origin of the infantile words 'Papa' and 'Mama' to the act of sucking.

levels of organization are comprehended under the primacy of the genital fixations. I think this process, which enables perverse fixations to be discharged, must surely be demonstrable in all sublimations. Owing to the operation of complexes, various intensifications and displacements arise, which are of the nature of regression or reaction. These afford an unlimited number of possibilities in the individual, as appears, to keep the example of speech, both in his own special peculiarities of speech and in the development of languages in general.

In Fritz I found that speaking, which undoubtedly is one of the earliest sublimations, was inhibited from the outset. During the analysis this child, who had begun to speak unusually late and subsequently seemed to be of a silent disposition, turned into a remarkably talkative little fellow. He never tired of telling stories which he made up himself, and in these there was a development of phantasy to which he had shown no tendency before the analysis. But it was plain, too, that he took a delight in the actual speaking and that he stood in a special relation to words in themselves. Hand in hand with this, too, went a strong interest in grammar. As an illustration I will quote briefly what he said grammar meant to him. He told me that 'the root of the word itself does not move, only its termination'. He wanted to give his sister on her birthday a notebook in which he wrote everything that a thing did. What does a thing do? 'A thing jumps, a thing runs, a thing flies', etc. It was the representation of what the penis can do that he wanted to write in the book and also to do in the mother.

The significance of speaking as a genital activity, as reported also by Abraham in a case of pseudologia, I found at work in a greater or lesser degree in every case. In my opinion both this and the anal determination are typical. This was peculiarly evident to me in the case of a girl with a stammer, who had strong homosexual fixations. This girl, Grete, who was nine years old, looked upon speaking and singing as the male activity and the movement of the tongue as that of the penis. She took a special delight when lying on the couch in reciting certain French sentences. She said it was 'such fun when her voice went up and down like someone on a ladder'. Her association to this was that the ladder was set up in a snail. But would there be room for it in a snail? (A snail, however, was her name for her genitals.) The comma and the full stop, like the pause corresponding to them in speaking, meant that one had gone 'up and down' once and was beginning again. A single word stood for the penis and a sentence for the thrust of the penis in coitus and also for coitus as a whole.

In a number of cases it became clear that theatres and concerts, in fact any performance where there is something to be seen or heard, always stand for parental coitus—listening and watching standing for observation in fact or phantasy—while the falling curtain stands for objects which hinder observations, such as bed-clothes, the side of the bed, etc. I will quote an example. Little Grete told me about a play at the theatre. At first she had been distressed at not having a good enough seat and having to be at some distance from the stage. But she made out that she saw better than the people who sat quite near the stage, for they could not see all over it. Her associations then led to the position of the children's beds, which were placed in their parents' bedroom in such a way that her younger brother slept close to his parents' bed, but the backs of the beds made it difficult for him to see them. Her bed, however, was further off and she could see theirs perfectly.

In Felix, who was thirteen years old and up till then had shown no musical talent, a marked love of music gradually developed during analysis. This came about as the analysis was bringing into consciousness his fixation to early infantile observations of coitus. We found that sounds, some of which he had heard proceeding from his parents' bed and the rest of which he had phantasied, had formed the basis of a very strong (and very early inhibited) interest in music, an interest which was liberated again during analysis. This determination of the interest in and gift for music I found present (side by side with the anal determination) in other cases as well, and I believe it to be typical.

In Mrs H I found that a marked artistic appreciation of colours, forms and pictures was similarly determined, with this difference, that in her the early infantile observations and phantasies were concerned with what was to be *seen*. For instance, in this case a certain bluish tinge in pictures directly represented the male element; it was a fixation of the analysand to the colour of the penis in erection. These fixations resulted from observations of coitus, which had led to comparisons with the colour and form of the penis when not in erection, and further to observations of a certain change in colouring and form in different lights, the contrast with the pubic hair and so forth. Here the anal basis of the interest in colour was always present. One can repeatedly establish the fact of this libidinal cathexis of pictures as representing penis or child (the same applies to works of art in general), and further, of painters, virtuosi and creative artists, as standing for the father.

I will give only one more example of the significance of pictures as child and penis—a meaning which I repeatedly come across in analysis. Fritz, aged five and a half, said that he would like to see his mother naked, adding: 'I should like to see your tummy and the picture in it.' When she asked: 'Do you mean where you once were?' he replied: 'Yes, I should like to look in your tummy and see if there isn't a child there.' At this time, under the influence of analysis, his sexual curiosity manifested itself more freely and his theory of the 'anal child' came into the foreground.

To sum up what I have said, I have found that artistic and intellectual fixations, as well as those which subsequently lead to neurosis, have as some of their most powerful determining factors the primal scene or phantasies of it. An important point is which of the senses is more strongly excited: whether the interest applies more to what is to be seen or to what is to be heard. This will probably also determine, and on the other hand will also depend upon, whether ideas present themselves to the subject visually or auditorily. No doubt constitutional factors play a great part here.

In Fritz it was the movement of the penis to which he was fixated, in Felix the sounds which he heard, in others the colour-effects. Of course, for the talent or bent to develop, those special factors which I have already discussed in detail must come into play. In fixation to the primal scene (or phantasies) *the degree of activity*, which is so important for sublimation itself, undoubtedly also determines whether the subject develops a talent for creation or reproduction. For the degree of activity certainly influences the mode of identification. I mean it is a question whether it will spend itself in the admiration, study and imitation of the masterpieces of others or whether there will be an endeavour to excel these by the subject's own performances. In Felix I found that the first interest in music which manifested itself in analysis was exclusively concerned with criticism of composers and conductors. As his activity was gradually released he began to try himself to imitate what he heard. But at a further stage of still greater activity phantasies made their appearance in which the young composer was compared to older men. Although apparently there was no question of creative talent in this case, my observation of the way in which his activity, as it became freer, influenced his attitude in all his sublimations gave me some insight into the importance of activity in the development of talent. His analysis showed me what other analyses confirmed: that criticism always has its origin in the observation and criticism of the paternal genital activities. In Felix it was clear that he was onlooker and critic in one and that in his phantasy he also took part as a member of an orchestra in what he saw and heard. It was only at a much later stage of released activity that he could trust himself with the paternal rôle — that is, it was only then that he would have been able to summon up courage to become a composer himself, if he had had sufficient talent.

Let me sum up. Speech and pleasure in motion have always a libidinal cathexis which is also of a genital-symbolic nature. This is effected by means of the early identification of the penis with foot, hand, tongue, head and body, whence it proceeds to the activities of these members, which thus acquire the significance of coitus. After the use made by the sexual instincts of the self-preservative instincts in respect of the function of nutrition, the next ego-activities to which they turn are those of speech and pleasure in motion. Hence, speech may be assumed not only to have assisted the formation of symbols and sublimation, but to be itself the result of one of the earliest sublimations. It seems then that, where the necessary conditions for the capacity to sublimate are present, the fixations, beginning with these most primary sublimations and in connection with them, continually proceed to a sexual-symbolic cathexis of further ego-activities and interests. Freud demonstrates that that which seems to be an impulsion towards perfection in human beings is the result of the tension arising out of the disparity between man's desire for gratification (which is not to be appeased by all possible kinds of reactive substitutive formations and of sublimations) and the gratification which in reality he obtains. I think that we may put down to this motive not only that which Groddeck (1922) calls the compulsion to make symbols but also a constant development of the symbols. Accordingly the impulsion constantly to effect by means of fixations a libidinal cathexis of fresh ego-activities and interests genetically (*i.e.* by means of sexual symbolism) connected with one another, and to create new activities and interests, would be the driving force in the cultural evolution of mankind. This explains, too, how it is that we find symbols at work in increasingly complicated inventions and activities, just as the child constantly advances from his original primitive symbols, games and activities to others, leaving the former ones behind.

Further, in this paper I have tried to point out the great importance of those inhibitions which cannot be called neurotic. There are some which in themselves do not seem of any practical importance and can be recognized as inhibitions only in analysis (in their full implication possibly only if *infant-analysis* is undertaken). Such are an apparent lack of certain interests, insignificant dislikes—in short, the inhibitions of the healthy person, which assume the most varied disguises. Yet we shall come to attribute to these a very great importance when we consider at how big a sacrifice of instinctual energy the normal man purchases his health. 'If, however, we turn our attention not to an extension of the concept of psychical impotence, but to the gradations in its symptomatology, we cannot escape the conclusion that the behaviour in love of men in the civilized world today bears the stamp altogether of psychical impotence.'[1]

There is a passage in the *Introductory Lectures* in which Freud discusses what possibilities of prophylaxis can be held out to educationists. He comes to the conclusion that even rigid protection of childhood (in itself a very difficult thing) is probably powerless against the constitutional factor, but that it would also be dangerous if such protection succeeded too well in attaining its aim. This statement was fully confirmed in the case of little Fritz. The child had from his early days had a careful up-bringing by persons who had been influenced by analytic views, but this did not prevent inhibitions and neurotic character-traits from arising. On the other hand, his analysis showed me that the very fixations which had led to the inhibitions might form the basis of splendid capacities.

On the one hand, then, we must not rate too highly the importance of so-called analytical up-bringing, though we must do everything in our power to avoid mental injury to the child. On the other hand, the argument of this paper shows the necessity of analysis in early childhood as a help to all education. We cannot alter the factors which lead to the development of sublimation or of inhibition and neurosis, but early analysis makes it possible for us, at a time when this development is still going on, to influence its direction in a fundamental manner.

I have tried to show that the libidinal fixations determine the genesis of neurosis and also of sublimation and that for some time the two follow the same path. It is the force of repression which determines whether this path will lead to sublimation or turn aside to neurosis. It is at this point that early analysis has possibilities, for it can to a great extent substitute sublimation for repression and thus divert the path to neurosis into that which leads to the development of talents.

[1] Freud: 'On the Universal Tendency to Debasement in the Sphere of Love', *S.E.* **11**.

5

A CONTRIBUTION TO
THE PSYCHOGENESIS OF TICS[1]

(1925)

IN the following abstract of a somewhat lengthy case-history I propose primarily to examine those factors which have a bearing on
the psychogenesis of tics. In this case the tic appeared to be merely
a secondary symptom and for a considerable time it hardly entered
into the material. In spite of this, the part it played in the whole
personality of the patient, in the development of his sexuality, his
neurosis and his character was so fundamental that, once analysis
succeeded in curing it, the treatment was fairly near its end.

When the thirteen-year-old Felix was brought to me for analysis,
he illustrated strikingly what Alexander has termed the 'neurotic
character'. Though free from actual neurotic symptoms he was very
inhibited in his intellectual interests and social relations. His mental
ability was good, yet he had no interest in anything except games.
He held himself very much aloof from his parents, brother and
schoolfellows. His lack of emotions, too, was striking. His mother
mentioned only by the way that for some months he had had a tic,
which appeared only occasionally and to which she—and for that
matter I too, at least for a period—did not attach special importance.

As he came to analysis only three times a week, and as his treatment was repeatedly interrupted, the analysis of 370 hours was
drawn out over three and a quarter years. When the boy came to me
he was still in the pre-pubertal stage, and the long duration of the
treatment enabled me to gain an insight into the way in which all his
difficulties were intensified by the onset of puberty.

Here are some essential points concerning his development. At
the age of three a stretching of the foreskin was performed on him,
and the connection between this stretching and masturbation was
specially impressed on him. His father, too, had repeatedly given
warnings and even threatened the boy; and as a result of these
threats Felix was determined to give up masturbation. But even

[1] Note, 1947. I have to thank Miss D. J. Barnett for the help she gave me in the
translation of this paper.

during the latency period he only occasionally succeeded in carrying out this resolution. When he was eleven, a nasal examination became necessary and this reactivated his trauma connected with the surgical manipulation when he was three and led to a renewal of the struggle against masturbation, this time with complete success. The return of his father from the war and his renewed threats contributed materially to this result. Castration anxiety and the ensuing incessant struggle against masturbation dominated the development of the boy. Of great importance was the circumstance that up to his sixth year he had shared his parents' bedroom and his observations of parental intercourse had left a lasting impression on him.

The trauma of the surgical manipulation at the age of three— the age at which infantile sexuality reaches its climax—strengthened his castration complex and led him to turn from a heterosexual to a homosexual attitude. But even the inverted Oedipus situation was wrecked by castration anxiety. His sexual development was thrown back to the anal-sadistic level and showed a tendency to further regression to narcissism. Thus the foundation was laid for a rejection of the external world, an attitude which became increasingly clear in his rather asocial attitude.

As a very young child he had enjoyed singing, but at about the age of three he had given it up. It was not until he was being analysed that his musical talent and interest in music revived. Excessive physical restlessness already appeared at this early age and tended to increase. In school it was impossible for him to keep his legs still; he fidgeted unceasingly in his seat, pulled faces, rubbed his eyes, etc.

When Felix was seven, the birth of a baby brother intensified his difficulties in many ways. His craving for tenderness grew stronger, yet his aloofness from his parents and his environment became more marked.

During his first years at school Felix was a good scholar. Games and gym however roused strong anxiety in him and he showed a great aversion to them. When he was eleven his father, newly returned from the war, threatened him with punishment for his physical cowardice. The boy succeeded in overcoming his anxiety. He even swung over to the other extreme,[1] became an ardent footballer and took up gymnastics and swimming, although from time to time relapses occurred. On the other hand, he responded to his father's insistence on supervising his homework by losing his interest in schoolwork. An increasing aversion to learning gradually made school a torture. At this period the struggle against masturbation was revived

[1] For the alternation between love of games and love of learning—which I have also met with, even if not so marked, in other cases—see my chapter 'Early Analysis'.

with great energy. The analysis of his passion for games which, together with his dislike of school-work, was very much in the foreground during the first part of his treatment, showed clearly that games and other physical activities were to him a substitute for masturbation. At the beginning of his analysis the only masturbation phantasy of which he could still recall scraps was as follows: *He is playing with some little girls; he caresses their breasts and they play football together. In this game he is continually disturbed by a hut which can be seen behind the little girls.*

Analysis revealed that this hut was a lavatory which stood for his mother, expressed his anal fixation to her, and also had the significance of degrading her. The game of football was shown to represent an acting out of his coitus phantasies and took the place of masturbation as a permissible form of release of sexual tension, one which was encouraged, even exacted by his father. At the same time games afforded him an opportunity to utilize the excessive mobility which was closely associated with his struggle against masturbation. But this sublimation was only partially successful.[1]

The equation of games with sexual intercourse had, under the pressure of castration anxiety, been the cause of the former inhibition of his love of games. In consequence of his father's threats he had then succeeded in displacing a part of this anxiety on to his school-work, which also had some unconscious connection with sexual intercourse and now became a forbidden activity, as the games had been before. In my paper 'The Rôle of the School in the Libidinal Development of the Child' I have explained this connection more specifically with regard to this particular case as well as to its wider applications. Here I shall only mention that for Felix a successful dealing with anxiety by means of games, learning and other sublimations was not possible. Anxiety came up again and again. It became increasingly clear to him in the course of the analysis that games were an unsuccessful over-compensation for anxiety, an unsuccessful substitute for masturbation; and correspondingly his interest in games diminished. At the same time he developed—also gradually—an interest in various school subjects. Simultaneously his 'Berührungsangst' (the fear of touching his genital) diminished and after many unsuccessful efforts he gradually overcame his long-standing fears of masturbation.

An increase in the frequency of the tic was to be noticed at this time. It had first appeared a few months prior to the analysis, the precipitating factor being that Felix had clandestinely witnessed sexual intercourse between his parents. Immediately afterwards the

[1] In my chapter 'Early Analysis', I made a contribution to the theory of sublimation and also discussed this same case and the factors underlying the abandonment of an unsuccessful sublimation such as this.

symptoms, out of which the tic developed, appeared: a twitching of the face and a throwing back of the head. The tic comprised three phases. At the beginning Felix had a feeling as though the depression in his neck, under the back of his head, were being torn. In consequence of this feeling he felt constrained first to throw his head back and then to rotate it from right to left. The second movement was accompanied by a feeling that something was cracking loudly. The concluding phase consisted of a third movement in which the chin was pressed as deeply as possible downwards. This gave Felix a feeling of drilling into something. For a time he performed these three movements three times over consecutively. One meaning of the 'three' was that in the tic—I shall return to this later in detail—Felix played three rôles: the passive rôle of his mother, the passive rôle of his own ego, and the active rôle of his father. The passive rôles were represented predominantly by the first two movements; though in the feeling of 'cracking' was contained also the sadistic element representing the active rôle of the father, an element which came to fuller expression in the third movement, that of drilling into something.

In order to bring the tic within the scope of the analysis, it was necessary to obtain the patient's free associations to his sensations associated with the tic and to the circumstances which gave rise to the tic. It had developed after some time into a symptom that occurred with increasing frequency but at first at irregular intervals. Not until the analysis had succeeded in penetrating the deeper layers of his repressed homosexuality, the material for which had first appeared in his accounts of games and the phantasies associated with them, did its significance begin to emerge. Later his homosexuality found expression in the form of a hitherto unrevealed interest in concerts, particularly in conductors and individual musicians. A love of music came to light and developed into a real and lasting understanding of music.

Felix had already in this third year revealed by his singing an identification with his father. After the trauma this interest, in conformity with the rest of his unfavourable development, became repressed. Its re-emergence in the course of the analysis was preceded by screen memories of early childhood. He remembered as a small boy getting up in the morning and seeing his face reflected in the polished surface of the grand piano, noticing that it was a distorted reflection, and feeling afraid. Another screen memory was that of hearing his father snore in the night and seeing horns growing out of his forehead. His associations led from a dark piano, which he had seen at the house of a friend, to his parents' bed, and showed that the sounds which he had heard emanating from the bed had first contributed largely to his interest in sounds and music and had later caused their inhibition. After attending a concert he complained, during analysis, that the grand piano had completely concealed the artist, and in this connection he produced a memory: the position of his cot at the foot of his parents' bed had been such that the end piece of the bed had obstructed his view of what was taking place, but had not prevented him listening and making observations. It became increasingly clear that his interest in conductors was determined by the equation of the conductor with his father in the act of copulating. The wish to participate actively in what was taking place, while still an onlooker, came to light in the following association: he would very much like to know how the conductor manages to make the players follow his beat with such precision. To Felix that seemed extremely difficult, because while the conductor had a fairly large baton, the musicians use only their fingers.[1] Phantasies of being a musician and playing in time with the conductor constituted an essential part of his repressed masturbation phantasies. The already developing sublimation of his masturbation phantasies into an interest in the rhythmic and motor elements of music became impeded by the premature and violent onset of repression, and in this connection the trauma of the surgical manipulation when he was three was significant. The need for motor activity therefore was discharged in excessive restlessness and, in the course of his development, was expressed in other ways as well, of which I shall speak later.

With this boy the phantasy of taking his mother's place in relation to his father, that is the passive homosexual attitude, was concealed by the active homosexual phantasy of taking the place of his father in intercourse with a boy. This phantasy was the expression of his homosexual object choice at the narcissistic level; he chose himself as his love object. It was the castration anxiety arising from the trauma which determined the narcissistic development of his homosexuality. Further, the turning away first from his mother and then from his father as loved objects was the outcome of his narcissistic regression and formed the basis of his asocial behaviour. But behind this homosexual content of his masturbation phantasies it was possible to discern in numerous details (as for instance in his interest in the grand piano and in musical scores) Felix's original identification with his father, that is, the heterosexual phantasy of sexual intercourse with the mother. In his third year Felix had given expression to this identification by his singing, which he later gave up.

The anal components of his masturbation phantasies also became clear. For example, his wish to know whether it was due to the orchestra being placed below the stage in the theatre that the music

---

[1] This desire to keep time was expressed also in other ways, for instance in his emotional reaction when a bigger boy outstripped him in walking.

sounded so muffled was determined by the anal interpretation of the sounds emanating from his parents' bed. His criticism of one of the younger composers for making too much use of the wind instruments led us back to his infantile interest in the sounds of flatus. He himself, into whose musical sensibility the anal components entered so strongly, was the young composer who felt that he was only capable of anal achievement as compared with his father's genital achievement. It is significant that this intensified interest in sound was partly the result of repression of interest in the visual sphere. At a very early stage of his development his scoptophilia, which was intensified by the experience of the primal scene, had become subject to repression. This became again evident in the course of the analysis. Following a visit to the opera he had produced a phantasy based on the black dots and lines on the conductor's score, which from his seat near the stage he had tried to decipher. (Here again we had a link with his heterosexual desires, for the music lying in front of the conductor was identified by Felix with his mother's genitals.) We shall understand this better when we come to discuss the transitory symptoms of blinking and rubbing his eyes.

When he first came to analysis, Felix had a very pronounced tendency not to see the things that were nearest to him. A dislike of the cinema,[1] which he conceded to be of value only for scientific purposes, was connected with the repression of scoptophilia which was heightened by the primal scene.

In Felix's admiration for the conductor, who, unmoved by the audience and their applause was able 'simultaneously to conduct and so rapidly to turn over the pages of the music that it sounded like tearing' (*herumreissen*), we find an illustration of his sadistic conception of sexual intercourse. He claimed that even from his seat he could hear the sound of the pages being turned—a sound which so much interested him and which reminded him of revolution and violence—but he doubted that this could have been possible at that distance. The feeling of having heard it connected with the original situation in infancy. This violent tearing sound which to him stood for forceful tearing and penetrating revealed itself as an important sadistic element in his masturbation phantasies. We shall deal with this later when we analyse the tic.

[1] Similarly in another case of tic—that of a fifteen-year-old boy in whom the tic also appeared to be merely an unimportant symptom—aversion to the cinema was connected with repression of scoptophilia stimulated by observation of sexual intercourse. In addition he suffered from severe fears for his eyes. I was not able to analyse this boy sufficiently because, following an early improvement, his analysis was stopped. His tic—also consisting of movements of the head—had not entered into the analysis. Nevertheless I gained some data which were consistent with the material discussed in the present paper.

The increasing interest which he came to take at the same time in poets, writers and composers was connected with his early admiration for his father, which later was deeply repressed. In this connection he experienced for the first time a direct homosexual interest after reading a book which contained a description of a man's love for a boy. He developed a romantic 'crush' for a schoolfellow. This boy, besides being adored by a large number of the other boys, was the favourite of one of the masters, and the whole class assumed, apparently with good reason, that there was a love affair between teacher and pupil. It was largely this relation to the master which determined Felix's object choice. The analysis showed that this boy, A., represented on the one hand an idealization of Felix himself and, on the other, something between male and female, the mother with a penis. A.'s relation to the master stood for the realization of Felix's own unfulfilled longing to be loved as a son by his father, as well as to take the mother's place in the relation to his father. His love for A. was principally based on identification and corresponded to a narcissistic object relation. This love remained unrequited. It is true, Felix scarcely dared to approach the loved boy. He came to share this unhappy love with another school-fellow, B., and then chose B. as a loved object. The material showed that B., by his colouring and in various other ways, recalled Felix's father and was meant to replace him. This relation led to mutual masturbation, and in view of all the complications I felt that in the interest of the analysis I had to put a stop to this relation between the two boys.

Simultaneously with those developments—reawakening interest in music, manifest homosexuality and revived masturbation—there was a marked diminution in the frequency of the tic, and when on occasions it did appear, we were able to grasp its unconscious meaning. At the time when Felix told me that he felt he had overcome his love for both A. and B. the tic reappeared with increased severity. This showed clearly what the tic had been standing for—namely for the repressed homosexual impulses, or rather for the discharge of these impulses in phantasies or in masturbation. During the period of early childhood conflicts Felix had felt impelled by castration anxiety to repress his desires directed towards his mother and father. Now, partly at my request, he had repeated the process by turning away from A. and B. Thus the tic appeared as a substitute, in the same way as formerly excessive physical restlessness had taken the place of masturbation and masturbation phantasies. A more extensive analysis of his homosexual tendencies now became possible. Direct homosexuality declined to a marked degree and sublimations appeared, particularly friendships with other boys began at this period.

Further analysis of the tic took us back again and again to its sources in early childhood. On one occasion, when Felix was doing his homework together with a friend, he made up his mind to be the first in solving a mathematical problem, but the friend solved it first, and then the tic appeared. Associations showed that this defeat in the rivalry with his friend brought up again the father's superiority and revived Felix's castration complex. As a result he felt thrown back into adopting the feminine rôle in relation to his father. On another occasion the tic occurred when he had to confess to the English master that he had not been able to keep up with the work and wished to have some private lessons to make good the deficiency. For him this, too, had the significance of an admission of defeat in relation to his father.

The following incident was particularly characteristic. Felix had tried to obtain admission to a concert that was sold out; he was standing with many other people in the entrance to the concert hall, when in the crush a man broke a pane of glass and a policeman had to be summoned. At that moment the tic appeared. Analysis revealed that this particular situation represented a repetition of the eaves-dropping scene in early childhood which was closely bound up with the origin of the tic. He identified himself with the man who broke the window for, like him, he too in that early situation had wanted to force admission to a 'concert', i.e. the sexual intercourse between the parents. The policeman stood for the father detecting him in this attempt.

The further diminution of the tic took place along two lines: the tic became less frequent, and the three movements of the tic were reduced to two and then to one movement. First the feeling that something at the back of his neck was being torn, which occasioned the first movement of the tic, came to an end; then the feeling of loud cracking, which ushered in the second movement, also came to an end. All that remained was the feeling of drilling into something, which had the two-fold significance of pressure in the anal sense and a penetration by his penis. Phantasies of destroying his father's penis as well as that of his mother by this drilling into them by his penis were associated with this feeling. At this stage the tic movements were condensed into one, in which traces of the first two movements could still be detected.

The disappearance of the feelings of tearing and cracking, which were determined by passive homosexual factors, went side by side with a similar alteration in the masturbation phantasies; their homo-sexual content changed from passive to active. The rhythm of sexual intercourse, however, was implied in the tearing as well as in the cracking and drilling. When Felix, despite the urgency of these feel-ings, refrained from the tic movements, he experienced a strong sense of tension, an increase and then a diminution of these feelings, for a time predominantly that of tearing, then of cracking, later only of drilling. After some time the tic disappeared altogether, but its place was taken by a movement which consisted in pushing back both shoulders. The meaning of this was revealed by the following incident: while talking to the headmaster, Felix was suddenly seized with an irresistible urge to scratch his back and this was followed by an irritation of the anus and contraction of the sphincter. It became clear that he had also experienced the repressed wish to insult the master with coprophilic language and to smear him with faeces. This again took us back to the primal scene when the same wish had arisen with regard to his father and had been expressed by passing a motion and screaming.

At a later stage in the analysis of the tic, eye-rubbing and blinking appeared as substitutes for the tic, a transformation which was explained as follows: a medieval inscription had been written on the blackboard in school and Felix had the feeling—quite without justification—that he could not decipher it properly. He thereupon began to rub his eyes violently and to blink. Associations revealed that the blackboard[1] and the writing on it signified—as on many other occasions during the analysis—his mother's genital as the unknowable, incomprehensible element in the coitus situation which he had observed. There is an analogy between this inscription on the blackboard and the conductor's score, the black lines of which he had tried to decipher from his seat in the theatre. From both instances it would appear that repressed scoptophilia led to the blinking and that, particularly in the eye-rubbing, a wish to masturbate—which arose at the same time—obtained expression by means of displacement. We were also able in the analysis to come to understand fully the connection between these situations and states of withdrawal which frequently came over him at school. The staring into vacancy was associated with phantasies of which the following is an instance: he is watching and listening to a thunderstorm; that reminds him of a thunderstorm in his early childhood; after the storm was over he had leaned out of the window to see if the landlord and his wife, who had previously been in the garden, were injured. This memory, however, proved to be a screen memory which again led to the primal scene.

Further progress was made in the analysis of the tic and its substitute formations, so that eventually even the blinking and eye-rubbing came to an end, and it was only the thought about the tic which appeared in his mind on special occasions. When these, too, had revealed their connection with the repressed masturbation wishes and

[1] For this symbolical meaning of table, desk, penholder, writing, etc., see my chapter on 'The Rôle of the School in the Libidinal Development of the Child'.

the primal scene, even the thought about the tic disappeared and with this a complete and lasting cure of the tic was effected. At the same time a notable change in other directions had taken place in the analysis. For the first time heterosexual desires appeared and took the form of admiration for an actress. This object choice was in line with Felix's consistent identification[1] of the theatre, concerts, etc., with sexual intercourse and the performers with the parents. He himself then figured, as I have already shown, as an onlooker and auditor and, simultaneously through identification with his parents, as a performer in the different rôles.

Once, after he had had to wait for me in the consulting-room for a few moments, Felix informed me that he had looked through the window at the flats opposite and in so doing had experienced a peculiar sensation. At the numerous windows he had seen shadows and forms and had tried to imagine what they were doing. It seemed to him like being in a theatre where one sees various rôles being played and at the same time has the feeling of sharing what is going on.

Felix's first heterosexual object choice was much influenced by his homosexual attitude. For him this actress possessed male attributes, she was the mother with a penis. This attitude persisted still in his relation to his second heterosexual love object. He fell in love with a girl who was older than himself and had taken the initiative in the matter. She personified his early childhood picture of his mother as a prostitute, at the same time also that of the mother with a penis who was superior to him. The transference proved strong enough for me to impose a temporary break in this relation,[2] particularly since Felix had already reached the insight that feelings of anxiety were bound up with these relationships. This object choice served the purpose of a flight from the phantasies and wishes directed towards me, and which only at this stage came more fully to the fore in the analysis. It could now be seen that the turning away from the originally loved but forbidden mother had participated in the strengthening of the homosexual attitude and the phantasies about the dreaded castrating mother.

The change from homosexual to heterosexual tendencies, and the modification within the latter, also found expression in the development and modification of Felix's masturbation phantasies. The analysis took us back to the earliest masturbation phantasies directly

[1] I have found the equation of theatre, concert, cinema and every kind of performance with the primal scene characteristic of all child analyses. It is described in my chapter 'Early Analysis'.

[2] Contrary to my usual custom, I had to impose a prohibition in this case, as well as in the previous relation, in order to render the continuation of the analysis at all possible.

connected with his observation of parental sexual intercourse. I shall now describe in broad outline the development of these phantasies in their actual chronological order.

As a small boy, while still sharing his parents' bedroom, which he did up to the age of six, Felix had pictured in front of him the trunk of a big tree pointing in the opposite direction to that of his parents' bed. A little man was sliding down this tree towards him, and was half an old man and half a child—a condensation of his father and himself; this expressed his narcissistic homosexual object choice. Later on it was men's heads, in particular the heads of Greek heroes, which he saw flying towards him and which also were in his mind projectiles and heavy objects. This was already the material for his later football phantasies and for his later method of over-compensating for his fear of his castrating father by skill in football.

With the onset of psychic puberty a fresh effort to effect a hetero-sexual object choice appeared in the masturbation phantasies concerning the little girls with whom he played football. In this phantasy too he changed the heads (of the little girls), just as earlier he had introduced the heads of heroes, in order to make the real loved objects unrecognizable. In the course of the analysis, and with the gradual resumption of masturbation which increased as the tic diminished, his masturbation phantasies developed step by step to the following content: he had phantasies of a woman lying on top of him, then of a woman lying sometimes on top of him and occasionally also under him, finally of one exclusively in the latter position. Various details of the associated phantasies of sexual intercourse corresponded to these different positions.

The analysis of the masturbation phantasies had in Felix's case proved to be the decisive factor in the cure of the tic. His giving up masturbation had led to motor discharge along other lines, these being, as we have seen, pulling faces, blinking and eye-rubbing, excessive mobility in the most diverse forms, games and finally the tic.

But if we now consider the vicissitudes of the specific repressed masturbation phantasies, we find that they were partly connected with these motor discharges and were partly contained in all his attempts at sublimation. At the basis of his love of sport lay the same masturbation phantasies which had proved to be associated with the tic: namely the identification, based on the primal scene, with both parents in the act of sexual intercourse when in his mind he participated both as an onlooker and as a loved object. Since in his analysis the interest in games and reports about them played a great part, I had ample material to substantiate that the same identification was underlying his phantasies connected with games. His opponent in football, etc., was always his father who was threatening to castrate him and against whom he had to defend himself. But the goal into which the ball is thrown and the playing field represented his mother. In other ways too analysis made it possible to see the figure of the mother even behind the homosexual tendencies, in the same way as was later the case with the phantasies associated with the tic. Games and excessive mobility also served as a flight from the tic, or rather from masturbation. It was due primarily to the constantly recurring castration anxiety that this sublimation was only imperfectly achieved and that the boy's relation to games remained unstable. But we find that these masturbation phantasies were also the cause of his ambivalent attitude towards learning, being intimately bound up also with that activity.

One day, while the master was leaning against his desk during a lesson, the wish came to Felix that the master should knock the desk over, break it and, in so doing, injure himself. To Felix this represented a new version of his father having sexual intercourse with the mother while Felix looked on. His relation to the master was, from the beginning, a repetition of his relation to his father, and in the same way was determined by repressed homosexuality. Every answer he gave in class, all the work he did at school, had the significance of homosexual intercourse with his father. But here too, just as in his relation to his partner or opponent in games, the original relation to his mother—however well concealed—appeared behind the homosexual tendency. The form on which he sat in school, the desk on which the master leaned and the blackboard on which he wrote, the class-room, the school building—all of these stood, in relation to the master, for the mother with whom the master (father) has sexual intercourse, in exactly the same way as did the goal into which the ball falls, the playground at school, the playing fields, etc. Castration anxiety accounted both for his inhibition in learning and in games. We can, therefore, understand how it came about that Felix, in spite of certain inhibitions, was a good scholar for the first few years, for that period corresponded with the absence of the father owing to the war, so that the anxiety associated with learning was at any rate diminished. It was on the father's return that the aversion to school arose. On the other hand, Felix then for a time sublimated his masturbation phantasies in the physical activities demanded by his father; it is true this was partly by over-compensating for his anxiety.

The same changing content of masturbation phantasies could be found, as I have shown, in his love for music—a sublimation which had been even more strongly repressed but was gradually released in the course of the analysis. It was again due to anxiety aroused by his masturbation phantasies that this even stronger and earlier inhibition had developed.

117

In Felix's case it became quite clear that there was a close connection of the tic with the whole personality of the patient, with his sexuality as well as with his neurosis, with the fate of his sublimations, with the development of his character and with his social attitude. This connection was rooted in his masturbation phantasies; and in Felix's case it became particularly clear that these phantasies materially influenced his sublimations, his neurosis and his personality.

Similarly in the case of another patient I found that the development of the tic was determined by the significance and structure of masturbation phantasies. It was a question not of a pronounced tic but of motor discharges which, in many important respects, were very similar to a tic. Werner, who came to me at the age of nine, was a neurotic boy. Already at the age of a year and a half he displayed an excessive physical restlessness which was constantly increasing. At the age of five he developed the peculiar habit of moving his hands and feet to imitate the the movements of an engine. From this game there developed what he himself and those around him termed 'fidgeting' and which increasingly came to dominate all his play activities. The original engine game soon ceased to be the sole content of his play. At the age of nine he often fidgeted for hours on end. He said: 'Fidgeting is fun, but it isn't always fun, you can't leave off when you want to—as, for instance, when you ought to do your lessons.'

In the analysis it became evident that suppression of the movement called up not anxiety but a feeling of tension—it is then that he always had to think of fidgeting—just as with Felix suppression of the tic had released not anxiety but tension. Further important resemblances are found in the content of the phantasies. In the course of the analysis I found out what Werner called his 'fidgeting thoughts'. He told me that he fidgeted about Tarzan's animals.[1] The monkeys are walking through the jungle; in his phantasy he walks behind them and adapts himself to their gait. Associations showed clearly his admiration for his father who copulates with his mother (monkey = penis) and his wish to participate as a third person. This identification, again with both mother and father, also formed the basis of his other numerous 'fidgeting' thoughts, all of which could be recognized as masturbation phantasies. It was significant that while fidgeting he had to twirl a pencil or ruler between the fingers of his right hand, and also that he could not 'fidget properly' in the presence of other people.

The following is another of the phantasies which accompanied the fidgeting; he saw in front of him a boat built of particularly hard wood and equipped with quite strong ladders on which a person

[1] The reference is to one of the Tarzan books, the frontispiece of which he had seen and then used as the subject of his phantasy.

could climb up and down with perfect safety. On the lower part there were stores of provisions and a large balloon filled with gas. Seaplanes could alight on this 'ship of rescue' (as he called it) if they were in distress. This phantasy expressed the castration anxiety arising from his adoption of a feminine attitude towards his father as well as the defence against that attitude. The seaplanes in distress represented himself, the ship's hull his mother—the balloon and stores of provisions, his father's penis. In this case, as in that of Felix, castration anxiety led to a narcissistic turning back on to the self as a loved object, In his phantasies a 'Little One' who joins in as well as competes, and proves himself more skilled than a 'Big One', played a great part; as for instance, a smaller engine and particularly a smaller clown. The 'Little One' is not only the penis but he, himself, in comparison with his father; and the admiration for himself, which he expressed in this way, showed the narcissistic disposal of his libido.

A further resemblance between the two cases was the important part played by sound in Werner's phantasies. Werner had not yet developed a marked feeling for music but showed a strong interest in sounds which, as the analysis showed, was closely associated with his phantasies arising from his observations of the sexual intercourse of his parents. He shared his parents' bedroom temporarily when he was five months old. Nothing can be established—at any rate at the present stage of his analysis[1]—concerning his observations at this early age. On the other hand, the analysis has proved beyond question the importance of what he repeatedly overheard through the open door leading into his parents' room at about the age of eighteen months. It was during this period that the excessive mobility appeared. The following illustrates the important part played by the acoustic factor in his masturbation phantasies: he told me that he had 'fidgeted' about a gramophone which he wants to get; the fidgeting was, as usual, an imitation of certain movements, in this case those of winding up the gramophone and of the needle moving over the disc. He then passed on to phantasies about a motor-cycle which he would like to possess and in the same way described the movements of it by 'fidgeting'. He made drawings of his phantasies. The motor-cycle had an enormous motor, clearly drawn as a penis and, like the balloon on the 'rescue ship', it was well filled, in this case with petrol. On the motor sat a woman who sets the motor-cycle in motion. The sounds produced by cranking fell in the form of pointed rays on a 'poor little man' who was very frightened by them. In connection with this Werner produced a phantasy about a jazz band, the sounds of which he imitated, and said that he was 'fidgeting'

---

[1] *Note, 1947*—When I was writing this paper, Werner's analysis was still in progress; in fact it had, at that time, only lasted about three months.

about it. He showed me how the trumpeter plays his instrument, how the leader conducts and the man with the big drum beats. On my asking him what in this connection he was 'fidgeting' about, he replied that he was taking part in all these activities. He then drew on paper a giant with huge eyes and a head containing aerials and wireless sets. A diminutive manikin wanted to see the giant and for that purpose climbed up the Eiffel Tower which on the drawing was connected with a skyscraper. His admiration for his father was here expressed through the admiration for his mother; behind the passive homosexual attitude the heterosexual one could be discerned.

With Werner, as in the case of Felix, the strong acoustic interest which has to find rhythmic expression was associated with repression of scoptophilia. Following the phantasies which I have just described, about a jazz band which was represented by a giant, Werner told me about the cinemas he had been to. It is true he did not have such a marked aversion to the cinema as had Felix, but I noticed signs of repressed scoptophilia when I had a chance to observe him one day with other children during a theatrical performance. He turned his eyes away from the stage for fairly long periods and afterwards said it was all boring and untrue. In between he sat as though enchanted, his gaze riveted to the scene on the stage, but then relapsed again into the former attitude.

In Werner's case, too, the castration complex was extraordinarily strong; the struggle against masturbation had failed, yet the boy sought a substitute in other motor discharges. What the traumatic impressions were which led to the development of so strong a castration complex and to fear of masturbation, his analysis has not yet been able to ascertain. Without doubt auditory observation of coitus at the age of five—again through the open door—then probably visual observation of it as well between the ages of six and seven, when he shared his parents' bedroom for a short time, served to intensify all his difficulties, including the 'fidgeting' which had already developed by then. The analogy between 'fidgeting' and a tic is unquestionable. Possibly one would be justified in regarding the motor symptom as a kind of preliminary stage in the development of an actual tic. In the case of Felix, too, a diffuse excessive mobility had been apparent from early childhood, and was only replaced by a tic at puberty, after a particular experience which served as a precipitating factor. Perhaps it often happens that a tic finally develops only in puberty when so many difficulties are brought to a head.

I shall now compare the conclusions from my material with the psycho-analytic publications on the tic. I wish to refer to the comprehensive 'Psycho-analytical Observations on Tic' by Ferenczi (1921) and Abraham's (1921) paper read to the Berlin Psycho-analytical Society. One of Ferenczi's conclusions—namely that the tic is an equivalent of masturbation—is confirmed in both cases I have described. The tendency to work off the tic in seclusion, which was also stressed by Ferenczi, could be seen in the case of Werner, where we were able to observe the condition in a state of development; to be alone became necessary for his being able to 'fidget'. Ferenczi's conclusions that in the analysis the tic does not play the same rôle as other symptoms, that it—to some extent—eludes analysis, I can also confirm, though only up to a certain point. For a considerable time I, too, had the impression in Felix's analysis that there was something quite different about his tic in comparison to other symptoms which revealed their meaning much earlier and more clearly. Also I found with Felix that he did not mind the tic, and this again is in keeping with Ferenczi's conclusions. I also agree with Ferenczi that the reasons for all these differences are to be found in the narcissistic nature of the tic.

Here, however, some essential disagreement with Ferenczi arises. He regards the tic as a primary narcissistic symptom having a common source with the narcissistic psychoses. Experience has convinced me that the tic is not accessible to therapeutic influence as long as the analysis has not succeeded in uncovering the object relations on which it is based. I found that underlying the tic there were genital, anal- and oral-sadistic impulses towards the object. The analysis, it is true, had to penetrate to the earliest stages of childhood development, and the tic did not disappear completely until the predisposing fixations of the infantile period had been thoroughly explored.[1] Ferenczi's contention that in the case of a tic no object relations at all appear to be concealed behind the symptom, cannot be sustained. The original object relations became quite clear during the course of the analysis in both cases I described; they had merely, under the pressure of the castration complex, undergone regression to the narcissistic stage.

[1] This seems to me to explain also why, in the analysis of adults, the tic, as Ferenczi says, 'does not appear at the end of the analysis to belong within the framework of the complicated structure of the neurosis'. With adults it might frequently not be possible to carry the analysis to the depth required to uncover the earliest fixations and object relations which determine the tic. So long as this is not done, the tic—by virtue of what I would call its semi-narcissistic character—will always elude analysis. In the case of Felix, analysis succeeded not only in reconstructing the details of his earliest development which determined the form of his masturbation phantasies and of his tic, but also, with the aid of memories, in making them fully conscious again. We may assume that it is the narcissistic element in the tic which is responsible for the difficulty in gaining access to this symptom in analysis, a difficulty which increases in proportion to the age of the patient. One would conclude that treatment of a tic should be undertaken at an early age, as soon as possible after the appearance of the symptom.

The anal-sadistic object relations to which Abraham pointed were also apparent in my cases. With Felix, the contraction of the shoulders which followed the tic was a substitute for contraction of the sphincter, which also formed the basis of the rotary movement in the tic. In connection with this there arose the urge to hurl abuse at the headmaster. The 'drilling' movement in the tic, the third phase, is compatible not only with drilling in but also with drilling out—defaecation.

At the time when the tic was replaced by diffuse excessive mobility, Felix had the habit of swinging his feet in such a way that he repeatedly kicked the master as he passed. He was unable to overcome this habit despite the trouble it caused him. This aggressive component in his physical restlessness, which was again represented later in the tic, also evinced itself quite plainly in the case of Werner in such a significant connection that it showed clearly the fundamental meaning of the sadistic impulses in the tic-like discharges. During the analytic sessions a series of passionate and compulsive questions, which proved to be an expression of curiosity connected with the primal scene—for the details of which the one-and-a-half-year-old child could find no explanation—was repeatedly followed by violent outbursts of rage. At such times Werner dirtied the window-sill and the table with coloured pencils, made attempts to dirty me as well, threatened me with his fists and with scissors, tried to kick me, produced flatus-like sounds by blowing out his cheeks, abused me in all kinds of ways, pulled faces and whistled; in between whiles he repeatedly put his fingers into his ears[1] and suddenly announced that he could hear a peculiar sound, as from a distance, but did not know what it was.

I shall mention one other fact which provides unequivocal proof that this scene was a repetition of the aggressive motor discharges provoked by the primal scene. During the outburst of rage Werner used to go out of the room to see whether he could hit me with a ball thrown from the hall through the open door—an obvious repetition of the situation when, at the age of eighteen months, he wanted to abuse and injure his parents through the open door.[2]

Numerous phantasies shown to be connected with the tic, for instance that of the wind instruments with which Felix felt he wanted

[1] Whistling, covering the ears, etc., was in his case an ever-recurring sign of resistance during analysis; but he also made use of it at home.

[2] His parents confirmed that at the time these auditory observations took place, that is at the age of eighteen months, the child used repeatedly to disturb them during the night and in the morning was frequently found lying in his excreta. At this time, as I have already mentioned, the first hints of his excessive mobility made their appearance and first took the form of continuously running to and fro with pieces of wood he picked up in an adjacent timber yard.

to participate in the parental intercourse, bear witness to the anal object relation. Werner, too, 'fidgeted' to imitate the trumpeter in the jazz band—who stood for his father in the act of copulating—and expressed it also by whistling and imitating the sounds of flatus.

The way in which these anal-sadistic components not merely entered but proved to be important factors in the whole construction of the tic, seems to me to confirm Abraham's view that the tic is a conversion symptom at the anal-sadistic level. Ferenczi in replying to Abraham expressed agreement with this view, and he also drew attention in his paper to the importance of the anal-sadistic components for the tic and to their connection with coprolalia.

The genital object relations were clearly seen in the above material. The coitus phantasies associated with the tic had originally found expression in masturbatory activities. This became apparent when in the course of the analysis the homosexual object choice reappeared in connection with masturbation which so long had been avoided under pressure of anxiety. The heterosexual object choice, which was the last to be uncovered, was accompanied by further changes in the masturbation phantasies, and with these the return to the masturbation of early childhood was clearly re-established.

Here I can point to a passage in Ferenczi's paper which seems to bridge the difference of view between Ferenczi and myself. Ferenczi writes: 'In the case of a tic occurring in a "constitutional narcissist" the primacy of the genital zone appears, on the whole, to be not quite firmly established, so that ordinary stimulations or unavoidable disturbances give rise to such a displacement. Masturbation would be then a kind of semi-narcissistic sexual activity from which both the transition to normal gratification with another object as well as a return to auto-erotism are possible.'

My material shows that a retreat from the object relations already achieved to a secondary narcissism had taken place by means of masturbation; for certain reasons, to be discussed in detail, masturbation again became an auto-erotic activity. This, however, seems to me to clarify the difference between Ferenczi's view and mine. According to my findings, the tic is not a primary narcissistic but a secondary narcissistic symptom. As I have already pointed out, the disappearance of the tic in my cases was succeeded not by anxiety but by a feeling of tension—which is in keeping with Abraham's statements.

To some extent my conclusions may be regarded as complementary to the views of Ferenczi and Abraham. I found that the tic was a secondary narcissistic symptom, and it was the uncovering of the original anal-sadistic and genital object relations on which it was based which led me to this conclusion. It appeared, moreover, that the tic is not merely an equivalent of masturbation but that masturbation phantasies are also bound up with it. The analytic exploration and dissolution of the tic only became possible after the most searching analysis of the masturbation phantasies, and these I had to trace back to their earliest appearance, which entailed uncovering the whole sexual development of childhood. Thus the analysis of the masturbation phantasies proved to be the key to an understanding of the tic.

At the same time I came to see that the tic, which at the beginning had seemed to be an incidental and detached symptom, was closely and organically connected with very severe inhibitions and asocial development of character. I have repeatedly pointed out that when sublimation is successful, every talent and every interest is partly based on masturbation phantasies. In the case of Felix, his masturbation phantasies were bound up very closely with his tic. The sublimation of his masturbation phantasies in numerous interests went parallel with the disintegration and disappearance of the tic. The final result of the analysis was the far-reaching diminution both of inhibitions and of characterological defects. In Werner's case, too, analysis revealed the central significance of the 'fidgeting' and its connection with his severe inhibitions and asocial behaviour. Despite the fact that Werner's analysis has not yet penetrated deeply enough to exert a therapeutic effect on the symptom, it is already clear how far the whole of his rich phantasy life has been put into the service of this symptom and consequently withdrawn from other interests. His analysis also shows that the inhibition of his personality had been progressive.

These facts, it seems to me, point to the necessity of examining the significance of the tic from this angle, *i.e.* to discover how far it is not merely an indication of inhibition and asocial development but is of fundamental importance for the development of these disturbances.

I should like once more to point out the specific factors underlying the psychogenesis of the tic as they appeared to me in the material presented. The masturbation phantasies underlying the tic are certainly not specific, for we know that they have the same importance for nearly every neurotic symptom and, as I have repeatedly attempted to show, for phantasy life and sublimations. But even the special content of masturbation phantasies which was common to my two cases—simultaneous identification with both father and mother while the self participates—does not seem in itself specific. This type of phantasy is certainly to be met with in many other patients who have no tic.

But a more specific factor seems to me to lie in the development which this form of identification took in both cases. At first identification with the father was covered up by identification with the mother (passive homosexual attitude); owing to a particularly intense castration anxiety this attitude then gave way to a renewed onset of an active attitude. A kind of identification with the father again took place, but was no longer successful because his characteristics were fused with the patient's own ego, and the patient's ego, loved by the father, emerges as the new loved object.

There is however one definite specific factor which favoured both the narcissistic regression, arising out of the castration complex, and the tic which was based on this regression. In the case of Felix, as in that of Werner, observations of sexual intercourse were carried out in such a way that the principal interest was directed to the accompanying sounds, In Felix this interest in sound was intensified by a very considerable repression of scoptophilia. In Werner's case, there is no doubt that the fact that his observations were made from the adjoining room, and were therefore primarily auditory observations, led to the development of his interest in sound. An increase of mobility, probably of constitutional origin (Ferenczi, *loc cit.*) appears in connection with this interest.[1] He imitated,[2] first by representation in rhythmic masturbation movements, what he had heard. When masturbation was given up under pressure of castration anxiety, then the sounds had to be reproduced by other motor discharges. For instance in both cases I described the phantasy of keeping time in music with the conductor. We may assume that this acoustic interest was not only influenced by circumstances but was derived from a constitutional factor which in these two cases had shown itself to be connected with strong anal-sadistic components. These came to light in an interest in the sounds of flatus and in the aggression underlying the heightened mobility.

Whether the specific factors which were operative in the cases I observed are of importance in the psychogenesis of tics in other cases as well, only further experience can decide.

APPENDIX ADDED ON CORRECTING THE PROOFS (1925)

Since writing this paper I have begun the analysis of a boy, Walter, five and a half years old, whose principal symptom consisted

---

[1] The connection between auditory impressions and their reproduction in movement is seen as a normal phenomenon in the urge to dance which is aroused by listening to dance music.

[2] With Felix and Werner it was a matter of imitating the father in sexual intercourse. The urge to imitate, to act, in patients suffering from a tic is also mentioned by Ferenczi.

in a stereotyped movement. The patient's youth and the progress made in the analysis (so far lasting six weeks) made it possible to explore thoroughly the interacting factors underlying the symptom and very favourably to influence the recently developed symptom. An obsessional neurosis and incipient characterological deformation in the boy render further deep analysis necessary. This case also reveals the operation of the factors which were shown to be decisive in the first two cases. For the sake of brevity I shall single out that of overhearing coitus from an adjacent room in the second year of life. At this age excessive mobility and a fear of knocking noises made their appearance. Week after week during the analysis Walter gives a compulsive repetition with variations of a 'Kasperle' show (similar to a Punch and Judy show). In these performances I have to start as the conductor and with a stick or similar object I have to knock, which is meant to be music; keeping time with this knocking he did acrobatic tricks. Many details prove the 'Kasperle' show to be sexual intercourse in which he takes the place of his mother. His fear of masturbation, which was associated with a traumatic event at the age of three, was obvious. So far the theatrical performance is always succeeded by an outburst of rage, accompanied by aggressive motor discharges, and a representation of anal and urethral dirtying attacks—all directed against the parents in sexual intercourse. The anal-sadistic foundation of the motor symptoms could be clearly seen. My conclusions are confirmed at all points by this third case, and it is particularly instructive to note that the cases belong to different and very important periods of development. It now seems clearly proved that a tic has its basis in the fidgeting and physical restlessness so frequently seen in early childhood, which therefore calls for serious consideration. Whether this diffuse, excessive mobility is invariably conditioned by auditory observations of coitus, even when it does not develop into a tic, can be decided only after further experience. At any rate, they were a fundamental factor in the three cases which I analysed and in which the excessive mobility did develop into a tic or tic-like movements. With Walter, as with Werner, the condensation into motor symptoms occurred in the sixth year. I refer to the fact mentioned by Ferenczi that in the latency period tics frequently occur as a transitory symptom. In two out of my three cases traumatic impressions certainly contributed to a failure to overcome the Oedipus and castration complexes, while the third case has not yet been sufficiently analysed in that direction. This gave rise, after the decline of the Oedipus complex, to a particularly intense struggle against masturbation for which the motor symptom then became the immediate substitute. It may be assumed that in other cases too the—frequently transitory—tics and stereotyped movements of the latency period may develop further into a genuine tic when a recrudescence of the conflicts of early childhood or of traumatic experiences— especially at puberty, or even later—supervene as precipitating factors.

6

THE PSYCHOLOGICAL PRINCIPLES
OF EARLY ANALYSIS

(1926)

In the following paper I propose to discuss in detail certain differences between the mental life of young children and that of adults. These differences require us to use a technique adapted to the mind of the young child, and I shall try to show that there is a certain analytical *play-technique* which fulfils this requirement. This technique is planned in accordance with certain points of view which I shall discuss in some detail in this paper.

As we know, children form relations with the outside world by directing to objects from which pleasure is obtained the libido that was originally attached exclusively to the child's own ego. A child's relation to these objects, whether they be living or inanimate, is in the first instance purely narcissistic. It is in this way, however, that children arrive at their relations with reality. I should now like to illustrate the relation of young children to reality by means of an example.

Trude, a child of three and a quarter, went on a journey with her mother, having previously had a single hour's analysis. Six months later the analysis was continued. It was only after some considerable time that she spoke of anything that had happened to her in the interval, the occasion of her touching on it being a dream which she related to me. She dreamt that she was with her mother again in Italy, in a familiar restaurant. The waitress did not give her any raspberry-syrup, for there was none left. The interpretation of this dream showed, amongst other things, that the child was still suffering from the deprivation of the mother's breast when she was weaned; further, it revealed her envy of her little sister. As a rule Trude told me all sorts of apparently irrelevant things, and also repeatedly mentioned details of her first hour's analysis six months previously, but it was only the connection with the deprivation she had experienced which caused her to think of her travels, otherwise they were of no interest to her.

At a very early age children become acquainted with reality through the deprivations which it imposes on them. They defend themselves against reality by repudiating it. The fundamental thing, however, and the criterion of all later capacity for adaptation to reality, is the degree in which they are able to tolerate the deprivations that result from the Oedipus situation. Hence, even in little children, an exaggerated repudiation of reality (often disguised under an apparent 'adaptability' and 'docility') is an indication of neurosis and differs from the flight from reality of adult neurotics only in the forms in which it manifests itself. Even in the analysis of young children, therefore, one of the final results to be attained is successful adaptation to reality. One way in which this shows itself in children is in the modification of the difficulties encountered in their education. In other words, such children have become capable of tolerating real deprivations.

We can observe that children often show, as early as the beginning of their second year, a marked preference for the parent of the opposite sex and other indications of incipient Oedipus tendencies. *When* the ensuing conflicts begin, that is, at what point the child actually becomes dominated by the Oedipus complex, is less clear; for we infer its existence only from certain changes which we notice in the child.

The analysis of one child of two years and nine months, another of three years and a quarter, and several children of about four years old, has led me to conclude that, in them, the Oedipus complex exercised a powerful influence as early as their second year.[1] I will illustrate this from the development of a little patient. Rita

[1] With this conclusion is very closely connected a second, which I can only indicate here.

In a number of children's analyses I discovered that the little girl's choice of the father as love-object ensued on weaning. This deprivation, which is followed by the training in cleanliness (a process which presents itself to the child as a new and grievous withdrawal of love), loosens the bond to the mother and brings into operation the heterosexual attraction, reinforced by the father's caresses, which are now construed as a seduction. As a love-object the father, too, subserves in the first instance the purpose of oral gratification. In the paper which I read at the Salzburg Congress in April, 1924, I gave examples to show that children at first conceive of, and desire, coitus as an oral act.

I think that the effect of these deprivations on the development of the Oedipus complex in *boys* is at once inhibitory and promotive. The *inhibitory* effect of these traumas is seen in the fact that it is they to which the boy subsequently reverts whenever he tries to escape from his mother-fixation and which reinforce his inverted Oedipus attitude. The circumstance that these traumas, which pave the way for the castration complex, proceed from the mother is also, as I have seen, the reason why in both sexes it is the mother who in the deepest strata of the unconscious is specially dreaded as castrator.

On the other hand, however, the oral and anal deprivation of love appears to *promote* the development of the Oedipus situation in boys, for it compels them to change their libido-position and to desire the mother as a genital love-object.

showed a preference for her mother up to the beginning of her second year; after that she showed a striking preference for her father. For instance, at the age of fifteen months she would repeatedly demand to stay alone in the room with him and, sitting on his knee, look at books with him. At the age of eighteen months, however, her attitude changed again, and once more she preferred her mother. Simultaneously she began to suffer from *pavor nocturnus* and a dread of animals. She developed an excessive fixation to her mother and a very pronounced father-identification. At the beginning of her third year she displayed increasing ambivalence, and was so extremely difficult to bring up that when she was two years and nine months she was brought for analytic treatment. At this time she had for some months shown very considerable inhibition in play, as well as an inability to tolerate deprivations, an excessive sensitivity to pain, and marked moodiness. The following experiences had contributed to this development. Up till the age of nearly two years Rita had slept in her parents' room, and the effects of the primal scene showed plainly in her analysis. The occasion of the outbreak of her neurosis, however, was the birth of her little brother. Soon after this, still greater difficulties manifested themselves which rapidly increased. There can be no doubt that there is a close connection between neurosis and such profound effects of the Oedipus complex experienced at so early an age. I cannot determine whether it is neurotic children whom the early working of the Oedipus complex affects so intensely, or if children become neurotic when this complex sets in too soon. It is, however, certain that experiences such as I have mentioned here make the conflict more severe and therefore either increase the neurosis or cause it to break out.

I shall now select from this case the features which the analysis of children of different ages has taught me are typical. They are seen most directly in the analysis of *little* children. In several cases in which I analysed anxiety-attacks in very young children, these attacks proved to be the repetition of a *pavor nocturnus* which had occurred in the second half of the child's second year and at the beginning of its third year. This fear was at once an effect and a neurotic elaboration of the Oedipus complex. There are a great many elaborations of this sort and they lead us to certain positive conclusions as to the effects of the Oedipus complex.[1]

Amongst such elaborations, in which the connection with the Oedipus situation was quite clear, are to be reckoned the way in which children frequently fall and hurt themselves, their exaggerated

---

[1] The close connection of such elaborations with anxiety has already been demonstrated by me in my chapter on 'Early Analysis', where I discussed the relation between anxiety and inhibition.

sensitivity, their incapacity to tolerate deprivations, their inhibitions in play, their highly ambivalent attitude towards festive occasions and presents, and finally, various difficulties in upbringing which often make their appearance at a surprisingly early age. But I found that the cause of these very common phenomena was a particularly strong sense of guilt, the development of which I will now examine in detail.

I will show from an example how strongly the sense of guilt operates even in *pavor nocturnus*. Trude, at the age of four and a quarter, constantly played in the analytic hour that it was night. We both had to go to sleep. Then she came out of the particular corner which she called her room, stole up to me and made all sorts of threats. She would stab me in the throat, throw me into the courtyard, burn me up, or give me to the policeman. She tried to tie my hands and feet, she lifted the sofa-cover and said she was making '*po-kaki-kucki*'.[1]

It turned out that she was looking into the mother's 'popo' for the kakis, which to her represented children. Another time she wanted to hit me on the stomach and declared that she was taking out the 'a-a's' (faeces) and making me poor. She then pulled down the cushions, which she repeatedly called 'children', and hid herself with them in the corner of the sofa, where she crouched down with vehement signs of fear, covered herself up, sucked her thumb and wetted herself. This situation always followed her attacks on me. Her attitude was, however, similar to that which, at the age of not quite two she had adopted in bed when she began to suffer from intense *pavor nocturnus*. At that time, too, she used repeatedly to run into her parents' bedroom in the night without being able to tell them what she wanted. When her sister was born she was two years old, and the analysis succeeded in revealing what was in her mind at the time and also what were the causes of her anxiety and of her wetting and dirtying her bed. Analysis also succeeded in getting rid of these symptoms. At that time she had already wished to rob her mother, who was pregnant, of her children, to kill her and to take her place in coitus with the father. These tendencies to hate and aggression were the cause of her fixation to her mother (which, at the age of two years, was becoming particularly strong), as well as of her feelings of anxiety and guilt. At the time when these phenomena were so prominent in Trude's analysis, she managed to hurt herself almost always just before the analytic hour. I found out that the objects against which she hurt herself (tables, cupboards, stoves, etc.), signified to her (in accordance with the primitive infantile identification) her mother, or at times her father, who was punishing her. In general

---

[1] *Popo* = buttocks. *Kaki* = faeces. *Kucki, Kucken* = look.

I have found, especially in very young children, that constantly 'being in the wars' and falling and hurting themselves is closely connected with the castration complex and the sense of guilt.

Children's games enable us to form certain special conclusions about the very early sense of guilt. As early as her second year, those with whom Rita came into contact were struck by her remorse for every naughtiness, however small, and her hyper-sensitiveness to any sort of blame. For instance, she burst into tears when her father playfully threatened a bear in a picture-book. Here, what determined her identification with the bear was her fear of blame from her *real* father. Again, her inhibition in play proceeded from her sense of guilt. When she was two and a quarter she repeatedly declared, when playing with her doll (a game which she did not much enjoy), that she was not the baby-doll's mother. Analysis showed that she did not *dare* to play at being the mother because the baby-doll stood to her amongst other things for the little brother whom she had wanted to take away from her mother, even during the pregnancy. But here the prohibition of the childish wish no longer emanated from the *real* mother, but from an introjected mother, whose rôle she enacted for me in many ways and who exercised a harsher and more cruel influence upon her than her real mother had ever done. One obsessional symptom which Rita developed at the age of two was a sleep-ceremonial which wasted a great deal of time. The main point of this was that she insisted on being tightly rolled up in the bed-clothes for fear that 'a mouse or a butty might come through the window and bite off her butty (genital)'.[1] Her games revealed other determinants: the doll had always to be rolled up in the same way as Rita herself, and on one occasion an elephant was put beside its bed. This elephant was supposed to prevent the baby-doll from getting up; otherwise it would steal into the parents' bedroom and do them some harm or take something away from them. The elephant (a father-imago) was intended to take over the part of hinderer. This part the introjected father had played within her since the time when, between the ages of fifteen months and two years, she had wanted to usurp her mother's place with her father, to steal from her mother the child with which she was pregnant, and to injure and castrate the parents. The reactions of rage and anxiety which followed on the punishment of the 'child' during such games showed, too, that Rita was inwardly playing both parts: that of the authorities who sit in judgement and that of the child who is punished.

[1] Rita's castration complex manifested itself in a number of neurotic symptoms as well as in the development of her character. Her games, too, showed clearly her very strong father-identification and her fear of failing in the male rôle—an anxiety which had its origin in the castration complex.

A fundamental and universal mechanism in the game of acting a part serves to separate those different identifications at work in the child which are tending to form a single whole. By the division of rôles the child succeeds in expelling the father and mother whom, in the elaboration of the Oedipus complex, it has absorbed into itself and who are now tormenting it inwardly by their severity. The result of this expulsion is a sensation of relief, which contributes in great measure to the pleasure derived from the game. Though this game of acting often appears quite simple and seems to represent only primary identifications, this is only the surface appearance. To penetrate behind this appearance is of great importance in the analysis of children. It can, however, have its full therapeutic effect only if the investigation reveals all the underlying identifications and determinations and, above all, if we have found our way to the sense of guilt which is here at work.

In the cases which I have analysed the inhibitory effect of feelings of guilt was clear at a very early age. What we here encounter corresponds to that which we know as the super-ego in adults. The fact that we assume the Oedipus complex to reach its zenith round about the fourth year of life and that we recognize the development of the super-ego as the end-result of the complex, seems to me in no way to contradict these observations. Those definite, typical phenomena, the existence of which in the most clearly developed form we can recognize when the Oedipus complex has reached its zenith and which precede its waning, are merely the termination of a development which occupies *years*. The analysis of very young children shows that, as soon as the Oedipus complex arises, they begin to work it through and thereby to develop the super-ego.

The effects of this infantile super-ego upon the child are analogous to those of the super-ego upon the adult, but they weigh far more heavily upon the weaker, infantile ego. As the analysis of children teaches us, we strengthen that ego when the analytic procedure curbs the excessive demands of the super-ego. There can be no doubt that the ego of little children differs from that of older children or of adults. But, when we have freed the little child's ego from neurosis, it proves perfectly equal to such demands of reality as it encounters —demands as yet less serious than those made upon adults.[1]

---

[1] Children cannot change the circumstances of their lives, as adults often do at the end of an analysis. But a child has been very greatly helped if, as a result of analysis, we enable him to feel more at ease in the existing circumstances and to develop better. Moreover, the clearing-up of neurosis in children often diminishes the difficulties of their *milieu*. For instance, I have repeatedly proved that the mother's reactions were much less neurotic when favourable changes took place in her children after analysis.

Just as the minds of little children differ from those of older children, so their reaction to psycho-analysis is different in early childhood from what it is later. We are often surprised at the facility with which on some occasions our interpretations are accepted: sometimes children even express considerable pleasure in them. The reason why this process is different from that met with in the analysis of adults is that in certain strata of the child-mind there is a much easier communication between Cs and Ucs, and therefore it is much simpler to retrace the steps from the one to the other. This accounts for the rapid effect of our interpretation, which of course is never given except on the basis of adequate material. Children, however, often produce such material surprisingly quickly and in great variety. The effect, also, is often astonishing, even when the children have not seemed at all receptive of the interpretation. The play which was interrupted owing to the setting-up of resistances is resumed; it alters, expands and expresses deeper strata of the mind; the contact between the child and the analyst is re-established. The pleasure in play, which visibly ensues after an interpretation has been given, is also due to the fact that the expenditure necessitated by a repression is no longer required after the interpretation. But soon we once more encounter resistances for a time, and here matters are no longer made easy in the way I have described. In fact, at such times we have to wrestle with very great difficulties. This is especially the case when we encounter the sense of guilt.

In their play children represent symbolically phantasies, wishes and experiences. Here they are employing the same language, the same archaic, phylogenetically acquired mode of expression as we are familiar with from dreams. We can only fully understand it if we approach it by the method Freud has evolved for unravelling dreams. Symbolism is only a part of it; if we want rightly to comprehend children's play in connection with their whole behaviour during the analytic hour, we must take into account not only the symbolism which often appears so clearly in their games, but also all the means of representation and the mechanisms employed in dream-work, and we must bear in mind the necessity of examining the whole nexus of phenomena.[1]

[1] My analyses again and again reveal how many different things, dolls, for example, can mean in play. Sometimes they stand for the penis, sometimes for the child stolen from the mother, sometimes for the little patient itself, etc. It is only by examining the minutest details of the game and their interpretation that the connections are made clear to use and the interpretation becomes effective. The *material* that children produce during an analytic hour, as they pass from play with toys to dramatization in their own person and, again, to playing with water, cutting out paper, or drawing; the *manner* in which they do this; the *reason* why they change from one to another; the *means* they choose for their representations

If we employ this technique we soon find that children produce no fewer associations to the separate features of their games than do adults to the elements of their dreams. The details of the play point the way for an attentive observer; and, in between, the child tells all sorts of things which must be given their full weight as associations.

Besides this archaic mode of representation children employ another primitive mechanism, that is to say, they substitute actions (which were the original precursors of thoughts) for words: with children, *acting* plays a prominent part.

In 'From the History of an Infantile Neurosis',[1] Freud says: 'An analysis which is conducted upon a neurotic child itself must, as a matter of course, appear to be more trustworthy, but it cannot be very rich in material; too many words and thoughts have to be lent to the child, and even so the deepest strata may turn out to be impenetrable to consciousness.'

If we approach children with the technique appropriate to the analysis of adults we shall assuredly not succeed in penetrating to the deepest layers of the child's mental life. But it is precisely these layers which are of moment for the value and success of an analysis. If, however, we take into account the psychological differences between children and adults and bear in mind the fact that in children we find Ucs still in operation side by side with Cs, the most primitive tendencies side by side with those most complicated developments known to us, such as the super-ego—if, that is to say, we rightly understand the child's mode of expression, all these doubtful points and unfavourable factors vanish. For we find that, as regards the depth and scope of the analysis, we may expect as much from children as from adults. And still more, in the analysis of children we can go back to experiences and fixations which in analysing adults we can only *reconstruct*, while in children they are *directly* represented.[2] Take for instance, the case of Ruth who, as an infant,

---

—all this medley of factors, which so often seems confused and meaningless, is seen to be consistent and full of meaning and the underlying sources and thoughts are revealed to us if we interpret them just like dreams. Moreover, in their play children often represent the same thing as has appeared in some dream which they have narrated before and they often produce associations to a dream by means of the play which follows it and which is their most important mode of expressing themselves.

[1] *S.E.* 17.

[2] At the Eighth International Psycho-Analytical Congress, held in Salzburg in 1924, I showed that a fundamental mechanism in children's play and in all subsequent sublimations is the discharge of masturbation-phantasies. This underlies all play-activity and serves as a constant stimulus to play (compulsion to repetition). Inhibitions in play and in learning have their origin in an exaggerated repression of these phantasies and, with them, of all phantasy. Sexual experiences

had gone hungry for some time because her mother had little milk to give her. At the age of four years and three months, when playing with the wash-basin, she called the water-tap a milk-tap. She declared that the milk was running into mouths (the holes of the waste-pipe), but that only a very little was flowing. This unsatisfied oral desire made its appearance in countless games and dramatizations and showed itself in her whole attitude. For instance, she asserted that she was poor, that she only had one coat, and that she had very little to eat—none of these statements being in the least in accordance with reality.

Another little patient (who suffered from obsessional neurosis) was the six-year-old Erna, whose neurosis was based on impressions received during the period of training in cleanliness.[1] These impressions she dramatized for me in the minutest detail. Once she placed a little doll on a stone, pretended that it was defaecating and stood other dolls round it which were supposed to be admiring it. After this dramatization Erna brought the same material into a game of acting. She wanted me to be a baby in long clothes which made itself dirty, while she was the mother. The baby was a spoilt child and an object of admiration. This was followed by a reaction of rage in Erna, and she played the part of a cruel teacher who knocked the child about. In this way Erna enacted before me one of the first traumata in her experience: the heavy blow her narcissism received when she imagined that the measures taken to train her meant the loss of the excessive affection bestowed on her in her infancy.

In general, in the analysis of children we cannot over-estimate the importance of phantasy and of translation into action at the bidding of the compulsion to repetition. Naturally, *little* children use the vehicle of action to a far greater extent, but even older ones constantly have recourse to this primitive mechanism, especially when

---

are associated with the masturbation-phantasies and, with these, find representation and abreaction in play. Amongst the experiences dramatized, representations of the primal scene play a prominent part and they regularly appear in the foreground of the analyses of young children. It is only after a considerable amount of analysis, which has partially revealed the primal scene and the genital development, that we come on representations of pregenital experiences and phantasies.

[1] This training, which Erna had felt as a most cruel act of coercion, was in reality accomplished without any sort of harshness and so easily that, at the age of one year, she was perfectly clean in her habits. A strong incentive was her unusually early developed ambition, which, however, caused her to face all the measures taken to train her from the very beginning as an outrage. This early ambition was the primary condition of her sensitiveness to blame and of the precocious and marked development of her sense of guilt. But it is a common thing to see these feelings of guilt already playing a very big part in the training in cleanliness, and we can recognize in them the first beginnings of the super-ego.

analysis has removed some of their repressions. It is indispensable for carrying on the analysis that children should have the pleasure that is bound up with this mechanism, but the pleasure must always remain only a means to the end. It is just here that we see the predominance of the pleasure-principle over the reality-principle. We cannot appeal to the sense of reality in little patients as we can in older ones.

Just as children's means of expression differ from those of adults, so the analytic situation in the analysis of children appears to be entirely different. It is, however, in both cases *essentially* the same. Consistent interpretations, gradual solving of resistances and persistent tracing of the transference to earlier situations—these constitute in children as in adults the correct analytic situation.

I have said that in the analysis of young children I have again and again seen how rapidly the interpretations take effect. It is a striking fact that, though there are numerous unmistakable indications of this effect: the development of play, the consolidating of the transference, the lessening of anxiety, etc., nevertheless for quite a long time the child does not consciously elaborate the interpretations. I have been able, however, to prove that this elaboration does set in later. For instance, children begin to distinguish between the 'pretence' mother and the real mother and between the wooden baby-doll and the live baby brother. They then firmly insist that they wanted to do this or that injury to the toy-baby only—the real baby, they say, of course they love. Only when very powerful and long-standing resistances have been overcome do children realize that their aggressive acts were directed against the *real* objects. When this admission is made, however, the result, even in quite little children, is generally a notable step forward in adaptation to reality. My impression is that the interpretation is at first only unconsciously assimilated. It is not till later that its relation to reality gradually penetrates the child's understanding. The process of enlightenment is analogous. For a long time analysis brings to light only the material for sexual theories and birth-phantasies and interprets this material without any 'explanation'. Thus, enlightenment takes place bit by bit with the removal of the unconscious resistances which operate against it.

Hence, the first thing that happens as a result of psycho-analysis is that the emotional relation to the parents improves; conscious understanding only comes when this has taken place. This understanding is admitted at the bidding of the super-ego, whose demands are modified by analysis so that it can be tolerated and complied with by an ego which is less oppressed and therefore stronger. Thus the child is not *suddenly* confronted with the situation of admitting a new knowledge of its relation to the parents or, in general, of being obliged to absorb knowledge which burdens it. It has always been my experience that the effects of such knowledge, gradually elaborated, is in fact to *relieve* the child, to establish a fundamentally more favourable relation to the parents and thus to increase its power of social adaptation.

When this has taken place children also are quite able to replace repression to some extent by reasoned rejection. We see this from the fact that at a later stage of the analysis children have advanced so far from various anal-sadistic or cannibalistic cravings (which at an earlier stage were still so powerful) that they can now at times adopt an attitude of humorous criticism towards them. When this happens I hear even very little children making jokes to the effect, for instance, that some time ago they really wanted to eat up their mummy or cut her into bits. When this change takes place, not only is the sense of guilt inevitably lessened, but at the same time the children are enabled to *sublimate* the wishes which previously were wholly repressed. This manifests itself in practice in the disappearance of inhibitions in play and in a beginning of numerous interests and activities.

To sum up what I have said: the special primitive peculiarities of the mental life of children necessitate a special technique adapted to them, consisting of the analysis of their play. By means of this technique we can reach the deepest repressed experience and fixations and this enables us fundamentally to influence the children's development.

It is a question only of a difference of *technique*, not of the *principles* of treatment. The criteria of the psycho-analytic method proposed by Freud, namely, that we should use as our starting-point the facts of transference and resistance, that we should take into account infantile impulses, repression and its effects, amnesia and the compulsion to repetition and, further, that we should discover the primal scene, as he requires in the 'History of an Infantile Neurosis'—all these criteria are maintained in their entirety in the play-technique. The method of play preserves all the principles of psycho-analysis and leads to the same results as the classic technique. Only it is adapted to the minds of children in the technical means employed.

7

SYMPOSIUM ON CHILD-ANALYSIS[1]

(1927)

[Note, 1947. — The following paper represents my contribution to a discussion on problems of child analysis in which special attention was paid to Anna Freud's book Introduction to the Technique of the Analysis of Children, *published in 1927 in Vienna. In an expanded version published in London in 1946 under the title* The Psycho-Analytical Treatment of Children *(Imago Publishing Co.), Anna Freud has moved as regards some points closer to my views. These modifications of her opinions are discussed in a postscript at the end of this paper, which latter, however, still stands as an exposition of my own views. (The page references are to the 1946 Imago edition.)]*

I SHALL begin my remarks with a short retrospect of the development of child-analysis in general. Its beginnings date from the year 1909, when Freud published the 'Analysis of a Phobia in a Five-year-old Boy'. This publication was of the greatest theoretical importance, confirming as it did in the person of the child who was its subject the truth of what Freud, proceeding from the analysis of adults, had discovered to exist in children. The paper had, however, yet another significance, the greatness of which could not at that time at all be gauged. This analysis was destined to be the foundation-stone of subsequent child-analysis. For not only did it show the presence and the evolution of the Oedipus complex in children and demonstrate the forms in which it operates in them; it showed also that these unconscious tendencies could safely and most profitably be brought into consciousness. Freud himself describes this discovery as follows:[2] 'But I must now inquire what harm was done to Hans by dragging to light in him complexes such as are not only repressed by children but dreaded by their parents. Did the little boy proceed to take some serious action as regards what he wanted from his mother? or did his evil intentions against his father give place to evil deeds? *Such misgivings will no doubt have occurred to many doctors, who misunderstand the nature of psycho-analysis and think that wicked instincts are strengthened by being made conscious.*' (My italics.)

And again, next paragraph; 'On the contrary, the only results of

---

[1] Held before the British Psycho-Analytical Society, May 4 and 18, 1927.
[2] *S.E.* **10**, p. 144.

the analysis were that Hans recovered, that he ceased to be afraid of horses, and that he got on to rather familiar terms with his father, as the latter reported with some amusement. But whatever his father may have lost in the boy's respect he won back in his confidence: "I thought," said Hans, "you knew everything as you knew that about the horse." For analysis does not undo the *effects* of repression. The instincts which were formerly suppressed remain suppressed; but the same effect is produced in a different way. Analysis replaces the process of repression, which is an automatic and excessive one, by a temperate and purposeful control on the part of the highest mental faculty. In a word, *analysis replaces repression by condemnation*. This seems to bring us the long-looked-for evidence that consciousness has a biological function, and that with its entrance upon the scene an important advantage is secured.'

H. Hug-Hellmuth, who had the honourable distinction of having been the first to undertake the systematic analysis of children, approached her task with certain preconceptions in her mind, which she also retained to the last. In her paper entitled 'On the Technique of Child-Analysis' (Hug-Hellmuth, 1921), written after four years' work in this field, which gives us the clearest idea of her principles and her technique, she makes it very clear that she deprecated the idea of analysing very young children, that she considered it necessary to content oneself with 'partial success' and not to penetrate too deep in analysis with children, for fear of stirring up too powerfully the repressed tendencies and impulses or of making demands which their powers of assimilation are unable to meet.

From this paper, as well as from her other writings, we know that she shrank from penetrating at all deeply into the Oedipus complex. Another assumption to which she held in her work was that in the case of children not only analytic treatment but also a definite educative influence is required of the analyst.

As early as 1921, when I published my first paper, 'The Development of a Child', I had arrived at very different conclusions. In my analysis of a boy of five and a quarter I found (as all my later analyses confirmed) that it was perfectly possible and also salutary to probe the Oedipus complex to its depths and that by so doing one could obtain results at least equal to those of adult analysis. But, side by side with this, I found out that in an analysis so conducted not only was it unnecessary for the analyst to endeavour to exert an educative influence but that the two things were incompatible. I took these discoveries as the guiding principles in my work and advocated them in all my writings, and this is how I have come to attempt the analysis of quite little children, that is, from three to six years old, and to find it both successful and full of promise.

Let us now first of all select from Anna Freud's book what seem to be her four principal points. Here we meet again with the fundamental idea which we have already mentioned as being also Hug-Hellmuth's, namely, the conviction that the analysis of children should not be pressed too far. By this, as is clear also from the more immediate conclusions drawn, is meant that the child's relation to the parents should not be too much handled, that is, that the Oedipus complex must not be searchingly examined. The examples which Anna Freud gives do in fact show no analysis of the Oedipus complex.

The second leading idea is, here again, that the analysis of children should be combined with exerting an educational influence upon them.

It is remarkable and should give food for thought that, though child-analysis was first attempted some eighteen years ago and has been practised ever since, we have to face the fact that its most fundamental principles have not yet been clearly enunciated. If we compare with this fact the development of adult psycho-analysis we shall find that, within a similar period of time, all the basic principles for the latter work were not only laid down but were empirically tested and proved beyond refutation, and that a technique was evolved the details of which had certainly to be perfected but whose fundamental principles have remained unshaken.

What is the explanation of the fact that just the analysis of children should have been so much less fortunate in its development? The argument often heard in analytical circles that children are not suitable objects for analysis does not seem to be valid. Hug-Hellmuth was indeed very sceptical about the results to be obtained with children. She said she 'had to content herself with partial success and also to reckon with relapses'. Moreover she restricted the treatment to a limited range of cases. Anna Freud also sets very definite limits to its applicability, but on the other hand she takes a more optimistic view than did Hug-Hellmuth of the potentialities of child-analysis. At the end of her book she says: 'In child-analysis, in spite of all the difficulties I have enumerated, we do bring about changes, improvements and cures such as we dare not even dream of in analysing adults' (p. 86).

In order to answer the question I have suggested, I want now to make certain statements which it will be my business to prove as I go on. I think that child-analysis, as compared with that of adults, has developed so much less favourably in the past because it was not approached in a spirit of free and unprejudiced enquiry, as adult analysis was, but was hampered and burdened from the outset by certain preconceptions. If we look back at that first child-analysis, the foundation of all others (that of little Hans), we discover that it did not suffer from this limitation. Certainly there was as yet no special technique: the child's father, who carried out this partial analysis under Freud's directions, was quite unversed in the practice of analysis. In spite of this he had the courage to go quite a long way in the analysis and his results were good. In the summary to which I referred earlier in this article Freud says that he himself would have liked to go further. What he says shows, too, that he did not see any danger in a thorough analysis of the Oedipus complex, so evidently he did not think that this complex should on grounds of principle be left unanalysed in children. But Hug-Hellmuth, who for so many years was almost alone and certainly pre-eminent in this field of work, approached it from the outset with principles which were bound to limit it and therefore make it less fruitful, not only in respect of its practical results, the number of cases in which analysis was to be used, etc., but also in respect of theoretical findings. For, during all these years, child-analysis, which might reasonably have been expected to contribute directly to the development of psycho-analytical theory, has done nothing in this direction worth speaking of. Anna Freud, as well as Hug-Hellmuth, has the idea that in analysing children we can discover not only no more, but actually *less* about the early period of life than when we analyse adults.

Here I come upon another pretext which is put forward as a reason for the slow progress made in the field of child-analysis. It is said that a child's behaviour in analysis is obviously different from that of an adult, and that therefore a different technique must be used. I think this argument is incorrect. If I may adapt the saying, 'It is the spirit which builds the body', I should like to maintain that it is the attitude, the inner conviction which finds the necessary technique. I must reiterate what I have said: if one approaches child-analysis with an open mind one will discover ways and means of probing to the deepest depths. And then, from the results of the procedure one will realize what is the child's *true nature* and will perceive that there is no need to impose any restriction on the analysis, either as to the depth to which it may penetrate or the method by which it may work.

In what I have now said I have already touched on the principal point in my criticism of Anna Freud's book.

A number of technical devices employed by Anna Freud may, I think, be explained from two points of view: (1) she assumes that the analytic situation cannot be established with children; and (2) in the case of children she regards pure analysis without any pedagogic admixture as unsuitable or questionable.

The first thesis follows directly from the assumption of the second.

If we compare this with the technique of adult analysis, we perceive that we assume unconditionally that a true *analytic* situation can be brought about only by *analytic* means. We should regard it as a grave error to ensure for ourselves a positive transference from the patient by employing measures such as Anna Freud describes in Chapter I of her book, or to utilize his anxiety in order to make him submissive, or otherwise to intimidate or win him over by means of authority. We should think that even if such an introduction as this secured for us partial access to the patient's Ucs, we yet could never expect to establish a true analytic situation and to carry through a complete analysis which should penetrate the deeper layers of the mind. We know that we constantly have to analyse the fact that patients wish to see us as an authority—whether a hated or a loved one—and that only by analysing this attitude do we gain access to these deeper layers.

All the means which we should regard as incorrect in the analysis of adults are specially stressed by Anna Freud as valuable in analysing children, the object being that introduction to the treatment which she believes to be necessary and which she calls the 'breaking-in' to analysis. It would appear obvious that after this 'breaking-in' she will never wholly succeed in establishing a true analytic situation. Now I think it surprising and illogical that Anna Freud, who does not use the necessary measures to establish the analytic situation but substitutes others at variance with these, yet continually refers to her assumption, and tries to prove it theoretically, that it is *not possible* to establish an analytic situation with children nor, therefore, to carry through with them a pure analysis in the sense of adult analysis.

Anna Freud gives a number of reasons to justify the elaborate and troublesome means which she considers it necessary to employ with children in order to bring about a situation which shall make analytic work possible. These reasons do not seem to me sound. She departs in so many respects from the proved analytic rules, because she thinks that children are such *different* beings from adults. Yet the sole purpose of all these elaborate measures is to make the child like the adult in his attitude to analysis. This seems contradictory and I think is to be explained by the fact that in her comparisons Anna Freud puts the Cs and the ego of the child and the adult in the foreground, while we (though we give all necessary consideration to the ego) surely have to work first and foremost with the Ucs. But in the Ucs (and here I am basing my statement on deep analytical work with both children and adults) the former are by no means so fundamentally different from the latter. It is only that in children the ego has not yet attained to its full development, and therefore they are very much more under the sway of their Ucs. It is this which we must approach and this that we must regard as the central point of our work if we want to learn to know children as they really are and to analyse them.

I do not attach any special value to the goal which Anna Freud so ardently strives after—that of bringing about in children an attitude towards analysis analogous to the attitude of adults. I think, too, that if Anna Freud does attain this goal by the means which she describes (and this can be only in a certain limited number of cases) the result is not that towards which her work is directed but something very different. The 'acknowledgement of illness or of naughtiness' which she has succeeded in awaking in the child emanates from the anxiety which she has mobilized in him for her own purposes: castration-anxiety and the sense of guilt. (I will not here go into the question how far in adults too the reasonable and conscious desire to get well is simply a façade screening this anxiety.) With children we cannot expect to find any lasting basis for our analytic work in a conscious purpose which, as we know, even in adults, would not long hold firm as the sole support for the analysis.

Anna Freud too, it is true, thinks that this purpose is necessary in the first instance as a preparation for the work, but she further believes that, when once the purpose is there, she can rely upon it as the analysis progresses. I think this idea is mistaken and that whenever she appeals to this insight she is really having recourse to the child's anxiety and sense of guilt. In itself there would be nothing objectionable about this, for feelings of anxiety and guilt are undoubtedly most important factors in the possibility of our work. Only I think it necessary for us to be clear *what* are the supports upon which we are relying and *how* we are using them. Analysis is not in itself a gentle method: it cannot spare the patient *any suffering*, and this applies equally to children. In fact, it must force the suffering into consciousness and bring about abreaction if the patients are to be spared permanent and more fatal suffering later. So my criticism is not that Anna Freud *activates* anxiety and the sense of guilt, but on the contrary that she does not *resolve* them *sufficiently*. It seems to me an unnecessary harshness towards a child when, as for instance she describes on pages 11–12, she brings into his consciousness the anxiety lest he should go mad, without immediately attacking this anxiety at its unconscious roots and thus as far as possible allaying it again.

But if it is really to feelings of anxiety and guilt that we have to appeal in our work, why should we not regard these two as factors to be reckoned with and work with them systematically from the outset?

I myself always do this, and I have found that I can place complete reliance in a technique which goes on the principle of taking into account and working analytically with the quantities of anxiety and of feelings of guilt which are so strong in all children and are much clearer and more easily laid hold of than in adults.

Anna Freud states (p. 34) that a hostile or anxious attitude towards me in a child does not justify me in concluding immediately that there is a negative transference at work, for 'the more tenderly a little child is attached to its own mother, the fewer friendly impulses it has towards strangers'. I do not think we can draw a comparison, as she does, with tiny infants who reject what is strange to them. We do not know a great deal about tiny infants, but it is possible to learn a great deal from an early analysis about the mind of a child of, say, three years old, and there we see that it is only very ambivalent neurotic children who manifest fear or hostility towards strangers. My experience has confirmed my belief that if I construe this dislike at once as anxiety and negative transference feeling, and interpret it as such in connection with material which the child at the same time produces and then trace it back to its original object, the mother, I can at once observe that the anxiety diminishes. This manifests itself in the beginning of a more positive transference and, with it, of more vigorous play. In older children the situation is analogous though it differs in detail. Of course, my method presupposes that I have from the beginning been willing to attract to myself the negative as well as the positive transference and, further, to investigate it to its source in the Oedipus situation. Both these measures are in full agreement with analytical principles, but Anna Freud rejects them for reasons which I think are unfounded.

I believe then that a radical difference between our attitudes to anxiety and a sense of guilt in children is this: that Anna Freud makes use of these feelings to attach the child to herself, while I from the outset enlist them in the service of the analytic work. There cannot in any case be any very large number of children in whom one can stir up anxiety without its proving an element which will most painfully disturb or even make impossible the progress of the work, unless one immediately proceeds to resolve it analytically.

Anna Freud, moreover, as far as I can understand from her book, employs this means only in particular cases. In others she tries by every means to bring about a positive transference, in order to fulfil the condition, which she regards as necessary for her work, of attaching the child to her own personality.

This method, again, seems to me unsound, for surely we could work more certainly and more effectually by purely analytic means. It is not every child who responds to us from the beginning with fear and dislike. My experience bears me out when I say that if a child's attitude to us is friendly and playful we are justified in assuming that there is a positive transference and in at once making use of this in our work. And we have another excellent and well-tried weapon which we use in an analogous fashion to that in which we employ it in the analyses of adults, though there, it is true, we do not have so speedy and so plain an opportunity to intervene. I mean that we *interpret* this positive transference; that is, in both children's as in adults' analyses we trace it back to the original object. In general, we shall probably notice both the positive and the negative transference and we shall be given every opportunity for analytic work if we handle both from the outset analytically. By resolving some part of the negative transference we shall then obtain, just as with adults, an increase in the positive transference and this, in accordance with the ambivalence of childhood, will soon in its turn be succeeded by a re-emerging of the negative. Now this is true analytic work and an analytic situation has been established. Moreover, we have then found the basis upon which to build in the child itself, and we can often be to a great extent independent of a knowledge of its surroundings. In short, we have achieved the conditions necessary for analysis and not only are we spared the laborious, difficult and unreliable measures described by Anna Freud, but (and this seems even more important) we can ensure for our work the full value and success of an analysis in every sense equivalent to adult analysis.

At this point, however, I encounter an objection raised by Anna Freud in the second chapter of her book, entitled 'The Means Employed in Child-Analysis'. To work in the way I have described we must get material from the child's associations. Anna Freud and I and probably everyone who analyses children agree that they neither can nor will give associations in the same way as grown-ups and so sufficient material cannot be collected by means of speech alone. Amongst the means which Anna Freud suggests as useful for making up for the lack of verbal associations are some which I too have found valuable in my experience. If we examine these means rather more closely—take, for instance, drawing, or telling day-dreams, etc.— we shall see that their object is to collect material in some other way than that of association according to rule, and that it is above all important with children to set their phantasy free and to induce them to phantasy. In one of Anna Freud's statements we have a clue, which must be carefully considered, as to how this is to be done. She states that 'there is nothing easier than to make children understand dream-interpretation'. And again (p. 19) 'even unintelligent children, who in all other points were as inept as possible for analysis, did not fail in dream-interpretation'. I think that these children would perhaps not have been so unsuitable for analysis at all if Anna Freud had made more use, in other ways as well as in dream-interpretation, of the understanding of symbolism which they so plainly manifested. For it is my experience that, if this is done, no child, not even the least intelligent, is unfit for analysis.

For this is just the lever which we must make use of in child-analysis. A child will bring us an abundance of phantasies if we follow him along this path with the conviction that what he recounts is symbolic. In Chapter III Anna Freud puts forward a number of theoretical arguments against the play-technique which I have devised, at least when it is applied for the purpose of analysis and not merely of observation. She thinks it doubtful whether one is justified in interpreting the content of the drama enacted in children's play as symbolic and thinks that they might very likely be occasioned simply by actual observations or experiences of daily life. Here I must say that from Anna Freud's illustrations of my technique, I can see that she misunderstands it. 'If the child overturns a lamp-post or a toy figure she interprets it as something of an aggressive impulse against the father; a deliberate collision between two cars as evidence of an observation of sexual union between the parents' (p. 29). I should never attempt any such 'wild' symbolic interpretations of children's play. On the contrary I emphasized this very specially in my last paper, 'Early Analysis'. Supposing that a child gives expression to the same psychic material in various repetitions—often actually through various media, *i.e.* toys, water, by cutting-out, drawing, etc.—and supposing that, besides, I can observe that these particular activities are mostly accompanied at the time by a sense of guilt, manifesting itself either as anxiety or in representations which imply over-compensation, which are the expression of reaction-formations —supposing, then, that I have arrived at an insight into certain connections: then I interpret these phenomena and link them up with the Ucs and the analytic situation. The practical and theoretical conditions for the interpretation are precisely the same as in the analysis of adults.

The little toys I use are only one means I provide; paper, pencils, scissors, string, balls, bricks and, above all, water are others. They are at the child's disposal to use if he likes and the purpose of them all is simply to gain access to and to liberate his phantasy. There are some children who for a long time will not touch a toy or perhaps for weeks on end will only cut things out. In the case of children altogether inhibited in play the toys may possibly simply be a means of studying more closely the reasons for their inhibition. Some children, often the very little ones, as soon as the playthings have given them the opportunity of dramatizing some of the phantasies or experiences by which they are dominated, often put ṭhe toys aside altogether and pass on to every imaginable kind of game in which they themselves, various objects in my room and I have to take part.

I have gone into this detail of my technique at some length because I want to make clear the principle which, in my experience, makes it possible to handle children's associations in the greatest abundance and to penetrate into the deepest strata of the unconscious.

We can establish a quicker and surer contact with the Ucs of children if, acting on the conviction that they are much more deeply under the sway of the Ucs and their instinctual impulses than are adults, we shorten the route which adult analysis takes by way of contact with the ego and *make direct connection with the child's Ucs*. It is obvious that, if this preponderance of the Ucs is a fact, we should also expect that the mode of representation by symbols which prevails in the Ucs would be much more natural to children than to adults, in fact, that the former will be dominated by it. Let us follow them along this path, that is to say, let us come into contact with their Ucs, making use of its language through our interpretation. If we do this we shall have won access to the children themselves. Of course this is not all so easily and quickly to be accomplished as it appears; if it were, the analysis of little children would take only a short time, and this is not by any means the case. In child-analysis, we shall again and again detect resistance no less markedly than in that of adults, in children very often in the form still the more natural to them, namely, in anxiety.

This, then, is the second factor which seems to me so essential if we wish to penetrate into the child's Ucs. If we watch the alterations in his manner of representing what is going on within him (whether it is that he changes his game or gives it up or that there is a direct onset of anxiety) and try to see what there is in the nexus of the material to cause these alterations, we shall be convinced that we are always coming up against the sense of guilt and have to interpret this in its turn.

These two factors, which I have found to be the most reliable aids in the technique of child-analysis, are mutually dependent and complementary. Only by *interpreting* and so *allaying* the child's anxiety whenever we can reach it shall we gain access to his Ucs and get him *to phantasy*. Then, if we follow out the symbolism that his phantasies contain, we shall soon see anxiety reappear, and thus we shall ensure the progress of the work.

The account given of my technique and the importance attributed by me to the symbolism contained in children's actions might be misconstrued as implying that in child-analysis one has to do without the help of free association in the true sense.

In an earlier passage of my paper I pointed out that Anna Freud and I and all of us who work at child-analysis are agreed that children cannot and will not associate in the same way as adults. I should like here to add that probably it is chiefly that children *cannot*, not because they lack the capacity to put their thoughts into words (to some degree this would apply only to quite small children), but because *anxiety* resists verbal associations. It does not lie within the scope of this paper to discuss this interesting special question in greater detail: I will just briefly mention some facts of experience.

Representation by means of toys—indeed, symbolic representation in general, as being to some extent removed from the subject's own person—is less invested with anxiety than is confession by word of mouth. If, then, we succeed in allaying anxiety and in getting in the first instance more indirect representations, we shall be able to convince ourselves that we can elicit for analysis the fullest verbal expression of which the child is capable. And then we find repeatedly that at times when anxiety becomes more marked the indirect representations once more occupy the foreground. Let me give a brief illustration. When I had advanced quite a long way in the analysis of a five-year-old boy, he produced a dream the interpretation of which went very deep and was fruitful in results. This interpretation occupied the whole analytic hour, all the associations being *exclusively verbal*. On the two following days he again brought dreams which turned out to be continuations of the first. But verbal associations to the second dream could be elicited only with great difficulty and one at a time. The resistance was plain and the anxiety markedly greater than on the day before. But the child turned to the box of toys and by means of dolls and other playthings depicted for me his associations, helping himself out with words again whenever he overcame some resistance. On the third day the anxiety was even greater, on account of the material which had come to light on the two previous days. The associations were given almost exclusively by means of play with toys and water.

If we are logical in our application of the two principles that I have emphasized, namely, that we should follow up the child's symbolic mode of representation and that we should take into account the facility with which anxiety is roused in children, we shall be able also to count on their associations as a very important means in analysis, but, as I have said, only at times and as one means amongst several.

I think therefore that Anna Freud's statement is incomplete when she says: 'Here and there, and more frequently than these deliberate and invited associations, others, unintentional and uninvited, come to our help' (p. 25). Whether associations appear or not depends quite regularly on certain definite attitudes in the analysand and in no way on chance. In my opinion we can make use of this means to a far greater extent than seems likely. Over and over again it bridges the gulf to reality, and this is one reason why it is more closely associated with anxiety than is the unreal, indirect mode of representation. On this account I would not regard any child-analysis, not even that of a quite little child, as terminated unless I could finally succeed in its being expressed in speech, to the degree to which the child is capable of this, and so of linking it up with reality.

We have then a perfect analogy with the technique of adult analysis. The only difference is that with children we find that the Ucs prevails to a far greater extent and that therefore its mode of expression is far more predominant than in adults, and further that we have to take into account the child's greater tendency to anxiety.

But this is also very decidedly true of analysis during the latency and prepubertal periods and even to some extent during puberty. In a number of analyses in which the subjects were at one or other of these phases of development I was forced to adopt a modified form of the same technique as I use with children.

I think that what I have now said robs of their force Anna Freud's two main objections to my play-technique. She questioned (1) whether we were justified in assuming that the symbolic content of children's play is its main motive, and (2) whether we could regard children's play as equivalent to verbal association in adults. For, she argues, such play lacks the idea of purpose which the adult brings to his analysis and which 'enables him when associating to exclude all conscious directing and influencing of his trains of thought'.

To this latter objection I should like to reply further that these intentions in adult patients (which in my experience are not so effective as Anna Freud supposes even with them) are quite superfluous for children, and by this I do not mean very little children.

It is clear from what I have said that children are so much dominated by their Ucs that it is really unnecessary for them deliberately to exclude conscious ideas.[1] Anna Freud herself too has weighed this possibility in her mind (p. 49).

I have devoted so much space to the question of the technique to be employed with children because this seems to me fundamental in the whole problem of child-analysis. When Anna Freud rejects the

---

[1] I must go yet a step further. I do not think that the problem is to induce a child in the analytic hour 'to exclude all conscious directing and influencing of his trains of thought', but rather that we must aim at inducing him to recognize all that lies outside his Ucs, not only in the analytic hour, but also in life in general. The special relation of children to reality rests (as I showed in greater detail in my last paper already quoted: 'The Psychological Principles of Early Analysis' 1926) on the fact that they endeavour to exclude and repudiate everything which is not in accordance with their Ucs impulses, and in this is included reality in the broader sense.

play-technique, her argument applies not only to the analysis of little children, but also in my opinion to the basic principle of the analysis of older children as I understand it. The play-technique provides us with a rich abundance of material and gives us access to the deepest strata of the mind. If we make use of it we arrive unconditionally at the analysis of the Oedipus complex, and once arrived, we cannot mark out limits for analysis in any direction. If then we really wish to avoid analysing the Oedipus complex we must not make use of the play-technique, even in its modified application to older children.

It follows that the question is not whether the analysis of children *can* go so deep as that of adults, but whether it *ought* to go so deep. To answer this question we must examine the reasons which Anna Freud gives, in Chapter IV of her book, *against* penetrating so far.

Before we do this, however, I should like to discuss Anna Freud's conclusions, given in Chapter III of her book, about the part played by the transference in child-analysis.

Anna Freud describes certain essential differences between the transference situation in adults and in children. She comes to the conclusion that in the latter there may be a satisfactory transference, but that no transference-neurosis is produced. In support of this statement she adduces the following theoretical argument. Children, she says, are not ready like adults to enter upon a new edition of their love-relations, because the original love-objects, the parents, still exist as objects in reality.

In order to refute this statement, which I believe to be incorrect, I should have to enter into a detailed discussion of the structure of the super-ego in children. But as this is contained in a later passage I will content myself here with a few statements which are supported by my subsequent exposition.

The analysis of very young children has shown me that even a three-year-old child has left behind him the most important part of the development of his Oedipus complex. Consequently he is already far removed, through repression and feelings of guilt, from the objects whom he originally desired. His relations to them have undergone distortion and transformation so that the present love-objects are now *imagos* of the original objects.

Hence in reference to the analyst children can very well enter upon a new edition of their love-relations in all the fundamental and therefore decisive points. But here we encounter a second theoretical objection. Anna Freud considers that in analysing children the analyst is not, as he is when the patient is an adult, 'impersonal, shadowy, a blank page upon which the patient can inscribe his phantasies', one who avoids imposing prohibitions and permitting gratifications. But according to my experience it is exactly thus that a children's analyst

151

can and ought to behave, when once he has established the analytic situation. His activity is only apparent, for even when he throws himself wholly into all the play-phantasies of the child, conforming to the modes of representation peculiar to children, he is doing just the same as the analyst of adults, who, we know, also willingly follows the phantasies of his patients. But beyond this I do not permit child-patients any personal gratifications, either in the form of presents or caresses or personal encounters outside analysis and so forth. In short, I keep on the whole to the approved rules of adult analysis. What I give to the child-patient is analytic help and relief, which he feels comparatively quickly even if he has not had any sense of illness before. Besides this, in response to his trust in me he can absolutely rely on perfect sincerity and honesty on my part towards him.

I must, however, contest Anna Freud's conclusion no less than her premises. In my experience a full transference-neurosis does occur in children, in a manner analogous to that in which it arises with adults. When analysing children I observe that their symptoms change, are accentuated or lessened in accordance with the analytic situation. I observe in them the abreaction of affects in close connection with the progress of the work and in relation to myself. I observe that anxiety arises and that the children's reactions work themselves out on this analytic ground. Parents who watch their children carefully have often told me that they have been surprised to see habits, etc., which had long disappeared, come back again. I have not found that children work off their reactions when they are at home as well as when with me: for the most part they are reserved for abreaction in the analytic hour. Of course it does happen that at times, when very powerful affects are violently emerging, something of the disturbance becomes noticeable to those with whom the children are associated, but this is only temporary and it cannot be avoided in the analysis of adults either.

On this point, therefore, my experience is in complete contradiction to Anna Freud's observations. The reason for this difference in our findings is easy to see: it depends on the different way in which she and I handle the transference. Let me sum up what I have already said. Anna Freud thinks that a *positive* transference is a necessary condition for all analytic work with children. She regards a negative transference as undesirable. 'But with a child', she writes, 'negative impulses towards the analyst'—however revealing they may be in many respects'—are essentially inconvenient, and should be dealt with as soon as possible. The really fruitful work always takes place with a positive attachment' (p. 31).

We know that one of the principal factors in analytic work is the handling of the transference, strictly and objectively, in accordance with the facts, in the manner which our analytic knowledge has taught us to be the right one. A thorough resolution of the transference is regarded as one of the signs that an analysis has been satisfactorily concluded. On this basis psycho-analysis has laid down a number of important rules which prove necessary in every case. Anna Freud sets aside these rules for the most part in child-analysis. With her the transference, the clear recognition of which we know to be an important condition of our work, becomes an uncertain and doubtful concept. She says that the analyst '*probably* has to share with the parents the child's love or hate'. And I do not understand what is intended by 'demolishing or modifying' the inconvenient negative tendencies.

Here premises and conclusions move in a circle. If the analytic situation is not produced by analytic means, if the positive and the negative transference are not handled logically, then neither shall we bring about a transference-neurosis nor can we expect the child's reactions to work themselves out in relation to analysis and the analyst. Later in this paper I will deal with this point more thoroughly, but at present I will just briefly sum up what I have already said by stating that Anna Freud's method of attracting the positive transference by all possible means to herself, and of lessening the negative transference when it is directed against herself, seems to me not only technically incorrect but, in effect, to militate far more against the parents than my method. For it is only natural that the negative transference will then remain directed against those with whom the child is associated in daily life.

In her fourth lecture Anna Freud comes to a number of conclusions which seem to me again to display this vicious circle, this time specially clearly. The term 'vicious circle' I have explained elsewhere as meaning that from certain premises conclusions are drawn which are then used to confirm those same premises. As one of the conclusions which seem to me erroneous I would instance Anna Freud's statement that in child-analysis it is impossible to surmount the barrier of the child's imperfect mastery of speech. It is true she makes a reservation: 'As far as my experience goes up till now, with the technique I have described.' But the very next sentence contains an explanation of a general theoretical nature. She says that what we discover about early childhood when we are analysing adults 'is revealed by these very methods of free association and interpretation of the transference-reactions, *i.e.* by those means which fail us in child-analysis'. In various passages in her book Anna Freud stresses the idea that child-analysis, adapting itself to the child's mind, must alter its methods. Yet she bases her doubts of the technique which I have evolved on a number of theoretical considerations, without having submitted it to a practical test. But I have proved by practical application that this technique helps us to get the child's associations in even greater abundance than we get in adult analysis and thus to penetrate far deeper than we can in the latter.

From what my own experience has taught me, then, I really can only emphatically combat Anna Freud's statement that both the methods used in adult analysis (namely, free association and the interpretation of the transference-reactions), in order to investigate the patient's early childhood, fail us in analysing children. I am even convinced that it is the special province of child-analysis, particularly that of quite young children, to make valuable contributions to our theory, just because with children analysis can go far deeper and therefore can bring to light details which do not appear so clearly in the case of adults.

Anna Freud compares the situation of an analyst of children with that of an ethnologist 'who would also seek in vain for a short cut to prehistory in studying a primitive people instead of a cultured race' (p. 39). This again strikes me as a theoretical statement which contradicts practical experience. The analysis of little children, as well as that of older children, if it is carried far enough, gives a very clear picture of the enormous complexity of development which we find even in very little ones and shows that children of the age of, say, three years, just because they are already so much the products of civilization, have gone and are going through severe conflicts. To keep to Anna Freud's illustration, I should say that precisely from the standpoint of research a children's analyst finds himself in a fortunate situation which is never vouchsafed to an ethnologist, namely that of finding the civilized people in closest association with the primitive and, in consequence of this rare association, of receiving the most valuable information about both the earliest and later times.

I will now deal in greater detail with Anna Freud's conceptions of the child's super-ego. In Chapter IV of her book are certain statements which have special significance, both because of the importance of the theoretical question to which they relate and also because of the wide conclusions which Anna Freud draws from them.

The deep analysis of children, and particularly of little children, has led me to form quite a different picture of the super-ego in early childhood from that painted by Anna Freud principally as a result of theoretical considerations. It is certain that the ego of children is not comparable to that of adults. The super-ego, on the other hand, approximates closely to that of the adult and is not radically influenced by later development as is the ego. The dependence of children on external objects is naturally greater than that of adults and this fact produces results which are indisputable, but which I think Anna

Freud very much over-estimates, and therefore does not rightly interpret. For these external objects are certainly not identical with the already developed super-ego of the child, even though they have at one time contributed to its development. It is only thus that we can explain the astonishing fact that in children of three, four or five years old we encounter a super-ego of a severity which is often in the sharpest contradiction to the real love-objects, the parents. I should like to instance the case of a four-year-old boy whose parents have not only never punished or threatened him but who are really unusually kind and loving. The conflict between the ego and the super-ego in this case (and I am taking it only as one example of many) shows that the super-ego is of a phantastic severity. On account of the well-known formula which prevails in the Ucs this child anticipates, by reason of his own cannibalistic and sadistic impulses, such punishments as castration, being cut to pieces, eaten up, etc., and lives in perpetual dread of them. The contrast between his tender and loving mother and the punishment threatened by the child's super-ego is actually grotesque and is an illustration of the fact that we must on no account identify the real objects with those which children introject.

We know that the formation of the super-ego takes place on the basis of various identifications. My results show that this process, which terminates with the passing of the Oedipus complex, *i.e.* with the beginning of the latency period, commences at a very early age. In my last paper I have indicated, basing my remarks on my findings in the analysis of very young children, that the Oedipus complex ensues upon the deprivation experienced at weaning, that is, at the end of the first or the beginning of the second year of life. But, hand in hand with this, we see the beginnings of the formation of the super-ego. The analyses both of older and of quite young children give a clear picture of the various elements out of which the super-ego develops and the different strata in which the development takes place. We see how many stages there are in this evolution before it terminates with the beginning of the latency period. It is really a case of *terminating*, for, in contrast to Anna Freud, I am led to believe from the analysis of children that their super-ego is a highly resistant product, at heart unalterable, and is not essentially different from that of adults. The difference is only that the *maturer ego* of adults is better able to come to terms with their super-ego. This, however, is often only *apparently* the case. Further, adults can defend themselves better against those authorities which represent the super-ego in the outside world; children are inevitably more dependent on these. But this does not imply, as Anna Freud concludes, that the child's super-ego is still 'too immature, too dependent on its object, spontaneously to control the demands of the instincts, when analysis has got rid of the neurosis'. Even in children these objects—the parents—are not identical with the super-ego. Their influence on the child's super-ego is entirely analogous to that which we can prove to be at work on adults when life places them in somewhat similar situations, *e.g.* in a position of peculiar dependence. The influence of dreaded authorities in examinations, of officers in military service, and so forth, is quite comparable to the effect which Anna Freud perceives in the 'constant correlations in children between the super-ego and the love-objects, which may be likened to those of two vessels with a communicating duct'. Under the pressure of those situations in life such as I have mentioned, or others similar to them, adults, like children, react with an increase in their difficulties. This is because the old conflicts are reactivated or reinforced through the harshness of reality, and here a predominant part is played precisely by the intensified operation of the super-ego. Now this is exactly the same process as that to which Anna Freud refers, namely, the influencing of the (child's) super-ego by objects still actually present. It is true that good and bad influences on character and all the other dependent relations of childhood exert a stronger pressure on children than is undergone by adults. Yet in adults too such things are undoubtedly important.[1]

Anna Freud quotes an example (pp. 42-43) which she thinks illustrates particularly well the weakness and dependence of the claims of the ego-ideal in children. A boy in the period of life immediately preceding puberty, when he had an uncontrollable impulse to steal, found that the highest agency which influenced him was his fear of his father. She regards this as a proof that here the father who actually existed could still be substituted for the super-ego.

Now I think that quite often we can find in adults similar developments of the super-ego. There are many people who (often all through their lives) ultimately control their asocial instincts only through fear of a 'father' in a somewhat different guise: the police, the law, loss of caste, etc. The same is true too of the 'double morality' which Anna Freud observes in children. It is not only children who keep one moral code for the world of adults and another for themselves and their boon companions. Many grown-ups behave in just the same way and adopt one attitude when they are alone or with their equals, and another towards superiors and strangers.

[1] In his 'Psycho-Analytical Studies on Character Formation', Abraham (1921-1925) says. 'But the dependence of character-traits on the general fate of the libido is not confined to one particular period of life but is universally valid for the whole of life. The proverb *"Jugend kennt keine Tugend"* ("youth knows no virtue") voices the fact that at a tender age character is immature and lacking in firmness. We should, however, not over-estimate the stability of character even in later years.'

I think that one reason for the difference of opinion between Anna Freud and myself on this very important point is the following. By the super-ego I understand (and here I am in complete agreement with what Freud has taught us of its development) the faculty which has resulted from the Oedipus development through the introjection of the Oedipus objects, and, with the passing of the Oedipus complex, has assumed a lasting and unalterable form. As I have already explained, this faculty, both during its evolution and still more when it is completely formed, differs fundamentally from those objects which really initiated its development. Of course children (but also adults) will set up all kinds of ego-ideals, installing various 'super-egos', but this surely takes place in the more superficial strata and is at bottom determined by that one super-ego which is firmly rooted in the child and whose nature is immutable. The super-ego which Anna Freud thinks is still operative in the persons of the parents is not identical with this inner super-ego in the true sense, though I do not dispute its influence in itself. If we wish to reach the real super-ego, to reduce its power of operation and to influence it, our only means of doing so is analysis. But by this I mean an analysis which investigates the whole development of the Oedipus complex and the structure of the super-ego.

To return to Anna Freud's illustration which I mentioned before. In the boy whose highest weapon against the onslaught of his instincts was his fear of his father we encounter a super-ego which was certainly immature. I would rather not call such a super-ego typically 'childish'. To take another example: The four-year-old boy of whom I reported that he suffered from the pressure of a castrating and cannibalistic super-ego, in complete contrast to his kind and loving parents, has certainly not only this one super-ego. I discovered in him identifications which corresponded more closely to his real parents, though not by any means identical with them. These figures, who appeared good and helpful and ready to forgive, he called his 'fairy papa and mamma', and, when his attitude towards me was positive, he allowed me in the analysis to play the part of the 'fairy mamma' to whom everything could be confessed. At other times— always when the negative transference was reappearing—I played the part of the wicked mamma from whom everything evil that he phantasied was anticipated. When I was the fairy mamma he was able to make the most extraordinary demands and gratify wishes which could have no possible fulfilment in reality. I was to help him by bringing him as a present, in the night, an object which represented his father's penis, and this was then to be cut up and eaten. That he and she should kill his father together was one of the wishes which the 'fairy mamma' was to gratify. When I was the 'fairy papa', we were to do the same sort of things to his mother, and, when he took over the rôle himself and I enacted that of the son, he not only gave me leave to have coitus with his mother but gave me information about it, encouraged me and also showed me how the phantasied coitus could be performed with the mother by father and son simultaneously. A whole series of most varied identifications, which were in opposition to one another, originated in widely different strata and periods and differed fundamentally from the real objects, had in this child resulted as a whole in a super-ego which actually gave the impression of being normal and well developed. An additional reason for selecting this case from many analogous ones is that it was that of a child who would be called *perfectly normal* and who was having analytic treatment only for prophylactic reasons. It was only after we had done analysis for some time and the development of his Oedipus complex had been probed to the depths that I was able to recognize the complete structure and the different parts of this child's super-ego. He showed the reactions of a sense of guilt on a really high level ethically. He condemned anything that he regarded as wrong or ugly in a manner which, while appropriate to the ego of a child, was analogous to the functioning of the super-ego of an adult on a high ethical level.

The development of the child's super-ego, but not less that of the adult, depends on various factors which need not here be discussed in greater detail. If for any reason this development has not been fully accomplished and the identifications are not wholly successful, then anxiety, in which the whole formation of the super-ego originated, will preponderate in its functioning.

The case which Anna Freud quotes does not seem to me to prove anything but that such developments of the super-ego exist. I do not think it shows that this is an instance of a specifically childish development, for we meet with the same phenomenon in those adults in whom the super-ego is undeveloped. And so I think that the conclusions which she draws from this case are erroneous.

What Anna Freud says in this connection gives me the impression that she believes the development of the super-ego, with reaction-formations and screen-memories, to take place to a large extent during the period of latency. My analytic knowledge of little children forces me to differ from her quite definitely on this point. My observations have taught me that all these mechanisms are set going when the Oedipus complex arises and are activated by that complex. With its passing they have accomplished their fundamental work; the subsequent developments and reactions are rather the super-structure on a substratum which has assumed a fixed form and persists unchanged. At certain times and in certain circumstances the reaction-formations are accentuated, and, again, when the pressure from without is more powerful, the super-ego will operate more powerfully.

These, however, are phenomena which are not peculiar to childhood.

That which Anna Freud regards as a further extension of the super-ego and reaction-formations in the periods of latency and immediately before puberty is simply an apparent outward adaptation to the pressure and requirements of the outside world, and has nothing to do with the true development of the super-ego. As they grow older, children (like adults) learn how to handle the 'double-moral code' more skilfully than little children who are as yet less conventional and more honest about things.

Let us now pass on to the deductions which the author makes from her statements about the dependent nature of the super-ego of children and their double moral code in relation to the emotions of shame and disgust.

On p. 45 of her book Anna Freud argues that children differ from adults in this respect: that when the child's instinctual tendencies have been brought into consciousness the super-ego by itself should not be expected to assume complete responsibility for their direction. For she believes that children, left to themselves on this point, can only discover 'one single short and convenient path—that of direct gratification'. Anna Freud is reluctant—and gives good reasons for her reluctance—that the decision as to the way in which the instinctual forces liberated from repression are to be employed should be left to the persons responsible for the child's training. She therefore considers that the only thing to be done is that the analyst should 'guide the child at this important point'. She gives an example to illustrate the necessity for educational intervention on the part of the analyst. Let us see what she says. If my objections to her theoretical propositions are valid they must stand the test of a practical example.

The case in question is one which she discusses in several passages of her book: that of a six-year-old girl who suffered from an obsessional neurosis. This child, who before treatment displayed inhibitions and obsessional symptoms, became for the time being naughty and lacking in restraint. Anna Freud drew the inference that at this point she ought to have intervened in the rôle of educator. She thought she recognized that the fact that the child gratified its anal impulses outside analysis, when once they were free from repression, indicated that she herself had made a mistake and had relied too much on the strength of the childish ego-ideal. She felt that this as yet insufficiently established super-ego had needed temporary educative influence on the part of the analyst and therefore was not at that point capable of controlling the child's impulses un-aided.

I think it will be a good thing if I too select an illustration in support of my view, which is contrary to Anna Freud's. The case which I shall cite was a very severe one, that of a six-year-old girl who, at the beginning of the analysis, was suffering from an obsessional neurosis.[1]

Erna, whose behaviour at home was unbearable and who dis-played marked asocial tendencies in all her relations, suffered from great sleeplessness, excessive obsessional onanism, complete inhibi-tion in learning, moods of deep depression, obsessive brooding, and a number of other serious symptoms. She was treated analytically for two years, and that the result was a cure is evident from the fact that for more than a year now she has been at a school which on principle takes only 'normal children' and that she is standing the test of the life there. As goes without saying, in such a severe case of obsessional neurosis the child suffered from excessive inhibitions and deep remorse. She displayed the characteristic cleavage of per-sonality into 'devil and angel', 'good and wicked princess', etc. In her, too, analysis naturally liberated enormous quantities of affect as well as anal-sadistic impulses. During the analytic hours extra-ordinary abreactions took place: rages which were vented on objects in my room, such as cushions, etc.; dirtying and destroying of play-things, smearing paper with water, plasticine, pencils and so forth. In all this the child gave the impression of a very considerable free-dom from inhibition and seemed to take a remarkable pleasure in this often quite wild behaviour. But I discovered that it was not simply a case of 'uninhibited' gratification of her anal fixations, but that other factors were playing a decisive part. She was not by any means so 'happy' as might have been thought at first sight and as those with whom the child was associated assumed to be the case in the instance quoted by Anna Freud. To a great extent what lay behind Erna's 'lack of restraint' was anxiety and also the need for punishment which compelled her to repeat her behaviour. In it, too, there was clear evidence of all the hate and defiance which dated from the period when she was being trained in cleanliness. The situation changed completely when we had analysed these early fixations, their connection with the development of the Oedipus complex, and the sense of guilt associated with it.

In these periods when anal-sadistic impulses were being liberated

---

[1] I discussed this case-history in greater detail at the Würzburger Tagung Deutscher Analytiker (autumn 1924) and in one of my lectures in London in the summer of 1925. I propose later to publish the history. As the analysis went on I discovered that the severe obsessional neurosis masked a paranoia.

in such force Erna showing a passing inclination to abreact and gratify these outside analysis. I came to the same conclusion as Anna Freud: that the analyst must have made a mistake. Only—and here is probably one of the most salient and fundamental differences in our views—I concluded that I had failed somehow on the *analytic* side, and not on the educational. I mean that I realized that I had failed to resolve the resistances completely in the analytic hour and to release in its fullness the negative transference. I have found in this and in every other case that if we want to make it possible for children to control their impulses better without fretting themselves in a laborious struggle with them, the Oedipus development must be laid bare analytically as completely as possible, and the feelings of hate and guilt which result from it must be investigated down to their earliest beginnings.[1]

Now if we look to see at what point Anna Freud found it necessary to substitute educational for analytic measures we find that the little patient herself gives us quite exact information about it. After Anna Freud had clearly demonstrated to her (p. 25) that people could only behave so badly to some one they hated, the child asked 'the reason for such a hostile feeling towards her apparently well-loved mother'. This question was well justified and shows that good understanding of the essence of analysis that we often find in even quite little patients of a certain obsessional type. The question points the way which the analysis ought to have taken; it should have penetrated deeper. Anna Freud, however, did not take this way, for we read 'Here I declined to give further information, for I too was at the end of my knowledge.' The little patient then tried herself to help to find the way which should lead them further. She repeated a dream which she had already mentioned, the meaning of which was a reproach against her mother for always going away just when the child needed her most. Some days later she produced another dream which clearly indicated jealousy of her younger brothers and sisters.

Anna Freud then stopped and ceased to press the analysis any further just at the point where she would have had to analyse the child's hatred against her mother, that is, where it really meant first clearing up the whole Oedipus situation. We see that it is true that she had liberated and brought to abreaction some of the anal-sadistic impulses, but she did not follow up the connection of these impulses

---

[1] Anna Freud's little patient recognized this too quite correctly when, after recounting how she had come off victorious in a fight with her devil, she defined the object of her analysis thus: 'You have to help me not to be so unhappy at having to be stronger than it' (p. 13). I think, however, that this object can be fully attained only when we have been able to clear up the earliest oral and anal-sadistic fixations and the feelings of guilt connected with them.

with the Oedipus development; on the contrary she confined her investigations to superficial conscious or pre-conscious strata, for, as far as one can judge from what she writes, she seems also to have omitted to follow up the child's jealousy of her brothers and sisters to her unconscious death-wishes against them. Had Anna Freud done so this would again have led on to the death-wishes against the mother. Moreover, up till then she must also have avoided analysing the attitude of rivalry with the mother, for otherwise both patient and analyst must by this time have known something of the causes of the child's hatred of her mother.

In the fourth chapter of her book, where Anna Freud quotes this analysis as an illustration of the necessity for the analyst to intervene for a time in the educational rôle, she is apparently considering that turning-point in the analysis which I have just discussed. But I picture the situation as follows: the child became partially conscious of her anal-sadistic tendencies but was not given the opportunity through a further analysis of her Oedipus situation to become largely and fundamentally free of them. In my view it was not a question of directing her to a painful mastery and control of the impulses liberated fron repression. What was needed was rather to subject to a further and fuller analysis the motive-force behind these impulses.

But I have the same criticism to make of certain other illustrations given by Anna Freud. She refers several times to confessions of onanism which she received from patients. The nine-year-old girl who made such admissions in two dreams which she related (p. 20) was, I think, telling much more that that and something very important. Her dread of fire and the dream of the explosion in the geyser, which took place on account of wrong-doing on her part and was visited with punishment, seem to me clearly to indicate observations of parental coitus. This is evident in the second dream as well. In it there were 'two bricks of different colours' and a house which 'was going to catch fire'. These, as my experience of child-analysis enables me to say quite generally, regularly represent the primal scene. That this was true in the case of this little girl, with her dreams of fire, is to my mind plain from her drawings of the monster (described by Anna Freud, p. 23) which she called 'Bitey' and of the witch pulling out a giant's hair. Anna Freud is certainly right in interpreting these drawings as indicating the child's castration anxiety, as well as her masturbation. But I have no doubt that the witch, who castrates the giant, and the 'biter' represent parental coitus, construed by the child as a sadistic act of castration; and further that, when she received this impression, she herself conceived sadistic desires against her parents (the explosion of the geyser caused by her in the dream); that her masturbation was associated with these and that therefore, from its connection with the Oedipus complex, it involved a deep sense of guilt and, on that account, involved the compulsion to repetition and part of the fixation.

What then was left out in Anna Freud's interpretation? Everything which would have led deeper into the Oedipus situation. But this means that she omitted to explain the deeper causes of the sense of guilt and of the fixation, and made it impossible to reduce the latter. I am compelled to draw the same conclusion as in the case of the little obsessional neurotic: If Anna Freud had submitted the instinctual impulses to a more thorough analysis, there would have been no necessity to teach the child how to control them. And at the same time the cure would have been more complete. For we know that the Oedipus complex is the nuclear complex in neurosis; hence analysis, if it shrinks from analysing that complex, cannot resolve the neurosis either.

Now what are Anna Freud's reasons for refraining from thorough analysis, which should without reservation investigate the child's relation to his parents and to the Oedipus complex? There are a number of important arguments which we come upon in different passages of the book. Let us summarize them and consider what they amount to.

Anna Freud had the feeling that she ought not to intervene between child and parents and that the home training would be endangered and conflicts aroused in the child if his opposition to his parents were brought into consciousness.

Now I think that this is the point which chiefly determines the difference between Anna Freud's and my views and our opposite methods of work. She herself says (p. 8) that she feels uneasy in relation to the child's parents as her employers if she, as she calls it, sets herself against them. In the case of a nurse who was hostile to her (p. 13) she did everything she could to prejudice the child against the woman and to detach the positive feeling from her and attach it to herself. She hesitates to do this where the parents are in question, and I think she is entirely right. The difference in our point of view is this: that I never attempt in any way to prejudice a child against those with whom he is associated. But if his parents have entrusted him to me to analyse, either in order to cure a neurosis or for other reasons, I think I am justified in taking the line which seems to me in the child's interest the most advantageous and the only possible one. I mean that of analysing without reservation his relation to those about him, and therefore in particular to his parents and brothers and sisters.

There are several dangers which Anna Freud apprehends from

163

analysis of the relation to the parents and which she thinks would arise from that weakness assumed by her to characterize the child's super-ego. Let me mention some of them. —When the transference is successfully resolved, the child could no longer find his way back to the proper love-objects, and he might be forced to take 'either once more the path to neurosis or if this is closed to it by the successful outcome of the analytical treatment, the opposite line of open rebellion' (p. 37). Or again: if the parents use their influence in opposition to the analyst, the result would be, 'since the child is emotionally attached to both, a situation similar to that in an unhappy marriage where the child has become an object of contention' (p. 46). And again: 'Where a child's analysis cannot be organically grafted onto the rest of its life, but is intruded like a disturbing foreign body into its other relationships, more conflicts for the child may be created than can be resolved by the treatment' (p. 50).

In so far as it is the idea that the child's super-ego is as yet not strong enough which makes the author fear that, when he is freed from neurosis, he will no longer adapt himself satisfactorily to the necessary demands of education and of the persons with whom he is associated, I would reply as follows:

My experience has taught me that, if we analyse a child *without any preconceptions* whatever in our minds, we shall form a different picture of him, just because we are able to penetrate further into that critical period before the age of two years. There is then revealed in a far greater degree the severity of the child's super-ego, a feature Anna Freud herself has on occasion discovered. We find that what is needed is not to reinforce this super-ego but to tone it down. Let us not forget that educational influences and cultural demands are not suspended during analysis, even if the analyst, who acts as a quite unbiased third person, does not assume responsibility for them. If the super-ego has been strong enough to lead to conflict and to neurosis, it will surely retain sufficient influence, even if in the analysis we modify it little by little.

I have never finished an analysis with the feeling that this faculty had become too much weakened; on the other hand there have been a good many at the conclusion of which I have wished that its exaggerated power could be still further reduced.

Anna Freud justly emphasizes the fact that, if we secure a positive transference, children will contribute much in the way of co-operation and in other kinds of sacrifice. But I think this surely proves that, besides the strictness of the super-ego, this craving for love is an adequate security that the child will have a strong enough motive to comply with reasonable cultural requirements, if only his capacity for love is liberated by analysis.

We must not forget that the demands made by reality on the adult ego are far heavier than the much less exacting demands with which the much weaker ego of the child is confronted.

Of course it is possible that, if the child has to associate with people lacking in insight, neurotic, or otherwise harmful to him, the result may be that we cannot completely clear up his own neurosis or that it may be evoked again by his surroundings. According to my experience, however, we can even in these cases do much to mitigate matters and to induce a better development. Moreover, the neurosis on its reappearance will be milder and easier to cure in the future. Anna Freud's fears that a child who has been analysed and remains in surroundings wholly adverse to analysis will, on account of his detachment from his love-objects, become more opposed to them, and hence more of a prey to conflicts, seem to me theoretical considerations which are refuted by experience. Even in such cases I have found that the children were enabled by analysis to adapt themselves better and therefore better to stand the test of an unfavourable *milieu* and to suffer less than before being analysed.

And I have proved repeatedly that when a child becomes less neurotic it becomes less tiresome to those around it who are themselves neurotic or lacking in insight, and in this way too analysis will exercise only a favourable influence on their relationships.

In the last eight years I have analysed a large number of children; and my findings in regard to this point, which is crucial in the question of child-analysis, have been constantly confirmed. I would summarize them by saying that the danger apprehended by Anna Freud, that the analysis of a child's negative feelings to its parents will spoil their relationship, is always and in all circumstances non-existent. Rather, the exact opposite is the case. Exactly the same thing takes place as with adults: the analysis of the Oedipus situation not only releases the negative feelings of the child towards its parents and brothers and sisters but it also in part resolves them, and thus makes it possible for the positive impulses to be greatly strengthened. It is just the analysis of the earliest period which brings to light the hate-tendencies and feelings of guilt originating in the early oral deprivation, the training in cleanliness and the deprivation connected with the Oedipus situation. And it is this bringing of them to light which largely frees the child from them. The final result is a deeper and better relation to those around him, and by no means a detachment in the sense of an estrangement. The same applies to the age of puberty, only that at this period the capacity for detachment and transference necessary in that particular phase of development is powerfully reinforced by analysis. So far I have never had complaints from the family, after the analysis terminated or even while it was going on, that the child's relation to those around him had become worse. Now this means a good deal when we remember the ambivalence of the relations. On the other hand I have frequently received assurances that children have become much more social and amenable to training. So in the end I do the parents as well as the child a great service in this very matter of *improving* the relation between them.

Undoubtedly it is desirable and helpful that the parents should support us in our work both during and after the analysis. I must, however, say that such gratifying instances are decidedly in the minority: they represent the *ideal case*, and upon this we cannot base our method. Anna Freud says (p. 50), '[the indications for analysis] are not comprised solely in the fact of the child having a certain malady. The analysis of children belongs essentially in the analytical milieu and must for the present be confined to the children of analysts or of people who have been analysed or regard analysis with a certain confidence and respect.'

In reply I would say that we must discriminate very clearly between the Cs and the Ucs attitudes of the parents themselves, and I have repeatedly found that the Ucs attitude is by no means guaranteed by the conditions desiderated by Anna Freud. Parents may be theoretically entirely convinced of the necessity of analysis and may consciously wish to help us with all their might and yet for unconscious reasons they may hinder us in our work all the way along. On the other hand I have constantly found that people who knew nothing about analysis—sometimes just a homely nurse who met me with personal confidence—have been most helpful owing to a favourable Ucs attitude. However, in my experience, anyone who analyses children has to reckon with a certain hostility and jealousy in nurses, governesses and even mothers, and has to try to accomplish the analysis in spite of and against these feelings. At first sight this seems impossible and it certainly is a special and very considerable difficulty in child-analysis. Nevertheless in most cases I have not found it insuperable. Of course I presuppose that we have not 'to share with the parents in the child's love and hate', but that we handle both positive and negative transference in such a way as to enable us to establish the analytic situation and to rely upon it. It is amazing how children, even little children, then support us by their insight and their need for help and how we are able to include in our work the resistances caused by those with whom the little patients are associated.

My experience, therefore, has gradually led me to emancipate myself in my work as far as possible from these persons. Valuable as their communications at times may be, when they tell us about important changes which are taking place in the children and afford us insight into the real situation, we must of necessity be able to manage without this aid. I do not of course imply that an analysis may never come to grief through the fault of those associated with the child, but I can only say that so long as the parents send their children to be analysed at all I see no particular reason why it should be impossible to carry the analysis through simply because their attitude shows a lack of insight or is otherwise unfavourable.

From all that I have said it will be clear that my position with regard to the advisability of analysis in various cases is in many respects entirely different from that of Anna Freud. I consider analysis helpful not only in every case of obvious mental disturbance and faulty development, but also as a means of diminishing the difficulties of normal children. The way may be indirect, but I am sure that it is not too hard, too costly, or too tedious.

In this second part of my paper my intention was to prove that it is impossible to combine in the person of the analyst analytical and educational work, and I hoped to show why this is so. Anna Freud describes these functions (p. 49) as 'two difficult and diametrically opposed functions'. And again she says: 'To analyse and educate, that is to say in the same breath [the analyst] must allow and forbid, loosen and bind again.' I may sum up my arguments by saying that the one activity in effect cancels the other. If the analyst, even only temporarily, becomes the representative of the educative agencies, if he assumes the rôle of the super-ego, at that point he blocks the way of the instinctual impulses to Cs: he becomes the representative of the repressing faculties. I will go a step further and say that, in my experience, what we have to do with children as well as with adults is not simply to establish and maintain the analytic situation by every analytic means and to refrain from all *direct* educative influence, but, more than that, a children's analyst must have the same Ucs attitude as we require in the analyst of adults, if he is to be successful. It must enable him to be really willing *only to analyse* and not to wish to mould and direct the minds of his patients. If anxiety does not prevent him, he will be able calmly to wait for the development of the correct issue, and in this way that issue will be achieved.

If he does this, however, he will prove the validity of the second principle which I represent in opposition to Anna Freud: namely, that we must analyse completely and without reservation the child's relation to his parents and his Oedipus complex.

*   *   *   *   *   *   *

Postscript, May 1947.

Both in the Preface and in Part 3 of her new book Anna Freud presents various modifications of her technique. Some of these modifications concern points with which I dealt in the above paper.

One divergence of our views arose through her use of educational methods in the analysis of children. She explained that this technique was necessary in view of the weak and underdeveloped superego of children, even in the latency period (which at that time was the only age at which she considered children should be analysed). She now states in her Preface that the educational side in the work of the child analyst is no longer necessary (because parents and educational authorities have become much more enlightened) and that the analyst 'can now, with rare exceptions, concentrate his energies on the purely analytic side of the task' (Preface, p. xi).

Again, when Anna Freud published her book in 1926, she not only criticized play-technique (which I had evolved for the analysis of young children), but also objected on principle to young children below the latency age being analysed. She has now, as she puts it in her Preface, lowered the age range 'from the latency period, as originally suggested, to two years . . .' and has also, it appears, to some extent accepted play-technique as a necessary part of the analysis of children. Furthermore she has extended the range of her patients, not only where age is concerned, but also as regards the type of illness, and now considers children analysable 'whose abnormalities are of a schizophrenic type' (p. x).

The following issue is a more complicated one because an important difference remains even though some similarity in approach has come about. Anna Freud says about her 'introductory phase' in the analysis of children that her study of the defence mechanisms of the ego has led her to find 'ways and means to uncover and penetrate the first resistances in the analysis of children, whereby the introductory phase of the treatment is shortened, and, in some instances, rendered unnecessary' (Preface, pp. xi–xii). A consideration of my contribution to the Symposium will show that the essence of my argument against Anna Freud's 'introductory phase' was as follows: if the analyst deals with the child's immediate anxiety and resistance by analytic means from the beginning, the transference situation is at once established, and no measures other than psychoanalytic ones are needed or advisable. Our views on this problem have therefore now in common that an introductory phase is unnecessary (though Anna Freud only seems to allow this for certain cases) if analytic ways and means are found to penetrate first resistances. In my contribution to the Symposium I dealt with this problem mainly from the angle of the young child's acute anxiety.

Many instances, however, in my *Psycho-Analysis of Children* show that in those cases in which the anxiety is less acute, I attribute great significance to the analysis of defences from the beginning. In fact it is not possible to analyse resistances without analysing defences. However, even though Anna Freud does not refer to the analysis of acute anxiety but seems to lay the main emphasis on the analysis of defences, our views coincide on the possibility of conducting an analysis from the beginning by analytic means.

These alterations in Anna Freud's views, which I give only as instances, amount in fact, though she does not state this, to a lessening of some important divergencies between her and myself as regards the psycho-analysis of children.

There is another point I should mention, because it concerns fundamentally my approach to the principles and technique of early analysis, which I illustrate in the present book. Anna Freud states (p. 71): 'Melanie Klein and her followers repeatedly expressed the opinion that, with the help of the play-technique, children can be analysed at almost any age, from earliest infancy onwards.' I do not know on what grounds this statement was made, and the reader of this volume as of *The Psycho-Analysis of Children* will find no passages to substantiate it, nor material from the analysis of children younger than two and three-quarter years of age. I do of course attach great importance to the study of infant behaviour, especially in the light of my findings concerning early mental processes, but such analytic observation is essentially different from carrying out psycho-analytic treatment.

I would here also draw attention to the fact that in this new edition of her book (pp. 69–71) Anna Freud repeats the erroneous description of my technique she gave twenty years ago, for she infers that I rely predominantly on symbolic interpretations and make very little use—if any—of the child's speech, day-dreams, night-dreams, stories, imaginative play, drawings, his emotional reactions and his relations to external reality, *e.g.* in his home. This misconception has been explicitly corrected by me in the above contribution to the Symposium, and it is hard to understand how it could have been maintained in the face of my *Psycho-Analysis of Children* and of my various publications since.

8

CRIMINAL TENDENCIES IN NORMAL CHILDREN

(1927)

ONE of the bases of psycho-analysis is Freud's discovery that we find in the adult all the stages of his early childish development. We find them in the unconscious which contains all repressed phantasies and tendencies. As we know, the mechanism of repression is mostly directed by the judging, criticizing faculties—the super-ego. It is evident that the deepest repressions are those which are directed against the most unsocial tendencies.

As the individual repeats biologically the development of mankind, so also does he do it psychically. We find, repressed and unconscious, the stages which we still observe in primitive people: cannibalism and murderous tendencies of the greatest variety. This primitive part of a personality entirely contradicts the cultured part of the personality, which is the one that actually engenders the repression.

Child-analysis and especially early analysis, by which is meant the analysis of children between three and six, gives a very illuminating picture of how early this fight between the cultured part of the personality and the primitive one starts. The results I have obtained in my analytical work with small children have proved to me that as early as the second year we find the super-ego already at work.

At this age the child has already passed through most important stages of its psychical development; it has gone through its oral fixations, wherein we must distinguish between the oral-*sucking* fixation and the oral-*biting* fixation. The latter is very much connected with cannibalistic tendencies. The fact that we can observe often enough that babies bite the mother's breast is one of the evidences of this fixation.

In the first year, too, a great part of the anal-sadistic fixations take place. This term, anal-sadistic erotism, is used to denote the pleasure derived from the anal erotogenic zone and the excretory function, together with the pleasure in cruelty, mastery, or possession, etc., which has been found to be closely connected with anal pleasures. The oral-sadistic and the anal-sadistic impulses play the greatest part in those tendencies which I intend to examine in this paper.

I have just mentioned that as early as in the second year we find the super-ego at work, certainly in its developing stage. What calls this into being is the advent of the Oedipus complex. Psycho-analysis has shown that the Oedipus complex plays the largest part in the entire development of a personality, as much in persons who will become normal as in those who will become neurotic. Psycho-analytic work has demonstrated more and more that the whole of character formation, too, is derived from the Oedipus development, that all shades of difficulties of character, from the slightly neurotic to the criminalistic, are determined by it. In this direction—the study of the criminal—only the first steps have been made, but they are steps which promise far-reaching developments.[1]

It is the subject of my present paper to show you how we can see criminal tendencies at work in every child and to make some suggestions as to what it is which determines whether those tendencies will assert themselves in the personality or not.

I have to go back now to the point from which I started. When the Oedipus complex sets in, which, according to the results of my work, happens at the end of the first or the commencement of the second year, the early stages I mentioned—the oral-sadistic and the anal-sadistic—are fully at work. They become connected with the Oedipus tendencies, and are directed towards the objects around which the Oedipus complex develops: the parents. The little boy, who hates the father as a rival for the love of the mother, will do this with the hate, the aggression and the phantasies derived from his oral-sadistic and anal-sadistic fixations. Phantasies of penetrating into the bedroom and killing the father are not lacking in any boy's analysis, even in the case of a normal child. I should like to mention a special case, that of a very normal and in every respect satisfactorily developed boy of four years, named Gerald. This case is very illuminating in many respects. Gerald was a very lively and seemingly happy child in whom no anxiety had ever been noticed, and he was only brought for analysis for prophylactic reasons.

During the course of the analysis I found that the child had undergone intense anxiety and was still under the stress of this anxiety. I shall show later on how it is possible for a child to hide his fears and difficulties so well. One of his anxiety-objects we ascertained during the analysis was a beast which only had the habits of a beast, but in reality was a man. This beast, which made big noises in the next room, was the father from whom the noises emanated in the

[1] See Freud, 'Some Character-Types met with in Psycho-Analytic Work: III Criminals from a Sense of Guilt' *S.E.* **14**; and Reik (1925).

adjoining bedroom. The desire of Gerald to penetrate there, to blind the father, to castrate and to kill him caused a dread that he would be treated in the same way by the beast. Certain passing habits, such as a movement of the arms, which analysis proved to be a pushing off of the beast, were due to this anxiety. Gerald had a little tiger and his great affection for this animal was partly due to the hope that it would protect him from the beast. But this tiger proved sometimes to be not only a defender but an aggressor. Gerald proposed to send it into the next room to carry out his aggressive desires on the father. In this case too the father's penis was to be bitten off, cooked and eaten, which desire derived partly from the boy's oral fixations and partly as a means of fighting the enemy; for a child, having no other weapon, in a primitive manner uses his teeth as a weapon. This primitive part of the personality was in this case represented by the tiger, which, as I ascertained later on, was Gerald himself, but a part of him which he would have liked not to realize. But Gerald also had phantasies of cutting his father and mother into pieces, these phantasies being connected with anal actions, with dirtying his father and mother with his faeces. A dinner party he arranged after such phantasies proved to be a meal in which he and his mother were eating the father. It is difficult to illustrate how such a warm-hearted child, as this one was, in particular suffers through such phantasies, which the cultivated part of his personality strongly condemns. This boy could not show enough love and kindness to his father; and here we see a strong reason for his repressing his love for his mother, who somehow is the cause of such phantasies, and remaining attached to the father in a redoubled fixation which might form the basis for a permanent homosexual attitude later on.

To mention briefly the analogous case of a little girl. The rivalry for the father, the wish to take the mother's place in his love, also leads to sadistic phantasies of the most varied nature. Here the wish to destroy the beauty of the mother, to mutilate her face and her body, to appropriate the mother's body for herself—this very primitive phantasy of biting and cutting and so on—is connected with a strong feeling of guilt, which strengthens the fixation to the mother. At this age, between two and five years, we often see little girls excessively affectionate to their mothers, but this affection is partly based on anxiety and a feeling of guilt, and is followed by a turning away from the father. Thus this complicated psychical situation becomes still more complicated by the fact that, in defending itself against those tendencies which its super-ego condemns, the child appeals to its homosexual tendencies, strengthens them and develops what we call the 'inverted' Oedipus complex. This is the development which shows itself by a very strong fixation in the little girl to her mother, in the little boy to his father. Just one step more, and we arrive at the stage where this relation, too, cannot be maintained and the child withdraws from both. This is surely the basis of an unsocial personality, for the relation to father and mother determines all subsequent relations in life. There is another relation which plays a fundamental rôle. This is the relation to brothers and sisters; every analysis proves that all children suffer great jealousy of younger sisters and brothers as well as of older ones. Even the quite small child, which seemingly knows nothing about birth, has a very distinct *unconscious* knowledge of the fact that children grow in the mother's womb. A great hate is directed against this child in the mother's womb for reasons of jealousy, and—as typical of the phantasies of a child during the mother's expectancy of another one —we find desires to mutilate the mother's womb and to deface the child in it by biting and cutting it.

Against the new-born child, too, sadistic desires are directed. Moreover, these sadistic desires are also directed against older sisters and brothers, because the child feels itself slighted in comparison with the elder children, even when this is not actually the case. But these feelings of hate and jealousy also give the child a strong feeling of guilt, which is apt to influence its relationship to brother and sister for ever. Little Gerald, for example, possessed a small doll which he nursed most tenderly and often bandaged. It represented his small brother, whom, according to his strict super-ego, he had mutilated and castrated while the brother was in his mother's womb.

In all these situations, so far as his feelings are negative, the child reacts with all the power and intensity of the hatred characteristic of the early sadistic stages of development. But, since the objects it hates are at the same time objects of its love, the conflicts which arise become very soon unbearably burdensome to the weak ego; the only escape is flight through repression, and the whole conflicting situation, which is thus never cleared up, remains active in the unconscious mind. Although psychology and pedagogy have always maintained the belief that a child is a happy being without any conflicts, and have assumed that the sufferings of adults are the result of the burdens and hardships of reality, it must be asserted that *just the opposite is true*. What we learn about the child and the adult through psycho-analysis shows that all the sufferings of later life are for the most part repetitions of these early ones, and that every child in the first years of its life goes through an immeasurable degree of suffering.

It is not to be denied that appearances speak against these statements. Even though on close observation one can note signs of difficulties, the child seems to overcome these more or less easily. The question how the difference between appearances and the actual psychical situation is to be explained will be answered later, when we are dealing with the various ways and means the child uses to overcome its difficulties.

I have to return to the point where I spoke about the negative feelings of the child. These are directed against the parent of the *same* sex and the brothers and sisters. But, as I mentioned, the situation is more complicated through the fact that negative feelings are also directed against the parent of the opposite sex, partly because of the frustration this parent too imposes, and partly because in its efforts to escape the conflict the child withdraws from his love-object and changes the love into aversion. But the situation is still more complicated through the fact that the child's love-tendencies are coloured by sexual theories and phantasies typical of the pre-genital stages, just as its negative feelings are. A great deal about the infantile sexual theories has been discovered from the analysis of adults; but to the analyst who deals with *children themselves* an astonishing variety of sexual theories is revealed. I will just say a few words about the way in which this material is obtained from the child. When from our psycho-analytic point of view we watch the child at play and use special technical measures to diminish its inhibition, we can bring out these phantasies and theories, find out the experiences the child has had, and see all the child's impulses and its reacting criticizing faculties at work. This technique is not an easy one; it requires a great deal of identification with the phantasies of the child and a special attitude towards the child, but it is extremely productive. This technique leads us to depths of the unconscious which are surprising even to the analyst of the adult. Slowly the analyst, by interpreting to the child what his play, drawings and whole behaviour means, resolves the repressions against the phantasies behind the play and liberates those phantasies. Tiny dolls, men, women, animals, cars, trains and so on, enable the child to represent various persons, mother, father, brothers and sisters, and by means of the toys to act all its most repressed unconscious material. It is not possible within the limits of this paper to enter more fully into the details of my technique. I must confine myself to the statement that I get this material in so many different performances and in such variety that an error about its meaning is impossible; which is proved, too, through the resolving and liberating effect of the interpretations. Both the primitive and the reacting judging tendencies become clear. If the child has shown in a game, for example, that a tiny man fighting against a bigger one was able to overcome him, it very often happens that the big man when dead is put in a carriage and brought to the butcher who cuts him to pieces and cooks him. The little man eats the meat with pleasure, even inviting to this feast a lady who sometimes represents the mother. She has accepted the little murderer instead of the killed father. The situation can be quite different, of course. The homosexual fixation may stand in the foreground and we might as well see the mother cooked and eaten and the two brothers dividing the meal between them. As I mentioned, an innumerable variety of phantasies, differing even in the same child at different stages of its analysis, manifests itself. But such a manifestation of primitive tendencies is invariably followed by anxiety, and by performances which show how the child now tries to make good and to atone for that which he has done. Sometimes he tries to mend the very same men, trains and so on he has just broken. Sometimes drawing, building and so on express the same reactive tendencies.

I want to make a point clear. The games I have described, through which the child gives me the material I discussed, differ greatly from the games which children are usually observed to play. This is to be explained as follows: The analyst gets his material in a very specific way. The attitude he shows to the child's associations and games is entirely free from ethical and moral criticism. This is indeed one of the ways in which a transference can be established and analysis set going. Thus the child will show to the analyst what it never would reveal to its mother or nurse. For good reasons: as they would be very much shocked to notice aggression and unsocial tendencies against which education is mostly directed. Moreover, it is just the analytical work which resolves repressions and in this way brings about the manifestations of the unconscious. This is obtained slowly, step by step, and some of the games I mentioned have occurred in the course of the analysis, and not at the beginning. It must be added, however, that the children's games, even outside of analysis, are very instructive and give evidence of many of those impulses which are discussed here. But it requires a specially trained observer, a knowledge of symbolism and psycho-analytic methods in order to ascertain these.

The sexual theories are the basis of a variety of most sadistic and primitive fixations. We know from Freud that there is some unconscious knowledge which the child obtains, apparently in a phylogenetic way. To this belongs the knowledge about parental intercourse, birth of children, etc.; but it is of a rather vague and confused nature. According to the oral- and anal-sadistic stage which he is going through himself, intercourse comes to mean to the child a performance in which eating, cooking, exchange of faeces and sadistic acts of every kind (beating, cutting, and so on) play the principal part. I wish to emphasize *how important the connection between these phantasies and sexuality is bound to become in later life*. All these phantasies will then apparently have disappeared, but their unconscious effect will be of far-reaching importance in frigidity, in impotence and in other sexual disturbances. This may be quite distinctly seen in the small child in analysis. The little boy who has demonstrated his wishes about the mother, showing in this respect most sadistical phantasies, tries to escape by choosing instead of the mother-object the father-imago; and will then withdraw from this too, if his oral-sadistic phantasies prove to be connected with this object of love also. Here we find the basis of all the perversions which Freud has discovered to have their origin in the early development of the child. Phantasies of the father, or of himself, ripping up the mother, beating, scratching her, cutting her into pieces, are some instances of childish conception of intercourse. I will refer here to the fact that phantasies of this nature are really carried into action by criminals, to mention only the instance of Jack the Ripper. In the homosexual relation these phantasies change to castrating the father, by cutting or biting off the penis, and all sorts of violent acts. Birth is very often connected with phantasies of cutting open the body, and taking the babies out from different places in the body. These are but a few examples of the abundant variety of sexual phantasies which are to be found *in every normal child*—a point which I wish particularly to emphasize. I can assert this, as I have been lucky enough to have several normal children for analysis, from the prophylactic point of view. This repulsive aspect of a child's phantasy-life changes entirely when we become more familiar with the depths of the child's mind. A child is entirely dominated by his impulses, which, however, we see to be the foundation of all the attractive and socially important creative tendencies. I must say that the impression I get of the way in which even the quite small child fights his unsocial tendencies is rather touching and impressive. One moment after we have seen the most sadistic impulses, we meet with performances showing the greatest capacity for love and the wish to make all possible sacrifices to be loved. We cannot apply any ethical standards to these impulses; we have to take their existence for granted, without any criticism, and help the child to deal with them; whereby we at the same time diminish his sufferings, strengthen his capacities, his mental equilibrium, and in the final result accomplish a work of notable social importance. It is impressive to see in analysis how these destructive tendencies can be used for sublimation when we resolve the fixations—how the phantasies can be liberated for most artistic and constructive work. This is done in analysis only through purely analytical measures, not at all by advising or encouraging the child. From my experience, the latter way, which is the pedagogical one, cannot be combined with analytical work in the person of the analyst, but analysis prepares the ground for very productive pedagogical work.

In a communication made some years ago to the Berlin Analytical Society, I pointed out an analogy between some very horrible crimes which had recently happened, and corresponding phantasies which I had found in the analysis of some small children. One was a case which really was a combination of perversion and crime. By acting in a very skilful way, so that he was not discovered for a long time, the man was able to carry out the following acts on a great number of persons: the criminal in question, whose name was Harmann, became intimate with young men, whom he first of all used for his homosexual tendencies, then cut off their heads, either burnt or disposed of the parts of the body in some way or other, and even sold their clothes afterwards. Another very horrible case was that of a man who killed various people, using the parts of the bodies for making sausages. The analogous phantasies in children which I mentioned before had in all details the same features as these crimes. The persons on whom they were committed were, for instance, the father and brother of a little boy between four and five, to whom he was bound by a very strong sexual fixation. After having expressed the desired mutual masturbation and other actions, he cut off the head of the little doll, selling the body to a pretended butcher, who was to sell it for food. For himself he kept the head, which he wanted to eat himself, finding it the most tempting portion. But he likewise appropriated the belongings of the victim.

I will enter more fully into this special case, as I think it will be more illuminating if I give you more details about one case, rather than enumerate more examples. This little boy, Peter, when he came to me for analysis, was a most inhibited, extremely apprehensive child, very difficult to educate, entirely incapable of playing; he could do nothing with his toys but break them. His inhibition of play, as well as his anxiety, were closely connected with his oral-sadistic and anal-sadistic fixations. As phantasies are really the motive power of play, he could not play, for his cruel phantasies had to be kept in repression. Being afraid of what he unconsciously felt the desire to do, he expected always the same things to be done to himself. The sadistic wishes connected with his desire in regard to the mother led to a withdrawal from her and to rather bad relations with her. The libido was directed towards the father, but as he was also very much frightened of his father, the only real relationship he could maintain was with his little brother. This was naturally very ambivalent too. The way this child was always expecting a punishment may be best shown by the following example: he once played, representing himself and his little brother by two tiny dolls, that they were expecting punishment for their naughtiness to the mother; she comes, finds them dirty, punishes them and goes away. The two children repeat their dirty acts again, are again punished, and so on. At last, the dread of punishment becomes so strong that the two children determine to kill the mother, and he executes a little doll. They then cut and eat the body. But the father appears to help the mother, and is killed too in a very cruel manner and also cut up and eaten. Now the two children seem to be happy. They can do what they like. But after a very short time great anxiety sets in, and it appears that the killed parents are again alive and come back. When the anxiety started the little boy had hidden the two dolls under the sofa, so that the parents should not find them, and then happened what the boy called 'becoming educated'. The father and mother find the two dolls, the father cuts *his* head off, the mother that of the brother, and then they, too, get cooked and eaten.

But it is characteristic, and I wish to emphasize this point, that after a short time the bad acts are again repeated, it may be even in different performances; the aggression against the parents starts again and the children are again and again punished. The mechanism, which expresses itself in this circle, will occupy our attention later.

Just a few words regarding the result of this case. Although the child, while it was still being analysed, had to live through some hard experiences, as the parents were divorced during that time, and both remarried under straitened circumstances, his neurosis was entirely resolved during analysis. He lost his anxiety and his play-inhibition and became good at his school-work, socially well adapted and happy.

Perhaps the question will arise: why, as the title of my paper promises to deal with normal children, have I entered in such detail into a case of a distinctly obsessional-neurotic child? As I have mentioned several times, the same material is to be found in normal children too. A neurotic only shows more clearly what is found with less intensity in the normal child as well. This is one important factor in explanation of the problem how the same psychical fundamentals can lead to such different results. In the case of little Peter, the intensity of the oral-sadistic and anal-sadistic fixation was so great that his whole development was dominated by it. Certain experiences were also a determining factor in bringing out his obsessional neurosis. The child changed in a very striking manner at about two years of age. The parents mentioned it without being able to account for it. At that time, the child had a great relapse to the habit of dirtying himself, he stopped all playing, started breaking his toys, and became very difficult to manage.

Analysis revealed that in that summer when the change appeared, the child shared the parents' bedroom and witnessed intercourse. The impression he received was of a very oral and sadistic act and it strengthened his fixations. He had at this time already reached the genital stage to some extent, and under this impression he regressed to the pre-genital stages. Thus his whole sexual development remained really under the domination of these stages. The birth of a little brother, six months later, increased still more his conflicts and likewise his neurosis. But there is yet another factor, which is of the greatest importance in the development of the obsessional neurosis generally, and particularly in this case. This is the feeling of guilt engendered by the super-ego. In Peter already at a very early age, a super-ego not less sadistic than his own tendencies was at work. The intensity of this fight, unbearable for the weak ego, led to a very strong repression. Another factor is of importance too: there are children who can bear very little anxiety and feeling of guilt. This child could bear very little; the struggle between his sadistic impulses and his sadistic super-ego, threatening him with the same acts as a punishment, was a terrific burden for him. In the unconscious the Biblical precept 'an eye for an eye' is at work. This explains how it is that we find in children such fantastic ideas of *what the parents might do to them*: kill them, cook them, castrate them and so on.

As we know, the parents are the source of the super-ego, in that their commands, prohibitions, and so on become absorbed by the child itself. But this super-ego is not identical with the parents; it is partly formed upon the child's own sadistic phantasies. But such strong repressions only stabilize the fight, without ever bringing it to an end. Moreover, by shutting off phantasies, repression makes it impossible for the child to abreact these phantasies in play, and in other ways to use them for sublimations, so that the whole weight of these fixations is left in a never-ending circle. It remains a circle, for repression, as I mentioned, does not end this process. The feeling of guilt, repressed too, is no less burdensome; thus the child repeats over and over a variety of actions, expressing both his desires and his wish to be punished. This desire for punishment, which is a determining factor when the child constantly repeats naughty acts, finds an analogy in the repeated misdeeds of the criminal, as I shall indicate later in my paper. I will remind you what little Peter did in his game where he represented himself and his little brother as dolls; they were naughty and were punished, they killed their parents and their parents killed them, and then the whole thing started over again. We see here a repetition-compulsion derived from various causes, but influenced very much by the feeling of guilt demanding punishment. Here we can already see some differences between the normal and the neurotic child: the intensity of the fixations, the way and the time at which those fixations become connected with experiences, the degree of severity and whole manner of development of the super-ego, which is again dependent on inner and outside causes; and, furthermore, the child's capacity for bearing anxiety and conflict, are some of the most important factors which determine either normal or neurotic development.

The normal child, as well as the abnormal child, uses repression to deal with his conflicts, but since these are less intense the whole circle will not be so strong. There are other mechanisms, too, which both the normal and the neurotic child use, and again only the degree will determine the issue: one is the flight from reality. Much more than would appear on the surface, the child resents the unpleasantness of reality and tries *to adapt it to his phantasies* and not *his phantasies to reality*. Here we have the answer I put off at one point, how it is possible that the child does not show its inward suffering much outwardly. We see that a child is very often soon consoled after it has wept bitterly; we see it sometimes enjoying the most insignificant trifles and conclude that it is happy. It can do this because it has a refuge which is more or less denied to the grown-up: this is the flight from reality. Those who are familiar with the play-life of children know that this play-life is concerned entirely with the child's impulse-life and desires, performing them and fulfilling them through his phantasies. From reality, to which it is more or less apparently well adapted, the child takes only as much as is absolutely essential. Therefore we see that a number of difficulties arise at periods in the child's life when the demands of reality become more urgent, as for example, when school is begun.

I have already mentioned that this mechanism, the flight from reality, is to be found at work in all types of development, but that the difference is chiefly a question of degree. Where some of the factors which I mentioned as determining the development of the obsessional neurosis are at work, besides other special ones, we see this flight from reality developed to a dominating extent, and preparing the basis for a psychosis. We can sometimes perceive these factors in some child who on the surface makes rather a normal impression, often not showing more than a very intensive phantasy-life and capacity for playing. The mechanism of escaping from reality and falling back on phantasy is connected with another very usual form of reaction on the part of the child: namely its ability to comfort itself constantly for the frustration of its desires, proving to itself again through its play and its fancies that all is well and will be well.

This attitude in children is very apt to give the impression to adults that the child is much happier than it actually is.

To come back to little Gerald. His happiness and liveliness were partly designed to hide his anxiety and unhappiness from himself and others. This changed very much through analysis, which helped him to rid himself of the anxiety and to substitute a much better-founded contentment for this partly artificial one. It is in this respect that analysis of normal children finds its greatest opportunity. There is *no* child without difficulties, fears and feelings of guilt, and even when these seem to be of small importance, they cause much greater suffering than would appear, and are in addition the early indication of much greater disturbances in later life.

I mentioned in the case of Peter that the feeling of guilt plays a great part in the compulsion to repeat forbidden acts again and again, although in time these acts assume quite a different character. One may regard it as a rule that in every so-called 'naughty' child the desire to be punished is at work too. I should like to quote Nietzsche and what he called his 'pale criminal'; he knew much about the criminal driven by his sense of guilt. Here we come to the most difficult part of my paper: the problem of what development these fixations have to undergo in order to make the criminal. This point is difficult to answer, for the reason that psycho-analysis has not yet occupied itself much with this particular problem. Unfortunately I have not a great deal of experience to which I can refer in this very interesting and important field of work. But certain cases which approximated somewhat to the criminal type have given me some idea of the way in which this development comes about. I will quote one case which seems to me to be very instructive. A boy of twelve years of age who was to be sent to a reformatory was brought for analysis to me. His delinquencies were breaking open the school cupboard and a tendency to steal in general, but mostly breaking up things, and sexual attacks on little girls. He had no relationship to anyone but a destructive one; his boy friendships had mostly this purpose too. He had no special interests and even seemed indifferent to punishments and rewards. The intelligence of this child was much under normal, but this did not prove a hindrance to the analysis, which went on quite well and seemed to promise good results. I was told after a few weeks that the child began to change favourably. Unfortunately I had to make a long break for personal reasons, when I had had the child for two months in analysis. In those two months the child was to have come three times a week, but I saw him only fourteen times, as his foster-mother did her best to keep him from coming to me. During this very disturbed analysis the child nevertheless did not commit any act of delinquency, but began them again during the time of the break, whereupon he was at once sent to a reformatory, and all my attempts after my return to get him back for analysis failed. From the whole situation, I do not doubt in the least that he has started on the path of a criminal career.

I will now give a brief survey of the causes of his development as far as I could gather them from the analysis. The child grew up under the most desolate circumstances. The older sister had forced him and his smaller brother at a very early age to sexual acts. The father died during the war; the mother fell ill; the sister dominated the whole family; things altogether were in a sorry state. When the mother was dead he came under the care of various foster-mothers and grew from bad to worse. The main point in his development seemed to be fear and hatred of his sister. He hated his sister, who represented for him the principle of evil, on account of this sexual relation, but also because she ill-treated him, was unkind to the dying mother and so on. On the other hand, however, he was bound to the sister by a dominating fixation which apparently was based only on hatred and anxiety. But there were still deeper-reaching causes for his delinquencies. Throughout his childhood this boy had shared the bedroom of his parents and obtained a very sadistic impression from their intercourse. As I pointed out earlier, this experience strengthened his own sadism. His desire for intercourse both with his father and his mother remained under the domination of his sadistic fixations, and was connected with great anxiety. The violence of the sister under these circumstances took in his unconscious the place both of the violent father and, alternately, the mother. In both cases it was castration and punishment he had to expect, and again the punishment corresponded to his own very sadistic and primitive super-ego. It was plain that he repeated on the little girls the attacks he had suffered himself, only changing the situation in so far that now he was the aggressor. His breaking open of cupboards and taking out articles, as well as his other destructive tendencies, had the same unconscious causes and symbolic meaning as his sexual assaults. This boy, feeling overwhelmed and castrated, had to change the situation by proving to himself that he could be the *aggressor* himself. One important motive for these destructive tendencies was to prove to himself again and again that he *was still a man*, besides abreacting his hatred against his sister on other objects.

It was however no less his feeling of guilt which drove him to repeat again and again acts which were to be punished by a cruel father or mother, or even both. His apparent indifference to punishment, his apparent lack of fear were completely misleading. The child was overwhelmed by fear and feeling of guilt. Now arises the question wherein his development differed from that of the neurotic child I described earlier. I can only throw out some suggestions. It may have been that through his experiences with the sister this very primitive and cruel super-ego had remained fixated on the one hand in the stage of development it had then reached; on the other hand it was bound to this experience and always dealing with it. Thus this child was inevitably more overwhelmed with anxiety than little Peter. Connected with this a still stronger repression shut off all outlets for phantasy and sublimation, so that no other way remained than to repeat desire and fear continually *in the same acts*. Compared with the neurotic child he had actually had experience of an overwhelming super-ego, which the other child had only evolved from inner causes. Thus it was also with his hatred, which, in consequence of his *real* experience, found expression in his destructive acts.

I mentioned that in this case, as probably in others of the same nature, the very strong and early repression, shutting off the phantasies, deprived him of the possibility of working off his fixations through other ways and means, that is to sublimate them. In sublimations of the most varied kind we find aggressive and sadistic fixations playing a part too. I wish to indicate just one means by which, even physically, much aggression and sadism can be worked through, namely sport. Thus attacks on the hated object can be made in a manner socially permissible; at the same time it serves as overcompensation for anxiety, as it proves to the individual that he will not succumb to the aggressor.

In the case of the little criminal it was very interesting to see, as the repression was weakened through analysis, what sublimation took place. The boy, who had no interest but a destructive one of breaking and spoiling things, showed an entirely new interest in the construction of lifts and every form of locksmith's work. It may be assumed that this would have proved a good way of sublimating his aggressive tendencies, and that thus analysis might have turned him into a good locksmith, instead of becoming a criminal as may now be expected.

It seems to me that one main cause for the deviation of the development of this child from that of the neurotic child lies in the greater anxiety caused by the traumatic experience with his sister. I see the effects of this greater anxiety in different directions. A greater fear caused a greater repression at a stage where the way to sublimation was not yet opened, so that no other outlet or possibility of working off remained. Furthermore, the greater fear increased the cruelty of the super-ego, and fixated it at this point through this experience.

There is still another effect of this greater anxiety I would suggest, but to explain this I must make a brief digression. When I mentioned the different possibilities of development, based on the same grounds, I quoted the normal, the obsessional neurotic, the psychotic, and endeavoured to come nearer to the criminal. I did not speak of the pervert.

We know that Freud called neurosis the negative of the perversions. An important addition to the psychology of the perversions was made by Sachs, who arrived at the conclusion that the pervert does not simply permit himself, owing to lack of conscience, what the neurotic represses in consequence of his inhibitions. He found that the conscience of the pervert is not less strict but is simply working in a different way. It permits one part only of the forbidden tendencies to be retained in order to escape from other parts which seem still more objectionable to the super-ego. What it rejects are desires belonging to the Oedipus complex, and the apparent absence of inhibition in the pervert is only the effect of a super-ego not less strict, but working in a different way.

I arrived at an analogous conclusion concerning the criminal some years ago, in the report mentioned at the beginning of my paper, in which I gave details of the analogy between criminal acts and childish phantasies.

In the case of the child I have described and in other not quite so pronounced but yet instructive cases, I found that the criminal disposition was not due to a less strict super-ego but to a super-ego working in a different direction. It is just anxiety and the feeling of guilt which drive the criminal to his delinquencies. In committing these he also partly tries to escape from his Oedipus situation. In the case of my little criminal the breaking open of cupboards and attacks on little girls were substituted for attacks on his mother.

These views naturally require to be further examined and worked out. In my opinion everything seems to point to the conclusion that it is not the lack of a super-ego but a different development of the super-ego—probably the fixation of the super-ego at a very early stage—which will prove to be the main factor.

If these suppositions prove true, practical prospects of great importance are opened out. If it is not a deficiency in the super-ego and conscience, but a different development of these which causes a criminal development, analysis should be able to modify the latter as well as it removes neuroses. Just as with perversions and with psychoses, it may be impossible to find ways of approaching adult criminals. But as regards analyses in childhood the position is different. A child does not need special motives for analysis; it is a question of technical measures to establish the transference and to keep the analysis going. *I do not believe in the existence of a child in whom it is impossible to obtain this transference, or in whom the capacity for love cannot be brought out.* In the case of my little criminal, he was apparently utterly devoid of any capacity for love, but analysis proved that this was not so. He had a good transference to me, good enough to make analysis possible, although he had no motives for it, since he even did not show any special aversion to being sent to the reformatory. Moreover, analysis showed that this dull boy had a deep and sincere love for his mother. The mother died in terrible circumstances from cancer, which in the last stage of her illness led to complete decay. The daughter did not like to go near her, and it was *he* who looked after her. As she lay dead, the family was leaving. He could not be found for some time: he had locked himself up with his dead mother in the room.

It may be objected that in childhood the tendencies are not yet clearly defined, so that we may often be unable to recognize when a child is on the way to becoming a criminal. This is undoubtedly true, but precisely this statement leads me to my concluding remarks. It is undoubtedly not easy to know to what results the tendencies of a child will lead, whether to the normal, the neurotic, the psychotic, the pervert, or the criminal. But precisely because we do not know we must seek to know. Psycho-analysis gives us this means. And it does more; it can not only ascertain the future development of the child, but it can also change it, and direct it into better channels.

9

EARLY STAGES OF THE OEDIPUS
CONFLICT

(1928)

In my analyses of children, especially of children between the ages of three and six, I have come to a number of conclusions of which I shall here present a summary.

I have repeatedly alluded to the conclusion that the Oedipus complex comes into operation earlier than is usually supposed. In my paper, 'The Psychological Principles of Early Analysis', I discussed this subject in greater detail. The conclusion which I reached there was that the Oedipus tendencies are released in consequence of the frustration which the child experiences at weaning, and that they make their appearance at the end of the first and the beginning of the second year of life; they receive reinforcement through the anal frustrations undergone during training in cleanliness. The next determining influence upon the mental processes is that of the anatomical difference between the sexes.

The boy, when he finds himself impelled to abandon the oral and anal positions for the genital, passes on to the aim of *penetration* associated with possession of the penis. Thus he changes not only his libido-position, but its *aim*, and this enables him to retain his original love-object. In the girl, on the other hand, the *receptive* aim is carried over from the oral to the genital position: she changes her libido-position, but retains its aim, which has already led to disappointment in relation to her mother. In this way receptivity for the penis is produced in the girl, who then turns to the father as her love-object.

The very onset of the Oedipus wishes, however, already becomes associated with incipient dread of castration and feelings of guilt.

The analysis of adults, as well as of children, has familiarized us with the fact that the pregenital instinctual impulses carry with them a sense of guilt, and it was thought at first that the feelings of guilt were of subsequent growth, displaced back on to these tendencies, though not originally associated with them. Ferenczi assumes that, connected with the urethral and anal impulses, there is a 'kind of physiological forerunner of the super-ego', which he terms 'sphincter-morality'. According to Abraham, anxiety makes its appearance on the cannibalistic level, while the sense of guilt arises in the succeeding early anal-sadistic phase.

My findings lead rather further. They show that the sense of guilt associated with pregenital fixation is already the direct effect of the Oedipus conflict. And this seems to account satisfactorily for the genesis of such feelings, for we know the sense of guilt to be in fact a result of the introjection (already accomplished or, as I would add, in process of being accomplished) of the Oedipus love-objects: that is, a sense of guilt is a product of the formation of the super-ego.

The analysis of little children reveals the structure of the super-ego as built up of identifications dating from very different periods and strata in the mental life. These identifications are surprisingly contradictory in nature, excessive goodness and excessive severity existing side by side. We find in them, too, an explanation of the severity of the super-ego, which comes out specially plainly in these infant analyses. It does not seem clear why a child of, say, four years old should set up in his mind an unreal, phantastic image of parents who devour, cut and bite. But it *is* clear why in a child of about *one year* old the anxiety caused by the beginning of the Oedipus conflict takes the form of a dread of being devoured and destroyed. The child himself desires to destroy the libidinal object by biting, devouring and cutting it, which leads to anxiety, since awakening of the Oedipus tendencies is followed by introjection of the object, which then becomes one from which punishment is to be expected. The child then dreads a punishment corresponding to the offence: the super-ego becomes something which bites, devours and cuts.

The connection between the formation of the super-ego and the pregenital phases of development is very important from two points of view. On the one hand, the sense of guilt attaches itself to the oral- and anal-sadistic phases, which as yet predominate; and, on the other, the super-ego comes into being while these phases are in the ascendant, which accounts for its sadistic severity.

These conclusions open up a new perspective. Only by strong repression can the still very feeble ego defend itself against a super-ego so menacing. Since the Oedipus tendencies are at first chiefly expressed in the form of oral and anal impulses, the question of which fixations will predominate in the Oedipus development will be mainly determined by the degree of the repression which takes place at this early stage.

Another reason why the direct connection between the pregenital phase of development and the sense of guilt is so important is that the oral and anal frustrations, which are the prototypes of all later frustrations in life, at the same time signify *punishment* and give rise to anxiety. This circumstance makes the frustration more acutely felt, and this bitterness contributes largely to the hardship of all subsequent frustrations.

We find that important consequences ensue from the fact that the ego is still so little developed when it is assailed by the onset of the Oedipus tendencies and the incipient sexual curiosity associated with them. The infant, still undeveloped intellectually, is exposed to an onrush of problems and questions. One of the most bitter grievances which we come upon in the unconscious is that these many overwhelming questions, which are apparently only partly conscious and even when conscious cannot yet be expressed in words, remain unanswered. Another reproach follows hard upon this, namely, that the child could not understand words and speech. Thus his first questions go back beyond the beginnings of his understanding of speech.

In analysis both these grievances give rise to an extraordinary amount of hate. Singly or in conjunction they are the cause of numerous inhibitions of the epistemophilic impulse: for instance, the incapacity to learn foreign languages, and, further, hatred of those who speak a different tongue. They are also responsible for direct disturbances in speech, etc. The curiosity which shows itself plainly later on, mostly in the fourth or fifth year of life, is not the beginning, but the climax and termination, of this phase of development, which I have also found to be true of the Oedipus conflict in general.

The early feeling of *not knowing* has manifold connections. It unites with the feeling of being incapable, impotent, which soon results from the Oedipus situation. The child also feels this frustration the more acutely because he *knows nothing* definite about sexual processes. In both sexes the castration complex is accentuated by this feeling of ignorance.

The early connection between the epistemophilic impulse and sadism is very important for the whole mental development. This instinct, activated by the rise of the Oedipus tendencies, at first mainly concerns itself with the mother's body, which is assumed to be the scene of all sexual processes and developments. The child it still dominated by the anal-sadistic libido-position which impels him to wish to *appropriate* the contents of the body. He thus begins to be curious about what it contains, what it is like, etc. So the epistemophilic instinct and the desire to take possession come quite early to be most intimately connected with one another and at the same time with the sense of guilt aroused by the incipient Oedipus conflict. This significant connection ushers in a phase of development in both sexes which is of vital importance, hitherto not sufficiently recognized. It consists of a very early identification with the mother.

The course run by this 'femininity' phase must be examined separately in boys and in girls, but, before I proceed to this, I shall show its connection with the previous phase, which is common to both sexes.

In the early anal-sadistic stage the child sustains his second severe trauma, which strengthens his tendency to turn away from the mother. She has frustrated his oral desires, and now she also interferes with his anal pleasures. It seems as though at this point the anal deprivations cause the anal tendencies to amalgamate with the sadistic tendencies. The child desires to get possession of the mother's faeces, by penetrating into her body, cutting it to pieces, devouring and destroying it. Under the influence of his genital impulses, the boy is beginning to turn to his mother as a love-object. But his sadistic impulses are fully at work, and the hate originating in earlier frustrations is powerfully opposed to his object-love on the genital level. A still greater obstacle to his love is his dread of castration by the father, which arises with the Oedipus impulses. The degree to which he attains the genital position will partly depend on his capacity for tolerating this anxiety. Here the intensity of the oral-sadistic and anal-sadistic fixations is an important factor. It affects the degree of hatred which the boy feels towards the mother; and this, in its turn, hinders him to a greater or lesser extent in attaining a positive relation to her. The sadistic fixations exercise also a decisive influence upon the formation of the super-ego, which is coming into being whilst these phases are in the ascendant. The more cruel the super-ego the more terrifying will be the father as castrator, and the more tenaciously, in the child's flight from his genital impulses, will he cling to the sadistic levels, from which levels his Oedipus tendencies, too, in the first instance, take their colour.

In these early stages all the positions in the Oedipus development are cathected in rapid succession. This, however, is not noticeable, because the picture is dominated by the pregenital impulses. Moreover, no rigid line can be drawn between the active heterosexual attitude which finds expression on the anal level and the further stage of identification with the mother.

We have now reached that phase of development of which I spoke before under the name of the 'femininity-phase'. It has its basis on the anal-sadistic level and imparts to that level a new content, for faeces are now equated with the child that is longed for, and the desire to rob the mother now applies to the child as well as to faeces. Here we can discern two aims which merge with one another. The one is directed by the desire for children, the

intention being to appropriate them, while the other aim is moti-
vated by jealousy of the future brothers and sisters whose appearance
is expected, and by the wish to destroy them in the mother. (A
third object of the boy's oral-sadistic tendencies inside the mother
is the father's penis.)

As in the castration complex of girls, so in the femininity complex
of the male, there is at bottom the frustrated desire for a special organ.
The tendencies to steal and destroy are concerned with the organs
of conception, pregnancy and parturition, which the boy assumes
to exist in the mother, and further with the vagina and the breasts,
the fountain of milk, which are coveted as organs of receptivity
and bounty from the time when the libidinal position is purely oral.

The boy fears punishment for his destruction of his mother's
body, but, besides this, his fear is of a more general nature, and
here we have an analogy to the anxiety associated with the castration-
wishes of the girl. He fears that his body will be mutilated and
dismembered, and this dread also means castration. Here we have a
direct contribution to the castration complex. In this early period of
development the mother who takes away the child's faeces signifies
also a mother who dismembers and castrates him. Not only by
means of the anal frustrations which she inflicts does she pave the
way for the castration complex: in terms of psychic reality she *is* also
already the *castrator*.

This dread of the mother is so overwhelming because there is
combined with it an intense dread of castration by the father. The
destructive tendencies whose object is the womb are also directed
with their full oral- and anal-sadistic intensity against the father's
penis, which is supposed to be located there. It is upon this penis
that the dread of castration by the father is focused in this phase.
Thus the femininity-phase is characterized by anxiety relating to the
womb and the father's penis, and this anxiety subjects the boy to the
tyranny of a super-ego which devours, dismembers and castrates
and is formed from the image of father and mother alike.

The incipient genital positions are thus from the beginning criss-
crossed by and intermingled with the manifold pregenital tendencies. The greater the preponderance of sadistic fixations, the
more does the boy's identification with his mother correspond to an
attitude of rivalry towards the woman, with its blending of envy and
hatred; for, on account of his wish for a child, he feels himself at a
disadvantage and inferior to the mother.

Let us now consider why the femininity complex of men seems so
much more obscure than the castration complex in women, with
which it is equally important.

The amalgamation of the desire for a child with the epistemophilic impulse enables a boy to effect a displacement on to the intellectual plane; his sense of being at a disadvantage is then concealed and over-compensated by the superiority he deduces from his possession of a penis, which is also acknowledged by girls. This exaggeration of the masculine position results in excessive protestations of masculinity. In her paper, 'Die Wurzel des Wissbegierde', Mary Chadwick (1925), too, has traced the man's narcissistic over-estimation of the penis, and his attitude of intellectual rivalry towards women, to the frustration of his wish for a child and to the displacement of this desire on to the intellectual plane.

A tendency in boys to express excessive aggression, which very frequently occurs, has its source in the femininity complex. It goes with an attitude of contempt and 'knowing better', and is highly asocial and sadistic; it is partly determined by an attempt to mask the anxiety and ignorance which lie behind it. In part it coincides with the boy's protest (originating in his fear of castration) against the feminine rôle, but it is rooted also in his dread of his mother, whom he intended to rob of the father's penis, her children and her female sexual organs. This excessive aggression unites with the pleasure in attack which proceeds from the direct, genital Oedipus situation, but it represents that part of the situation which is by far the more asocial factor in character-formation. This is why a man's rivalry with women will be far more asocial than his rivalry with his fellow-men, which is largely prompted through the genital position. Of course, the quantity of sadistic fixations will also determine the relationship of a man to other men when they are rivals. If, on the contrary, the identification with the mother is based on a more securely established genital position, on the one hand his relation to women will be positive in character, and on the other the desire for a child and the feminine component, which play so essential a part in men's work, will find more favourable opportunities for sublimation.

In both sexes one of the principal roots of inhibitions in work is the anxiety and sense of guilt associated with the femininity phase. Experience has taught me, however, that a thorough analysis of this phase is, for other reasons as well, important from a therapeutic point of view, and should be of help in some obsessional cases which seem to have reached a point where nothing more could be resolved.

In the boy's development the femininity-phase is succeeded by a prolonged struggle between the pregenital and the genital positions of the libido. When at its height, in the third to the fifth year of life, this struggle is plainly recognizable as the Oedipus conflict. The anxiety associated with the femininity-phase drives the boy back to identification with the father; but this stimulus in itself does not provide a firm foundation for the genital position, since it leads mainly to repression and over-compensation of the anal-sadistic instincts, and not to overcoming them. The dread of castration by the father strengthens the fixation to the anal-sadistic levels. The degree of constitutional genitality also plays an important part as regards a favourable issue, *i.e.* the attainment of the genital level. Often the outcome of the struggle remains undecided, and this gives rise to neurotic troubles and disturbances of potency.[1] Thus the attainment of complete potency and reaching the genital position will in part depend upon the favourable issue of the femininity-phase.

I will now turn to the development of girls. As a result of the process of weaning, the girl-child has turned from the mother, being impelled more strongly to do so by the anal deprivations she has undergone. Genital trends now begin to influence her mental development.

I entirely agree with Helene Deutsch (1925), who holds that the genital development of the woman finds its completion in the successful displacement of oral libido on to the genital. Only, my results lead me to believe that this displacement begins with the first stirrings of the genital impulses and that the oral, receptive aim of the genitals exercises a determining influence in the *girl's turning to the father*. Also I am led to conclude that not only an unconscious awareness of the vagina, but also sensations in that organ and the rest of the genital apparatus, are aroused as soon as the Oedipus impulses make their appearance. In girls, however, onanism does not afford anything like so adequate an outlet for these quantities of excitation as it does in boys. Hence the accumulated lack of gratification provides yet another reason for more complications and disturbances of female sexual development. The difficulty of obtaining full gratification by masturbation may be another cause, besides those indicated by Freud, for the girl's repudiation of onanism, and this may partly explain why, during her struggle to give it up, manual masturbation is generally replaced by pressing the legs together.

Besides the receptive quality of the genital organ, which is brought into play by the intense desire for a new source of gratification, envy and hatred of the mother who possesses the father's penis seem, at the period when these first Oedipus impulses are stirring, to be a further motive for the little girl's turning to the father. His caresses have now the effect of a seduction and are felt as 'the attraction of the opposite sex'.[2]

---

[1] Cf. here W. Reich: 'Die Funktion des Orgasmus' (1927).

[2] We regularly come across the unconscious reproach that the mother has seduced the child whilst tending it. This reproach goes back to the period when genital desires come to the fore and the Oedipus tendencies are awakening.

In the girl, identification with the mother results directly from the Oedipus impulses: the whole struggle caused in the boy by his castration anxiety is absent in her. In girls as well as boys this identification coincides with the anal-sadistic tendencies to rob and destroy the mother. If identification with the mother takes place predominantly at a stage when oral- and anal-sadistic tendencies are very strong, dread of a primitive maternal super-ego will lead to the repression and fixation of this phase and interfere with further genital development. Dread of the mother, too, impels the little girl to give up identification with her, and identification with the father begins.

The little girl's epistemophilic impulse is first roused by the Oedipus complex; the result is that she discovers her lack of a penis. She feels this lack to be a fresh cause of hatred of the mother, but at the same time her sense of guilt makes her regard it as a punishment. This embitters her frustration in this direction, and, in its turn, exercises a profound influence on the whole castration complex.

This early grievance about the lack of a penis is greatly magnified later on, when the phallic phase and the castration complex are fully active. Freud has stated that the discovery of the lack of a penis causes the turning from the mother to the father. My findings show, however, that this discovery operates only as a reinforcement in this direction: it is made at a very early stage in the Oedipus conflict, and penis-envy succeeds the wish for a child, which again replaces penis-envy in later development. I regard the deprivation of the breast as the most fundamental cause of the turning to the father.

Identification with the father is less charged with anxiety than that with the mother; moreover, the sense of guilt towards her impels to over-compensation through a fresh love-relation with her. Against this new love-relation with her there operates the castration complex which makes a masculine attitude difficult, and also the hatred of her which sprang from the earlier positions. Hate and rivalry of the mother, however, again lead to abandoning the identification with the father and turning to him as the object to love and be loved by.

The girl's relation to her mother causes her relation to her father to take both a positive and a negative direction. The frustration undergone at his hands has as its very deepest basis the disappointment already suffered in relation to the mother; a powerful motive in the desire to possess him springs from the hatred and envy against the mother. If the sadistic fixations remain predominant, this hatred and its over-compensation will also materially affect the woman's relation to men. On the other hand, if there is a more positive relation to the mother, built up on the genital position, not only will the woman be freer from a sense of guilt in her relation to her children, but her love for her husband will be strongly reinforced, since for the woman he always stands at one and the same time for the mother who gives what is desired and for the beloved child. On this very significant foundation is built up that part of the relation which is connected exclusively with the father. At first it is focused on the act of the penis in coitus. This act, which also promises gratification of the desires that are now displaced on to the genital, seems to the little girl a most consummate performance.

Her admiration is, indeed, shaken by the Oedipus frustration, but unless it is converted into hate, it constitutes one of the fundamental features of the woman's relation to the man. Later, when full satisfaction of the love-impulses is obtained, there is joined with this admiration the great gratitude ensuing from the long-pent-up deprivation. This gratitude finds expression in the greater feminine capacity for complete and lasting surrender to one love-object, especially to the 'first love'.

One way in which the little girl's development is greatly handicapped is the following. Whilst the boy does in reality *possess* the penis, in respect of which he enters into rivalry with the father, the little girl has only the *unsatisfied* desire for motherhood, and of this, too, she has but a dim and uncertain, though a very intense, awareness.

It is not merely this uncertainty which disturbs her hope of future motherhood. It is weakened far more by anxiety and sense of guilt, and these may seriously and permanently damage the maternal capacity of a woman. Because of the destructive tendencies once directed by her against the mother's body (or certain organs in it) and against the children in the womb, the girl anticipates retribution in the form of destruction of her own capacity for motherhood or of the organs connected with this function and of her own children. Here we have also one root of the constant concern of women (often so excessive) for their personal beauty, for they dread that this too will be destroyed by the mother. At the bottom of the impulse to deck and beautify themselves there is always the motive of *restoring* damaged comeliness, and this has its origin in anxiety and sense of guilt.[1]

It is probable that this deep dread of the destruction of internal organs may be the psychic cause of the greater susceptibility of women, as compared with men, to conversion-hysteria and organic diseases.

[1] Cf. Hárnik's (1928) paper at the Innsbruck Psycho-Analytical Congress: 'Die ökonomischen Beziehungen zwischen dem Schuldgefühl und dem weiblichen Narzissmus'.

It is this anxiety and sense of guilt which is the chief cause of the repression of feelings of pride and joy in the feminine rôle, which are originally very strong. This repression results in depreciation of the capacity for motherhood, at the outset so highly prized. Thus the girl lacks the powerful support which the boy derives from his possession of the penis, and which she herself might find in the anticipation of motherhood.

The girl's very intense anxiety about her womanhood can be shown to be analogous to the boy's dread of castration, for it certainly contributes to the checking of her Oedipus impulses. The course run by the boy's castration anxiety concerning the penis which *visibly* exists is, however, different; it might be termed more *acute* than the more chronic anxiety of the girl concerning her internal organs, with which she is necessarily less familiar. Moreover, it is bound to make a difference that the boy's anxiety is determined by the paternal and the girl's by the maternal super-ego.

Freud has said that the girl's super-ego develops on different lines from that of the boy. We constantly find confirmation of the fact that jealousy plays a greater part in women's lives than in men's, because it is reinforced by deflected envy of the male on account of the penis. On the other hand, however, women especially possess a great capacity, which is not based merely on an over-compensation, for disregarding their own wishes and devoting themselves with self-sacrifice to ethical and social tasks. We cannot account for this capacity by the blending of masculine and feminine traits which, because of the human being's bisexual disposition, does in individual cases influence the formation of character, for this capacity is so plainly maternal in nature. I think that in order to explain how women can run so wide a gamut from the most petty jealousy to the most self-forgetful loving-kindness, we have to take into consideration the peculiar conditions of the formation of the feminine super-ego. From the early identification with the mother in which the anal-sadistic level so largely preponderates, the little girl derives jealousy and hatred and forms a cruel super-ego after the maternal imago. The super-ego which develops at this stage from a father-identification can also be menacing and cause anxiety, but it seems never to reach the same proportions as that derived from the mother-identification. But the more the identification with the mother becomes stabilized on the genital basis, the more will it be characterized by the devoted kindness of a bountiful mother-ideal. Thus this positive affective attitude depends on the extent to which the maternal mother-ideal bears the characteristics of the pregenital or of the genital stage. But when it comes to the active conversion of the emotional attitude into social or other activities, it would seem that it is the paternal ego-ideal which is at work. The deep admiration felt by the little girl for the father's genital activity leads to the formation of a paternal super-ego which sets before her active aims to which she can never fully attain. If, owing to certain factors in her development, the incentive to accomplish these aims is strong enough, their very impossibility of attainment may lend an impetus to her efforts which, combined with the capacity for self-sacrifice which she derives from the maternal super-ego, gives a woman, in individual instances, the capacity for very exceptional achievements on the intuitive plane and in specific fields.

The boy, too, derives from the feminine phase a maternal super-ego which causes him, like the girl, to make both cruelly primitive and kindly identifications. But he passes through this phase to resume (it is true, in varying degrees) identification with the father. However much the maternal side makes itself felt in the formation of the super-ego, it is yet the *paternal* super-ego which from the beginning is the decisive influence for the man. He too sets before himself a figure of an exalted character upon which to model himself, but, because the boy *is* 'made in the image of' his ideal, it is not unattainable. This circumstance contributes to the more sustained and objective creative work of the male.

The dread of injury to her womanhood exercises a profound influence on the castration complex of the little girl, for it causes her to over-estimate the penis which she herself lacks; this exaggeration is then much more obvious than is the underlying anxiety about her own womanhood. I would remind you here of the work of Karen Horney, who was the first to examine the sources of the castration complex in women in so far as those sources lie in the Oedipus situation.

In this connection I must speak of the importance for sexual development of certain early experiences in childhood. In the paper which I read at the Salzburg Congress in 1924, I mentioned that when observations of coitus take place at a later stage of development they assume the character of traumata, but that if such experiences occur at an early age they become fixated and form part of the sexual development. I must now add that a fixation of this sort may hold in its grip not only that particular stage of development, but also the super-ego which is then in process of formation, and may thus injure its further development. For the more completely the super-ego reaches its zenith in the genital stage, the less prominent will be the sadistic identifications in its structure and the more likely will be the securing of mental health and the development of a personality on an ethically high level.

There is another kind of experience in early childhood which strikes me as typical and exceedingly important. These experiences often follow closely in time upon the observations of coitus and are induced or fostered by the excitations set up thereby. I refer to the sexual relations of little children with one another, between brothers and sisters or playmates, which consist in the most varied acts: looking, touching, performing excretion in common, fellatio, cunnilingus and often direct attempts at coitus. They are deeply repressed and have a cathexis of profound feelings of guilt. These feelings are mainly due to the fact that this love-object, chosen under the pressure of the excitation due to the Oedipus conflict, is felt by the child to be a substitute for the father or mother or both. Thus these relations, which seem so insignificant and which apparently no child under the stimulus of the Oedipus development escapes, take on the character of an Oedipus relation actually realized, and exercise a determining influence upon the formation of the Oedipus complex, the subject's detachment from that complex and upon his later sexual relations. Moreover, an experience of this sort forms an important fixation-point in the development of the super-ego. In consequence of the need for punishment and the repetition-compulsion, these experiences often cause the child to subject himself to sexual traumata. In this connection I would refer you to Abraham (1927), who showed that experiencing sexual traumata is one part of the sexual development of children. The analytic investigation of these experiences, during the analysis of adults as well as of children, to a great extent clears up the Oedipus situation in its connection with early fixations, and is therefore important from the therapeutic point of view.

To sum up my conclusions: I wish first of all to point out that they do not, in my opinion, contradict the statements of Professor Freud. I think that the essential point in the additional considerations which I have advanced is that I date these processes earlier and that the different phases (especially in the initial stages) merge more freely into one another than was hitherto supposed.

The early stages of the Oedipus conflict are so largely dominated by pregenital phases of development that the genital phase, when it begins to be active, is at first heavily shrouded and only later, between the third and fifth years of life, becomes clearly recognizable. At this age the Oedipus complex and the formation of the super-ego reach their climax. But the fact that the Oedipus tendencies begin so much earlier than we supposed, the pressure of the sense of guilt which therefore falls upon the pregenital levels, the determining influence thus exercised so early upon the Oedipus development on the one hand and that of the super-ego on the other, and accordingly upon character-formation, sexuality and all the rest of the subject's development,—all these things seem to me of great and hitherto unrecognized importance. I found out the therapeutic value of this knowledge in the analyses of children, but it is not confined to these. I have been able to test the resulting conclusions in the analysis of adults and have found not only that their theoretical correctness was confirmed but that their therapeutic importance was established.

10

PERSONIFICATION IN THE PLAY
OF CHILDREN

(1929)

IN an earlier paper, 'The Psychological Principles of Early Analysis',
(1926) I gave an account of some of the mechanisms which I have
found in my analysis of children to be fundamental in their play.
I pointed out that the specific content of their play, which recurs
again and again in the most varied forms, is identical with the nucleus
of the masturbation-phantasies and that it is one of the principal
functions of children's play to provide a discharge for these phantasies.
Further, I discussed the very considerable analogy which exists
between the means of representation used in play and in dreams and
the importance of wish-fulfilment in both forms of mental activity. I
also drew attention to one principal mechanism in games in which
different 'characters' are invented and allotted by the child. My
object in the present paper is to discuss this mechanism in more
detail and also to illustrate by a number of examples of different
types of illness the relation between the 'characters' or personifications introduced by children into these games and the element of
wish-fulfilment.

My experience so far is that schizophrenic children are not
capable of play in the proper sense. They perform certain monotonous actions, and it is a laborious piece of work to penetrate from
these to the Ucs. When we do succeed, we find that the wish-fulfilment associated with these actions is pre-eminently the negation of
reality and the inhibition of phantasy. In these extreme cases
personification does not succeed.

In the case of my little patient, Erna, who was six years old when
we began the treatment, a severe obsessional neurosis masked a
paranoia which was revealed after a considerable amount of analysis.
In her play Erna often made me be a child, while she was the mother
or a teacher. I then had to undergo fantastic tortures and humiliations. If in the game anyone treated me kindly, it generally turned
out that the kindness was only simulated. The paranoiac traits
showed in the fact that I was constantly spied upon, people divined
my thoughts, and the father or teacher allied themselves with the

mother against me—in fact, I was always surrounded with perse-cutors. I myself, in the rôle of the child, had constantly to spy upon and torment the others. Often Erna herself played the part of the child. Then the game generally ended in her escaping the persecu-tions (on these occasions the 'child' was good), becoming rich and powerful, being made a queen and taking a cruel revenge on her persecutors. After her sadism had spent itself in these phantasies, apparently unchecked by any inhibition (all this came about after we had done a good deal of analysis), reaction would set in in the form of deep depression, anxiety and bodily exhaustion. Her play then reflected her incapacity to bear this tremendous oppression, which manifested itself in a number of serious symptoms.[1] In this child's phantasies all the rôles engaged could be fitted into one formula: that of two principal parts—the persecuting super-ego and the id or ego, as the case might be, threatened, but by no means less cruel.

In these games the wish-fulfilment lay principally in Erna's endeavour to identify herself with the stronger party, in order thus to master her dread of persecution. The hard-pressed ego tried to influence or deceive the super-ego, in order to prevent its over-powering the id, as it threatened to do. The ego tried to enlist the highly sadistic id in the service of the super-ego and to make the two combine in the fight with a common enemy. This necessitated extensive use of the mechanisms of projection and displacement. When Erna played the part of the cruel mother, the naughty child was the enemy; when she herself was the child who was persecuted but soon became powerful, the enemy was represented by the wicked parents. In each case there was a motive, which the ego attempted to render plausible to the super-ego, for indulging in unrestrained sadism. By the terms of this 'compact' the super-ego was to take action against the enemy as though against the id. The id, however, in secret, continued to pursue its predominantly sadistic gratification, the objects being the primal ones. Such narcissistic satisfaction as accrued to the ego through its victory over foes both without and within helped also to appease the super-ego and thus was of considerable value in diminishing anxiety. This compact between the two forces may in less extreme cases be relatively successful: it may not be noticeable to the outside world nor lead to an outbreak of illness. But in Erna's case it broke down completely because of the excessive sadism of both id and super-ego. Thereupon the ego joined forces with the super-ego and tried by punishing the id to extract a certain gratification, but this in its turn was inevitably

[1] I hope before long to publish a book in which a more detailed account of this case-history will be found.

a failure. Reactions of intense anxiety and remorse set in again and again, showing that none of these contradictory wish-fulfilments could be sustained for long.

The next example shows how difficulties analogous to Erna's were dealt with differently in certain particulars.

George, who at the time was six years old, brought me for months on end a series of phantasies in which he, as the mighty leader of a band of savage huntsmen and wild animals, fought, conquered and cruelly put to death his enemies, who also had wild beasts to support them. The animals were then devoured. The battle never came to an end as new enemies always appeared. A considerable course of analysis had revealed in this child not only neurotic but markedly paranoiac traits. George had always consciously[1] felt himself surrounded and threatened (by magicians, witches and soldiers), but, in contrast to Erna, he had tried to defend himself against them by the aid of helping figures, also it is true, highly phantastic creatures.

The wish-fulfilment in his phantasies was to some extent analogous to that in Erna's play. In George's case too the ego tried to ward off anxiety by identifying itself with the stronger party in phantasies of being great. Again George too endeavoured to change the enemy into a 'bad' enemy, in order to appease the super-ego. In him, however, sadism was not such an overpowering factor as in Erna, and so the primary sadism underlying his anxiety was less artfully concealed. His ego identified itself more thoroughly with the id and was less ready to make terms with the super-ego. Anxiety was warded off by a noticeable exclusion of reality.[2] Wish-fulfilment clearly predominated over recognition of reality—a tendency which is one of Freud's criteria of psychosis. The fact that in George's phantasies parts were played by *helpful figures* distinguished his type of personifications from those of Erna's play. Three principal parts were represented in his games: that of the id and those of the super-ego in its persecuting and its helpful aspects.

The play of a child with a severe obsessional neurosis may be illustrated by the following game of my little patient, Rita, aged two and three-quarters. After a ceremonial which was plainly obsessional, her doll was tucked up to go to sleep and an elephant was placed by the doll's bed. The idea was that the elephant should prevent the 'child' from getting up; otherwise the latter would steal

[1] Like so many children, George had invariably kept the content of his anxiety a secret from those around him. Nevertheless he clearly bore the impress of it.

[2] As George had developed, this withdrawal from reality became more and more marked in him. He was completely enmeshed in his phantasies.

into its parents' bedroom and either do them some harm or take something away from them. The elephant (a father-imago) was to act the part of a figure who *prevents*. In Rita's mind her father, by introjection, had filled this rôle of 'preventer' ever since, at the time she was a year and a quarter to two years old, she had wished to usurp her mother's place with him, to steal away the child with which her mother was pregnant and to injure and castrate both parents. The reactions of rage and anxiety which took place when the 'child' was punished in these games showed that in her own mind Rita was enacting both parts: that of the authorities who inflicted punishment and that of the child who received it.

The only wish-fulfilment apparent in this game lay in the fact that the elephant succeeded for a time in preventing the 'child' from getting up. There were only two main 'characters': that of the doll, which embodied the id, and that of the deterring elephant, which represented the super-ego. The wish-fulfilment consisted in the defeat of the id by the super-ego. This wish-fulfilment and the allotting of the action to *two* 'characters' are interdependent, for the game represents the struggle between super-ego and id which in severe neuroses almost entirely dominates the mental processes. In Erna's games too we saw the same personifications, consisting of the influence of a dominating super-ego and the absence of any helpful imagos. But while in Erna's play the wish-fulfilment lay in the compact with the super-ego, and in George's mainly in the id's defiance against the super-ego (by means of withdrawal from reality), in Rita it consisted of the defeat of the id by the super-ego. It was because some analytic work had already been done that this hardly maintained supremacy of the super-ego was possible at all. The excessive severity of the super-ego at first hindered all phantasy, and it was not until the super-ego became less severe that Rita began to play phantasy-games of the sort described. Compared with the preceding stage in which play was completely inhibited, this was progress, for now the super-ego did not *merely threaten* in a meaningless and terrifying way but tried with menaces to *prevent* the forbidden actions. The failure in the relation between the super-ego and the id gave place to that forcible suppression of instinct which consumes the subject's whole energy and is characteristic of severe obsessional neurosis in adults.[1]

[1] Rita suffered from an obsessional neurosis unusual at her age. It was characterized by a complicated sleep-ceremonial and other grave obsessional symptoms. My experience is that when little children suffer from such illnesses, which bear the stamp of obsessional neurosis as we see it in adults, it is very serious. On the other hand, isolated obsessional features in the general picture of neurosis in children are, I think, a regular phenomenon.

Let us now consider a game which originated in a less serious phase of obsessional neurosis. Later on in Rita's analysis (when she had reached the age of three), a 'journey-game', which went on through nearly the whole analysis, took the following form. Rita and her toy bear (who then represented the penis) went in a train to see a good woman who was to entertain them and give them presents. At the beginning of this part of the analysis this happy ending was generally spoilt. Rita wanted to drive the train herself and get rid of the driver. He, however, either refused to go or came back and threatened her. Sometimes it was a bad woman who hindered the journey, or when they got to the end they found not a good woman but a bad one. The difference between the wish-fulfilment in this game (much disturbed as it is) and that in the examples mentioned earlier is obvious. In this game the libidinal gratification is positive and sadism does not play so prominent a part in it as in the earlier examples. The 'characters', as in George's case, consist of three principal rôles: that of the ego or the id, that of a figure who helps and that of a figure who threatens or frustrates.

The helping figures thus invented are mostly of an extremely phantastic type, as the example of George shows. In the analysis of a boy of four and a half there appeared a 'fairy-mamma', who used to come at night and bring nice things to eat, which she shared with the little boy. The food stood for the father's penis, which she had secretly stolen from him. In another analysis the fairy-mamma used to heal with a magic wand all the wounds which the boy's harsh parents had inflicted on him; then he and she together killed these harsh parents in some cruel way.

I have come to realize that the operation of such imagos, with phantastically good and phantastically bad characteristics, is a general mechanism in adults as well as children.[1] These figures represent intermediate stages between the terrible menacing super-ego, which is wholly divorced from reality and the identifications which approximate more closely to reality. These intermediate figures, whose gradual evolution into the maternal and paternal helpers (who are nearer again to reality) may constantly be observed in play-analyses, and seem to me very instructive for our knowledge of the formation of the super-ego. My experience is that at the onset of the Oedipus conflict and the start of its formation the super-ego is of a tyrannical character, formed on the pattern of the pregenital stages, which are then in the ascendant. The influence of the genital has already begun to make itself felt, but at first it is hardly

[1] We have an example of this in the phantastic belief in a God who would assist in the perpetration of every sort of atrocity (as lately as in the recent war) in order to destroy the enemy and his country.

203

perceptible. The further evolution of the super-ego towards genitality depends ultimately upon whether the prevailing oral fixation has taken the form of sucking or of biting. *The primacy of the genital phase in relation both to sexuality and to the super-ego requires a sufficiently strong fixation to the oral-sucking stage.* The further from the pregenital levels both the development of the super-ego and the libidinal development progress towards the genital level, the more closely to the figures of the real parents will the phantastic, wish-fulfilling identifications (whose source is the image of a mother who provides oral gratification[1]) approximate.

The imagos adopted in this early phase of ego-development bear the stamp of the pregenital instinctual impulses, although they are actually constructed on the basis of the real Oedipus objects. These early levels are responsible for the phantastic imagos which devour, cut to pieces, and overpower and in which we see a mixture of the various pregenital impulses at work. Following the evolution of the libido, these imagos are introjected under the influence of the libidinal fixation-points. But the super-ego as a whole is made up of the various identifications adopted on the different levels of development whose stamp they bear. When the latency-period sets in, the development of both super-ego and libido terminates.[2] Already during the process of its construction the ego employs its tendency to synthesis by endeavouring to form a whole out of these various identifications. The more extreme and sharply contrasting the imagos, the less successful will be the synthesis and the more difficult will it be to maintain it. The excessively strong influence exerted by these extreme types of imagos, the intensity of the need for the kindly figures in opposition to the menacing, the rapidity with which allies will change into enemies (which is also the reason why the wish-fulfilment in play so often breaks down)—all this indicates that the process of synthesizing the identifications has failed. This failure manifests itself in the ambivalence, the tendency to anxiety, the lack of stability or the readiness with which this is overthrown, and the

[1] In my two earlier papers I had come to the conclusion that in both sexes the turning away from the mother as an oral love-object results from the oral frustrations undergone through her and that the mother who frustrates persists in the child's mental life as the mother who is feared. I would refer here to Radó (1928) who traces to the same source the splitting-up of the mother-imago into a good and a bad mother and makes it the basis of his views about the genesis of melancholia.

[2] Fenichel, in his account of my contributions to the problem of super-ego formation (1928, p. 596) is not correct in assuming that I hold that the development of the super-ego terminates in the second or third year of life. In my writings I have suggested that the formation of the super-ego and the development of the libido terminate simultaneously.

defective relation to reality characteristic of neurotic children.[1] The necessity for a synthesis of the super-ego arises out of the difficulty experienced by the subject in coming to an understanding with a super-ego made up of imagos of such opposite natures.[2] When the latency period sets in and the demands of reality are increased, the ego makes even greater efforts to effect a synthesis of the super-ego, in order that on this basis a balance may be struck between super-ego, id and reality.

I have come to the conclusion that this splitting of the super-ego into the primal identifications introjected at different stages of development is a mechanism analogous to and closely connected with projection. I believe these mechanisms (splitting-up and projection) are a principal factor in the tendency to personification in play. By their means the synthesis of the super-ego, which can be maintained only with more or less effort, can be given up for the time being and, further, the tension of maintaining the truce between the super-ego as a whole and the id is diminished. The intrapsychic conflict thus becomes less violent and can be displaced into the external world. The pleasure gained thereby is increased when the ego discovers that this displacement into the external world affords it various real proofs that the psychic processes, with their cathexis of anxiety and guilt, may have a favourable issue and anxiety be greatly reduced.

I have already mentioned that in play the child's attitude to reality reveals itself. I want now to make clear how the attitude to reality is related to the factors of wish-fulfilment and personification which we have so far used as our criterion of the mental situation.

In Erna's analysis it was for a long time impossible to establish a relation to reality. There seemed to be no bridge over the gulf which separated the loving and kindly mother of real life and the monstrous persecutions and humiliations which 'she' inflicted on the child in play. But, when the analysis reached the stage in which the paranoiac traits became more prominent, there was an increasing number of details which reflected the real mother in a grotesquely distorted form. At the same time there was revealed the child's attitude to reality, which had, to be sure, undergone much distortion.

[1] The further the analysis progresses the less powerful does the influence of the threatening figures become and the more strongly and lastingly do the wish-fulfilling figures appear in play; at the same time there is a proportionate increase in the desire to play and in the satisfaction of the ending of the games. Pessimism has diminished; optimism has increased.

[2] Children often have quite a range of parent-figures, from the terrifying 'Giant-mummy', 'Squashing-mummy' up to the all-bountiful 'Fairy-mummy'. I also meet with a 'Medium-mummy' or a 'Three-quarters-mummy', who represent a compromise between the other extreme examples.

With a remarkably keen faculty of observation Erna took in all the details of the actions and motives of those around her, but in *an unreal way* she worked all these into her system of being persecuted and spied upon. For instance, she believed that intercourse between her parents (which she imagined as invariably taking place whenever her parents were alone) and all the tokens of their mutual affection were mainly prompted by her mother's wish to excite jealousy in her (Erna). She assumed the same motive in all her mother's pleasures, and indeed, in everybody's enjoyment, especially in the case of women. They wore pretty clothes to cause her chagrin and so on. But she was conscious that there was something peculiar in these ideas of hers and took great care to keep them secret.

In George's play the isolation from reality was, as I have already said, considerable. Rita's play also, in the first part of the analysis, when the threatening and punishing imagos were in the ascendant, showed scarcely any relation to reality. Let us now consider that relation as revealed in the second part of Rita's analysis. We may regard it as typical of neurotic children, even of children rather older than Rita. In her play at this period there appeared, in contrast to the attitude of the paranoiac child, the tendency to recognize reality only in so far as it related to the frustrations which she had undergone but had never got over.

We may compare here the extensive withdrawal from reality which was revealed in George's play. It afforded him great freedom in his phantasies, which were liberated from the sense of guilt just because they were so remote from reality. In his analysis every step forward in adaptation to reality involved the releasing of large quantities of anxiety and the stronger repression of phantasies. It was always a great advance in the analysis[1] when this repression was, in its turn, lifted and the phantasies became free as well as more closely linked with reality.

In neurotic children a 'compromise' arises: a very limited amount of reality is recognized; the rest is denied. At the same time there is extensive repression of the masturbation-phantasies, which the sense of guilt inhibits, and the result is the inhibition in play and learning which is common in neurotic children. The obsessional symptom in which they take refuge (at first, in play) reflects the compromise

---

[1] Such an advance was always accompanied also by a considerable increase in the capacity for sublimation. The phantasies, released from the sense of guilt, could now be sublimated in a manner more in accordance with reality. I may say here that the results of analysis in children far surpass what analysis can accomplish in adults in the way of increased capacity for sublimation. Even in quite little children we constantly see that, when the sense of guilt is taken away, new sublimations appear and those which already exist are strengthened.

between the extensive inhibition of phantasy and the defective relation to reality and affords on this basis only the most limited forms of gratification.

The play of normal children shows a better balance between phantasy and reality.

I will now summarize the different attitudes to reality revealed in the play of children suffering from various types of illness. In paraphrenia there is the most extensive repression of phantasy and withdrawal from reality. In paranoiac children the relation to reality is subordinated to the lively workings of phantasy, the balance between the two being weighted on the side of *unreality*. The experiences which neurotic children represent in their play are obsessively coloured by their need for punishment and their dread of an unhappy issue. Normal children, however, are able to master reality in better ways. Their play shows that they have more power to influence and live out reality in conformity with their phantasies. Moreover, where they cannot alter the real situation they are better able to bear it, because their freer phantasy provides them with a refuge from it and also because the fuller discharge that they have for their masturbation-phantasies in an ego-syntonic form (play and other sublimations) gives them greater opportunities of gratification.

Let us now review the relation between the attitude to reality and the processes of personification and wish-fulfilment. In the play of normal children these latter processes testify to the stronger and more lasting influence of identifications originating on the genital level. In proportion as the imagos approximate to the real objects a good relation to reality (characteristic of normal people) becomes more marked. The diseases (psychosis and severe obsessional neurosis) which are characterized by a disturbed or displaced relation to reality are also those in which the wish-fulfilment is negative and extremely cruel types are impersonated in play. I have tried to demonstrate from these facts that here a super-ego is in the ascendant which is still in its early phases of super-ego formation, and I draw this conclusion: the ascendancy of a terrifying super-ego which has been introjected in the earliest stages of ego-development is a basic factor in psychotic disturbance.

In this paper I have discussed in detail the important function of the mechanism of personification in children's play. I have now to point out the significance of this mechanism in the mental life of adults also. I have come to the conclusion that it is the basis of a phenomenon of great and universal significance, one which is also essential to analytic work in both children and adults, namely, of the transference. If a child's phantasy is free enough, he will assign to the analyst, during a play-analysis, the most varied and contradictory rôles. He will make me, for example, assume the part of the id, because in this projected form his phantasies can be given outlet without inspiring so much anxiety. Thus, the boy Gerald, for whom I represented the 'fairy-mamma' who brought him the father's penis, repeatedly made me act the part of a boy who crept by night into the cage of a mother-lioness, attacked her, stole her cubs and killed and ate them. Then he himself was the lioness who discovered me and killed me in the cruellest manner. The rôles alternated in accordance with the analytic situation and the amount of latent anxiety. At a later period, for instance, the boy himself enacted the part of the miscreant who penetrated into the lion's cage, and he made me be the cruel lioness. But in this case the lions were soon replaced by a helpful fairy-mamma whose part I also had to play. At this time the boy was able to represent the id himself (which indicated an advance in his relation to reality), for his anxiety had to some extent diminished, as was shown in the appearance of the fairy-mamma.

We see then that a weakening of the conflict or its displacement into the external world by means of the mechanisms of splitting up and projection, is one of the principal incentives to transference and a driving force in analytic work. A greater activity of phantasy and more abundant and positive capacity for personification are, moreover, the prerequisite for a greater capacity for transference. The paranoiac possesses, it is true, a rich phantasy-life, but the fact that in the structure of his super-ego the cruel, anxiety-inspiring identifications predominate, causes the types he invents to be pre-eminently negative and susceptible only of reduction to the rigid types of persecutor and persecuted. In schizophrenia, in my opinion, the capacity for personification and for transference fails, amongst other reasons, through the defective functioning of the projection-mechanism. This interferes with the capacity for establishing or maintaining the relation to reality and the external world.

From the conclusion that the transference is based on the mechanism of character-representation I have taken a hint as regards technique. I have already mentioned how very rapid the change often is from 'enemy' to 'helper', from the 'bad' mother to the 'good'. In such games involving personification this change is constantly to be observed following upon the release of quantities of anxiety in consequence of interpretations. But, as the analyst assumes the hostile rôles required by the play-situation and thus subjects them to analysis, there is a constant progress in the development of the anxiety-inspiring imagos towards the kindlier identifications with their closer approximations to reality. In other words: One of the principal aims of analysis—the gradual modification of the excessive severity of the super-ego—is attained by the analyst's assumption of the rôles which the analytic situation causes to be assigned to him. This statement merely expresses what we know to be a requirement in the analysis of adults, namely, that the analyst must simply be a medium in relation to whom the different imagos can be activated and the phantasies lived through, in order to be analysed. When the child in his play directly assigns to him certain rôles, the task of the children's analyst is clear. He will of course assume, or at least give a suggestion of playing, the rôles assigned to him;[1] otherwise he would interrupt the progress of the analytic work. But only in certain phases of child-analysis, and even then by no means invariably, do we come to personification in this open form. Far more frequently, with children as well as with adults, we have to infer from the analytic situation and material the details of the hostile rôle attributed to us, which the patient indicates through the negative transference. Now what is true of personification in its open form I have found to be also indispensable for the more disguised and obscure forms of the personifications underlying transference. The analyst who wishes to penetrate to the earliest, anxiety-inspiring imagos, *i.e.* to strike at the roots of the super-ego's severity, must have no preference for any particular rôle; he must accept that which comes to him from the analytic situation.

In conclusion, I wish to say a few words on the subject of therapy. In this paper I have tried to show that the severest and most pressing anxiety proceeds from the super-ego introjected at a very early stage of ego-development, and that the supremacy of this early super-ego is a fundamental factor in the genesis of psychosis.

My experience has convinced me that with the help of play-technique it is possible to analyse the early phases of super-ego-formation in little children and in older ones. Analysis of these strata diminishes the most intense and overwhelming anxiety and thus opens out the way for developments of the kindly imagos, which originate on the oral-sucking level, and therewith for attainment of genital primacy in sexuality and super-ego-formation. In this we may see a fair prospect for the diagnosis[2] and cure of the psychoses in childhood.

[1] When children ask me to play parts which are too difficult or disagreeable I meet their wishes by saying that I am 'pretending I am doing it'.

[2] It is only in the most extreme cases that psychosis in children bears the character of psychosis in adults. In the less extreme cases it is generally brought to light only by a searching analysis lasting over a considerable period.

11

INFANTILE ANXIETY-SITUATIONS REFLECTED IN A WORK OF ART AND IN THE CREATIVE IMPULSE

(1929)

M Y first subject is the highly interesting psychological material underlying an opera of Ravel's, now being revived in Vienna. My account of its content is taken almost word for word from a review by Eduard Jakob in the *Berliner Tageblatt*.

A child of six years old is sitting with his homework before him, but he is not doing any work. He bites his pen-holder and displays that final stage of laziness, in which *ennui* has passed into *cafard*. 'Don't want to do the stupid lessons,' he cries in a sweet soprano. 'Want to go for a walk in the park! I'd like best of all to eat up all the cake in the world, or pull the cat's tail or pull out all the parrot's feathers! I'd like to scold every one! Most of all I'd like to put mama in the corner!' The door now opens. Everything on the stage is shown very large—in order to emphasize the smallness of the child—so all that we see of his mother is a skirt, an apron and a hand. A finger points and a voice asks affectionately whether the child has done his work. He shuffles rebelliously on his chair and puts out his tongue at his mother. She goes away. All that we hear is the rustle of her skirts and the words: 'You shall have dry bread and no sugar in your tea!' The child flies into a rage. He jumps up, drums on the door, sweeps the tea-pot and cup from the table, so that they are broken into a thousand pieces. He climbs on to the window-seat, opens the cage and tries to stab the squirrel with his pen. The squirrel escapes through the open window. The child jumps down from the window and seizes the cat. He yells and swings the tongs, pokes the fire furiously in the open grate, and with his hands and feet hurls the kettle into the room. A cloud of ashes and steam escapes. He swings the tongs like a sword and begins to tear the wallpaper. Then he opens the case of the grandfather-clock and snatches out the copper pendulum. He pours the ink over the table. Exercise-books and other books fly through the air. Hurrah! . . .

The things he has maltreated come to life. An armchair refuses to let him sit in it or have the cushions to sleep on. Table, chair, bench and sofa suddenly lift up their arms and cry: 'Away with the dirty little creature!' The clock has a dreadful stomach-ache and begins to strike the hours like mad. The tea-pot leans over the cup, and they begin to talk Chinese. Everything undergoes a terrifying change. The child falls back against the wall and shudders with fear and desolation. The stove spits out a shower of sparks at him. He hides behind the furniture. The shreds of the torn wallpaper begin to sway and stand up, showing shepherdesses and sheep. The shepherd's pipe sounds a heartbreaking lament; the rent in the paper, which separates Corydon from his Amaryllis, has become a rent in the fabric of the world! But the doleful tale dies away. From under the cover of a book, as though out of a dog's kennel, there emerges a little old man. His clothes are made of numbers, and his hat is like a pi. He holds a ruler and clatters about with little dancing steps. He is the spirit of mathematics, and begins to put the child through an examination: millimetre, centimetre, barometer, trillion—eight and eight are forty. Three times nine is twice six. The child falls down in a faint!

Half suffocated he takes refuge in the park round the house. But there again the air is full of terror, insects, frogs (lamenting in muted thirds), a wounded tree-trunk, which oozes resin in long-drawn-out bass notes, dragon-flies and oleander-flies all attack the newcomer. Owls, cats and squirrels come along in hosts. The dispute as to who is to bite the child becomes a hand-to-hand fight. A squirrel which has been bitten falls to the ground, screaming beside him. He instinctively takes off his scarf and binds up the little creature's paw. There is great amazement amongst the animals, who gather together hesitatingly in the background. The child has whispered: 'Mama!' He is restored to the human world of helping, 'being good'. 'That's a good child, a very well-behaved child,' sing the animals very seriously in a soft march—the finale of the piece—as they leave the stage. Some of them cannot refrain from themselves calling out 'Mama'.

I will now examine more closely the details in which the child's pleasure in destruction expresses itself. They seem to me to recall the early infantile situation which in my most recent writings I have described as being of fundamental importance both for neurosis in boys and for their normal development. I refer to the attack on the mother's body and on the father's penis in it. The squirrel in the cage and the pendulum wrenched out of the clock are plain symbols of the penis in the mother's body. The fact that it is the *father's* penis and that it is in the act of coitus with the mother is indicated by the rent in the wallpaper 'which separates Corydon from his Amaryllis', of which it has been said that to the boy it has become 'a rent in the fabric of the world'. Now what weapons does the child employ in this attack on his united parents? The ink poured over the table, the emptied kettle, from which a cloud of ashes and steam escapes, represent the weapon which very little children have at their disposal: namely the device of soiling with excrement.

Smashing things, tearing them up, using the tongs as a sword—these represent the other weapons of the child's primary sadism, which employs his teeth, nails, muscles and so on.

In my paper at the last Congress (Klein, 1928) and on other occasions in our Society, I have described this early phase of development, the content of which is the attack made on the mother's body with all the weapons that the child's sadism has at its disposal. Now, however, I can add to this earlier statement and say more exactly where this phase is to be inserted in the scheme of sexual development proposed by Abraham. My result leads me to conclude that the phase in which sadism is at its zenith in all the fields whence it derives, precedes the earlier anal stage and acquires a special significance from the fact that it is also the stage of development at which the Oedipus tendencies first appear. That is to say, that the Oedipus conflict begins under the complete dominance of sadism. My supposition that the formation of the super-ego follows closely on the beginning of the Oedipus tendencies, and that, therefore, the ego falls under the sway of the super-ego even at this early period, explains, I think, why this sway is so tremendously powerful. For, when the objects are introjected, the attack launched upon them with all the weapons of sadism rouses the subject's dread of an analogous attack upon himself from the external and the internalized objects. I wanted to recall these concepts of mine to your minds because I can make a bridge from them to a concept of Freud's: one of the most important of the new conclusions which he has put before us in *Inhibitions, Symptoms, and Anxiety* (1926), namely the hypothesis of an early infantile situation of anxiety or danger. I think that this places analytic work on a yet more exactly defined and firmer basis than heretofore, and thus gives our methods an even plainer direction. But in my view it also makes a fresh demand upon analysis. Freud's hypothesis is that there is an infantile danger-situation which undergoes modification in the course of development, and which is the source of the influence exercised by a series of *anxiety-situations*. Now the new demand upon the analyst is this—that analysis should fully uncover these anxiety-situations right back to that which lies deepest of all. This demand for a *complete* analysis is allied to that which Freud suggests as a new demand at the conclusion of his 'History of an Infantile Neurosis', where he says that a complete analysis must reveal the primal scene. This latter requirement can have its full effect only in conjunction with that which I have just put forward. If the analyst succeeds in the task of discovering the infantile danger-situations, working at their resolution and elucidating in each individual case the relations between the anxiety-situations and the neurosis on the one hand and the ego-development on the other—then, I think, he will achieve more completely the main aim of psycho-analytic therapy: removal of the neuroses. It seems to me, therefore, that everything that can contribute to the elucidation and exact description of the infantile danger-situations is of great value, not only from the theoretical, but also from the therapeutic point of view.

Freud assumes that the infantile danger-situation can be reduced ultimately to the loss of the beloved (longed-for) person. In girls, he thinks, the loss of the object is the danger-situation which operates most powerfully; in boys it is castration. My work has proved to me that both these danger-situations are a modification of yet earlier ones. I have found that in boys the dread of castration by the father is connected with a very special situation which, I think, proves to be the earliest anxiety-situation of all. As I pointed out, the attack on the mother's body, which is timed psychologically at the zenith of the sadistic phase, implies also the struggle with the father's penis in the mother. A special intensity is imparted to this danger-situation by the fact that a union of the two parents is in question. According to the early sadistic super-ego, which has already been set up, these united parents are extremely cruel and much dreaded assailants. Thus the anxiety-situation relating to castration by the father is a modification, in the course of development, of the earliest anxiety-situation as I have described it.

Now I think that the anxiety engendered in this situation is plainly represented in the libretto of the opera which was the starting-point of my paper. In discussing the libretto, I have already dealt in some detail with the *one* phase—that of the sadistic attack. Let us now consider what happens after the child has given rein to his lust for destruction.

At the beginning of his review the writer mentions that all the things on the stage are made very large, in order to emphasize the smallness of the child. But the child's anxiety makes things and people seem gigantic to him—far beyond the actual difference in size. Moreover, we see what we discover in the analysis of every child: that things represent human beings, and therefore are objects of anxiety. The writer of the review writes as follows: 'The maltreated things begin to live.' The armchair, the cushion, table, chair, etc., attack the child, refuse to serve him, banish him outside. We find that things to sit and lie upon, as well as beds, occur regularly in children's analyses as symbols for the protecting and loving mother. The strips of the torn wallpaper represent the injured interior of the mother's body, while the little old number-man who comes out of the book-cover is the father (represented by his penis), now in the character of judge, and about to call the child, who faints with anxiety, to his reckoning for the damage he has done and the theft he had committed in the mother's body. When the boy flees into the world of nature, we see how it takes on the rôle of the mother whom he has assaulted. The hostile animals represent a multiplication of the father, whom he has also attacked, together with the children assumed to be in the mother. We see the incidents which took place inside the room now reproduced on a bigger scale in a wider space and in larger numbers. The world, transformed into the mother's body, is in hostile array against the child and persecutes him.

In ontogenetic development sadism is overcome when the subject advances to the genital level. The more powerfully this phase sets in, the more capable does the child become of object-love, and the more able is he to conquer his sadism by means of pity and sympathy. This step in development is also shown in the libretto of Ravel's opera; when the boy feels pity for the wounded squirrel and comes to its aid, the hostile world changes into a friendly one. The child has learnt to love and believes in love. The animals conclude: 'That is a good child—a very well-behaved child.' The profound psychological insight of Colette—the author of the libretto of the opera—is shown in the way in which the conversion in the child's attitude takes place. As he cares for the wounded squirrel, he whispers: 'Mama.' The animals round him repeat this word. It is this redeeming word which has given the opera its title: 'The Magic Word' (*Das Zauberwort*). But we also learn from the text what is the factor which has ministered to the child's sadism. He says: 'I want to go for a walk in the park! I want most of all to eat up all the cakes in the world!' But his mother threatens to give him tea without sugar and dry bread. The oral frustration which turns the indulgent 'good mother' into the 'bad mother' stimulates his sadism.

I think we can now understand why the child, instead of peaceably doing his homework, has become involved in such an unpleasant situation. It *had* to be so, for he was driven to it by the pressure of the old anxiety-situation which he had never mastered. His anxiety enhances the repetition-compulsion, and his need for punishment ministers to the compulsion (now grown very strong) to secure for himself actual punishment in order that the anxiety may be allayed by a chastisement less severe than that which the anxiety-situation causes him to anticipate. We are quite familiar with the fact that children are naughty because they wish to be punished, but it seems of the greatest importance to find out what part anxiety plays in this craving for punishment and what is the ideational content at the bottom of this urgent anxiety.

I will now illustrate from another literary example the anxiety which I have found connected with the earliest danger-situation in a girl's development.

In an article entitled 'The Empty Space', Karin Michaelis gives an account of the development of her friend, the painter Ruth Kjär. Ruth Kjär possessed remarkable artistic feeling, which she employed especially in the arrangement of her house, but she had no pronounced creative talent. Beautiful, rich and independent, she spent a great part of her life travelling, and was constantly leaving her house upon which she had expended so much care and taste. She was subject at times to fits of deep depression, which Karin Michaelis describes as follows: 'There was only one dark spot in her life. In the midst of the happiness which was natural to her, and seemed so untroubled, she would suddenly be plunged into the deepest melancholy. A melancholy that was suicidal. If she tried to account for this, she would say something to this effect: "There is an empty space in me, which I can never fill!" '

The time came when Ruth Kjär married, and she seemed perfectly happy. But after a short time the fits of melancholy recurred. In Karin Michaelis's words: 'The accursed empty space was once more empty.' I will let the writer speak for herself: 'Have I already told you that her home was a gallery of modern art? Her husband's brother was one of the greatest painters in the country, and his best pictures decorated the walls of the room. But before Christmas this brother-in-law took away one picture, which he had only lent to her. The picture was sold. This left an empty space on the wall, which in some inexplicable way seemed to coincide with the empty space within her. She sank into a state of the most profound sadness. The blank space on the wall caused her to forget her beautiful home, her happiness, her friends, everything. Of course, a new picture could be got, and would be got, but it took time; one had to look about to find just the right one.

'The empty space grinned hideously down at her.

'The husband and wife were sitting opposite one another at the breakfast table. Ruth's eyes were clouded with hopeless despair. Suddenly, however, her face was transfigured with a smile: "I'll tell you what! I think I will try to daub a little on the wall myself, until we get a new picture!" "Do, my darling," said her husband. It was quite certain that whatever daub she made would not be too monstrously ugly.

'He had hardly left the room when, in a perfect fever, she had rung up the colour-shop to order the paints which her brother-in-law generally used, brushes, palette, and all the rest of the "gear", to be sent up at once. She herself had not the remotest idea of how to begin. She had never squeezed paint out of a tube, laid the ground-colour on a canvas or mixed colours on a palette. Whilst the things were coming, she stood before the empty wall with a piece of black chalk in her hand and made strokes at random as they came into her head. Should she have the car and rush wildly to her brother-in-law to ask how one paints? No, she would rather die!

'Towards evening her husband returned, and she ran to meet him with a hectic brilliance in her eyes. She was not going to be ill, was she? She drew him with her, saying: "Come, you will see!" And he saw. He could not take his eyes from the sight; could not take it in, did not believe it, *could* not believe it. Ruth threw herself on a sofa in a state of deadly exhaustion: "Do you think it at all possible?"

'The same evening they sent for the brother-in-law. Ruth palpitated with anxiety as to the verdict of the connoisseur. But the artist exclaimed immediately: "You don't imagine you can persuade me that you painted that! What a damned lie! This picture was painted by an old and experienced artist. Who the devil is he? I don't know him!"

'Ruth could not convince him. He thought they were making game of him. And when he went, his parting words were: "If *you* painted that, *I* will go and conduct a Beethoven Symphony in the Chapel Royal to-morrow, though I don't know a note of music!"

'That night Ruth could not sleep much. The picture on the wall had been painted, that was certain—it was not a dream. But how had it happened? And what next?

'She was on fire, devoured by ardour within. She must prove to herself that the divine sensation, the unspeakable sense of happiness that she had felt could be repeated.'

Karin Michaelis then adds that after this first attempt, Ruth Kjär painted several masterly pictures, and had them exhibited to the critics and the public.

Karin Michaelis anticipates one part of my interpretation of the anxiety relating to the empty space on the wall when she says: 'On the wall there was an empty space, which in some inexplicable way seemed to coincide with the empty space within her.' Now, what is the meaning of this empty space within Ruth, or rather, to put it more exactly, of the feeling that there was something lacking in her body?

Here there has come into consciousness one of the ideas connected with that anxiety which, in my last paper, already mentioned

(1928), I described as the most profound anxiety experienced by girls. It is the equivalent of castration-anxiety in boys. The little girl has a sadistic desire, originating in the early stages of the Oedipus conflict, to rob the mother's body of its contents, namely, the father's penis, faeces, children, and to destroy the mother herself. This desire gives rise to anxiety lest the mother should in her turn rob the little girl herself of the contents of her body (especially of children) and lest her body should be destroyed or mutilated. In my view, this anxiety, which I have found in the analyses of girls and women to be the deepest anxiety of all, represents the little girl's earliest danger-situation. I have come to see that the dread of being alone, of the loss of love and loss of the love-object, which Freud holds to be the basic infantile danger-situation in girls, is a modification of the anxiety-situation I have just described. When the little girl who fears the mother's assault upon her body cannot *see* her mother, this intensifies the anxiety. The presence of the real, loving mother diminishes the dread of the terrifying mother, whose introjected image is in the child's mind. At a later stage of development the content of the dread changes from that of an attacking mother to the dread that the real, loving mother may be lost and that the girl will be left solitary and forsaken.

In seeking the explanation of these ideas, it is instructive to consider what sort of pictures Ruth Kjär has painted since her first attempt, when she filled the empty space on the wall with the life-sized figure of a naked negress. Apart from one picture of flowers, she had confined herself to portraits. She has twice painted her younger sister, who came to stay with her and sat for her, and, further, the portrait of an old woman and one of her mother. The two last are described by Karin Michaelis as follows: 'And now Ruth cannot stop. The next picture represents an old woman, bearing the mark of years and disillusionments. Her skin is wrinkled, her hair faded, her gentle, tired eyes are troubled. She gazes before her with the disconsolate resignation of old age, with a look that seems to say: "Do not trouble about me any more. My time is so nearly at an end!"

'This is not the impression we receive from Ruth's latest work — the portrait of her Irish-Canadian mother. This lady has a long time before her before she must put her lips to the cup of renunciation. Slim, imperious, challenging, she stands there with a moonlight-coloured shawl draped over her shoulders: she has the effect of a magnificent woman of primitive times, who could any day engage in combat with the children of the desert with her naked hands. What a chin! What force there is in the haughty gaze!

'The blank space has been filled.'

It is obvious that the desire to make reparation, to make good the injury psychologically done to the mother and also to restore herself was at the bottom of the compelling urge to paint these portraits of her relatives. That of the old woman, on the threshold of death, seems to be the expression of the primary, sadistic desire to destroy. The daughter's wish to destroy her mother, to see her old, worn out, marred, is the cause of the need to represent her in full possession of her strength and beauty. By so doing the daughter can allay her own anxiety and can endeavour to restore her mother and make her new through the portrait. In the analyses of children, when the representation of destructive wishes is succeeded by an expression of reactive tendencies, we constantly find that drawing and painting are used as means to restore people. The case of Ruth Kjär shows plainly that this anxiety of the little girl is of greatest importance in the ego-development of women, and is one of the incentives to achievement. But, on the other hand, this anxiety may be the cause of serious illness and many inhibitions. As with the boy's castration-dread, the effect of his anxiety on his ego-development depends on the maintenance of a certain optimum and a satisfactory interplay between the separate factors.

12

THE IMPORTANCE OF
SYMBOL-FORMATION IN THE
DEVELOPMENT OF THE EGO

(1930)

My argument in this paper is based on the assumption that there is an early stage of mental development at which sadism becomes active at all the various sources of libidinal pleasure.[1] In my experience sadism reaches its height in this phase, which is ushered in by the oral-sadistic desire to devour the mother's breast (or the mother herself) and passes away with the earlier anal stage. At the period of which I am speaking, the subject's dominant aim is to possess himself of the contents of the mother's body and to destroy her by means of every weapon which sadism can command. At the same time this phase forms the introduction to the Oedipus conflict. Genital trends now begin to exercise an influence, but this is as yet not evident, for the pregenital impulses hold the field. My whole argument depends on the fact that the Oedipus conflict begins at a period when sadism predominates.

The child expects to find within the mother (a) the father's penis, (b) excrement, and (c) children, and these things it equates with edible substances. According to the child's earliest phantasies (or 'sexual theories') of parental coitus, the father's penis (or his whole body) becomes incorporated in the mother during the act. Thus the child's sadistic attacks have for their object both father and mother, who are in phantasy bitten, torn, cut or stamped to bits. The attacks give rise to anxiety lest the subject should be punished by the united parents, and this anxiety also becomes internalized in consequence of the oral-sadistic introjection of the objects and is thus already directed towards the early super-ego. I have found these anxiety-situations of the early phases of mental development to be the most profound and overwhelming. It is my experience that in the phantasied attack on the mother's body a considerable part is played by the urethral and anal sadism which is very soon added to the oral and muscular sadism. In phantasy the excreta are transformed into dangerous weapons: wetting is regarded as cutting, stabbing,

[1] Cf. my 'Early Stages of the Oedipus Conflict' (1928).

burning, drowning, while the faecal mass is equated with weapons and missiles. At a later stage of the phase which I have described, these violent modes of attack give place to hidden assaults by the most refined methods which sadism can devise, and the excreta are equated with poisonous substances.

The excess of sadism gives rise to anxiety and sets in motion the ego's earliest modes of defence. Freud (1926a, p. 164) writes: 'It may well be that before its sharp cleavage into an ego and an id, and before the formation of a super-ego, the mental apparatus makes use of different methods of defence from those which it employs after it has reached these stages of organization.' According to what I have found in analysis, the earliest defence set up by the ego has reference to two sources of danger: the subject's own sadism and the object which is attacked. This defence, in conformity with the degree of the sadism, is of a violent character and differs fundamentally from the later mechanism of repression. In relation to the subject's own sadism the defence implies expulsion, whereas in relation to the object it implies destruction. The sadism becomes a source of danger because it offers an occasion for the liberation of anxiety and also because the weapons employed to destroy the object are felt by the subject to be levelled at his own self as well. The object of the attack becomes a source of danger because the subject fears similar — retaliatory — attacks from it. Thus, the wholly undeveloped ego is faced with a task which at this stage is quite beyond it—the task of mastering the severest anxiety.

Ferenczi holds that identification, the forerunner of symbolism, arises out of the baby's endeavour to rediscover in every object his own organs and their functioning. In Jones's view the pleasure-principle makes it possible for two quite different things to be equated because of a similarity marked by pleasure or interest. Some years ago I wrote a paper, based on these concepts, in which I drew the conclusion that symbolism is the foundation of all sublimation and of every talent, since it is by way of symbolic equation that things, activities and interests become the subject of libidinal phantasies.

I can now add to what I said then (1923b) and state that, side by side with the libidinal interest, it is the anxiety arising in the phase that I have described which sets going the mechanism of identification. Since the child desires to destroy the organs (penis, vagina, breasts) which stand for the objects, he conceives a dread of the latter. This anxiety contributes to make him equate the organs in question with other things; owing to this equation these in their turn become objects of anxiety, and so he is impelled constantly to make other and new equations, which form the basis of his interest in the new objects and of symbolism.

Thus, not only does symbolism come to be the foundation of all phantasy and sublimation but, more than that, it is the basis of the subject's relation to the outside world and to reality in general. I pointed out that the object of sadism at its height, and of the desire for knowledge arising simultaneously with sadism, is the mother's body with its phantasied contents. The sadistic phantasies directed against the inside of her body constitute the first and basic relation to the outside world and to reality. Upon the degree of success with which the subject passes through this phase will depend the extent to which he can subsequently acquire an external world corresponding to reality. We see then that the child's earliest reality is wholly phantastic; he is surrounded with objects of anxiety, and in this respect excrement, organs, objects, things animate and inanimate are to begin with equivalent to one another. As the ego develops, a true relation to reality is gradually established out of this unreal reality. Thus, the development of the ego and the relation to reality depend on the degree of the ego's capacity at a very early period to tolerate the pressure of the earliest anxiety-situations. And, as usual, it is a question of a certain optimum balance of the factors concerned. A sufficient quantity of anxiety is the necessary basis for an abundance of symbol-formation and of phantasy; an adequate capacity on the part of the ego to tolerate anxiety is essential if anxiety is to be satisfactorily worked over, if this basic phase is to have a favourable issue and if the development of the ego is to be successful.

I have arrived at these conclusions from my general analytical experience, but they are confirmed in a remarkably striking way by a case in which there was an unusual inhibition of ego-development.

This case, of which I will now give some details, is that of a four-year-old boy who, as regards the poverty of his vocabulary and of his intellectual attainments, was on the level of a child of about fifteen or eighteen months. Adaptation to reality and emotional relations to his environment were almost entirely lacking. This child, Dick, was largely devoid of affects, and he was indifferent to the presence or absence of mother or nurse. From the very beginning he had only rarely displayed anxiety, and that in an abnormally small degree. With the exception of one particular interest, to which I will return presently, he had almost no interests, did not play, and had no contact with his environment. For the most part he simply strung sounds together in a meaningless way, and constantly repeated certain noises. When he did speak he generally used his meagre vocabulary incorrectly. But it was not only that he was unable to make himself intelligible: he had no wish to do so. More than that, Dick's mother could at times clearly sense in the boy a strong negative attitude which expressed itself in the fact that he often did the very *opposite* of what was expected of him. For instance, if she succeeded in getting him to say different words after her, he often entirely altered them, though at other times he could pronounce the same words perfectly. Again, sometimes he would repeat the words correctly, but would go on repeating them in an incessant, mechanical way until everyone round him was sick and tired of them. Both these modes of behaviour are different from that of a neurotic child. When the neurotic child expresses opposition in the form of defiance and when he expresses obedience (even accompanied by an excess of anxiety), he does so with a certain understanding and some sort of reference to the thing or person concerned. But Dick's opposition and obedience lacked both affect and understanding. Then too, when he hurt himself, he displayed very considerable insensibility to pain and felt nothing of the desire, so universal with little children, to be comforted and petted. His physical awkwardness, also, was quite remarkable. He could not grip knives or scissors, but it was noteworthy that he could handle quite normally the spoon with which he ate.

The impression his first visit left on me was that his behaviour was quite different from that which we observe in neurotic children. He had let his nurse go without manifesting any emotion, and had followed me into the room with complete indifference. There he ran to and fro in an aimless, purposeless way, and several times he also ran round me, just as if I were a piece of furniture, but he showed no interest in any of the objects in the room. His movements as he ran to and fro seemed to be without co-ordination. The expression of his eyes and face was fixed, far-away and lacking in interest. Compare once more the behaviour of children with severe neuroses. I have in mind children who, without actually having an anxiety-attack, would on their first visit to me withdraw shyly and stiffly into a corner or sit motionless before the little table with toys on it or, without playing, lift up one object or another, only to put it down again. In all these modes of behaviour the great latent anxiety is unmistakable. The corner or the little table is a place of refuge from me. But Dick's behaviour had no meaning or purpose, nor was any affect or anxiety associated with it.

I will now give some details of his previous history. He had had an exceptionally unsatisfactory and disturbed time as a sucking infant, for his mother kept up for some weeks a fruitless attempt to nurse him, and he nearly died of starvation. Artificial foods were then resorted to. At last, when he was seven weeks old, a wet-nurse was found for him, but by then he did not thrive on breast-feeding. He suffered from digestive upsets, *prolapsus ani* and, later, from haemorrhoids. Possibly his development was affected by the fact that, though he had every care, no real love was lavished on him, his mother's attitude to him being from the very beginning over-anxious.

As, moreover, neither his father nor his nurse showed him much affection, Dick grew up in an environment rather poor in love. When he was two years old he had a new nurse, who was skilful and affectionate, and, shortly afterwards, he was for a considerable time with his grandmother, who was very loving to him. The influence of these changes was observable in his development. He had learnt to walk at about the normal age, but there was a difficulty in training him to control his excretory functions. Under the new nurse's influence he acquired habits of cleanliness much more readily. At the age of about three he had mastered them, and on this point he actually showed a certain amount of ambition and apprehensiveness. In one other respect he showed himself in his fourth year sensitive to blame. The nurse had found out that he practised masturbation and had told him it was 'naughty' and he must not do it. This prohibition clearly gave rise to apprehension and to a sense of guilt. Moreover, in his fourth year Dick did in general make a greater attempt at adaptation, but principally in relation to external things, especially to the mechanical learning of a number of new words. From his earliest days the question of feeding had been abnormally difficult. When he had the wet-nurse he showed no desire at all to suck, and this disinclination persisted. Next, he would not drink from a bottle. When the time came for him to have more solid food, he refused to bite it up and absolutely rejected everything that was not of the consistency of pap; even this he had almost to be forced to take. Another good effect of the new nurse's influence was some improvement in Dick's willingness to eat, but even so, the main difficulties persisted.[1] Thus, although the kindly nurse had made a difference to his development in certain respects, the fundamental defects remained untouched. With her, as with everyone else, Dick had failed to establish emotional contact. Thus neither her tenderness nor that of his grandmother had succeeded in setting in train the lacking object-relation.

I found from Dick's analysis that the reason for the unusual inhibition in his development was the failure of those earliest steps of which I spoke at the beginning of this paper. In Dick there was a complete and apparently constitutional incapacity of the ego to tolerate anxiety. The genital had begun to play its part very early; this caused a premature and exaggerated identification with the object attacked and had contributed to an equally premature

[1] By the end of his first year it struck her that the child was abnormal, and some such feeling may have affected her attitude towards him.

defence against sadism. The ego had ceased to develop phantasy-life and to establish a relation with reality. After a feeble beginning, symbol-formation in this child had come to a standstill. The early attempts had left their mark in one interest, which, isolated and unrelated to reality, could not form the basis for further sublimations. The child was indifferent to most of the objects and playthings around him, and did not even grasp their purpose or meaning. But he was interested in trains and stations and also in door-handles, doors and the opening and shutting of them.

The interest in these things and actions had a common source: it really had to do with the penetration of the penis into the mother's body. Doors and locks stood for the ways in and out of her body, while the door-handles represented the father's penis and his own. Thus what had brought symbol-formation to a standstill was the dread of what would be done to him (particularly by the father's penis) after he had penetrated into the mother's body. Moreover, his defences against his destructive impulses proved to be a fundamental impediment to his development. He was absolutely incapable of any act of aggression, and the basis of this incapacity was clearly indicated at a very early period in his refusal to bite up food. At four years old he could not hold scissors, knives or tools, and was remarkably clumsy in all his movements. The defence against the sadistic impulses directed against the mother's body and its contents—impulses connected with phantasies of coitus—had resulted in the cessation of the phantasies and the standstill of symbol-formation. Dick's further development had come to grief because he could not bring into phantasy the sadistic relation to the mother's body.

The unusual difficulty I had to contend with in the analysis was not his defective capacity for speech. In the play-technique, which follows the child's symbolic representations and gives access to his anxiety and sense of guilt, we can, to a great extent, dispense with verbal associations. But this technique is not restricted to an analysis of the child's play. Our material can be derived (as it has to be in the case of children inhibited in play) from the symbolism revealed in details of his general behaviour.[1] But in Dick symbolism had not developed. This was partly because of the lack of any affective relation to the things around him, to which he was almost entirely indifferent. He had practically no special relations with particular objects, such as we usually find in even severely inhibited children.

[1] This applies only to the introductory phase of the analysis and to other limited portions of it. When once access to the Ucs has been gained and the degree of anxiety has been diminished, play-activities, speech-associations and all the other modes of representation begin to make their appearance, alongside the ego-development which is made possible by the analytic work.

Since no affective or symbolic relation to them existed in his mind, any chance actions of his in relation to them were not coloured by phantasy, and it was thus impossible to regard them as having the character of symbolic representations. His lack of interest in his environment and the difficulty of making contact with his mind were, as I could perceive from certain points in which his behaviour differed from that of other children, only the effect of his lack of a symbolic relation to things. The analysis, then, had to begin with this, the *fundamental* obstacle to establishing contact with him.

The first time Dick came to me, as I said before, he manifested no sort of affect when his nurse handed him over to me. When I showed him the toys I had put ready, he looked at them without the faintest interest. I took a big train and put it beside a smaller one and called them 'Daddy-train' and 'Dick-train'. Thereupon he picked up the train I called 'Dick' and made it roll to the window and said 'Station'. I explained: 'The station is mummy; Dick is going into mummy.' He left the train, ran into the space between the outer and inner doors of the room, shut himself in, saying 'dark' and ran out again directly. He went through this performance several times. I explained to him: 'It is dark inside mummy. Dick is inside dark mummy.' Meantime he picked up the train again, but soon ran back into the space between the doors. While I was saying that he was going into dark mummy, he said twice in a questioning way: 'Nurse?' I answered: 'Nurse is soon coming,' and this he repeated and used the words later quite correctly, retaining them in his mind. The next time he came, he behaved in just the same way. But this time he ran right out of the room into the dark entrance hall. He put the 'Dick' train there too and insisted on its staying there. He kept repeatedly asking: 'Nurse coming?' In the third analytic hour he behaved in the same way, except that besides running into the hall and between the doors, he also ran behind the chest of drawers. There he was seized with anxiety, and for the first time called me to him. Apprehension was now evident in the way in which he repeatedly asked for his nurse, and, when the hour was over, he greeted her with quite unusual delight. We see that simultaneously with the appearance of anxiety there had emerged a sense of dependence, first on me and then on the nurse, and at the same time he began to be interested in the soothing words 'Nurse is coming soon' and, contrary to his usual behaviour, had repeated and remembered them. During the third hour, however, he also, for the first time, looked at the toys with interest, in which an aggressive tendency was evident. He pointed to a little coal-cart and said: 'Cut.' I gave him a pair of scissors, and he tried to scratch the little pieces of black wood which represented coal, but he could not hold the scissors. Acting on a glance which he gave me, I cut the pieces of wood out of the cart, whereupon he threw the damaged cart and its contents into the drawer and said, 'Gone.' I told him that this meant that Dick was cutting faeces out of his mother. He then ran into the space between the doors and scratched on the doors a little with his nails, thus showing that he identified the space with the cart and both with the mother's body, which he was attacking. He immediately ran back from the space between the doors, found the cupboard and crept into it. At the beginning of the next analytic hour he cried when the nurse left him—an unusual thing for him to do. But he soon calmed down. This time he avoided the space between the doors, the cupboard and the corner, but concerned himself with the toys, examining them more closely and with obviously dawning curiosity. Whilst doing this he came across the cart which had been damaged the last time he came and upon its contents. He quickly pushed both aside and covered them with other toys. After I had explained that the damaged cart represented his mother, he fetched it and the little bits of coal out again and took them into the space between the doors. As his analysis progressed it became clear that in thus throwing them out of the room he was indicating an expulsion, both of the damaged object and of his own sadism (or the means employed by it), which was in this manner projected into the external world. Dick had also discovered the wash-basin as symbolizing the mother's body, and he displayed an extraordinary dread of being wetted with water. He anxiously wiped it off his hand and mine, which he had dipped in as well as his own, and immediately afterwards he showed the same anxiety when urinating. Urine and faeces represented to him injurious and dangerous substances.[1]

It became clear that in Dick's phantasy faeces, urine and penis stood for objects with which to attack the mother's body, and were therefore felt to be a source of injury to himself as well. These phantasies contributed to his dread of the contents of his mother's body, and especially of his father's penis which he phantasied as being in her womb. We came to see this phantasied penis and a

---

[1] Here I found the explanation of a peculiar apprehensiveness which Dick's mother had noticed in him when he was about five months old and again from time to time at later periods. When the child was defecating and urinating, his expression was one of great anxiety. Since the faeces were not hard, the fact that he suffered from *prolapsus ani* and haemorrhoids did not seem enough to account for his apprehensiveness, especially as it manifested itself in just the same way when he was passing urine. During the analytic hour this anxiety reached such a pitch that when Dick told me he wanted to urinate or defecate he did so—in either case—only after long hesitation, with every indication of deep anxiety and with tears in his eyes. After we had analysed this anxiety his attitude towards both these functions was very different and is now almost normal.

growing feeling of aggression against it in many forms, the desire to eat and destroy it being specially prominent. For example, on one occasion Dick lifted a little toy man to his mouth, gnashed his teeth and said 'Tea daddy,' by which he meant 'Eat daddy.' He then asked for a drink of water. The introjection of the father's penis proved to be associated with the dread both of it, as of a primitive, harm-inflicting super-ego, and of being punished by the mother thus robbed: dread, that is, of the external and the introjected objects. And at this point there came into prominence the fact which I have already mentioned, and which was a determining factor in his development, namely, that the genital phase had become active in Dick prematurely. This was shown in the circumstance that such representations as I have just spoken of were followed not by anxiety only, but by remorse, pity and a feeling that he must make restitution. Thus he would proceed to place the little toy men on my lap or in my hand, put everything back in the drawer, and so on. The early operation of the reactions originating on the genital level was a result of premature ego-development, but further ego-development was only inhibited by it. This early identification with the object could not as yet be brought into relation with reality. For instance, once when Dick saw some pencil shavings on my lap he said 'Poor Mrs Klein.' But on a similar occasion he said in just the same way, 'Poor curtain.' Side by side with his incapacity for tolerating anxiety, this premature *empathy* became a decisive factor in his warding-off of all destructive impulses. Dick cut himself off from reality and brought his phantasy-life to a standstill by taking refuge in the phantasies of the dark, empty mother's body. He had thus succeeded in withdrawing his attention also from the different objects in the outside world which represented the contents of the mother's body—the father's penis, faeces, children. His own penis, as the organ of sadism, and his own excreta were to be got rid of (or denied) as being dangerous and aggressive.

It had been possible for me, in Dick's analysis, to gain access to his unconscious by getting into contact with such rudiments of phantasy-life and symbol-formation as he displayed. The result was a diminution of his latent anxiety, so that it was possible for a certain amount of anxiety to become manifest. But this implied that the working-over of this anxiety was beginning by way of the establishment of a symbolic relation to things and objects, and at the same time his epistemophilic and aggressive impulses were set in action. Every advance was followed by the releasing of fresh quantities of anxiety and led to his turning away to some extent from the things with which he had already established an affective relation and which had therefore become objects of anxiety. As he turned away from these he turned towards new objects, and his aggressive and episte-mophilic impulses were directed to these new affective relations in their turn. Thus, for instance, for some time Dick altogether avoided the cupboard, but thoroughly investigated the wash-basin and the electric radiator, which he examined in every detail, again mani-festing destructive impulses against these objects. He then transferred his interest from them to fresh things or, again, to things with which he was already familiar and which he had given up earlier. He occupied himself once more with the cupboard, but this time his interest in it was accompanied by a far greater activity and curiosity and a stronger tendency to aggression of all kinds. He beat on it with a spoon, scratched and hacked it with a knife and sprinkled water on it. He examined in a lively way the hinges of the door, the way in which it opened and shut, the lock, etc., climbed up inside the cupboard and asked what the different parts were called. Thus as his interests developed he at the same time enlarged his vocabulary, for he now began to take more and more interest not only in the things themselves but in their names. The words which before he had heard and disregarded he now remembered and applied correctly.

Hand in hand with this development of interests and an in-creasingly strong transference to myself, the hitherto lacking object-relation has made its appearance. During these months his attitude to his mother and nurse has become affectionate and normal. He now desires their presence, wants them to take notice of him and is distressed when they leave him. With his father, too, his relation reveals growing indications of the normal Oedipus attitude, and there is an increasingly firm relation to objects in general. The desire to make himself intelligible, which was lacking before, is now in full force. Dick tries to make himself understood by means of his still meagre but growing vocabulary which he diligently endeavours to enlarge. There are many indications, moreover, that he is beginning to establish a relation to reality.

So far we have spent six months over his analysis, and his develop-ment, which has begun to take place at all the fundamental points during this period, justifies a favourable prognosis. Several of the peculiar problems which arose in his case have proved soluble. It has been possible to get into contact with him with the help of quite a few words, to activate anxiety in a child in whom interest and affect were wholly lacking, and it has further been possible gradually to resolve and to regulate the anxiety released. I would emphasize the fact that in Dick's case I have modified my usual technique. In general I do not interpret the material until it has found expression in various representations. In this case, however, where the capacity to represent it was almost entirely lacking, I found myself obliged to make my interpretations on the basis of my general knowledge, the representations in Dick's behaviour being relatively vague. Finding access in this way to his unconscious, I succeeded in activating anxiety and other affects. The representations then became fuller and I soon acquired a more solid foundation for the analysis, and so was able gradually to pass over to the technique that I generally employ in analysing little children.

I have already described how I succeeded in causing the anxiety to become manifest by diminishing it in its latent state. When it did manifest itself, I was able to resolve part of it by interpretation. At the same time, however, it became possible for it to be worked over in a better way, namely, by its distribution amongst new things and interests; in this manner it became so far mitigated as to be tolerable for the ego. Whether, if the quantities of anxiety are thus regulated, the ego can become capable of tolerating and working over normal quantities, only the further course of the treatment can show. In Dick's case, therefore, it is a question of modifying a fundamental factor in his development by means of analysis.

The only possible thing to do in analysing this child, who could not make himself intelligible and whose ego was not open to influence, was to try to gain access to his unconscious and, by diminishing the unconscious difficulties, to open up a way for the development of the ego. Of course, in Dick's case, as in every other, access to the unconscious had to be by way of the ego. Events proved that even this very imperfectly developed ego was adequate for establishing connection with the unconscious. From the theoretical point of view I think it is important to note that, even in so extreme a case of defective ego-development, it was possible to develop both ego and libido only by analysing the unconscious conflicts, without bringing any educational influence to bear upon the ego. It seems plain that, if even the imperfectly developed ego of a child who had no relation at all with reality can tolerate the removal of repressions by the aid of analysis, without being overwhelmed by the id, we need not fear that in neurotic children (*i.e.* in very much less extreme cases) the ego might succumb to the id. It is also noteworthy that, whereas the educational influence exercised by those about him previously glided off Dick without any effect, now, when owing to analysis his ego is developing, he is increasingly amenable to such influence, which can keep pace with the instinctual impulses mobilized by analysis and quite suffices to deal with them.

There still remains the question of diagnosis. Dr Forsyth diagnosed the case as one of dementia praecox and he thought it might be worth while attempting analysis. His diagnosis would seem to be corroborated by the fact that the clinical picture agreed in many important points with that of advanced dementia praecox in adults. To summarize it once again: it was characterized by an almost complete absence of affect and anxiety, a very considerable degree of withdrawal from reality, and of inaccessibility, a lack of emotional *rapport*, negativistic behaviour alternating with signs of automatic obedience, indifference to pain, perseveration—all symptoms which are characteristic of dementia praecox. Moreover, this diagnosis is further corroborated by the fact that the presence of any organic disease can be certainly excluded, firstly because Dr Forsyth's examination revealed none and, secondly because the case has proved amenable to psychological treatment. The analysis showed me that the idea of a psycho-neurosis could be definitely dismissed.

Against the disgnosis of dementia praecox is the fact that the essential feature of Dick's case was an inhibition in development and not a regression. Further, dementia praecox is of extraordinarily rare occurrence in early childhood, so that many psychiatrists hold that it does not occur at all at this period.

From this standpoint of clinical psychiatry I will not commit myself on the subject of diagnosis, but my general experience in analysing children enables me to make some observations of a general nature on psychosis in childhood. I have become convinced that schizophrenia is much commoner in childhood than is usually supposed. I will give some of the reasons why it is not in general recognized: (1) Parents, especially in the poorer classes, mostly consult a psychiatrist only when the case is desperate, that is, when they can do nothing with the child themselves. Thus a considerable number of cases never come under medical observation. (2) In the patients whom the physician does see, it is often impossible for him in a single rapid examination to establish the presence of schizophrenia. So that many cases of this sort are classified under indefinite headings, such as 'arrested development', 'mental deficiency', 'psychopathic condition', 'asocial tendency', etc. (3) Above all, in children schizophrenia is less obvious and striking than in adults. Traits which are characteristic of this disease are less noticeable in a child because, in a lesser degree, they are natural in the development of normal children. Such things, for instance, as a marked severance from reality, a lack of emotional *rapport*, an incapacity to concentrate on any occupation, silly behaviour and talking nonsense do not strike us as so remarkable in children and we do not judge of them as we should if they occurred in adults. An excess of mobility and stereotyped movements are quite common in children and differ only in degree from the hyperkinesis and stereotypy of schizophrenia. Automatic obedience must be very marked indeed for the parents to regard it as anything but 'docility'. Negativistic behaviour is usually looked upon as 'naughtiness', and dissociation is a phenomenon which generally escapes observation in a child altogether. That the phobic anxiety of children often contains ideas of persecution which are of a paranoid character[1] and hypochondriacal fears is a fact which requires very close observation and can often be revealed only through analysis. (4) Even more commonly than psychoses in children, we meet psychotic traits which, in unfavourable circumstances, lead to disease in later life.

Thus, in my opinion, fully developed schizophrenia is more common, and especially the occurrence of schizophrenic traits is a far more general phenomenon in childhood, than is usually supposed. I have come to the conclusion—for which I must give my full reasons elsewhere—that the concept of schizophrenia in particular and of psychosis in general as occurring in childhood must be extended, and I think that one of the foremost tasks of child analysis is the discovery and cure of psychoses in childhood. The theoretical knowledge thus acquired would doubtless be a valuable contribution to our understanding of the structure of the psychoses and would also help us to reach a more accurate differential diagnosis between the various diseases.

If we extend the use of the term in the manner which I propose, I think we shall be justified in classifying Dick's illness under the heading schizophrenia. It is true that it differs from the typical schizophrenia of childhood in that in him the trouble was an inhibition in development, whereas in most such cases there is a regression after a certain stage of development has been successfully reached.[2] Moreover the severity of the case adds to the unusual character of the clinical picture. Nevertheless, I have reason to think that even so it is not an isolated one, for recently I have become acquainted with two analogous cases in children of about Dick's age. One is therefore inclined to conjecture that, if we observed with a more penetrating eye, more cases of the kind would come to our knowledge.

I will now sum up my theoretical conclusions. I have drawn them not from Dick's case only but from other, less extreme, cases of schizophrenia in children between the ages of five and thirteen and from my general analytic experience.

The early stages of the Oedipus conflict are dominated by sadism.

---

[1] Cf. my paper on 'Personification in the Play of Children' (1929).

[2] The fact, however, that analysis made it possible to establish contact with Dick's mind and brought about some advance in so comparatively short a time suggests the possibility that there had already been some latent development as well as the slight development outwardly manifest. But, even if we suppose this, the total development was so abnormally meagre that the hypothesis of a regression from a stage already successfully reached will hardly meet the case.

They take place during a phase of development which is inaugurated by oral sadism (with which urethral, muscular and anal sadism associate themselves) and terminate when the ascendancy of anal sadism comes to an end.

It is only in the later stages of the Oedipus conflict that the defence against the libidinal impulses makes its appearance: in the earlier stages it is against the accompanying *destructive* impulses that the defence is directed. The earliest defence set up by the ego is directed against the subject's own sadism and the object attacked, both of these being regarded as sources of danger. This defence is of a violent character, different from the mechanism of repression. In the boy this strong defence is also directed against his penis as the executive organ of his sadism and it is one of the deepest sources of all disturbances of potency.

Such are my hypotheses with regard to the development of normal persons and neurotics; let us now turn to the genesis of the psychoses.

The first part of the phase when sadism is at its height is that in which the attacks are conceived of as being made by violence. This I have come to recognize as the fixation-point in dementia praecox. In the second part of this phase the attacks are imagined as being made by poisoning, and the urethral and anal-sadistic impulses predominate. This I believe to be the fixation-point in paranoia.[1] I may recall that Abraham maintained that in paranoia the libido regresses to the earlier anal stage. My conclusions are in agreement with Freud's hypotheses, according to which the fixation-points of dementia praecox and paranoia are to be sought in the narcissistic stage, that of dementia praecox preceding that of paranoia.

The ego's excessive and premature defence against sadism checks the establishing of a relation to reality and the development of phantasy-life. The further sadistic appropriation and exploration of the mother's body and of the outside world (the mother's body in an extended sense) are brought to a standstill, and this causes the more or less complete suspension of the symbolic relation to the things and objects representing the contents of the mother's body and hence of the relation to the subject's environment and to reality. This withdrawal becomes the basis of the lack of affect and anxiety, which is one of the symptoms of dementia praecox. In this disease, therefore, the regression would go right back to the early phase of development in which the sadistic appropriation and destruction of the interior of the mother's body, as conceived of by the subject in phantasy, together with the establishing of the relation to reality, was prevented or checked owing to anxiety.

[1] I will cite elsewhere (in *The Psycho-Analysis of Children, Writings,* **2**) the material upon which I am basing this view and will give more detailed reasons for it.

13

THE PSYCHOTHERAPY OF THE PSYCHOSES

(1930)

IF one studies the diagnostic criteria of psychiatrists, one is impressed with the fact that, although these appear to be very complicated and to cover a wide clinical ground, yet in essence they mostly centre on one special point, namely, the relationship to reality. But evidently the reality the psychiatrist has in mind is the reality, both subjective and objective, of the normal adult. Whilst this is justifiable from the social point of view of insanity, it ignores the most important fact: that the foundations of reality relations in early childhood are of an entirely different order. The analysis of small children between two and a half and five years clearly shows that for all children in the beginning external reality is mainly a mirror of the child's own instinctual life. Now, the earliest phase of human relationship is one dominated by oral-sadistic urges. These sadistic urges are accentuated by experiences of frustration and deprivation, and the result of this process is that every other instrument of sadistic expression the child possesses, to which we give the labels urethral sadism, anal sadism, muscle sadism, are in turn activated and directed towards objects. The fact is that at this phase external reality is peopled in the child's imagination with objects who are expected to treat the child in precisely the same sadistic way as the child is impelled to treat the objects. This relationship is really the very young child's primitive reality.

In the earliest reality of the child it is no exaggeration to say that the world is a breast and a belly which is filled with dangerous objects, dangerous because of the child's own impulse to attack them. Whilst the normal course of development for the ego is gradually to assess external objects through a reality scale of values, for the psychotic, the world—and that in practice means objects—is valued at the original level; that is to say, that for the psychotic the world is still a belly peopled with dangerous objects. If, therefore, I were asked to give in a few words a valid generalization for the psychoses, I would say that the main groupings correspond to defences against the main developmental phases of sadism.

233

One of the reasons why these relationships are not generally appreciated is that, though there are of course cases where there are quite close resemblances, generally the diagnostic features of psychosis in childhood are essentially different from those of the classical psychoses. For example, I would say that the most sinister feature in a child of four would be the undiminished activity of systems of phantasy characteristic of a child of one year; in other words, a fixation which clinically gives rise to arrest of development. Although the phantasy fixation is only uncovered by analysis, nevertheless there are many clinical evidences of retardation which are seldom or never adequately appreciated.

In the patients whom the physician does see, it is often impossible for him in a single rapid examination to establish the presence of schizophrenia. So that many cases of this sort are classified under indefinite headings, such as 'arrested development', 'psychopathic condition', 'asocial tendency', etc. Above all, in children schizophrenia is less obvious and striking than in adults. Traits which are characteristic of this disease are less noticeable in a child because, in a lesser degree, they are natural in the development of normal children. Such things, for instance, as a marked severance from reality, a lack of emotional *rapport*, an incapacity to concentrate on any occupation, silly behaviour and talking nonsense do not strike us as so remarkable in children and we do not judge of them as we should if they occurred in adults. An excess of activity and stereotyped movements are quite common in children and differ only in degree from the hyperkinesis and stereotypy of schizophrenia. Automatic obedience must be very marked indeed for the parents to regard it as anything but 'docility'. Negativistic behaviour is usually looked upon as 'naughtiness', and dissociation is a phenomenon which generally escapes observation in a child altogether. That the phobic anxiety of children often contains ideas of persecution which are of a paranoid character and hypochondriacal fears is a fact which requires very close observation and can often be revealed only through analysis. Even more commonly than psychoses we meet in children with psychotic traits which, in unfavourable circumstances, lead to disease in later life. (Cf. 'Symbol Formation' (1930a).

I could give an example of a case in which stereotyped actions were entirely based on a foundation of psychotic anxiety, but which would not have in any way given rise to such suspicions. A boy of six would play for hours at being a policeman directing the traffic, in which he takes up certain attitudes again and again, and remains transfixed in some of them for quite a time. Thus he showed indications of catatonia as well as of stereotypy, and analysis revealed the characteristic overwhelming fear and dread which we meet with in cases of a psychotic nature. It is our experience that this over-whelming psychotic dread is typically barricaded off by various devices with which the symptoms are connected.

Then there is the child who lives in phantasy, and we can see how in their play such children must shut out reality completely and can only maintain their phantasies by excluding it altogether. These children find any frustration very intolerable because it reminds them of reality; and they are quite unable to concentrate on any occupation connected with reality. For instance, a boy of six of this type would repeatedly play that he was the mighty leader of a band of savage huntsmen and wild animals; he fought, conquered and cruelly put to death his enemies, who also had wild beasts to support them. The animals were then eaten up. The battle never came to an end, as new animals always appeared. A considerable course of analysis had revealed in this child not only a severe neurosis but also markedly paranoid traits. He had always consciously felt himself surrounded and threatened by magicians, soldiers, witches, etc. Like so many children, this boy had invariably kept the content of his anxiety a complete secret from those around him.

Further, I found, for example, in an apparently normal child who had an unusually tenacious belief in the constant presence round him at all times of fairies and friendly figures like Father Christmas, that these figures were a cover for his anxiety of being always surrounded by terrifying animals threatening to attack and swallow him up.

In my opinion fully developed schizophrenia is more common—and especially the occurrence of schizophrenic traits is a far more general phenomenon—in childhood than is usually supposed. I have come to the conclusion that the concept of schizophrenia in particular and of psychosis in general as occurring in childhood must be extended, and I think that one of the chief tasks of the children's analyst is to discover and cure psychoses in children. The theoretical knowledge thus acquired would doubtless be a valuable contribution to our understanding of the structure of the psychoses and would also help us to reach a more accurate differential diagnosis between the various diseases.

14

A CONTRIBUTION TO THE THEORY
OF INTELLECTUAL INHIBITION

(1931)

I INTEND to deal here with some mechanisms of intellectual in-hibition and will begin with a short abstract from an analysis of a seven-year-old boy, dealing with the principal points of two consecutive analytic sessions. The boy's neurosis consisted partly of neurotic symptoms, partly of character-difficulties, and also of quite severe intellectual inhibitions. At the time when the two hours with which I propose to deal occurred, the child had had more than two years' treatment and the material in question had already undergone considerable analysis. The intellectual inhibitions in general had diminished gradually to some extent during this period; but it was only in these two hours that the connection of this material with one of his special difficulties in regard to learning became clear. This led to a remarkable improvement where his intellectual inhibitions were concerned.

The boy complained to me that he could not distinguish certain French words from one another. There was a picture in the school of various objects to help the children to understand the words. The words were: *poulet*, chicken; *poisson*, fish; *glace*, ice. Whenever he was asked what any of these words meant he invariably answered with the meaning of one of the other two—for instance, asked *poisson*, he would answer ice; *poulet*, fish; and so on. He felt quite hopeless and despairing about it, saying he would never learn it, etc. I obtained the material from him by ordinary association, but at the same time he was also playing about idly in the room.

I asked him first to tell me what *poulet* made him think of. He lay on his back on the table, kicking his legs about and drawing on a piece of paper with a pencil. He thought of a fox breaking into a chicken-house. I asked him when this would happen and instead of saying 'in the night,' he answered, 'At four o'clock in the afternoon,' which I knew to be a time when his mother was often out. 'The fox breaks in and kills a little chicken,' and while he said this he cut off what he had drawn. I asked him what it was and he said, 'I don't know.' When we looked at it, it was a house, of which he had cut off the roof. He said that was the way the fox got into the house. He realized that he was himself the fox, that the chicken was his little brother and that the time at which the fox broke in was precisely when his mother was out.

We had already done a lot of work in connection with his strong aggressive impulses and phantasies of attacking his little brother inside his mother while she was pregnant and after his birth, together with the intensely heavy weight of guilt relating to them.[1] The brother is now nearly four years old. When he was a baby it had been an appalling temptation for my patient John to be left alone with him even for a minute, and even now when the mother is out we see that his wishes are still active. This was partly due to his extreme jealousy of the baby enjoying the mother's breast.

I asked him about *poisson* and he began to kick more violently and to thrust the scissors near his eyes and to try to cut his hair, so that I had to ask him to let me have the scissors. He answered about *poisson* that fried fish was very nice and he liked it. He then began to draw again, this time a seaplane and a boat. I could not get any more associations to a fish and went on to the ice. To this he said, 'A big piece of ice is nice and white, and it gets first pink and then red.' I asked why it does this and he said, 'It melts.' 'How is that?' 'The sun shone on it.' He had a good deal of anxiety here and I could get no more. He cut out the boat and seaplane and tried to see if they would float in water.

The next day he showed anxiety and said he had had a bad dream. 'The fish was a crab. He was standing on a pier at the seaside where he has often been with his mother. He was supposed to kill an enormous crab which came out of the water on to the pier. He shot it with his little gun and killed it with his sword, which was not very efficient. As soon as he killed the crab, he had to kill more and more of them which kept on coming out of the water.' I asked him why he had to do this and he said to stop them going into the world, because they would kill the whole world. As soon as we began on this dream he got into the same position on the table as the day before and kicked harder than ever. I then asked him why he kicked, and he answered, 'I am lying on the water and crabs are all round me.' The scissors the day before had represented the crabs nipping and cutting him, and this was why he had drawn a boat and a seaplane in which to escape from them. I said he had been on a pier, and he answered, 'O yes, but I fell down into the water long ago.' The crabs wanted most of all to get into a joint of meat on the water which

[1] These tendencies in regard to his younger brother contributed in no small measure towards disturbing his relations with his elder brother, who was four years his senior, in whom he presupposed the existence of similar intentions towards himself.

looked like a house. It was mutton, his favourite meat. He said they had never been inside yet, but they might get in by the doors and windows. The whole scene on the water was the inside of his mother —the world. The meat-house represented both her body and his. The crabs stood for his father's penis and their numbers were legion. They were as big as elephants and were black outside and red inside. They were black because someone had made them black, and so everything had turned black in the water. They had got into the water from the other side of the sea. Someone who had wanted to turn the water black had put them in there. It turned out that the crabs represented not only his father's penis but his own faeces. One of them was no bigger than a lobster and was red outside as well as inside. This represented his own penis. There was much material as well to show that he identified his faeces with dangerous animals which would at his command (by a sort of magic) enter into his mother's body and damage and poison both her and his father's penis.

This material throws, I think, some light on the theory of paranoia. I can only allude to this point very briefly here; but we know that Van Ophuijsen (1920) and Stärcke (1919) have referred the 'persecutor' to the paranoic's unconscious idea of his own scybalum in his bowels, which he has identified with the penis of his persecutor. Analysis of many children and adults, as well as of the case under discussion, has led me to the view that a person's fear of his faeces as a persecutor is ultimately derived from his sadistic phantasies, in which he employs his urine and faeces as poisonous and destructive weapons in his attacks upon his mother's body. In these phantasies he turns his own faeces into things that persecute his objects; and by a kind of magic (which, in my opinion, is the basis of black magic) he pushes them secretly and by stealth into the anus and other orifices of the objects and lodges them inside their bodies. Because he has done this he becomes afraid of his own excrements as a substance that is dangerous and damaging to his own body; and he also becomes afraid of the excrements, introjected within him, of his objects, since he expects the latter to make similar secret attacks on him by means of their dangerous faeces. These fears give rise to a terror of having a number of persecutors inside his body and of being poisoned, as well as to hypochondriacal fears. The point of fixation for paranoia is situated, I believe, in that period of the phase when sadism is at its height, when the child carries out his attacks upon his mother's inside, and his father's penis which he supposes to be there, by means of his faeces, transformed into poisonous and dangerous animals or substances.[1]

[1] Cf. my paper, 'The Importance of Symbol-formation in the Development of the Ego' (1930a). The view put forward there is in agreement with Abraham's

Since, as a result of his urethral-sadistic impulses, the child regards urine as something dangerous that burns, cuts and poisons, the way is already prepared for him to think of the penis as a sadistic and dangerous thing. And his phantasies of the scybalum as a persecutor—phantasies formed under the dominance of anal-sadistic tendencies and, as far as can be seen, preceding ideas of the dangerous penis as a persecutor—also tend in the same direction, in virtue of the fact that he equates pieces of stool with the penis. In consequence of the equation of the two, the dangerous properties of faeces serve to enhance the dangerous and sadistic character of the penis, and of the persecuting object which is identified with them.

In the present case the crabs represented a combination of the dangerous faeces and penis of the boy and of his father. At the same time the boy felt responsible for the employment of all those instruments and sources of destruction, for it was his own sadistic wishes against his copulating parents which transformed his father's penis and excrements into dangerous animals, so that his father and mother should destroy one another. In his imagination John had also attacked his father's penis with his own faeces and had thus rendered it more dangerous than before; and he had put his own dangerous faeces into his mother's body.

I asked him again about *glace* (ice) and he began to talk about a glass and went to the water-tap and drank a glass of water. He said it was barley-water—which he likes—and talked about a glass which had 'little pieces' broken out of it, meaning cut-glass. He said the sun had spoilt this glass, as it had spoilt the big block of ice about which he had spoken yesterday. It shot at the glass, he said, and spoilt all the barley-water as well. When I asked how it had shot at the glass, he said, 'With its heat.'

As he was saying this, he chose a yellow pencil from a number of pencils that were lying before him, and began making dots on a piece of paper, and then punching holes in it, until he finally reduced

theory that in paranoiacs the libido has regressed to the earlier anal stage; for the phase of development in which sadism reaches its height begins, in my opinion, with the emergence of the oral-sadistic instincts and ends with the decline of the earlier anal stage. That period of the phase which has been described above and which, in my view, forms the basis of paranoia, would occur, therefore, at a time when the earlier anal stage is in the ascendant. In this way Abraham's theory would be extended in two directions. In the first place we see what an intensive co-operation of the various instruments of the child's sadism there is in this phase, and especially, besides his oral sadism, what enormous importance attaches to his hitherto little recognized urethral-sadistic tendencies in reinforcing and elaborating his anal-sadistic ones. In the second place, we get a more detailed understanding of the structure of those phantasies in which his anal-sadistic impulses belonging to the earlier stage find expression.

it to ribbons. Then he started to cut the pencil with a knife, slicing off its yellow outside. The yellow pencil stood for the sun, which symbolized his own burning penis and urine. (The word 'sun' stood for himself, the 'son', through verbal association as well.) In many of his analytic hours he had burnt bits of paper, match-boxes and matches in the fire, and at the same time, or in alternation with this, had torn them up or poured water over them and soaked them or cut them in pieces. These objects represented his mother's breast or her whole person. He had also repeatedly broken tumblers in the play-room. They stood for his mother's breast and also for his father's penis.

The sun had a further significance as his father's sadistic penis. As he was cutting up the pencil, he said a word that turned out to be made up of the word 'go' and his father's christian name. Thus the glass was being destroyed both by the son and the father; it meant the breast, and the barley-water meant milk. The big block of ice which was the same size as the meat-house represented his mother's body; it was melted and ruined by the heat of his own and his father's penis and urine; and when it turned crimson this symbolized the blood of his injured mother.

John showed me a Christmas card with a bull-dog on it near a dead chicken, which it had obviously killed. Both were painted brown. He said: 'I know, they are all the same, chicken, ice, glass and crabs.' I asked why they were all the same, and he said, 'Because they are all brown and broken and dead.' This is why he could not distinguish between these things, because all were dead; he killed all the crabs, but the chicken, representing the babies, and the ice and glass representing the mother, were all dirtied and injured, or killed too.

After this he began in the same hour to draw parallel lines getting narrower and wider. It was the clearest possible vagina symbol. He then put his own little engine on it and let it go up the lines to the station. He was very relieved and happy. He felt now that he could symbolically have intercourse with his mother; whereas before this analysis her body was a place of horrors. This seems to show what one can see confirmed in every man's analysis, that his dread of the woman's body as a place full of destruction might be one of the main causes of impaired potency. This anxiety is also, however, a basic factor in inhibitions of the desire for knowledge, since the inside of the mother's body is the first object of this impulse; in phantasy it is explored and investigated, as well as attacked with all the sadistic armoury, including the penis as a dangerous offensive weapon, and this is another cause of subsequent impotence in men: penetrating and exploring are to a great extent synonymous in the unconscious. For this reason, after the analysis of his anxiety relating to his own and his father's sadistic penis—the piercing yellow pencil equated with the burning sun—John was much more able to represent himself symbolically as having coitus with his mother and investigating her body. The next day he could look attentively and with interest at the picture on the wall at school and could distinguish the words from one another easily.

J. Strachey (1930) has shown that reading has the unconscious significance of taking knowledge out of the mother's body, and that the fear of robbing her is an important factor for inhibitions in reading. I should like to add that it is essential for a favourable development of the desire for knowledge that the mother's body should be felt to be well and unharmed. It represents in the unconscious the treasure-house of everything desirable which can only be got from there; therefore if it is not destroyed, not so much in danger and therefore not so dangerous itself, the wish to take food for the mind from it can more easily be carried out.

When I described the fight which in phantasy John had inside the mother's body with his father's penises (crabs)—actually with a swarm of them—I pointed out that the meat-house, which had apparently not been broken into and which John was trying to prevent them from getting into, represented not only the inside of his mother's body but his own inside. His defences against anxiety were here expressed in elaborate displacements and reversals. At first, what he ate was a nice fried fish. Then it changed into a crab. In the first version about the crab he stood on the pier and tried to keep the crabs from crawling out of the water. It appeared, however, that he actually felt himself to be lying in the water, and there—inside his mother—to be at the mercy of his father. In this version he still tried to keep hold of the idea that he was preventing the crabs from getting into the meat-house, but his deepest dread was that the crabs *had* got into it and were destroying it, and his efforts were to drive them out again. Both the sea and the meat-house represented his mother's body.

I must now point out another source of anxiety which is closely connected with that of destroying the mother, and must show how it influences the intellectual inhibitions and disturbances in ego-development. This is connected with the fact that the meat-house was not only his mother's body but his own. Here we have a representation of the early anxiety-situations which arise in both sexes from the oral-sadistic impulse to devour the contents of the mother's body, and especially the penises imagined to be in it. The father's penis, which from the sucking oral point of view is equated with the breast, and so becomes an object of desire,[1] is thus incorporated and

---

[1] This is shown by his association about the nice fried fish which he liked

in the boy's phantasy very rapidly transforms itself, in consequence of his sadistic attacks against it, into a terrifying internal aggressor and becomes equated with dangerous, murderous animals or weapons. In my view it is the introjected father's penis which forms the kernel of the paternal super-ego.

The example of John's case shows: (a) that the destruction imagined to have been wrought in the mother's body is also anticipated and imagined as having occurred in his own body; and (b) how the dread of attacks on the inside of one's own body by the internalized penises of the father and by faeces is experienced.

Just as the excessive anxiety in regard to the destruction wrought in the mother's body inhibits the capacity to obtain any *clear conception* of its contents, so in an analogous way the anxiety in regard to the terrible and dangerous things that are happening inside one's own body can suppress all investigation into it; and this again is a factor in intellectual inhibition.[1] To illustrate this from John's case: the day after the analysis of the crab-dream, *i.e.* the day on which he found himself suddenly able to distinguish the French words, John began his analysis by saying, 'I am going to turn out my drawer.' This was the drawer in which he kept the toys he used in his analysis; for months he had thrown every possible sort of rubbish into it, scraps of paper, things sticky with glue, scraps of soap, bits of string, etc., without ever having been able to make up his mind to tidy it.

He now sorted out its contents and threw away the useless or broken articles. On the same day he discovered in a drawer at home his fountain-pen which he had been unable to find for months. Thus he had in a symbolic way looked into his mother's body and restored it, and had also found his penis again. But the drawer also represented his own body; and his now less inhibited impulse to become acquainted with its contents found expression, as the course of his analysis showed, in a much greater co-operation on his part in analytic work and in a deeper insight into his own difficulties. This deeper insight was the result of an advance in the development

---

[1] In a paper which appeared some years ago ('Early Analysis', 1923b) I discussed a special form of inhibition of the capacity to develop a picture of the inside of the mother's body with its special functions of conception, pregnancy and birth; namely, disturbance of the sense of orientation and of interest in geography. I then pointed out, however, that the effect of this inhibition can go very much further and affect the whole attitude to the external world and impair orientation in its widest and most metaphorical sense. Since then, further investigation has shown me that this inhibition is due to fear of the mother's body, in consequence of sadistic attacks upon it; and has also demonstrated that the early sadistic phantasies about the mother's body and a capacity to work these over successfully form the bridge to object-relationships and adaptation to reality, thus fundamentally influencing the subject's later relation to the external world.

of his ego which followed from this particular piece of analysis of his threatening super-ego. For, as we know from our experience with children, especially very young ones, analysis of the early stages of super-ego formation promotes the development of the ego by lessening the sadism of the super-ego and the id.

But what I wish to draw attention to here, in addition to this fact, is the connection, which is observable over and over again in analysis, between a diminution of anxiety on the part of the ego in respect of the super-ego and an increased capacity in the child to become acquainted with its own intrapsychic processes and to control them more efficiently through its ego. In the present instance tidying represented making an inspection of intrapsychic reality. When John tidied his drawer he was tidying his own body and separating his own possessions from the things he had stolen out of his mother's body, as well as separating 'bad' faeces from 'good' faeces, and 'bad' objects from 'good' ones. In doing this John likened the broken, damaged and dirty things to the 'bad' object, 'bad' faeces and 'bad' children, in accordance with the workings of the unconscious, where the damaged object becomes a 'bad' and dangerous one.

In that John was now able to examine the different objects and see what use could be made of them or what damage they had suffered, and so on, he showed himself as daring to face the imagined havoc wrought by his super-ego and id; that is, he was carrying out a test by reality. This enabled his ego to function better in making decisions about what the things could be used for, whether they could be repaired or should be thrown away, and so on; his super-ego and id were at the same time brought more into harmony and thus could be better dealt with by the stronger ego.

In this connection I should like to return once more to the matter of his rediscovery of his fountain-pen. So far, we have interpreted it in the sense that his fear of the destructive and dangerous qualities of his penis—ultimately his sadism—had been lessened and he was enabled to recognize the possession of such an organ.

This line of interpretation discloses to us the underlying causes of sexual potency and of the instinct for knowledge as well, since to discover and to penetrate into things are activities which are equated in the unconscious. In addition to this, potency in the male (or, in the case of the young boy, the psychological conditions for it) is the basis for the development of a large number of activities and creative interests and capacities.

But—and this is the point I want to make—such a development hinges on the fact that the penis has become the representative of the person's ego. In the earliest stages of his life the male child looks upon his penis as the executive organ of his sadism, and consequently it becomes the vehicle of his primary feelings of omnipotence. For this reason, and because, being an external organ, it can be examined and put to the proof in various ways, it takes on the significance of his ego, his ego-functions and his consciousness; while the internalized and invisible penis of his father—his super-ego—about which he can know nothing, becomes the representative of his unconscious. If the child's fear of his super-ego and id is too powerful, he will not only be unable to know about the contents of his body and his mental processes, but will also be incapable of using his penis in its psychological aspect as a regulating and executive organ of the ego, so that his ego-functions will be subjected to inhibitions along these lines as well.

In John's case, finding the fountain-pen meant not only that he had acknowledged the existence of his penis and the pride and pleasure he took in it, but had also recognized the existence of his own ego—an attitude which found expression in a further advance of his ego-development and an enlargement of his ego-functions, as well as in a diminution of the power of his super-ego, which, up till now, had dominated the situation.

To sum up what has been said: While the improvement in John's capacity to conceive the condition of the inside of his *mother's body* led to a greater ability to understand and appreciate the outer world, the reduction of his inhibition against really knowing about the inside of his *own* body at the same time led to a deeper understanding and better control over his own mental process; he could then clear up and bring order into his own mind. The first resulted in a greater capacity to take in knowledge; the second entailed a better ability to work over, organize and correlate the knowledge obtained, and also to give it out again, *i.e.* return it, formulate it or express it—an advance in ego-development. These two fundamental contents of anxiety (relating to one's mother's body and one's own body) condition each other and react on each other in every detail, and in the same way the greater freedom of the two functions of introjection and extrajection (or projection), resulting from a reduction in the anxiety from these sources, allows both to be employed in a more appropriate and less compulsive way.

When, however, the super-ego exerts a too extensive domination over the ego, the latter frequently, in its attempts to maintain control over the id and the internalized objects by repression, shuts itself off from the influences of the outer world and objects there, and thus deprives itself of all sources of stimulus which would form the basis of ego-interests and achievements, both those from the id and those from external sources.

In those cases in which the significance of reality and real objects as reflections of the dreaded internal world and imagos has retained its preponderance, the stimuli from the external world may be felt to be nearly as alarming as the phantasied domination of the internalized objects, which have taken possession of all initiative and to which the ego feels compulsively bound to surrender the execution of all activities and intellectual operations, together of course with the responsibility for them. In certain cases, severe inhibitions in regard to learning are combined with great general intractability and ineducability and an attitude of knowing better; what I have then found is that the ego feels itself oppressed and paralysed on the one hand by the influences of the super-ego, which it feels to be tyrannical and dangerous, and on the other by its distrust of accepting the influences of the real objects, often because they are felt to be in complete opposition to the demands of the super-ego, but more often because they are too closely identified with the dreaded internal ones. The ego then tries (by means of projection on to the outer world) to demonstrate its independence from the imagos by rebelling against all the influences emanating from *real objects*. The degree to which a reduction of the sadism and anxiety and of the operation of the super-ego can be achieved, so that the ego acquires a broader basis on which to function, determines the degree of improvement in the patient's accessibility to influence by the external world, together with a progressive resolution of his intellectual inhibitions.

We have seen that the mechanisms we have been discussing lead to certain definite kinds of intellectual inhibitions. But when they enter into a clinical picture they take on the character of psychotic traits. We know already that John's fear of crabs as persecutors inside him was of a paranoid character. This anxiety of his, moreover, caused him to shut himself off from outside influences, objects and external reality—a state of mind which we regard as one of the indications of psychotic disturbance, though in this instance the main result was a lowering of the patient's intellectual capacities. But that even in cases like these the operation of such mechanisms is not confined to the production of intellectual inhibitions is seen from the great changes that take place in the person's whole being and character, no less than from the diminution of neurotic traits that can be observed, as the analysis of intellectual inhibition goes forward, especially if the patient is a child or young person.

In John, for instance, I was able to establish the fact that a marked apprehensiveness, secrecy and untruthfulness, as well as a very strong distrust of everything, which were part of his mental make-up, entirely disappeared in the course of his analysis, and that both his character and his ego-development underwent a very great change for the better. In his case the paranoid traits had for the most part been modified into certain distortions of character and intellectual inhibitions; but they had also, as it proved, led to a number of neurotic symptoms in him.

I will here mention one or two more mechanisms of intellectual inhibition, this time of a definitely obsessional-neurotic character, which appear as a result of the strong operation of early anxiety-situations. In alternation with an inhibition of the kind described above, we sometimes see the opposite extreme result—a craving to take in everything that offers itself, together with an inability to distinguish between what is valuable and what is worthless. In several cases I have noticed that these mechanisms would begin to set in and make their influence felt when analysis had succeeded in lessening those mechanisms of a psychotic type which we have just been discussing. This appetite for intellectual nourishment, which took the place of the child's former incapacity to take in anything, was accompanied by other obsessional impulses, in particular a desire to collect things and accumulate them, and by the corresponding compulsions to give things away indiscriminately, *i.e.* to eject them. Obsessional taking-in of this sort often goes with a feeling of empti-ness in the body, of impoverishment, etc.—a sensation which my patient John used to have very strongly—and rests upon the child's anxiety, derived from the deepest levels of its mind, lest its inside should have been destroyed or filled with 'bad' and dangerous substances, should be poor or quite lacking in 'good' substances. This anxiety-causing material undergoes a greater degree of re-modelling and alteration from the obsessional mechanisms than it does from the psychotic ones.

My observations of this case, as well as of other obsessional neurotics, have led me to certain conclusions about the special obsessional mechanisms concerned with the phenomenon of intel-lectual inhibition which is interesting us at present. Before stating them briefly, let me say that in my view, as I shall shortly set out in detail, obsessional mechanisms and symptoms in general serve the purpose of binding, modifying and warding-off anxiety belonging to the earliest levels of the mind; so that obsessional neuroses are built up upon the anxiety of the first danger-situations.

To return to the point: I think that the child's compulsive, almost greedy, collection and accumulation of things (including knowledge as a substance) is based, among other factors which need not be mentioned here, upon its ever-renewed attempt (*a*) to get hold of 'good' substances and objects (ultimately, 'good' milk, 'good' faeces, a 'good' penis and 'good' children) and with their help to paralyse the action of the 'bad' objects and substances inside its body; and (*b*) to amass sufficient reserves inside itself to be able to resist attacks made upon it by its external objects, and if necessary to restore to its mother's body, or rather, to its objects, what it has stolen from them. Since its endeavours to do this by means of obsessional actions are continually being disturbed by onsets of anxiety from many counter-sources (for instance, its doubt whether what it has just taken into itself is really 'good' and whether what it has cast out was really the 'bad' part of its inside; or its fear that in putting more material into itself it has once more been guilty of robbing its mother's body) we can understand why it is under a constant obligation to repeat its attempts and how that obligation is in part responsible for the compulsive character of its behaviour.

In the present case we have already seen how, in proportion as the influence of the child's ferocious and phantastic super-ego— ultimately, that is, his own sadism—was diminished, the mechanisms which we have recognized as psychotic and which gave rise to his intellectual inhibitions lost their effectiveness. A diminution of this kind in the severity of the super-ego seems to me to weaken those mechanisms of intellectual inhibition which are of the obsessional-neurotic type as well. If this is so, then it would show that the presence of excessively strong early anxiety-situations and the predominance of a threatening super-ego derived from the first stages of its formation are fundamental factors, not only in the genesis of the psychoses,[1] but in the production of disturbances of ego-development and intellectual inhibitions.

[1] For an exposition of this theory, cf. my papers 'Personification in the Play of Children', p. 199, and 'The Importance of Symbol-formation in the Development of the Ego', p. 219; also my *Psycho-Analysis of Children*.

THE EARLY DEVELOPMENT OF
CONSCIENCE IN THE CHILD

(1933)

ONE of the most important contributions of psycho-analytic research has been the discovery of the mental processes which underlie the development of conscience in the individual. In his work of bringing to light unconscious instinctual tendencies, Freud has also recognized the existence of those forces which serve as a defence against them. According to his findings, which psycho-analytic practice has borne out in every instance, the person's conscience is a precipitate or representative of his early relations to his parents. He has in some sense internalized his parents—has taken them into himself. There they become a differentiated part of his ego—his super-ego—and an agency which advances against the rest of his ego certain require-ments, reproaches, and admonitions, and which stands in opposition to his instinctual impulses.

Freud has since shown that the operation of this super-ego is not limited to the conscious mind, is not only what is meant by con-science, but also exerts an unconscious and often very oppressive influence which is an important factor both in mental illness and in the development of normal personality. This new discovery has brought the study of the super-ego and its origins more and more into the focus of psycho-analytic investigation.

In the course of my analysis of small children, as I began to get a direct knowledge of the foundations upon which their super-ego was built, I came upon certain facts which seemed to allow of an en-largement in some directions of Freud's theory on this subject. There could be no doubt that a super-ego had been in full operation for some time in my small patients of between two and three-quarters and four years of age, whereas according to the accepted view the super-ego would not begin to be activated until the Oedipus complex had died down—*i.e.* until about the fifth year of life. Furthermore, my data showed that this early super-ego was im-measurably harsher and more cruel than that of the older child or adult, and that it literally crushed down the feeble ego of the small child.

In the adult, it is true, we find a super-ego at work which is a great deal more severe than the subject's parents were in reality, and which is in other ways by no means identical with them.[1] Nevertheless it approximates to them more or less. But in the small child we come across a super-ego of the most incredible and phantastic character. And the younger the child is, or the deeper the mental level we penetrate to, the more this is the case. We get to look upon the child's fear of being devoured, or cut up, or torn to pieces, or its terror of being surrounded and pursued by menacing figures, as a regular component of its mental life; and we know that the man-eating wolf, the fire-spewing dragon, and all the evil monsters out of myths and fairy-stories flourish and exert their unconscious influence in the phantasy of each individual child, and it feels itself persecuted and threatened by those evil shapes. But I think we can know more than this. I have no doubt from my own analytic observations that the real objects behind those imaginary, terrifying figures are the child's own parents, and that those dreadful shapes in some way or other reflect the features of its father and mother, however distorted and phantastic the resemblance may be.

If we accept these facts of early analytic observation and recognize that the things the child fears are these internalized wild beasts and monsters which it equates with its parents, we are led to the following conclusions: (1) The super-ego of the child does not coincide with the picture presented by its real parents, but is created out of imaginary pictures or imagos of them which it has taken into itself; (2) its fear of real objects—its phobic anxiety—is based upon its fear both of its unrealistic super-ego and of objects which are real in themselves, but which it views in a phantastic light under the influence of its super-ego.

This brings us to the problem which seems to me to be the central one in the whole question of super-ego formation. How does it come about that the child creates such a phantastic image of its parents— an image that is so far removed from reality? The answer is to be found in the facts elicited in early analysis. In penetrating to the deepest layers of the child's mind and discovering those enormous quantities of anxiety—those fears of imaginary objects and those terrors of being attacked in all sorts of ways—we also lay bare a corresponding amount of repressed impulses of aggression, and can observe the causal connection which exists between the child's fears and its aggressive tendencies.

[1] In 'Symposium on Child-Analysis' (1927), similar views, based on adult analysis and seen from somewhat different angles, were put forward by Ernest Jones, Joan Riviere, Edward Glover and Nina Searl. Nina Searl has also had her view confirmed in her experience of child-analysis.

In his book, *Beyond the Pleasure Principle*, Freud (1920) put forward a theory according to which at the outset of the life of the human organism the instinct of aggression, or the death-instinct, is being opposed and bound by the libido, or life-instinct—the eros. A fusion of the two instincts ensues, and gives rise to sadism. In order to escape from being destroyed by its own death-instinct, the organism employs its narcissistic, or self-regarding libido to force the former outward, and direct it against its objects. Freud considers this process as fundamental for the person's sadistic relations to his objects. I should say, moreover, that parallel with this deflection of the death-instinct outward against objects, an intra-psychic reaction of defence goes on against that part of the instinct which could not be thus externalized. For the danger of being destroyed by this instinct of aggression sets up, I think, an excessive tension in the ego, which is felt by it as an anxiety,[1] so that it is faced at the very beginning of its development with the task of mobilizing libido against its death-instinct. It can, however, only imperfectly fulfil this task, since, owing to the fusion of the two instincts, it can no longer, as we know, effect a separation between them. A division takes place in the id, or instinctual levels of the psyche, by which one part of the instinctual impulses is directed against the other.

This apparently earliest measure of defence on the part of the ego constitutes, I think, the foundation-stone of the development of the super-ego, whose excessive violence in this early stage would thus be accounted for by the fact that it is an offshoot of very intense destructive instincts, and contains, along with a certain proportion of libidinal impulses, very large quantities of aggressive ones.[2]

This view of the matter makes it also less puzzling to understand why the child should form such monstrous and phantastic images of his parents. For he perceives his anxiety arising from his aggressive instincts as fear of an external object, both because he has made that object their outward goal, and because he has projected them on to it so that they seem to be initiated against himself from that quarter.[3]

He thus displaces the source of his anxiety outwards and turns his objects into dangerous ones; but, ultimately, that danger belongs to

---

[1] This tension is, it is true, felt as a libidinal tension as well, since the destructive and libidinal instincts are fused together; but its effect of causing anxiety is referable, in my opinion, to the destructive components in it.

[2] In his *Civilization and its Discontents* (*S.E.* **20**), Freud says: '. . . that the original severity of the super-ego does not—or does not so much—represent the severity which one has experienced from it [the object] or which one attributes to it; it represents rather one's own aggressiveness towards it' (pp. 129–30).

[3] The infant has, incidentally, some real grounds for fearing its mother, since it becomes growingly aware that she has the power to grant or withhold the gratification of its needs.

his own aggressive instincts. For this reason his fear of his objects will always be proportionate to the degree of his own sadistic impulses.

It is not, however, simply a question of converting a given amount of sadism into a corresponding amount of anxiety. The relation is one of content as well. The child's fear of its object and the imaginary attacks it will suffer from it adhere in every detail to the particular aggressive impulses and phantasies which it harbours against its environment. In this way each child develops parental imagos that are peculiar to itself; though in every case they will be of an unreal and terrifying character.

According to my observations, the formation of the super-ego begins at the same time as the child makes its earliest oral intro-jection of its objects.[1] Since the first imagos it thus forms are endowed with all the attributes of the intense sadism belonging to this stage of its development, and since they will once more be projected on to objects of the outer world, the small child becomes dominated by the fear of suffering unimaginable cruel attacks, both from its real objects and from its super-ego. Its anxiety will serve to increase its own sadistic impulses by urging it to destroy those hostile objects so as to escape their onslaughts. The vicious circle that is thus set up, in which the child's anxiety impels it to destroy its object, results in an increase of its own anxiety, and this once again urges it on against its object, and constitutes a psychological mechanism which, in my view, is at the bottom of asocial and criminal tendencies in the individual. Thus, we must assume that it is the excessive severity and overpowering cruelty of the super-ego, not the weakness or want of it, as is usually supposed, which is responsible for the be-haviour of asocial and criminal persons.

In a somewhat later stage of development, fear of the super-ego will cause the ego to turn away from the anxiety-arousing object. This defensive mechanism can lead to a defective or impaired object-relation on the part of the child.

As we know, when the genital stage sets in, the child's sadistic instincts have normally been overcome, and its relationship to objects has acquired a positive character. In my view such an advance in its development accompanies, and interacts with, alterations in the nature of its super-ego. For the more the child's sadism is lessened, the more the influence of its unreal and frightening

[1] This view is also based on my belief that the child's Oedipus tendencies, too, begin much earlier than has hitherto been thought, *i.e.* while it is still in the suckling stage, long before its genital impulses have become paramount. In my opinion the child incorporates its Oedipus objects during the oral-sadistic stage, and it is at this time, in close connection with its earliest Oedipus impulses, that its super-ego begins to develop.

imagos recedes into the background, since they are the offshoots of its own aggressive tendencies. And as its genital impulses grow in strength there emerge beneficent and helpful imagos, based upon its fixations, in the oral-sucking stage, on its generous and kindly mother, which approximate more closely to the real objects; and its super-ego, from being a threatening, despotic force issuing senseless and self-contradictory commands which the ego is totally unable to satisfy, begins to exert a milder and more persuasive rule and to make requirements which are capable of being fulfilled. In fact, it becomes transformed into conscience in the true sense of the word.

As the character of the super-ego changes, moreover, so will its effect upon the ego and the defensive mechanism it sets in motion there. We know from Freud that pity is a reaction to cruelty. But reactions of this kind do not set in until the child has attained some degree of positive object-relationship—until, in other words, its genital organization has come to the fore. If we place this fact side by side with the facts concerning the formation of the super-ego, as I see them, we shall be able to come to the following conclusions: so long as the function of the super-ego is mainly to arouse anxiety it will call out those violent defensive mechanisms in the ego which I have described above, and which are unethical and asocial in their nature. But as soon as the child's sadism is diminished and the character and function of its super-ego changed so that it arouses less anxiety and more sense of guilt, those defensive mechanisms which form the basis of a moral and ethical attitude are activated, and the child begins to have consideration for its objects and to be amenable to social feeling.[1]

Numerous analyses of children of all ages have borne out this view. In play-analysis we are able to follow the course of our patients' phantasies as represented in their games and play, and to establish a connection between those phantasies and their anxiety. As we proceed to analyse the content of their anxiety, we see the aggressive tendencies and phantasies which give rise to it come forward more and more, and grow to huge proportions, both in amount and intensity. The ego of the small child is in danger of being overwhelmed by their elemental force and enormous extent, and is engaged in a perpetual struggle to maintain itself against them with the help of its libidinal impulses, either by holding them under, or calming them down, or rendering them innocuous.

This picture exemplifies Freud's thesis of the life-instinct (eros)

---

[1] In analysing adults it was for the most part only these later functions and attributes of the super-ego that came under notice. Analysts were therefore inclined to regard them as constituting its specific character; and, indeed, only recognized the super-ego as such in so far as it appeared in this character.

at war with the death-instinct, or instinct of aggression. But we also recognize that there is the closest union and interaction between those two forces at every point, so that analysis can only succeed in tracing the child's aggressive phantasies in all their details, and thus diminishing their effect, in so far as it can follow up the libidinal ones and uncover their earliest sources as well—and vice versa.

Concerning the actual contents and aims of those phantasies, we know from Freud and Abraham that in the earliest, pregenital stages of libidinal organization, in which this fusion of libido and destructive instinct takes place, the sadistic impulses of the child are paramount. As the analysis of every grown-up person demonstrates, in the oral-sadistic stage which follows upon the oral-sucking one, the small child goes through a cannibalistic phase with which are associated a wealth of cannibalistic phantasies. These phantasies, although they are still centred on eating up the mother's breast or her whole person, are not solely concerned with the gratification of a primitive desire for nourishment. They also serve to gratify the child's destructive impulses. The sadistic phase which succeeds this —the anal-sadistic phase—is characterized by a dominating interest in excretory processes—in faeces and the anus; and this interest, too, is closely allied to extremely strong destructive tendencies.[1]

We know that the ejection of faeces symbolizes a forcible ejection of the incorporated object and is accompanied by feelings of hostility and cruelty, and by destructive desires of various kinds, the buttocks receiving importance as an object of these activities. In my opinion, however, the anal-sadistic tendencies contain more profound and deeply repressed aims and objects still. The data I have been able to collect from early analyses reveal that between the oral-sadistic and anal-sadistic stages there exists another stage in which urethral-sadistic tendencies make themselves felt, and that the anal and urethral tendencies are a direct continuation of the oral-sadistic ones as regards the specific aim and object of attack. In its oral-sadistic phantasies the child attacks its mother's breast, and the means it employs are its teeth and jaws. In its urethral and anal phantasies it seeks to destroy the inside of the mother's body, and uses its urine and faeces for this purpose. In this second group of phantasies the excrements are regarded as burning and corroding substances, wild animals, weapons of all kinds, etc.; and the child enters a phase in which it directs every instrument of its sadism to the one purpose of destroying its mother's body and what is contained in it.

[1] Besides Freud, the chief contributors to our knowledge of the influence this alliance has exerted upon character-formation and neurosis in the individual have been Jones, Abraham and Ferenczi.

As regards choice of object, the child's oral-sadistic impulses are still the underlying factor, so that it thinks of sucking out and eating up the inside of its mother's body as though it were a breast. But those impulses receive an extension from the child's first sexual theories, which it develops during this phase. We already knew that when its genital instincts awakened it began to have unconscious theories about copulation between its parents, birth of children, etc. But early analysis has shown that it develops such theories much earlier than this, at a time when its pregenital impulses still predominantly determine the picture though its as yet concealed genital impulses have some say in the matter. These theories are to the effect that in copulation the mother is continually incorporating the father's penis via the mouth, so that her body is filled with a great many penises and babies. All these the child desires to eat up and destroy.

In attacking its mother's inside, therefore, the child is attacking a great number of objects, and is embarking on a course which is fraught with consequences. The womb first stands for the world; and the child originally approaches this world with desires to attack and destroy it, and is therefore prepared from the outset to view the real, external world as more or less hostile to itself, and peopled with objects ready to make attacks upon it.[1] Its belief that in thus attacking its mother's body it has also attacked its father and its brothers and sisters, and, in a wider sense the whole world, is, in my experience, one of the underlying causes of its sense of guilt, and of the development of its social and moral feelings in general.[2] For when the excessive severity of the super-ego has become somewhat lessened, its visitations upon the ego on account of those imaginary attacks induce feelings of guilt which arouse strong tendencies in the child to make good the imaginary damage it has done to its objects. And now the individual content and details of its destructive phantasies help to determine the development of its sublimations, which indirectly subserve its restitutive tendencies,[3] or to produce even more direct desires to help other people.

[1] An excessive strength of such early anxiety-situations is, in my opinion, a fundamental factor in the production of psychotic disorders.

[2] Owing to the child's belief in the omnipotence of thought (cf. Freud, *Totem and Taboo*, 1913; Ferenczi, *Development of the Sense of Reality*, 1916)—a belief dating from an earlier stage of development—it confuses its imaginary attacks with real ones; and the consequences of this can still be seen at work in adult life.

[3] In my 'Infantile Anxiety Situations Reflected in a Work of Art and in the Creative Impulse' (1929) I have maintained that the person's sense of guilt and desire to restore the damaged object are a universal and fundamental factor in the development of his sublimations. Ella Sharpe in her paper, 'Certain Aspects of Sublimation and Delusion' (1930) has come to the same conclusion.

Play-analyses show that when the child's aggressive instincts are at their height it never tires of tearing and cutting up, breaking, wetting and burning all sorts of things like paper, matches, boxes, small toys, all of which represent its parents and brothers and sisters, and its mother's body and breasts, and that this rage for destruction alternates with attacks of anxiety and a sense of guilt. But when, in the course of analysis, anxiety slowly diminishes, his constructive tendencies begin to come to the fore.[1] For instance, where before a small boy has done nothing but chop bits of wood to pieces, he will now begin to try and make those bits of wood into a pencil. He will take pieces of lead got from pencils he has cut up, and put them in a crack in the wood, and then sew a piece of stuff round the rough wood to make it look nicer. That this home-made pencil represents his father's penis, which he has destroyed in phantasy, and his own, whose destruction he dreads as a measure of retaliation, is evident, furthermore, from the general context of the material he presents and from the associations he gives to it.

When, in the course of its analysis, the child begins to show stronger constructive tendencies in all sorts of ways in its play and its sublimations—painting or writing or drawing things instead of smearing everything with ashes, or sewing and designing where it used to cut up or tear to pieces—it also exhibits changes in its relation to its father or mother, or to its brothers and sisters; and these changes mark the beginning of an improved object-relationship in general, and a growth of social feeling. What channels of sublimation will become open to the child, how powerful will be its impulses to make restitution, and what forms they will assume—these things are determined not only by the extent of its primary aggressive tendencies, but by the interplay of a number of other factors, which we have no room to discuss in these pages. But our knowledge of child-analysis allows us to say this much, that analysis of the deepest layers of the super-ego invariably leads to a considerable betterment in the child's object-relationship, its capacity for sublimation, and its powers of social adaptation—that it makes the child not only happier and healthier in itself, but more capable of social and ethical feeling.

This brings us to the consideration of a very obvious objection that may be raised against child-analysis. It might be asked, would not too great a reduction in the severity of the super-ego—a reduction below a certain favourable level—have an opposite result and lead to the abolition of social and ethical sentiments in the child? The answer to this is, in the first place, that so great a diminution

[1] In analysis the resolution of anxiety is effected gradually and evenly, so that both it and the aggressive instincts are set free piecemeal.

has never, as far as I know, happened in fact; and, in the second place, that there are theoretical reasons for believing that it never can happen. As far as actual experience goes, we know that in analysing the pre-genital libidinal fixations we can only succeed in converting a certain amount of the libidinal quantities involved into genital libido, even in favourable circumstances, and that the remainder, and no unimportant remainder, continues to be operative as pre-genital libido and sadism; although, since the genital level has now more firmly established its supremacy, it can be better dealt with by the ego, either by receiving satisfaction, or by being kept down, or by undergoing modification or sublimation. In the same way analysis can never entirely do away with the sadistic nucleus of the super-ego which has been formed under the primacy of the pre-genital levels; but it can mitigate it by increasing the strength of the genital level, so that the now more powerful ego can deal with its super-ego, as it does with its instinctual impulses, in a manner that shall be more satisfactory both for the individual himself and for the world about him.

So far we have been concerned to establish the fact that the social and moral feelings of the person develop from a super-ego of a milder type, governed by the genital level. Now we must consider the inferences that follow from this. The deeper analysis penetrates into the lower levels of the child's mind, the more will it succeed in mitigating the severity of the super-ego by lessening the operation of its sadistic constituents that arise from the earliest stages of development. In doing this, analysis prepares the way not only for the achievement of social adaptability in the child, but for the development of moral and ethical standards in the adult; for a development of this kind depends upon both super-ego and sexuality having satisfactorily attained to a genital level at the close of the expansion of the child's sexual life.[1] so that the super-ego shall have developed the character and function from which the person's sense of guilt in so far as it is socially valuable — *i.e* his conscience — is derived.

Experience has already for some time shown that psycho-analysis, though originally devised by Freud as a method of curing mental disease, accomplishes a second purpose as well. It puts right disturbances of character-formation, especially in children and adolescents, where it is able to effect very considerable alterations. Indeed we may say that after it has been analysed, every child exhibits radical changes of character; nor can we avoid the conviction, based on observation of fact, that character-analysis is no less important than analysis of neuroses as a therapeutic measure.

[1] That is, when the latency-period sets in—approximately between the ages of five and six.

In view of these facts, one cannot help wondering whether psycho-analysis is not destined to go beyond the single individual in its range of operation and influence the life of mankind as a whole. The repeated attempts that have been made to improve humanity—in particular to make it more peaceable—have failed, because nobody has understood the full depth and vigour of the instincts of aggression innate in each individual. Such efforts do not seek to do more than encourage the positive, well-wishing impulses of the person while denying or suppressing his aggressive ones. And so they have been doomed to failure from the beginning. But psycho-analysis has different means at its disposal for a task of this kind. It cannot, it is true, altogether do away with man's aggressive instinct as such; but it can, by diminishing the anxiety which accentuates those instincts, break up the mutual reinforcement that is going on all the time between his hatred and his fear. When, in our analytic work, we are always seeing how the resolution of early infantile anxiety not only lessens and modifies the child's aggressive impulses, but leads to a more valuable employment and gratification of them from a social point of view; how the child shows an ever-growing, deeply rooted desire to be loved and to love, and to be at peace with the world about it; and how much pleasure and benefit, and what a lessening of anxiety it derives from the fulfilment of this desire—when we see all this, we are ready to believe that what would now seem a Utopian state of things may well come true in those distant days when, as I hope, child-analysis will become as much a part of every person's upbringing as school education is now. Then perhaps, that hostile attitude, springing from fear and suspicion, which is latent more or less strongly in each human being, and which intensifies a hundredfold in him every impulse of destruction, will give way to kindlier and more trustful feelings towards his fellow-men, and people may inhabit the world together in greater peace and good-will than they do now.

16

ON CRIMINALITY

(1934)

MR CHAIRMAN, Ladies and Gentlemen: When your Secretary asked me a day or two ago to speak to-night in the discussion I replied that I would do so with pleasure, but that I could not at such short notice work up anything like a paper or a contribution to this topic. I point this out as I am actually only going to put together loosely a few conclusions which I have formulated in other connections.[1]

In a paper[2] which I read to this Section in 1927 I endeavoured to show that criminal tendencies are also at work in normal children, and I threw out a few suggestions as to the factors which underlie an asocial or criminal development. I had found that children would show asocial and criminal tendencies, and act them out (of course in their childish way) over and over again, the more they were dreading a cruel retaliation from their parents as a punishment for their aggressive phantasies directed against those parents. Children who, unconsciously, were expecting to be cut to pieces, beheaded, devoured and so on, would feel compelled to be naughty and to get punished, because the real punishment, however severe, was reassuring in comparison with the murderous attacks which they were continuously expecting from fantastically cruel parents. I came to the conclusion in the paper to which I have just referred, that it is not (as is usually supposed) the weakness or lack of a super-ego, it is not in other words the lack of conscience, but the overpowering strictness of the super-ego, which is responsible for the characteristic behaviour of asocial and criminal persons.

Further work in the field of child-analysis has confirmed these suggestions and given a deeper insight into the mechanisms at work in such cases. The small child first harbours against its parents aggressive impulses and phantasies, it then projects these on to them, and thus it comes about that it develops a phantastic and distorted picture of the people around it. But the mechanism of introjection operates at the same time, so that these unreal imagos become internalized,

[1] *The Psycho-Analysis of Children* (1932) and 'Early Development of Conscience in the Child' (1933).
[2] 'Criminal Tendencies in Normal Children' (1927).

258

with the result that the child feels itself to be ruled by phantastically dangerous and cruel parents—the super-ego within itself.

In the early sadistic phase, which every individual normally passes through, the child protects himself against his fear of his violent objects, both introjected and external, by redoubling his attacks upon them in his imagination; his aim in thus getting rid of his objects is in part to silence the intolerable threats of his super-ego. A vicious circle is set up, the child's anxiety impels it to destroy its objects, this leads to an increase of its own anxiety, and this once again urges it on against its objects; this vicious circle constitutes the psychological mechanism which seems to be at the bottom of asocial and criminal tendencies in the individual.

When in the normal course of development both sadism and anxiety diminish, the child finds better and more social means and ways for mastering its anxiety. The better adaptation to reality enables the child to get more support against the phantastic imagos through its relation to the real parents. While in the earliest stages of development its aggressive phantasies against its parents, brothers and sisters aroused anxiety mainly lest those objects should turn against him, those tendencies now become the basis for feelings of guilt and the wish to make good what it has done in its imagination. Changes of the same kind come about as a result of analysis.

Play-analyses show that when the child's aggressive instincts and its anxiety are very strong, it goes on and on, tearing and cutting up, breaking, wetting, and burning all sorts of things such as paper, matches, boxes, small toys, which represent its parents, brothers and sisters, and its mother's body and breasts, and we also find that these aggressive activities alternate with severe anxiety. But when in analysis anxiety gradually gets resolved and thus sadism diminishes, feelings of guilt and constructive tendencies come to the fore, *e.g.* where formerly a small boy has done nothing but chop bits of wood to pieces, he will now begin to try and make those bits of wood into a pencil. He will take pieces of lead got from pencils which he has cut up, and put them in a crack in the wood and then sew a piece of stuff round the rough wood to make it look nicer. It is evident, from the general context of the material he presents and from the associations he gives, that this home-made pencil represents his father's penis, which he has destroyed in phantasy, and his own, whose destruction he dreads as a measure of retaliation.

The more the tendency and capacity to restitute increases and the more the belief and trust in those around him grows, the milder does the super-ego become, and vice versa. But in those cases in which, as a result of a strong sadism and an overwhelming anxiety (I can only briefly mention here some of the more important factors), the vicious

259

circle between hatred, anxiety and destructive tendencies cannot be broken, the individual remains under the stress of the early anxiety situations and retains the defensive mechanisms belonging to that early stage. If then fear of the super-ego, either for external or intrapsychic reasons, oversteps certain bounds, the individual may be compelled to destroy people and this compulsion may form the basis for the development either of a criminal type of behaviour or of a psychosis.

Thus we see that the same psychological roots may develop into paranoia, or into criminality. Certain factors will in the latter case lead to a greater tendency in the criminal to suppress unconscious phantasies and to act them out in reality. Phantasies of persecution are common to both conditions; it is because the criminal feels persecuted that he goes about destroying others. Naturally, in cases where children, not only in phantasy, but also in reality, experience some degree of persecution through unkind parents and miserable surroundings, the phantasies will be greatly reinforced. There is a common tendency to over-estimate the importance of unsatisfactory surroundings, in the sense that the internal psychological difficulties, which partly result from the surroundings, are not sufficiently appreciated. It depends, therefore, on the degree of the intrapsychical anxiety, whether or not it will avail much merely to improve the child's environment.

One of the great problems about criminals, which has always made them incomprehensible to the rest of the world, is their lack of natural human good feelings; but this lack is only apparent. When in analysis one reaches the deepest conflicts from which hate and anxiety spring, one also finds there the love as well. Love is not absent in the criminal, but it is hidden and buried in such a way that nothing but analysis can bring it to light; since the hated persecuting object was originally to the tiny baby the object of all its love and libido, the criminal is now in the position of hating and persecuting his own loved object; as this is an intolerable position all memory and consciousness of any love for any object must be suppressed. If there is nothing in the world but enemies, and that is how the criminal feels, his hate and destructiveness are, in his view, to a great extent justified—an attitude which relieves some of his unconscious feelings of guilt. Hate is often used as the most effective cover for love; but one must not forget that to the person who is under the continuous stress of persecution, the safety of his own ego is the first and only consideration.

Thus, to sum up: In cases where the function of the super-ego is mainly to arouse anxiety it will call out violent defensive mechanisms in the ego, which are unethical and asocial in their nature; but as soon as the child's sadism diminishes and the character and function of its super-ego changes so that it arouses less anxiety and more sense of guilt, those defensive mechanisms which form the basis of a moral and ethical attitude are activated, and the child begins to have consideration for its objects, and to be amenable to social feelings.

One knows how difficult it is to approach the adult criminal and to cure him, though we have no reason to be too pessimistic about it; but experience shows that one can approach and cure both criminal and psychotic children. It seems, therefore, that the best remedy against delinquency would be to analyse children who show signs of abnormality in the one direction or the other.

17

A CONTRIBUTION
TO THE PSYCHOGENESIS OF
MANIC-DEPRESSIVE STATES

(1935)

M Y earlier writings[1] contain the account of a phase of sadism at its height, through which children pass during the first year of life. In the very first months of the baby's existence it has sadistic impulses directed, not only against its mother's breast, but also against the inside of her body: scooping it out, devouring the contents, destroying it by every means which sadism can suggest. The development of the infant is governed by the mechanisms of introjection and projection. From the beginning the ego introjects objects 'good' and 'bad', for both of which the mother's breast is the prototype—for good objects when the child obtains it, for bad ones when it fails him. But it is because the baby projects its own aggression on to these objects that it feels them to be 'bad' and not only in that they frustrate its desires: the child conceives of them as actually dangerous—persecutors who it fears will devour it, scoop out the inside of its body, cut it to pieces, poison it—in short, compassing its destruction by all the means which sadism can devise. These imagos, which are a phantastically distorted picture of the real objects upon which they are based, become installed not only in the outside world but, by the process of incorporation, also within the ego. Hence, quite little children pass through anxiety-situations (and react to them with defence-mechanisms), the content of which is comparable to that of the psychoses of adults.

One of the earliest methods of defence against the dread of persecutors, whether conceived of as existing in the external world or internalized, is that of scotomization, the *denial of psychic reality*; this may result in a considerable restriction of the mechanisms of introjection and projection and in the denial of external reality, and forms the basis of the most severe psychoses. Very soon, too, the ego tries to defend itself against internalized persecutors by the processes of expulsion and projection. At the same time, since the

---

[1] *The Psycho-Analysis of Children,* chapters viii and ix.

dread of internalized objects is by no means extinguished with their projection, the ego marshals against the persecutors inside the body the same forces as it employs against those in the outside world. These anxiety-contents and defence-mechanisms form the basis of paranoia. In the infantile dread of magicians, witches, evil beasts, etc., we detect something of this same anxiety, but here it has already undergone projection and modification. One of my conclusions, moreover, was that infantile psychotic anxiety, in particular paranoid anxiety, is bound and modified by the obsessional mechanisms which make their appearance very early.

In the present paper I propose to deal with depressive states in their relation to paranoia on the one hand and to mania on the other. I have acquired the material upon which my conclusions are based from the analysis of depressive states in cases of severe neurosis, border-line cases and in patients, both adults and children, who displayed mixed paranoiac and depressive trends.

I have studied manic states in various degrees and forms, including the slightly hypomanic states which occur in normal persons. The analysis of depressive and manic features in normal children and adults also proved very instructive.

According to Freud and Abraham, the fundamental process in melancholia is the loss of the loved object. The real loss of a real object, or some similar situation having the same significance, results in the object becoming installed within the ego. Owing, however, to an excess of cannibalistic impulses in the subject, this introjection miscarries and the consequence is illness.

Now, why is it that the process of introjection is so specific for melancholia? I believe that the main difference between incorporation in paranoia and in melancholia is connected with changes in the relation of the subject to the object, though it is also a question of a change in the constitution of the introjecting ego. According to Edward Glover (1932), the ego, at first but loosely organized, consists of a considerable number of ego-nuclei. In his view, in the first place an oral ego-nucleus and later an anal ego-nucleus predominates over the others. In this very early phase, in which oral sadism plays a prominent part and which in my view is the basis of schizophrenia,[1] the ego's power of identifying itself with its objects is as yet small, partly because it is itself still unco-ordinated and partly because the introjected objects are still mainly partial objects, which it equates with faeces.

[1] I would refer the reader to my account of the phase in which the child makes onslaughts on the mother's body. This phase is initiated by the onset of oral sadism and in my view it is the basis of paranoia (cf. *The Psycho-Analysis of Children*, chapter viii).

In paranoia the characteristic defences are chiefly aimed at annihilating the 'persecutors', while anxiety on the ego's account occupies a prominent place in the picture. As the ego becomes more fully organized, the internalized imagos will approximate more closely to reality and the ego will identify itself more fully with 'good' objects. The dread of persecution, which was at first felt on the ego's account, now relates to the good object as well and from now on preservation of the good object is regarded as synonymous with the survival of the ego.

Hand in hand with this development goes a change of the highest importance; namely, from a partial object-relation to the relation to a complete object. Through this step the ego arrives at a new position, which forms the foundation of the situation called the loss of the loved object. Not until the object is loved *as a whole* can its loss be felt as a whole.

With this change in the relation to the object, new anxiety-contents make their appearance and a change takes place in the mechanisms of defence. The development of the libido also is decisively influenced. Paranoid anxiety lest the objects sadistically destroyed should themselves be a source of poison and danger inside the subject's body causes him, in spite of the vehemence of his oral-sadistic onslaughts, at the same time to be profoundly mistrustful of the objects while yet incorporating them.

This leads to a weakening of oral desires. One manifestation of this may be observed in the difficulties very young children often have in taking food; these difficulties I think have a paranoid root. As a child (or an adult) identifies himself more fully with a good object, the libidinal urges increase; he develops a greedy love and desire to devour this object and the mechanism of introjection is reinforced. Besides, he finds himself constantly impelled to repeat the incorporation of a good object—*i.e.* the repetition of the act is designed to test the reality of his fears and disprove them—partly because he dreads that he has forfeited it by his cannibalism and partly because he fears internalized persecutors against whom he requires a good object to help him. In this stage the ego is more than ever driven both by love and by need to introject the object.

Another stimulus for an increase of introjection is the phantasy that the loved object may be preserved in safety inside oneself. In this case the dangers of the inside are projected on to the external world.

If, however, consideration for the object increases, and a better acknowledgement of psychic reality sets in, the anxiety lest the object should be destroyed in the process of introjecting it leads—as Abraham has described—to various disturbances of the function of introjection.

In my experience there is, furthermore, a deep anxiety as to the dangers which await the object inside the ego. It cannot be safely maintained there, as the inside is felt to be a dangerous and poisonous place in which the loved object would perish. Here we see one of the situations which I described above, as being fundamental for 'the loss of the loved object'; the situation, namely, when the ego becomes fully identified with its good internalized objects, and at the same time becomes aware of its own incapacity to protect and preserve them against the internalized persecuting objects and the id. This anxiety is psychologically justified.

For the ego, when it becomes fully identified with the object, does not abandon its earlier defence-mechanisms. According to Abraham's hypothesis, the annihilation and expulsion of the object —processes characteristic of the earlier anal level—initiate the depressive mechanism. If this be so, it confirms my concept of the genetic connection between paranoia and melancholia. In my opinion, the paranoiac mechanism of destroying the objects (whether inside the body or in the outside world), by every means derived from oral, urethral and anal sadism, persists, but still in a lesser degree and with a certain modification due to the change in the subject's relation to his objects. As I have said, the dread lest the *good* object should be expelled along with the *bad* causes the mechanisms of expulsion and projection to lose value. We know that, at this stage, the ego makes a greater use of introjection of the *good* object as a mechanism of defence. This is associated with another important mechanism: that of making reparation to the object. In certain of my earlier works[1] I discussed in detail the concept of restoration and showed that it is far more than a mere reaction-formation. The ego feels impelled (and I can now add, impelled by its identification with the good object) to make restitution for all the sadistic attacks that it has launched on that object. When a well-marked cleavage between good and bad objects has been attained, the subject attempts to restore the former, making good in the restoration every detail of his sadistic attacks. But the ego cannot as yet believe enough in the benevolence of the object and in its own capacity to make restitution. On the other hand, through its identification with a good object and through the other mental advances which this implies, the ego finds itself forced to a fuller recognition of psychic reality, and this exposes it to fierce conflicts. Some of its objects (an indefinite number) are persecutors to it, ready to devour it and do violence to it. In all sorts of ways they endanger both the ego and the good object. Every injury inflicted in phantasy by the

[1] 'Infantile Anxiety Situations Reflected in a Work of Art and in the Creative Impulse' (1929); also *The Psycho-Analysis of Children*.

child upon its parents (primarily from hate and secondarily in self-defence), every act of violence committed by one object upon another (in particular the destructive, sadistic coitus of the parents, which the child regards as yet another result of its own sadistic wishes) — all this is played out, both in the outside world and, since the ego is constantly absorbing into itself the whole external world, within the ego as well. Now, however, all these processes are viewed as a perpetual source of danger both to the good object and to the ego.

It is true that, now that good and bad objects are more clearly differentiated, the subject's hate is directed rather against the latter, while his love and his attempts at reparation are more focused on the former; but the excess of his sadism and anxiety acts as a check to this advance in his mental development. Every internal or external stimulus (*e.g.* every real frustration) is fraught with the utmost danger: not only bad objects but also the good ones are thus menaced by the id, for every access of hate or anxiety may temporarily abolish the differentiation and thus result in a 'loss of the loved object'. And it is not only the vehemence of the subject's uncontrollable hatred but that of his love too which imperils the object. For at this stage of his development loving an object and devouring it are very closely connected. A little child which believes, when its mother disappears, that it has eaten her up and destroyed her (whether from motives of love or of hate) is tormented by anxiety both for her and for the good mother which it has absorbed into itself.

It now becomes plain why, at this phase of development, the ego feels itself constantly menaced in its possession of internalized good objects. It is full of anxiety lest such objects should die. Both in children and adults suffering from depression, I have discovered the dread of harbouring dying or dead objects (especially the parents) inside one and an identification of the ego with objects in this condition.

From the very beginning of psychic development there is a constant correlation of real objects with those installed within the ego. It is for this reason that the anxiety which I have just described manifests itself in a child's exaggerated fixation to its mother or whoever looks after it.[1] The absence of the mother arouses in the child anxiety lest it should be handed over to bad objects, external and internalized, either because of her *death* or because of her return in the guise of a '*bad*' mother.

[1] For many years now I have supported the view that the source of a child's fixation to its mother is not simply its dependence on her, but also its anxiety and sense of guilt, and that these feelings are connected with its early aggression against her.

Both cases mean to the child the loss of the loved mother, and I would particularly draw attention to the fact that dread of the loss of the 'good', internalized object becomes a perpetual source of anxiety lest the real mother should die. On the other hand, every experience which suggests the loss of the real loved object stimulates the dread of losing the internalized one too.

I have already stated that my experience has led me to conclude that the loss of the loved object takes place during that phase of development in which the ego makes the transition from partial to total incorporation of the object. Having now described the situation of the ego in that phase, I can express myself with greater precision on this point. The processes which subsequently become clear as the 'loss of the loved object' are determined by the subject's sense of failure (during weaning and in the periods which precede and follow it) to secure his *good, internalized* object, *i.e.* to possess himself of it. One reason for his failure is that he has been unable to overcome his paranoid dread of internalized persecutors.

At this point we are confronted with a question of importance for our whole theory. My own observations and those of a number of my English colleagues have led us to conclude that the direct influence of the early processes of introjection upon both normal and pathological development is very much more momentous, and in some ways differs from what has hitherto commonly been accepted in psycho-analytical circles.

According to our views, even the earliest incorporated objects form the basis of the super-ego and enter into its structure. The question is by no means a merely theoretical one. As we study the relations of the early infantile ego to its internalized objects and to the id, and come to understand the gradual changes these relations undergo, we obtain a deeper insight into the specific anxiety-situations through which the ego passes and the specific defence-mechanisms which it develops as it becomes more highly organized. Viewing them from this standpoint in our experience, we find that we arrive at a more complete understanding of the earliest phases of psychic development, of the structure of the super-ego and of the genesis of psychotic diseases. For where we deal with aetiology it seems essential to regard the libido-disposition not merely as such, but also to consider it in connection with the subject's earliest relations to his internalized and external objects, a consideration which implies an understanding of the defence mechanisms developed gradually by the ego in dealing with its varying anxiety-situations.

If we accept this view of the formation of the super-ego, its relentless severity in the case of the melancholic becomes more intelligible. The persecutions and demands of bad internalized objects; the attacks of such objects upon one another (especially that represented by the sadistic coitus of the parents); the urgent necessity to fulfil the very strict demands of the 'good objects' and to protect and placate them within the ego, with the resultant hatred of the id; the constant uncertainty as to the 'goodness' of a good object, which causes it so readily to become transformed into a bad one— all these factors combine to produce in the ego a sense of being a prey to contradictory and impossible claims from within, a condition which is felt as a bad conscience. That is to say: the earliest utterances of conscience are associated with persecution by bad objects. The very word 'gnawing of conscience' (*Gewissensbisse*) testifies to the relentless 'persecution' by conscience and to the fact that it is originally conceived of as devouring its victim.

Among the various internal demands which go to make up the severity of the super-ego in the melancholic, I have mentioned his urgent need to comply with the very strict demands of the 'good' objects. It is this part of the picture only—namely, the cruelty of the 'good', *i.e.* loved, objects within—which has been recognized by general analytic opinion; it became clear in the relentless severity of the super-ego in the melancholic. But in my view it is only by looking at the whole relation of the ego to its phantastically bad objects as well as to its good objects, only by looking at the whole picture of the internal situation which I have tried to outline in this paper, that we can understand the slavery to which the ego submits when complying with the extremely cruel demands and admonitions of its loved object which has become installed within the ego. As I have mentioned before, the ego endeavours to keep the good apart from the bad, and the real from the phantastic objects. The result is a conception of extremely bad and *extremely perfect* objects, that is to say, its loved objects are in many ways intensely moral and exacting. At the same time, as the infant cannot fully keep his good and bad objects apart in his mind,[1] some of the cruelty of the bad objects and of the id becomes attached to the good objects and this then again increases the severity of their demands.[2] These strict demands serve the purpose of supporting the ego in its fight against its uncontrollable hatred and its bad attacking objects, with which the

---

[1] I have explained that, gradually, by unifying and then splitting up the good and bad, the phantastic and the real, the external and the internal objects, the ego makes its way towards a more realistic conception both of the external and the internal objects and thus obtains a satisfactory relation to both. (Cf. *The Psycho-Analysis of Children.*)

[2] In *The Ego and the Id*, Freud (1923) has shown that in melancholia the destructive component has become concentrated in the super-ego and is directed against the ego.

ego is partly identified.[1] The stronger the anxiety is of losing the loved objects, the more the ego strives to save them, and the harder the task of restoration becomes, the stricter will grow the demands which are associated with the super-ego.

I have tried to show that the difficulties which the ego experiences when it passes on to the incorporation of whole objects proceed from its as yet imperfect capacity for mastering, by means of its new defence-mechanisms, the fresh anxiety-contents arising out of this advance in its development.

I am aware how difficult it is to draw a sharp line between the anxiety-content and feelings of the paranoiac and those of the depressive since they are so closely linked up with each other. But they can be distinguished one from the other if, as a criterion of differentiation, one considers whether the persecution-anxiety is mainly related to the preservation of the ego—in which case it is paranoiac—or to the preservation of the good internalized objects with which the ego is identified as a whole. In the latter case—which is the case of the depressive—the anxiety and feelings of suffering are of a much more complex nature. The anxiety lest the good objects and with them the ego should be destroyed, or that they are in a state of disintegration, is interwoven with continuous and desperate efforts to save the good objects both internalized and external.

It seems to me that only when the ego has introjected the object as a whole, and has established a better relationship to the external world and to real people, is it able fully to realize the disaster created through its sadism and especially through its cannibalism, and to feel distressed about it. This distress is related not only to the past but to the present as well, since at this early stage of development sadism is at its height. It requires a fuller identification with the loved object, and a fuller recognition of its value, for the ego to become aware of the state of disintegration to which it has reduced and is continuing to reduce its loved object. The ego then finds itself confronted with the psychic reality that its loved objects are in a state of dissolution.—in bits—and the despair, remorse and anxiety deriving from this recognition are at the bottom of numerous anxiety-situations. To quote only a few of them: there is anxiety how to put the bits together in the right way and at the right time; how to pick out the good bits and do away with the bad ones; how to bring the object to life when it has been put together; and there is the anxiety of being interfered with in this task by bad objects and by one's own hatred, etc.

[1] It is well known that some children display an urgent need to be kept under strict discipline and thus to be stopped by an external agency from doing wrong.

Anxiety-situations of this kind I have found to be at the bottom not only of depression, but of all inhibitions of work. The attempts to save the loved object, to repair and restore it, attempts which in the state of depression are coupled with despair, since the ego doubts its capacity to achieve this restoration, are determining factors for all sublimations and the whole of the ego-development. In this connection I shall only mention the specific importance for sublimation of the bits to which the loved object has been reduced and the effort to put them together. It is a 'perfect' object which is in pieces; thus the effort to undo the state of disintegration to which it has been reduced presupposes the necessity to make it beautiful and 'perfect'. The idea of perfection is, moreover, so compelling because it disproves the idea of disintegration. In some patients who had turned away from their mother in dislike or hate, or used other mechanisms to get away from her, I have found that there existed in their minds nevertheless a beautiful picture of the mother, but one which was felt to be a *picture* of her only, not her real self. The real object was felt to be unattractive—really an injured, incurable and therefore dreaded person. The beautiful picture had been dissociated from the real object but had never been given up, and played a great part in the specific ways of their sublimations.

It appears that the desire for perfection is rooted in the depressive anxiety of disintegration, which is thus of great importance in all sublimations.

As I have pointed out before, the ego comes to a realization of its love for a good object, a whole object and in addition a real object, together with an overwhelming feeling of guilt towards it. Full identification with the object based on the libidinal attachment, first to the breast, then to the whole person, goes hand in hand with anxiety for it (of its disintegration), with guilt and remorse, with a sense of responsibility for preserving it intact against persecutors and the id, and with sadness relating to expectations of the impending loss of it. These emotions, whether conscious or unconscious, are in my view among the essential and fundamental elements of the feelings we call love.

In this connection I may say we are familiar with the self-reproaches of the depressive which represent reproaches against the introjected object. But the ego's hate of the id, which is paramount in this phase, accounts even more for its feelings of unworthiness and despair than do its reproaches against the object. I have often found that these reproaches and the hatred against bad objects are secondarily increased as a defence against the hatred of the id, which is even more unbearable. In the last analysis it is the ego's unconscious knowledge that the hate is indeed also there, as well as the love, and that it may at any time get the upper hand (the ego's anxiety of being carried away by the id and so destroying the loved object), which brings about the sorrow, feelings of guilt and the despair which underlie grief. This anxiety is also responsible for the doubt in the goodness of the loved object. As Freud has pointed out, doubt is in reality a doubt of one's own love and 'a man who doubts his own love may, or rather *must*, doubt every lesser thing'.[1]

The paranoiac, I should say, has also introjected a whole and real object, but has not been able to achieve a full identification with it, or, if he has got as far as this, has not been able to maintain it. To mention a few of the reasons which are responsible for this failure: the persecution-anxiety is too great; suspicions and anxieties of a phantastic nature stand in the way of a full and stable introjection of a good object and a real one. In so far as it has been introjected, there is little capacity to maintain it as a good object, since doubts and suspicions of all kinds will soon turn the loved object again into a persecutor. Thus his relationship to whole objects and to the real world is still influenced by his early relation to internalized part-objects and faeces as persecutors and may again give way to the latter.

It seems to me characteristic of the paranoiac that, though, on account of his persecution-anxiety and his suspicions, he develops a very strong and acute power of observation of the external world and of real objects, this observation and his sense of reality are nevertheless distorted, since his persecution-anxiety makes him look at people mainly from the point of view of whether they are persecutors or not. Where the persecution-anxiety for the ego is in the ascendant, a full and stable identification with another object, in the sense of looking at it and understanding it as it really is, and a full capacity for love, are not possible.

Another important reason why the paranoiac cannot maintain his whole-object relation is that while the persecution-anxieties and the anxiety for himself are still so strongly in operation he cannot endure the additional burden of anxieties for a loved object, and, besides, the feelings of guilt and remorse which accompany this depressive position. Moreover, in this position he can make far less use of projection, for fear of expelling his good objects and so losing them, and, on the other hand, for fear of injuring good external objects by expelling what is bad from within himself.

Thus we see that the sufferings connected with the depressive position thrust him back to the paranoiac position. Nevertheless, though he has retreated from it, the depressive position has been

---

[1] 'Notes upon a Case of Obsessional Neurosis', *S.E.* **10**, p. 241.

reached and therefore the liability to depression is always there. This accounts, in my opinion, for the fact that we frequently meet depression along with severe paranoia as well as in milder cases.

If we compare the feelings of the paranoiac with those of the depressive in regard to disintegration, we can see that characteristically the depressive is filled with sorrow and anxiety for the object, which he would strive to unite again into a whole, while to the paranoiac the disintegrated object is mainly a multitude of persecutors, since each piece is growing again into a persecutor.[1] This conception of the dangerous fragments to which the object is reduced seems to me to be in keeping with the introjection of part-objects which are equated with faeces (Abraham), and with the anxiety of a multitude of internal persecutors to which, in my view,[2] the introjection of many part-objects and the multitude of dangerous faeces gives rise.

I have already considered the distinctions between the paranoiac and the depressive from the point of view of their different relations to loved objects. Let us take inhibitions and anxieties about food in this connection. The anxiety of absorbing dangerous substances destructive to one's inside will thus be paranoiac, while the anxiety of destroying the external good objects by biting and chewing, or of endangering the internal good object by introducing bad substances from outside into it, will be depressive. Again, the anxiety of leading an external good object into danger within oneself by incorporating it is a depressive one. On the other hand, in cases with strong paranoiac features I have met phantasies of luring an external object into one's inside, which was regarded as a cave full of dangerous monsters, etc. Here we can see the paranoiac reasons for an intensification of the introjection-mechanism, while the depressive employs this mechanism so characteristically, as we know, for the purpose of incorporating a *good* object.

Considering now hypochondriacal symptoms in this comparative way, the pains and other manifestations which in phantasy result from the attacks of persecuting objects within against the ego are typically paranoid.[3] The symptoms which derive, on the other hand, from the attacks of bad internal objects and the id against good ones,

[1] As Melitta Schmideberg has pointed out, cf. 'The Rôle of Psychotic Mechanisms in Cultural Development' (1931).

[2] *The Psycho-Analysis of Children.*

[3] Dr Clifford Scott mentioned in his course of lectures on Psychoses, at the Institute of Psycho-Analysis, in the autumn of 1934, that in his experience, in schizophrenia clinically the hypochondriacal symptoms are more manifold and bizarre and are linked to persecutions and part-object functions. This may be seen even after a short examination. In depressive reactions clinically the hypochondriacal symptoms are less varied and more related in their expression to ego-functions.

i.e. an internal warfare in which *the ego is identified with the sufferings of the good objects*, are typically depressive.

For instance, patient X, who had been told as a child that he had tapeworms (which he himself never saw) connected the tapeworms inside him with his greediness. In his analysis he had phantasies that a tapeworm was eating its way through his body and a strong anxiety of cancer came to the fore. The patient, who suffered from hypochondriacal and paranoid anxieties, was very suspicious of me, and, among other things, suspected me of being allied with people who were hostile towards him. At this time he dreamt that a detective was arresting a hostile and persecuting person and putting this person in prison. But then the detective proved unreliable and became the accomplice of the enemy. The detective stood for myself and the whole anxiety was internalized and was also connected with the tapeworm-phantasy. The prison in which the enemy was kept was his own inside—actually the special part of his inside where the persecutor was to be confined. It became clear that the dangerous tapeworm (one of his associations was that the tapeworm is bisexual) represented the two parents in a hostile alliance (actually in intercourse) against him.

At the time when the tapeworm-phantasies were being analysed the patient developed diarrhoea which—as X wrongly thought— was mixed with blood. This frightened him very much; he felt it as a confirmation of dangerous processes going on inside him. This feeling was founded on phantasies in which he attacked his bad united parents in his inside with poisonous excreta. The diarrhoea meant to him poisonous excreta, as well as the bad penis of his father. The blood which he thought was in his faeces represented me (this was shown by associations in which I was connected with blood). Thus the diarrhoea was felt to represent dangerous weapons with which he was fighting his bad internalized parents, a well as his poisoned and broken-up parents themselves—the tapeworm. In his early childhood he had in phantasy attacked his real parents with poisonous excreta and actually disturbed them in intercourse by defaecating. Diarrhoea had always been something very frightening to him. Along with these attacks on his real parents his whole warfare became internalized and threatened his ego with destruction. I may mention that this patient remembered during his analysis that at about ten years of age he had definitely felt that he had a little man inside his stomach who controlled him and gave him orders, which he, the patient, had to execute, although they were always perverse and wrong (he had had similar feelings about his real father's requests).

When the analysis progressed and distrust in me had diminished, the patient became very much concerned about me. X had always worried about his mother's health; but he had not been able to develop real love towards her, though he did his best to please her. Now, together with the concern for me, strong feelings of love and gratitude came to the fore, together with feelings of unworthiness, sorrow and depression. The patient had never felt really happy, his depression had been spread out, one might say, over his whole life, but he had not suffered from actual depressed states. In his analysis he went through phases of deep depression with all the symptoms characteristic of this state of mind. At the same time the feelings and phantasies connected with his hypochondriacal pains changed. For instance, the patient felt anxiety that the cancer would make its way through the lining of his stomach; but now it appeared that, while he feared for his stomach, he really wanted to protect 'me' inside him—actually the internalized mother—who he felt was being attacked by the father's penis and by his own id (the cancer). Another time the patient had phantasies (connected with physical discomfort) about an internal haemorrhage from which he would die. It became clear that I was identified with the haemorrhage, the good blood representing me. We must remember that, when the paranoid anxieties dominated and I was mainly felt as a persecutor, I had been identified with the *bad* blood which was mixed with the diarrhoea (with the bad father). Now the precious *good* blood represented me—losing it meant my death, which would imply his death. It became clear now that the cancer which he made responsible for the death of his loved object, as well as for his own, and which stood for the bad father's penis, was even more felt to be his own sadism, especially his greed. That is why he felt so unworthy and so much in despair.

While the paranoid anxieties predominated and the anxiety of his bad united objects prevailed, X felt only hypochondriacal anxieties for his own body. When depression and sorrow had set in, the love and the concern for the good object came to the fore and the anxiety-contents as well as the whole feelings and defences altered. In this case, as well as in others, I have found that *paranoid fears and suspicions were reinforced as a defence against the depressive position* which was overlaid by them. I shall now quote another case, Y, with strong paranoiac and depressive features (paranoia predominating) and with hypochondria. His complaints about manifold physical troubles, which occupied a large part of the hours, alternated with strong feelings of suspicion about people in his environment and often became directly related to them, since he made them reponsible for his physical troubles in one way or another. When, after hard analytic work, distrust and suspicion diminished, his relation to me improved more and more. It became clear that, buried under the continuous paranoid accusations, complaints and criticisms of others, there existed a very profound love for his mother and concern for his parents as well as for other people. At the same time sorrow and severe depression came more and more to the fore. During this phase the hypochondriacal complaints altered, both in the way they were presented to me and in the content which underlay them. For instance, the patient complained about different physical troubles and then went on to say what medicines he had taken—enumerating what he had done for his chest, his throat, his nose, his ears, his intestines, etc. It sounded rather as if he were nursing these parts of his body and his organs. He went on to speak about his concern for some young people under his care (he is a teacher) and then about the worry he was feeling for some members of his family. It became quite clear that the different organs he was trying to cure were identified with his internalized brothers and sisters, about whom he felt guilty and whom he had to be perpetually keeping alive. It was his *over-anxiousness* to put them right, because he had damaged them in phantasy, and his *excessive* sorrow and despair about it, which had led to such an increase of the paranoid anxieties and defences that love and concern for people and identification with them became buried under hate. In this case, too, when depression came to the fore in full force and the paranoid anxieties diminished, the hypochondriacal anxieties became related to the internalized loved objects and thus to the ego, while before they had been experienced in reference to the ego only.

After having attempted to differentiate between the anxiety-contents, feelings and defences at work in paranoia and those in the depressive states, I must again make clear that in my view the depressive state is based on the paranoid state and genetically derived from it. I consider the depressive state as being the result of a mixture of paranoid anxiety and of those anxiety-contents, distressed feelings and defences which are connected with the impending loss of the whole loved object. It seems to me that to introduce a term for those specific anxieties and defences might further the understanding of the structure and nature of paranoia as well as of the manic-depressive states.[1]

---

[1] This brings me to another question of terminology.

In my former work I have described the psychotic anxieties and mechanisms of the child in terms of phases of development. The genetic connection between them, it is true, is given full justice by this description, and so is the fluctuation which goes on between them under the pressure of anxiety until more stability is reached; but since in normal development the psychotic anxieties and mechanisms never solely

In my view, wherever a state of depression exists, be it in the normal, the neurotic, in manic-depressives or in mixed cases, there is always in it this specific grouping of anxieties, distressed feelings and different varieties of these defences, which I have here described and called the depressive position.

If this point of view proves correct, we should be able to understand those very frequent cases where we are presented with a picture of mixed paranoiac and depressive trends, since we could then isolate the various elements of which it is composed.

The considerations that I have brought forward in this paper about depressive states may lead us, in my opinion, to a better understanding of the still rather enigmatic reaction of suicide. According to the findings of Abraham and James Glover, a suicide is directed against the introjected object. But, while in committing suicide the ego intends to murder its bad objects, in my view at the same time it also always aims at saving its loved objects, internal or external. To put it shortly: in some cases the phantasies underlying suicide aim at preserving the internalized good objects and that part of the ego which is identified with good objects, and also at destroying the other part of the ego which is identified with the bad objects and the id. Thus the ego is enabled to become united with its loved objects.

In other cases, suicide seems to be determined by the same type of phantasies, but here they relate to the external world and real objects, partly as substitutes for the internalized ones. As already stated, the subject hates not only his 'bad' objects, but his id as well and that vehemently. In committing suicide, his purpose may be to make a clean breach in his relation to the outside world because he desires to rid some real object—or the 'good' object which that whole world represents and which the ego is identified with—of himself, or of that part of his ego which is identified with his bad objects and his id.[1] At bottom we perceive in such a step his reaction to his own sadistic attacks on his mother's body, which to a little child is the first representative of the outside world. Hatred and revenge against the real (good) objects also always play an important part in such a step, but it is precisely the uncontrollable danger-

---

predominate (a fact which, of course, I have emphasized) the term psychotic phases is not really satisfactory. I am now using the term 'position' in relation to the child's early developmental psychotic anxieties and defences. It seems to me easier to associate with this term, than with the words 'mechanisms' or 'phases', the differences between the developmental psychotic anxieties of the child and the psychoses of the adult: *e.g.* the quick change-over that occurs from a persecution-anxiety or depressed feeling to a normal attitude—a change-over that is so characteristic for the child.

[1] These reasons are largely responsible for that state of mind in the melancholic in which he breaks off all relations with the external world.

ous hatred, which is perpetually welling up in him, from which the melancholic by his suicide is in part struggling to preserve his real objects.

Freud has stated that mania has for its basis the same contents as melancholia and is, in fact, a way of escape from that state. I would suggest that in mania the ego seeks refuge not only from melancholia but also from a paranoiac condition which it is unable to master. Its torturing and perilous dependence on its loved objects drives the ego to find freedom. But its identification with these objects is too profound to be renounced. On the other hand, the ego is pursued by its dread of bad objects and of the id and, in its effort to escape from all these miseries, it has recourse to many different mechanisms, some of which, since they belong to different phases of development, are mutually incompatible.

The *sense of omnipotence*, in my opinion, is what first and foremost characterizes mania and, further (as Helene Deutsch, 1933, has stated) mania is based on the mechanism of *denial*. I differ, however, from Helene Deutsch in the following point. She holds that this 'denial' is connected with the phallic phase and the castration complex (in girls it is a denial of the lack of the penis); while my observations have led me to conclude that this mechanism of denial originates in that very early phase in which the undeveloped ego endeavours to defend itself from the most overpowering and profound anxiety of all, namely, its dread of internalized persecutors and of the id. That is to say, that which is *first of all denied is psychic reality* and the ego may then go on to deny a great deal of external reality.

We know that scotomization may lead to the subject's becoming entirely cut off from reality, and to his complete inactivity. In mania, however, denial is associated with an overactivity, although this excess of activity, as Helene Deutsch points out, often bears no relation to any actual results achieved. I have explained that in this state the source of the conflict is that the ego is unwilling and unable to renounce its good internal objects and yet endeavours to escape from the perils of dependence on them as well as from its bad objects. Its attempt to detach itself from an object without at the same time completely renouncing it seems to be conditioned by an increase in the ego's own strength. It succeeds in this compromise by *denying the importance* of its good objects and also of the dangers with which it is menaced from its bad objects and the id. At the same time, however, it endeavours ceaselessly to *master and control* all its objects, and the evidence of this effort is its hyperactivity.

What in my view is quite specific for mania is the *utilization of the sense of omnipotence* for the purpose of *controlling and mastering* objects.

This is necessary for two reasons: (*a*) in order to deny the dread of them which is being experienced, and (*b*) so that the mechanism (acquired in the previous—the depressive—position) of making reparation to the object may be carried through.[1] By mastering his objects the manic person imagines he will prevent them not only from injuring himself but from being a danger to one another. His mastery is to enable him particularly to prevent dangerous coitus between the parents he has internalized and their death within him.[2] The manic defence assumes so many forms that it is, of course, not easy to postulate a general mechanism. But I believe that we really have such a mechanism (though its varieties are infinite) in this mastery of the internalized parents, while at the same time the existence of this internal world is being depreciated and denied. Both in children and in adults I have found that, where obsessional neurosis was the most powerful factor in the case, such mastery betokened a forcible separation of two (or more) objects; whereas, where mania was in the ascendant, the patient had recourse to methods more violent. That is to say, the objects were killed but, since the subject was omnipotent, he supposed he could also immediately call them to life again. One of my patients spoke of this process as 'keeping them in suspended animation'. The killing corresponds to the defence-mechanism (retained from the earliest phase) of destruction of the object; the resuscitation corresponds to the reparation made to the object. In this position the ego effects a similar compromise in its relation to real objects. The hunger for objects, so characteristic of mania, indicates that the ego has retained one defence-mechanism of the depressive position: the introjection of good objects. The manic subject *denies* the different forms of anxiety associated with this introjection (anxiety, that is to say, lest either he should introject bad objects or else destroy his good objects by the process of introjection); his denial relates not merely to the impulses of the id but to his own concern for the object's safety. Thus we may suppose that the process by which the ego and ego-ideal comes to coincide (as Freud has shown that they do in mania) is as follows. The ego incorporates the object in a cannibalistic way (the 'feast', as Freud calls it in his account of mania) but denies that it feels any concern for it. 'Surely,' argues the ego, 'it is not a matter of such great importance if this particular object is destroyed. There are so many others to be incorporated.' This *disparagement of the object's importance and the contempt for it* is, I think, a specific charac-

---

[1] This 'reparation', in accordance with the phantastic character of the whole position, is nearly always of a quite unpractical and unrealizable nature.

[2] Bertram Lewin (1933) reported about an acute manic patient who identified herself with both parents in intercourse.

teristic of mania and enables the ego to effect that partial detachment which we observe side by side with its hunger for objects. Such detachment, which the ego cannot achieve in the depressive position, represents an advance, a fortifying of the ego in relation to its objects. But this advance is counteracted by those earlier mechanisms described which the ego at the same time employs in mania.

Before I go on to make a few suggestions about the part which the paranoid, depressive and manic positions play in normal development, I shall speak about two dreams of a patient which illustrate some of the points I have put forward in connection with the psychotic positions. Various symptoms of which I shall here only mention severe states of depression and paranoid and hypochondriacal anxieties, had induced the patient C to come for analysis. At the time he dreamt these dreams his analysis was well advanced. He dreamt that he was travelling with his parents in a railway-carriage, probably without a roof, since they were in the open air. The patient felt that he was 'managing the whole thing', taking care of the parents, who were much older and more in need of his care than in reality. The parents were lying in bed, not side by side, as they usually did, but with the ends of the beds joined together. The patient found it difficult to keep them warm. Then the patient urinated, while his parents were watching him, into a basin in the middle of which there was a cylindrical object. The urination seemed complicated, since he had to take special care not to urinate into the cylindrical part. He felt this would not have mattered had he been able to aim exactly into the cylinder and not to splash anything about. When he had finished urinating he noticed that the basin was overflowing and felt this as unsatisfactory. While urinating he noticed that his penis was very large and he had an uncomfortable feeling about this—as if his father ought not to see it, since he would feel beaten by him and he did not want to humiliate his father. At the same time he felt that by urinating he was sparing his father the trouble of getting out of bed and urinating himself. Here the patient stopped, and then said that he really felt as if his parents were a part of himself. In the dream the basin with the cylinder was supposed to be a Chinese vase, but it was not right, because the stem was not underneath the basin, as it should have been, it was 'in the wrong place', since it was above the basin—really inside it. The patient then associated the basin to a glass bowl, as used for gas-burners in his grandmother's house, and the cylindrical part reminded him of a gas-mantle. He then thought of a dark passage, at the end of which there was a low-burning gas-light, and said that this picture evoked in him sad feelings. It made him think of poor and dilapidated houses, where there seemed to be nothing alive but this low-burning gas-light. It is true, one had only to pull the string and then the light would burn fully. This reminded him that he had always been frightened of gas and that the flames of a gas-ring made him feel that they were jumping out at him, biting him, as if they were a lion's head. Another thing which frightened him about gas was the 'pop' noise it made, when it was put out. After my interpretation that the cylindrical part in the basin and the gas-mantle were the same thing and that he was afraid to urinate into it because he did not want for some reason to put the flame out, he replied that of course one cannot extinguish a gas-flame in this way, as then poison remains behind—it is not like a candle which one can simply blow out.

The night after this the patient had the following dream: he heard the frizzling sound of something which was frying in an oven. He could not see what it was, but he thought of something brown, probably a kidney which was frying in a pan. The noise he heard was like the squeaking or crying of a tiny voice and his feeling was that a live creature was being fried. His mother was there and he tried to draw her attention to this, and to make her understand that to fry something alive was much the worst thing to do, worse than boiling or cooking it. It was more torturing since the hot fat prevented it from burning altogether and kept it alive while skinning it. He could not make his mother understand this and she did not seem to mind. This worried him but in a way it reassured him, as he thought it could not be so bad after all if she did not mind. The oven, which he did not open in the dream—he never saw the kidney and the pan—reminded him of a refrigerator. In a friend's flat he had repeatedly mixed up the refrigerator door with the oven door. He wonders whether heat and cold are, in a way, the same thing for him. The torturing hot fat in the pan reminds him of a book about tortures which he had read as a child; he was especially excited by beheadings and by tortures with hot oil. Beheading reminded him of King Charles. He had been very excited over the story of his execution and later on developed a sort of devotion towards him. As regards tortures with hot oil, he used to think a great deal about them, imagining himself in such a situation (especially his legs being burnt), and trying to find out how, if it had to be done, it could be done so as to cause the least possible pain.

On the day the patient told me this second dream, he had first remarked on the way I struck my match for lighting a cigarette. He said it was obvious that I did not strike the match in the right way as a bit of the top had flown towards him. He meant I did not strike it at the right angle, and then went on to say, 'like his father, who served the balls the wrong way at tennis'. He wondered how often it had happened before in his analysis that the top of the match had flown towards him. (He had remarked once or twice before that I must have silly matches, but now the criticism applied to my way of striking them.) He did not feel inclined to talk, complaining that he had developed a heavy cold in the last two days; his head felt very heavy and his ears were blocked up, the mucus was thicker than it had been at other times when he had a cold. Then he told me the dream which I have already given, and in the course of the associations once again mentioned the cold and that it made him so disinclined to do anything.

Through the analysis of these dreams a new light was thrown on some fundamental points in the patient's development. These had already come out and been worked through before in his analysis, but now they appeared in new connections and then became fully clear and convincing to him. I shall now single out only the points bearing on the conclusions arrived at in this paper; I may mention that I have no space to quote all the important associations given.

The urination in the dream led on to the early aggressive phantasies of the patient towards his parents, especially directed against their sexual intercourse. He had phantasied biting them and eating them up, and among other attacks, urinating on and into his father's penis, in order to skin and burn it and to make his father set his mother's inside on fire in their intercourse (the torturing with hot oil). These phantasies extended to babies inside his mother's body, which were to be killed (burnt). The kidney burnt alive stood both for his father's penis—equated with faeces—and for the babies inside his mother's body (the stove which he did not open). Castration of the father was expressed by the associations about beheading. Appropriation of the father's penis was shown by the feeling that his penis was so large and that he urinated both for himself and for his father (phantasies of having his father's penis inside his own or joined on to his own had come out a great deal in his analysis). The patient's urinating into the bowl meant also his sexual intercourse with his mother (whereby the bowl and the mother in the dream represented her both as a real and as an internalized figure). The impotent and castrated father was made to look on at the patient's intercourse with his mother—the reverse of the situation the patient had gone through in phantasy in his childhood. The wish to humiliate his father is expressed by his feeling that he ought not to do so. These (and other) sadistic phantasies had given rise to different anxiety-contents: the mother could not be made to understand that she was endangered by the burning and biting penis inside her (the burning and biting lion's head, the gas-ring which he had lit), and that her babies were in danger of being burnt, at the same time being a danger to herself (the kidney in the oven). The patient's feeling that the cylindrical stem was 'in the wrong place' (inside the bowl instead of outside) expressed not only his early hate and jealousy that his mother took his father's penis into herself, but also his anxiety about this dangerous happening. The phantasy of keeping the kidney and the penis alive while they were being tortured expressed both the destructive tendencies against the father and the babies, and, to a certain degree the wish to preserve them. The special position of the beds—different from the one in the actual bedroom— in which the parents were lying, showed not only the primary aggressive and jealous drive to separate them in their intercourse, but also the anxiety lest they should be injured or killed by intercourse which in his phantasies the son had arranged to be so dangerous. The death-wishes against the parents had led to an overwhelming anxiety about their death. This is shown by associations and feelings about the low-burning gas-light, the advanced age of the parents in the dream (older than in reality), their helplessness and the necessity for the patient to keep them warm.

One of the defences against his feelings of guilt and his responsibility for the disaster he had arranged was brought out by the association of the patient that I am striking the matches, and that his father serves tennis balls, in the wrong way. Thus he makes the parents responsible for their own wrong and dangerous intercourse, but the fear of retaliation based on projection (my burning him) is expressed by his remark that he wondered how often during his analysis tops of my matches had flown towards him, and all the other anxiety-contents related to attacks against him (the lion's head, the burning oil).

The fact that he had internalized (introjected) his parents is shown in the following: (1) the railway-carriage, in which he was travelling with his parents, continuously taking care of them, 'managing the whole thing', represented his own body; (2) the carriage was open, in contrast to his feeling, representing their internalization, that he could not free himself from his internalized objects, but its being open was a denial of this; (3) that he had to do everything for his parents, even to urinate for his father; (4) the definite expression of a feeling that they were a part of himself.

But through the internalization of his parents all the anxiety-situations which I have mentioned before in regard to the real parents became internalized and thus multiplied, intensified and, partly, altered in character. His mother containing the burning penis and the dying children (the oven with frying pan) is inside him. Furthermore there are his parents having dangerous intercourse inside him and the necessity to keep them separated. This necessity became the source of many anxiety-situations and was found in his analysis to be at the bottom of his obsessional symptoms. At any time the parents may have dangerous intercourse, burn and eat each other, and, since his ego has become the place where all these danger-situations are acted out, destroy him as well. Thus he has at the same time to bear great anxiety both for them and for himself. He is full of sorrow about the impending death of the internalized parents, but at the same time he dare not bring them back to full life (he dare not pull the string of the gas-burner), since intercourse would be implied in their coming fully to life and this would then result in their death and his.

Then there are the dangers threatening from the id. If jealousy and hate stirred by some real frustration are welling up in him, he will again in his phantasy attack the internalized father with his burning excreta, disturbing the parents' intercourse, which gives rise to renewed anxiety. Either external or internal stimuli may increase his paranoid anxieties of internalized persecutors. If he then kills his father inside him altogether, the dead father becomes a persecutor of a special kind. We see this from the patient's remark (and his subsequent associations) that if the gas is extinguished by liquid, poison remains behind. Here the paranoid position comes to the fore and the dead object within becomes equated with faeces and flatus.[1] However, the paranoid position, which had been very strong in the patient at the beginning of his analysis, but was then greatly diminished, did not appear much in the dreams.

What dominates the dreams are the distressed feelings which are connected with anxiety for his loved objects and, as I have pointed out before, are characteristic for the depressive position. In the dreams the patient deals with the depressive position in different ways. He uses the sadistic manic control over his parents by keeping them separated from each other and thus stopping them in pleasurable as well as in dangerous intercourse. At the same time, the way in which he takes care of them is indicative of obsessional mechanisms. But his main way of overcoming the depressive position is reparation. In the dream he devotes himself entirely to his parents in order to keep them alive and comfortable. His concern for his mother goes back to his earliest childhood, and the drive to put her right and to restore her as well as his father, and to make babies

---

[1] In my experience the paranoiac conception of a dead object within is one of a secret and uncanny persecutor. He is felt as not being fully dead and perhaps reappearing at any time in cunning and plotting ways, and seeming all the more dangerous and hostile because the subject tried to do away with him by killing him (the concept of a dangerous ghost).

grow, plays an important part in all his sublimations. The connection between the dangerous happenings in his inside and his hypochondriacal anxieties is shown by the patient's remarks about the cold he had developed at the time he had the dreams. It appeared that the mucus, which was so extraordinarily thick, was identified with the urine in the bowl—with the fat in the pan—at the same time with his semen, and that in his head which he felt so heavy, he carried the genitals of his parents (the pan with the kidney). The mucus was supposed to preserve his mother's genital from contact with that of his father and at the same time it implied sexual intercourse with his mother within. The feeling which he had in his head was that of its being blocked up, a feeling which corresponded to the blocking off of one parent's genital from the other, and so separating his internal objects. One stimulus for the dream had been a real frustration which the patient experienced shortly before he had these dreams; though this experience did not lead to a depression, it influenced his emotional balance unconsciously: this became evident from the dreams. In the dreams the strength of the depressive position appears increased and the effectiveness of the patient's strong defences is, to a certain amount, reduced. This was not so in his actual life. It is interesting that another stimulus for the dreams was of a very different kind. It happened after this painful experience that he went recently with his parents on a short journey which he very much enjoyed. Actually the dream started in a way which reminded him of this pleasant journey, but then the depressive feelings overshadowed the gratifying ones. As I pointed out before, the patient used formerly to worry a great deal about his mother, but this attitude has changed during his analysis, and he has now quite a happy and care-free relation to his parents.

The points which I stressed in connection with the dreams seem to me to show that the process of internalization, which sets in in the earliest stage of infancy, is instrumental for the development of the psychotic positions. We see how, as soon as the parents become internalized, the early aggressive phantasies against them lead to the paranoid fear of external and, still more, internal persecutions, produce sorrow and distress about the impending death of the incorporated objects, together with hypochondriacal anxieties, and give rise to an attempt to master in an omnipotent manic way the unbearable sufferings within, which are imposed on the ego. We also see how the masterful and sadistic control of the internalized parents becomes modified as the tendencies to restoration increase.

Space does not permit me to deal here in detail with the ways in which the normal child works through the depressive and manic positions, which in my view make up a part of normal development.[1] I shall confine myself therefore to a few remarks of a general nature

In my former work I have brought forward the view which I referred to at the beginning of this paper, that in the first few months of its life the child goes through paranoid anxieties related to the 'bad' denying breasts, which are felt as external and internalized persecutors.[2] From this relation to part-objects, and from their equation with faeces, springs at this stage the phantastic and unrealistic nature of the child's relation to all objects; to parts of its own body, people and things around it, which are at first but dimly perceived. The object-world of the child in the first two or three months of its life could be described as consisting of hostile and persecuting, or else of gratifying parts and portions of the real world. Before long the child perceives more and more of the whole person of the mother, and this more realistic perception extends to the world beyond the mother. (The fact that a good relation to its mother and to the external world helps the baby to overcome its early paranoid anxieties throws a new light on the importance of its earliest experiences. From its inception analysis has always laid stress on the importance of the child's early experiences, but it seems to me that only since we know more about the nature and contents of its early anxieties, and the continuous interplay between its actual experiences and its phantasy-life, can we fully understand *why* the external factor is so important.) But when this happens its sadistic phantasies and feelings, especially its cannibalistic ones, are at their height. At the same time the child now experiences a change in its emotional attitude towards its mother. Its libidinal fixation to the breast develops into feelings towards her as a person. Thus feelings both of a destructive and of a loving nature are experienced towards one and the same object and this gives rise to deep and disturbing conflicts in the child's mind.

In the normal course of events the ego is faced at this point of its development—roughly between four and five months of age—with the necessity to acknowledge psychic reality as well as the external reality to a certain degree. It is thus made to realize that

[1] Edward Glover (1932) makes the suggestion that the child in its development goes through phases which provide the foundation for the psychotic disorders of melancholia and mania.

[2] Dr Susan Isaacs (1934) has suggested in her remarks on 'Anxiety in the First Year of Life', that the child's earliest experiences of painful external and internal stimuli provide a basis for phantasies about hostile external and internal objects and that they largely contribute to the building up of such phantasies. It seems that in the very earliest stage every unpleasant stimulus is related to the 'bad', denying, persecuting breasts, every pleasant stimulus to the 'good', gratifying breasts.

the loved object is at the same time the hated one; and, in addition to this, that the real objects and the imaginary figures, both external and internal, are bound up with each other. I have pointed out elsewhere that in the very young child there exist, side by side with its relations to real objects—but on a different plane, as it were— relations to its unreal imagos, both as excessively good and excessively bad figures,[1] and that these two kinds of object-relations intermingle and colour each other to an ever-increasing degree in the course of development.[2] The first important steps in this direction occur, in my view, when the child comes to know its mother as a whole person and becomes identified with her as a whole, real and loved person. It is then that the depressive position—the characteristics of which I have described in this paper—come to the fore. This position is stimulated and reinforced by the 'loss of the loved object' which the baby experiences over and over again when the mother's breast is taken away from it, and this loss reaches its climax during weaning. Sandor Radó (1923) has pointed out that 'the deepest fixation-point in the depressive disposition is to be found in the situation of threatened loss of love (Freud), more especially in the hunger situation of the suckling baby'. Referring to Freud's statement that in mania the ego is once more merged with the super-ego in unity, Radó comes to the conclusion that 'this process is the faithful intrapsychic repetition of the experience of that fusing with the mother that takes place during drinking at her breast'. I agree with these statements, but my views differ in important points from the conclusions which Radó arrives at, especially about the indirect and circuitous way in which he thinks that guilt becomes connected with these early experiences. I have pointed out before that, in my view, already during the sucking period, when it comes to know its mother as a whole person and when it progresses from the introjection of part-objects to the introjection of the whole object, the infant experiences some of the feelings of guilt and remorse, some of the pain which results from the conflict between love and uncontrollable hatred, some of the anxieties of the impending death of the loved internalized and external objects—that is to say, in a lesser and milder degree the sufferings and feelings which we find fully developed in the adult melancholic. Of course these feelings are experienced in a different setting. The whole situation and the defences of the baby, who obtains reassurance over and over again in the love of the mother, differ greatly from those in the adult melancholic. But the important point is that these sufferings, conflicts, and feelings

[1] Cf. 'Early Stages of the Oedipus Conflict', and 'Personification in the Play of Children'.
[2] *The Psycho-Analysis of Children*, chapter viii.

of remorse and guilt, resulting from the relation of the ego to its internalized object, are already active in the baby. The same applies, as I suggested, to paranoid and manic positions. If the infant at this period of life fails to establish its loved object within—if the introjection of the 'good' object miscarries—then the situation of the 'loss of the loved object' arises already in the same sense as it is found in the adult melancholic. This first and fundamental external loss of a real loved object, which is experienced through the loss of the breast before and during weaning, will only result in later life in a depressive state if at this early period of development the infant has failed to establish its loved object within its ego. In my view it is also at this early stage of development that the manic phantasies, first of controlling the breast, and very soon after, of controlling the internalized parents as well as the external ones, set in with all the characteristics of the manic position which I have described, and are made use of to combat the depressive position. At any time that the child finds the breast again, after having lost it, the manic process by which the ego and ego-ideal come to coincide (Freud) is set going; for the child's gratification at being fed is not only felt to be a cannibalistic incorporation of external objects (the 'feast' in mania, as Freud calls it), but also sets going cannibalistic phantasies relating to the internalized loved objects and connects with the control over these objects. No doubt, the more the child can at this stage develop a happy relationship to its real mother, the more will it be able to overcome the depressive position. But all depends on how it is able to find its way out of the conflict between love and uncontrollable hatred and sadism. As I have pointed out before, in the earliest phase the persecuting and the good objects (breasts) are kept wide apart in the child's mind. When, along with the introjection of the whole and real object, they come closer together, the ego has over and over again recourse to that mechanism—so important for the development of the relations to objects—namely, a splitting of its imagos into loved and hated, that is to say, into good and dangerous ones.

One might think that it is actually at this point that ambivalence which, after all, refers to object-relations—that is to say, to whole and real objects—sets in. Ambivalence, carried out in a splitting of the imagos, enables the young child to gain more trust and belief in its real objects and thus in its internalized ones—to love them more and to carry out in an increasing degree its phantasies of restoration of the loved object. At the same time the paranoid anxieties and defences are directed towards the 'bad' objects. The support which the ego gets from a real 'good' object is increased by a flight-mechanism, which alternates between its external and internal good objects.

It seems that at this stage of development the unification of external and internal, loved and hated, real and imaginary objects is carried out in such a way that each step in the unification leads again to a renewed splitting of the imagos. But, as the adaptation to the external world increases, this splitting is carried out on planes which gradually become increasingly nearer and nearer to reality. This goes on until love for the real and the internalized objects and trust in them are well established. Then ambivalence, which is partly a safeguard against one's own hate and against the hated and terrifying objects, will in normal development again diminish in varying degrees.

Along with the increase in love for one's good and real objects goes a greater trust in one's capacity to love and a lessening of the paranoid anxiety of the bad objects—changes which lead to a decrease of sadism and again to better ways of mastering aggression and working it off. The reparation-tendencies which play an all-important part in the normal process of overcoming the infantile depressive position are set going by different methods, of which I shall just mention two fundamental ones: the manic and the obsessional defences and mechanisms.

It would appear that the step from the introjection of part-objects to whole loved objects with all its implications is of the most crucial importance in development. Its success—it is true—depends largely on how the ego has been able to deal with its sadism and its anxiety in the preceding stage of development and whether or not it has developed a strong libidinal relation to part-objects. But once the ego has made this step it has, as it were, arrived at a crossroads from which the ways determining the whole mental make-up radiate in different directions.

I have already considered at some length how a failure to maintain the identification with both internalized and real loved objects may result in psychotic disorders, such as depressive states, mania, or paranoia.

I shall now mention one or two other ways by which the ego attempts to make an end to all the sufferings which are connected with the depressive position, namely: (a) by a 'flight to the "good", internalized object', a mechanism to which Melitta Schmideberg (1930) has drawn attention in connection with schizophrenia. The ego has introjected a whole loved object, but owing to its immoderate dread of internalized persecutors, which are projected on to the external world, the ego takes refuge in an extravagant belief in the benevolence of his internalized objects. The result of such a flight may be denial of psychic and external reality and the deepest psychosis.

(*b*) By a flight to external 'good' objects as a means to disprove all anxieties—internal as well as external. This is a mechanism which is characteristic for neurosis and may lead to a slavish dependence on objects and to a weakness of the ego.

These defence-mechanisms, as I pointed out before, play their part in the normal working-through of the infantile depressive position. Failure to work successfully through this position may lead to the predominance of one or another of the flight-mechanisms referred to and thus to a severe psychosis or a neurosis.

I have emphasized in this paper that, in my view, the infantile depressive position is the central position in the child's development. The normal development of the child and its capacity for love would seem to rest largely on how the ego works through this nodal position. This again depends on the modification undergone by the earliest mechanisms (which remain at work in normal persons) in accordance with the changes in the ego's relations to its objects, and especially on a successful interplay between the depressive, the manic and the obsessional positions and mechanisms.

18

WEANING

(1936)

ONE of the most fundamental and far-reaching discoveries ever made in human history was Freud's finding that there exists an unconscious part of the mind and that the nucleus of this unconscious mind is developed in earliest infancy. Infantile feelings and phantasies leave, as it were, their imprints on the mind, imprints which do not fade away but get stored up, remain active, and exert a continuous and powerful influence on the emotional and intellectual life of the individual. The earliest feelings are experienced in connection with external and internal stimuli. The first gratification which the child derives fron the external world is the satisfaction experienced in being fed. Analysis has shown that only one part of this satisfaction results from the alleviation of hunger and that another part, no less important, results from the pleasure which the baby experiences when his mouth is stimulated by sucking at his mother's breast. This gratification is an essential part of the child's sexuality, and is indeed its initial expression. Pleasure is experienced also when the warm stream of milk runs down the throat and fills the stomach.

The baby reacts to unpleasant stimuli, and to the frustration of his pleasure, with feelings of hatred and aggression. These feelings of hatred are directed towards the same objects as are the pleasurable ones, namely, the breasts of the mother.

Analytic work has shown that babies of a few months of age certainly indulge in phantasy-building. I believe that this is the most primitive mental activity and that phantasies are in the mind of the infant almost from birth. It would seem that every stimulus the child receives is immediately responded to by phantasies, the unpleasant stimuli, including mere frustration, by phantasies of an aggressive kind, the gratifying stimuli by those focusing on pleasure.

As I said before, the object of all these phantasies is, to begin with, the breast of the mother. It may seem curious that the tiny child's interest should be limited to a part of a person rather than to the whole, but one must bear in mind first of all that the child has an extremely undeveloped capacity for perception, physical and mental, at this stage, and then we must remember the all-important fact that the tiny child is only concerned with his immediate gratification or the lack of it; Freud called this the 'pleasure-pain principle'. Thus the breast of the mother which gives gratification or denies it becomes, in the mind of the child, imbued with the characteristics of good and evil. Now, what one might call the 'good' breasts become the prototype of what is felt throughout life to be good and beneficent, while the 'bad' breasts stand for everything evil and persecuting. The reason for this can be explained by the fact that, when the child turns his hatred against the denying or 'bad' breast, he attributes to the breast itself all his own active hatred against it.—a process which is termed *projection*.

But there is another process of great importance going on at the same time, namely, that of *introjection*. By this is meant the mental activity in the child, by which, in his phantasy, he takes into himself everything which he perceives in the outside world. We know that at this stage the child receives his main satisfaction through his mouth, which therefore becomes the main channel through which the child takes in not only his food, but also, in his phantasy, the world outside him. Not only the mouth, but to a certain degree the whole body with all its senses and functions, performs this 'taking in' process—for instance, the child breathes in, takes in through his eyes, his ears, through touch and so on. To begin with, the breast of the mother is the object of his constant desire, and therefore this is the first thing to be introjected. In phantasy the child sucks the breast into himself, chews it up and swallows it; thus he feels that he has actually got it there, that he possesses the mother's breast within himself, in both its good and in its bad aspects.

The child's focusing on and attachment to a part of the person is characteristic of this early stage of development, and accounts in great measure for the phantastic and unrealistic nature of his relation to everything, for example, to parts of his own body, to people and to inanimate objects, all of which are at first of course only dimly perceived. The object world of the child in the first two or three months of its life could be described as consisting of gratifying or of hostile and persecuting parts or portions of the real world. At about this age he begins to see his mother and others about him as 'whole people', his realistic perception of her (and them) coming gradually as he connects her face looking down at him with the hands that caress him and with the breast that satisfies him, and the power to perceive 'wholes' (once the pleasure in 'whole persons' is assured and he has confidence in them) spreads to the external world beyond the mother.

At this time other changes too are taking place in the child. When the baby is a few weeks old, one can observe that he begins definitely to enjoy periods in his waking life; judging by appearances, there are times when he feels quite happy. It seems that at about the age just mentioned localized overstrong stimuli diminish (in the beginning, for instance, defaecation is often felt as unpleasant), and a much better co-ordination begins to be established in the exercise of the different bodily functions. This leads not only to a better physical but also to a better mental adaptation to external and internal stimuli. One can surmise that stimuli which at first were felt as painful, no longer are so and some of them have even become pleasant. The fact that lack of stimuli can now be felt as an enjoyment in itself, indicates that he is no longer so much swayed by painful feelings, caused by unpleasant stimuli, or so avid for pleasurable ones in connection with the immediate and full gratification given by feeding; his better adaptation towards stimuli renders the necessity for immediate and strong gratification less urgent.[1]

I have referred to the early phantasies and fears of persecution in connection with the hostile breasts, and I have explained how they are connected with the phantastic object-relationship of the tiny child. The child's earliest experiences of painful external and internal stimuli provide a basis for phantasies about hostile external and internal objects, and they contribute largely to the building up of such phantasies.[2]

In the earliest stage of mental development every unpleasant stimulus is apparently related in the baby's phantasy to the 'hostile' or denying breasts, every pleasant stimulus on the other hand to the 'good', gratifying breasts. It seems that here we have two circles, the one benevolent and the other vicious, both of which are based on the interplay of external or environmental and internal psychical factors; thus any lessening of the amount or intensity of painful stimuli or any increase in the capacity to adjust to them should help to diminish the strength of phantasies of a frightening nature, and a decrease of frightening phantasies in its turn enables the child to take steps towards a better adaptation to reality, and this helps to diminish the frightening phantasies.

It is important for the proper development of the mind that the child should come under the influence of the benevolent circle I have just outlined; when this happens he is greatly assisted in forming an image of his mother as a person; this growing perception of the mother as a whole implies not only very important changes in his intellectual, but also in his emotional development.

[1] In this connection I am reminded of a comment made recently by Dr Edward Glover; he pointed out that the abrupt change between very painful and very pleasurable sensations might be felt as painful in itself.

[2] Dr Susan Isaacs emphasized the importance of this point in a paper to the British Psycho-Analytical Society (January, 1934).

I have already mentioned that phantasies and feelings of an aggressive and of a gratifying, erotic nature, which are to a large extent fused together (a fusion which is called sadism), play a dominant part in the child's early life. They are first of all focused on the breasts of his mother, but gradually extend to her whole body. Greedy, erotic and destructive phantasies and feelings have for their object the inside of the mother's body. In his imagination the child attacks it, robbing it of everything it contains and eating it up.

At first the destructive phantasies are more of a sucking nature. Something of this is shown in the powerful way with which some children will suck, even when milk is plentiful. The nearer the child comes to the time of cutting teeth, the more the phantasies take on the nature of biting, tearing, chewing up and thus destroying their object. Many mothers find that long before the child cuts his teeth these biting tendencies show themselves. Analytic experience has proved that these tendencies go along with phantasies of a definitely cannibalistic nature. The destructive quality of all these sadistic phantasies and feelings, as we find from the analysis of small children, is in full swing when the child begins to perceive his mother as a whole person.

At the same time he now experiences a change in his emotional attitude towards the mother. The child's pleasurable attachment to the breast develops into feelings towards her as a person. Thus feelings both of a destructive and of a loving nature are experienced towards one and the same person and this gives rise to deep and disturbing conflicts in the child's mind.

It is, in my view, very important for the child's future that he should be able to progress from the early fears of persecution and a phantastic object-relationship to the relation to the mother as a whole person and a loving being. When, however, he succeeds in doing this, feelings of guilt arise in connection with the child's own destructive impulses, which he now fears to be a danger to his loved object. The fact that at this stage of development the child is unable to control his sadism, as it wells up at any frustration, still further aggravates the conflict and his concern for the loved one. Again it is very important that the child should deal satisfactorily with these conflicting feelings—love, hatred and guilt—which are aroused in this new situation. If the conflicts prove unbearable the child cannot establish a happy relationship with his mother, and the way lies open for many failures in subsequent development. I wish especially to mention states of undue or abnormal depression which, in my view, have their deepest source in the failure to deal satisfactorily with these early conflicts.

But let us now consider what happens when the feelings of guilt and fear of the death of his mother (which is dreaded as a result of his unconscious wishes for her death) are dealt with adequately. These feelings have, I think, far-reaching effects on the child's future mental well-being, his capacity for love and his social development. From them springs *the desire to restore*, which expresses itself in numerous phantasies of saving her and making all kinds of reparation. These tendencies to make reparation I have found in the analysis of small children to be the driving forces in all constructive activities and interests, and for social development. We find them at work in the first play-activities and at the basis of the child's satisfaction in his achievements, even those of the most simple kind for example, in putting one brick on top of another, or making a brick stand upright after it had been knocked down—all this is partly derived from the unconscious phantasy of making some kind of restoration to some person or several persons whom he has injured in phantasy. But more than this, even the much earlier achievements of the baby, such as playing with his fingers, finding something which had rolled aside, standing up and all sorts of voluntary movements—these too, I believe, are connected with phantasies in which the reparation element is already present.

The analysis of quite small children—in recent years children of even between one and two years have been analysed—show that babies of a few months connect their faeces and urine with phantasies in which these materials are regarded as presents. Not only are they presents, and as such are indications of love towards their mother or nurse, but they are also regarded as being able to effect a restoration. On the other hand, when the destructive feelings are dominant the baby will in his phantasy defaecate and urinate in anger and hatred, and use his excrements as hostile agents. Thus the excrements produced with friendly feelings are, in fantasy, used as a means of making good the injuries inflicted also by the agency of faeces and urine in moments of anger.

It is impossible within the scope of this paper to deal adequately with the connection between aggressive phantasies, fears, feelings of guilt and the wish to make reparation; nevertheless, I have touched on this topic because I wanted to indicate that aggressive feelings, which lead to so much disturbance in the child's mentality, are at the same time of the highest value for his development.

I have already mentioned that the child mentally takes into himself—introjects—the outside world as far as he can perceive it. First he introjects the good and bad breasts, but gradually it is the whole mother (again conceived as a good and bad mother) which he takes into himself. Along with this the father and the other people in the child's surroundings are taken in as well, to begin with in a lesser degree but in the same manner as the relation to the mother; these figures grow in importance and acquire independence in the child's mind as time goes on. If the child succeeds in establishing within himself a kind and helpful mother, this internalized mother will prove a most beneficial influence throughout his whole life. Though this influence will normally change in character with the development of the mind, it is comparable with the vitally important place that the real mother has in the tiny child's very existence. I do not mean that the 'internalized' good parents will consciously be felt as such (even in the small child the feeling of possessing them inside is deeply unconscious), they are not felt consciously to be there, but rather as something within the personality having the nature of kindness and wisdom; this leads to confidence and trust in oneself and helps to combat and overcome the feelings of fear of having bad figures within one and of being governed by one's own uncontrollable hatred; and furthermore, this leads to trust in people in the outside world beyond the family circle.

As I have pointed out above, the child feels any frustration very acutely; though some progress towards adaptation to reality is normally going on all the time, the child's emotional life seems dominated by the cycle of gratification and frustration; but the feelings of frustration are of a very complicated nature. Dr Ernest Jones found that frustration is always felt as deprivation: if the child cannot obtain the desired thing, he feels that it is being withheld by the nasty mother, who has power over him.

Coming to our main problem, we find that the child feels, when the breast is wanted but is not there, as if it were lost for ever; since the conception of the breast extends to that of the mother, the feelings of having lost the breast lead to the fear of having lost the loved mother entirely, and this means not only the real mother, but also the good mother within. In my experience this fear of the total loss of the good object (internalized and external) is interwoven with feelings of guilt at having destroyed her (eaten her up), and then the child feels that her loss is a punishment for his dreadful deed; thus the most distressing and conflicting feelings become associated with frustration, and it is these which make the pain of what seems like a simple thwarting so poignant. The actual experience of weaning greatly reinforces these painful feelings or tends to substantiate these fears; but in so far as the baby never has uninterrupted possession of the breast, and over and over again is in the state of lacking it, one could say that, in a sense, he is in a constant state of being weaned or at least in a state leading up to weaning. Nevertheless, the crucial point is reached at the actual weaning when the loss is complete and the breast or bottle is gone irrevocably.

I might quote from my experience a case in which the feelings connected with this loss were very clearly shown. Rita, aged two years and nine months when she came for analysis, was a very neurotic child with fears of all kinds, and most difficult to bring up; her quite unchildlike depressions and feelings of guilt were very striking. She was very much tied to her mother, displaying at times an exaggerated love and at others antagonism. She was, at the time she came to me, still having one bottle at night-time and the mother told me that she had had to continue this, since she had found that the child showed too much distress when she attempted to stop giving it to her. Rita's weaning had been very difficult. She had been breast fed for a few months, had then been given bottles which at first she did not want to accept; then she got used to them, and displayed again great difficulties when the bottles were replaced by ordinary food. When, during her analysis with me, she was weaned from this last bottle, she fell into a state of despair. She lost her appetite, refused food, clung more than ever to her mother, asking her constantly whether she loved her, if she had been naughty, and so on. It could not have been a question of food in itself, as the milk was only part of her diet, and moreover the same amount of milk was given to her, but out of a glass. I had advised the mother to give Tita the milk herself, adding a biscuit or two, and sitting at her bed-side or taking her on her lap. But the child did not want to have the milk. Her analysis revealed that her despair was due to her anxiety lest her mother die or to the fear of her mother punishing her cruelly for her badness. What she felt as 'badness' was actually her unconscious wishes for her mother's death both in the present and in the past. She was overwhelmed by anxiety of having destroyed, and especially of having eaten up her mother, and the loss of the bottle was felt as the confirmation that she had done so. Even looking at her mother did not disprove these fears until they were resolved by analysis. In this case the early fears of persecution had not been sufficiently overcome, and the personal relation to the mother had never been well established. This failure was on the one hand due to the child's inability to deal with her overstrong conflicts, and on the other hand—and this again becomes part of the internal conflict— to the actual conduct of her mother who was a highly neurotic person.

It is evident that a good human relationship between the child and his mother at the time when these basic conflicts set in and are largely worked through is of the highest value. We must remember that at the critical time of weaning the child, as it were, loses his 'good' object, that is, he loses what he loves most. Anything which makes the loss of an external good object less painful and diminishes the fear of being punished, will help the child to preserve the belief in his good object within. At the same time it will prepare the way for the child to keep up, in spite of the frustration, a happy relation to his real mother and to establish pleasurable relations with people other than his parents. Then he will succeed in obtaining satisfactions, which will replace the all-important one which he is just about to lose.

Now, what can we do to help the child in this difficult task? The preparations for this task start at birth. From the very beginning the mother must do everything she can to help the child to establish a happy relationship with her. So often we find that the mother does everything in her power for the child's physical condition; she concentrates on this as if the child were a material thing which needs constant upkeep, like a valuable machine rather than a human being. This is the attitude of many paediatricians who are mostly concerned with the physical development of the child, and are only interested in his emotional reactions in so far as they indicate something about his physical or intellectual state. Mothers often do not realize that a tiny baby is already a human being whose emotional development is of highest importance.

A good contact between mother and child may be jeopardized at the first or at the first few feeds by the fact that the mother does not know how to induce the baby to take the nipple; if, for example, instead of dealing patiently with the difficulties as they arise, the nipple is pushed rather roughly into the baby's mouth, he may fail to develop a strong attachment to the nipple and to the breast, and become a difficult feeder. On the other hand, one can observe how babies who show this initial difficulty develop under patient assistance into quite as good feeders as those who have no initial difficulty at all.[1]

There are many other occasions than just at the breast when the baby will feel and unconsciously record his mother's love, patience and understanding—or the contrary. As I have already pointed out, the earliest feelings are experienced in connection with internal and external stimuli—pleasant or unpleasant—and are associated with phantasies. The way in which the baby is handled even from the time of delivery from the womb is bound to leave impressions on his mind.

Though the infant in the earliest stage of his development cannot yet relate the pleasant feelings, which the care and patience of the mother rouse in him, to her as a 'whole person', it is of vital importance that these pleasurable feelings and the sense of trust should be experienced. Everything which makes the baby feel that it is

[1] I have to thank Dr D. Winnicott for many illuminating details on this subject.

surrounded with friendly objects, though these are, to begin with, conceived of, for the most part, as 'good breasts', prepares the ground for and contributes to the building up of a happy relation to the mother and later on to other people around him.

A balance must be kept between physical and psychical necessities. The regularity of feeding has proved to be of great value for the baby's physical well-being, and this again influences the psychical development; but there are many children who, in the early days at any rate, cannot easily sustain breaks of too long duration between the feeds; in these cases it is better not to keep rigidly to rules, and to feed the baby every three hours or even under this, and, if necessary, to give a sip of dill-water or sugar water in between times.

I think the use of the comforter is helpful. It is true that it has a disadvantage—not of a hygienic nature, for that can be overcome—but of a psychological nature, namely the disappointment for the baby, when in sucking he does not receive the desired milk; but at any rate he has the partial gratification in being able to suck. If he is not allowed the comforter he will probably all the more suck his fingers; as the use of the comforter can be better regulated than the sucking of the fingers, the baby can better be weaned from the comforter. One might begin the weaning gradually, e.g., to give it only before the child settles down to sleep, or if he is not quite well, and so on.

As regards the question of weaning from thumb-sucking, Dr Middlemore (1936) expresses the opinion that on the whole the child should not be weaned from sucking his thumb. There is something to be said in favour of this view. Frustrations which can be avoided should not be inflicted on the child. Furthermore, there is the fact to be considered that overstrong frustrations of the mouth may lead to an intensified need for compensatory genital pleasure, for example, compulsive masturbation, and that some of the intrinsic frustrations experienced at the mouth are carried over to the genital.

But there are other aspects to be considered as well. In unbridled sucking of the thumb or the comforter there is a danger of overstrong mouth-fixation; (I mean by this that the libido is hindered in its natural movement from the mouth to the genital), while mild frustration of the mouth would have the desirable effect of distributing the sensual urges.

Continual sucking may act inhibitively upon speech development. Furthermore, the sucking of the thumbs, if excessive, has this disadvantage: the child often hurts himself, and then he not only experiences physical pain, but the connection between the pleasure in sucking and the pain in his fingers is psychologically disadvantageous.

With regard to masturbation I should say definitely that it ought not to be interfered with, the child should be left to deal with this in his own way.[1] With regard to the thumb-sucking, I should say that it can in many cases be replaced without pressure partly and gradually with other oral gratifications, such as sweets, fruit and specially favoured foods. These one should provide for the child *ad libitum*, while at the same time, with the help of the comforter, one softens the process of weaning.

Another point I want to stress is the mistake of attempting too early to get the child used to habits of cleanliness in regard to his excretory functions. Some mothers are proud of having achieved this task very early, but they do not realize the bad psychological effects to which it may give rise. I don't mean to say that there is any harm in holding the baby from time to time over a chamber and thus begin to accustom him gently to it. The point in question is that the mother ought not to be over-anxious, and ought not to try to prevent the child from ever dirtying or wetting himself. The baby senses this attitude towards his excrements and feels disturbed by it, for he takes a strong sexual pleasure in his excretory functions and he likes his excrements as a part and product of his own body. On the other hand, as I pointed out before, he feels that his faeces and urine are hostile agents when he defaecates and urinates with angry feelings. If the mother anxiously tries to prevent him from getting into contact with them altogether, the baby feels this behaviour as a confirmation that his excrements are evil and hostile agents of which the mother is afraid: her anxiety increases his. This attitude to his own excrements is psychologically detrimental, and plays a great part in many neuroses.

Of course I do not mean to say that the baby ought to be allowed to lie dirty indefinitely; what to my mind should be avoided is making his cleanliness a matter of such importance, because then the child senses how anxious the mother is over it. The whole thing should be taken easily and signs of disgust or disapproval while cleaning the baby should be avoided. I think that a *systematic* training

[1] If the masturbation is done obtrusively or excessively—and the same applies to prolonged and excessively hard thumb-sucking—one may find that something is wrong with the child's relation to his environment. For instance, he may feel afraid of his nurse without this ever coming to the knowledge of his parents. He may feel unhappy at school because he feels backward or because he is on bad terms with a certain teacher or afraid of another child. In analyses one discovers that such things can account for an increased strain on the child's mind which finds relief in increased and compulsive sensual gratification. Naturally, the removal of external factors will not always alleviate the strain, but with such children a reprimand for the excessive masturbation can only add to the underlying difficulties. When these are so great, they can be removed only by a psychological treatment.

in cleanliness is better postponed until after weaning. This training is certainly a considerable strain both mentally and physically
on the baby and one that ought not to be imposed on him while he
is coping with the difficulties of weaning. Even later on this training
should not be carried out with any strictness, as Dr Isaacs shows in
her paper on 'Habit' (Isaacs, 1936).

It is a great asset for the future relationship between mother and
child if the mother not only feeds but nurses her baby as well. If
circumstances prevent her from doing so she may still be able to
establish a strong bond between herself and her baby, if she has
insight into the baby's mentality.

The baby can enjoy his mother's presence in so many ways. He
will often have a little play with her breast after feeding, he will take
pleasure in her looking at him, smiling at him, playing with him
and talking to him long before he understands the meaning of words.
He will get to know and to like her voice, and her singing to him
may remain a pleasurable and stimulating memory in his unconscious. Soothing him in this way, how often she can avert tension
and avoid an unhappy state of mind, and thus put him to sleep instead of letting him fall asleep exhausted with crying!

A really happy relationship between mother and child can be
established only when nursing and feeding the baby is not a matter
of duty but a real pleasure to the mother. If she can enjoy it thoroughly, her pleasure will be unconsciously realized by the child,
and this reciprocal happiness will lead to a full emotional understanding between mother and child.

But there is another side to the picture. The mother must realize
that the baby is not actually her possession, and that, though he is
so small and utterly dependent on her help, he is a separate entity
and ought to be treated as an individual human being; she must not
tie him too much to herself, but assist him to grow up to independence. The earlier she can take up this attitude the better; she will
thus not only help the child, but preserve herself from future disappointment.

The child's development ought not to be unduly interfered with.
It is one thing to watch with enjoyment and understanding his
mental and physical growth, and another thing to try to accelerate
it. The baby ought to be left to grow quietly in his own way. As Ella
Sharpe (1936) has mentioned, the desire to impose a rate of growth
upon the child, to make it fit into a prearranged plan, is detrimental
to the child and to his relationship to the mother. Her desire to
speed on progress is often due to anxiety, which is one of the main
sources of disturbance in the mother–child relationship.

There is another matter in which the mother's attitude is of highest importance, and that is in regard to the sexual development of the child, that is, his experiences of bodily sexual sensations and the accompanying desires and feelings. It is not yet generally realized that the infant from birth onwards has strong sexual feelings, which, to begin with, manifest themselves through the pleasure experienced in his mouth activities and excretory functions, but which very soon get connected with the genitals as well (masturbation); nor is it generally and sufficiently realized that these sexual feelings are essential for the proper development of the child, and that his personality and character, as well as a satisfactory adult sexuality, depend on his sexuality being established in childhood.

I have already pointed out that one should not interfere with the child's masturbation, nor exert pressure in weaning him from thumb-sucking, and that one should be understanding about the pleasure he takes in his excretory functions and his excreta. But that alone is not sufficient. The mother must have a really friendly attitude towards these manifestations of his sexuality. So often she is apt to show disgust, harshness or scorn which is both humiliating and detrimental to the child. Since all his erotic trends are directed first and foremost towards his mother and father, their reactions will influence his whole development in these matters. On the other hand, there is also the question of too great indulgence to be considered. Though the child's sexuality is not to be interfered with, the mother might have to restrain him—of course in a friendly way—if he should attempt to take too much liberty with her person. Neither must the mother allow herself to become involved in his sexuality. A really friendly acceptance of sexuality in her child constitutes the limit of her rôle. Her own erotic needs must be well controlled where he is concerned. She must not become passionately excited by any of her activities in tending the child. When washing, drying or powdering him restraint is necessary, particularly in connection with the genital regions. The mother's lack of self-control may easily be felt by the child as a seduction, and this would set up undue complications in his development. Yet the child should by no means be deprived of love. The mother certainly can and ought to kiss and caress him and take him on her lap, all of which he needs and is only to his good.

This leads me to another important point. It is essential that the baby should not sleep in his parents' bedroom and be present during sexual intercourse. People often think that this is not harmful for the baby, because, for one thing, they do not realize that his sexual feelings, his aggression and fears get too much stirred through such an experience, and they further ignore the fact that the baby takes in unconsciously what he seems unable to grasp intellectually. Often, when the parents think the baby is asleep, he is awake or half awake, and even when he seems to be asleep he is able to sense what is going on around him. Though everything is perceived only in a dim way, a vivid, but distorted memory remains active in his unconscious mind, and has harmful effects on his development. Especially bad is the effect when this experience coincides with others which also put a strain on the child, for example, an illness, an operation or—to come back to the topic of my chapter—the weaning.

I should like to say now a few words about the actual process of the weaning from the breast. It seems to me of great importance to do this slowly and gently. If the baby is to be completely weaned, let us say, at eight or nine months—which seems the right age—at about five or six months, for one breast-feeding a day a bottle should be substituted, and every subsequent month another bottle should take the place of a breast-feeding. At the same time other suitable food should be introduced, and when the child has got used to this, one can begin to wean him from the bottle, which then will be replaced partly by other food and partly by milk drunk out of a glass. The weaning will be greatly facilitated if patience and gentleness are exercised in accustoming the child to new food. The child ought not to be made to eat more than he wants, or to eat food he dislikes—on the contrary, he should be provided with the food he likes in plenty—nor should table manners play any part at this period.

So far I have said nothing about upbringing where the baby is not breast-fed. I hope I have made clear the great psychological importance of the mother feeding her child; let us now consider the eventuality of the mother's being unable to do this.

The bottle is a substitute for the mother's breast, for it allows the baby to have the pleasure of sucking and thus to establish to a certain degree the breast–mother relationship in connection with the bottle given by the mother or nurse.

Experience shows that often children who have not been breast-fed develop quite well.[1] Still, in analysis one will always discover in such people a deep longing for the breast which has never been fulfilled, and though the breast–mother relationship has been established to a certain degree, it makes all the difference to the psychic development that the earliest and fundamental gratification has been

[1] More than this, even children who have gone through very difficult experiences in this early period, such as illnesses, sudden weaning or an operation, often develop quite satisfactorily, though such experiences are always in one way or another a handicap and should, of course, if possible be avoided.

obtained-from a substitute, instead of from the real thing which was desired. One may say that although children can develop well without being breast-fed, the development would have been different and better in one way or another had they had a successful breast-feeding. On the other hand, I infer from my experience that children whose development goes wrong, even though they have been breast-fed, would have been more ill without it.

To summarize: successful breast-feeding is always an important asset for development; some children, though they have missed this fundamentally favourable influence, develop very well without it.

In this chapter I have discussed the methods which might help to make the sucking period and the weaning successful; I am now in the rather difficult position of having to tell you that what may seem to be a success is not necessarily a complete one. Although some children appear to have gone through the weaning quite well and even for some time progress satisfactorily, deep down they have been unable to deal with the difficulties arising out of this situation; only an outward adaptation has taken place. This outward adaptation results from the child's urge to please those around him, upon whom he is so dependent, and from his desire to be on good terms with them. This drive in the child manifests itself to a certain degree even as early as in the weaning period; I believe that babies have altogether much more intellectual capacity than is assumed. There is another important reason for this mainly outward adaptation, namely, that it serves as an escape from the deep inner conflicts which the child is unable to deal with. In other cases, there are more obvious signs of the failure of true adaptation; for instance, in many character defects, such as jealousy, greed and resentfulness. In this connection I would mention Dr Karl Abraham's work on the relation between early difficulties and the formation of character.

We all know people who go about in life with constant grievances. For instance, they resent even the bad weather as a thing especially inflicted upon them by a hostile fate. Again, there are others who turn away from every gratification if it does not come immediately when it is wanted; in the words of the popular song of a few years ago, 'I want what I want when I want it, or I don't want it at all.'

I have endeavoured to show you that frustration is so difficult for the infant to bear because of the deep inner conflicts which are connected with it. A really successful weaning implies that the baby has not only got used to new food, but that it has actually made the first and fundamental steps towards dealing with its inner conflicts and fears, and that it is thus finding adjustment to frustration in its true sense.

If this adjustment has been made, then weaning in the obsolete sense of the word can here be applied. I understand that in old English the word weaning was used not only in the sense of 'weaning from' but also of 'weaning to'. Applying these two senses of the word, we may say that when real adaptation to frustration has taken place, the individual is weaned not only from his mother's breasts, but towards substitutes—towards all those sources of gratification and satisfaction which are needed for building up a full, rich and happy life.

POSTSCRIPT[1]

RECENT research has added considerably to our knowledge of the earliest stage of infancy—roughly the first three or four months of life—and it is from this angle that I am writing this postscript.

As was described in detail in my paper on Weaning, the very young infant's emotions are particularly powerful and are dominated by extremes. There are vigorous dividing processes between the two aspects (good and bad) of his first and most important object, the mother, and between his emotions (love and hatred) towards her. These divisions enable him to cope with his fears. The earliest fears derive from his aggressive impulses (which are easily stirred up by any frustration and discomfort) and take the form of feeling abandoned, injured, attacked—that is to say, intensely persecuted. Such persecutory fears, which focus on the mother, are prevalent in the infant until he develops a more integrated relation to her (and thereby to other people) which also implies an integration of his ego.

Recent investigations have been particularly concerned with the earliest stage of infancy. It has been recognized that the cleavage between love and hatred, usually described as a splitting of emotions, varies in intensity and takes many forms. These variations are bound up with the strength of persecutory fears in the infant. If splitting is excessive, the fundamentally important relation to the mother cannot be securely achieved and normal progress towards integration of the ego is disturbed. This may result in later mental illness. Another possible consequence is inhibition of intellectual development which may contribute to mental backwardness and—in extreme cases—to mental deficiency. Even in normal development there are temporary disturbances in the relation to the mother which are due to states of withdrawal both from her and from the experience of emotions. Should such states be too frequent or prolonged, they can be taken as an indication of abnormal development.

[1] Added in 1952.

If the difficulties in the first phase are normally overcome, the infant is likely to succeed in dealing with the depressive feelings arising in the crucial stage which follows at the age of about four to six months.

The theoretical findings concerning the first year of life, which were derived from the analysis of young children (generally speaking from about two years onwards) have been confirmed in the analysis of older children and of adults as well. They have been increasingly applied to the observation of infantile behaviour, and the field has been widened to include even very young babies. Since this book first appeared, depressive feelings in young children have been more generally observed and recognized. Some of the phenomena now understood to be characteristic of the first three or four months of life are also in some degree observable. For instance, the states of withdrawal by which the infant cuts himself off from emotions imply an absence of response to his surroundings. In such states the infant may appear apathetic and without interest in his environment. This condition is more easily overlooked than other disturbances such as excessive crying, restlessness and refusal of food.

The growing understanding of the anxieties babies experience should also make it easier for all who have the care of young children to find ways in which these difficulties can be alleviated. Frustrations are up to a point unavoidable and the fundamental anxieties I have described cannot in any case be completely eradicated. A better understanding of the infant's emotional needs, however, is bound to influence favourably our attitude towards his problems and thereby help him on the road to stability. In expressing this hope I am summing up the main purpose of the present study.

19

LOVE, GUILT AND REPARATION

(1937)

THE two parts of this book[1] discuss very different aspects of human emotions. The first, 'Hate, Greed and Aggression,' deals with the powerful impulses of hate which are a fundamental part of human nature. The second, in which I am attempting to give a picture of the equally powerful force of love and the drive to reparation, is complementary to the first, for the apparent division implied in this mode of presentation does not actually exist in the human mind. In separating our topic in this way we cannot perhaps clearly convey the constant *interaction* of love and hate; but the division of this vast subject was necessary, for only when consideration has been given to the part that destructive impulses play in the interaction of hate and love, is it possible to show the ways in which feelings of love and tendencies to reparation develop in connection with aggressive impulses and in spite of them.

Joan Riviere's chapter made it clear that these emotions first appear in the early relation of the child to his mother's breasts, and that they are experienced fundamentally in connection with the desired person. It is necessary to go back to the mental life of the baby in order to study the interaction of all the various forces which go to build up this most complex of all human emotions which we call love.

The Emotional Situation of the Baby

The baby's first object of love and hate—his mother—is both desired and hated with all the intensity and strength that is characteristic of the early urges of the baby. In the very beginning he loves his mother at the time that she is satisfying his needs for nourishment, alleviating his feelings of hunger, and giving him the sensual pleasure which he experiences when his mouth is stimulated by sucking at her breast. This gratification is an essential part of the child's sexuality, and is indeed its initial expression. But when the baby is hungry and his desires are not gratified, or when he is feeling bodily pain or discomfort, then the whole situation suddenly alters. Hatred and aggressive feelings are aroused and he becomes dominated by the impulses

---

[1] *Love, Hate and Reparation* (see Explanatory Note p. 435).

to destroy the very person who is the object of all his desires and who in his mind is linked up with everything he experiences—good and bad alike. In the baby hatred and aggressive feelings give rise, moreover, as Joan Riviere has shown in detail, to most painful states, such as choking, breathlessness and other sensations of the kind, which are felt to be destructive to his own body; thus aggression, unhappiness and fears are again increased.

The immediate and primary means by which relief is afforded to a baby from these painful states of hunger, hate, tension and fear is the satisfaction of his desires by his mother. The temporary feeling of security which is gained by receiving gratification greatly enhances the gratification itself; and thus a feeling of security becomes an important component of the satisfaction whenever a person receives love. This applies to the baby as well as to the adult, to the more simple forms of love and to its most elaborate manifestations. Because our mother first satisfied all our self-preservative needs and sensual desires and gave us security, the part she plays in our minds is a lasting one, although the various ways in which this influence is effected and the forms it takes may not be at all obvious in later life. For instance, a woman may apparently have estranged herself from her mother, yet still unconsciously seek some of the features of her early relation to her in her relation to her husband or to a man she loves. The very important part which the father plays in the child's emotional life also influences all later love relations, and all other human associations. But the baby's early relation to him, in so far as he is felt as a gratifying, friendly and protective figure, is partly modelled on the one to the mother.

The baby, to whom his mother is primarily only an object which satisfies all his desires—a good breast,[1] as it were—soon begins to

[1] In order to simplify my description of the very complicated and unfamiliar phenomena that I present in this lecture, I am throughout, in speaking of the feeding situation of the baby, referring to breast-feeding only. Much of what I am saying in connection with breast-feeding and the inferences I am drawing apply to bottle-feeding also, though with certain differences. In this connection I will quote a passage from my paper on 'Weaning' (1936): 'The bottle is a substitute for the mother's breast, for it allows the baby to have the pleasure of sucking and thus to establish to a certain degree the breast–mother relationship in connection with the bottle given by the mother or nurse. Experience shows that often children who have not been breast-fed develop quite well. Still, in analysis one will always discover in such people a deep longing for the breast which has never been fulfilled, and though the breast–mother relationship has been established to a certain degree, it makes all the difference to the psychic development that the earliest and fundamental gratification has been obtained from a substitute, instead of from the real thing which was desired. One may say that although children can develop well without being breast-fed, the development would have been different and better in one way or another had they had a successful breast-feeding. On the

respond to these gratifications and to her care by developing feelings of love towards her as a person. But this first love is already disturbed at its roots by destructive impulses. Love and hate are struggling together in the baby's mind; and this struggle to a certain extent persists throughout life and is liable to become a source of danger in human relationships.

The baby's impulses and feelings are accompanied by a kind of mental activity which I take to be the most primitive one: that is phantasy-building, or more colloquially, imaginative thinking. For instance, the baby who feels a craving for his mother's breast when it is not there may imagine it to be there, *i.e.* he may imagine the satisfaction which he derives from it. Such primitive phantasying is the earliest form of the capacity which later develops into the more elaborate workings of the imagination.

The early phantasies which go along with the baby's feelings are of various kinds. In the one just mentioned he imagines the gratification which he lacks. Pleasant phantasies, however, also accompany actual satisfaction; and destructive phantasies go along with frustration and the feelings of hatred which this arouses. When a baby feels frustrated at the breast, in his phantasies he attacks this breast; but if he is being gratified by the breast, he loves it and has phantasies of a pleasant kind in relation to it. In his aggressive phantasies he wishes to bite up and to tear up his mother and her breasts, and to destroy her also in other ways.

A most important feature of these destructive phantasies, which are tantamount to death-wishes, is that the baby feels that what he desires in his phantasies has really taken place; that is to say he feels that he *has really destroyed* the object of his destructive impulses, and is going on destroying it: this has extremely important consequences for the development of his mind. The baby finds support against these fears in omnipotent phantasies of a restoring kind: that too has extremely important consequences for his development. If the baby has, in his aggressive phantasies, injured his mother by biting and tearing her up, he may soon build up phantasies that he is putting the bits together again and repairing her.[1] This, however, does not quite do away with his fears of having destroyed the object which,

---

other hand, I infer from my experience that children whose development goes wrong, even though they have been breast-fed, would have been more ill without it.'

[1] The psycho-analysis of small children, which enabled me to draw conclusions also as to the workings of the mind at an earlier stage, has convinced me that such phantasies are already active in babies. Psycho-analysis of adults has shown me that the effects of this early phantasy-life are lasting, and profoundly influence the unconscious mind of the grown-up person.

as we know, is the one whom he loves and needs most, and on whom he is entirely dependent. In my view, these basic conflicts profoundly influence the course and the force of the emotional lives of grown-up individuals.

Unconscious Sense of Guilt

We all know that if we detect in ourselves impulses of hate towards a person we love, we feel concerned or guilty. As Coleridge puts it:

> . . . to be wroth with one we love,
> Doth work like madness in the brain.

We tend very much to keep these feelings of guilt in the background, because of their painfulness. They express themselves, however, in many disguised ways, and are a source of disturbance in our personal relations. For instance, some people readily experience distress through lack of appreciation, even from persons who mean but little to them; the reason is that in their unconscious minds they feel unworthy of man's regard, and a cold reception confirms their suspicion of this unworthiness. Others are dissatisfied with themselves (not on objective grounds) in the most various ways, for example, in connection with their appearance, their work, or their abilities in general. Some of these manifestations are quite commonly recognized and have been popularly termed an 'inferiority complex'.

Psycho-analytic findings show that feelings of this kind are more deeply rooted than is usually supposed and are always connected with unconscious feelings of guilt. The reason why some people have so strong a need for general praise and approval lies in their need for evidence that they are lovable, worthy of love. This feeling arises from the unconscious fear of being incapable of loving others sufficiently or truly, and particularly of not being able to master aggressive impulses toward others: they dread being a danger to the loved one.

Love and Conflicts in Relation to the Parents

The struggle between love and hate, with all the conflicts to which it gives rise, sets in, as I have tried to show, in early infancy, and is active all through life. It begins with the child's relationship to both parents. In the relation of the suckling to his mother, sensual feelings are already present and express themselves in the pleasurable mouth sensations connected with the sucking process. Soon genital feelings come to the fore and the craving for the mother's nipples diminishes. It does not altogether vanish, however, but remains active in the unconscious and partly also in the conscious mind. Now in the case of the little girl the concern with the nipple passes over to an interest, which is for the most part unconscious, in the father's genital, and this becomes the object of her libidinal wishes and phantasies. As development proceeds, the little girl desires her father more than her mother, and has conscious and unconscious phantasies of taking her mother's place, winning her father for herself and becoming his wife. She is also very jealous of the children her mother possesses, and wishes her father to give her babies of her own. These feelings, wishes and phantasies go along with rivalry, aggression and hatred against her mother, and are added to the grievances which she felt against her because of the earliest frustrations at the breast. Nevertheless sexual phantasies and desires towards her mother do remain active in the little girl's mind. Under the influence of these she wants to take her father's place in connection with her mother, and in certain cases these desires and phantasies may develop more strongly even than those towards the father. Thus besides the love to both of them there are also feelings of rivalry to both, and this mixture of feelings is carried further in her relation to brothers and sisters. The desires and phantasies in connection with mother and sisters are the basis for direct homosexual relationships in later life, as well as for homosexual feelings which express themselves indirectly in friendship and affection between women. In the ordinary course of events these homosexual desires recede into the background, become deflected and sublimated, and the attraction towards the other sex predominates.

A corresponding development takes place in the small boy, who soon experiences genital desires towards his mother and feelings of hatred against his father as a rival. But in him, too, genital desires towards his father develop, and this is the root of homosexuality in men. These situations give rise to many conflicts—for the little girl, although she hates her mother, also loves her; and the little boy loves his father and would spare him the danger arising from his—the boy's—aggressive impulses. Moreover, the main object of all sexual desires—in the girl, the father, in the boy, the mother—also rouses hate and revenge, because these desires are disappointed.

The child is also intensely jealous of brothers and sisters, in so far as they are rivals for the parents' love. He also loves them, however, and thus again in this connection strong conflicts between aggressive impulses and feelings of love are aroused. This leads to feelings of guilt and again to wishes to make good: a mixture of feelings which has an important bearing not only on our relations with brothers and sisters but, since relations to people in general are modelled on the same pattern, also on our social attitude and on feelings of love and guilt and the wish to make good in later life.

Love, Guilt and Reparation

I said before that feelings of love and gratitude arise directly spontaneously in the baby in response to the love and care of his mother. The power of love — which is the manifestation of the forces which tend to preserve life — is there in the baby as well as the destructive impulses, and finds its first fundamental expression in the baby's attachment to his mother's breast, which develops into love for her as a person. My psycho-analytic work has convinced me that when in the baby's mind the conflicts between love and hate arise, and the fears of losing the loved one become active, a very important step is made in development. These feelings of guilt and distress now enter as a new element into the emotion of love. They become an inherent part of love, and influence it profoundly both in quality and quantity.

Even in the small child one can observe a concern for the loved one which is not, as one might think, merely a sign of dependence upon a friendly and helpful person. Side by side with the destructive impulses in the unconscious mind both of the child and of the adult, there exists a profound urge to make sacrifices, in order to help and to put right loved people who in phantasy have been harmed or destroyed. In the depths of the mind, the urge to make people happy is linked up with a strong feeling of responsibility and concern for them, which manifests itself in genuine sympathy with other people and in the ability to understand them, as they are and as they feel.

Identification and Making Reparation

To be genuinely considerate implies that we can put ourselves in the place of other people: we 'identify' ourselves with them. Now this capacity for identification with another person is a most important element in human relationships in general, and is also a condition for real and strong feelings of love. We are only able to disregard or to some extent sacrifice our own feelings and desires, and thus for a time to put the other person's interests and emotions first, if we have the capacity to identify ourselves with the loved person. Since in being identified with other people we share, as it were, the help or satisfaction afforded to them by ourselves, we regain in one way what we have sacrificed in another.[1] Ultimately, in making sacrifices for

---

[1] As I said at the beginning there is a constant interaction of love and hate in all of us. My topic, however, is concerned with the ways in which feelings of love develop and become strengthened and stabilized. Since I am not entering much into questions of aggression I must make clear that it is also active, even in people whose capacity for love is strongly developed. Generally speaking, in such people both aggression and hatred (the latter diminished and to some degree counterbalanced by the capacity for love) is used very greatly in constructive ways

311

somebody we love and in identifying ourselves with the loved person, we play the part of a good parent, and behave towards this person as we felt at times the parents did to us—or as we wanted them to do. At the same time, we also play the part of the good child towards his parents, which we wished to do in the past and are now acting out in the present. Thus, by reversing a situation, namely in acting towards another person as a good parent, in phantasy we re-create and enjoy the wished-for love and goodness of our parents. But to act as good parents towards other people may also be a way of dealing with the frustrations and sufferings of the past. Our grievances against our parents for having frustrated us, together with the feelings of hate and revenge to which these have given rise in us, and again, the feelings of guilt and despair arising out of this hate and revenge because we have injured the parents whom at the same time we loved—all these, in phantasy, we may undo in retrospect (taking away some of the grounds for hatred), by playing at the same time the parts of loving parents and loving children. At the same time, in our unconscious phantasy we make good the injuries which we did in phantasy,

---

('sublimated,' as it has been termed). There is actually no productive activity into which some aggression does not enter in one way or another. Take, for instance, the housewife's occupation: cleaning and so on certainly bear witness to her desire to make things pleasant for others and for herself, and as such is a manifestation of love for other people and for the things she cares for. But at the same time she also gives expression to her aggression in destroying the enemy, dirt, which in her unconscious mind has come to stand for 'bad' things. The original hatred and aggression derived from the earliest sources may break through in women whose cleanliness becomes obsessional. We all know the type of women who make life miserable for the family by continuously 'tidying up'; there the hatred is actually turned against the people she loves and cares for. To hate people and things which are felt to be worthy of hate—be they people we dislike or principles (political, artistic, religious or moral) with which we disagree, is a general way of giving vent, in a manner which is felt to be permissible and can actually be quite constructive, to our feelings of hatred, aggression, scorn and contempt, if it does not go to extremes. These emotions, though made use of in adult ways, are at bottom the ones we experienced in childhood when we hated the people whom at the same time we also loved—our parents. Even then we attempted to keep our love towards our parents, and to turn the hatred on to other people and things, a process which is more successful when we have developed and stabilized our capacity for love and also extended our range of interests, affections and hatreds in adult life. To give a few more examples: the work of lawyers, politicians and critics involves combating opponents, but in ways which are felt to be allowable and useful; and here again the foregoing conclusions would apply. One of the many ways in which aggression can be expressed legitimately and even laudably is in games, in which the opponent is temporarily—and this fact of its being temporary also helps to diminish the sense of guilt—attacked with feelings that again derive from early emotional situations. There are thus many ways—sublimated and direct—in which aggression and hatreds find expression in people who are at the same time very kind-hearted and capable of love.

and for which we still unconsciously feel very guilty. This *making reparation* is, in my view, a fundamental element in love and in all human relationships; I shall therefore refer to it frequently in what follows.

A Happy Love Relationship

Bearing in mind what I have said about the origins of love, let us now consider some particular relationships of adults, taking first, as an example, a satisfactory and stable love relationship between a man and a woman, as it may be found in a happy marriage. This implies a deep attachment, a capacity for mutual sacrifice, a sharing—in grief as well as in pleasure, in interests as well as in sexual enjoyment. A relationship of this nature affords the widest scope for the most varied manifestations of love.[1] If the woman has a maternal attitude towards the man, she satisfies (as far as can be) his earliest wishes for the gratifications he desired from his own mother. In the past, these wishes have never been quite satisfied, and have never been quite given up. The man has now, as it were, this mother for his own, with relatively little feeling of guilt. (I shall go into the reason for this in more detail later.) If the woman has a richly developed emotional life, besides possessing these maternal feelings, she will also have kept something of the child's attitude towards her father, and some of the features of this old relationship will enter into her relation to her husband; for instance, she will trust and admire her husband, and he will be a protective and helpful figure to her as her father was. These feelings will be a foundation for a relation in which the woman's desires and needs as a grown-up person can find full satisfaction. Again, this attitude of his wife's gives the man the opportunity to be protective and helpful to her in various ways—that is, in his unconscious mind, to play the part of a good husband to his mother.

If the woman is capable of strong feelings of love both towards her husband and towards her children, one can infer that she has most probably had a good relationship in childhood to both parents, and to her brothers and sisters; that is to say, that she has been able to deal satisfactorily with her early feelings of hate and revenge against them. I have mentioned before the importance of the little girl's unconscious wish to receive a baby from her father, and of the sexual

[1] In considering adult emotions and relationships I shall throughout this paper deal mainly with the bearing the child's early impulses and unconscious feelings and phantasies have upon the later manifestations of love. I am aware that this necessarily leads to a somewhat concentrated and schematic presentation, for in this way I cannot do justice to the multiple factors that in the life-long interaction between influences coming from the outer world and the individual's inner forces work together to build up an adult relationship.

desires towards him which are connected with this wish. The father's frustration of her genital desires gives rise to intense aggressive phantasies in the child, which have an important bearing upon the capacity for sexual gratification in adult life. Sexual phantasies in the little girl thus become connected with hatred which is specifically directed against her father's penis, because she feels that it denies her the gratification which it affords to her mother. In her jealousy and hatred she wishes it to be a dangerous and evil thing—one which could not gratify her mother either—and the penis thus, in her phantasy, acquires destructive qualities. Because of these unconscious wishes, which focus on her parents' sexual gratifications, in some of her phantasies sexual organs and sexual gratification take on a bad and dangerous character. These aggressive phantasies are again followed in the child's mind by wishes to make good—more specifically, by phantasies of healing the father's genital which, in her mind, she has injured or made bad. The phantasies of a curative nature are also connected with sexual feelings and desires. All these unconscious phantasies influence greatly the woman's feelings towards her husband. If he loves her and also gratifies her sexually, her unconscious sadistic phantasies will lose in strength. But since these are not entirely put out of action (though in a woman who is fairly normal, they are not present in a degree that inhibits the tendency to blend with more positive or friendly erotic impulses), they lead to a stimulation of phantasies of a restoring nature; thus once more the drive to make reparation is brought into action. Sexual gratification affords her not only pleasure, but reassurance and support against the fears and feelings of guilt which were the result of her early sadistic wishes. This reassurance enhances sexual gratification and gives rise in the woman to feelings of gratitude, tenderness and increased love. Just because there is somewhere in the depths of her mind a feeling that her genital is dangerous and could injure her husband's genital—which is a derivative of her aggressive phantasies towards her father—one part of the satisfaction she obtains comes from the fact that she is capable of giving her husband pleasure and happiness, and that her genital thus proves to be good.

Because the little girl had phantasies of her father's genital being dangerous, these still have a certain influence upon the woman's unconscious mind. But if she has a happy and sexually gratifying relation with her husband, his genital is felt to be good, and thus her fears of the bad genital are disproved. The sexual gratification thus works as a double reassurance: of her own goodness and of her husband's, and the feeling of security gained in this way adds to the actual sexual enjoyment. The circle of reassurance thus provided is still wider. The woman's early jealousy and hatred of her mother as a rival for her father's love has played an important part in her aggressive phantasies. The mutual happiness provided both by sexual gratification and by a happy and loving relation to her husband will also be felt partly as an indication that her sadistic wishes against her mother have not taken effect, or that reparation has succeeded.

The emotional attitude and the sexuality of a man in his relation to his wife are of course also influenced by his past. The frustration by his mother of his genital desires in his childhood aroused phantasies in which his penis became an instrument which could give pain and cause injury to her. At the same time jealousy and hatred of his father as a rival for his mother's love set going phantasies of a sadistic nature against his father also. In the sexual relation to his love-partner the man's early aggressive phantasies, which led to a fear of his penis being destructive, come into play to some extent, and by a transmutation similar in kind to that described for the woman, the sadistic impulse, when it is in manageable quantity, stimulates phantasies of reparation. The penis is then felt to be a good and curative organ, which shall afford the woman pleasure, cure her injured genital and create babies in her. A happy and sexually gratifying relationship with the woman affords him proofs of the goodness of his penis, and also unconsciously gives him the feeling that his wishes to restore her have succeeded. This not only increases his sexual pleasure and his love and tenderness for the woman, but here again it leads to feelings of gratitude and security. In addition, these feelings are apt to increase his creative powers in other ways and to influence his capacity for work and for other activities. If his wife can share in his interests (as well as in love and in sexual satisfaction), she affords him proofs of the value of his work. In these various ways his early wish to be capable of doing what his father did for his mother, sexually and otherwise, and to receive from her what his father received, can be fulfilled in his relation to his wife. His happy relation to her has also the effect of diminishing his aggression against his father, which was greatly stimulated by his being unable to have his mother as a wife, and this may reassure him that his long-standing sadistic tendencies against his father have not been effective. Since grievances and hatred against his father have influenced his feelings towards men who have come to stand for his father, and grievances against his mother have affected his relation to women who stand for her, a satisfactory love relationship alters his outlook on life and his attitude to people and activities in general. To possess his wife's love and appreciation gives him a feeling of being fully grown-up and thus of being equal to his father. The hostile and aggressive rivalry with him diminishes and gives way to a more friendly competition with his father—or rather with admired father-figures—in productive functions and achievements, and this is very likely to enhance or increase his productivity.

Similarly, when a woman in a happy love relationship with a man unconsciously feels that she can take, as it were, the place that her mother took with *her* husband, and now gains satisfactions that her mother enjoyed and that she, as a child, was denied—then she is able to feel equal to her mother, to enjoy the same happiness, rights and privileges as her mother did, but without injuring and robbing her. The effects upon her attitude and the development of her personality are analogous to the changes which take place in the man when he finds himself, in a happy married life, equal to his father.

Thus in both partners a relationship of mutual sexual gratification and love will be felt as a happy re-creation of their early family lives. Many wishes and phantasies can never be satisfied in childhood,[1] not only because they are impracticable, but also because there are simultaneously contradictory wishes in the unconscious mind. It seems a paradoxical fact that, in a way, fulfilment of many infantile wishes is possible only when the individual has grown up. In the happy rela-

---

[1] In the case of the boy, for example, the child wishes to have his mother to himself the whole twenty-four hours of the day, to have sexual intercourse with her, to give her babies, to kill his father because he is jealous of him, to deprive his brothers and sisters of everything they have, and turn them out too if they get in his way. It is obvious that if these impracticable wishes were fulfilled they would cause him the deepest feelings of guilt. Even the realization of much less far-reaching destructive desires is apt to arouse deep conflicts. For instance many a child will feel guilty if he becomes his mother's favourite, because his father and brothers and sisters will be correspondingly neglected. This is what I mean by saying there are simultaneously contradictory wishes in the unconscious mind. The child's desires are unlimited and so are his destructive impulses in connection with these desires, but at the same time he also has—unconsciously and consciously—opposite tendencies; he also wishes to give them love and make reparation. He himself actually wants to be restrained by the adults around him in his aggression and selfishness, because if these are given free rein he is caused suffering by the pain of remorse and unworthiness; and in fact he relies on obtaining this help from grown-ups, like any other help he needs. Consequently it is psychologically quite inadequate to attempt to solve children's difficulties by not frustrating them at all. Naturally, frustration which is in reality unnecessary or arbitrary and shows nothing but lack of love and understanding is very detrimental. It is important to realize that the child's development depends on, and to a large extent is formed by, his capacity to find the way to bear inevitable and necessary frustrations and the conflicts of love and hate which are in part caused by them: that is, to find his way between his hate which is increased by frustrations, and his love and wish for reparation which bring in their train the sufferings of remorse. The way the child adapts himself to these problems in his mind forms the foundation for all his later social relationships, his adult capacity for love and cultural development. He can be immensely helped in childhood by the love and understanding of those around him, but these deep problems can neither be solved for him nor abolished.

tionship of grown-up people the early wish to have one's mother or father all to oneself is still unconsciously active. Of course, reality does not allow one to be one's mother's husband or one's father's wife; and had it been possible, feelings of guilt towards others would have interfered with the gratification. But only if one has been able to develop such relationships with the parents in unconscious phantasy, and has been able to overcome to some extent one's feelings of guilt connected with these phantasies, and gradually to detach oneself from as well as remain attached to the parents, is one capable of transferring these wishes to other people, who then stand for desired objects of the past, though they are not identical with them. That is to say, only if the individual has grown up in the real sense of the word can his infantile phantasies be fulfilled in the adult state. What is more, guilt due to these infantile wishes then becomes relieved, just because a situation phantasied in childhood has now become real in a permissible way, and in a way which proves that the injuries of various kinds, which in phantasy were connected with this situation, have not actually been inflicted.

A happy adult relationship, such as I have described, can thus, as I said before, mean a re-creation of the early family situation, and this will be the more complete, and therefore the whole circle of reassurance and security will be wider still, through the relation of the man and woman to their children. This brings us to the subject of parenthood.

Parenthood: On Being a Mother

We will consider first a really loving relationship of a mother to her baby, as it develops if the woman has attained a fully maternal personality. There are many threads which link the relationship of the mother to her child with that of her own relation to her mother in babyhood. A very strong conscious and unconscious wish for babies exists in small children. In the little girl's unconscious phantasies, her mother's body is full of babies. These she imagines have been put into her by her father's penis, which is to her the symbol of all creativeness, power and goodness. This predominant attitude of admiration towards her father and his sexual organs as creative and life-giving goes along with the little girl's intense desire to possess children of her own and to have babies inside her, as the most precious possession.

It is an everyday observation that little girls play with dolls as if these were their babies. But a child will often display a passionate devotion to the doll, for it has become to her a live and real baby, a companion, a friend, which forms part of her life. She not only carries it about with her, but constantly has it in her mind, starts the day with it and gives it up unwillingly if she is made to do something else. These wishes experienced in childhood persist into womanhood and contribute greatly to the strength of the love that a pregnant woman feels for the child growing inside her, and then for the baby to which she has given birth. The gratification of at last having it relieves the pain of the frustration experienced in childhood when she wanted a baby from her father and could not have it. This long-postponed fulfilment of an all-important wish tends to make her less aggressive and to increase her capacity for loving her child. Further-more, the child's helplessness and its great need for its mother's care call for more love than can be given to any other person, and thus all the mother's loving and constructive tendencies now have scope. Some mothers, as we know, exploit this relationship for the gratifica-tion of their own desires, *i.e.* their possessiveness and the satisfaction of having somebody dependent upon them. Such mothers want their children to cling to them, and they hate them to grow up and to acquire individualities of their own. With others, the child's helpless-ness calls out all the strong wishes to make reparation, which are derived from various sources and which can now be related to this most wished-for baby, who is the fulfilment of her early longings. Gratitude towards the child who affords his mother the enjoyment of being able to love him enhances these feelings, and may lead to an attitude where the mother's first concern will be for the baby's good, and her own gratification will become bound up with his welfare.

The nature of the relations of the mother to her children alters, of course, as they grow up. Her attitude to her older children will be more or less influenced by her attitude to her brothers and sisters, cousins, etc., in the past. Certain difficulties in these past relationships may easily interfere with her feelings for her own child, especially if it develops reactions and traits which tend to stir these difficulties in her. Her jealousy and rivalry towards her brothers and sisters gave rise to death-wishes and aggressive phantasies, in which in her mind she injured or destroyed them. If her sense of guilt and the conflicts derived from these phantasies are not too strong, then the possibility of making reparation can have more scope and her maternal feelings can come more fully into play.

One element in this maternal attitude seems to be that the mother is capable of putting herself in the child's place and of looking at the situation from his point of view. Her being able to do so with love and sympathy is closely bound up, as we have seen, with feelings of guilt and the drive to reparation. If, however, the sense of guilt is over-strong, this identification may lead to an entirely self-sacrificing attitude which is very much to the child's disadvantage. It is well known that a child who has been brought up by a mother who showers love on him and expects nothing in return often becomes a selfish person. Lack of capacity for love and consideration in a child is, to a certain extent, a cover for over-strong feelings of guilt. A mother's over-indulgence tends to increase feelings of guilt, and moreover does not allow enough scope for the child's own tendencies to make reparation, to make sacrifices sometimes, and to develop true consideration for others.[1]

If, however, the mother is not too closely wrapped up in the child's feelings and is not too much identified with him, she is able to use her wisdom in guiding the child in the most helpful way. She will then get full satisfaction from the possibility of furthering the child's development—a satisfaction which is again enhanced by phantasies of doing for her child what her own mother did for her, or what she wished her mother to do. In achieving this, she also repays her mother and makes good the injuries done, in phantasy, to her mother's children, and this again lessens her feelings of guilt.

A mother's capacity to love and to understand her children will be especially tested when they come to the stage of adolescence. At this period, children normally tend to turn away from their parents and to free themselves to a certain degree from their old attachments to them. The children's striving to find their way towards new objects of love creates situations which are apt to be very painful for parents. If the mother has strong maternal feelings, she can remain unshaken in her love, can be patient and understanding, give help and advice where this is necessary, and yet allow the children to work out their problems for themselves—and she may be able to do all this without asking much for herself. This is only possible, however, if her capacity for love has developed in such a way that she can make a strong identification both with her child, and with a wise mother of her own whom she keeps in her mind.

The mother's relations to her children will again alter in character and her love may manifest itself in different ways when her children are grown up, have made lives of their own and freed themselves from old ties. The mother may now find that she has not a large part to play in their lives. But she may find some satisfaction in keeping her love prepared for them whenever it is needed. She thus feels unconsciously that she affords them security, and is forever the mother of the early days, whose breast gave them full gratification and who satisfied their needs and their desires. In this situation, the mother has identified herself fully with her own helpful mother, whose

---

[1] A similar detrimental effect (though this comes about in a different way) is produced by harshness or lack of love on the part of parents—This touches on the important problem of how the environment influences the child's emotional development in a favourable or unfavourable way. This, however, is beyond the scope of the present paper.

protective influence has never ceased to function in her mind. At the same time she is also identified with her own children: she is, in her phantasy, as it were, again a child, and shares with her children the possession of a good and helpful mother. The unconscious minds of the children very often correspond to the mother's unconscious mind, and whether or not they make much use of this store of love prepared for them, they often gain great inner support and comfort through the knowledge that this love exists.

Parenthood: On Being a Father

Although his children do not on the whole mean so much to the man as to the woman, they do play an important part in his life, especially if he and his wife are in harmony. To go back to deeper sources of this relationship, I have already referred to the gratification which a man derives from giving a baby to his wife, in so far as this means making up for his sadistic wishes towards his mother and making restoration to her. This increases the actual satisfaction of creating a baby and of fulfilling his wife's wishes. An additional source of pleasure is the gratification of his feminine wishes by his sharing the maternal pleasure of his wife. As a small boy he had strong desires to bear children as his mother did, and these desires increased his tendencies to rob her of her children. As a man, he can *give* children to his wife, can see her happy with them, and is then able, without feeling guilty, to identify himself with her in her bearing and suckling of their children, and again in her relation to the older children.

There are many satisfactions, however, which he derives from being able to be a *good father* to his children. All his protective feelings, which have been stimulated by feelings of guilt in connection with the early family life when he was a child, find full expression. Again, there is the identification with the good father—either with his actual father or with his ideal of a father. Another element in his relationship with his children is his strong identification with them, for he shares in his mind their enjoyments; and, moreover, in helping them in their difficulties and promoting their development he is renewing his own childhood in a more satisfactory way.

Much of what I have said about the mother's relation to her children in different stages of their development applies also to the father's. He plays a different part from that of the mother, but their attitudes complement each other; and if (as is assumed in this whole discussion) their married life is based upon love and understanding, the husband also enjoys his wife's relation with their children, whilst she takes pleasure in his understanding and helping them.

Difficulties in Family Relationships

A fully harmonious family life such as that implied in my description is, as we know, not an everyday occurrence. It depends upon a happy coincidence of circumstances and psychological factors, first of all upon a well-developed faculty for love in both partners. Difficulties of all kinds may occur, both in the relation between husband and wife and in their relations to the children, and I will give a few examples of these.

The individuality of the child may not correspond to what the parents wished it to be. Either partner may unconsciously want the child to be like a brother or a sister of the past; and this wish obviously cannot be satisfied in both parents—and may not be fulfilled even in one. Again, if there has been strong rivalry and jealousy in relation to brothers and sisters in either or both partners, this may be repeated in connection with the achievements and the development of their own children. Another situation of difficulty arises when the parents are over-ambitious and wish, by means of the achievements of their children, to gain reassurances for themselves and to lessen their own fears. Then, again, some mothers are not able to love and to enjoy the possession of their children because they feel too guilty of taking, in phantasy, their own mother's place. A woman of this type may not be able to tend her children herself, but has to leave them to the care of nurses or other people—who in her unconscious mind stand for her own mother, to whom she is thus returning the children whom she wished to take away from her. This fear of loving the child, which of course disturbs the relationship with the child, may occur in men as well as in women, and will probably affect the mutual relations of husband and wife.

I have said that feelings of guilt and the drive to make reparation are intimately bound up with the emotion of love. If, however, the early conflict between love and hate has not been satisfactorily dealt with, or if guilt is too strong, this may lead to a turning away from loved people or even to a rejection of them. In the last analysis it is the fear that the loved person—to begin with, the mother—may die because of the injuries inflicted upon her in phantasy, which makes it unbearable to be dependent upon this person. We can observe the satisfaction small children gain from their early achievements, and from everything which increases their independence. There are many obvious reasons for this, but a deep and important one is, in my experience, that the child is driven towards weakening his attachment to the all-important person, his mother. She originally kept his life going, supplied all his needs, protected him and gave him security; she is therefore felt as the source of all goodness and of life; in unconscious phantasy she becomes an inseparable part of oneself; her death would therefore imply one's own death. Where these feelings and phantasies are very strong, the attachment to loved people may become an overwhelming burden.

Many people find their way out of these difficulties by lessening their capacity for love, *denying* or suppressing it, and by avoiding strong emotions altogether. Others have found an escape from the dangers of love by having displaced it predominantly from people to something else but people. The displacement of love to things and interests (which I discuss in connection with the explorer and the man struggling with the hardships of nature) is part of normal growth. But with some people this displacement to objects other than human has become their main mode of dealing with, or rather escaping from, conflicts. We all know the type of animal lover, passionate collector, scientist, artist, and so on, who is capable of a great love, and often self-sacrifice, for the objects of his devotion or his chosen work, but has little interest and love to spare for his fellow-men.

A quite different development takes place in people who become entirely dependent upon those to whom they are strongly attached. With them, the unconscious fear that the loved one will die leads to over-dependence. Greed, which is increased by fears of the kind, is one element in such an attitude, and is expressed in making as much use as possible of the person on whom one is dependent. Another constituent in this attitude of over-dependence is the shirking of responsibility: the other person is made responsible for one's actions, and sometimes even for one's opinions and thoughts. (This is one of the reasons why people accept without criticism the views of a leader and act with blind obedience to his commands.) With people who are so over-dependent, love is very much needed as a support against the sense of guilt and fears of various kinds. The loved person, by signs of affection, must prove to them over and over again that they are not bad, not aggressive, and that their destructive impulses have not taken effect.

These over-strong ties are especially disturbing in the relation of a mother to her child. As I have pointed out before, the attitude of a mother to her child has much in common with her feelings as a child towards her own mother. We know already that this early relationship is characterized by the conflicts between love and hate. Unconscious death-wishes which the child bears towards her mother are carried over to her own child when she becomes a mother. These feelings are increased by the conflicting emotions in childhood towards brothers and sisters. If as the result of unsolved conflict in the past the mother feels too guilty in relation to her own child, she may need its love so intensely that she uses various devices to tie it closely to herself and to make it dependent upon her; or again, she may devote herself too much to the child, making him the centre of her whole life.

Let us consider now, though only from one basic aspect, a very different mental attitude—infidelity. The manifold forms and manifestations of infidelity (being the outcome of the most varied ways of development and expressing in some people mainly love, in others mainly hatred, with all degrees in between) have one phenomenon in common: the repeated turning away from a (loved) person, which partly springs from the fear of dependence. I have found that the typical Don Juan in the depths of his mind is haunted by the dread of the death of loved people, and that this fear would break through and express itself in feelings of depression and in great mental sufferings if he had not developed this particular defence—his infidelity—against them. By means of this he is proving to himself over and over again that his *one* greatly loved object (originally his mother, whose death he dreaded because he felt his love for her to be greedy and destructive), is not after all indispensable since he can always find another woman to whom he has passionate but shallow feelings. In contrast to those people whom a great dread of the death of the loved person drives to rejecting her or to stifling and denying love, he is, for various reasons, incapable of doing so. But through his attitude towards women an unconscious compromise finds expression. By deserting and rejecting some women he unconsciously turns away from his mother, saves her from his dangerous desires and frees himself from his painful dependence on her, and by turning to other women and giving them pleasure and love he is in his unconscious mind retaining the loved mother or re-creating her.

In reality he is driven from one person to another, since the other person soon comes to stand again for his mother. His original love object is thus replaced by a succession of different ones. In unconscious phantasy he is re-creating or healing his mother by means of sexual gratifications (which he actually gives to other women), for only in one aspect is his sexuality felt to be dangerous; in another aspect it is felt to be curative and to make her happy. This twofold attitude is part of the unconscious compromise which resulted in his infidelity and is one condition for his particular way of development.

This leads me to another type of difficulty in love relationships. A man may restrict his affectionate, tender and protective feelings to one woman, who may be his wife, but he is unable to get sexual enjoyment in this relationship, and has either to repress his sexual desires or to turn them towards some other woman. Fears of the destructive nature of his sexuality, fears of his father as a rival and feelings of guilt in this connection are deep reasons for such a separation of feelings of a tender kind from specifically sexual ones. The loved and highly valued woman, who stands for his mother, has to be saved from his sexuality, which in phantasy is felt to be dangerous.

Choice of Love-Partner

Psycho-analysis shows that there are deep unconscious motives which contribute to the choice of a love-partner, and make two particular people sexually attractive and satisfactory to each other. The feelings of a man towards a woman are always influenced by his early attachment to his mother. But here again this will be more or less unconscious, and may be very much disguised in its manifestations. A man may choose as a love-partner a woman who has some characteristics of an entirely opposite kind to those of his mother—perhaps the loved woman's appearance is quite different, but her voice or some characteristics of her personality are in accordance with his early impressions of his mother and have a special attraction for him. Or again, just because he wanted to get away from too strong an attachment to his mother, he may choose a love-partner who is in absolute contrast to her.

Very often, as development proceeds, a sister or a cousin takes the mother's place in the boy's sexual phantasies and feelings of love. It is obvious that an attitude based on such feelings will differ from that of a man who seeks mainly maternal traits in a woman; although a man whose choice is influenced by his feelings for a sister may also seek some traits of a maternal kind in his love-partner. A great variety of possibilities is created by the early influence of various people in the child's environment: a nurse, an aunt, a grandmother, may play an important part in this respect. Of course, in considering the bearing early relationships have upon the later choice, we must not forget that it is the impression of the loved person that the child had at the time, and the phantasies he connected with her then, which he wishes to rediscover in his later love relationship. Furthermore, the unconscious mind does associate things on grounds other than those the conscious mind is aware of. Completely forgotten—repressed—impressions of various kinds for this reason contribute to make one person more attractive, sexually and otherwise, than another to the individual concerned.

Similar factors are at work in the woman's choice. Her impressions of her father, her feelings towards him—admiration, trust, and so on—may play a predominant part in her choosing of a love companion. But her early love to her father may have been shaken. Perhaps she soon turned away from him because of over-strong conflicts, or because he disappointed her too much, and a brother, a cousin or a playmate, let us say, may have become a very important person to her; she may have had sexual desires and phantasies as well as maternal feelings towards him. She would then seek a lover or husband agreeing with this image of a brother rather than one who had qualities of a more fatherly kind. In a successful love relationship, the unconscious minds of the love-partners correspond. Taking the case of the woman who has mainly maternal feelings and is seeking a partner of a brotherly nature, then the man's phantasies and desires would correspond if he is looking for a predominantly maternal woman. If the woman is strongly tied to her father, then she unconsciously chooses a man who needs a woman to whom he can play the part of a good father.

Although love-relationships in adult life are founded upon early emotional situations in connection with parents, brothers and sisters, the new relationships are not necessarily mere repetitions of early family situations. Unconscious memories, feelings and phantasies enter into the new love-relationship or friendship in quite disguised ways. But besides early influences there are many other factors at work in the complicated processes that build up a love-relationship or a friendship. Normal adult relationships always contain fresh elements which are derived from the new situation—from circumstances and the personalities of the people we come in contact with, and from their response to our emotional needs and practical interests as grown-up people.

Achieving Independence

So far I have spoken mainly of intimate relationships between people. We now come to the more general manifestations of love and the ways in which it enters into interests and activities of all kinds. The child's early attachment to his mother's breast and to her milk is the foundation of all love relations in life. But if we consider the mother's milk merely as a healthy and suitable food, we may conclude that it could easily be replaced by other equally suitable food. The mother's milk, however, which first stills the baby's pangs of hunger and is given to him by the breast which he comes to love more and more, acquires for him an emotional value which cannot be overrated. The breast and its product, which first gratify his self-preservative instinct as well as his sexual desires, come to stand in his mind for love, pleasure and security. The extent to which he is *psychologically* able to replace this first food by other foods is therefore a matter of supreme importance. The mother may succeed with greater or lesser difficulty in accustoming the child to other foods; but, even so, the baby may not have given up his intense desire for his first food, may not have got over the grievances and hatred at having been deprived of it, nor have adapted himself in the real sense to this frustration — and if this be so, he may not be able to adapt himself truly to any other frustrations which follow in life.

If, by exploring the unconscious mind, we come to understand the strength and depth of this first attachment to the mother and to her food, and the intensity with which it persists in the unconscious mind of the grown-up person, we may wonder how it can come about that the child detaches himself more and more from his mother, and gradually achieves independence. Already in the small baby there is, it is true, a keen interest in things that go on around him, a growing curiosity, an enjoyment in getting to know new people and things, and pleasure in his various achievements, all of which seem to enable the child to find new objects of love and interest. But these facts do not altogether explain the child's ability to detach himself from his mother, since in his unconscious mind he is so closely tied to her. The very nature of this over-strong attachment, however, tends to drive him away from her because (frustrated greed and hatred being inevitable) it gives rise to the fear of losing this all-important person, and consequently to the fear of dependence upon her. There is thus in the unconscious mind a tendency to give her up, which is counteracted by the urgent desire to keep her for ever. These conflicting feelings, together with the emotional and intellectual growth of the child which enable him to find other objects of interest and pleasure, result in the capacity to transfer love, replacing the first loved person by other people and things. It is because the child experiences so much love in connection with his mother that he has so much to draw upon for his later attachments. This process of displacing love is of the greatest importance for the development of the personality and of human relationships; indeed, one may say, for the development of culture and civilization as a whole.

Along with the process of displacing love (and hate) from one's mother to other people and things, and thus distributing these emotions on to the wider world, goes another mode of dealing with early impulses. Sensual feelings which the child experiences in connection with his mother's breast develop into love towards her as a whole person; feelings of love are from their very beginning fused with sexual desires. Psycho-analysis has drawn attention to the fact that sexual feelings towards the parents, brothers and sisters not only exist but can be observed to a certain extent in young children; it is only by exploring the unconscious mind, however, that the strength and fundamental importance of these sexual feelings can be understood.

Sexual desires are, as we already know, closely linked up with aggressive impulses and phantasies, with guilt and the fear of the

326

death of the loved people, all of which drive the child to lessen his attachments to his parents. There is also a tendency in the child to repress these sexual feelings, *i.e.* they become unconscious, and are, so to speak, buried in the depths of the mind. Sexual impulses also get disconnected from the first loved people, and thus the child acquires the capacity to love some people in a predominantly affectionate way.

The psychological processes just described—replacing one loved person by others, dissociating to a certain extent sexual from tender feelings, and repressing sexual impulses and desires—are an integral part of the child's capacity for establishing wider relationships. It is, however, essential for a successful all-round development that the repression of sexual feelings in connection with the first loved people should not be too strong,[1] and that the displacing of the child's feelings from the parents to other people should not be too complete. If enough love remains available for those nearest to the child, if his sexual desires in connection with them are not too deeply repressed, then in later life love and sexual desires can be revived and brought together again, and they then play a vital part in happy love relationships. In a really successfully developed personality some love for the parents remains, but love for other people and things will be added. This is not, however, a mere extension of love but, as I have stressed, a diffusion of emotions, which lessens the burden of the child's conflicts and guilt connected with the attachment to and dependence on the first people he loves.

By turning to other people his conflicts are not done away with, for he transfers them from the first and most important people in a less intense degree to these new objects of love (and hate) which partly stand for the old ones. Just because his feelings towards these new people are less intense, his drive to make reparation, which may be impeded if the feelings of guilt are over-strong, can now come more fully into play.

It is well known that a child's development is helped by his having brothers and sisters. His growing up with them allows him to detach himself more from his parents and to build up a new type of relationship with brothers and sisters. We know, however, that he not only loves them, but has strong feelings of rivalry, hate and jealousy towards them. For this reason, relationships to cousins, playmates and

---

[1] Sexual phantasies and desires remain active in the unconscious mind and are also expressed to a certain extent in the child's behaviour and in his play and other activities. If repression is too strong, if the phantasies and desires remain too deeply buried and can find no expression, this may not only have the effect of inhibiting strongly the working of his imagination (and with this of activities of all kinds), but also of seriously impeding the individual's later sexual life.

other children still further removed from the nearest family situation, allow divergences from the relationships to brothers and sisters — divergences which again are of great importance as a foundation for later social relationships.

Relationships in School Life

School life affords an opportunity for developing the experience already gained of relationship to people, and provides a field for new experiments in this line. Among a greater number of children the child may find one or two or several who respond better to his special make-up than his brothers and sisters did. These new friendships, among other satisfactions, give him an opportunity for revising and improving, as it were, the early relationships with his brothers and sisters, which may have been unsatisfactory. He may actually have been aggressive towards, let us say, a brother who was weaker or younger; or it may have been mainly his unconscious sense of guilt because of hatred and jealousy which disturbed the relationship — a disturbance which may persist into grown-up life. This unsatisfactory state of affairs may have a profound effect later upon his emotional attitudes towards people in general. Some children are, as we know, incapable of making friends at school, and this is because they carry their early conflicts into a new environment. With others who can detach themselves sufficiently from their first emotional entanglements and can make friends with schoolmates, it is often found that the actual relation to brothers and sisters then improves. The new companionships prove to the child that he is able to love and is lovable, that love and goodness *exist*, and this is unconsciously felt also as a proof that he can repair harm which he has done to others in his imagination or in actual fact. Thus new friendships help in the solution of earlier emotional difficulties, without the person being aware either of the exact nature of those early troubles or of the way in which they are being solved. By all of these means the tendencies for making reparation find scope, the sense of guilt is lessened, and trust in oneself and in others is increased.

School life also gives opportunity for a greater separation of hate from love than was possible in the small family circle. At school, some children can be hated, or merely disliked, while others can be loved. In this way, both the repressed emotions of love and hate — repressed because of the conflict about hating a loved person — can find fuller expression in more or less socially accepted directions. Children ally themselves in various ways, and develop certain rules as to how far they can go in their expressions of hatred or dislike of others. Games and the team spirit associated with them are a regulating factor in these alliances and in the display of aggression.

Jealousy and rivalry for the teacher's love and appreciation, though they may be quite strong, are experienced in a setting different from that of home life. Teachers are, on the whole, further removed from the child's feelings, they bring less emotion into the situation than parents do, and they also divide their feelings among many children.

Relationships in Adolescence

As the child grows to adolescence, his tendency to hero-worship often finds expression in his relation to some teachers, while he may dislike, hate or scorn others. This is another instance of the process of separating hatred from love, a process which affords relief, both because the 'good' person is spared and because there is satisfaction in hating someone who is thought to be worthy of it. The loved and hated father, the loved and hated mother, are, as I have already said, originally the objects of both admiration and of hatred and devaluation. But these mixed feelings, which are, as we know, too conflicting and burdensome for the young child's mind and therefore likely to be impeded or buried, find part expression in the child's relations with other people—for instance, nurses, aunts, uncles and various relatives. Later on, in adolescence, most children manifest a strong tendency to turn away from their parents; and this is largely because sexual desires and conflicts connected with the parents are once more gaining in strength. The early feelings of rivalry and hatred against the father or the mother, as the case may be, are revived and experienced with full force, though their sexual motive remains unconscious. Young people tend to be very aggressive and unpleasant to their parents, and to other people who lend themselves to it, such as servants, a weak teacher, or disliked schoolmates. But when hatred reaches such strength, the necessity to preserve goodness and love within and without becomes all the more urgent. The aggressive youth is therefore driven to find people whom he can look up to and idealize. Admired teachers can serve this purpose; and inner security is derived from the feelings of love, admiration and trust towards them, because, among other reasons, in the unconscious mind these feelings seem to confirm the existence of good parents and of a love relation to them, thus disproving the great hatred, anxiety and guilt which at this period of life have become so strong. There are, of course, children who can keep love and admiration for the parents themselves even while they are going through these difficulties, but they are not very common. I think that what I have said goes a little way to explain the peculiar position in the minds of people generally of idealized figures such as famous men and women, authors, athletes, adventurers, imaginary characters taken from literature—people towards whom is turned the love and

329

admiration without which all things would take on the gloom of hate and lovelessness, a state that is felt to be dangerous to the self and to others.

Together with the idealization of certain people goes the hatred against others, who are painted in the darkest colours. This applies especially to imaginary people, *i.e.* certain types of villains in films and in literature; or to real people somewhat removed from oneself, such as political leaders of the opposite party. It is safe to hate these people, who are either unreal or further removed, than to hate those nearer to one—safer for them and for oneself. This applies also to a certain extent to the hatred against some teachers or headmasters, for the general school discipline and the whole situation tends to make a greater barrier between pupil and teacher than often exists between son and father.

This division between love and hate towards people not too close to oneself also serves the purpose of keeping loved people more secure, both actually and in one's mind. They are not only remote from one physically and thus inaccessible, but the division between the loving and hating attitude fosters the feeling that one can keep love unspoilt. The feeling of security that comes from being able to love is, in the unconscious mind, closely linked up with keeping loved people safe and undamaged. The unconscious belief seems to run: I am able to keep some loved people intact, then I have really not damaged any of my loved people and I keep them all for ever in my mind. In the last analysis the image of the loved parents is preserved in the unconscious mind as the most precious possession, for it guards its possessor against the pain of utter desolation.

The Development of Friendships

The child's early friendships change in character during adolescence. The strength of impulses and feelings, which is so characteristic of this stage of life, brings about very intense friendships between young people, mostly between members of the same sex. Unconscious homosexual tendencies and feelings underlie these relationships and very often lead to actual homosexual activities. Such relationships are partly an escape from the drive towards the other sex, which is often too unmanageable at this stage, for various internal and external reasons. To speak of internal ones and to take the case of the boy: his desires and phantasies are still very much connected with his mother and sisters, and the struggle of turning away from them and finding new love objects is at its very height. The impulses towards the other sex, with both boys and girls at this stage, are often felt to be fraught with so many dangers that the drive towards people of the same sex tends to become intensified. The love, admiration and adulation which can be put into these friendships are also, as I pointed out before, a safeguard against hatred, and for these various reasons young people cling all the more to such relationships. At this stage of development, the increased homosexual tendencies, whether conscious or unconscious, also play a great part in the adulation of teachers of the same sex. Friendships in adolescence, as we know, are very often unstable. A reason for this is to be found in the strength of the sexual feelings (unconscious or conscious) which enter into them and disturb them. The adolescent is not yet emancipated from the strong emotional ties of infancy and is still—more than he knows—swayed by them.

Friendships in Adult Life

In adult life, though unconscious homosexual tendencies play their part in friendships between people of the same sex, it is characteristic of friendship—as distinct from a homosexual love relationship[1]—that affectionate feelings can be partially dissociated from sexual ones, which recede into the background, and though remaining to a certain extent active in the unconscious mind, for practical purposes they disappear. This separation of sexual from affectionate feelings can apply also to friendships between men and women, but since the vast topic of friendship is only one part of my subject, I shall confine myself here to speaking of friendships between people of the same sex, and even then I shall make only a few general remarks.

Let us take as an instance a friendship between two women who are not too dependent upon each other. Protectiveness and helpfulness may still be needed, at times by the one, at other times by the other, as situations arise. This capacity to give and take emotionally is one essential for true friendship. Here, elements of early situations are expressed in adult ways. Protection, help and advice were first afforded to us by our mothers. If we grow up emotionally and become self-sufficient, we shall not be too dependent upon maternal support and comfort, but the wish to receive them when painful and difficult situations arise will remain until we die. In our relation to a friend we may at times receive and give some of a mother's care and love. A successful blending of a mother-attitude and a daughter-attitude seems to be one of the conditions for an emotionally rich feminine personality and for the capacity for friendship. (A fully developed feminine personality implies a capacity for good relations

[1] The subject of homosexual love relations is a wide and very complicated one. To deal with it adequately would necessitate more space than I have at my disposal, and I restrict myself, therefore, to mentioning that much love can be put into these relationships.

with men, as far as both affectionate and sexual feelings are concerned; but in speaking of friendship between women I am referring to the sublimated homosexual tendencies and feelings.) We may have had an opportunity in our relations to sisters to experience and express both the motherly care and the daughter's response; and then we can easily carry them further into adult friendships. But there may not have been a sister, or none with whom these feelings could be experienced, and in that case, if we come to develop a friendship with another woman, this will bring to realization, modified by adult needs, a strong and important wish of childhood.

We share interests and pleasures with a friend, but we may also be capable of enjoying her happiness and success even when we ourselves lack these. Feelings of envy and jealousy may recede into the background if our capacity to identify ourselves with her, and thus to share in her happiness, is strong enough.

The element of guilt and reparation is never missing in such an identification. Only if we have successfully dealt with our hatred and jealousy, dissatisfaction and grievance against our mother, and have succeeded in being happy in seeing her happy, in feeling that we have not injured her or that we can repair the injury done in phantasy, are we capable of true identification with another woman. Possessiveness and grievance, which lead to over-strong demands, are disturbing elements in friendship; indeed, over-strong emotions altogether are likely to undermine it. Whenever this happens, one finds, on psycho-analytical investigation, that early situations of unsatisfied desires, of grievance, of greed or jealousy, have broken through, *i.e.* though current episodes may have started the trouble, an unresolved conflict from infancy plays an important part in the break-up of the friendship. A balanced emotional atmosphere, which does not at all exclude strength of feeling, is a basis for success in friendship. It is not so likely to succeed if we expect too much of it, *i.e.* expect the friend to make up for our early deprivations. Such undue demands are for the most part unconscious, and therefore cannot be dealt with rationally. They expose us necessarily to disappointment, pain and resentment. If such excessive unconscious demands lead to disturbances in our friendships, exact repetitions—however different the external circumstances may be—of early situations have come about, when in the first place intense greed and hatred disturbed our love for our parents and left us with feelings of dissatisfaction and loneliness. When the past does not press so strongly upon the present situation, we are more able both to make the right choice of friends and to satisfy ourselves with what they have to give.

Much of what I have said about friendship between women— though there are also important differences by reason of the differ-

ence between the man's and the woman's psychology—applies to
the development of friendship between men. The separation of affectionate from sexual feelings, the sublimation of homosexual tendencies and identification, are also the foundation for male friendships. Although elements and new gratifications corresponding to
adult personality enter—fresh—into a man's friendship with another
man, he also is seeking partly for a repetition of his relation to his
father or brother, or trying to find a new affinity which fulfils past
desires, or to improve on the unsatisfactory relations to those who
once stood nearest to him.

Wider Aspects of Love

The process by which we displace love from the first people we
cherish to other people is extended from earliest childhood onwards
to things. In this way we develop interests and activities into which
we put some of the love that originally belonged to people. In the
baby's mind, one part of the body can stand for another part, and
an object for parts of the body or for people. In this symbolical way,
any round object may, in the child's unconscious mind, come to stand
for his mother's breast. By a gradual process, anything that is felt to
give out goodness and beauty, and that calls forth pleasure and satisfaction, in the physical or in the wider sense, can in the unconscious
mind take the place of this ever-bountiful breast, and of the whole
mother. Thus we speak of our own country as the 'motherland' because in the unconscious mind our country may come to stand for
our mother, and then it can be loved with feelings which borrow
their nature from the relation to her.

To illustrate the way in which the first relationship enters into
interests that seem very remote from it, let us take as an instance the
explorers who set out for new discoveries, undergoing the greatest
deprivations and encountering grave dangers and perhaps death in
the attempt. Besides stimulating external circumstances, there are
very many psychological elements that underlie the interest and the
pursuit of exploring. Here I can mention only one or two specific unconscious factors. In his greed, the little boy has desires to attack his
mother's body, which is felt as an extension of her good breast. He
also has phantasies of robbing her of the contents of her body—
among other things of babies, which are felt to be precious possessions— and in his jealousy he also attacks the babies. These aggressive
phantasies of penetrating her body are soon linked up with his genital
desires to have intercourse with her. In psycho-analytic work it has
been found that phantasies of exploring the mother's body, which
arise out of the child's aggressive sexual desires, greed, curiosity and
love, contribute to the man's interest in exploring new countries.

In discussing the emotional development of the small child, I pointed out that his aggressive impulses give rise to strong feelings of guilt and to fear of the death of the loved person, all of which form part of feelings of love and reinforce and intensify them. In the explorer's unconscious mind, a new territory stands for a new mother, one that will replace the loss of the real mother. He is seeking the 'promised land'—the 'land flowing with milk and honey'. We have already seen that fear of the death of the most loved person leads to the child's turning away from her to some extent; but at the same time it also drives him to re-create her and to find her again in whatever he undertakes. Here both the escape from her and the original attachment to her find full expression. The child's early aggression stimulates the drive to restore and to make good, to put back into his mother the good things he had robbed her of in phantasy, and these wishes to make good merge into the later drive to explore, for by finding new land the explorer gives something to the world at large and to a number of people in particular. In his pursuit the explorer actually gives expression to both aggression and the drive to reparation. We know that in discovering a new country aggression is made use of in the struggle with the elements, and in overcoming difficulties of all kinds. But sometimes aggression is shown more openly; especially was this so in former times when ruthless cruelty against native populations was displayed by people who not only explored, but conquered and colonized. Some of the early phantasied attacks against the imaginary babies in the mother's body, and actual hatred against new-born brothers and sisters, were here expressed in reality by the attitude towards the natives. The wished-for restoration, however, found full expression in repopulating the country with people of their own nationality. We can see that through the interest in exploring (whether or not aggression is openly shown) various impulses and emotions—aggression, feelings of guilt, love and the drive to reparation—can be transferred to another sphere, far away from the original person.

The drive to explore need not be expressed in an actual physical exploration of the world, but may extend to other fields, for instance, to any kind of scientific discovery. Early phantasies and desires to explore his mother's body enter into the satisfaction which the astronomer, for example, derives from his work. The desire to re-discover the mother of the early days, whom one has lost actually or in one's feelings, is also of the greatest importance in creative art and in the ways people enjoy and appreciate it.

To illustrate some of the processes I have just been discussing, I will take the well-known sonnet by Keats, 'On First Looking into Chapman's Homer'.

For convenience I am quoting the whole poem, though it is so well known:

> Much have I travell'd in the realms of gold,
>   And many goodly states and kingdoms seen;
>   Round many western islands have I been
> Which bards in fealty to Apollo hold.
> Oft of one wide expanse had I been told
>   That deep-brow'd Homer ruled as his demesne:
>   Yet did I never breathe its pure serene
> Till I heard Chapman speak out loud and bold:

Keats is speaking here from the point of view of one who enjoys a work of art. Poetry is compared to 'goodly states and kingdoms' and 'realms of gold'. He himself, on reading Chapman's Homer, is first the astronomer who watches the skies when 'a new planet swims into his ken'. But then Keats becomes the explorer who discovers 'with a wild surmise' a new land and sea. In Keats's perfect poem the world stands for art, and it is clear that to him scientific and artistic enjoyment and exploration are derived from the same source—from the love for the beautiful lands—the 'realms of gold'. The exploration of the unconscious mind (by the way, an unknown continent discovered by Freud) shows that, as I have pointed out before, the beautiful lands stand for the loved mother, and the longing with which these lands are approached is derived from our longings for her. Going back to the sonnet, one may suggest—without any detailed analysis of it—that the 'deep-browed Homer' who rules over the land of poetry stands for the admired and powerful father, whose example the son (Keats) follows when he too enters the country of his desire (art, beauty, the world—ultimately his mother).

Similarly, the sculptor who puts life into his object of art, whether or not it represents a person, is unconsciously restoring and re-creating the early loved people, whom he has in phantasy destroyed.

> Then felt I like some watcher of the skies
>   When a new planet swims into his ken;
> Or like stout Cortez, when with eagle eyes
>   He stared at the Pacific—and all his men
> Look'd at each other with a wild surmise—
>   Silent, upon a peak in Darien.

Sense of Guilt, Love and Creativeness

Feelings of guilt, which as I have endeavoured to show, are a fundamental incentive towards creativeness and work in general (even of the simplest kinds) may however, if they are too great, have the effect of inhibiting productive activities and interests. These complex connections have first become clear through the psycho-analysis of small children. In children, creative impulses which have hitherto been dormant awaken and express themselves in such activities as drawing, modelling, building and in speech, when by means of psycho-analysis fears of various kinds become lessened. These fears had brought about an increase of the destructive impulses, and therefore when fears are diminished, destructive impulses also are lessened. Along with these processes, feelings of guilt and the anxiety about the death of the loved person, with which the child's mind had been unable to cope because they were overwhelming, gradually diminish, become less intense and are then manageable. This has the effect of increasing the child's concern for other people, of stimulating pity and identification with them, and thus love altogether is increased. The wish to make reparation, so intimately bound up with the concern for the loved one and the anxiety about his death, can now be expressed in creative and constructive ways. In the psycho-analysis of adults, too, these processes and changes can be observed.

I have suggested that any source of joy, beauty and enrichment (whether internal or external) is, in the unconscious mind, felt to be the mother's loving and giving breast and the father's creative penis, which in phantasy possesses similar qualities—ultimately, the two kind and generous parents. The relation to nature which arouses such strong feelings of love, appreciation, admiration and devotion, has much in common with the relation to one's mother, as has long been recognized by poets. The manifold gifts of nature are equated with whatever we have received in the early days from our mother. But she has not always been satisfactory. We often felt her to be ungenerous and to be frustrating us; this aspect of our feelings towards her is also revived in our relation to nature which often is unwilling to give.

The satisfaction of our self-preservative needs and the gratification of our desire for love are forever linked up with each other, because they are first derived from one and the same source. Security was first of all afforded to us by our mother, who not only stilled the pangs of hunger, but also satisfied our emotional needs and relieved anxiety. Security attained by satisfaction of our essential requirements is therefore linked up with emotional security, and both are all the more needed because they counteract the early fears of losing the loved mother. To be sure of our livelihood also implies, in the unconscious phantasy, not being deprived of love and not losing our mother altogether. The man who is out of work and who struggles to find some has in mind first of all his essential material needs. I am not underrating the actual sufferings and distress, direct and indirect, which result from poverty; but the actual painful situation is made more poignant by the sorrow and despair springing from his earliest emotional situations, when he not only felt deprived of food because his mother did not satisfy his needs, but also felt he was losing both her and her love and protection.[1] Being out of work deprives him also of giving expression to his constructive tendencies, one most important way of dealing with his unconscious fears and sense of guilt— *i.e.* of making reparation. Harshness of circumstances (though this may be partly due to an unsatisfactory social system, and thus give actual ground for the person living in misery to blame other people for it) has something in common with the relentlessness of dreaded parents, in which children, under stress of anxiety, believe. Conversely, help—material or mental—afforded to poor or unemployed people, in addition to its actual value, is unconsciously felt to prove the existence of loving parents.

To go back to the relation to nature. In some parts of the world nature is cruel and destructive, but nevertheless the inhabitants defy the dangers of the elements, whether these be drought, floods, cold, heat, earthquakes or plagues, rather than give up their land. External circumstances, it is true, play an important part, for these tenacious people may have no facilities for moving away from the place where they have grown up. This, however, does not seem to me to explain fully the phenomenon that so much hardship can sometimes be borne in order to keep to the native land. With people who are living under such hard conditions of nature, the struggle for a livelihood serves other (unconscious) purposes as well. Nature represents to him a grudging and exacting mother, whose gifts must be forcibly extolled from her, whereby early violent phantasies are repeated and acted out (though in a sublimated and socially adaptive way); feeling unconsciously guilty for his aggressive impulses towards his mother, he expected (and still unconsciously expects now in his relation to nature) that she would be harsh with him. This feeling of guilt acts as an incentive to making reparation. The struggle with nature is therefore partly felt to be a struggle to *preserve nature*, because it expresses also the wish to make reparation to her (mother). People who

[1] In the psycho-analysis of children I frequently discovered—of course in varying degrees—fears of being turned out of the home as a punishment for unconscious aggression (wishing to turn others out) and for actual harm which had been done. This anxiety sets in very early and may prey very strongly on the child's mind. A special case of it is the fear of being either a poor orphan or a beggar, and having no home and no food. Now these fears of being destitute, in the children in whom I have observed them, were quite independent of the parents' financial situation. In later life, fears of this kind have the effect of increasing the actual difficulties which arise from such things as loss of money or having to give up a house, or loss of one's work; they add an element of poignancy and deepen despair.

strive with the severity of nature thus not only take care of themselves, but also serve nature herself. In not severing their connection with her they keep alive the image of the mother of the early days. They preserve themselves and her in phantasy by remaining close to her — actually by not leaving their country. In contrast with this, the explorer is seeking in phantasy a new mother in order to replace the real one from whom he feels estranged, or whom he is unconsciously afraid to lose.

The Relationship to Ourselves and to Others

I have dealt in this section with some aspects of the individual's love and relations towards other people. I cannot conclude, however, without attempting to throw some light upon the most complicated relationship of all, and that is the one we have to ourselves. But what are our selves? Everything, good or bad, that we have gone through from our earliest days onwards; all that we have received from the external world and all that we have felt in our inner world, happy and unhappy experiences, relationships to people, activities, interests and thoughts of all kinds — that is to say, everything we have lived through — makes part of our selves and goes to build up our personalities. If some of our past relationships, with all the associated memories, with the wealth of feelings they called forth, could be suddenly wiped out of our lives, how impoverished and empty we should feel! How much love, trust, gratification, comfort and gratitude, which we experienced and returned, would be lost! Many of us would not even want to have missed some of our painful experiences, for they have also contributed to the enrichment of our personalities. I have referred many times in this paper to the important bearing our early relationships have on our later ones. Now I want to show that these earliest emotional situations fundamentally influence our relationships to *ourselves*. We keep enshrined in our minds our loved people; we may feel in certain difficult situations that we are guided by them, and may find ourselves wondering how *they* would behave, and whether or not they would approve of our actions. From what I have already said, we may conclude that these people to whom we look up in this way ultimately stand for the admired and loved parents. We have seen, however, that it is by no means easy for the child to establish harmonious relationships to them, and that early feelings of love are seriously inhibited and disturbed by impulses of hatred and by the unconscious sense of guilt to which these give rise. It is true, the parents may have been lacking in love or understanding, and this would tend to increase difficulties all round. Destructive impulses and phantasies, fears and distrust, which are always to some extent active in the small child even in the most favourable circumstances, are necessarily very much increased by unfavourable conditions and unpleasant experiences. Moreover—and this is also very important—if the child is not afforded enough happiness in his early life, his capacity for developing a hopeful attitude as well as love and trust in people will be disturbed. It does not follow from this, however, that the capacity for love and happiness which develops in the child is in direct proportion to the amount of love afforded him. Indeed there are children who develop extremely harsh and stern parent-figures in their unconscious minds—which disturb the relation to the actual parents and to people in general—even though the parents have been kind and loving to them. On the other hand, the child's mental difficulties are often not in direct proportion to the unfavourable treatment he receives. If, for internal reasons, which from the outset vary in different individuals, there is little capacity to tolerate frustration, and if aggression, fears and feelings of guilt are very strong, then the actual shortcomings of the parents, and especially their motives for doing the wrong thing, may become grossly exaggerated and distorted in the child's mind, and his parents and other people around him may be felt to be predominantly harsh and stern. For our own hatred, fear and distrust tend to create in our unconscious minds frightening and exacting parent-figures. Now these processes are in varying degrees active in all of us, since we all have to struggle—in one way or another and more or less—with feelings of hatred and fears. Thus we see that the *quantities* of aggressive impulses, fears and feelings of guilt (which arise partly for internal reasons) have an important bearing upon the predominant mental attitude which we develop.

In contrast to those children who, in response to an unfavourable treatment, develop, in their unconscious minds, such harsh and stern parent-figures and whose whole mental attitude is so disastrously affected by this, there are many children who are much less adversely affected by the mistakes or lack of understanding of their parents. Children who—for internal reasons—are from the beginning more capable of bearing frustrations (whether avoidable or unavoidable), that is to say, can do so without being so dominated by their own impulses of hatred and suspicion—such children will be much more tolerant of mistakes their parents make in dealing with them. They can rely more upon their own friendly feelings, and are therefore more secure in themselves and less easily shaken by what comes to them from the outer world. No child's mind is free from fears and suspicions, but if the relation to our parents is built predominantly upon trust and love, we can establish them firmly in our minds as guiding and helpful figures, which are a source of comfort and harmony and the prototype for all friendly relationships in later life.

I tried to throw light on some of our adult relationships by saying that we behave towards certain people as our parents behaved towards us, when they were loving, or as we wanted them to behave, and that thus we reverse early situations. Or again, with some people, we have the attitude of a loving child towards his parents. Now this interchangeable child-parent relation which we manifest in our attitude to people is also *experienced within ourselves to these helpful, guiding figures whom we keep in our minds*. We unconsciously feel these people who form part of our inner world to be loving and protective parents towards us, and we return this love, we feel like parents towards them. These phantasy-relationships, based on real experiences and memories, form part of our continuous, active life of feeling and of imagination, and contribute to our happiness and mental strength. If, however, the parent-figures, which are maintained in our feelings and in our unconscious minds, are predominantly harsh, then we cannot be at peace with ourselves. It is well known that too harsh a conscience gives rise to worry and unhappiness. It is less well known, but proved by psycho-analytic findings, that the strain of such phantasies of internal warfare and the fears connected with it are at the bottom of what we recognize as a vindictive conscience. Incidentally these stresses and fears can be expressed in deep mental disturbances and lead to suicide.

I have used the rather odd phrase 'the relation to ourselves'. Now I should like to add that this is a relation to all that we cherish and love and to all that we hate in ourselves. I have tried to make clear that one part of ourselves that we cherish is the wealth we have accumulated through our relations to external people, for these relations and also the emotions that are bound up with them have become an inner possession. We hate in ourselves the harsh and stern figures who are also part of our inner world, and are to a large extent the result of our own aggression towards our parents. At the bottom our strongest hatred, however, is directed against the hatred within ourselves. We so much dread the hatred in ourselves that we are driven to employ one of our strongest measures of defence by putting it on to other people—to project it. But we also displace love into the outer world; and we can do so genuinely only if we have established good relations with the friendly figures within our minds. Here is a benign circle, for in the first place we gain trust and love in relation to our parents, next we take them, with all this love and trust, as it were, into ourselves; and then we can give from this wealth of loving feelings to the outer world again. There is an analogous circle in regard to our hatred; for hatred, as we have seen, leads to our establishing frightening figures in our minds, and then we are apt to endow other people with unpleasant and malevolent qualities. Incidentally, such an attitude of mind has an actual effect in making other people unpleasant and suspicious towards us, while a friendly and trusting attitude on our part is apt to call forth trust and benevolence from others.

We know that some people, especially when growing old, get more and more bitter; that others become milder, and more understanding and tolerant. It is well known also that such variations are due to a difference in attitude and character, and do not simply correspond to the adverse or favourable experiences which are met with in life. From what I have said we may conclude that bitterness of feeling, be it towards people or towards fate—and this bitterness is usually felt in relation to both,—is fundamentally established in childhood and may become strengthened or intensified in later life.

If love has not been smothered under resentment, grievances and hatred, but has been firmly established in the mind, trust in other people and belief in one's own goodness are like a rock which withstands the blows of circumstance. Then when unhappiness arises, the person whose development has followed lines such as these is capable of preserving in himself those good parents, whose love is an unfailing help in his unhappiness, and can find once more in the outer world people who, in his mind, stand for them. With the capacity for reversing situations in phantasy, and identifying himself with others, a capacity which is a great characteristic of the human mind, a man can distribute to others the help and love of which he himself is in need, and in this way can gain comfort and satisfaction for himself.

I started out by describing the emotional situation of the baby, in his relation to his mother, who is the original and paramount source of the goodness that he receives from the outer world. I went on to say that it is an extremely painful process for the baby to do without the supreme satisfaction of being fed by her. If, however, his greed and his resentment at being frustrated are not too great, he is able to detach himself gradually from her and at the same time to gain satisfaction from other sources. The new objects of pleasure are linked up in his unconscious mind with the first gratifications received from his mother, and that is why he can accept other enjoyments as substitutes for the original ones. This process could be described as retaining the primary goodness as well as replacing it, and the more successfully it is carried through, the less ground is left in the baby's mind for greed and hatred. But, as I have frequently stressed, the unconscious feelings of guilt which arise in connection with the phantasied destruction of a loved person play a fundamental part in these processes. We have seen that the baby's feelings of guilt and sorrow, arising from his phantasies of destroying his mother in his greed and hate, set going the drive to heal these imaginary injuries, and to make reparation to her. Now these emotions have an important bearing upon the baby's wish and capacity to accept substitutes for his mother. For feelings of guilt give rise to the fear of being dependent upon this loved person whom the child is afraid of losing, since as soon as aggression wells up he feels he is injuring her. This fear of dependence is an incentive to his detaching himself from her—to his turning to other people and things and thus enlarging the range of interests. Normally, the drive to make reparation can keep at bay the despair arising out of feelings of guilt, and then hope will prevail, in which case the baby's love and his desire to make reparation are unconsciously carried over to the new objects of love and interest. These, as we already know, are in the baby's unconscious mind linked up with the first loved person, whom he rediscovers or re-creates through his relation to new people and through constructive interests. Thus making reparation—which is such an essential part of the ability to love—widens in scope, and the child's capacity to accept love and, by various means, to take into himself goodness from the outer world steadily increases. This satisfactory balance between 'give' and 'take' is the primary condition for further happiness.

If in our earliest development we have been able to transfer our interest and love from our mother to other people and other sources of gratification, then, and only then, are we able in later life to derive enjoyment from other sources. This enables us to compensate for a failure or a disappointment in connection with one person by establishing a friendly relationship to others, and to accept substitutes for things we have been unable to obtain or to keep. If frustrated greed, resentment and hatred within us do not disturb the relation to the outer world, there are innumerable ways of taking in beauty, goodness and love from without. By doing this we continuously add to our happy memories and gradually build up a store of values by which we gain a security that cannot easily be shaken, and contentment which prevents bitterness of feeling. Moreover all these satisfactions have in addition to the pleasure they afford, the effect of diminishing frustrations (or rather the feeling of frustration) past and present, back to the earliest and fundamental ones. The more true satisfaction we experience, the less do we resent deprivations, and the less shall we be swayed by our greed and hatred. Then we are actually capable of accepting love and goodness from others and of giving love to others; and again receiving more in return. In other words, the essential capacity for 'give and take' has been developed in us in a way that ensures our own contentment, and contributes to the pleasure, comfort or happiness of other people.

In conclusion, a good relation to ourselves is a condition for love, tolerance and wisdom towards others. This good relation to ourselves has, as I have endeavoured to show, developed in part from a friendly, loving and understanding attitude towards other people, namely, those who meant much to us in the past, and our relationship to whom has become part of our minds and personalities. If we have become able, deep in our unconscious minds, to clear our feelings to some extent towards our parents of grievances, and have forgiven them for the frustrations we had to bear, then we can be at peace with ourselves and are able to love others in the true sense of the word.

20

MOURNING AND ITS RELATION TO
MANIC-DEPRESSIVE STATES

(1940)

An essential part of the work of mourning is, as Freud points out in 'Mourning and Melancholia', the testing of reality. He says that 'in mourning time is needed for the command of reality-testing to be carried out in detail, and that when this work has been accomplished the ego will have succeeded in freeing its libido from the lost object' (*S.E.* **14**, p. 252). And again, 'Each single one of the memories and expectations in which the libido is bound to the object is brought up and hypercathected, and detachment of the libido is accomplished in respect of it. Why this compromise by which the command of reality is carried out piecemeal should be so extraordinarily painful is not at all easy to explain in terms of economics. It is remarkable that this painful unpleasure is taken as a matter of course by us' (*ibid.*, p. 245). And in another passage: '. . . we do not even know the economic means by which mourning carries out its task. Possibly, however, a conjecture will help us here. Each single one of the memories and situations of expectancy which demonstrate the libido's attachment to the lost object is met by the verdict of reality that the object no longer exists; and the ego, confronted as it were with the question whether it shall share this fate, is persuaded by the sum of the narcissistic satisfactions it derives from being alive to sever its attachment to the object that has been abolished. We may perhaps suppose that this work of severance is so slow and gradual that by the time it has been finished the expenditure of energy necessary for it is also dissipated' (*ibid.*, p. 255).

In my view there is a close connection between the testing of reality in normal mourning and early processes of the mind. My contention is that the child goes through states of mind comparable to the mourning of the adult, or rather, that this early mourning is revived whenever grief is experienced in later life. The most important of the methods by which the child overcomes his states of mourning, is, in my view, the testing of reality; this process, however, as Freud stresses, is part of the work of mourning.

In my paper 'A Contribution to the Psychogenesis of Manic-

Depressive States',[1] I introduced the conception of the *infantile depressive position* and showed the connection between that position and manic-depressive states. Now in order to make clear the relation between the infantile depressive position and normal mourning I must first briefly refer to some statements I made in that paper, and shall then enlarge on them. In the course of this exposition I also hope to make a contribution to the further understanding of the connection between normal mourning, on the one hand, and abnormal mourning and manic-depressive states, on the other.

I said there that the baby experiences depressive feelings which reach a climax just before, during and after weaning. This is the state of mind in the baby which I termed the 'depressive position', and I suggested that it is a melancholia in *statu nascendi*. The object which is being mourned is the mother's breast and all that the breast and the milk have come to stand for in the infant's mind: namely, love, goodness and security. All these are felt by the baby to be lost, and lost as a result of his own uncontrollable greedy and destructive phantasies and impulses against his mother's breasts. Further distress about impending loss (this time of both parents) arises out of the Oedipus situation, which sets in so early and in such close connection with breast frustrations that in its beginnings it is dominated by oral impulses and fears. The circle of loved objects who are attacked in phantasy, and whose loss is therefore feared, widens owing to the child's ambivalent relations to his brothers and sisters. The aggression against phantasied brothers and sisters, who are attacked inside the mother's body, also gives rise to feelings of guilt and loss. The sorrow and concern about the feared loss of the 'good' objects, that is to say, the depressive position, is, in my experience, the deepest source of the painful conflicts in the Oedipus situation, as well as in the child's relations to people in general. In normal development these feelings of grief and fears are overcome by various methods.

Along with the child's relation, first to his mother and soon to his father and other people, go those processes of internalization on which I have laid so much stress in my work. The baby, having incorporated his parents, feels them to be live people inside his body in the concrete way in which deep unconscious phantasies are experienced —they are, in his mind, 'internal' or 'inner' objects, as I have termed them. Thus an inner world is being built up in the child's unconscious mind, corresponding to his actual experiences and the impressions he gains from people and the external world, and yet altered by his own phantasies and impulses. If it is a world of people predominantly at

[1] See p. 262. The present paper is a continuation of that paper, and much of what I have now to say will of necessity assume the conclusions I arrived at there.

peace with each other and with the ego, inner harmony, security and integration ensue.

There is a constant interaction between anxieties relating to the 'external' mother—as I will call her here in contrast to the 'internal' one—and those relating to the 'internal' mother, and the methods used by the ego for dealing with these two sets of anxieties are closely inter-related. In the baby's mind, the 'internal' mother is bound up with the 'external' one, of whom she is a 'double', though one which at once undergoes alterations in his mind through the very process of internalization; that is to say, her image is influenced by his phantasies, and by internal stimuli and internal experiences of all kinds. When external situations which he lives through become internalized —and I hold that they do, from the earliest days onwards—they follow the same pattern: they also become 'doubles' of real situations, and are again altered for the same reasons. The fact that by being internalized, people, things, situations and happenings—the whole inner world which is being built up—becomes inaccessible to the child's accurate observation and judgement, and cannot be verified by the means of perception which are available in connection with the tangible and palpable object-world, has an important bearing on the phantastic nature of this inner world. The ensuing doubts, uncertainties and anxieties act as a continuous incentive to the young child to observe and make sure about the external object-world,[1] from which this inner world springs, and by these means to understand the internal one better. The visible mother thus provides continuous proofs of what the 'internal' mother is like, whether she is loving or angry, helpful or revengeful. The extent to which external reality is able to disprove anxieties and sorrow relating to the internal reality varies with each individual, but could be taken as one of the criteria for normality. In children who are so much dominated by their internal world that their anxieties cannot be sufficiently disproved and counteracted even by the pleasant aspects of their relationships with people, severe mental difficulties are unavoidable. On the other hand, a certain amount even of unpleasant experiences is of value in this testing of reality by the child if, through overcoming them, he feels that he can retain his objects as well as their love for him and his love for them, and thus preserve or re-establish internal life and harmony in face of dangers.

All the enjoyments which the baby lives through in relation to his

[1] Here I can only refer in passing to the great impetus which these anxieties afford to the development of interests and sublimations of all kinds. If these anxieties are over-strong, they may interfere with or even check intellectual development. (Cf. 'A Contribution to the Theory of Intellectual Inhibition', p. 236.)

mother are so many proofs to him that the loved object *inside as well as outside* is not injured, is not turned into a vengeful person. The increase of love and trust, and the diminishing of fears through happy experiences, help the baby step by step to overcome his depression and feeling of loss (mourning). They enable him to test his inner reality by means of outer reality. Through being loved and through the enjoyment and comfort he has in relation to people his confidence in his own as well as in other people's goodness becomes strengthened, his hope that his 'good' objects and his own ego can be saved and preserved increases, at the same time as his ambivalence and acute fears of internal destruction diminish.

Unpleasant experiences and the lack of enjoyable ones, in the young child, especially lack of happy and close contact with loved people, increase ambivalence, diminish trust and hope and confirm anxieties about inner annihilation and external persecution; moreover they slow down and perhaps permanently check the beneficial processes through which in the long run inner security is achieved.

In the process of acquiring knowledge, every new piece of experience has to be fitted into the patterns provided by the psychic reality which prevails at the time; whilst the psychic reality of the child is gradually influenced by every step in his progressive knowledge of external reality. Every such step goes along with his more and more firmly establishing his inner 'good' objects, and is used by the ego as a means of overcoming the depressive position.

In other connections I have expressed the view that every infant experiences anxieties which are psychotic in content,[1] and that the infantile neurosis[2] is the normal means of dealing with and modifying these anxieties. This conclusion I can now state more precisely, as a result of my work on the infantile depressive position, which has led me to believe that it is the central position in the child's development. In the infantile neurosis the early depressive position finds expression, is worked through and gradually overcome; and this is an important part of the process of organization and integration which, together with the sexual development,[3] characterizes the first years of life.

[1] *The Psycho-Analysis of Children*, 1932; in particular, chapter viii.

[2] In the same book (*Writings*, 2, pp. 100–01, fn), referring to my view that every child passes through a neurosis differing only in degree from one individual to another, I added: 'This view, which I have maintained for a number of years now, has lately received valuable support. In his book, *The Question of Lay Analysis* (*S.E.* 20), Freud writes "since we have learnt how to look more sharply, we are tempted to say that neurosis in children is not the exception but the rule, as though it could scarcely be avoided on the path from the innate disposition of infancy to civilized society" (p. 215).'

[3] At every juncture the child's feelings, fears and defences are linked up with his libidinal wishes and fixations, and the outcome of his sexual development in

Normally the child passes through the infantile neurosis, and among other achievements arrives step by step at a good relation to people and to reality. I hold that this satisfactory relation to people depends upon his having succeeded in his struggles against the chaos inside him (the depressive position) and having securely established his 'good' internal objects.

Let us now consider more closely the methods and mechanisms by which this development comes about.

In the baby, processes of introjection and projection, since they are dominated by aggression and anxieties which reinforce each other, lead to fears of persecution by terrifying objects. To such fears are added those of losing his loved objects; that is to say, the depressive position has arisen. When I first introduced the concept of the depressive position, I put forward the suggestion that the introjection of the whole loved object gives rise to concern and sorrow lest that object should be destroyed (by the 'bad' objects and the id), and that these distressed feelings and fears, in addition to the paranoid set of fears and defences, constitute the depressive position. There are thus two sets of fears, feelings and defences, which, however varied in themselves and however intimately linked together, can, in my view, for purposes of theoretical clearness, be isolated from each other. The first set of feelings and phantasies are the persecutory ones, characterized by fears relating to the destruction of the ego by internal persecutors. The defences against these fears are predominantly the destruction of the persecutors by violent or secretive and cunning methods. With these fears and defences I have dealt in detail in other contexts. The second set of feelings which go to make up the depressive position I formerly described without suggesting a term for them. I now propose to use for these feelings of sorrow and concern for the loved objects, the fears of losing them and the longing to regain them, a simple word derived from everyday language—namely the 'pining' for the loved object. In short—persecution (by 'bad' objects) and the characteristic defences against it, on the one hand, and pining for the loved ('good') object, on the other, constitute the depressive position.

When the depressive position arises, the ego is forced (in addition to earlier defences) to develop methods of defence which are essentially directed against the 'pining' for the loved object. These are

---

childhood is always interdependent with the processes I am describing in this paper. I think that new light will be thrown on the child's libidinal development if we consider it in connection with the depressive position and the defences used against that position. It is, however, a subject of such importance that it needs to be dealt with fully, and is therefore beyond the scope of this paper.

fundamental to the whole ego-organization. I formerly termed some of these methods *manic defences*, or the *manic position*, because of their relationship to the manic-depressive illness.[1]

The fluctuations between the depressive and the manic position are an essential part of normal development. The ego is driven by depressive anxieties (anxiety lest the loved objects as well as itself should be destroyed) to build up omnipotent and violent phantasies, partly for the purpose of controlling and mastering the 'bad', dangerous objects, partly in order to save and restore the loved ones. From the very beginning these omnipotent phantasies, both the destructive and the reparative ones, stimulate and enter into all the activities, interests and sublimations of the child. In the infant the extreme character both of his sadistic and of his constructive phantasies is in line with the extreme frightfulness of his persecutors—and, at the other end of the scale, the extreme perfection of his 'good' objects.[2] Idealization is an essential part of the manic position and is bound up with another important element of that position, namely denial. Without partial and temporary denial of psychic reality the ego cannot bear the disaster by which it feels itself threatened when the depressive position is at its height. Omnipotence, denial and idealization, closely bound up with ambivalence, enable the early ego to assert itself to a certain degree against its internal persecutors and against a slavish and perilous dependence upon its loved objects, and thus to make further advances in development. I will here quote a passage from my former paper [pp. 287–88]:

'. . . in the earliest phase the persecuting and the good objects (breasts) are kept wide apart in the child's mind. When, along with

---

[1] 'A Contribution to the Psychogenesis of Manic-Depressive States,' p. 262.

[2] I have pointed out in various connections (first of all in 'Early Stages of the Oedipus Complex', p. 186) that the fear of phantastically 'bad' persecutors and the belief in phantastically 'good' objects are bound up with each other. Idealization is an essential process in the young child's mind, since he cannot yet cope in any other way with his fears of persecution (a result of his own hatred). Not until early anxieties have been sufficiently relieved owing to experiences which increase love and trust, is it possible to establish the all-important process of bringing together more closely the various aspects of objects (external, internal, 'good' and 'bad', loved and hated), and thus for hatred to become actually mitigated by love—which means a decrease of ambivalence. While the separation of these contrasting *aspects*—felt in the unconscious as contrasting *objects*—operates strongly, feelings of hatred and love are also so much divorced from each other that love cannot mitigate hatred.

The flight to the internalized 'good' object, which Melitta Schmideberg (1930) has found to be a fundamental mechanism in schizophrenia, thus also enters into the process of idealization which the young child normally resorts to in his depressive anxieties. Melitta Schmideberg has also repeatedly drawn attention to the connections between idealization and distrust of the object.

the introjection of the whole and real object, they come closer together, the ego has over and over again recourse to that mechanism
—so important for the development of the relations to objects—
namely, a splitting of its imagos into loved and hated, that is to say,
into good and dangerous ones.

'One might think that it is actually at this point that ambivalence
which, after all, refers to object-relations—that is to say, to whole
and real objects—sets in. Ambivalence, carried out in a splitting of
the imagos, enables the young child to gain more trust and belief in
its real objects and thus in its internalized ones—to love them more
and to carry out in an increasing degree its phantasies of restoration
of the loved object. At the same time the paranoid anxieties and
defences are directed towards the "bad" objects. The support which
the ego gets from a real "good" object is increased by a flight-
mechanism, which alternates between its external and internal good
objects. [Idealization.]

'It seems that at this stage of development the unification of external and internal, loved and hated, real and imaginary objects is
carried out in such a way that each step in the unification leads again
to a renewed splitting of the imagos. But as the adaptation to the
external world increases, this splitting is carried out on planes which
gradually become increasingly nearer and nearer to reality. This goes
on until love for the real and the internalized objects and trust in
them are well established. Then ambivalence, which is partly a safeguard against one's own hate and against the hated and terrifying
objects, will in normal development again diminish in varying
degrees.'[1]

As has already been stated, omnipotence prevails in the early
phantasies, both the destructive and the reparative ones, and influences sublimations as well as object relations. Omnipotence, however,
is so closely bound up in the unconscious with the sadistic impulses
with which it was first associated that the child feels again and again
that his attempts at reparation have not succeeded, or will not succeed. His sadistic impulses, he feels, may easily get the better of him.
The young child, who cannot sufficiently trust his reparative and
constructive feelings, as we have seen, resorts to manic omnipotence.
For this reason, in an early stage of development the ego has not adequate means at its disposal to deal efficiently with guilt and anxiety.
All this leads to the need in the child—and for that matter to some
extent in the adult also—to repeat certain actions obsessionally (this,
in my view, is part of the repetition compulsion);[2] or—the contrasting method—omnipotence and denial are resorted to. When the

[1] 'A Contribution to the Psychogenesis of Manic-Depressive States', p. 262.
[2] *The Psycho-Analysis of Children, Writings,* **2,** pp. 116 and 202.

defences of a manic nature fail (defences in which dangers from various sources are in an omnipotent way denied or minimized) the ego is driven alternately or simultaneously to combat the fears of deterioration and disintegration by attempted reparations carried out in obsessional ways. I have described elsewhere[1] my conclusion that the obsessional mechanisms are a defence against paranoid anxieties as well as a means of modifying them, and here I will only show briefly the connection between obsessional mechanisms and manic defences in relation to the depressive position in normal development.

The very fact that manic defences are operating in such close connection with the obsessional ones contributes to the ego's fear that the reparation attempted by obsessional means has also failed. The desire to control the object, the sadistic gratification of overcoming and humiliating it, of getting the better of it, the *triumph* over it, may enter so strongly into the act of reparation (carried out by thoughts, activities or sublimations) that the 'benign' circle started by this act becomes broken. The objects which were to be restored change again into persecutors, and in turn paranoid fears are revived. These fears reinforce the paranoid defence mechanisms (of destroying the object) as well as the manic mechanisms (of controlling it or keeping it in suspended animation, and so on). The reparation which was in progress is thus disturbed or even nullified—according to the extent to which these mechanisms are activated. As a result of the failure of the act of reparation, the ego has to resort again and again to obsessional and manic defences.

When in the course of normal development a relative balance between love and hate is attained, and the various aspects of objects are more unified, then also a certain equilibrium between these contrasting and yet closely related methods is reached, and their intensity is diminished. In this connection I wish to stress the importance of *triumph*, closely bound up with contempt and omnipotence, as an element of the manic position. We know the part rivalry plays in the child's burning desire to equal the achievements of the grown-ups. In addition to rivalry, his wish, mingled with fears, to 'grow out' of his deficiencies (ultimately to overcome his destructiveness and his bad inner objects and to be able to control them) is an incentive to achievements of all kinds. In my experience, the desire to reverse the child-parent relation, to get power over the parents and to triumph over them, is always to some extent associated with desires directed to the attainment of success. A time will come, the child phantasies, when he will be strong, tall and grown up, powerful, rich and potent,

---

[1] *ibid.*, chapter ix.

and father and mother will have changed into helpless children, or again, in other phantasies, will be very old, weak, poor and rejected. The triumph over the parents in such phantasies, through the guilt to which it gives rise, often cripples endeavours of all kinds. Some people are obliged to remain unsuccessful, because success always implies to them the humiliation or even the damage of somebody else, in the first place the triumph over parents, brothers and sisters. The efforts by which they seek to achieve something may be of a highly constructive nature, but the implicit triumph and the ensuing harm and injury done to the object may outweigh these purposes, in the subject's mind, and therefore prevent their fulfilment. The effect is that the reparation to the loved objects, which in the depths of the mind are the same as those over which he triumphs, is again thwarted, and therefore guilt remains unrelieved. The subject's triumph over his objects necessarily implies to him their wish to triumph over him, and therefore leads to distrust and feelings of persecution. Depression may follow, or an increase in manic defences and more violent control of his objects, since he has failed to reconcile, restore, or improve them, and therefore feelings of being persecuted by them again have the upper hand. All this has an important bearing on the infantile depressive position and the ego's success or failure in overcoming it. The triumph over his internal objects which the young child's ego controls, humiliates and tortures is a part of the destructive aspect of the manic position which disturbs the reparation and re-creating of his inner world and of internal peace and harmony; and thus triumph impedes the work of early mourning.

To illustrate these developmental processes let us consider some features which can be observed in hypomanic people. It is characteristic of the hypomanic person's attitude towards people, principles and events that he is inclined to exaggerated valuations: over-admiration (idealization) or contempt (devaluation). With this goes his tendency to conceive of everything on a large scale, to think in *large numbers*, all this in accordance with the greatness of his omnipotence, by which he defends himself against his fear of losing the one irreplaceable object, his mother, whom he still mourns at bottom. His tendency to minimize the importance of details and small numbers, and a frequent casualness about details and contempt of conscientiousness contrast sharply with the very meticulous methods, the concentration on the smallest things (Freud), which are part of the obsessional mechanisms.

This contempt, however, is also based to some extent on denial. He must deny his impulse to make extensive and detailed reparation because he has to deny the cause for the reparation; namely, the injury to the object and his consequent sorrow and guilt.

Returning to the course of early development, we may say that every step in emotional, intellectual and physical growth is used by the ego as a means of overcoming the depressive position. The child's growing skills, gifts and arts increase his belief in the psychic reality of his constructive tendencies, in his capacity to master and control his hostile impulses as well as his 'bad' internal objects. Thus anxieties from various sources are relieved, and this results in a diminution of aggression and, in turn, of his suspicions of 'bad' external and internal objects. The strengthened ego, with its greater trust in people, can then make still further steps towards unification of its imagos—external, internal, loved and hated—and towards further mitigation of hatred by means of love, and thus to a general process of integration.

When the child's belief and trust in his capacity to love, in his reparative powers and in the integration and security of his good inner world increase as a result of the constant and manifold proofs and counter-proofs gained by the testing of external reality, manic omnipotence decreases and the obsessional nature of the impulses towards reparation diminishes, which means in general that the infantile neurosis has passed.

We have now to connect the infantile depressive position with normal mourning. The poignancy of the actual loss of a loved person is, in my view, greatly increased by the mourner's unconscious phantasies of having lost his *internal* 'good' objects as well. He then feels that his internal 'bad' objects predominate and his inner world is in danger of disruption. We know that the loss of a loved person leads to an impulse in the mourner to reinstate the lost loved object in the ego (Freud and Abraham). In my view, however, he not only takes into himself (reincorporates) the person whom he has just lost, but also reinstates his internalized good objects (ultimately his loved parents), who became part of his inner world from the earliest stages of his development onwards. These too are felt to have gone under, to be destroyed, whenever the loss of a loved person is experienced. Thereupon the early depressive position, and with it anxieties, guilt and feelings of loss and grief derived from the breast situation, the Oedipus situation and from all other sources, are reactivated. Among all these emotions, the fears of being robbed and punished by both dreaded parents—that is to say, feelings of persecution—have also been revived in deep layers of the mind.

If, for instance, a woman loses her child through death, along with sorrow and pain her early dread of being robbed by a 'bad' retaliating mother is reactivated and confirmed. Her own early aggressive phantasies of robbing her mother of babies gave rise to fears and feelings of being punished, which strengthened ambivalence and led to hatred and distrust of others. The reinforcement of feelings or persecution in the state of mourning is all the more painful because, as a result of an increase in ambivalence and distrust, friendly relations with people, which might at that time be so helpful, become impeded.

The pain experienced in the slow process of testing reality in the work of mourning thus seems to be partly due to the necessity, not only to renew the links to the external world and thus continuously to re-experience the loss, but at the same time and by means of this to rebuild with anguish the inner world, which is felt to be in danger of deteriorating and collapsing.[1] Just as the young child passing through the depressive position is struggling, in his unconscious mind, with the task of establishing and integrating his inner world, so the mourner goes through the pain of re-establishing and reintegrating it.

In normal mourning early psychotic anxieties are reactivated. The mourner is in fact ill, but because this state of mind is common and seems so natural to us, we do not call mourning an illness. (For similar reasons, until recent years, the infantile neurosis of the normal child was not recognized as such.) To put my conclusions more precisely: I should say that in mourning the subject goes through a modified and transitory manic-depressive state and overcomes it, thus repeating, though in different circumstances and with different manifestations, the processes which the child normally goes through in his early development.

The greatest danger for the mourner comes from the turning of his hatred against the lost loved person himself. One of the ways in which hatred expresses itself in the situation of mourning is in feelings of triumph over the dead person. I refer in an earlier part of this paper to triumph as part of the manic position in infantile development. Infantile death-wishes against parents, brothers and sisters are actually fulfilled whenever a loved person dies, because he is necessarily to some extent a representative of the earliest important figures, and therefore takes over some of the feelings pertaining to them. Thus his death, however shattering for other reasons, is to some extent also felt as a victory, and gives rise to triumph, and therefore all the more to guilt.

At this point I find that my view differs from that of Freud, who stated: 'In the first place, normal mourning, too, overcomes the loss of the object, and it, too, while it lasts, absorbs all the energies of the

---

[1] These facts I think go some way towards answering Freud's question which I have quoted at the beginning of this paper: 'Why this compromise by which the command of reality is carried out piecemeal should be so extraordinarily painful is not at all easy to explain in terms of economics. It is remarkable that this painful unpleasure is taken as a matter of course by us.'

ego. Why, then, after it has run its course, is there no hint in its case of the economic condition for a phase of triumph? I find it impossible to answer this objection straight away' (*S.E.* **14**, p. 255). In my experience, feelings of triumph are inevitably bound up even with normal mourning, and have the effect of retarding the work of mourning, or rather they contribute much to the difficulties and pain which the mourner experiences. When hatred of the lost loved object in its various manifestations gets the upper hand in the mourner, this not only turns the loved lost person into a persecutor, but shakes the mourner's belief in his good inner objects as well. The shaken belief in the good objects disturbs most painfully the process of idealization, which is an essential intermediate step in mental development. With the young child, the idealized mother is the safeguard against a retaliating or a dead mother and against all bad objects, and therefore represents security and life itself. As we know, the mourner obtains great relief from recalling the lost person's kindness and good qualities, and this is partly due to the reassurance he experiences from keeping his loved object for the time being as an idealized one.

The passing states of elation[1] which occur between sorrow and distress in normal mourning are manic in character and are due to the feeling of possessing the perfect loved object (idealized) inside. At any time, however, when hatred against the lost loved person wells up in the mourner, his belief in him breaks down and the process of idealization is disturbed. (His hatred of the loved person is increased by the fear that by dying the loved one was seeking to inflict punishment and deprivation upon him, just as in the past he felt that his mother, whenever she was away from him and he wanted her, had died in order to inflict punishment and deprivation upon him.) Only gradually, by regaining trust in external objects and values of various kinds, is the normal mourner able once more to strengthen his confidence in the lost loved person. Then he can again bear to realize that this object was not perfect, and yet not lose trust and love for him, nor fear his revenge. When this stage is reached, important steps in the work of mourning and towards overcoming it have been made.

To illustrate the ways in which a normal mourner re-established connections with the external world I shall now give an instance. Mrs A, in the first few days after the shattering loss of her young son, who had died suddenly while at school, took to sorting out

---

[1] Abraham (1924) writes of a situation of this kind: 'We have only to reverse [Freud's] statement that "the shadow of the lost love-object falls upon the ego" and say that in this case it was not the shadow but the bright radiance of his loved mother which was shed upon her son.'

letters, keeping his and throwing others away. She was thus unconsciously attempting to restore him and keep him safe inside herself,
and throwing out what she felt to be indifferent, or rather hostile —
that is to say, the 'bad' objects, dangerous excreta and bad feelings.

Some people in mourning tidy the house and rearrange furniture,
actions which spring from an increase of the obsessional mechanisms
which are a repetition of one of the defences used to combat the
infantile depressive position.

In the first week after the death of her son she did not cry much,
and tears did not bring her the relief which they did later on. She
felt numbed and closed up, and physically broken. It gave her some
relief, however, to see one or two intimate people. At this stage
Mrs A, who usually dreamed every night, had entirely stopped
dreaming because of her deep unconscious denial of her actual loss.
At the end of the week she had the following dream:

*She saw two people, a mother and son. The mother was wearing a black
dress. The dreamer knew that this boy had died, or was going to die. No
sorrow entered into her feelings, but there was a trace of hostility towards the
two people.*

The associations brought up an important memory. When Mrs A.
was a little girl, her brother, who had difficulties in his school-work,
was going to be tutored by a schoolfellow of his own age (I will call
him B). B's mother had come to see Mrs A's mother to arrange about
the coaching, and Mrs A remembered this incident with very strong
feelings. B's mother behaved in a patronizing way, and her own
mother appeared to her to be rather dejected. She herself felt that
a fearful disgrace had fallen upon her very much admired and beloved brother and the whole family. This brother, a few years older
than herself, seemed to her full of knowledge, skill and strength — a
paragon of all the virtues, and her ideal was shattered when his deficiencies at school came to light. The strength of her feelings about
this incident as being an irreparable misfortune, which persisted in
her memory, was, however, due to her unconscious feelings of guilt.
She felt it to be the fulfilment of her own harmful wishes. Her brother
himself was very much chagrined by the situation, and expressed
great dislike and hatred of the other boy. Mrs A at the time identified
herself strongly with him in these resentful feelings. In the dream, the
two people whom Mrs A saw were B and his mother, and the fact
that the boy was dead expressed Mrs A's early death wishes against
him. At the same time, however, the death wishes against her own
brother and the wish to inflict punishment and deprivation upon her
mother through the loss of her son — very deeply repressed wishes —
were part of her dream thoughts. It now appeared that Mrs A, with
all her admiration and love for her brother, had been jealous of him

on various grounds, envying his greater knowledge, his mental and physical superiority, and also his possession of a penis. Her jealousy of her much beloved mother for possessing such a son had contributed towards her death wishes against her brother. One dream-thought, therefore, ran: 'A mother's son has died, or will die. It is this unpleasant woman's son, who hurt my mother and brother, who should die.' But in deeper layers, the death wish against her brother had also been reactivated, and this dream-thought ran: 'My mother's son died, and not my own.' (Both her mother and her brother were in fact already dead.) Here a contrasting feeling came in—sympathy with her mother and sorrow for herself. She felt: 'One death of the kind was enough. My mother lost her son; she should not lose her grandson also.' When her brother died, besides great sorrow, she unconsciously felt triumph over him, derived from her early jealousy and hatred, and corresponding feelings of guilt. She had carried over some of her feelings for her brother into her relation to her son. In her son, she also loved her brother; but at the same time, some of the ambivalence towards her brother, though modified through her strong motherly feelings, was also transferred on to her son. The mourning for her brother, together with the sorrow, the triumph and the guilt experienced in relation to him, entered into her present grief, and was shown in the dream.

Let us now consider the interplay of defences as they appeared in this material. When the loss occurred, the manic position became reinforced, and denial in particular came especially into play. Unconsciously, Mrs A strongly rejected the fact that her son had died. When she could no longer carry on this denial so strongly—but was not yet able to face the pain and sorrow—triumph, one of the other elements of the manic position, became reinforced. 'It is not at all painful', the thought seemed to run, as the associations showed, 'if *a* boy dies. It is even satisfactory. Now I get my revenge against this unpleasant boy who injured my brother.' The fact that triumph over her brother had also been revived and strengthened became clear only after hard analytic work. But this triumph was associated with control of the *internalized* mother and brother, and triumph over them. At this stage the *control* over her internal objects was reinforced, the misfortune and grief were *displaced* from herself on to her internalized mother. Here denial again came into play—denial of the psychical reality that she and her internal mother were one and suffered together. Compassion and love for the internal mother were denied, feelings of revenge and triumph over the internalized objects and control of them were reinforced, partly because, through her own revengeful feelings, they had turned into persecuting figures.

In the dream there was only one slight hint of Mrs A's growing unconscious knowledge (indicating that the denial was lessening) that it was she *herself* who lost her son. On the day preceding the dream she was wearing a black dress with a white collar. The woman in the dream had something white round her neck on her black dress.

Two nights after this dream she dreamt again: *She was flying with her son, and he disappeared. She felt that this meant his death—that he was drowned. She felt as if she, too, were to be drowned—but then she made an effort and drew away from the danger, back to life.*

The associations showed that in the dream she had decided that she would not die with her son, but would survive. It appeared that even in the dream she felt that it was good to be alive and bad to be dead. In this dream the unconscious knowledge of her loss is much more accepted than in the one of two days earlier. Sorrow and guilt had drawn closer. The feeling of triumph had apparently gone, but it became clear that it had only diminished. It was still present in her satisfaction about remaining alive—in contrast to her son's being dead. The feelings of guilt which already made themselves felt were partly due to this element of triumph.

I am reminded here of the passage in Freud's 'Mourning and Melancholia': 'Each single one of the memories and situations of expectancy which demonstrate the libido's attachment to the lost object is met by the verdict of reality that the object no longer exists; and the ego, confronted as it were with the question of whether it shall share this fate, is persuaded by the sum of the narcissistic satisfactions it derives from being alive to sever its attachment to the object that has been abolished' (*S.E.* **14**, p. 255). In my view, this 'narcissistic satisfaction' contains in a milder way the element of triumph which Freud seemed to think does not enter into normal mourning.

In the second week of her mourning Mrs A found some comfort in looking at nicely situated houses in the country, and in wishing to have such a house of her own. But this comfort was soon interrupted by bouts of despair and sorrow. She now cried abundantly, and found relief in tears. The solace she found in looking at houses came from her rebuilding her inner world in her phantasy by means of this interest and also getting satisfaction from the knowledge that other people's houses and good objects existed. Ultimately this stood for re-creating her good parents, internally and externally, unifying them and making them happy and creative. In her mind she made reparation to her parents for having, in phantasy, killed their children, and by this she also averted their wrath. Thus her fear that the death of her son was a punishment inflicted on her by retaliating parents lost in strength, and also the feeling that her son frustrated and punished her by his death was lessened. The diminution of hatred and fear in this way allowed the sorrow itself to come out in full strength. Increase of distrust and fears had intensified her feeling of being persecuted and mastered by her internal objects and strengthened her need to master them. All this had expressed itself by a hardening in her internal relationships and feelings—that is to say, in an increase in manic defences. (This was shown in the first dream.) If these again diminish through the strengthening of the subject's belief in goodness—his own and others'—and fears decrease, the mourner is able to surrender fully to his feelings, and to cry out his sorrow about the actual loss.

It seems that the processes of projecting and ejecting, which are closely connected with giving vent to feelings, are held up in certain stages of grief by an extensive manic control, and can again operate more freely when that control relaxes. Through tears, the mourner not only expresses his feelings and thus eases tension, but, since in the unconscious they are equated with excrements, he also expels his 'bad' feelings and his 'bad' objects, and this adds to the relief obtained through crying. This greater freedom in the inner world implies that the internalized objects, being less controlled by the ego, are also allowed more freedom: that these objects themselves are allowed in particular, greater freedom of feeling. In the mourner's state of mind, the feelings of his internal objects are also sorrowful. In his mind, they share his grief, in the same way as actual kind parents would. The poet tells us that 'Nature mourns with the mourner.' I believe that 'Nature' in this connection represents the internal good mother. This experience of mutual sorrow and sympathy in internal relationships, however, is again bound up with external ones. As I have already stated, Mrs A's greater trust in actual people and things, and help received from the external world, contributed to a relaxing of the manic control over her inner world. Thus introjection (as well as projection) could operate still more freely, more goodness and love could be taken in from without, and goodness and love increasingly experienced within. Mrs A, who at an earlier stage of her mourning had to some extent felt that her loss was inflicted on her by revengeful parents, could now in phantasy experience the sympathy of these parents (dead long since), their desire to support and to help her. She felt that they also suffered a severe loss and shared her grief, as they would have done had they lived. In her internal world harshness and suspicion had diminished, and sorrow had increased. The tears which she shed were also to some extent the tears which her internal parents shed, and she also wanted to comfort them as they—in her phantasy —comforted her.

If greater security in the inner world is gradually regained, and feelings and inner objects are therefore allowed to come more to life again, re-creative processes can set in, and hope return.

As we have seen, this change is due to certain movements in the two sets of feelings which make up the depressive position: persecution decreases and the pining for the lost loved object is experienced in full force. To put it in other words: hatred has receded and love is freed. It is inherent in the feeling of persecution that it is fed by hatred and at the same time feeds hatred. Furthermore, the feeling of being persecuted and watched by internal 'bad' objects, with the consequent necessity for constantly watching them, leads to a kind of dependence which reinforces the manic defences. These defences, in so far as they are used predominantly against persecutory feelings (and not so much against the pining for the loved object), are of a very sadistic and forceful nature. When persecution diminishes, the hostile dependence on the object, together with hatred, also diminishes, and the manic defences relax. The pining for the lost loved object also implies dependence on it, but dependence of a kind which becomes an incentive to reparation and preservation of the object. It is creative because it is dominated by love, while the dependence based on persecution and hatred is sterile and destructive.

Thus while grief is experienced to the full and despair is at its height, the love for the object wells up and the mourner feels more strongly that life inside and outside will go on after all, and that the lost loved object can be preserved within. At this stage in mourning, suffering can become productive. We know that painful experiences of all kinds sometimes stimulate sublimations, or even bring out quite new gifts in some people, who may take to painting, writing or other productive activities under the stress of frustrations and hardships. Others become more productive in a different way—more capable of appreciating people and things, more tolerant in their relation to others—they become wiser. Such enrichment is in my view gained through processes similar to those steps in mourning which we have just investigated. That is to say, any pain caused by unhappy experiences, whatever their nature, has something in common with mourning. It reactivates the infantile depressive position; the encountering and overcoming of adversity of any kind entails mental work similar to mourning.

It seems that every advance in the process of mourning results in a deepening in the individual's relation to his inner objects, in the happiness of regaining them after they were felt to be lost ('Paradise Lost and Regained'), in an increased trust in them and love for them because they proved to be good and helpful after all. This is similar to the ways in which the young child step by step builds up his relations to external objects, for he gains trust not only from pleasant experiences, but also from the ways in which he overcomes frustrations and unpleasant experiences, nevertheless retaining his good objects (externally and internally). The phases in the work of mourning when manic defences relax and a renewal of life inside sets in, with a deepening in internal relationships, are comparable to the steps which in early development lead to greater independence from external as well as internal objects.

To return to Mrs A. Her relief in looking at pleasant houses was due to the setting in of some hope that she could re-create her son as well as her parents; life started again inside herself and in the outer world. At this time she could dream again and unconsciously begin to face her loss. She now felt a stronger wish to see friends again, but only one at a time and only for a short while. These feelings of greater comfort, however, again alternated with distress. (In mourning as well as in infantile development, inner security comes about not by a straightforward movement but in waves.) After a few weeks of mourning, for instance, Mrs A went for a walk with a friend through the familiar streets, in an attempt to re-establish old bonds. She suddenly realized that the number of people in the street seemed overwhelming, the houses strange and the sunshine artificial and unreal. She had to retreat into a quiet restaurant. But there she felt as if the ceiling were coming down, and the people in the place became vague and blurred. Her own house suddenly seemed the only secure place in the world. In analysis it became clear that the frightening indifference of these people was reflected from her internal objects, who in her mind had turned into a multitude of 'bad' persecuting objects. The external world was felt to be artificial and unreal, because real trust in inner goodness had temporarily gone.

Many mourners can only make slow steps in re-establishing the bonds with the external world because they are struggling against the chaos inside; for similar reasons the baby develops his trust in the object-world first in connection with a few loved people. No doubt other factors as well, e.g. his intellectual immaturity, are partly responsible for this gradual development in the baby's object relations, but I hold that this is also due to the chaotic state of his inner world.

One of the differences between the early depressive position and normal mourning is that when the baby loses the breast or bottle, which has come to represent to him a 'good', helpful, protective object inside him, and experiences grief, he does this even though his mother is there. With the grown-up person, however, the grief is brought about by the actual loss of an actual person; yet help comes to him against this overwhelming loss through his having established in his early life his 'good' mother inside himself. The young child, however, is at the height of his struggles with fears of losing her internally and externally, for he has not yet succeeded in establishing her securely inside himself. In this struggle, the child's relation to his mother, her actual presence, is of the greatest help. Similarly, if the mourner has people whom he loves and who share his grief, and if he can accept their sympathy, the restoration of the harmony in his inner world is promoted, and his fears and distress are more quickly reduced.

Having described some of the processes which I have observed at work in mourning and in depressive states, I wish now to link up my contribution with the work of Freud and Abraham.

Based on Freud's and his own discoveries about the nature of the archaic processes at work in melancholia, Abraham found that such processes also operate in the work of normal mourning. He concluded that in this work the individual succeeds in establishing the lost loved person in his ego, while the melancholic has failed to do so. Abraham also described some of the fundamental factors upon which that success or failure depends.

My experience leads me to conclude that, while it is true that the characteristic feature of normal mourning is the individual's setting up the lost loved object inside himself, he is not doing so for the first time but, through the work of mourning, is reinstating that object as well as all his loved *internal* objects which he feels he has lost. He is therefore *recovering* what he had already attained in childhood.

In the course of his early development, as we know, he establishes his parents within his ego. (It was the understanding of the processes of introjection in melancholia and in normal mourning which, as we know, led Freud to recognize the existence of the super-ego in normal development.) But, as regards the nature of the super-ego and the history of its individual development, my conclusions differ from those of Freud. As I have often pointed out, the processes of introjection and projection from the beginning of life lead to the institution inside ourselves of loved and hated objects, who are felt to be 'good' and 'bad', and who are interrelated with each other and with the self: that is to say, they constitute an inner world. This assembly of internalized objects becomes organized, together with the organization of the ego, and in the higher strata of the mind it becomes discernible as the super-ego. Thus, the phenomenon which was recognized by Freud, broadly speaking, as the voices and the influence of the actual parents established in the ego is, according to my findings, a complex object-world, which is felt by the individual, in deep layers of the unconscious, to be concretely inside himself, and for which I and some of my colleagues therefore use the term 'internalized objects' and an 'inner world'. This inner world consists of in-

362

numerable objects taken into the ego, corresponding partly to the multitude of varying aspects, good and bad, in which the parents (and other people) appeared to the child's unconscious mind throughout various stages of his development. Further, they also represent all the real people who are continually becoming internalized in a variety of situations provided by the multitude of ever-changing external experiences as well as phantasied ones. In addition, all these objects are in the inner world in an infinitely complex relation both with each other and with the self.

If I now apply this description of the super-ego organization, as compared with Freud's super-ego, to the process of mourning, the nature of my contribution to the understanding of this process becomes clear. In normal mourning the individual reintrojects and reinstates, as well as the actual lost person, his loved parents who are felt to be his 'good' inner objects. His inner world, the one which he has built up from his earliest days onwards, in his phantasy was destroyed when the actual loss occurred. The rebuilding of this inner world characterizes the successful work of mourning.

An understanding of this complex inner world enables the analyst to find and resolve a variety of early anxiety-situations which were formerly unknown, and is therefore theoretically and therapeutically of an importance so great that it cannot yet be fully estimated. I also believe that the problem of mourning can only be more fully understood by taking account of these early anxiety situations.

I shall now illustrate in connection with mourning one of these anxiety-situations which I have found to be of crucial importance also in manic-depressive states. I refer to the anxiety about the internalized parents in destructive sexual intercourse; they as well as the self are felt to be in constant danger of violent destruction. In the following material I shall give extracts from a few dreams of a patient, D, a man in his early forties, with strong paranoid and depressive traits. I am not going into details about the case as a whole, but am here concerned only to show the ways in which these particular fears and phantasies were stirred in this patient by the death of his mother. She had been in failing health for some time, and was, at the time to which I refer, more or less unconscious.

One day in analysis, D spoke of his mother with hatred and bitterness, accusing her of having made his father unhappy. He also referred to a case of suicide and one of madness which had occurred in his mother's family. His mother, he said, had been 'muddled' for some time. Twice he applied the term 'muddled' to himself and then said: 'I know you are going to drive me mad and then lock me up.' He spoke about an animal being locked up in a cage. I interpreted that his mad relative and his muddled mother were now felt to be inside himself, and that the fear of being locked up in a cage partly implied his deeper fear of containing these mad people inside himself and thus of going mad himself. He then told me a dream of the previous night: *He saw a bull lying in a farmyard. It was not quite dead, and looked very uncanny and dangerous. He was standing on one side of the bull, his mother on the other. He escaped into a house, feeling that he was leaving his mother behind in danger and that he should not do so; but he vaguely hoped that she would get away.*

To his own astonishment, my patient's first association to the dream was of the blackbirds which had disturbed him very much by waking him up that morning. He then spoke of buffaloes in America, the country where he was born. He had always been interested in them and attracted by them when he saw them. He now said that one could shoot them and use them for food, but that they are dying out and should be preserved. Then he mentioned the story of a man who had been kept lying on the ground, with a bull standing over him for hours, unable to move for fear of being crushed. There was also an association about an actual bull on a friend's farm; he had lately seen this bull, and he said it looked ghastly. This farm had associations for him by which it stood for his own home. He had spent most of his childhood on a large farm his father owned. In between, there were associations about flower seeds spreading from the country and taking root in town gardens. D saw the owner of this farm again the same evening and urgently advised him to keep the bull under control. (D had learnt that the bull had recently damaged some buildings on the farm.) That very evening the patient received news of his mother's death.

In the following hour, D did not at first mention his mother's death, but expressed his hatred of me—my treatment was going to kill him. I then reminded him of the dream of the bull, interpreting that in his mind his mother had become mixed up with the attacking bull-father—half-dead himself—and had become uncanny and dangerous. I myself and the treatment were at the moment standing for this combined parent-figure. I pointed out that the recent increase of hatred against his mother was a defence against his sorrow and despair about her approaching death. I referred to his aggressive phantasies by which, in his mind, he had changed his father into a dangerous bull which would destroy his mother; hence his feeling of responsibility and guilt about this impending disaster. I also referred to the patient's remark about eating buffaloes, and explained that he had incorporated the combined parent-figure and so felt afraid of being crushed internally by the bull. Former material had shown his fear of being controlled and attacked internally by dangerous beings, fears which had resulted among other things in his taking up at times a very rigid and immobile posture. His story of the man who was in danger of being crushed by the bull, and who was kept immobile and controlled by it, I interpreted as a representation of the dangers by which he felt threatened internally.[1]

I now showed the patient the sexual implications of the bull's attacking his mother, connecting this with his exasperation about the birds waking him that morning (this being his first association to the bull-dream). I reminded him that in his associations birds often stood for people, and that the noise the birds made—a noise to which he was quite accustomed—represented to him the dangerous sexual intercourse of his parents, and was so unendurable on this particular morning because of the bull-dream, and owing to his acute state of anxiety about his dying mother. Thus his mother's death meant to him her being destroyed by the bull inside him, since—the work of mourning having already started—he had internalized her in this most dangerous situation.

I also pointed out some hopeful aspects of the dream. His mother might save herself from the bull. Blackbirds and other birds he is actually fond of. I showed him also the tendencies to reparation and re-creation present in the material. His father (the buffaloes) should be preserved, *i.e.* protected against his—the patient's—own greed. I reminded him, among other things, of the seeds which he wanted to spread from the country he loved to the town, and which stood for new babies being created by him and by his father as a reparation to his mother—these live babies being also a means of keeping her alive.

It was only *after* this interpretation that he was actually able to tell me that his mother had died the night before. He then admitted, which was unusual with him, his full understanding of the internalization process which I had interpreted to him. He said that after he had received the news of his mother's death he felt sick, and that he thought, even at the time, that there could be no physical reason for this. It now seemed to him to confirm my interpretation that he had internalized the whole imagined situation of his fighting and dying parents.

During this hour he had shown great hatred, anxiety and tension,

---

[1] I have often found that processes which the patient unconsciously feels are going on inside him are represented as something happening on top of or closely round him. By means of the well-known principle of representation by the contrary, an external happening can stand for an internal one. Whether the emphasis lies on the internal or the external situation becomes clear from the whole context—from the details of associations and the nature and intensity of affects. For instance, certain manifestations of very acute anxiety and the specific defence mechanisms against this anxiety (particularly an increase in denial of psychic reality) indicate that an internal situation predominates at the time.

but scarcely any sorrow; towards the end, however, after my interpretation, his feelings softened, some sadness appeared, and he experienced some relief.

The night after his mother's funeral, D dreamt that X (a father-figure) and another person (who stood for me) were trying to help him, but actually he had to fight for his life against us; as he put it: 'Death was claiming me.' In this hour he again spoke bitterly about his analysis as disintegrating him. I interpreted that he felt the helpful external parents to be at the same time the fighting, disintegrating parents, who would attack and destroy him—the half-dead bull and the dying mother inside him—and that I myself and analysis had come to stand for the dangerous people and happenings inside himself. That his father was also internalized by him as dying or dead was confirmed when he told me that at his mother's funeral he had wondered for a moment whether his father was not also dead. (In reality the father was still alive.)

Towards the end of this hour, after a decrease of hatred and anxiety, he again became more co-operative. He mentioned that the day before, looking out of the window of his father's house into the garden and feeling lonely, he disliked a jay he saw on a bush. He thought that this nasty and destructive bird might possibly interfere with another bird's nest with eggs in it. Then he associated that he had seen, some time previously, bunches of wild flowers thrown on the ground—probably picked and thrown away by children. I again interpreted his hatred and bitterness as being in part a defence against sorrow, loneliness and guilt. The destructive bird, the destructive children—as often before—stood for himself who had, in his mind, destroyed his parents' home and happiness and killed his mother by destroying her babies inside her. In this connection his feelings of guilt related to his *direct* attacks in phantasy on his mother's body; whilst in connection with the bull-dream the guilt was derived from his *indirect* attacks on her, when he changed his father into a dangerous bull who was thus carrying into effect his—the patient's—own sadistic wishes.

On the third night after his mother's funeral, D had another dream:

He saw a bus coming towards him in an uncontrolled way—apparently driving itself. It went towards a shed. He could not see what happened to the shed, but knew definitely that the shed 'was going to blazes'. Then two people, coming from behind him, were opening the roof of the shed and looking into it. D did not 'see the point of their doing this', but they seemed to think it would help.

Besides showing his fear of being castrated by his father through a homosexual act which he at the same time desired, this dream expressed the same internal situation as the bull-dream—the death of his mother inside him and his own death. The shed stood for his mother's body, for himself, and also for his mother inside him. The dangerous sexual intercourse represented by the bus destroying the shed happened in his mind to his mother as well as to himself; but in addition, and that is where the predominant anxiety lay, to his mother *inside* him.

His not being able to see what happened in the dream indicated that in his mind the catastrophe was happening internally. He also knew, without seeing it, that the shed was 'going to blazes'. The bus 'coming towards him', besides standing for sexual intercourse and castration by his father, also meant 'happening inside him'.[1]

The two people opening the roof from behind (he had pointed to my chair) were himself and myself, looking into his inside and into his mind (psycho-analysis). The two people also meant myself as the 'bad' combined parent-figure, myself containing the dangerous father—hence his doubts whether looking into the shed (analysis) could help him. The uncontrolled bus represented also himself in dangerous sexual intercourse with his mother, and expressed his fears and guilt about the badness of his own genitals. Before his mother's death, at a time when her fatal illness had already begun, he accidentally ran his car into a post—without serious consequences. It appeared that this was an unconscious suicidal attempt, meant to destroy the internal 'bad' parents. This accident also represented his parents in dangerous sexual intercourse inside him, and was thus an acting out as well as an externalization of an internal disaster.

The phantasy of the parents combined in 'bad' intercourse—or rather, the accumulation of emotions of various kinds, desires, fears and guilt, which go with it—had very much disturbed his relation to both parents, and had played an important part not only in his illness but in his whole development. Through the analysis of these emotions referring to the actual parents in sexual intercourse, and particularly through the analysis of these internalized situations, the patient became able to experience real mourning for his mother. All his life, however, he had warded off the depression and sorrow about losing her, which were derived from his infantile depressive feelings, and had denied his very great love for her. Unconsciously he had reinforced his hatred and feelings of persecution, because he could not bear the fear of losing his *loved* mother. When his anxieties about his own destructiveness decreased and confidence in his power to restore and preserve her became strengthened, persecution lessened

[1] An attack on the outside of the body often stands for one which is felt to happen internally. I have already pointed out that something represented as being on top of or tightly round the body often has the deeper meaning of being inside.

and love for her came gradually to the fore. But together with this he increasingly experienced the grief and longing for her which he had repressed and denied from his early days onward. While he was going through this mourning with sorrow and despair, his deeply buried love for his mother came more and more into the open, and his relation to both parents altered. On one occasion he spoke of them, in connection with a pleasant childhood memory, as 'my dear old parents'—a new departure in him.

I have shown here and in my previous paper the deeper reasons for the individual's incapacity to overcome successfully the infantile depressive position. Failure to do so may result in depressive illness, mania or paranoia. I pointed out (*op. cit.*) one or two other methods by which the ego attempts to escape from the sufferings connected with the depressive position, namely either the flight to internal good objects (which may lead to severe psychosis) or the flight to external good objects (with the possible outcome of neurosis). There are, however, many ways, based on obsessional, manic and paranoid defences, varying from individual to individual in their relative proportion, which in my experience all serve the same purpose, that is, to enable the individual to escape from the sufferings connected with the depressive position. (All these methods, as I have pointed out, have a part in normal development also.) This can be clearly observed in the analyses of people who fail to experience mourning. Feeling incapable of saving and securely reinstating their loved objects inside themselves, they must turn away from them more than hitherto and therefore deny their love for them. This may mean that their emotions in general become more inhibited; in other cases it is mainly feelings of love which become stifled and hatred is increased. At the same time, the ego uses various ways of dealing with paranoid fears (which will be the stronger the more hatred is reinforced). For instance, the internal 'bad' objects are manically subjugated, immobilized and at the same time denied, as well as strongly projected into the external world. Some people who fail to experience mourning may escape from an outbreak of manic-depressive illness or paranoia only by a severe restriction of their emotional life which impoverishes their whole personality.

Whether some measure of mental balance can be maintained in people of this type often depends on the ways in which these various methods interact, and on their capacity to keep alive in other directions some of the love which they deny to their lost objects. Relations to people who do not in their minds come too close to the lost object, and interest in things and activities, may absorb some of this love which belonged to the lost object. Though these relations and sublimations will have some manic and paranoid qualities, they may nevertheless offer some reassurance and relief from guilt, for through them the lost loved object which has been rejected and thus again destroyed is to some extent restored and retained in the unconscious mind.

If, in our patients, analysis diminishes the anxieties of destructive and persecuting internal parents, it follows that hate and thus in turn anxieties decrease, and the patients are enabled to revise their relation to their parents—whether they be dead or alive—and to rehabilitate them to some extent even if they have grounds for actual grievances. This greater tolerance makes it possible for them to set up 'good' parent-figures more securely in their minds, alongside the 'bad' internal objects, or rather to mitigate the fear of these 'bad' objects by the trust in 'good' objects. This means enabling them to experience emotions—sorrow, guilt and grief, as well as love and trust—to go through mourning, but to overcome it, and ultimately to overcome the infantile depressive position, which they have failed to do in childhood.

To conclude. In normal mourning, as well as in abnormal mourning and in manic-depressive states, the infantile depressive position is reactivated. The complex feelings, phantasies and anxieties included under this term are of a nature which justifies my contention that the child in his early development goes through a transitory manic-depressive state as well as a state of mourning, which become modified by the infantile neurosis. With the passing of the infantile neurosis, the infantile depressive position is overcome.

The fundamental difference between normal mourning on the one hand, and abnormal mourning and manic-depressive states on the other, is this: the manic-depressive and the person who fails in the work of mourning, though their defences may differ widely from each other, have this in common, that they have been unable in early childhood to establish their internal 'good' objects and to feel secure in their inner world. They have never really overcome the infantile depressive position. In normal mourning, however, the early depressive position, which had become revived through the loss of the loved object, becomes modified again, and is overcome by methods similar to those used by the ego in childhood. The individual is reinstating his actually lost loved object; but he is also at the same time re-establishing inside himself his first loved objects—ultimately the 'good' parents—whom, when the actual loss occurred, he felt in danger of losing as well. It is by reinstating inside himself the 'good' parents as well as the recently lost person, and by rebuilding his inner world, which was disintegrated and in danger, that he overcomes his grief, regains security, and achieves true harmony and peace.

21

THE OEDIPUS COMPLEX IN THE LIGHT OF EARLY ANXIETIES

(1945)

INTRODUCTION

I HAVE two main objectives in presenting this paper. I intend to single out some typical early anxiety situations and show their connection with the Oedipus complex. Since these anxieties and defences are part of the infantile depressive position as I see it, I hope to throw some light on the relation between the depressive position and libidinal development. My second purpose is to compare my conclusions about the Oedipus complex with Freud's views on that subject.

I shall exemplify my argument by short extracts from two case histories. Many more details could be adduced about both analyses, about the patients' family relationships and about the technique used. I shall, however, confine myself to those details of the material which are most essential from the point of view of my subject-matter.

The children whose case histories I shall use to illustrate my argument were both suffering from severe emotional difficulties. In making use of such material as a basis for my conclusions about the normal course of the Oedipus development, I am following a method well tried in psycho-analysis. Freud justified this angle of approach in many of his writings. For instance in one place, he says: 'Pathology has always done us the service of making discernible by isolation and exaggeration conditions which would remain concealed in a normal state.' (*S.E.* **22**, p. 121).

EXTRACTS FROM CASE HISTORY ILLUSTRATING THE BOY'S OEDIPUS DEVELOPMENT

The material on which I shall draw to illustrate my views about the boy's Oedipus development is taken from the analysis of a boy of ten. His parents felt impelled to seek help for him since some of his symptoms had developed to such an extent that it became impossible for him to attend school. He was very much afraid of children and because of this fear he more and more avoided going out by himself. Moreover, for some years a progressive inhibition of his faculties and interests caused great concern to his parents. In addition to these symptoms, which prevented him from attending school, he was excessively preoccupied with his health and was frequently subject to depressed moods. These difficulties showed themselves in his appearance, for he looked very worried and unhappy. At times, however—and this became striking during analytic sessions—his depression lifted and then sudden life and sparkle came into his eyes and transformed his face completely.

Richard was in many ways a precocious and gifted child. He was very musical and showed this already at an early age. He had a pronounced love of nature, but only of nature in its pleasant aspects. His artistic gifts showed, for instance, in the ways in which he chose his words and in a feeling for the dramatic which enlivened his conversation. He could not get on with children and was at his best in adult company, particularly in the company of women. He tried to impress them by his conversational gifts and to ingratiate himself with them in a rather precocious way.

Richard's suckling period had been short and unsatisfactory. He had been a delicate infant and had suffered from colds and illnesses from infancy onwards. He had undergone two operations (circumcision and tonsillectomy) between his third and sixth year. The family lived in modest but not uncomfortable circumstances. The atmosphere in the home was not altogether happy. There was a certain lack of warmth and of common interests between his parents, though no open trouble. Richard was the second of two children, his brother being a few years his senior. His mother, though not ill in a clinical sense, was a depressive type. She was very worried about any illness in Richard, and there was no doubt that her attitude had contributed to his hypochondriacal fears. Her relation to Richard was in some ways not satisfactory; while his elder brother was a great success at school and absorbed most of the mother's capacity for love, Richard was rather a disappointment to her. Though he was devoted to her, he was an extremely difficult child to deal with. He had no interests and hobbies to occupy him. He was over-anxious and over-affectionate towards his mother and clung to her in a persistent and exhausting way.

His mother lavished much care on him and in some ways pampered him, but she had no real appreciation of the less obvious sides of his character, such as a great inherent capacity for love and kindness. She failed to understand that the child loved her very much, and she had little confidence in his future development. At the same time she was on the whole patient in dealing with him; for instance she did not attempt to press the company of other children on him or to force him to attend school.

371

Richard's father was fond of him and very kind to him, but he seemed to leave the responsibility for the boy's upbringing predominantly to his mother. As the analysis showed, Richard felt that his father was too forbearing with him and exerted his authority in the family circle too little. His elder brother was on the whole friendly and patient with Richard, but the two boys had little in common.

The outbreak of the war had greatly increased Richard's difficulties. He was evacuated with his mother, and moved with her for the purpose of his analysis to the small town where I was staying at the time, while his brother was sent away with his school. Parting from his home upset Richard a good deal. Moreover the war stirred all his anxieties, and he was particularly frightened of air-raids and bombs. He followed the news closely and took a great interest in the changes in the war situation, and this preoccupation came up again and again during the course of the analysis.

Though there were difficulties in the family situation—as well as serious difficulties in Richard's early history—in my view the severity of his illness could not be explained by those circumstances alone. As in every case, we have to take into consideration the internal processes resulting from, and interacting with, constitutional as well as environmental factors; but I am unable to deal here in detail with the interaction of all these factors. I shall restrict myself to showing the influence of certain early anxieties on genital development.

The analysis took place in a small town some distance from London, in a house whose owners were away at the time. It was not the kind of playroom I should have chosen, since I was unable to remove a number of books, pictures, maps, etc. Richard had a particular, almost personal relation to this room and to the house, which he identified with me. For instance, he often spoke affectionately about it and to it, said good-bye to it before leaving at the end of an hour, and sometimes took great care in arranging the furniture in a way which he felt would make the room 'happy'.

In the course of the analysis Richard produced a series of drawings.[1] One of the first things he drew was a starfish hovering near a plant under water, and he explained to me that it was a hungry baby which wanted to eat the plant. An octopus, much bigger than the starfish and with a human face, entered into his drawings a day or

---

[1] The accompanying reproductions are traced from the originals and somewhat reduced in size. The originals were drawn in pencil and coloured with crayons. The different colours have as far as possible been indicated by different markings. In *Drawing III*, however, the submarines should be black, the flags red, and the fishes and starfish yellow.

two later. This octopus represented his father and his father's genital in their dangerous aspects and was later unconsciously equated with the 'monster' which we shall presently encounter in the material. The starfish shape soon led to a pattern drawing made up of different coloured sections. The four main colours in this type of drawing—black, blue, purple and red—symbolized his father, mother, brother and himself respectively. In one of the first drawings in which these four colours were used he introduced black and red by marching the pencils towards the drawing with accompanying noises. He explained that black was his father, and accompanied the movement of the pencil by imitating the sound of marching soldiers. Red came next, and Richard said it was himself and sang a cheerful tune as he moved up the pencil. When colouring the blue sections he said this was his mother, and when filling in the purple sections he said his brother was nice and was helping him.

The pattern represented an empire, the different sections standing for different countries. It is significant that his interest in the events of the war played an important part in his associations. He often looked up on the map the countries which Hitler had subjugated, and the connection between the countries on the map and his own empire drawings was evident. The empire drawings represented his mother, who was being invaded and attacked. His father usually appeared as the enemy; Richard and his brother figured in the drawings in various rôles, sometimes as allies of his mother, sometimes as allies of his father.

These pattern drawings, though superficially similar, varied greatly in detail—in fact we never had two exactly alike. The way he made these drawings, or for that matter most of his drawings, was significant. He did not start out with any deliberate plan and was often surprised to see the finished picture.

He used various sorts of play material; for instance the pencils and crayons with which he made his drawings also figured in his play as people. In addition he brought his own set of toy ships, two of which always stood for his parents, while the other ships appeared in varying rôles.

For purposes of exposition I have restricted my selection of material to a few instances, mainly drawn from six analytic hours. In these hours—partly owing to external circumstances which I shall discuss later—certain anxieties had temporarily come more strongly to the fore. They were diminished by interpretation, and the resulting changes threw light on the influence of early anxieties on genital development. These changes, which were only a step towards fuller genitality and stability, had already been fore-shadowed earlier on in Richard's analysis.

373

With regard to the interpretations adduced in this paper, it goes without saying that I have selected those which were most relevant to my subject matter. I shall make clear which interpretations were given by the patient himself. In addition to interpretations which I gave to the patient, the paper contains a number of conclusions drawn from the material, and I shall not at every point make a clear distinction between these two categories. A consistent demarcation of such a kind would involve a good deal of repetition and blur the main issues.

Early anxieties impeding Oedipus development

I take as my starting point the resumption of the analysis after a break of ten days. The analysis had by then lasted six weeks. During this break I was in London, and Richard went away on holiday. He had never been in an air-raid, and his fears of air-raids centred on London as the place most in danger. Hence to him my going to London meant going to destruction and death. This added to the anxiety which was stirred up in him by the interruption of the analysis.

On my return I found Richard very worried and depressed. During the whole first hour he hardly looked at me, and alternated between sitting rigidly on his chair without lifting his eyes and wandering out restlessly into the adjoining kitchen and into the garden. In spite of his marked resistance he did, however, put a few questions to me: Had I seen much of 'battered' London? Had there been an air-raid while I was there? Had there been a thunderstorm in London?

One of the first things he told me was that he hated returning to the town where the analysis took place, and called the town a 'pigsty' and a 'nightmare'. He soon went out into the garden, where he seemed more free to look round. He caught sight of some toadstools which he showed to me, shuddering and saying they were poisonous. Back in the room, he picked up a book from the shelf and particularly pointed out to me a picture of a little man fighting against an 'awful monster'.

On the second day after my return Richard told me with great resistance about a conversation he had had with his mother while I was away. He had told his mother that he was very worried about his having babies later on and had asked her whether it would hurt very much. In reply she had, not for the first time, explained the part played by the man in reproduction, whereupon he had said he would not like to put his genital into somebody else's genital: that would frighten him, and the whole thing was a great worry to him.

374

In my interpretation I linked this fear with the 'pig-sty' town; it stood in his mind for my 'inside' and his mother's 'inside', which had turned bad because of thunderstorms and Hitler's bombs. These represented his 'bad' father's penis entering his mother's body and turning it into an endangered and dangerous place. The 'bad' penis inside his mother was also symbolized by the poisonous toad-stools which had grown in the garden in my absence, as well as by the monster against which the little man (representing himself) was fighting. The phantasy that his mother contained the destructive genital of his father accounted in part for his fears of sexual inter-course. This anxiety had been stirred up and intensified by my going to London. His own aggressive wishes relating to his parents' sexual intercourse greatly added to his anxieties and feelings of guilt.

There was a close connection between Richard's fear of his 'bad' father's penis inside his mother and his phobia of children. Both these fears were closely bound up with the phantasies about his mother's 'inside' as a place of danger. For he felt he had attacked and injured the imaginary babies inside his mother's body and they had become his enemies. A good deal of this anxiety was transferred on to children in the external world.

The first thing Richard did with his fleet during these hours was to make a destroyer, which he named 'Vampire', bump into the battleship 'Rodney', which always represented his mother. Resistance set in at once and he quickly rearranged the fleet. However, he did reply—though reluctantly—when I asked him who the 'Vampire' stood for, and said it was himself. The sudden resistance, which had made him interrupt his play, threw some light on the repression of his genital desires towards his mother. The bumping of one ship against another had repeatedly in his analysis turned out to symbolize sexual intercourse. One of the main causes of the repression of his genital desires was his fear of the destructiveness of sexual intercourse because—as the name 'Vampire' suggests—he attributed to it an oral-sadistic character.

I shall now interpret *Drawing I*, which further illustrates Richard's anxiety situations at this stage of the analysis. In the pattern draw-ings, as we already know, red always stood for Richard, black for his father, purple for his brother and light blue for his mother. While colouring the red sections Richard said: 'These are the Russians.' Though the Russians had become our allies, he was very suspicious of them. Therefore, in referring to red (himself) as the suspect Russians, he was showing me that he was afraid of his own aggression. It was this fear which had made him stop the fleet game at the moment when he realized that he was being the 'Vampire' in his sexual approach to his mother. *Drawing I* expressed his anxieties

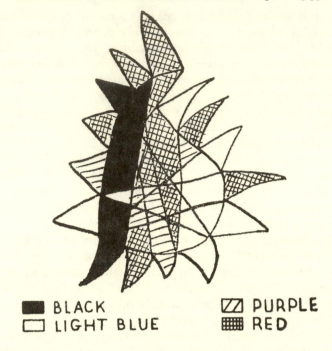

■ BLACK   ▨ PURPLE
☐ LIGHT BLUE   ▦ RED

I

about his mother's body, attacked by the bad Hitler-father (bombs, thunderstorms, poisonous toadstools). As we shall see when we discuss his associations to *Drawing II*, the whole empire represented his mother's body and was pierced by his own 'bad' genital. In *Drawing I*, however, the piercing was done by three genitals, representing the three men in the family: father, brother and himself. We know that during this hour Richard had expressed his horror of sexual intercourse. To the phantasy of destruction threatening his mother from his 'bad' father was added the danger to her from Richard's aggression, for he identified himself with his 'bad' father. His brother too appeared as an attacker. In this drawing his mother (light blue) contains the bad men, or ultimately their bad genitals, and her body is therefore endangered and a place of danger.

Some early defences

Richard's anxiety about his aggression, and particularly about his oral-sadistic tendencies, was very great and led to a sharp struggle in him against his aggression. This struggle could at times be plainly seen. It is significant that in moments of anger he ground his teeth and moved his jaws as if he were biting. Owing to the strength of his oral-sadistic impulses he felt in great danger of

376

harming his mother. He often asked, even after quite harmless remarks to his mother or to myself: 'Have I hurt your feelings?' The fear and guilt relating to his destructive phantasies moulded his whole emotional life. In order to retain his love for his mother, he again and again attempted to restrain his jealousy and grievances, denying even obvious causes for them.

However, Richard's attempts to restrain his hatred and aggressiveness and to deny his grievances were not successful. The repressed anger about frustrations in the past and present came out clearly in the transference situation—for instance, in his response to the frustration imposed on him by the interruption of the analysis. We know that by going to London I had become in his mind an injured object. I was not, however, injured only through being exposed to the danger of bombs, but also because by frustrating him I had aroused his hatred; in consequence he felt unconsciously that he had attacked me. In repetition of earlier situations of frustration, he had become—in his phantasied attacks on me—identified with the bombing and dangerous Hitler-father, and he feared retaliation. I therefore turned into a hostile and revengeful figure.

The early splitting of the mother figure into a good and bad 'breast mother' as a way of dealing with ambivalence had been very marked in Richard. This division developed further into a division between the 'breast mother' who was 'good' and the 'genital mother' who was 'bad'. At this stage of the analysis, his actual mother stood for the 'good breast mother', while I had become the 'bad genital mother', and I therefore aroused in him the aggression and fears connected with that figure. I had become the mother who is injured by the father in sexual intercourse, or is united with the 'bad' Hitler-father.

That Richard's genital interests had been active at that time was shown, for instance, by his conversation with his mother about sexual intercourse, though at the time he predominantly expressed horror. But it was this horror which made him turn away from me as the 'genital' mother and drove him to his actual mother as the good object. This he achieved by a regression to the oral stage. While I was in London, Richard was more than ever inseparable from his mother. As he put it to me, he was 'Mum's chick' and 'chicks do run after their Mums'. This flight to the breast mother, as a defence against anxiety about the genital mother, was not successful. For Richard added: 'But then chicks have to do without them, because the hens don't look after them any more and don't care for them.'

The frustration experienced in the transference situation through the interruption of the analysis had revived earlier frustrations and grievances, and fundamentally the earliest deprivation suffered in relation to his mother's breast. Therefore the belief in the good mother could not be maintained.

Immediately after the collision between 'Vampire' (himself) and 'Rodney' (his mother), which I have described in the previous section, Richard put the battleships 'Rodney' and 'Nelson' (his mother and father) side by side, and then, in a row lengthwise, some ships representing his brother, himself and his dog, arranged—as he said—in order of age. Here the fleet game was expressing his wish to restore harmony and peace in the family, by allowing his parents to come together and by giving way to his father's and brother's authority. This implied the need to restrain jealousy and hatred, for only then, he felt, could he avoid the fight with his father for the possession of his mother. In that way he warded off his castration fear and moreover preserved the good father and the good brother. Above all, he also saved his mother from being injured in the fight between his father and himself.

Thus Richard was not only dominated by the need to defend himself against the fear of being attacked by his rivals, his father and brother, but also by concern for his good objects. Feelings of love and the urge to repair damage done in phantasy—damage which would be repeated if he gave way to his hatred and jealousy—came out in greater strength.

Peace and harmony in the family, however, could only be achieved, jealousy and hatred could only be restrained, and the loved objects could only be preserved if Richard repressed his Oedipus wishes. The repression of his Oedipus wishes implied a partial regression to babyhood, but this regression was bound up with the *idealization* of the mother-and-baby relationship. For he wished to turn himself into an infant free from aggression, and in particular free from oral-sadistic impulses. The idealization of the baby presupposed a corresponding idealization of the mother, in the first place of her breasts: an ideal breast which never frustrates, a mother and child in a purely loving relation to each other. The bad breast, the bad mother, was kept widely apart in his mind from the ideal mother.

Drawing II illustrates some of Richard's methods of dealing with ambivalence, anxiety and guilt. He pointed out to me the red section 'which goes all through Mum's empire', but quickly corrected himself, saying: 'It's not Mum's empire, it's just an empire where all of us have some countries.' I interpreted that he was afraid to realize that he meant it to be his mother's empire because then the red section would be piercing his mother's inside. Thereupon Richard, looking at the drawing once more, suggested that this red section looked 'like a genital', and he pointed out that it divided the empire into two: in the West there were countries belonging to everybody, while the part in the East did not contain anything of his mother—but only himself, his father and his brother.

The left-hand side of the drawing represented the good mother in close association with Richard, for there was little of his father and relatively little of his brother on that side of the drawing. In contrast, on the right side (the 'dangerous East' which I had encountered before in his analysis) only the fighting men or rather their bad genitals appeared. His mother had disappeared from this side of the drawing because, as he felt it, she had been overwhelmed by the bad

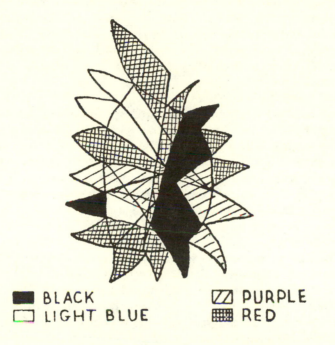

■■ BLACK   ▨ PURPLE
▢ LIGHT BLUE   ▦ RED

II

men. This drawing expressed the division into the endangered bad mother (the genital mother) and the loved and safe mother (the breast mother).

In the first drawing, which I have used to illustrate certain anxiety situations, we can already see something of the defence mechanisms which are more clearly shown in *Drawing II*. Though in *Drawing I* the light-blue mother is spread all over the picture, and the splitting into 'genital' mother and 'breast' mother has not come about as clearly as in *Drawing II*, an attempt at a division of this kind can be seen if we isolate the section on the extreme right.

It is illuminating that in *Drawing II* the division is effected by a particularly sharp and elongated section which Richard interpreted as a genital. In this way he expressed his belief that the male genital was piercing and dangerous. This section looks like a long sharp tooth or like a dagger, and in my view expresses both these meanings: the former symbolizing the danger to the loved object from the oral-sadistic impulses, the latter the danger pertaining, as he felt, to the genital function as such because of its penetrating nature.

These fears contributed again and again to his flight to the 'breast' mother. He could achieve relative stability only on a predominantly pre-genital level. The forward movement of the libido was impeded, because anxiety and guilt were too great and the ego was unable to evolve adequate defences. Thus the genital organization could not be sufficiently stabilized,[1] which implied a strong tendency to regression. The interplay between the phenomena of fixation and regression could be seen at every step of his development.

Diminished repression of Oedipus desires

The analysis of the various anxiety situations which I have described had the effect of bringing Richard's Oedipus desires and anxieties more fully to the fore. But his ego could only maintain those desires by the strengthened use of certain defences (which I shall deal with in this section). These defences, however, could only become effective because some anxiety had been lessened by analysis, and this also implied a lessening of fixations.

When the repression of Richard's genital desires was to some extent lifted, his castration fear came more fully under analysis and found expression in various' ways, with a corresponding modification in his methods of defence. In the third hour after my return Richard went out into the garden and spoke of his wish to climb mountains, particularly Snowdon, which he had mentioned earlier in the course of his analysis. While he was talking he noticed clouds in the sky and suggested that a dangerous storm was gathering. On such days, he said, he felt sorry for mountains which have a bad time when a storm breaks over them. This expressed his fear of the bad father, represented by bombs and thunderstorms in the earlier material. The wish to climb Snowdon, symbolizing his desire for

---

[1] Freud in his 'Infantile Genital Organization of the Libido', (*S.E.* 19), described the infantile genital organization as a 'phallic phase'. One of his main reasons for introducing this term was his view that during the infantile genital phase the female genital is not yet discovered or acknowledged, and that the whole interest centres on the penis. My experience does not confirm this point of view; and I do not think that the use of the term 'phallic' would cover the material under discussion in this paper. I am therefore keeping to Freud's original term 'genital phase' (or 'genital organization'). I shall give my reasons for this choice of terms more fully in the general theoretical summary later in this paper.

sexual intercourse with his mother, at once called up the fear of castration by the bad father, and the storm which was breaking thus meant a danger to his mother as well as to himself.

During the same hour Richard told me that he was going to make five drawings. He mentioned that he had seen a swan with four 'sweet' cygnets. In playing with the fleet, Richard allocated one ship to me and one to himself; I was going on a pleasure trip in my ship and so was he in his. At first he moved his ship away, but soon brought it round and put it quite close to mine. This touching of ships had in former material—particularly in relation to his parents—repeatedly symbolized sexual intercourse. In this play, therefore, Richard was expressing his genital desires as well as his hope for potency. The five drawings he said he was going to give me represented himself (the swan) giving me—or rather his mother—four children (the cygnets).

A few days earlier, as we have seen, there had been a similar incident in the fleet game: 'Vampire' (Richard) touching 'Rodney' (his mother). At that time it had led to an abrupt change of play caused by Richard's fear lest his genital desires should be dominated by his oral-sadistic impulses. During the following few days, however, anxiety was in some measure relieved, aggression was lessened, and concurrently some methods of defence became strengthened. Hence a similar play incident (his ship touching mine on the pleasure trip) could now take place without giving rise to anxiety and to the repression of his genital desires.

Richard's growing belief that he would achieve potency was bound up with a greater hope that his mother could be preserved. He was now able to allow himself the phantasy that she would love him as a man and permit him to take his father's place. This led to the hope that she would become his ally and protect him against all his rivals. For instance, Richard took the blue crayon and the red crayon (his mother and himself) and stood them up side by side on the table. Then the black crayon (his father) was marched towards them and was driven off by the red crayon, while the blue crayon drove off the purple one (his brother). This play expressed Richard's wish that his mother, in unison with himself, should drive off his dangerous father and brother. His mother as a strong figure, fighting against the bad men and their dangerous genitals, also appeared in an association to *Drawing II*, for he said that the blue mother in the West was preparing to fight the East and regain her countries there. As we know, on the right-hand side of *Drawing II* she had been overwhelmed by the genital attacks of the three men, his father, his brother and himself. In *Drawing IV*, which I shall describe a little later, Richard, by extending the blue over most of the drawing, expressed his hope that his mother would regain her lost territory. Then—restored and revived—she would be able to help and protect him. Because of this hope of restoring and reviving his good object, which implied his belief that he could cope more successfully with his aggression, Richard was able to experience his genital desires more strongly. Also, since his anxiety was lessened, he could turn his aggression outwards and take up in phantasy the fight with his father and brother for the possession of his mother. In his play with the fleet he arranged his ships to form one long row, with the smallest ship in front. The meaning of this game was that he had annexed his father's and brother's genitals and added them to his own. He felt that by this phantasied victory over his rivals he had achieved potency.

Drawing III is one of a series of drawings in which plants, starfishes, ships and fishes figured in various combinations, and which appeared frequently during the analysis. Just as in the type of drawing representing the empire, there was a great variation in details, but certain elements always represented the same object and situation. The plants underneath the water stood for his mother's genitals; there were usually two plants with a space in between. The plants also stood for his mother's breasts, and when one of the starfishes was in between the plants, this invariably meant that the child was in possession of his mother's breasts or having sexual intercourse with her. The jagged points in the shape of the starfish represented teeth and symbolized the baby's oral-sadistic impulses.

In starting *Drawing III* Richard first drew the two ships, then the large fish and some of the little ones around it. While drawing these, he became more and more eager and alive and filled in the space with baby fishes. Then he drew my attention to one of the baby fishes being covered by a fin of the 'Mum-fish' and said: 'This is the youngest baby.' The drawing suggests that the baby fish was being fed by the mother. I asked Richard whether he was among the little fishes, but he said he was not. He also told me that the starfish between the plants was a grown-up person and that the smaller starfish was a half-grown person, and explained that this was his brother; he also pointed out that the 'Sunfish' periscope was 'sticking into Rodney'. I suggested to him that the 'Sunfish' represented himself (the sun standing for the son) and that the periscope sticking into 'Rodney' (the mother) meant his sexual intercourse with his mother.

Richard's statement that the starfish between the plants was a grown-up person implied that it stood for his father, while Richard was represented by the 'Sunfish', the ship which was even bigger than 'Rodney' (his mother). In this way he expressed the reversal of

III

the father-son relation. At the same time he indicated his love for his father, and his wish to make reparation, by putting the starfish-father between the plants and thus allotting him the position of a gratified child.

The material presented in this section shows that the positive Oedipus situation and genital position had come more fully to the fore. Richard had, as we have seen, achieved this by various methods. One of them was to make his father into the baby—a baby which was not deprived of gratification and therefore would be 'good'— while he himself annexed his father's penis.

Until then Richard, who appeared in various rôles in this type of drawing, had always recognized himself in the rôle of the child as well. For under the stress of anxiety he retreated to the idealized rôle of the gratified and loving infant. Now he stated for the first time that he was not among the babies in the picture. This seemed to me another indication of the strengthening of his genital position. He now felt that he could grow up and become sexually potent. In phantasy he could therefore produce children with his mother and no longer needed to put himself into the part of the baby.

These genital desires and phantasies, however, gave rise to various anxieties, and the attempt to solve his Oedipus conflicts by taking his father's place without having to fight him was only partially successful. Side by side with this relatively peaceful solution we find evidence in the drawing of Richard's fears that his father suspected his genital desires towards his mother, kept close watch over Richard and would castrate him. For when I had interpreted to Richard his reversal of the father–son situation, he told me that the plane on top was British and was patrolling. It will be remembered that the periscope of the submarine sticking into 'Rodney' represented Richard's wish for sexual intercourse with his mother. This implied that he was trying to oust his father and therefore expected his father to be suspicious of him. I then interpreted to him that he meant that his father was not only changed into a child, but was present as well in the rôle of the paternal super-ego, the father who watched him, tried to prevent him from having sexual intercourse with his mother and threatened him with punishment. (The patrolling aeroplane.)

I furthermore interpreted that Richard himself had been 'patrolling' his parents, for he was not only inquisitive about their sexual life but unconsciously strongly desired to interfere with it and to separate his parents.

Drawing IV illustrates the same material in a different way. While colouring the blue sections Richard had been singing the National Anthem, and he explained that his mother was the Queen and he was the King. Richard had become the father and had acquired the potent father genital. When he had finished the drawing and looked at it, he told me that there was 'plenty of Mum' and of himself in it and that they 'could really beat Dad'. He showed me that there was little of the bad father there (black). Since the father had been made into a harmless infant, there seemed to be no need to beat him. However, Richard had not much confidence in this omnipotent solution, as was shown by his saying that together with his mother he could beat his father if necessary. The lessening of anxiety had enabled him to face the rivalry with his father and even the fight with him.

While colouring the purple sections, Richard sang the Norwegian and Belgian anthems and said 'he's all right'. The smallness of the

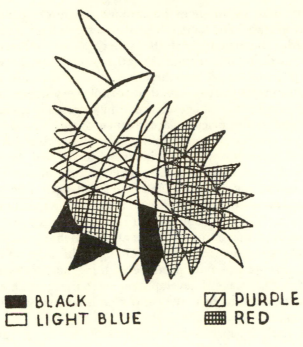

■ BLACK   ▨ PURPLE
☐ LIGHT BLUE   ▦ RED

IV

purple sections (in comparison with the blue and red) indicates that his brother too had been changed into a baby. The singing of the two anthems of small allied countries showed me that the 'he's all right' referred to both his father and brother, who had become harmless children. The repressed love for his father had at this juncture of the analysis come more into the open.[1] However, Richard felt he could not eliminate his father in his dangerous aspects. Moreover, his own faeces—in so far as they were unconsciously equated with the black father—appeared to him as a source of danger and could also not be eliminated. This acknowledgement of his psychic reality is shown in the fact that black was not left out of the picture, though Richard comforted himself by saying that there was only a little of the Hitler-father in it.

In the various ways which helped to strengthen Richard's genital position we see some of the compromises which the ego attempts to bring about between the demands of the super-ego and the id. While Richard's id-impulses were gratified by his phantasy of sexual

[1] It is significant that at the same time the libidinal desire for his father's penis, which had been strongly repressed, also came up, and in its most primary form. When looking again at the picture of the monster against which the little man was fighting, Richard said: 'The monster's awful to look at, but *its meat might be delicious* to eat.'

intercourse with his mother, the impulse to murder his father was circumvented and the reproaches of the super-ego were therefore diminished. The demands of the super-ego were, however, only partly satisfied, because though the father was spared, he was ousted from his position with the mother.

Such compromises are an essential part of every stage in the child's normal development. Whenever great fluctuations between libidinal positions occur, the defences are disturbed and new compromises have to be found. For instance, in the preceding section I have shown that, when Richard's oral anxieties were diminished, he attempted to cope with the conflict between his fears and desires by putting himself in phantasy into the rôle of an ideal baby who would not disturb the family peace. When the genital position was strengthened, however, and Richard could face his castration fear to a greater extent, a different compromise came about. Richard maintained his genital desires but avoided guilt by changing his father and brother into babies whom he would produce with his mother. Compromises of this kind at any stage of development can only bring about relative stability if the quantity of anxiety and guilt is not excessive in relation to the strength of the ego.

I have dealt in such detail with the influence of anxiety and defences on genital development because it does not seem to me possible fully to understand sexual development without taking into account the fluctuations between the different stages of libidinal organization and the particular anxieties and defences which characterize those stages.

Anxieties relating to the internalized parents

Drawings V and *VI* need some introduction. Richard had developed a sore throat and a slight temperature the evening before, but nevertheless came to analysis, since it was warm summer weather. As I pointed out earlier, sore throats and colds were among his symptoms and, even when they were slight, gave rise in him to great hypochondriacal anxiety. At the beginning of the hour during which he made *Drawings V* and *VI* he was extremely anxious and worried. He told me that his throat felt very hot and that he had some poison behind his nose. His next association, produced with great resistance, was his fear that his food might be poisoned—a fear of which he had been conscious for years, though it was only with difficulty that, on this occasion as well as on former ones, he could bring it up in the analysis.

During this hour Richard frequently looked out of the window in a suspicious way. When he saw two men talking to each other, he said that they were spying on him. This was one of the repeated indications of his paranoid fears which related to his watching and persecuting father and brother, but above all centred on his parents in a secret and hostile alliance against him. In my interpretation I linked this suspicion with the fear of internal persecutors spying on him and plotting against him—an anxiety which had come up earlier in his analysis. A little later Richard suddenly put his finger as far down as he could into his throat and seemed very worried. He explained to me that he was looking for germs. I interpreted to him that the germs also stood for Germans (the black Hitler-father in unison with myself) and were in his mind connected with the two spying men, ultimately his parents. Thus the fear of germs was closely connected with his fear of being poisoned which unconsciously referred to his parents, though he did not consciously suspect them. The cold had stirred up these paranoid fears.

During this hour Richard had been making *Drawings V* and *VI*, and the only association I could get on that day was that *VI* was the same empire as *V*. In fact these two drawings were made on the same piece of paper.

On the following day Richard had completely recovered from his sore throat and appeared in a very different mood. He described vividly how much he had enjoyed his breakfast, particularly the shredded wheat, and showed me how he had munched it up. (He had eaten very little during the previous two days.) His stomach, he said, had been quite small, thin and drawn in, and 'the big bones in it' had been 'sticking out' until he had his breakfast. These 'big bones' stood for his internalized father—or his father's genital— represented in earlier material at times by the monster, at times by the octopus. They expressed the bad aspect of his father's penis, while the 'delicious meat' of the monster expressed the desirable aspect of his father's penis. I interpreted the shredded wheat as standing for the good mother (the good breast and milk) since he had compared it on an earlier occasion to a bird's nest. Because his belief in the good internalized mother had increased, he felt less afraid of internal persecutors (the bones and the monster).

The analysis of the unconscious meaning of the sore throat had led to a diminution of anxieties with a corresponding change in the methods of defence. Richard's mood and associations during this hour clearly expressed this change. The world had suddenly become beautiful to him: he admired the countryside, my dress, my shoes, and said that I looked beautiful. He also spoke of his mother with great love and admiration. Thus, with the lessening of fears of internal persecutors, the external world appeared improved and more trustworthy to him and his capacity to enjoy it had increased. At the same time it was noticeable that his depression had given way to a hypomanic mood in which he denied his fears of persecution. In fact it was the lessening of anxiety which had allowed the manic defence against depression to come up. Richard's hypomanic mood did not, of course, last and in the further course of his analysis depression and anxiety appeared again and again.

I have so far mainly referred to Richard's relation to his mother as an external object. It had, however, become evident earlier in his analysis that the part she played as an external object was constantly interlinked with the part she played as an internal object. For the sake of clarity I have reserved this point to be illustrated by *Drawings V* and *VI*, which bring out vividly the rôle of the internalized parents in Richard's mental life.

In this hour Richard picked up *Drawings V* and *VI*, which he had made the day before, and freely associated to them. Now that his depression and hypochondriacal anxieties had diminished, he was able to face the anxieties which had been underlying his depression. He pointed out to me that *V* looked like a bird and a 'very horrid' one. The light blue on top was a crown, the purple bit was the eye, and the beak was 'wide open'. This beak, as can be seen, was formed by the red and purple sections on the right, that is to say by the colours which always stood for himself and his brother.

I interpreted to him that the light-blue crown showed that the bird was his mother—the Queen, the ideal mother of former material—who now appeared as greedy and destructive. The fact that her beak was formed by red and purple sections expressed Richard's projection on to his mother of his own (as well as his brother's) oral-sadistic impulses.

It appears from this material that Richard had made important progress in the direction of facing his psychic reality, for he had become able to express the projection of his oral-sadistic and cannibalistic impulses on to his mother. Furthermore, as shown in *Drawing V*, he had allowed the 'good' and 'bad' aspects of the mother to come together more closely. The prototypes of these two aspects, usually kept more widely apart from each other, were the good, loved breast and the bad, hated breast. In fact, the defences by means of splitting and isolating can also be seen in this drawing, for the left-hand side of the picture is completely blue. On the right-hand side of *Drawing V*, however, the mother appears simultaneously as the 'horrid' bird (open beak) *and* as the queen (light-blue crown). With the lessening of denial of his psychic reality, Richard had also become more able to face external reality, for this made it possible for him to recognize the fact that his mother had actually frustrated him and had therefore aroused his hatred.

Following my interpretations of *Drawing V*, Richard repeated emphatically that the bird looked 'horrid' and gave some associations about *Drawing VI*. It, too, looked like a bird, he said, but without a head; and the black at the bottom of it was 'big job' dropping out from it. He said it was all 'very horrid'.

V

VI

BLACK
LIGHT BLUE

PURPLE
RED

In my interpretation of *Drawing VI*, I reminded him that he had told me the day before that the two empires were the same. I suggested that *VI* represented himself, and that by internalizing the 'horrid bird' (*Drawing V*) he felt he had become like it. The open beak stood for his mother's greedy mouth, but also expressed his own desires to devour her, for the colours by which the beak was formed stood for himself and his brother (the greedy babies). In his mind he had devoured his mother as a destructive and devouring object. When in eating the breakfast food he had internalized the good mother, he felt that she was protecting him against the internalized bad father, the 'bones in his stomach'. When he internalized the 'horrid' bird mother he felt that she had become linked up with the monster father, and in his mind this terrifying combined parent figure was attacking him from within and eating him up as well as attacking him from without and castrating him.[1]

Thus Richard felt mutilated and castrated by the bad internal and external parents who retaliated for his attacks on them, and he expressed these fears in *Drawing VI*, for the bird appears there without a head. As a result of his oral-sadistic impulses towards his parents in the process of internalizing them, they had in his mind turned into correspondingly greedy and destructive enemies. Moreover, because he felt that by devouring his parents *he* had changed them into monster and bird, he experienced not only fear of these internalized persecutors but also guilt, all the more because he feared that he had exposed the good internal mother to the attacks of the internal monster. His guilt also related to his anal attacks on the external and internal parents which he had expressed by the 'horrid big job' dropping out of the bird.[2]

In the preceding hour, when Richard made these drawings, he had been so much under the sway of anxiety that he could not associate to them; now some relief of anxiety had made it possible for him to give associations.

An earlier drawing (*VII*) which expresses the internalization of his objects even more clearly than *Drawings V* and *VI* is of interest in this connection. When Richard finished this pattern drawing, he made a line round it and filled in the background with red. I found that this represented his 'inside', containing his father, mother, brother and himself in relation to each other. In his associations to this drawing he expressed his satisfaction about the increase of the light blue sections, *i.e.* his mother. He also spoke of his hope that his brother would be his ally. His jealousy of his brother often made him suspicious and frightened of his brother as a rival. But at this moment he stressed the alliance with his brother. Furthermore he pointed out that one of the black sections was completely surrounded by his mother, brother and himself. The implication was that he was allied

[1] It is relevant to recall here that he had been circumcised at the age of three and that ever since he had had a strong conscious fear of doctors and operations.

[2] Urethral impulses and anxieties were no less important in his phantasies, but do not specifically enter into this material.

with the loved internal mother against the dangerous internal father.[1]

In the light of the material presented in this section, it appears that the part which the good mother, so often idealized, played in Richard's emotional life referred to the internal mother as well as to the external mother. For instance, when he expressed the hope that the blue mother in the West would extend her territory (cf.

THIS ENCLOSED BACKGROUND AREA WAS CHALKED RED IN THE ORIGINAL

■ BLACK   ▨ PURPLE
☐ LIGHT BLUE   ▦ RED

VII

Drawing II), this hope applied to his inner world as well as to the outer world. The belief in the good internal mother was his greatest support. Whenever this belief was strengthened, hope and confidence and a greater feeling of security set in. When this feeling of confidence was shaken—either by illness or other causes—then depression and

[1] This drawing also represented his mother's 'inside', where the same struggle was going on. Richard and his brother appeared in the rôle of her protective inner objects and his father as her dangerous inner object.

hypochondriacal anxieties increased.[1] Moreover, when Richard's fears of persecutors, of the bad mother and the bad father, increased, he also felt that he could not protect his loved internal objects from the danger of destruction and death; and their death inevitably meant the end of his own life. Here we touch upon the fundamental anxiety of the depressive individual, which in my experience derives from the infantile depressive position.

A significant detail from his analysis illustrates Richard's fear of the death of his external and internal objects. As I said earlier, his almost personal relation to the playroom was one of the character-istic features in the transference situation. After my journey to London, which had strongly stirred up Richard's fear of air-raids and death, for some analytic sessions he could not bear having the electric stove turned off until the very moment when we left the house. In one of the hours which I have described in connection with the analysis of *Drawings III* and *IV* this obsession disappeared. In these hours, together with the strengthening of his genital desires and the diminution of anxiety and depression, the phantasy that he would be able to give 'good' babies to me and to his mother, and his love for babies, played a growing part in his associations. His obsessional insistence on keeping alight the stove in the room as long as possible was a measure of his depression.[2]

Summary of the boy's case history

Richard's failure to establish the genital position securely was largely caused by his incapacity to deal with anxiety in the early stages of his development. The great part which the bad breast played in Richard's emotional life was connected with his unsatis-factory feeding period and the strong oral-, urethral- and anal-sadistic impulses and phantasies which it stimulated. Richard's fears of the bad breast were to a certain extent counteracted by the idealization of the good breast, and in this way some of his love for his mother could be maintained. The bad qualities of the breast and his oral-sadistic impulses towards it were largely transferred to his father's penis. In addition, he experienced strong oral-sadistic impulses towards his father's penis, derived from jealousy and hatred in the early positive Oedipus situation. His father's genital therefore turned in his phantasy into a dangerous, biting and poisonous

---

[1] There is little doubt that such anxieties are apt in turn to produce colds or other physical illnesses, or at least to lower the resistance to them. This means that we are here confronted with a vicious circle, because these illnesses in turn reinforced all his fears.

[2] Keeping the stove alight also had the unconscious meaning of proving to himself that he was not castrated, and also that his father was not castrated.

object. The fear of the penis as an external and internal persecutor was so strong that trust in the good and productive qualities of the penis could not develop. In this way Richard's early feminine position was disturbed at the root by fears of persecution. These difficulties, experienced in the inverted Oedipus situation, interacted with the castration fear stimulated by his genital desires towards his mother. The hatred of his father which accompanied these desires, and expressed itself in the impulse to bite off his father's penis, led to the fear of being castrated in the same way, and therefore increased the repression of his genital desires.

One of the features of Richard's illness was a growing inhibition of all his activities and interests. This was linked with the severe repression of his aggressive tendencies, which was particularly marked in relation to his mother. In relation to his father and other men aggression was less repressed, though very much restrained by fear. Richard's predominant attitude to men was to pacify potential attackers and persecutors.

Richard's aggressiveness was least inhibited in relation to other children, though he was much too frightened to express it directly. His hatred of children, as well as his fear of them, was partly derived from the attitude towards his father's penis. The destructive penis and the destructive and greedy child who would exhaust the mother and ultimately destroy her were closely linked up with each other in his mind. For he unconsciously strongly maintained the equation 'penis = child'. He felt, too, that the *bad* penis could only produce *bad* children.

Another determining factor in his phobia of children was his jealousy of his brother and of any children his mother might have in the future. His unconscious sadistic attacks on the babies inside his mother's body were linked up with his hatred of his father's penis inside his mother. In one connection only could his love towards children show itself at times, and that was in a friendly attitude towards babies.

We know already that it was only by idealizing the mother–baby relationship that he could maintain his capacity for love. Because of his unconscious fear and guilt about his own oral-sadistic impulses, however, infants predominantly represented to him oral-sadistic beings. This was one of the reasons why he could not in phantasy fulfil his longing to give children to his mother. More fundamental still, oral anxiety had in his early development increased the fear connected with the aggressive aspects of the genital function and of his own penis. Richard's fear that his oral-sadistic impulses would dominate his genital desires and that his penis was a destructive organ was one of the main causes of his repression of his genital desires. Hence one essential means of making his mother happy, and making reparation for the babies which he felt he had destroyed, was barred to him. In all these various ways his oral-sadistic impu lse, phantasies and fears interfered again and again with his genital development.

In the preceding sections I have referred repeatedly to the regression to the oral stage as a defence against the additional anxieties arising in the genital position; it is, however, important not to overlook the part played by fixation in these processes. Because his oral-, urethral- and anal-sadistic anxieties were excessive, fixation to these levels was very strong; in consequence, the genital organization was weak and the tendency to repression marked. However, in spite of his inhibitions, he had developed some sublimated genital trends. Moreover, in so far as his desires were predominantly directed towards his mother, and his feelings of jealousy and hatred towards his father, he had achieved some main features of the positive Oedipus situation and of heterosexual development. This picture was, however, in some ways deceptive since his love for his mother could only be maintained by reinforcing the oral elements in his relation to her and by idealizing the 'breast' mother. We have seen that in his drawings the blue sections always stood for his mother; this choice of colour was connected with his love of the cloudless blue sky and expressed his longing for an ideal bountiful breast which would never frustrate him.

The fact that Richard was thus enabled in some ways to keep alive his love for his mother had given him what little measure of stability he possessed, and had also allowed him to develop his heterosexual tendencies to a certain extent. It was obvious that anxiety and feelings of guilt entered largely into his fixation to his mother. Richard was very devoted to her, but in a rather infantile way. He could hardly bear to leave her out of sight and showed few signs of developing an independent and manly relation to her. His attitude towards other women—though far from being truly manly and independent—was in striking contrast to his great love and even blind admiration for his mother. His behaviour with women was very precocious, in some ways like that of a grown-up Don Juan. He tried to ingratiate himself in various ways, even by blatant flattery. At the same time he was often critical and contemptuous of women and amused if they were taken in by his flattery.

Here we see two contrasting attitudes to women which bring to mind some conclusions Freud has drawn. Speaking of the 'disunion between the tender and sensual currents of erotic feeling' in some men who suffer, as Freud describes it, from 'psychical impotence', *i.e.* who can only be potent under certain circumstances, he says:

'The whole sphere of love in such people remains divided in the two directions personified in art as sacred and profane (or animal) love. Where they love, they do not desire and where they desire they cannot love' (*S.E.* **11,** p. 183).

There is an analogy between Freud's description and Richard's attitude to his mother. It was the 'genital' mother whom he feared and hated, while he turned his love and tenderness towards the 'breast' mother. This division between the two currents became apparent in the contrast between his attitude to his mother and to other women. While his genital desires towards his mother were strongly repressed and she therefore remained an object of love and admiration, these desires could become to some extent active towards women other than his mother. But those women were then objects of criticism and contempt to him. They stood for the 'genital' mother, and it appeared that his horror of genitality and his urge to repress it were reflected in his contempt towards objects which aroused his genital desires.

Among the anxieties which accounted for his fixation and regression to the 'breast' mother, Richard's fear of his mother's 'inside' as a place full of persecutors played a predominant part. For the 'genital' mother, who was to him the mother in sexual intercourse with the father, also contained the 'bad' father's genital—or rather a multitude of his genitals—thus forming a dangerous alliance with the father against the son; she also contained the hostile babies. In addition, there was the anxiety about his own penis as a dangerous organ which would injure and damage his loved mother.

The anxieties which disturbed Richard's genital development were closely linked with his relation to his parents as internalized figures. To the picture of his mother's 'inside' as a place of danger corresponded the feelings he had about his own 'inside'. In previous sections we have seen that the good mother (*e.g.* the good breakfast food) was protecting him internally against the father, 'the long bones sticking out' in his stomach. This picture of the mother protecting him against the internalized father corresponded to the mother-figure whom Richard felt urged to protect against the bad father—a mother endangered by the oral and genital attacks of the internal monster. Ultimately, however, he felt her to be endangered by his own oral-sadistic attacks on her. *Drawing II* showed the bad men (his father, brother and himself) overwhelming and swallowing up his mother. This fear derived from Richard's fundamental feeling of guilt about having destroyed (devoured) his mother and her breasts by his oral-sadistic attacks in the process of internalizing her. In addition, he expressed his guilt about his anal-sadistic attacks in *Drawing VI*, for he pointed out the 'horrid big job' dropping out from the bird. The equation between his own faeces and the black Hitler-father became apparent earlier on in his analysis when he began to make the empire drawings; for in the earliest drawing Richard had introduced the black as standing for himself, but soon decided that red stood for himself and black for his father; he afterwards maintained this arrangement throughout the drawings. This equation was further illustrated by some of the associations to *Drawings V* and *VI*. In *Drawing V* the black section represented the bad father. In *Drawing VI* it represented the 'horrid big job' dropping out of the mutilated bird.

To Richard's fear of his own destructiveness corresponded the fear of his mother as a dangerous and retaliating object. The 'horrid bird' with the open beak was a projection on to his mother of his oral-sadistic impulses. Richard's actual experiences of being frustrated by his mother could not by themselves account for his having built up in his mind a terrifying picture of an internal devouring mother. It becomes clear in *Drawing VI* how very dangerous he felt the 'horrid' bird-mother to be. For the bird without a head represented himself and corresponded to his fear of castration by this dangerous mother united with the monster father as external enemies. Moreover, in internal situations he felt threatened by the alliance of the internalized 'horrid' bird mother and the monster father. These internal danger situations were the main cause of his hypochondriacal and persecutory fears.

When Richard had become able during his analysis to face the psychological fact that his loved object was also his hated object and that the light-blue mother, the queen with the crown, was linked in his mind with the horrid bird with the beak, he could establish his love for his mother more securely. His feelings of love had become more closely linked with his feelings of hatred, and his happy experiences with his mother were no longer kept so widely apart from his experiences of frustration. He was therefore no longer driven on the one hand to idealize the good mother so strongly and on the other hand to form such a terrifying picture of the bad mother. Whenever he could allow himself to bring the two aspects of the mother together, this implied that the bad aspect was mitigated by the good one. This more secure good mother could then protect him against the 'monster' father. This again implied that at such times she was not felt to be so fatally injured by his oral greed and by the bad father, which in turn meant that he felt that both he and his father had become less dangerous. The good mother could come to life once more, and Richard's depression therefore lifted.

His increased hope of keeping the analyst and his mother alive as internal and external objects was bound up with the strengthening of his genital position and with a greater capacity to experience his Oedipus desires. Reproduction, the creation of good babies, which he unconsciously felt to be the most important means of combating death and the fear of death, had now become more possible to him in phantasy. Because he was less afraid of being carried away by his sadistic impulses, Richard believed that he would be able to produce good babies; for the creative and productive aspect of the male genital (his father's as well as his own) had come more strongly to the fore. The trust in his own constructive and reparative tendencies, as well as in his internal and external objects, had increased. His belief not only in the good mother but also in the good father had become strengthened. His father was no longer such a dangerous enemy that Richard could not face the fight with him as a hated rival. Thus he made an important step towards the strengthening of his genital position and towards facing the conflicts and fears bound up with his genital desires.

EXTRACTS FROM CASE HISTORY ILLUSTRATING THE GIRL'S OEDIPUS DEVELOPMENT

I have discussed some of the anxieties which disturb genital development in the boy and I shall now put forward some material from the case history of a little girl, Rita, which I have already described from various angles in earlier publications.[1] This material has certain advantages for purposes of presentation, for it is simple and straightforward. Most of this case material has been published previously; I shall however add a few details so far unpublished as well as some new interpretations which I could not have made at the time but which, in retrospect, seem to be fully borne out by the material.

My patient Rita, who was two years and nine months old at the beginning of her analysis, was a very difficult child to bring up. She suffered from anxieties of various kinds, from inability to tolerate frustration, and from frequent states of unhappiness. She showed marked obsessional features which had been increasing for some time, and she insisted on elaborate obsessional ceremonials. She alternated between an exaggerated 'goodness', accompanied by feelings of remorse, and states of 'naughtiness' when she attempted to dominate everybody around her. She also had difficulties over eating, was 'faddy', and frequently suffered from loss of appetite. Though she was a very intelligent child, the development and integration of her personality were held back by the strength of her neurosis.

[1] See the Lists of Patients at p. 444 of this volume and p. 292 of *Writings*, **2** (*The Psycho-Analysis of Children*).

She often cried, apparently without cause, and when asked by her mother why she was crying answered: 'Because I'm so sad.' To the question: 'Why are you so sad?' she replied: 'Because I'm crying.' Her feelings of guilt and unhappiness expressed themselves in constant questions to her mother: 'Am I good?' 'Do you love me?' and so on. She could not bear any reproach and, if reprimanded, either burst into tears or became defiant. Her feeling of insecurity in relation to her parents showed itself for instance in the following incident from her second year. Once, so I was told, she burst into tears because her father uttered a playful threat against a bear in her picture book with whom she had obviously identified herself.

Rita suffered from a marked inhibition in play. The only thing she could do with her dolls, for instance, was to wash them and change their clothes in a compulsive way. As soon as she introduced any imaginative element, she had an outbreak of anxiety and stopped playing.

The following are some relevant facts from her history. Rita was breast-fed for a few months; then she had been given the bottle, which she had at first been unwilling to accept. Weaning from the bottle to solid food was again troublesome, and she was still suffering from difficulties over eating when I began her analysis. Moreover, at that time she was still being given a bottle at night. Her mother told me that she had given up trying to wean Rita from this last bottle because every such attempt caused the child great distress. With regard to Rita's habit training, which was achieved early in her second year, I have reason to assume that her mother had been rather too anxious over it. Rita's obsessional neurosis proved to be closely connected with her early habit training.

Rita shared her parents' bedroom until she was nearly two, and she repeatedly witnessed sexual intercourse between her parents. When she was two years old, her brother was born, and at that time her neurosis broke out in full force. Another contributory circumstance was the fact that her mother was herself neurotic and obviously ambivalent towards Rita.

Her parents told me that Rita was much more fond of her mother than of her father until the end of her first year. At the beginning of her second year she developed a marked preference for her father, together with pronounced jealousy of her mother. At fifteen months Rita repeatedly and unmistakably expressed the wish, when she sat on her father's knee, to be left alone with him in the room. She could already put this into words. At the age of about eighteen months there was a striking change, which showed itself in an altered relation to both her parents, as well as in various symptoms such as night terrors and animal phobias (particularly of dogs). Her mother once again became the favourite, yet the child's relation to her showed strong ambivalence. She clung to her mother so much that she could hardly let her out of her sight. This went together with attempts to dominate her and with an often unconcealed hatred of her. Concurrently Rita developed an outspoken dislike of her father.

These facts were clearly observed at the time and reported to me by her parents. In the case of older children, parents' reports about the earlier years are often unreliable, since, as time goes on, the facts are apt to be increasingly falsified in their memory. In Rita's case the details were still fresh in her parents' minds, and the analysis fully confirmed all the essentials of their report.

Early relations to the parents

At the beginning of Rita's second year some important elements of her Oedipus situation were plainly observable, such as her preference for her father and jealousy of her mother, and even the wish to take her mother's place with her father. In assessing Rita's Oedipus development in her second year we have to consider some outstanding external factors. The child shared her parents' bedroom and had ample opportunity for witnessing sexual intercourse between them; there was therefore a constant stimulus for libidinal desires and for jealousy, hatred and anxiety. When she was fifteen months old her mother became pregnant, and the child unconsciously understood her mother's condition; thus Rita's desire to receive a baby from her father, as well as her rivalry with her mother, was strongly reinforced. As a consequence, her aggressiveness, and the ensuing anxiety and feelings of guilt increased to such an extent that her Oedipus desires could not be maintained.

The difficulties in Rita's development cannot be explained, however, by these external stimuli alone. Many children are exposed to similar, and even to much more unfavourable, experiences without becoming seriously ill in consequence. We have therefore to consider the internal factors which, in interaction with the influences from without, led to Rita's illness and to the disturbance of her sexual development.

As the analysis revealed, Rita's oral-sadistic impulses were exceedingly strong and her capacity to tolerate tension of any kind was unusually low. These were some of the constitutional characteristics which determined her reactions to the early frustrations she suffered and from the beginning strongly affected her relation to her mother. When Rita's positive Oedipus desires came to the fore at the end of her first year, this new relation to both parents reinforced Rita's feelings of frustration, hatred and aggressiveness, with their concomitants of anxiety and guilt. She was unable to cope with these manifold conflicts and therefore could not maintain her genital desires.

Rita's relation to her mother was dominated by two great sources of anxiety: persecutory fear and depressive anxiety. In one aspect her mother represented a terrifying and retaliating figure. In another aspect she was Rita's indispensable loved and good object, and Rita felt her own aggression as a danger to this loved mother. She was therefore overwhelmed by the fear of losing her. It was the strength of these early anxieties and feelings of guilt which largely determined Rita's incapacity to tolerate the additional anxiety and guilt arising from the Oedipus feelings—rivalry and hatred against her mother. In defence she repressed her hatred and over-compensated for it by excessive love, and this necessarily implied a regression to earlier stages of the libido. Rita's relation to her father was also fundamentally influenced by these factors. Some of the resentment she felt towards her mother was deflected on to her father and reinforced the hatred of him which derived from the frustration of her Oedipus desires and which, towards the beginning of her second year, strikingly superseded her former love for her father. The failure to establish a satisfactory relation to her mother was repeated in her oral and genital relation to her father. Strong desires to castrate him (partly derived from frustration in the feminine position, partly from penis envy in the male position) became clear in the analysis.

Rita's sadistic phantasies were thus closely bound up with grievances derived from frustration in various libidinal positions and experienced in the inverted as well as in the positive Oedipus situation. The sexual intercourse between her parents played an important part in her sadistic phantasies and became in the child's mind a dangerous and frightening event, in which her mother appeared as the victim of her father's extreme cruelty. In consequence, not only did her father turn in her mind into someone dangerous to her mother but—in so far as Rita's Oedipus desires were maintained in identification with her mother—into a person dangerous towards herself. Rita's phobia of dogs went back to the fear of the dangerous penis of her father which would bite her in retaliation for her own impulses to castrate him. Her whole relation to her father was profoundly disturbed because he had turned into a 'bad man'. He was all the more hated because he became the embodiment of her own sadistic desires towards her mother.

The following episode, reported to me by her mother, illustrates this last point. At the beginning of her third year Rita was out for a walk with her mother and saw a cabman beating his horses cruelly. Her mother was extremely indignant, and the little girl also expressed strong indignation. Later on in the day she surprised her mother by saying: 'When are we going out again to see the bad man beating the horses?' thus revealing the fact that she had derived sadistic pleasure from the experience and wished for its repetition. In her unconscious the cabman represented her father and the horses her mother, and her father was carrying out in sexual intercourse the child's sadistic phantasies directed against her mother. The fear of her father's bad genital, together with the phantasy of her mother injured and destroyed by Rita's hatred and by the bad father—the cabman—interfered both with her positive and with her inverted Oedipus desires. Rita could neither identify herself with such a destroyed mother, nor allow herself to play in the homosexual position the rôle of the father. Thus in these early stages neither position could be satisfactorily established.

Some instances from the analytic material

The anxieties Rita experienced when she witnessed the primal scene are shown in the following material.

On one occasion during the analysis she put a triangular brick on one side and said: 'That's a little woman.' She then took a 'little hammer', as she called an oblong brick, and she hit the brick-box with it saying: 'When the hammer hit hard, the little woman was *so* frightened.' The triangular brick stood for herself, the 'hammer' for her father's penis, the box for her mother, and the whole situation represented her witnessing the primal scene. It is significant that she hit the box exactly in a place where it happened to be stuck together only with paper, so that she made a hole in it. This was one of the instances when Rita showed me symbolically her unconscious knowledge of the vagina and the part it played in her sexual theories.

The next two instances relate to her castration complex and penis envy. Rita was playing that she was travelling with her Teddy-bear to the house of a 'good' woman where she was to be given 'a marvellous treat'. This journey, however, did not go smoothly. Rita got rid of the engine-driver and took his place. But he came back again and again and threatened her, causing her great anxiety. An object of contention between her and him was her Teddy-bear whom she felt to be essential for the success of the journey. Here the bear represented her father's penis, and her rivalry with her father was expressed by this fight over the penis. She had robbed her father of it, partly from feelings of envy, hatred and revenge, partly in order to take his place with her mother and—by means of her father's potent penis—to make reparation for the injuries done to her mother in phantasy.

The next instance is linked with her bed-time ritual, which had become more and more elaborate and compulsive as time went on and involved a corresponding ceremonial with her doll. The main point of it was that she (and her doll as well) had to be tightly tucked up in the bed clothes, otherwise—as she said—a mouse or a 'butzen' (a word of her own) would get in through the window and bite off her own 'butzen'. The 'butzen' represented both her father's genital and her own: her father's penis would bite off her own imaginary penis just as *she* desired to castrate *him*. As I see it now, the fear of her mother attacking the 'inside' of her body also contributed to her fear of someone coming through the window. The room also represented her body and the assailant was her mother retaliating for the child's attacks on her. The obsessional need to be tucked in with such elaborate care was a defence against all these fears.

Super-ego development

The anxieties and feelings of guilt described in the last two sections were bound up with Rita's super-ego development. I found in her a cruel and unrelenting super-ego, such as underlies severe obsessional neuroses in adults. This development I could in the analysis trace back definitely to the beginning of her second year. In the light of my later experience I am bound to conclude that the beginnings of Rita's super-ego reached back to the first few months of life.

In the travelling game I have described, the engine-driver represented her super-ego as well as her actual father. We also see her super-ego at work in Rita's obsessional play with her doll, when she went through a ritual similar to her own bed-time ceremonial, putting the doll to sleep and tucking her up very elaborately. Once during the analysis Rita placed an elephant by the doll's bedside. As she explained, the elephant was to prevent the 'child' (doll) from getting up, because otherwise the 'child' would steal into its parents' bedroom and either 'do them some harm or take something away from them'. The elephant represented her super-ego (her father and mother), and the attacks on her parents which it was to prevent were the expression of Rita's own sadistic impulses centring on her parents' sexual intercourse and her mother's pregnancy. The super-ego was to make it impossible for the child to rob her mother of the baby inside her, to injure or destroy her mother's body, as well as to castrate the father.

A significant detail from her history was that early in her third year Rita repeatedly declared, when she was playing with dolls, that she *was not the doll's mother*. In the context of the analysis it appeared that she could not allow herself to be the doll's mother because the doll stood for her baby brother whom she wanted and feared to take away from her mother. Her guilt also related to her aggressive phantasies during her mother's pregnancy. When Rita could not play at being her doll's mother, this inhibition derived from her feelings of guilt as well as from her fear of a cruel mother-figure, infinitely more severe than her actual mother had ever been. Not only did Rita see her *real* mother in this distorted light, but she felt in constant danger from a terrifying *internal* mother-figure. I have referred to Rita's phantasied attacks on her mother's body and the corresponding anxiety that her mother would attack her and rob her of her imaginary babies, as well as to her fear of being attacked and castrated by her father. I would now go further in my interpretations. To the phantasied attacks on her body by her parents as external figures corresponded fear of inner attacks by the internalized persecuting parent-figures who formed the cruel part of her super-ego.[1]

The harshness of Rita's super-ego often showed in her play during the analysis. For instance, she used to punish her doll cruelly; then would follow an outbreak of rage and fear. She was identified both with the harsh parents who inflict severe punishment and with the child who is being cruelly punished and bursts into a rage. This was not only noticeable in her play but in her behaviour in general. At certain times she seemed to be the mouthpiece of a severe and unrelenting mother, at other times of an uncontrollable, greedy and destructive infant. There seemed to be very little of her own ego to bridge these two extremes and to modify the intensity of the conflict. The gradual process of integration of her super-ego was severely interfered with, and she could not develop an individuality of her own.

Persecutory and depressive anxieties disturbing the Oedipus development

Rita's depressive feelings were a marked feature in her neurosis. Her states of sadness and crying without cause, her constant questions whether her mother loved her—all these were indications of her depressive anxieties. These anxieties were rooted in her relation to her mother's breasts. In consequence of her sadistic phantasies, in

---

[1] In my General Theoretical Summary below I deal with the girl's super-ego development and the essential part the good internalized father plays in it. With Rita this aspect of her super-ego formation had not appeared in her analysis. A development in this direction, however, was indicated by the improved relation to her father towards the end of her analysis. As I see it now, the anxiety and guilt relating to her mother so much dominated her emotional life that both the relation to the external father and to the internalized father-figure were interfered with.

which she had attacked the breast and her mother as a whole, Rita was dominated by fears which profoundly influenced her relation to her mother. In one aspect she loved her mother as a good and indispensable object and felt guilty because she had endangered her by her aggressive phantasies; in another aspect she hated and feared her as the bad, persecutory mother (in the first place, the bad breast). These fears and complex feelings, which related to her mother both as an external and internal object, constituted her infantile depressive position. Rita was incapable of dealing with these acute anxieties and could not overcome her depressive position.

In this connection some material from the early part of her analysis is significant.[1] She scribbled on a piece of paper and blackened it with great vigour. Then she tore it up and threw the scraps into a glass of water which she put to her mouth as if to drink from it. At that moment she stopped and said under her breath: 'Dead woman.' This material, with the same words, was repeated on another occasion.

The piece of paper blackened, torn up and thrown into the water represented her mother destroyed by oral, anal and urethral means, and this picture of a dead mother related not only to the external mother when she was out of sight but also to the *internal* mother. Rita had to give up the rivalry with her mother in the Oedipus situation because her unconscious fear of loss of the internal and external object acted as a barrier to every desire which would increase her hatred of her mother and therefore cause her mother's death. These anxieties, derived from the oral position, underlay the marked depression which Rita developed at her mother's attempt to wean her of the last bottle. Rita would not drink the milk from a cup. She fell into a state of despair; she lost her appetite in general, refused food, clung more than ever to her mother, asking her again and again whether she loved her, if she had been naughty, and so on. Her analysis revealed that the weaning represented a cruel punishment for her aggressive desires and death wishes against her mother. Since the loss of the bottle stood for the final loss of the breast, Rita felt when the bottle was taken away that she had actually destroyed her mother. Even the presence of her mother could do no more than temporarily alleviate these fears. The inference suggests itself that while the lost bottle represented the lost good breast, the cup of milk which Rita refused in her state of depression following the weaning represented the destroyed and dead mother, just as the glass of water with the torn paper had represented the 'dead woman'.

---

[1] This piece of material has not appeared in former publications.

As I have suggested, Rita's depressive anxieties about the death of her mother were bound up with persecutory fears relating to attacks on her own body by a retaliating mother. In fact such attacks always appear to a girl not only as a danger to her body, but as a danger to everything precious which in her mind her 'inside' contains: her potential children, the good mother and the good father.

The incapacity to protect these loved objects against external and internal persecutors is part of the most fundamental anxiety situation of girls.[1]

Rita's relation to her father was largely determined by the anxiety situations centring on her mother. Much of her hatred and fear of the bad breast had been transferred to her father's penis. Excessive guilt and fear of loss relating to her mother had also been transferred to her father. All this—together with the frustration suffered directly from her father—had interfered with the development of her positive Oedipus complex.

Her hatred of her father was reinforced by penis envy and by rivalry with him in the inverted Oedipus situation. Her attempts to cope with her penis envy led to a reinforced belief in her imaginary penis. However, she felt this penis to be endangered by a bad father who would castrate her in retaliation for her own desires to castrate him. When Rita was afraid of her father's 'butzen' coming into the room and biting off her own 'butzen', this was an instance of her castration fear.

Her desires to annex her father's penis and to play his part with her mother were clear indications of her penis envy. This was illustrated by the play material I have quoted: she travelled with her Teddy-bear, representing the penis, to the 'good woman' who was to give them a 'marvellous treat'. The wish to possess a penis of her own, however, was—as her analysis showed me—strongly reinforced by anxieties and guilt relating to the death of her loved mother. These anxieties, which early on had undermined her relation to her mother, largely contributed to the failure of the positive Oedipus development. They also had the effect of reinforcing Rita's desires to possess a penis, for she felt that she could only repair the damage done to her mother, and make up for the babies which in phantasy she had taken from her, if she possessed a penis of her own with which to gratify her mother and give her children.

Rita's excessive difficulties in dealing with her inverted and

---

[1] This anxiety situation entered to some extent into Rita's analysis, but at that time I did not realize fully the importance of such anxieties and their close connection with depression. This became clearer to me in the light of later experience.

positive Oedipus complex were thus rooted in her depressive position. Along with the lessening of these anxieties, she became able to tolerate her Oedipus desires and to achieve increasingly a feminine and maternal attitude. Towards the end of her analysis, which was cut short owing to external circumstances, Rita's relation to both parents, as well as to her brother, improved. Her aversion to her father, which had until then been very marked, gave place to affection for him; the ambivalence towards her mother decreased, and a more friendly and stable relationship developed.

Rita's changed attitude towards her Teddy-bear and her doll reflected the extent to which her libidinal development had progressed and her neurotic difficulties and the severity of her super-ego had been reduced. Once, near the end of the analysis, while she was kissing the bear and hugging it and calling it pet names, she said: 'I'm not a bit unhappy any more because now I've got such a dear little baby.' She could now allow herself to be the mother of her imaginary child. This change was not an altogether new development, but in some measure a return to an earlier libidinal position. In her second year Rita's desires to receive her father's penis and to have a child from him had been disturbed by anxiety and guilt relating to her mother; her positive Oedipus development broke down and there was a marked aggravation of her neurosis. When Rita said emphatically that she was not the mother of her doll, she clearly indicated the struggle against her desires to have a baby. Under the stress of her anxiety and guilt she could not maintain the feminine position and was driven to reinforce the male position. The bear thus came to stand predominantly for the desired penis. Rita could not allow herself the wish for a child from her father, and the identification with her mother in the Oedipus situation could not be established, until her anxieties and guilt in relation to both parents had lessened.

GENERAL THEORETICAL SUMMARY

(a) *Early stages of the Oedipus complex in both sexes*

The clinical pictures of the two cases I have presented in this paper differed in many ways. However, the two cases had some important features in common, such as strong oral-sadistic impulses, excessive anxiety and guilt, and a low capacity of the ego to tolerate tension of any kind. In my experience, these are some of the factors which, in interaction with external circumstances, prevent the ego from gradually building up adequate defences against anxiety. As a result, the working through of early anxiety situations is impaired and the child's emotional, libidinal and ego-development suffers.

Owing to the dominance of anxiety and guilt there is an over-strong fixation to the early stages of libidinal organization and, in interaction with this, an excessive tendency to regress to those early stages. In consequence, the Oedipus development is interfered with and the genital organization cannot be securely established. In the two cases referred to in this paper, as well as in others, the Oedipus complex began to develop on normal lines when these early anxieties were diminished.

The effect of anxiety and guilt on the course of the Oedipus development is to some extent illustrated by the two brief case histories I have given. The following survey of my theoretical conclusions on certain aspects of the Oedipus development is, however, based on the whole of my analytic work with child and adult cases, ranging from normality to severe illness.

A full description of the Oedipus development would have to include a discussion of external influences and experiences at every stage, and of their effect throughout childhood. I have deliberately sacrificed the exhaustive description of external factors to the need to clarify the most important issues.[1]

My experience has led me to believe that, from the very beginning of life, libido is fused with aggressiveness, and that the development of the libido is at every stage vitally affected by anxiety derived from aggressiveness. Anxiety, guilt and depressive feelings at times drive the libido forward to new sources of gratification, at times they check the development of the libido by reinforcing the fixation to an earlier object and aim.

In comparison with the later phases of the Oedipus complex, the picture of its earliest stages is necessarily more obscure, as the infant's ego is immature and under the full sway of unconscious phantasy; also his instinctual life is in its most polymorphous phase. These early stages are characterized by swift fluctuations between different objects and aims, with corresponding fluctuations in the nature of the defences. In my view, the Oedipus complex starts during the first year of life and in both sexes develops to begin with on similar lines. The relation to the mother's breast is one of the essential factors which determine the whole emotional and sexual development. I therefore take the breast relation as my starting

---

[1] My main purpose in this summary is to provide a clear presentation of my views on some aspects of the Oedipus complex. I also intend to compare my conclusions with certain of Freud's statements on the subject. I find it impossible, therefore, at the same time to quote other authors or to make references to the copious literature dealing with this subject. With regard to the girl's Oedipus complex, however, I should like to draw attention to chapter xi in my book, *The Psycho-Analysis of Children* (1932), in which I have referred to the views of various authors on this subject.

point in the following description of the beginnings of the Oedipus complex in both sexes.

It seems that the search for new sources of gratification is inherent in the forward movement of the libido. The gratification experienced at the mother's breast enables the infant to turn his desires towards new objects, first of all towards his father's penis. Particular impetus, however, is given to the new desire by frustration in the breast relation. It is important to remember that frustration depends on internal factors as well as on actual experiences. Some measure of frustration at the breast is inevitable, even under the most favourable conditions, for what the infant actually desires is *unlimited* gratification. The frustration experienced at the mother's breast leads both boy and girl to turn away from it and stimulates the infant's desire for oral gratification from the penis of the father. The breast and the penis are, therefore, the primary objects of the infant's oral desires.[1]

Frustration and gratification from the outset mould the infant's relation to a loved good breast and to a hated bad breast. The need to cope with frustration and with the ensuing aggression is one of the factors which lead to idealizing the good breast and good mother, and correspondingly to intensifying the hatred and fears of the bad breast and bad mother, which becomes the prototype of all persecuting and frightening objects.

The two conflicting attitudes to the mother's breast are carried over into the new relation to the father's penis. The frustration suffered in the earlier relation increases the demands and hopes from the new source and stimulates love for the new object. The inevitable disappointment in the new relation reinforces the pull-back to the first object; and this contributes to the lability and fluidity of emotional attitudes and of the stages of libidinal organization.

Furthermore, aggressive impulses, stimulated and reinforced by frustration, turn, in the child's mind, the victims of his aggressive phantasies into injured and retaliating figures which threaten him with the same sadistic attacks as he commits against the parents in phantasy.[2] In consequence, the infant feels an increased need for a

[1] In dwelling on the infant's fundamental relation to the mother's breast and to the father's penis, and on the ensuing anxiety situations and defences, I have in mind more than the relation to part-objects. In fact these part-objects are from the beginning associated in the infant's mind with his mother and father. Day-to-day experiences with his parents, and the unconscious relation which develops to them as inner objects, come increasingly to cluster round these primary part-objects and add to their prominence in the child's unconscious.

[2] Allowance must be made for the great difficulty of expressing a young child's feelings and phantasies in adult language. All descriptions of early unconscious

loved and loving object—a perfect, an ideal object—in order to satisfy his craving for help and security. Each object, therefore, is in turn liable to become at times good, at times bad. This movement to and fro between the various aspects of the primary imagos implies a close interaction between the early stages of the inverted and positive Oedipus complex.

Since under the dominance of the oral libido the infant from the beginning introjects his objects, the primary imagos have a counterpart in his inner world. The imagos of his mother's breast and of his father's penis are established within his ego and form the nucleus of his super-ego. To the introjection of the good and bad breast and mother corresponds the introjection of the good and bad penis and father. They become the first representatives on the one hand of protective and helpful internal figures, on the other hand of retaliating and persecuting internal figures, and are the first identifications which the ego develops.

The relation to internal figures interacts in manifold ways with the child's ambivalent relation to both parents as external objects. For to the introjection of external objects corresponds at every step the projection of internal figures on to the external world, and this interaction underlies the relation to the actual parents as well as the development of the super-ego. In consequence of this interaction, which implies an orientation outwards and inwards, there is a constant fluctuation between internal and external objects and situations. These fluctuations are bound up with the movement of the libido between different aims and objects, and thus the course of the Oedipus complex and the development of the super-ego are closely interlinked.

Though still overshadowed by oral, urethral and anal libido, genital desires soon mingle with the child's oral impulses. Early genital desires, as well as oral ones, are directed towards mother and father. This is in line with my assumption that in both sexes there is an inherent unconscious knowledge of the existence of the penis as well as of the vagina. In the male infant, genital sensations are the basis for the expectation that his father possesses a penis which the boy desires according to the equation 'breast = penis'. At the same time, his genital sensations and impulses also imply the search for an opening into which to insert his penis, *i.e.* they are directed towards his mother. The infant girl's genital sensations correspondingly prepare the desire to receive her father's penis into her vagina.

---

phantasies—and for that matter of unconscious phantasies in general—can therefore only be considered as pointers to the contents rather than to the form of such phantasies.

It appears therefore that the genital desires for the penis of the father, which mingle with oral desires, are at the root of the early stages of the girl's positive and of the boy's inverted Oedipus complex.

The course of libidinal development is at every stage influenced by anxiety, guilt and depressive feelings. In the two earlier papers I have repeatedly referred to the infantile depressive position as the central position in early development. I would now rather suggest the following formulation: the core of infantile depressive feelings, *i.e.* the child's fear of the loss of his loved objects, as a consequence of his hatred and aggression, enters into his object relations and Oedipus complex from the beginning.

An essential corollary of anxiety, guilt and depressive feelings is the urge for reparation. Under the sway of guilt the infant is impelled to undo the effect of his sadistic impulses by libidinal means. Thus feelings of love, which co-exist with aggressive impulses, are reinforced by the drive for reparation. Reparative phantasies represent, often in minute detail, the obverse of sadistic phantasies, and to the feeling of sadistic omnipotence corresponds the feeling of reparative omnipotence. For instance, urine and faeces represent agents of destruction when the child hates and gifts when he loves; but when he feels guilty and driven to make reparation, the 'good' excrements in his mind become the means by which he can cure the damage done by his 'dangerous' excrements. Again, both boy and girl, though in different ways, feel that the penis which damaged and destroyed the mother in their sadistic phantasies becomes the means of restoring and curing her in phantasies of reparation. The desire to give and receive libidinal gratification is thus enhanced by the drive for reparation. For the infant feels that in this way the injured object can be restored, and also that the power of his aggressive impulses is diminished, that his impulses of love are given free rein, and guilt is assuaged.

The course of libidinal development is thus at every step stimulated and reinforced by the drive for reparation, and ultimately by the sense of guilt. On the other hand, guilt which engenders the drive for reparation also inhibits libidinal desires. For when the child feels that his aggressiveness predominates, libidinal desires appear to him as a danger to his loved objects and must therefore be repressed.

(b) *The boy's Oedipus development*

So far I have outlined the early stages of the Oedipus complex in both sexes, and I shall now deal particularly with the boy's development. His feminine position—which vitally influences his attitude to both sexes—is arrived at under the dominance of oral, urethral and anal impulses and phantasies and is closely linked with his relation to his mother's breasts. If the boy can turn some of his love and libidinal desires from his mother's breast towards his father's penis, while retaining the breast as a good object, then his father's penis will figure in his mind as a good and creative organ which will give him libidinal gratification as well as give him children as it does to his mother. These feminine desires are always an inherent feature in the boy's development. They are at the root of his inverted Oedipus complex and constitute the first homosexual position. The reassuring picture of his father's penis as a good and creative organ is also a precondition for the boy's capacity to develop his positive Oedipus desires. For only if the boy has a strong enough belief in the 'goodness' of the male genital—his father's as well as his own—can he allow himself to experience his genital desires towards his mother. When his fear of the castrating father is mitigated by trust in the good father, he can face his Oedipus hatred and rivalry. Thus the inverted and positive Oedipus tendencies develop simultaneously, and there is a close interaction between them.

There are good grounds for assuming that as soon as genital sensations are experienced, castration fear is activated. Castration fear in the male, according to Freud's definition, is the fear of having the genital attacked, injured or removed. In my view this fear is first of all experienced under the dominance of oral libido. The boy's oral-sadistic impulses towards his mother's breast are transferred to his father's penis, and in addition rivalry and hatred in the early Oedipus situation find expression in the boy's desire to bite off his father's penis. This arouses his fear that his own genital will be bitten off by his father in retaliation.

There are a number of early anxieties from various sources which contribute to castration fear. The boy's genital desires towards his mother are from the beginning fraught with phantastic dangers because of his oral, urethral and anal phantasies of attack on the mother's body. The boy feels that her 'inside' is injured, poisoned and poisonous; it also contains in his phantasy his father's penis which—owing to his own sadistic attacks on it—is felt as a hostile and castrating object and threatens his own penis with destruction.

To this frightening picture of his mother's 'inside'—which co-exists with the picture of his mother as a source of all goodness and gratification—correspond fears about the inside of his own body. Outstanding among these is the infant's fear of internal attack by a dangerous mother, father or combined parental figure in retaliation for his own aggressive impulses. Such fears of persecution decisively influence the boy's anxieties about his own penis. For every injury done to his 'inside' by internalized persecutors implies to him an attack too on his own penis, which he fears will be mutilated, poisoned or devoured from within. It is, however, not only his penis he feels he must preserve, but also the good contents of his body, the good faeces and urine, the babies which he wishes to grow in the feminine position and the babies which—in identification with the good and creative father—he wishes to produce in the male position. At the same time he feels impelled to protect and preserve the loved objects which he internalized simultaneously with the persecuting figures. In these ways the fear of internal attacks on his loved objects is closely linked with castration fear and reinforces it.

Another anxiety contributory to castration fear derives from the sadistic phantasies in which his excrements have turned poisonous and dangerous. His own penis too, which is equated with these dangerous faeces, and in his mind is filled with bad urine, becomes therefore in his phantasies of copulation an organ of destruction. This fear is increased by the belief that he contains the bad penis of his father, *i.e.* by an identification with the bad father. When this particular identification gains in strength, it is experienced as an alliance with the bad internal father against his mother. In consequence, the boy's belief in the productive and reparative quality of his genital is diminished; he feels that his own aggressive impulses are reinforced and that the sexual intercourse with his mother would be cruel and destructive.

Anxieties of this nature have an important bearing on his actual castration fear and on the repression of his genital desires, as well as on the regression to earlier stages. If these various fears are excessive and the urge to repress genital desires is over-strong, difficulties in potency are bound to arise later. Normally such fears in the boy are counteracted by the picture of his mother's body as the source of all goodness (good milk and babies) as well as by his introjection of loved objects. When his love impulses predominate, the products and contents of his body take on the significance of gifts; his penis becomes the means of giving gratification and children to his mother and of making reparation. Also, if the feeling of containing the good breast of his mother and the good penis of his father has the upper hand, the boy derives from this a strengthened trust in himself which allows him to give freer rein to his impulses and desires. In union and identification with the good father he feels that his penis acquires reparative and creative qualities. All these emotions and phantasies enable him to face his castration fear and to establish the genital position securely. They are also the precondition for sublimated potency, which has an important bearing on the child's activities and interests; and at the same time the foundation is laid for the achievement of potency in later life.

(c) *The girl's Oedipus development*

I have already described the early stages of the girl's Oedipus development in so far as it is in line with the boy's development. I shall now point out some essential features which are specific to the girl's Oedipus complex.

When genital sensations in the infant girl gain in strength, in keeping with the receptive nature of her genitals, the desire to receive the penis arises.[1] At the same time she has an unconscious knowledge that her body contains potential children whom she feels to be her most precious possession. The penis of her father as the giver of children, and equated to children, becomes the object of great desire and admiration for the little girl. This relation to the penis as a source of happiness and good gifts is enhanced by the loving and grateful relation to the good breast.

Together with the unconscious knowledge that she contains potential babies, the little girl has grave doubts as to her future capacity to bear children. On many grounds she feels at a disadvantage in comparison with her mother. In the child's unconscious the mother is imbued with magic power, for all goodness springs from her breast and the mother also contains the father's penis and the babies. The little girl—in contrast to the boy, whose hope for potency gains strength from the possession of a penis which can be compared with his father's penis—has no means of reassuring herself about her future fertility. In addition, her doubts are increased by all the anxieties relating to the contents of her body. These anxieties intensify the impulses to rob her mother's body of her children as well as of the father's penis, and this in turn intensifies the fear lest her own inside be attacked and robbed of its 'good' contents by a retaliating external and internal mother.

Some of these elements are operative in the boy as well, but the fact that the girl's genital development centres on the feminine desire to receive her father's penis and that her main unconscious concern is for her imaginary babies, is a specific feature of the girl's development. In consequence, her phantasies and emotions are predominantly built round her inner world and inner objects; her Oedipus rivalry expresses itself essentially in the impulse to rob her mother of the father's penis and the babies; the fear of having her body attacked and her inner good objects injured or taken away by a bad retaliating mother plays a prominent and lasting part in her

---

[1] The analysis of young children leaves no doubt as to the fact that the vagina is represented in the unconscious of the child. Actual vaginal masturbation in early childhood is much more frequent than has been assumed, and this is corroborated by a number of authors.

anxieties. This, as I see it, is the leading anxiety situation of the girl.

Moreover, while in the boy the envy of his mother (who is felt to contain the penis of his father and the babies) is an element in his inverted Oedipus complex, with the girl this envy forms part of her positive Oedipus situation. It remains an essential factor throughout her sexual and emotional development, and has an important effect on her identification with her mother in the sexual relation with the father as well as in the maternal rôle.

The girl's desire to possess a penis and to be a boy is an expression of her bisexuality and is as inherent a feature in girls as the desire to be a woman is in boys. Her wish to have a penis of her own is secondary to her desire to receive the penis, and is greatly enhanced by the frustrations in her feminine position and by the anxiety and guilt experienced in the positive Oedipus situation. The girl's penis envy covers in some measure the frustrated desire to take her mother's place with the father and to receive children from him.

I can here only touch upon the specific factors which underlie the girl's super-ego formation. Because of the great part her inner world plays in the girl's emotional life, she has a strong urge to fill this inner world with good objects. This contributes to the intensity of her introjective processes, which are also reinforced by the receptive nature of her genital. The admired internalized penis of her father forms an intrinsic part of her super-ego. She identifies herself with her father in her male position, but this identification rests on the possession of an imaginary penis. Her main identification with her father is experienced in relation to the internalized penis of her father, and this relation is based on the feminine as well as on the male position. In the feminine position she is driven by her sexual desires, and by her longing for a child, to internalize her father's penis. She is capable of complete submission to this admired internalized father, while in the male position she wishes to emulate him in all her masculine aspirations and sublimations. Thus her male identification with her father is mixed with her feminine attitude, and it is this combination which characterizes the feminine super-ego.

To the admired good father in the girl's super-ego formation corresponds to some extent the bad castrating father. Her main anxiety object, however, is the persecuting mother. If the internalization of a good mother, with whose maternal attitude she can identify herself, counterbalances this persecutory fear, her relation to the good internalized father becomes strengthened by her own maternal attitude towards him.

In spite of the prominence of the inner world in her emotional life, the little girl's need for love and her relation to people show a great dependence on the outer world. This contradiction is, however, only apparent, because this dependence on the outer world is reinforced by her need to gain reassurance about her inner world.

(d) *Some comparisons with the classical concept of the Oedipus complex*

I now propose to compare my views with those of Freud on certain aspects of the Oedipus complex, and to clarify some divergences to which my experience has led me. Many aspects of the Oedipus complex, on which my work fully confirms Freud's findings, have been to some extent implied in my description of the Oedipus situation. The magnitude of the subject, however, makes it necessary for me to refrain from discussing these aspects in detail, and I have to limit myself to clarifying some of the divergences. The following summary represents in my opinion the essence of Freud's conclusions about certain essential features of the Oedipus development.[1]

According to Freud, genital desires emerge and a definite object choice takes place during the phallic phase, which extends from about three to five years of age, and is contemporaneous with the Oedipus complex. During this phase '. . . . only one genital, namely the male one, comes into account. What is present, therefore, is not a primacy of the genitals, but a primacy of the *phallus*' (*S.E.* **19**, p. 142).

In the boy, 'what brings about the destruction of the child's phallic organization is the threat of castration' (*S.E.* **19**, p. 175). Furthermore, his super-ego, the heir of the Oedipus complex, is formed by the internalization of the parental authority. Guilt is the expression of tension between the ego and the super-ego. It is only when the super-ego has developed that the use of the term 'guilt' is justified. Predominant weight is given by Freud to the boy's super-ego as the internalized authority of the father; and, though in some measure he acknowledges the identification with the mother as a factor in the boy's super-ego formation, he has not expressed his views on this aspect of the super-ego in any detail.

With regard to the girl, in Freud's view her long 'pre-Oedipal attachment' to her mother covers the period before she enters the Oedipus situation. Freud also characterizes this period as 'the phase of exclusive attachment to the mother, which may be called the pre-Oedipus phase' (*S.E.* **21**, p. 230). Subsequently during her phallic phase, the girl's fundamental desires in relation to her mother,

---

[1] This summary is mainly derived from the following of Freud's writings: *The Ego and the Id* (*S.E.* **19**), 'The Infantile Genital Organization' (*S.E.* **19**), 'The Dissolution of the Oedipus Complex' (*S.E.* **19**), 'Some Psychical Consequences of the Anatomical Distinction between the Sexes' (*S.E.* **19**), 'Female Sexuality' (*S.E.* **21**) and *New Introductory Lectures* (*S.E.* **22**).

maintained with the greatest intensity, focus on receiving a penis from her. The clitoris represents in the little girl's mind her penis, clitoris masturbation is the expression of her phallic desires. The vagina is not yet discovered and will only play its part in womanhood. When the girl discovers that she does not possess a penis, her castration complex comes to the fore. At this juncture the attachment to her mother is broken off with resentment and hatred because her mother has not given her a penis. She also discovers that even her mother lacks a penis, and this contributes to her turning away from her mother to her father. She first turns to her father with the wish to receive a penis, and only subsequently with the desire to receive a child from him, 'that is, a baby takes the place of a penis in accordance with an ancient symbolic equivalence' (*S.E.* **22,** p. 128). In these ways her Oedipus complex is ushered in by her castration complex.

The girl's main anxiety situation is the loss of love, and Freud connects this fear with the fear of the death of her mother.

The girl's super-ego development differs in various ways from the boy's super-ego development, but they have in common an essential feature, *i.e.* that the super-ego and the sense of guilt are sequels to the Oedipus complex.

Freud refers to the girl's motherly feelings derived from the early relation to her mother in the pre-Oedipal phase. He also refers to the girl's identification with her mother, derived from her Oedipus complex. But he has not linked these two attitudes, nor shown how the feminine identification with her mother in the Oedipus situation affects the course of the girl's Oedipus complex. In his view, while the girl's genital organization is taking shape, she values her mother predominantly in the phallic aspect.

I shall now summarize my own views on these essential issues. As I see it, the boy's and girl's sexual and emotional development *from early infancy onwards* includes genital sensations and trends, which constitute the first stages of the inverted and positive Oedipus complex; they are experienced under the primacy of oral libido and mingle with urethral and anal desires and phantasies. The libidinal stages overlap from the earliest months of life onwards. The positive and inverted Oedipus tendencies are from their inception in close interaction. It is during the stage of genital primacy that the positive Oedipus situation reaches its climax.

In my view, infants of both sexes experience genital desires directed towards their mother and father, and they have an unconscious knowledge of the vagina as well as of the penis.[1] For these

---

[1] This knowledge exists side by side with the infant's unconscious, and to some extent conscious, knowledge of the existence of the anus which plays a more frequently observed part in infantile sexual theories.

reasons Freud's earlier term 'genital phase' seems to me more adequate than his later concept of the 'phallic phase'.

The super-ego in both sexes comes into being during the oral phase. Under the sway of phantasy life and of conflicting emotions, the child at every stage of libidinal organization introjects his objects—primarily his parents—and builds up the super-ego from these elements.

Thus, though the super-ego corresponds in many ways to the actual people in the young child's world, it has various components and features which reflect the phantastic images in his mind. All the factors which have a bearing on his object relations play a part from the beginning in the building-up of the super-ego.

The first introjected object, the mother's breast, forms the basis of the super-ego. Just as the relation to the mother's breast precedes and strongly influences the relation to the father's penis, so the relation to the introjected mother affects in many ways the whole course of super-ego development. Some of the most important features of the super-ego, whether loving and protective or destructive and devouring, are derived from the early maternal components of the super-ego.

The earliest feelings of guilt in both sexes derive from the oral-sadistic desires to devour the mother, and primarily her breasts (Abraham). It is therefore in infancy that feelings of guilt arise. Guilt does not emerge when the Oedipus complex comes to an end, but is rather one of the factors which from the beginning mould its course and affect its outcome.

I wish now to turn specifically to the boy's development. In my view, castration fear starts in infancy as soon as genital sensations are experienced. The boy's early impulses to castrate his father take the form of wishing to bite off his penis, and correspondingly castration fear is first experienced by the boy as the fear lest his own penis should be bitten off. These early castration fears are to begin with overshadowed by anxieties from many other sources, among which internal danger situations play a prominent part. The closer development approaches to genital primacy, the more castration fear comes to the fore. While I thus fully agree with Freud that *castration fear is the leading anxiety situation in the male*, I cannot agree with his description of it as the *single factor* which determines the repression of the Oedipus complex. Early anxieties from various sources contribute all along to the central part which castration fear comes to play in the climax of the Oedipus situation. Furthermore, the boy experiences grief and sorrow in relation to his father as a loved object, because of his impulses to castrate and murder him. For in his good aspects the father is an indispensable source of strength, a friend and an ideal, to whom the boy looks for protection and guidance and whom he therefore feels impelled to preserve. His feelings of guilt about his aggressive impulses towards his father increase his urge to repress his genital desires. Again and again in the analyses of boys and men I have found that feelings of guilt in relation to the loved father were an integral element of the Oedipus complex and vitally influenced its outcome. The feeling that his mother too is endangered by the son's rivalry with the father, and that the father's death would be an irreparable loss to her, contributes to the strength of the boy's sense of guilt and hence to the repression of his Oedipus desires.

, Freud, as we know, arrived at the theoretical conclusion that the father, as well as the mother, is an object of the son's libidinal desires. (Cf. his concept of the inverted Oedipus complex.) Moreover, Freud in some of his writings (among his case histories particularly in the 'Analysis of a Phobia in a Five-Year-Old Boy', 1909) has taken account of the part which love for his father plays in the boy's positive Oedipus conflict. He has, however, not given enough weight to the crucial rôle of these feelings of love, both in the development of the Oedipus conflict and in its passing. In my experience the Oedipus situation loses in power not only because the boy is afraid of the destruction of his genital by a revengeful father, but also because he is driven by feelings of love and guilt to preserve his father as an internal and external figure.

I will now briefly state my conclusions about the girl's Oedipus complex. The phase in which, according to Freud, the girl is exclusively attached to her mother already includes, in my view, desires directed towards her father and covers the early stages of the inverted and positive Oedipus complex. While I therefore consider this phase as a period of fluctuation between desires directed towards mother and father in all libidinal positions, there is no doubt in my mind as to the far-reaching and lasting influence of every facet of the relation to the mother upon the relation to the father.

Penis envy and the castration complex play an essential part in the girl's development. But they are very much reinforced by frustration of her positive Oedipus desires. Though the little girl at one stage assumes that her mother possesses a penis as a male attribute, this concept does not play nearly as important a part in her development as Freud suggests. The unconscious theory that her mother contains the admired and desired penis of the father underlies, in my experience, many of the phenomena which Freud described as the relation of the girl to the phallic mother.

The girl's oral desires for her father's penis mingle with her first genital desires to receive that penis. These genital desires imply the wish to receive children from her father, which is also borne out by the equation 'penis=child'. The feminine desire to internalize the penis and to receive a child from her father invariably precedes the wish to possess a penis of her own.

While I agree with Freud about the prominence of the fear of loss of love and of the death of the mother among the girl's anxieties, I hold that the fear of having her body attacked and her loved inner objects destroyed essentially contributes to her main anxiety situation.

FINAL REMARKS

Throughout my description of the Oedipus complex I have attempted to show the interdependence of certain major aspects of development. The sexual development of the child is inextricably bound up with his object relations and with all the emotions which from the beginning mould his attitude to mother and father. Anxiety, guilt and depressive feelings are intrinsic elements of the child's emotional life and therefore permeate the child's early object relations, which consist of the relation to actual people as well as to their representatives in his inner world. From these introjected figures—the child's identifications—the super-ego develops and in turn influences the relation to both parents and the whole sexual development. Thus emotional and sexual development, object relations and super-ego development interact from the beginning.

The infant's emotional life, the early defences built up under the stress of the conflict between love, hatred and guilt, and the vicissitudes of the child's identifications—all these are topics which may well occupy analytic research for a long time to come. Further work in these directions should lead us to a fuller understanding of the personality, which implies a fuller understanding of the Oedipus complex and of sexual development as a whole.

EXPLANATORY NOTES[1]

THE DEVELOPMENT OF A CHILD (1921)

Melanie Klein gave her first paper, which was called 'The Development of a Child', to the Hungarian Psycho-Analytical Society in 1919. Two years later she read her second paper to the Berlin Psycho-Analytical Society on 'The Child's Resistance to Enlightenment'. These two papers form Part I and Part II of the whole now called 'The Development of a Child'. Each part complements the other: Part I shows how unenlightened upbringing may cause undue repression in a young mind, and Part II shows that a child's mind has its own powerful tendencies to repression.

Of course, both these conclusions were already known, but what was new was their exploration by the direct study of a child, a study Melanie Klein here describes as not a treatment but a case of 'upbringing with analytic features'. However, when some thirty-five years later she looked back at her work in 'The Psycho-Analytic Play Technique, Its History and Significance', she saw this case—and not her work of 1922 and 1932 as she says in her 1948 Preface to *The Psycho-Analysis of Children*—as the start of her psycho-analytic play technique.

The hallmarks of Melanie Klein's work are already apparent in the present paper. There is her serious commitment to Freud's discoveries; she believes in the extensive influence of the unconscious and unconscious phantasies, and she follows the principle of psychic continuity, and of the dual determination of development by constitution and environment. Also characteristic is her own unhesitating acceptance of speech, play, action and dreams as equally, often interchangeably, expressive of the unconscious, and the detail and abundance of her reports of the child's talk and play.

This, and her other first papers, are infused with very high hopes for child analysis to prevent and cure mental illness. In the Appendix to *The Psycho-Analysis of Children* ten years later her optimism is more tempered, and much later still it was further qualified in *Envy and Gratitude*.

INHIBITIONS AND DIFFICULTIES AT PUBERTY (1922)

Melanie Klein ignored this paper after publication; she did not translate it into English or include it in her volume of collected papers. Her reasons are not known, but the paper lacks anything distinctively hers and is without the dense thought characteristic of others of this period.

[1] See Preface, p. vii, and Introduction, p. x.

THE RÔLE OF THE SCHOOL IN THE LIBIDINAL
DEVELOPMENT OF THE CHILD (1923)

'The Development of a Child' (1921), this paper and 'Early Analysis' (1923) form a set. In the first the child is at home, this one studies him at school and the next relates childhood to adult life. All, but particularly this one, stress the psychic continuity in human life, always a governing idea in Melanie Klein's work.

Her approach here to the subject of intellectual inhibition, a topic she had written on in Part I of 'The Development of a Child', is of interest. Libido is the central concept, and the notions of progress, and inhibition through castration anxiety, take their place around it; aggression in its own right does not occur, and symbolic significance is always sexual symbolic significance. At the same time, the case material shows that in her clinical work Melanie Klein was already analysing the inhibitory effect of aggressive phantasies, and by the time she wrote 'A Contribution to the Theory of Intellectual Inhibition' in 1931, sadism rather than libido has moved to the centre of a new account of intellectual inhibition.

This paper also shows how her new play technique was providing a wealth of analytic material illustrating the child's phantasies and the symbolic significance of every aspect of school life, and indeed, this leads Melanie Klein to the general conclusion that *all* activities have a symbolic significance.

EARLY ANALYSIS (1923)

This paper, the title of which was formerly—for no ascertainable reason—translated as Infant Analysis, is complex in nature. This may partly be due to the fact that it is based on three unpublished papers, 'The Development and Inhibition of Abilities', 'Infantile Anxiety and Its Significance for the Development of the Personality' and 'On the Inhibition and Development of the Ability to Orient Oneself'. Furthermore, Melanie Klein is grappling with several basic concepts—anxiety, inhibition, symptoms, symbol formation and sublimation. She herself thought that the paper made a contribution to the theory of sublimation.

However, already in this paper Melanie Klein makes her first statement of what became one of her fundamental principles, viz,. that it is the resolution of anxiety which brings progress, both in analysis and in mental development. In an attempt to account for the anxiety in the *pavor nocturnus* of the small child, she is led to place the beginning of the Oedipus complex between the ages of two and three—the first of her succession of earlier dates. Three years later, however, in 'The Psychological Principles of Early Analysis' she gives an account of *pavor nocturnus* that is quite different from the one in the present paper and which marks the beginning of her exploration of the connection between anxiety and aggression.

Her views on symbolism, which culminate in 'The Importance of Symbol Formation in the Development of the Ego' (1930) are also developing rapidly. Earlier in the year, in 'The Rôle of the School in the Libidinal Development of the Child', she maintained that all activities have a symbolic significance. Here Melanie Klein says further that the symbolic significance of activities is the reason they give pleasure and also the cause of their inhibition. Furthermore, she posits that before symbol formation there is a prior stage of identification in which, as described by Ferenczi, the infant identifies objects with his own organs and activities. This type of identification later became part of her concept of projective identification in 'Notes on Some Schizoid Mechanisms' (1946).

A CONTRIBUTION TO THE PSYCHOGENESIS OF TICS
(1925)

This case study of a thirteen-year-old boy suffering from tic and related difficulties is markedly different from the tortuous paper which precedes it. With a new precision Melanie Klein traces and resolves the tic in the analysis in terms of identifications and masturbation phantasies. It is the first time that she considers identification with an object, in this instance the parents in intercourse, as a central phenomenon, and from now on, she always regards as of the utmost importance the identifications in the inner world. Indeed, her next paper presents new work on one of the most significant of all identifications, the super-ego. Although she never wrote specifically on masturbation phantasies, she plainly regarded them as fundamental; she states this in a footnote to the next paper (p. 135), and it can be seen throughout *The Psycho-Analysis of Children*.

At this stage, Melanie Klein takes for granted Freud's conception of a primary narcissistic phase. On the specific issue of tic, however, she disagrees with Ferenczi's view that it is an unanalysable primary narcissistic symbol, and maintains, with Abraham, that for a tic to be analysed the object relations on which it is based must be understood. This first uncovering of object relations underlying an apparently narcissistic phenomenon forecasts the direction of her subsequent work on psychosis and primary object relations. Her reasons for her later general rejection of the idea of a primary narcissistic phase will be found in 'The Origins of Transference' (1952).

An illustration of Melanie Klein's empirical approach to the technique of child analysis is the account of interfering and prohibiting two relationships in her patient's life, contrary to her usual custom, and indeed, two years later she marshalled strong arguments against such directive procedures in 'Symposium on Child Analysis'.

PSYCHOLOGICAL PRINCIPLES OF EARLY ANALYSIS
(1926)

This paper contains the first account of one of the most important of Melanie Klein's early findings; the super-ego exists in the child much earlier than Freud had supposed. This early super-ego—according to Melanie Klein a quite unexpected discovery—is composed of multiple identifications, is more cruel than its later form and is a heavy burden on the weak ego of the small child. These findings pose difficulties for Freud's view of the super-ego as the outcome of the Oedipus complex; at this stage Melanie Klein tries to accommodate to his conception. She moves— she has other reasons for this—the start of the Oedipus complex to the beginning of the child's second year, and she suggests that (p. 133) 'as soon as the Oedipus complex arises, they [young children] begin to work it through and thereby to develop the super-ego'. Later she departs from Freud and disconnects the super-ego's beginnings from the Oedipus complex; indeed, the super-ego is a subject Melanie Klein continually returned to and the reader will find a discussion of her main writings in the Explanatory Note to 'The Early Development of Conscience in the Child' (1933).

Melanie Klein had been using her psycho-analytic play technique for six or seven years. In the present paper she states its governing idea: the analytic situation and approach to treatment remain the same as in the analysis of adults, but adjusted to the child's mode of communication by play. She discusses this principle more fully and polemically in the next paper 'Symposium on Child Analysis'.

SYMPOSIUM ON CHILD ANALYSIS (1927)

In previous papers Melanie Klein had been concerned only to report her work. For this symposium with Anna Freud her tone alters and she argues forthrightly for her point of view. In one other place only, the Introduction to *The Psycho-Analysis of Children*, does Melanie Klein refer to the differences between herself and Anna Freud.

The issue between them is the nature of child analysis. Is it the counterpart of adult analysis? Melanie Klein contends, as she had the year before in 'The Psychological Principles of Early Analysis' that the analogue is perfect; a child forms a transference neurosis and gives in his play the equivalent of an adult's free associations to an analyst whose sole function is to analyse as fully as possible everything his small patient brings to him. Anna Freud had, at this time, opposite views on all these points, their disagreement deriving from divergencies in their conception of the child's mind and the nature of the bond between him and his parents.

Equally important is the discussion of the super-ego. In a preceding paper Melanie Klein put forward a conception of the super-ego which starts in a cruelly severe form at an early age and slowly develops into a more normal conscience. Here she offers an explanation of why the early super-ego should be so severe. Her contention is that the extreme, punitive and unreal nature of the super-ego comes from the child's own cannibalistic and sadistic impulses, a view which Freud, in one of his few published references to Melanie Klein, endorses in a footnote to *Civilization and its*

Discontents, *S.E.* **21**, p. 130. Melanie Klein goes on to draw a therapeutic implication. The task of child analysis cannot be to strengthen a feeble super-ego, as Anna Freud maintains, but rather its task must be to reduce the excessive strength of the early super-ego, and throughout the paper Melanie Klein emphasizes the overriding importance of analysing anxiety and guilt. An account of her writings on the super-ego is in the Explanatory Note to 'The Early Development of Conscience in the Child' (1933).

By this time Melanie Klein had eight years' experience of analysing children, and in the course of this symposium she gives her findings on technique in a discussion which continues and amplifies the account in the previous paper. She stresses the necessity of analysing not only the positive transference, but the negative transference also, this latter both for the sake of the analysis and for the protection of parents from unanalysed negative attitudes. She discusses the child's modes of communication, his abundant yield of material, and the relationship of the analyst to the parents of young patients. Melanie Klein also puts on record her views of methods she opposes. In particular, she assesses the adverse effects of the incomplete analysis of material and the use of unanalytic introductory techniques and educational or directive procedures. The fullest account of her play technique will be found in *The Psycho-Analysis of Children*. 'The Psycho-Analytic Play Technique' (1955) gives its history and the day-by-day clinical notes of *Narrative of a Child Analysis* (1961) show Melanie Klein at work.

This paper contains, in addition, new findings on the Oedipus complex. In a footnote in a previous paper (p. 129) Melanie Klein stated that the mother, by weaning and toilet-training her infant, initiates a turning to the father. Here in the text she says explicitly that the Oedipus complex, and therefore also super-ego formation, begin at weaning. She also times the zenith of the Oedipus complex differently, so that it no longer coincides with the end of early childhood and the approach of latency as in Freud's account, but, in her view, a three-year-old has achieved already the most important part of his oedipal development. For a discussion of Melanie Klein's work on the Oedipus complex the reader should consult the Explanatory Note to 'The Oedipus Complex in the Light of Early Anxieties' (1945).

CRIMINAL TENDENCIES IN NORMAL CHILDREN (1927)

This develops Freud's two seminal pages on 'Criminals from a Sense of Guilt', *S.E.* **14**, in which he put forward the thesis that guilt does not arise from crime, but rather, crime comes from guilt. This prior sense of guilt Melanie Klein here connects with her recent discovery of the early super-ego. Her thesis, in its turn as contrary to common assumption as Freud's, is that the criminal does not lack a conscience, but rather, has too cruel a conscience—an unmodified early super-ego which operates differently from the normal and drives him to crime by pressure of fear and guilt.

The present paper discusses both fear and guilt but without distinguishing their operation in the super-ego. In 1932 in *The Psycho-Analysis of Children* Melanie Klein differentiates the early super-ego from the developed super-ego. Her view is that the early super-ego is experienced in the psyche as anxiety or fear, and that it is the developed super-ego which arouses the sense of guilt, a view she expounds most clearly in 'The Early Development of Conscience in the Child' (1933). Her one other paper on the subject of criminality 'On Criminality', a brief paper written in 1934 at short notice, formulates the conclusions of the present paper in terms of this later differentiation. She there also connects criminality with psychosis.

Melanie Klein herself looked back to the year she wrote this paper as the year she realized the importance of aggression. Her other paper of 1927 'Symposium on Child Analysis' saw in the child's aggressive impulses the explanation of the cruelty of his early super-ego. And the present paper contains an important further thesis about crime. It links criminal acts with the criminal tendencies of normal children, and shows that crimes are the enactment in all detail of early sadistic phantasies which are part of normal development. Indeed, Melanie Klein stresses the normal child's numerous oral and anal sadistic phantasies, so adding to the two unconscious crimes of incest and parricide committed during the genital Oedipus complex that Freud mentions in relation to the inner sense of guilt. She also maintains that, traumatic experiences aside, it is sadistic phantasies that create distorted and frightening conceptions of sexual intercourse. In her next paper, 'Early Stages of the Oedipus Conflict', some of these sadistic phantasies are described in detail.

Lastly, throughout this paper which deals with the conflict between super-ego and id, the reader will discern Melanie Klein's interest in a different conflict, the conflict between love and hate, which later became the general governing idea of her work. It is interesting, in this connection, to notice her conviction that love, despite appearances to the contrary, exists in everyone, including every criminal.

EARLY STAGES OF THE OEDIPUS CONFLICT (1928)

This is one of Melanie Klein's most important papers. For some years she had already reported her view that the Oedipus complex begins earlier than Freud supposed; in 'Early Analysis' (1923) she suggests that it starts when a child is between two and three years old; in a footnote to 'The Psychological Principles of Early Analysis' (1926) she implies that it starts very much earlier—in the first year of life, at weaning, and she states this explicitly in 'Symposium on Child Analysis' (1927). But her findings from the analyses of small children go beyond mere earlier dating; in this relatively short paper she presents what amounts to a new conception of the Oedipus complex.

In her view the Oedipus complex starts at weaning in a confused and labile situation of intermingling impulses. Although genital feelings are emerging, oral and anal sadistic impulses first predominate; genital impulses dominate the scene only later when the child arrives at the Oedipal situation classically described by Freud. The positive and inverted Oedipus complexes interact closely, and the child's inner as well as his outer world is involved. Furthermore, the early onset of the Oedipus complex means that it starts when the ego is still little developed, and also, according to Melanie Klein's new researches on the super-ego, in the presence of an early severe super-ego. Both these facts are of considerable consequence. The infant is exposed to an onrush of contradictory sexual and sadistic impulses as well as sexual curiosity when he is still uncomprehending and inarticulate; Melanie Klein stresses the pain, hatred and anxiety of this situation and the consequences for sexual and epistemophilic development. Furthermore, the presence of the super-ego means that guilt about pregenital impulses is not displaced backwards from a super-ego formed at the genital level, but comes directly from the early severe super-ego.

She also thinks that the infant's early awareness of his mother's body and contents is of particular importance. So, in her view, is the femininity phase. Although she never linked it with her later ideas, the femininity phase did not lose its importance in her eyes; the envious and appropriative aspects of this relation to the mother were further investigated in *Envy and Gratitude* (1957), and the later concept of projective identification would appear to be the mechanism underlying the femininity phase.

In the present paper she traces successive identifications in early oedipal relations in an account that has links with Freud's discussions in *The Ego and the Id*, but on an earlier level. She describes the sexual development of the boy and the girl, and though she does not agree with Freud over the leading anxiety in either sex, she sees her work as a development of Freud's new ideas on anxiety in *Inhibitions, Symptoms and Anxiety, S.E.* **20**. The following year in 'Infantile Anxiety Situations Reflected, etc.' (1929) she illustrates the basic anxiety situations described in the present paper. In her view the deepest anxiety of both sexes comes from an imago formed through the attacks on the mother's body, the image of a hostile mother containing a hostile penis, the combined parent figure as she later called it. She contends that castration anxiety in the boy derives from this more primary anxiety and that fear of loss of love in the girl is secondary to the girl's anxiety about attacks on her inside from a hostile mother; she also gives a different account from Freud of castration anxiety and penis envy in the girl, and although she speaks of the phallic phase out of a manifest desire not to diverge from Freud, she none the less stresses the existence of early awareness of the vagina.

These are Melanie Klein's new findings on the Oedipus complex, It must be remembered that at this stage in her thinking anxiety is still a generic concept undifferentiated into persecutory and depressive anxiety, and also, and this is even more important, she still mainly investigates only hate. In 'The Oedipus Complex in the Light of Early Anxieties' written in 1945 after she had distinguished the two forms of anxiety, and had given the impulse of love its due place alongside hate, she changed her mind on several points. This and other matters are discussed in the Explanatory Note to the 1945 paper.

PERSONIFICATION IN THE PLAY OF CHILDREN (1929)

Melanie Klein's aim is to show that the characters or personifications in children's games originate, by splitting and projection, from internal imagos. In the course of the paper she shows that splitting and projection is also a defence against anxiety, and indeed, next year in 'The Importance of Symbol Formation in the development of the Ego' she examines this important defence in its own right. There is also in the present paper a new account of transference as the splitting and projection of inner figures onto the analyst.

Since 1926 Melanie Klein had conceived of the super-ego as a changing structure. Here she offers a first account of its successive stages; this brief account, however, is a medley of diverse ideas, and it is not until 1935 with the theory of the depressive position that she reached a clear view of psychic change. She also suggests in the present paper that the most intense anxiety comes from the very early super-ego, and that in psychosis this early super-ego is in the ascendent—a counterpart to her finding in 'Criminal Tendencies in Normal Children' (1927) that the early super-ego dominates the mind of the criminal.

INFANTILE ANXIETY-SITUATIONS REFLECTED IN A WORK OF ART AND IN THE CREATIVE IMPULSE (1929)

This is the first of the three papers in which Melanie Klein discusses literary material, the other two being 'On Identification' (1955) and 'Some Reflections on *The Oresteia*' (1963). Here she uses Colette's libretto for Ravel's opera 'The Magic Word' and an article by Karin Michaelis entitled 'The Empty Space' as illustrations of the anxiety situations she had described the year before in 'Early Stages of the Oedipus Conflict'.

For the first time Melanie Klein connects creativity with deep early anxieties; she sees the urge to create as arising from the impulse to restore and repair the injured object after a destructive attack. A few years later, this idea has an important place in her theory of the depressive position, and indeed, this paper foreshadows several future formulations. To give one instance: the statement on p. 217 that, in development, fear of an attacking mother gives way to fear of losing a real loving mother anticipates exactly Melanie Klein's later account of the change in anxiety content from the paranoid-schizoid to the depressive position.

In a late work, *Envy and Gratitude* (1957), Melanie Klein again approached the problem of creativity, but from another direction. There she posits that the first object experienced as manifesting creativity is the feeding breast, and she also describes the detrimental effect on creativity of excessive envy.

THE IMPORTANCE OF SYMBOL-FORMATION IN THE DEVELOPMENT OF THE EGO (1930)

The clinical material of this paper opens a new era. Historically, it is the first published report of an analysis of a psychotic child, and demonstrates that it is possible to make analytic contact and set development in train even where a child has no speech, or manifest emotion, and only a very rudimentary symbolism. Melanie Klein had been convinced of the occurrence of psychosis in childhood for several years now. Her preceding papers contain passages describing the form in which schizophrenia manifests itself in children, the play characteristic of the psychotic child and the nature of the super-ego in psychosis. This paper discusses the general question of psychosis in childhood and also contains the first of her attempts to specify the origins of schizophrenia. She suggests that the ego defends itself from intense anxiety by an excessive expulsion of its sadism so that there remains no experience of anxiety, no exploration of the world or formation of symbols, and normal development is brought to a halt. The evolution of Melanie Klein's ideas on schizophrenia is described in detail in the Explanatory Note to 'A Note on Depression in the Schizophrenic' (1960).

The present paper crystallizes several ideas. At the start Melanie Klein regarded anxiety chiefly as an inhibitor of capacities, but very soon, in 'Early Analysis' (1923), she viewed developmental progress as dependent on the resolution of anxiety. In 'Infantile Anxiety Situations Reflected in a Work of Art' published the same year as this paper she went further and saw in anxiety the spur to creativity. Here, from the analysis of psychotic processes in her child patient, she demonstrates that anxiety and its working through is the pre-condition of development—an idea which lies at the centre of her later theories. In addition, conceptions which ultimately find their place in her theory of the paranoid-schizoid position under the name of projective identification have their true beginning in the account given here of symbol formation and the ego's first mode of defence. She shows that the early forms of symbol formation, symbolic equations and identifications are the foundation of the relation to the external world. And she describes what she contends is the ego's first mode of defence, an expulsive mechanism, preceding and fundamentally different from repression; it is a defence against aggression and the anxiety it arouses: sadism is felt as dangerous to the self and attacked objects are feared as retaliatory, which leads the ego to expel its sadism into the object both to protect itself and to destroy the object. Melanie Klein's subsequent use of these ideas is described in the Explanatory Note to 'Notes on Some Schizoid Mechanisms' (1946).

THE PSYCHOTHERAPY OF THE PSYCHOSES (1930)

Melanie Klein contributed this short paper to a symposium on the rôle of psychotherapy in the psychoses. It is a recapitulation, in two places verbatim, of some of her findings about childhood schizophrenia and the anxiety situations at the root of psychoses she had described the year before in 'The Importance of Symbol Formation in the Development of the Ego'.

A CONTRIBUTION TO THE THEORY OF INTELLECTUAL INHIBITION (1931)

The subject of intellectual inhibition interested Melanie Klein from the first. Her early discussions in 'The Development of a Child' (1921(and 'The Rôle of the School in the Libidinal Development of the Child' (1923) follow Freud, and view intellectual capacity as a libidinal sublimation which can be inhibited by castration anxiety. However, already in the latter paper it is evident from the clinical material that she is aware of the inhibiting effect of aggressive phantasies and in 'Early Stages of the Oedipus Conflict' (1928) she contends that it is not libido which brings the epistemophilic instinct into being, but sadism, the early sadism with which the child attacks, and simultaneously comes to know, his mother's body. The mother's body is thus the first object of knowledge. In 'The Importance of Symbol Formation' (1930) she presents another finding. She shows that a massive defence against sadism, such as occurs in dementia praecox causes a general epistemophilic inhibition.

The present paper is the only one directly on the subject of intellectual inhibition. It gives a fuller account of the views put forward in 1928 and 1930 and contains as well some fresh discoveries. Melanie Klein describes two sets of contrasting anxieties which follow on sadistic attacks and inhibit intellectual functioning. Anxieties about the dangerous condition of the mother's body, and, by extension, external reality, interfere with the free exploration of the outside world, while fear of the dangers in the self, especially the forbidding presence of the early sadistic super-ego, prevents self-exploration. She shows, too, that specific intellectual inhibitions, no less than a generalized epistemophilic inhibition, may result from defences against sadism.

Up to this time Melanie Klein's original contribution to the problem of intellectual inhibition was through a study of sadism and its consequences. The next year, however, following her acceptance of Freud's theory of the life and death instincts as a fundamental principle, she no longer studies sadism in isolation but studies love and hate in interaction. Expressed in terms of her subsequent groupings of anxieties into persecutory and depressive, the anxieties so far investigated in connection with intellectual inhibition are persecutory anxieties. In 'A Contribution to the Psychogenesis of Manic-Depressive States' (1935) she draws attention to the other group of anxieties, the depressive anxieties, and shows how the capacity to learn and work may be hampered by depression and despair about damaged objects.

The reader who compares this paper with the first discussions of intellectual inhibition a little more than a decade ago will notice great changes. It would seem an appropriate point for Melanie Klein to present in book form her accumulated ideas. and, indeed, the following year saw the publication of *The Psycho-Analysis of Children*.

THE EARLY DEVELOPMENT OF CONSCIENCE IN THE CHILD (1933)

Freud's classic work on the super-ego *The Ego and the Id* appeared in 1923. Soon after, Melanie Klein began to contribute further findings gained largely from analysing children. She came across the unexpected phenomenon of guilt in very small children. This led her to postulate in 'Psychological Principles' (1926) that the super-ego exists very much earlier than Freud supposed; her view was that the super-ego is formed not at the end as the heir to the Oedipus complex but at the beginning of the Oedipus complex, and she also dated the onset of the Oedipus complex much earlier than Freud, namely, at weaning. She gave also her first description of the early super-ego; formed from the introjection of early oedipal figures it is composed of multiple identifications and is far more cruel and primitive than it is later. In 'Symposium on Child Analysis' (1927) and more completely in 'Early Stages of the Oedipus Conflict' (1928) she offered an explanation for the cruelty of the early super-ego which so exceeds the actual parents in severity. Her contention was that the oedipal introjects which form the super-ego are distorted into terrifying figures by the child's sadistic impulses. In 'Early Stages of the Oedipus Conflict' she also follows through an important corollary of the view that the super-ego is formed at the start rather than at the end of the Oedipus complex, namely, that the entire course of sexual development, as well as ego development and character formation, takes place in the presence of a super-ego. She demonstrated the early super-ego's terrifying and deforming hold on the psyche of the criminal and the psychotic in 'Criminal Tendencies in Normal Children' (1927) and 'Personification in the Play of Children' (1929) respectively, and the early super-ego's crippling rôle in intellectual inhibition in 'A Contribution to the Theory of Intellectual Inhibition' (1931). In 'Personification in the Play of Children' she also maintained that the source of greatest anxiety to the psyche is the very early super-ego.

Since 1927 Melanie Klein had differentiated between fear and guilt as two separate forces emanating from the super-ego. She did not, however, maintain this distinction consistently, until in *The Psycho-Analysis of Children* (1932) she confirmed and explained the significance of this difference by distinguishing the early super-ego from its developed form in terms of the anxiety of the early super-ego giving way to the guilt of the developed conscience. In the same work, while she still links the formation of the super-ego to the onset of the Oedipus complex at weaning, she also makes a brief statement about super-ego formation which implies contradictorily that it is an earlier structure than the Oedipus complex. She suggests (p. 127) that when the process of incorporation begins immediately after birth the incorporated object at once assumes the function of a super-ego.

These are the main steps so far in the development of Melanie Klein's views on the super-ego. In the present paper, in an exposition of great clarity, Melanie Klein presents these views, stressing the importance for society and the individual of the transformation of the early terrifying super-ego into the benign moral conscience. Curiously, though since 1927 she held the view that the cruelty of the early super-ego derives from the child's sadistic impulses, she did not until this paper use the word 'projection' in referring to this fact; she invoked the talion principle or used locutions such as that the early imagos 'take the imprint of' the child's sadistic impulses. Here she does say that the child *projects* his aggressive impulses onto his objects, and from now on she always expresses it in this way or in terms of the later concept of projective identification. She also repeats in amplified form her statements of 1932 about super-ego formation, saying that the super-ego is formed from a division in the id as a defence measure by the ego and begins when the infant makes its first oral introjections. This plainly dates super-ego formation earlier than the Oedipus complex; however, she puts a contradictory footnote on p. 251 affirming the view that the super-ego begins in close connection with early oedipal impulses, as if still reluctant to sever connection with so fundamental a tenet of Freud's theory which linked closely the origin of the super-ego and the Oedipus complex. However, two years later, in 'A Contribution to the Psychogenesis of Manic-Depressive States' the original forming of the super-ego is finally disconnected altogether from the Oedipus complex.

Her work on the super-ego raises in an acute form the problem of psychic change. How does the change from the early super-ego, felt as anxiety, and asocial in its effect, to the developed conscience, felt as guilt, and moral in outlook, come about? She often referred to this problem: 'Personification in the Play of Children' contains a particularly interesting discussion of one aspect of the developmental task, viz., the synthesizing of the polarised identifications which make up the super-ego. However, the dynamics of this change stay largely unexplained until 'A Contribution to the Psychogenesis of Manic-Depressive States' when the distinction between fear and guilt, which until then has only a descriptive significance, becomes a nodal differentiation in a new theory. Then the synthesizing of polarised figures, the growing assimilation of the super-ego by the ego and the change from fear to guilt can be explained and understood in terms of the processes of the depressive position. A short non-technical exposition of super-ego development is in 'A Comment by Mrs Melanie Klein' (1942) at the end of Volume IV of the *Writings* under 'Miscellaneous'. Later, in 'A Contribution to the Theory of Anxiety and Guilt'

(1948), Melanie Klein amends the view that guilt occurs only in the depressive position; she states that transiently it can be experienced earlier. In *Envy and Gratitude* (1957) she gives a description of the envious super-ego and also of premature guilt arising from envy.

Her final thoughts on the super-ego will be found in 'The Development of Mental Functioning' (1958). Melanie Klein abruptly departs from her tenet of forty years that the most terrifying and extreme figures form the basis of the super-ego. She states instead that the most extreme figures are not part of the super-ego, but occupy a region of their own, split off from the rest of the mind. This radical reclassification of internal figures is discussed more fully in the Explanatory Note to 'The Development of Mental Functioning'.

ON CRIMINALITY (1934)

This paper was given at short notice as part of a symposium on crime. In terms that take into account her work in the intervening years, Melanie Klein restates briefly the conclusions on criminality she formulated in 'Criminal Tendencies in Normal Children' (1927). New is a brief assertion of the common basis of psychosis and crime.

A CONTRIBUTION TO THE PSYCHOGENESIS OF MANIC-DEPRESSIVE STATES (1935)

With this paper begins the period of work in which Melanie Klein built a new theoretical structure. Her earlier work had prepared the ground. Over some fifteen years she accumulated a series of findings which not only altered her conception of the Oedipus complex and the super-ego, but also brought a gradual and fundamental conceptual shift. The notions of anxiety, internal object, unconscious phantasy, aggression, introjection and projection came to the fore, but in an unsystematic way. So that in *The Psycho-Analysis of Children*, published three years before the present paper, Melanie Klein is both accepting the classic account of development as a progression through psycho-sexual stages and at the same time using a terminology and describing phenomena requiring a different approach, viz., the ego's changing relations to its internalized and external objects and the fluctuations of early psychotic anxieties. Two things changed this situation of transition into the inauguration of a new theory. First, she based her work fully on the interaction of the life and death instincts expressed in love and hate; this not only rectified her former relative neglect of love and over-emphasis of aggression, but it also provided her with a basis for formulation. And second, there is in the present paper the *sine qua non* of all new theories—new scientific conceptions. Indeed, this paper contains an abundance of major new ideas, in terms of which it propounds two interwoven theories: a theory of early development and a theory of the origin of manic-depressive illness.

Briefly, the theory posits that in the first year at roughly four to five months a significant change occurs in the infant's object relations, a change from relation to a part-object to relation to a complete object. This change brings the ego to a new position in which it is able to identify with its object so that while formerly the infant's anxieties were of a paranoic kind about the preservation of his ego, he now has a more complicated set of ambivalent feelings and depressive anxieties about the condition of his object. He becomes afraid of losing his loved good object, and in addition to persecutory anxieties he experiences guilt for his aggression towards his object and has the urge out of love to repair it. A related change occurs in his defences: he mobilizes manic defences to annihilate persecutors and to deal with his newly experienced guilt and despair. This specific grouping of object relations, anxieties and defences Melanie Klein named the depressive position.

In this theory Melanie Klein distinguishes for the first time the two forms of anxiety, paranoic (which later she usually called persecutory) and depressive. This is a fundamental distinction. It brings order and clarification, and related concepts fall naturally into place around it. She also introduces a new opposition into object relations, namely, the difference between the relation to a part-object and the relation to a whole object. Of central importance is the new idea of position as the developmental unit in place of phase of stage.

Melanie Klein gives one reason for adopting the term 'position' in the 1948 Preface to the Third Edition of *The Psycho-Analysis of Children* (*Writings*, **2**, p. xiii) and at the end of Chapter Note 4 to 'Some Theoretical Conclusions Regarding the Emotional Life of the Infant' (1952) she gives an additional reason. The reader will notice the multiple use of the term 'position' in the present paper; as well as a depressive position, there is a manic position, obsessional position and paranoic position. 'Manic position' and 'obsessional position' disappear from use after 1940 and in 'Notes on Some Schizoid Mechanisms' (1946), the paper which completes her theory of early development, she renamed the paranoic position the paranoid-schizoid position. Reparation, first described in 'Infantile Anxiety Situations Reflected in a Work of Art and in the Creative Impulse' (1929) becomes here a key concept. Further, in place of successive libidinal stages, the course and outcome of development is expressed in terms of internal object relations.

The normal outcome of the depressive position, which in Melanie Klein's view is the central position in the child's development, on which both mental health and the capacity to love depend, is the secure internalization of the good object. If this fails to occur an abnormal situation has already arisen in the child, which constitutes the psychic setting for depressive illness. This is the second theory of the paper. In Melanie Klein's view the sufferings and psychotic anxieties of manic-depressive illness repeat the struggles of the infantile depressive position.

Earlier, in the 1920's, Melanie Klein had discovered infantile anxieties of a paranoid kind; here she uncovers a further category of infantile psychotic anxieties, depressive anxieties. Indeed, the paper makes a most considerable contribution to the general theory of psychosis. Though the focus of the paper is the infantile depressive position, it illumines by contrast the general nature of the preceding paranoic position as a time characterized by paranoid anxiety, relations to part objects and a splitting of objects and emotions. She compares paranoia and depression in detail and her theory that the infantile paranoiac position is succeeded by the infantile depressive position enables her to explain the observed clinical connection between the two illnesses by their original continuity and interplay in infancy. She offers a new account of manic-depressive illness in terms of the dread of containing dying or dead objects. She states her conception of manic defences, emphasizing omnipotence and denial; she shows the connection between manic and obsessional defences; and she shows that manic defences are used not only against depression but also against paranoid anxieties. Of course, not all the ramifications of the theory are worked out here. 'Mourning and Its Relation to Manic-Depressive States' published five years later continues the present paper and studies a further important process in the depressive position, the mourning for the lost object. It continues also the work of the present paper on manic defences, reparation and integrative processes in the ego, and stresses that the unification of objects—rather than repeated splitting on planes nearer reality which is emphasized in the present paper—is the all important process in the depressive position. The connection between the depressive position and the Oedipus complex is described in 'The Oedipus Complex in the Light of Early Anxieties' (1945) with some additions in 'Some Theoretical Conclusions Regarding the Emotional Life of the Infant' (1952). In the latter paper Melanie Klein also suggests that in the depressive position a split is made between an alive and un-injured object and an injured and dying object as a defence against depressive anxiety. A modification in the account of guilt given in the present paper will be found in 'Anxiety and Guilt' (1948) and in the account of depression in 'Depression in the Schizophrenic' (1960).

WEANING (1936)

This was Melanie Klein's contribution to a course of public lectures given by psycho-analysts. She added the preface and postscript in 1952 to the second edition of the small book *On the Bringing Up of Children*, in which the series of lectures was published.

Earlier, for example in 'The Psychological Principles of Early Analysis' (1926), Melanie Klein had viewed weaning as a trauma which in-augurates the Oedipus complex: frustration inflicted by the feeding mother causes the infant to turn away from her and move towards his father. However, her subsequent theory of the infantile depressive position in 'A Contribution to the Psychogenesis of Manic-Depressive

States' (1935) shed a different light on weaning. Weaning is seen pre-eminently as the total loss of the infant's first external good object which brings the emotions and conflicts of the depressive position to a height. At the same time, weaning, if successful, gives positive impetus to accepting substitutes and finding wider sources of gratification.

Melanie Klein gives a vivid and non-technical presentation of these new views and, as suits a practical guide to the upbringing of children, she includes psychological advice on problems in infant rearing. She compares briefly breast and bottle feeding, a subject discussed more fully in the first chapter note to 'On Observing the Behaviour of Young Infants' (1952). The second chapter note to the same paper discusses again the subject of weaning.

LOVE, GUILT AND REPARATION (1937)

Under the title 'The Emotional Life of Civilized Men and Women' Melanie Klein and Joan Riviere gave public lectures in 1936 which became the basis of a small volume *Love, Hate and Reparation* published the following year. They divided their subject: Joan Riviere spoke on 'Hate, Guilt and Aggression' and Melanie Klein on 'Love, Guilt and Reparation'. Melanie Klein presents the still very new ideas of the theory of the depressive position, which she had formulated only two years before. Of special interest, apart from the non-technical exposition, is the discussion of a wide range of human situations, indeed, more than in any other of her writings.

On one point her view was later different. The burden of reparation towards an object damaged by hate is here placed on the infant from the start. However, according to her later theory of the paranoid-schizoid position, splitting prevails in the first months and the need for reparation does not arise till later in the more integrated states of the depressive position.

MOURNING AND ITS RELATION TO MANIC-DEPRESSIVE STATES (1940)

Like 'A Contribution to the Psychogenesis of Manic-Depressive States' (1935) with which it is continuous, this is a work of the first rank. It places mourning among the phenomena of the depressive position. This enables Melanie Klein to elucidate the nature of mourning, and also to connect mourning with her work on manic-depressive states. Her main hypothesis is that the loss of a loved person reactivates the infantile depressive position, and that the ability in later life to mourn and recover from mourning is contingent upon the resolution of the depressive position in childhood.

435

She uncovers several processes not before known to be part of mourning, the chief of which is that the loss of an external good object brings with it an unconscious feeling of having lost also the internal good object. This means that the mourner's sufferings and the nature of his task are more extensive than had been thought; he is afflicted by the pain of the inner in addition to the outer loss and is left a prey to persecution from bad objects, *i.e.* the early persecutory and depressive anxieties of the depressive position are again aroused. Melanie Klein discusses also the special importance of reparation in overcoming states of mourning.

Throughout the paper she links her work to Freud's. She is not, however, in agreement with him over the relation between mourning and manic-depressive states. In her view, normal adult mourning involves manic and depressive states, which, as she showed in 1935, occur normally in the depressive position. In the present paper she extends her work on manic defences, particularly in the area of manic triumph; and shows how the excessive mobilization of manic defences interferes with the secure internal re-establishment of the good object.

From the point of view of her general theory of development, the paper completes the exposition of the depressive position begun in 1935. The depressive position is shown to include processes of mourning; the rôle of reparation in overcoming the depressive position is further described and two self-defeating forms of reparation, obsessional and manic reparation, are discussed for the first time. The paper, as remarked above, adds considerably to the account of manic defences given in 1935. Further, though Melanie Klein herself pays no explicit attention to it, there is in one respect a change of emphasis from 1935; there she stressed (p. 288, and requotes it here, p. 350) the importance in the depressive position of renewed splitting on more realistic planes after each step in the unification of imagos. Here, in a footnote she states (p. 349, note 2) that the unification of opposed aspects of the object is 'the all-important process'. In her later work, it becomes clear that the process of unification depends on more realistic splitting of the object. She also puts forward for the first time in the present paper the mitigation in the depressive position of hate by love.

THE OEDIPUS COMPLEX IN THE LIGHT OF EARLY ANXIETIES (1945)

This is Melanie Klein's final major statement on the Oedipus complex. Her previous principal discussions are in 'Early Stages of the Oedipus Complex' (1928) and *The Psycho-Analysis of Children* (1932). Since these were written, two considerable developments occurred in her work, one general, the other more specific. The general one is the acceptance in *The Psycho-Analysis of Children* of the interaction of love and hate as the basis of mental functioning. In that work itself, however, she had only begun to make use of this principle, so that her writings on the Oedipus complex in *The Psycho-Analysis of Children* were not affected by it. The more specific change is her new theory, formulated in 'A Contribution to the Psychogenesis of Manic-Depressive States' (1935), of the depressive position as the turning point of development in the first year of life. The present paper is a revised and enlarged account of the Oedipus complex in the light of both these changes.

Her distinctive conception of the Oedipus complex remains as in 1928—there exist earlier pregenital stages of the Oedipus complex in addition to the oedipal situation discovered by Freud; early phantasies about the mother's body containing the father's penis and about the child's own insides are part of the oedipal situation; and guilt is not only the outcome but is present from the start of the Oedipus complex, and affects its whole evolving course. Her account in *The Psycho-Analysis of Children* of the sexual development of the boy and the girl also still stands. But she now takes a different view of the onset of the Oedipus complex and of the cause of its decline, and she also makes certain important additions to the nature of the Oedipus complex itself.

Her new assumption that sadism declines rather than escalates in the first six months, taken together with her view that object relations are present from birth, means that her earlier statements that the Oedipus complex starts in the narcissistic phase, as she said in 1932, or when sadism is at its height, are incorrect and fall away. She no longer thinks that the oral frustration of weaning releases the oedipal impulses or, as she sometimes expressed it, that the Oedipus complex starts chiefly under the impulse of hate. On the contrary, she now holds that the onset of the Oedipus complex is coincident with the onset of the depressive position, when persecutory anxiety diminishes and feelings of love come strongly to the fore, and though deprivation may play a part in causing the child to turn away from the breast, this is secondary to the love which propels him forward and the libido's inherent search for new objects. With regard to the decline of the Oedipus complex she thought in 1932 that guilt was the chief factor; she now holds that positive emotions, the child's love for his parents and his wish to preserve them, are also reasons for the Oedipus complex losing its power.

When she connected the Oedipus complex with the depressive position in 1935 in 'A Contribution to the Psychogenesis of Manic-Depressive States' she did not go beyond the statement that the sorrow and concern about the feared loss of good objects in the depressive position was the source of the most painful oedipal conflicts. In the present paper she examines the interweaving of oedipal desires and depressive anxieties as the child struggles to integrate his love and hate, and she shows how sexual impulses gain a new dimension as a means of repairing the effects of aggression. This leads to the emergence of reparative sexual phantasies, of great significance for future sexuality. This more rounded picture of the oedipal situation is illustrated by material from two patients, Richard, the boy whose analysis is published in full in *Narrative of a Child Analysis* (1961), and Rita, a little girl much of whose material had already figured in previous papers.

In this paper there is a useful account by Melanie Klein of her disagreements with Freud on the Oedipus complex. It is of interest that, except for views which derive specifically from linking the Oedipus complex with the depressive position, all the divergences listed here were already present in her 1928 paper; but there she appeared to wish to avoid any emphasis on her differences with Freud.

A manifest clarification of her views of the very first months of life is evident in the present paper. The following year saw the publication of 'Notes on Some Schizoid Mechanisms', in which she suggests that in his earlier months the infant is in the paranoid-schizoid position. This does not, however, affect the views expressed here. Her own short statement of the changes since 1932 in her view of the Oedipus complex can be found in the preface to the Third Edition of *The Psycho-Analysis of Children*.

Melanie Klein added to her account of the Oedipus complex in two subsequent works. In the outline of the Oedipus complex in 'Some Theoretical Conclusions Regarding the Emotional Life of the Infant' (1952) she describes the reciprocal and beneficent relation between the Oedipus complex and the depressive position. Her last discussion of the Oedipus complex is in *Envy and Gratitude* (1957) where she describes the deleterious effect of envy on the oedipal situation.

To sum up: Melanie Klein furthered the understanding of the Oedipus complex in two main ways; first, she discovered the early stages of the complex, and then she connected the Oedipus complex—according to Freud the nuclear complex of the neuroses—with the depressive position, in her view the central position in the child's development.

BIBLIOGRAPHY

Abraham, K. (1914). 'A Constitutional Basis of Locomotor Anxiety.' In: *Selected Papers on Psycho-Analysis* (London: Hogarth, 1927).

—— (1920). 'Manifestations of the Female Castration Complex.' *ibid.*

—— (1921). 'A Contribution to a Discussion on Tic.' *ibid.*

—— (1921–25). 'Psycho-Analytical Studies on Character Formation.' *ibid.*

—— (1924). 'A Short Study of the Development of the Libido, Viewed in the Light of Mental Disorders.' *ibid.*

Alexander, F. (1923). 'The Castration Complex and the Formation of Character.' *Int. J. Psycho-Anal.*, **4.**

Boehm, F. (1922). 'Beiträge zur Psychologie der Homosexualität: ein Traum eines Homosexuellen.' *Int. Z. f. Psychoanal.*, **8.**

Chadwick, M. (1925). 'Uber die Wurzel der Wissbegierde.' *Int. Z. f. Psychoanal.*, **11.** Abstract in *Int. J. Psycho-Anal.*, **6.**

Deutsch, H. (1925). 'The Psychology of Women in Relation to the Functions of Reproduction.' *Int. J. Psycho-Anal.*, **6.**

—— (1933). 'Zur Psychologie der manisch-depressiven Zustände.' *Int. Z. f. Psychoanal.*, **19.**

Fenichel, O. (1928). 'Über organlibinöse Begleiterscheinunger der Triebabwehr.' *Int. Z. f. Psychoanal.*, **14.**

Ferenczi, S. (1912a). 'On Transitory Symptom-Constructions during the Analysis.' In: *First Contributions to Psycho-Analysis* (London: Hogarth, 1952).

—— (1912b). 'Symbolic Representation of the Pleasure and Reality Principles in the Oedipus Myth.' *ibid.*

—— (1913). 'Stages in the Development of the Sense of Reality.' *ibid.*

—— (1921a). 'The Symbolism of the Bridge.' *Further Contributions to the Theory and Technique of Psycho-Analysis* (London: Hogarth, 1926).

—— (1921b). 'Psycho-analytic Observations on Tic.' *ibid.*

—— (1924). *Thalassa: a Theory of Genitality* (New York: Psychoanalytic Quarterly, Inc., 1938).

Freud, A. (1927). *The Psychoanalytical Treatment of Children* (London: Imago, 1946).

Freud, S. (1900). *The Interpretation of Dreams. S.E.* **4–5.**

—— (1905). *Three Essays on the Theory of Sexuality. S.E.* **7.**

—— (1908). 'Hysterical Phantasies and their Relation to Bisexuality.' *S.E.* **9.**

—— (1909a). 'Analysis of a Phobia in a Five-Year-Old Boy.' *S.E.* **10.**

—— (1909b). 'Notes upon a Case of Obsessional Neurosis.' *S.E.* **10.**

Freud, S. (1910). *Leonardo da Vinci and a Memory of his Childhood. S.E.* **11**.

—— (1911). 'Formulations on the Two Principles of Mental Functioning.' *S.E.* **12**.

—— (1912). 'On the Universal Tendency to Debasement in the Sphere of Love.' *S.E.* **11**.

—— (1913). *Totem and Taboo. S.E.* **13**.

—— (1914). 'On Narcissism: an Introduction.' *S.E.* **14**.

—— (1915a). 'Repression.' *S.E.* **14**.

—— (1915b). 'The Unconscious.' *S.E.* **14**.

—— (1915c). 'Some Character-Types met with in Psycho-Analytic Work: III Criminals from a Sense of Guilt.' *S.E.* **14**.

—— (1916–17). *Introductory Lectures on Psycho-Analysis. S.E.* **15–16**.

—— (1917). 'Mourning and Melancholia.' *S.E.* **14**.

—— (1918). 'From the History of an Infantile Neurosis.' *S.E.* **17**.

—— (1920). *Beyond the Pleasure Principle. S.E.* **18**.

—— (1923). *The Ego and the Id. S.E.* **19**.

—— (1924). 'The Dissolution of the Oedipus Complex.' *S.E.* **19**.

—— (1925). 'Some Psychical Consequences of the Anatomical Distinction between the Sexes.' *S.E.* **19**.

—— (1926a). *Inhibitions, Symptoms and Anxiety. S.E.* **20**.

—— (1926b). *The Question of Lay Analysis. S.E.* **20**.

—— (1930). *Civilization and its Discontents. S.E.* **21**.

—— (1931). 'Female Sexuality.' *S.E.* **21**.

—— (1933). *New Introductory Lectures on Psycho-Analysis. S.E.* **22**.

Glover, E. (1932). 'A Psycho-Analytic Approach to the Classification of Mental Disorders.' In: *On the Early Development of Mind* (London: Baillière, 1956).

Groddeck, G. (1922). 'Der Symbolisierungszwang.' *Imago*, **8**.

Gross, O. (1902). *Die Cerebrale Sekundaerfunction.*

Hárnik, J. (1928). 'Die ökonomischen Beziehungen zwischen den Schuldgefühl und dem weiblichen Narzissmus.' *Int. Z. f. Psychoanal.*, **14**.

Hollós, I. (1922). 'Über das Zeitgefühl.' *Int. Z. f. Psychoanal.*, **8**.

Isaacs, S. (1934). 'Anxiety in the First Year of Life.' Unpublished paper read to the Brit. Psycho-Anal., Soc.

—— (1936). 'Habit.' In: *On the Bringing up of Children* ed. Rickman (London: Kegan Paul).

Jokl, R. (1922). 'Zur Psychogenese des Schreibkrampfes.' *Int. Z. f. Psychoanal.*, **8**.

Jones, E. (1916). 'The Theory of Symbolism.' In: *Papers on Psycho-Analysis* (London: Baillière, 2nd edn 1918–5th edn 1948).

Klein, M. [details of first publication of each paper/book are given here; the number of the volume in which they appear in *The Writings of Melanie Klein* is indicated in square brackets].

BIBLIOGRAPHY

Klein, M. (1921). 'The Development of a Child' *Imago*, **7**. [I]

—— (1922). 'Inhibitions and Difficulties in Puberty.' *Die neue Erziehung*, **4**. [I]

—— (1923a). 'The Role of the School in the Libidinal Development of the Child.' *Int. Z. f. Psychoanal.*, **9**. [I]

—— (1923b). 'Early Analysis.' *Imago*, **9**. [I]

—— (1925). 'A Contribution to the Psychogenesis of Tics.' *Int. Z. f. Psychoanal.*, **11**. [I]

—— (1926). 'The Psychological Principles of Early Analysis.' *Int. J. Psycho-Anal.*, **7**. [I]

—— (1927a). 'Symposium on Child Analysis.' *Int. J. Psycho-Anal.*, **8**. [I]

—— (1927b). 'Criminal Tendencies in Normal Children.' *Brit. J. med. Psychol.*, **7**. [I]

—— (1928). 'Early Stages of the Oedipus Conflict.' *Int. J. Psycho-Anal.*, **9**. [I]

—— (1929a). 'Personification in the Play of Children.' *Int. J. Psycho-Anal*, **10**. [I]

—— (1929b). 'Infantile Anxiety Situations Reflected in a Work of Art and in the Creative Impulse.' *Int. J. Psycho-Anal.*, **10**. [I]

—— (1930a). 'The Importance of Symbol-Formation in the Development of the Ego.' *Int. J. Psycho-Anal.*, **11**. [I]

—— (1930b). 'The Psychotherapy of the Psychoses.' *Brit. J. med. Psychol.*, **10**. [I]

—— (1931). 'A Contribution to the Theory of Intellectual Inhibition.' *Int. J. Psycho-Anal.*, **12**. [I]

—— (1932). *The Psycho-Analysis of Children* (London: Hogarth). [II]

—— (1933). 'The Early Development of Conscience in the Child.' In: *Psychoanalysis Today* ed. Lorand (New York: Covici-Friede). [I]

—— (1934). 'On Criminality.' *Brit. J. med. Psychol.*, **14**. [I]

—— (1935). 'A Contribution to the Psychogenesis of Manic-Depressive States.' *Int. J. Psycho-Anal.*, **16**. [I]

—— (1936). 'Weaning.' In: *On the Bringing Up of Children* ed. Rickman (London: Kegan Paul). [I]

—— (1937). 'Love, Guilt and Reparation.' In: *Love, Hate and Reparation* with Riviere (London: Hogarth). [I]

—— (1940). 'Mourning and its Relation to Manic-Depressive States.' *Int. J. Psycho-Anal.*, **21**. [I]

—— (1945). 'The Oedipus Complex in the Light of Early Anxieties.' *Int. J. Psycho-Anal.*, **26**. [I]

—— (1946). 'Notes on some Schizoid Mechanisms.' *Int. J. Psycho-Anal.*, **27**. [III]

—— (1948a). *Contributions to Psycho-Analysis 1921–1945* (London: Hogarth). [I]

—— (1948b). 'On the Theory of Anxiety and Guilt.' *Int. J. Psycho-Anal.*, **29**. [III]

Klein, M. (1950). 'On the Criteria for the Termination of a Psycho-Analysis.' *Int. J. Psycho-Anal.*, **31**. [III]

—— (1952a). 'The Origins of Transference.' *Int. J. Psycho-Anal.*, **33**. [III]

—— (1952b). 'The Mutual Influences in the Development of Ego and Id.' *Psychoanal. Study Child.* **7**. [III]

—— (1952c). 'Some Theoretical Conclusions regarding the Emotional Life of the Infant.' In: *Developments in Psycho-Analysis* with Heimann, Isaacs and Riviere (London: Hogarth). [III]

—— (1952d). 'On Observing the Behaviour of Young Infants.' *ibid.* [III]

—— (1955a). 'The Psycho-Analytic Play Technique: Its History and Significence.' In: *New Directions in Psycho-Analysis* (London: Tavistock). [III]

—— (1955b). 'On Identification.' *ibid.* [III]

—— (1957). *Envy and Gratitude* (London: Tavistock) [III]

—— (1958). 'On the Development of Mental Functioning.' *Int. J. Psycho-Anal.*, **29**. [III]

—— (1959). 'Our Adult World and its Roots in Infancy.' *Hum. Relations*, **12**. [III]

—— (1960a). 'A note on Depression in the Schizophrenic.' *Int. J. Psycho-Anal.*, **41**. [III]

—— (1960b). 'On Mental Health.' *Brit. J. med. Psychol.*, **33**. [III]

—— (1961). *Narrative of a Child Psycho-Analysis* (London: Hogarth). [IV]

—— (1963a). 'Some Reflections on *The Oresteia*.' In: *Our Adult World and Other Essays* (London: Heinemann Medical). [III]

—— (1963b). 'On the Sense of Loneliness.' *ibid.* [III]

Lewin, B. (1933). 'The Body as Phallus.' *Psychoanal. Quart.*, **2**.

Middlemore, M. P. (1936). 'The Uses of Sensuality.' In: *On the Bringing up of Children* ed. Rickman (London: Kegan Paul).

van Ophuijsen, J. H. W. (1920). 'On the Origin of the Feeling of Persecution.' *Int. J. Psycho-Anal.*, **1**.

Radó, S. (1928). 'The Problem of Melancholia.' *Int. J. Psycho-Anal.*, **9**.

Rank, O. (1912). *Das Inzestmotiv in Dichtung und Sage* (Leïpzig und Vienna: Deutike).

Rank, O. and Sachs, H. (1913). *Die Bedeutung der Psychoanalyse für die Geisteswissenschaften* (Wiesbaden: Bergmann).

Reich, W. (1927). 'Die Funktion des Orgasmus.' In: *The Discovery of the Orgone* (New York: Orgone Inst.).

Reik, T. (1925). *Geständniszwang und Strafbedürfnis* (Vienna: Int. Psychoanal. Vlg).

Riviere, J. (1937). 'Hate, Guilt and Aggression.' In: *Love, Hate and Reparation* with Klein (London: Hogarth).

Sadger, J. (1920). Über Prüfungsangst und Prüfungsträume.' *Int. Z. f. Psychoanal.*, **6**.

Schmideberg, M. (1930). 'The Rôle of Psychotic Mechanisms in Cultural Development.' *Int. J. Psycho-Anal.*, **11**.

—— (1931). 'A Contribution to the Psychology of Persecutory Ideas and Delusions.' *Int. J. Psycho-Anal.*, **12**.

Sharpe, E. (1930). 'Certain Aspects of Sublimation and Delusion.' In: *Collected Papers on Psycho-Analysis* (London: Hogarth, 1950).

—— (1936) Contribution to *On the Bringing up of Children* ed. Rickman (London: Kegan Paul).

Sperber, H. (1915). 'Über den Einfluss sexueller Momente auf Enstehung Entwicklung der Sprache.' *Imago*, **1**.

Spielrein, S. (1922). Die Entstehung der kindlichen Worte Papa und Mama.' *Imago.*, **8**.

Stärcke, A. (1919). 'Die Umkehrung des Libidovorzeichens beim Verfolgungswahn.' *Int. Z. f. Psychoanal.*, **5**.

Stekel, W. (1923). *Conditions of Nervous Anxiety and their Treatment* (London: Kegan Paul).

Strachey, J. (1930). 'Some Unconscious Factors in Reading.' *Int. J. Psycho-Anal.*, **11**.

Symposium on Child Analysis (1927). *Int. J. Psycho-Anal.*, **8**.

LIST OF PATIENTS

INDEX

Compiled by Barbara Forryan

445

breast, mothers—*contd*
disappearance of, as root of castration complex 48; and frustration 408; 'good' and 'bad' 262, 285 & *n*, 287, 291, 292, 294, 298, 307, 378, 388, 392, 404, 405, 408; idealization of 378, 392, 394, 408; introjection of, *see* introjection; libidinal attachment to 270; loved and hated 408; mourning for 345; and Oedipus complex 407; oral-sadistic attacks on in phantasy 253, 392, 417; and penis, *see* penis, father's; as persecutor(s) 285 & *n*, 287, 349; and super-ego, nucleus of 409, 147; and weaning, *see above* deprivation of; world as 233; *see also* nipple
breast-feeding 290–1, 297, 300, 306, 307 & *n*, 398, 435; and baby's fusion with mother 286; failed attempt at 222; *see also* sucking
breast-mother 379, 380, 395; good and bad 377; idealization of 394
British Psycho-Analytical Society 139*n*
brooding 160
brooding mania 87
brother(s) 327–8, ambivalence to 177–178, 345, 357; birth of, 107, 130, 179, 398, 403; and death of son 356–7; death-wish towards 162, 318; jealousy of 161–2, 173, 310, 318, 393; phantasied, inside mother's body, *see* mother's children inside; sadistic impulses against 173, 237
buttocks 253

C, *see* List of Patients, p. 444
cancer, fear of 273–4
cannibalism 170, 269
cannibalistic fixations 100, 170; impulses 423; —, and melancholia 263; phantasies 278, 287, 293
cannibalistic stage 71, 253
caricature 72*n*
castration 182; dread of by father 116, 189, 190, 192, 213, 366–7, 381, 403, 405; —, mitigated by trust in good father 411; of father in phantasy 65, 66, 172, 392*n*, 400, 402, 405, 417 (*see also* penis, father's); of mother 69; fear of by mother 62, 64, 115, 129*n*, 190, 396; need to disprove 392*n*; of parents by child, in phantasy 132, 202; primal/primitive 68*n*, 81; by super-ego, *see* super-ego
castration anxiety/dread/fear 59, 72*n*, 91*n*, 96, 100, 107, 110, 112, 116, 378, 380; in boy 393, 426; boy's

feminine attitude to father 119, 125; and faeces, loss of, as precursor 68*n*; and genital sensations 411; in girl 162, 405, 426; girl's equivalent of 217 (*see also* body, girl's; castration complex *s.v.* girl); and inhibitions 73–4; and narcissistic object choice 119; and oral-sadistic impulses 411; and school 59–60
castration complex 48, 98, 107, 113, 120; and falls/hurts 132; cleanliness training paves way for 129*n*; and feeling of ignorance 188; of girls 67, 190, 193, 196, 401, 416 (*see also* body, girl's; castration anxiety *s.v.* girl); and narcissistic regression 125; and trauma 126, 129*n*; weaning as root of 48, 129*n*
catatonia 234
cathexis: of Oedipus positions 189; sexual-symbolic, *see* sexual symbolic
ceremonial, sleep- 132, 202*n*, 402
Chadwick, Mary 191
character deformation 126
character formation: and analysis 256; and castration complex 73 & *n*; and Oedipus complex 171
character, stability of 156*n*; *see also* personality
'characters' in play 148, 152, 208–9; *see also* personification
child: pictures as 102; words as 100, 101; *see also* baby; boy; girl
child analysis: and analysis of child's relation to parents 163–7; and analytic situation, establishment of 137, 142, 143, 146, 152, 153, 166; broken off following early improvement 111*n*; child's attitude towards 144; of children aged one to two 294; direct representation of experiences/fixations in 135; difficulties of 49, 50; —, need for 47, 105; —, objections to 58, 168, 255; extent to which every child requires it 51–2, 257; fears of going deep 140, 141, 151; historical development of 139–41; need to go deep 94*n*, 96*nn*, 140; reaction differs in little children 134; and sublimation 206*n*; successful outcome 178
child analysis and adult analysis, x; differing means of expression in 135, 137; principles identical 138, 143, 423; slower development 141–2; techniques in, *see* technique
chimney-sweep 37*n*